The Workshop

The Workshop

SEVEN DECADES OF
THE IOWA
WRITERS' WORKSHOP
FORTY-THREE STORIES,
RECOLLECTIONS,
AND ESSAYS ON
IOWA'S PLACE IN
TWENTIETH-CENTURY
AMERICAN LITERATURE

EDITED BY TOM GRIMES

HYPERION / NEW YORK

Library of Congress Cataloging-in-Publication Data

Iowa Writers' Workshop.

The Workshop : seven decades of the Iowa Writers' Workshop : 42
stories, recollections & essays on Iowa's place in 20th-century
American literature / edited by Tom Grimes.

p.   cm.

ISBN 0-7868-6503-2 (hard cover)

1. Short stories, American.   2. American fiction—20th century.
3. United States—Social life and customs—20th century—Fiction.
4. Creative writing—Study and teaching (Higher)—Iowa—
History—20th century.   5. Iowa Writers' Workshop.   I. Grimes,
Tom, 1954–   .   II. Title.

PS648.S5I585   1999

813'.01089777—dc21   99-24268

                                                              CIP

Designed by Abby Kagan

FIRST EDITION

10   9   8   7   6   5   4   3   2   1

To writers everywhere
and
to their teachers

C O N T E N T S

1 9 8 0 s

1 9 9 0 s

P R E F A C E

THE IOWA WRITERS' WORKSHOP developed out of an idea, originally implemented in 1896 at the University of Iowa, to teach "Verse Making." By the 1920s, the university had taken the radical step of granting graduate degree credit for creative work. In 1941, the first Master of Fine Arts degree in Creative Writing was awarded. By the end of that decade, Flannery O'Connor was a member of the Workshop, which was fast becoming a national institution.

Being the first creative writing program in the country, Iowa acquired the reputation of also being the best, a reputation it maintains even as programs continue to be founded at other universities. In 1997, when *U.S. News & World Report* published its first ever ranking of creative writing programs, Iowa was voted number one.

The Iowa Writers' Workshop became the prototype for the now 300 programs in existence. Iowa was the first to incorporate writers into a university setting on a regular basis, a practice that has become commonplace. R. V. Cassill, who graduated in 1947 with Flannery O'Connor and later taught at Iowa, founded the Associated Writing Programs, an organization that now claims 17,000 members.

I have traced Iowa's decade-by-decade evolution, from the 1930s through the 1990s, in introductory essays and a coda that accompany the stories in this volume. The date given after each author's name in the table of contents indicates the writer's year of graduation on attendance. In addition, the opening essay on Iowa and the writing life, as well as recollections from Workshop graduates, allow the reader an inside look at the Workshop and its effect on writers who attend it.

The book may be read sequentially, as a narrative about the Workshop, or as an anthology of fiction with accompanying comments on writing. But for all of the importance of the Workshop as a twentieth-century literary institution, the diversity of voices and the human experiences that make up the place are its true legacy, and it is these qualities I've sought to capture here.

TOM GRIMES

INTRODUCTION

WHEN I WAS A KID of eighteen I went to Paris. I had very little money, lived in an Algerian slum, ate so badly I lost half the hair on the back of my head from a vitamin deficiency, got robbed, got beaten up, and endured various other hardships. Nevertheless I stayed, because I had read about prewar Paris—about Hemingway, Fitzgerald, Joyce, and all the others who used to hang out in "Boul-Miche" at The Dome or The Select. Surely it would all start up again now that the war was over. I wanted to meet artists, I wanted to connect with the literary ex-pats I assumed must be there. But of course I was too late. There was no doubt an artistic community, but it was no longer open and welcoming, if indeed it had ever been as open as I imagined. I met no American writers and made only a single friend, a young British painter who lived on boiled potatoes and *vinchaud*. Neither one of us did much more than survive that year, and then I came home.

Some time later—and I may have some of the details wrong since it was more than forty years ago—I read about the early training of an American writer who had gone on to write a book I admired. In his early twenties he'd fallen under the spell of a fat woman who ran a sort of camp/school/prison for writers way out in the boondocks. The regimen was rigid—up at dawn, no booze, no girlfriends, no phone calls. An existence entirely devoted to writing. Several hours each day were spent typing out whole books that the fat woman considered masterpieces. *Studs Lonigan, An American Tragedy, Grapes of Wrath,* and so on. Typed out in their entirety. It was nonsense of course, and yet I thought I understood why people put up with it. So they could stay, and talk about books and writing, so they could write themselves and show their writing to other writers. A sort of fascist version of what I had hoped for in Paris.

It has never surprised me that young American writers want to come to the Iowa Workshop. A place to read, write, and talk, a place to test ideas and to experiment. A literary community of some sophistication. Of course they want to come.

The wonderful stories in this book are only a small sample of the extraordinary outpouring of fine writing that has emerged from the Workshop over the last half century. The institution is a self-fulfilling prophecy. Very talented people are attracted (in part, I'm convinced, because older talented writers run the place and do the teaching, or, more accurately, the guiding), they arrive, do excellent work, publish, and attract the attention of even younger writers who want to come, and so on ad infinitum.

Writing fiction is, as E. L. Doctorow points out, "not a rational process," and I think he is almost right. Thus a good deal of humility is appropriate in teaching or guiding people. There are Zen aspects to the enterprise as Tom Grimes points out in his brilliant introduction. We can help people along only part of the way. After that they're on their own. But see what they have done!

FRANK CONROY

The Workshop

THE CULT OF GENIUS

THE QUESTION OF whether or not "creativity" can be learned, let alone taught, has nipped at the heels of writing workshops ever since their inception, which at Iowa dates back to 1896 when the first course in "creative" writing was offered. Detractors of the workshop idea prefer the noble savage or child-raised-by-wolves version of talent. To them, the creative spirit would thrive and emerge regardless of the conditions that shaped it. Genius was innate. It could no more be learned than breathing. You were either a genius, a sort of idiot savant like the version of Mozart depicted in *Amadeus,* or you weren't. Even Iowa Writers' Workshop graduate Flannery O'Connor claimed that "the ability to create life with words is essentially a gift. If you have it in the first place you can develop it; if you don't have it, you might as well forget it." As Stan Laurel and Oliver Hardy said, "You can lead a horse to water, but a pencil must be lead."

It isn't any surprise to recall that our modern notion of genius was developed by, well, geniuses, the German idealists Kant, Schiller, and Hegel. Schiller, in particular, assigned the creative imagination godlike powers, claiming that the sublime imaginings of genius superseded the limited imperfections of reality itself. The bearer of the genius gene became a sacred rather than mortal figure. Gone was the workmanlike figure of Shakespeare, who wrote plays to keep himself and his acting troupe employed. Forget the mere mnemonic devices employed in the oral telling of *The Iliad* or *The Odyssey* by Homer, whoever he was. The Romantic genius, usually a poet, had a red phone to the Muse, and whenever the spirit dialed, what could genius do but, in a state of rapture, take the call. Forget craft. Divinity was channeled into the work by "grace," which, according to *The Norton Anthology of English Literature*, in eighteenth-century literary terms meant "that ultimate, inexpressible charm which converts the merely formal and regular into vital and animated beauty, and which is the mysterious result of Nature and not of art, or rules." As a genius, you were the "Man," the "It Boy" of the Romantic movement in Europe.

The irony of this elitist sanctification of the human imagination is that while the French Revolution was abolishing monarchy and aristocracy, and Wordsworth began employing unheroic, autobiographical material in his poetry, Romanticism elevated genius to Olympian status. Geniuses were born, not made. Their work transcended the simple craftsmanship available to ordinary man. In other words, Romanticism ignored the democratic impulses in revolt throughout Europe and America and created a new elite in the form of the author. For a movement concerned with the power of humankind's imagination to conjure sublime experience through art, Romanticism turned out to be a pretty exclusive club.

Author worship flowered in the late eighteenth and nineteenth centuries. Byron, the clubfoot boy nonetheless beloved by women for his—what else?—genius, rates a 10 on the brooding poet scale and is the figure from whom all imitators take their cue. In part, this sentimentalization of the social outcast in search of beauty was a reaction against the dehumanizing effects of the Industrial Revolution. If the modern world was going to hell, the Romantic imagination alone held out the only hope of escaping it through Art. Those elected to wear this capital A on their chests became, along with their work, fetishes. Objects to be adored for their connection to beauty.

"The whole point of 'creative writing,' " Terry Eagleton noted in his study *Literary Theory: An Introduction*, "was that it was gloriously useless, an end in itself loftily removed from any sordid social purpose. Having lost his patron, the writer discovered a substitute in the poetic."

This fetishization peaked during the High Modernist period of the twentieth century when the "poetic" began to resemble the impenetrable. Anyone who has been subjected to reading Pound in college would probably sympathize with the position "Kill the critics." For who else could be responsible for defining as Art the often incomprehensible passages of the Cantos? The Romantic movement, Eagleton says, assumed "there was an unchanging object known as Art, or an isolatable experience called beauty or the aesthetic [that] was largely a product of the very alienation of art from social life." Yet what could possibly be more alienated from social life than Pound's work? So, ironically, rather than saving beauty, the endgame of Romanticism, found in High Modernism's often tortured sterility, buried it. In defense of this sweeping claim, remember four words: *Finnegan's Wake*, Gertrude Stein. A pose is a pose is a pose. Case closed.

If the extreme experiments of some Modernist writers introduced pain into the formerly pleasurable activity of reading, they certainly found willing and masochistic accomplices in the "lit. crit." industry. One of my American literature teachers once announced in class that he had spent his summer rereading Stein's *The Making of Americans*. His tone implied that his diligence was somehow noble, priestly, anointed, and separated him from us. All I could think was, "Why?"

Not unexpectedly, critical idolatry of Art, the artist, and the aesthetic soon brought about a demystifying reaction, something along the lines of stock market correction for geniuses. In tandem with this spirit, oddly enough, the creative writing workshop was born.

CRAFT VERSUS GENIUS

HENRY MILLER ONCE said that similar ideas tend to pop up at various points on the globe at the same time. Artists, of course, being the "antennae of the race," are aware of aesthetic developments taking place in regions as remote and disparate as Iowa City and Moscow, so the link between the beginnings of the Iowa Writers' Workshop and the Russian formalists should come as no surprise to these superior beings. The coincidental dovetailing of the two movements caused me, however, to experience that most crucial of workshop phenomena—the Joycean epiphany. What had begun in 1896 in Iowa City with that first class in "Verse Making," which laid emphasis on verse as a thing made, something that could be practiced, studied, and emulated, rather than channeled directly from the empyrean sublime, had by the 1920s led the University of Iowa to become one of the first institutions in the country to award a Master of Arts degree for creative work.

Meanwhile, back in the newly formed USSR, a rowdy group of "new" critics, fed up with the mandarin pretensions of symbolist poetry, reduced the task of literary creation and interpretation to something as methodical as building a car engine. If the Romantic artist had been a secular priest, the new twentieth-century author was no more than a mechanic. Literature could be taken apart and examined as easily as a V-8.

Just as Hemingway focused on how a story worked, rather than what it was about, the Russian formalists, according to Eagleton, believed that "[C]riticism should dissociate art from mystery and concern itself with how literary texts actually worked: literature was not a pseudo-religion or psychology or sociology but a particular organization of language. It had its own specific laws, structures and devices, which were to be studied for themselves." This manifesto could be posted on the door of any Iowa Workshop seminar room and not seem out of place.

"Abandon all hope all ye who enter here" would make an apt companion piece. For as surely as the formalists, demolished the mystical abstractions of the writing process, the Workshop, with its exclusive focus on the text, announced the death of the author, and it did so four decades ahead of French literary theorist Roland Barthes. Paul Engle, the Workshop's early director and the man most responsible for its development, aptly described the Workshop's paradoxical intentions when he said the Workshop's mission was to nurture the author, to give "the writer a place where he can be himself, confronting the hazards and hopes of his own talent," and at the same time to "knock, or persuade, or terrify the false tenderness toward his own work out of the beginning writer." It did so by concerning itself solely with the text and its mechanics. The author was separated from his or her work, observing Eliot's dictum that "the progress of an artist is a continual self-sacrifice, a continual extinction of personality."

Personality is exactly what the Russian formalists hoped to bleed from literary appreciation and criticism. Further proving Henry Miller's point about similar ideas blooming simultaneously in different parts of the world, a virtually identical disdain for artistic personality flowered in Great Britain, led by Cambridge critic F. R. Leavis, who, Eagleton notes, "stressed the centrality of rigorous critical analysis, a disciplined attention to 'the words on the page.'" The author was extraneous. Leavis advanced the concepts of "practical criticism" and "close reading," which detached literary texts from their personal and historical contexts and concentrated purely on the text's "organic unity." A continent away in Iowa, the first Workshop instructors had reached the same conclusions.

Where the Romantics had reified the artist, turning a simple craftsman into a deity, the text itself now assumed the qualities of sacred object. It reached the literary pantheon only by its relation to other texts, those "existing monuments" that, according to Eliot, "form an ideal order among themselves." In American literary circles, this ideal was championed most fervently by the New Critics, a group whose major work, *The New Criticism,* was published in 1941, not so coincidentally the very same year the University of Iowa awarded its first Master of Fine Arts degree in Creative Writing.

NEW CRITICISM AND THE IOWA WORKSHOP

THE NEW CRITICS took Eliot's idea, a rather demoralizing notion for any would-be writer to encounter—"Welcome to the Workshop, we're going to extinguish your personality!"—and combined it with Leavis's practice of "close reading" until the text revealed itself in Terry Eagleton's words "as a self-enclosed object, mysteriously intact in its own unique being." This unique being, it was claimed, "could not be paraphrased ... [because] each of its parts ... folded in on others in a complex organic unity which it would be a kind of blasphemy to violate." The New Critics insisted, according to Eagleton, "that the author's intentions in writing, even if they could be recovered, were of no relevance to the interpretation of his or her text."

Violating this mysterious unity or, more often, a text's lack thereof, proved to be the Workshop's reason for being. "A lot of people come for self-expression or therapy," Philip Roth said of his experience teaching at the Workshop in the early '60s. "We try to put a stop to that." Roth saw the Workshop as serving three purposes: giving young writers an audience, a sense of community, and an acceptable social category—student. "If a boy went to his father and said, 'I'm going to New York to be a writer,' his father would hit the ceiling. But who will quarrel with a Master's degree, or even a Ph.D.?" Ultimately, Roth concludes, "Part of our function is to discourage those without enough talent."

What is judged in Workshop, generally by the process of "close reading," is the executed result of the author's intentions. Workshop doesn't care about what you meant to say, or how you feel about what you said, it cares about what was said, the "words on the page." Like New Criticism, it examines texts without regard to authorial desire. If Workshop students enter the program believing "My book is my self," they, like Montaigne in his *Essays,* quickly discover that "In molding this figure upon myself, I have been so oft constrained to temper and compose myself in a right posture, that the copy is truly taken, and has in some sort form'd itself." As a writer, Montaigne saw that his virtual literary self was the product of communal and historical forces, rather than something produced by a unique, highly Romanticized individual imagination. Deconstruction theory, advanced by critics like Jacques Derrida, announced this identical insight about 400 years later. I don't mean to denigrate critics. As Eugene O'Neill said, "I love every bone in their heads." I just wish to point out that critical notions such as the death of the author or "Reception Theory's" bold claim that the reader completes the literary work by—my God!—imagining the illusory world conjured up by black marks on a page are only startling in their obviousness, proving once again that academics treat as revelation circumstances that which the rest of literate humankind takes for granted.

When a student enters a Workshop seminar room, any hope of being rescued by the abstractions of theory vanishes the moment discussion begins. If we arrive not believing in the death of the author, we often crawl away several hours later wishing for it. What's established instantly is the fact that Romanticism's deification of the writer is the single most idiotic aberration in the history of literature.

Writers are craftsmen, and as such all of our apprentice work is rough, inelegant, flawed. In fact, much of the time it isn't even functional. Sometimes we can't even begin discussing character or story, let alone structuralist notions that language creates the writer rather than the other way around, because actions described in the text defy the laws of physics. We enter the program possessing the skills of fledgling carpenters—if we're lucky—yet hoping to build palaces. It's this gap between ambition and mastery that the Workshop addresses and, if possible, tries to bridge, and it does so by concentrating on "the words on the page."

CAN WRITING AND CREATIVITY BE TAUGHT?

LET'S LEAVE BEHIND, for a moment, the historical vicissitudes of literary theory and return to the original question. Can creativity be learned, let alone taught? The answer depends on how you define creativity. If you believe in the largely discredited notion of genius, your answer will be no, it can't.

Also, for all its impact on twentieth-century American literature, the Iowa Workshop must be acknowledged not only for the great writers connected with it but for the writers not connected with it. If the Workshop were the only place to develop as a writer, how do we account for Toni Morrison, Thomas Pynchon, Saul Bellow, Don DeLillo, Robert Stone, Tim O'Brien, Richard Ford, E. Annie Proulx, and Cormac McCarthy, none of whom studied at Iowa or any other formalized version of a fiction-writing workshop? Nelson Algren's denunciatory 1971 essay, "At Play in the Fields of Hackademe," claimed that "for what it lacks in creativity, the Iowa Creative Workshop makes up in quietivity." He asked, "[W]hy has the Iowa Writers' Workshop, in its 35 years of existence, not produced a single novel, poem or short story worth rereading?" then answered, "Because its offer of painless creativity is based on self-deception." Was he on the money? Or was he still miffed about losing a rumored $34,000 playing poker while teaching at Iowa and simply biting the hand that bleeds? Can the Workshop be held accountable if Algren overestimated his gift for five-card stud?

John Barth, a novelist who taught creative writing for decades, noted that "not even in America can one major in Towering Literary Artistry." In lieu of the hackwork envisioned by Algren, Barth saw workshops producing "your average pretty-damn-good literary artifact as published by the *New Yorker* or *Esquire* . . . or one of the better New York trade-book publishing houses." Like his German idealist fore-fathers, Barth also believed in "genius," although he found it to be, "like matter in the universe, thinly distributed." Consequently, writing workshops such as those offered by Iowa were, to him, places where "those with any aptitude for [writing] . . . hone what skills they have."

Aptititude, however, is not easily detectable. As Flannery O'Connor discovered, those "who do have talent . . . flounder around because they don't really know what a story is."

If you think about it, storytelling is, outside of breathing, eating, and sleeping, the most fundamental and time-consuming human activity there is. We listen to and tell stories all our lives. So why should we have to learn how to do something we've been doing since childhood? Cormac McCarthy said teaching creative writing is a scam, and Kay Boyle declared that "all creative writing programs ought to be abolished by law." Were they right?

No. It's amazing to discover how difficult it is to write a good story. One often experiences a certain degree of shock upon first slipping into the Workshop's "hallowed" hallways, removing from its shelves copies of stories by other Workshoppers, and confronting how truly awful some of them are. The expectation of finding perfectly polished pieces ready for acceptance by *Best American Short Stories,* and these pop up as well, instantly yields thoughts of "Is my stuff this bad?" It must be, since the astoundingly terrible "words on the page" in your hands were written by someone who'd been accepted, like you, into the most prestigious creative writing program in the world. The thrill of being at Iowa momentarily vanishes, as does the delirium in which you've imagined immediate publication, praise, fame, riches, and that most elusive of all writerly qualities—validation. Street cred. Anointment. A word or nod from the published sage, the "real writer" at the workshop table in whose estimation and assessment you believe your literary fate begins and ends.

This, after all, is what you've come for. Not so much to be taught as initiated into the mysteries and thereby lifted out of that quivering, awkward bundle of doubt previously called "you." You've come seeking transcendence. You've come to slip into the skin of some idealized, immortal writerly you, a being as imaginary as ancient Crete's Minotaur. Ironically, what you stumble into is the labyrinth that is the writer's life. No workshop instructor or mentor will arrive like Theseus to slay the personal literary Minotaur pursuing you. Your trip through the labyrinth, you discover, turns out to be a private one. Your imagination and its sources are the deepest mysteries. Transcendence is a confrontation with your limitations and flaws. You arrive full of passion and, confoundingly, are introduced into the tedium of creation. "Writing is ultimately a test of character," Frank Conroy says. To ward off the confusions and uncertainties of the writing life, all you have, you soon find, is "the habit of art."

He had coffee and a sandwich at his desk. Then tapped on the keys, hearing an old watery moan deep in the body. How the day's first words set off physical alarms . . . Used to be that time rushed down on him when he started a book . . . Please Jesus just let me work . . . How typing mistakes became despair . . . He looked at the sentence, six disconsolate words . . . Took him all these years to realize this book was his hated adversary. Locked together in the forbidden room, had him in a choke hold. I'm between novels, he used to say, so I don't mind dying.

Don DeLillo's fictional description of the writer's life in *MAO II* should be enough to scare off any pretenders or glory-seekers, the millions waiting on inspiration, that Godot-like no-show. Or maybe Algren was right: the "Writer's Workshop . . . provides sanctuary from those very pressures in which creativity is forged." Because one has to ask: Can patience and humility be taught? Will attention to the "words on the page" mold and fire-harden a writer's character so that it might withstand the daily trials of the literary life?

"Habits have to be rooted deep in the whole personality," Flannery O'Connor warned. "They have to be cultivated like any other habit, over a long period of time, by experience; and teaching any kind of writing is largely a matter of helping the student develop the habit of art."

Can a workshop, in which the personality and often even the presence of the writer is ignored, address these singular, lifelong lessons?

Barth claims there are four "proper objects of study for serious writers—their material ('human life,' Aristotle says, 'its happiness and its misery'), their medium (language), their craft . . . and their art (the inspired and masterful application of their craft and medium to their material)." But he qualifies a workshop's ability to deal with "human life," which he doesn't believe to be its "province." He also says that art "is more the hope than the curricular goal of a sound writing program; it comes from mastery of the other three [objects of study] plus a dash of genius."

A "dash of genius"? At least the Romantics let their claims for genius rip. Barth applies it like baking powder to a cake recipe. Coupling the need for a "dash of genius" with a writing workshop's supposed aversion to "human life, its happiness and misery," what's left, we still have to ask, to be taught?

ZEN AND THE ART OF MANUSCRIPT MAINTENANCE

EVERYTHING AND NOTHING: this is what, I believe, the Iowa Writers' Workshop teaches.

When one arrives for Workshop in late August, Iowa seems to burst with abundance, rolling green fields stretching everywhere beyond the edges of town, corn piled high in markets, summer vegetables sold off the tailgates of pickup trucks by local farmers. The place spills over with a kind of fertile thrill that seems to match and accommodate your own barely contained enthusiasm. Anything could grow here, the land seems to whisper, even your own unsown talent.

Then come the Workshop discussions. The line edits that pick apart the imagined integrity of your story before the end of the first sentence. The declaration by others of utter mystification when it came to being able to say what your story was about. The lancing comparisons of your pale imitation to the work of obviously influential masters. The subtle and not so subtle assassinations of character that, even though directed at your fictional understudies, carry their sting back to their original flesh-and-blood source. Charges of sexism, misogyny, elitist tendencies. Too many metaphors! Too passive a protagonist. You read the word "Congratulations" on one of the written commentaries you receive, and your heart hums. Then you read the rest of the accolade—"you've created the most despicable narrator in American literature!" You take up pool at the Foxhead, the local writers' bar. You lose money you don't have playing poker, then realize you don't play poker!

Without quite understanding it, Workshop students expect validation as writers. When that isn't automatically bestowed we begin hungering after wisdom, then secrets, then tricks of the trade, and finally, in despair, a critical vocabulary we can call our own. We study everything there is to say about writing. We master the Workshop lingo, repeating "show, don't tell" like a mantra. We express our vague dissatisfactions with one another's work by claiming to want "more," and dread the news or rumor that someone else has sold a story or book because we fear this leaves us behind, somehow diminished.

Meanwhile, summer's abundance has quickly retreated, season's end stripping the heartland of all its lush promise, taking with it the brimming confidence you momentarily enjoyed. You came to the Workshop to get into the illusion-making business, and now your illusions about the writing life are as naked as the leafless trees you hike past in the woods where you hide, trying to recenter yourself. In the gray of early fall, Algren's resented "sanctuary" seems very far away, the small room you write in a babel of critical voices. You wanted the writing life, you got it. Doubt, anxiety, staying in the chair, wrestling with sentences one by one until they yield something you can call beautiful and true. Knowing everything there is to know about the craft of writing. Knowing more than you ever imagined there was to know.

So, why do you feel so incomplete? So uncertain? So alone?

Could it be that the intellectual lessons of Workshop have made you realize "What a job of heavy labor the writing of fiction is"? Or, as O'Connor also said, that "the materials of the fictional writer are the humblest."

"Fiction is about everything human and we are made out of dust," she wrote, and in the short days of fall and winter it is, as writers, to dust that we return. No longer believing we have arrived. No longer even believing in the notion of arrival. Emptied of certainty by everything we have come to learn.

Yet, as the surfaces of art dissolve, we begin to sense, as the *Tao Te Ching* puts it, the unnameable, the "darkness within darkness" that, paradoxically, is "the gateway to all understanding."

What the Workshop has done, strangely enough, is taught us what *not* to do. It has offered no prescriptions for "fixing" stories, no formulas for creating characters, no blueprint for surefire plotting. It seemingly hasn't a clue as to how to find a "voice" for one's work. If it possesses the secret to writing dialogue, the secret is well kept. If it knows which of us will fail and which will be successful, it isn't saying. Everything it teaches, essentially, is a form of No, a variation on wisdom that lies in knowing what not to do. Oddly, a process that seemed to begin with New Critical "close reading" has instead demanded something akin to Zen surrender.

"The Master leads," the Tao says in words that Paul Engle echoes, "by emptying people's minds and filling their cores, by weakening their ambition and toughening their resolve. He helps people lose everything they know, everything they desire, and creates confusion in those who think that they know. Practice not-doing, and everything will fall into place."

By the end of our first Workshop year, we realize we have learned everything in order to understand that we know nothing. It's a realization that is as tenaciously resisted and fitfully born as the rebirth of spring greenery and balmy temperatures in the place itself. After all, how could the path toward mastery yield nothing but anxiety and confusion? Cormac McCarthy was right, we angrily recall, teaching creative writing is a scam. Resentment for the entire notion of Workshop, its self-denying indifference and calm certainty, builds in us. A frustration with how the Workshop, the writing life, even literature itself sails on without us, ignoring our struggle. The expectation for glory we arrived with, diminished by the repeated No of Workshop, now coils into neediness, a sullen rejection of the life that seems to have rejected us. Traffic at the local mental health clinic increases. Love affairs flare into full burn, only to last a week. The Foxhead does end-of-the-world-style business, as dozens of us sit at the bar, heads hung over a whiskey, as dejected as Humphrey Bogart in *Casablanca,* while the friends still standing offer Dooley Wilson–like advice. "We'll get drunk. We'll go fishing." Flee, forget, quit.

(Raymond Carver actually did flee.)

The injustice, the blindness of the whole system, the entire writing life, has never been so apparent to us. "Screw Golden Boy!" we shout, alone in our rooms. (Where else?) Or, "How did she ever get a fellowship?" we want to know, suspecting nepotism, conspiracy, every sin but personal bias, every option but the probability of our inadequate work.

Unsurprisingly, a psychological survey of the Iowa Workshop showed that 80 percent of writers in the program reported evidence of manic-depression, alcoholism, or other lovely addictions in themselves or their immediate families. We're writers. Whoever claimed we were a tightly wrapped bunch?

What's going on actually, what we're still learning and struggling with, is the emotional rather than the intellectual meaning of not-doing, the impact of finally and fully knowing that we know nothing. This is more difficult than rationally accepting all the arguments about what constitutes literature. Because until the Workshop's resistance to our desire to "write literature" and to "become writers" touches the quivering, naked, three-o'clock-in-the-morning doubt-filled creature we all are, understanding cannot begin.

Still not wanting to face this ourselves, in desperation we lean on our teachers, blurting out in private conferences unanswerable questions. "Am I any good? Am I wasting my time? Am I going to be a real writer?" We're greeted with uncomfortable squirming, sighs, poker-faced admissions of ignorance on the subject. Everything but what we really still want—assurance. Short of that, and by now we're beginning to sense that assurance is probably about as tangible as Santa Claus, we'd happily settle for our conferee leaping out of his or her chair and knocking us to the floor with a Zen-master whack on the head so we could at least look up and say, "Thank you. I now have satori, and also grounds for a lawsuit." But even here we're frustrated, because the Workshop trains us for emotional growth and an understanding of the writing life by indirection, by turning us back on ourselves.

"Do you have the patience to wait till your mud settles and the water is clear?" the Tao asks. "Can you remain unmoving till the right action arises by itself?"

Can you take the pressure of the writing life, and the anxieties of producing art, is the question of character that is now yours alone to decide. Can you develop and maintain the "habit of art," which Maritain, via Flannery O'Connor, explained as "a certain quality or virtue of mind"?

How different this is from the Romantic myth of genius. To remain unmoving until right literary action arises isn't the same as expecting the Muse to arrive with a perfectly composed piece of work for you to jot down, a fairy tale that made the difficulties of composition seem about as arduous as having a pizza delivered.

No, a more useful Romantic notion than "genius" touches upon what is essential to surviving as a writer, Keats's "negative capability." Keats didn't set the idea out as literary theory or criticism. Instead, the notion arose in a personal letter to his brother. Keats lived with the "habit of art," the continual alertness to questions of form and imagination that a writer slowly learns to always keep in mind.

"Negative capability," he suggested, constitutes a writer's ability to survive and triumph over the difficulties and anxieties of composing a work of imagination "without any irritable grasping after fact."

Stress the word "irritable" and you detect the Taoist patience Keats proposed as a writer's cardinal virtue. But this ability to stop irritably grasping after facts while sifting for the right word, Flaubert's *le mot juste,* this the writer must discover and nurture on his or her own. The Workshop provides no direct help. Instead, once you've surrendered your desire to become a writer, the Workshop teaches you that in place of the cult of "genius" there is, more importantly, what Sartre calls, "a pact of generosity between author and reader."

WRITING FOR THE READER

CURIOUSLY, EVEN though we've all been readers long before we even considered being writers, most of us show up at the Workshop without giving too much thought to that abstract partner in our work, the "ideal reader," as Salinger calls him. That total stranger, who Nabokov imagines innocently plucking a work of fiction off some small town library shelf, completes the act of imagination each writer has begun. "Each one trusts the other," Sartre observed, "each one counts on the other, demands as much of the other as he demands of himself."

Nurturing this pact, and continually elevating the demands writers and readers place upon each other, goes to the heart of the Workshop's vision. It urges apprentice writers toward fulfilling and mastering this pact by comparing their "words on the page" to words set down on the page by writers who have mastered the writer/reader relationship before them.

Every writer, whether they attend a workshop or not, discovers that literature is one's true teacher. Imagination cannot be taught. Habits of art and virtues of mind can be encouraged, no more. But a serious study of literature can enable a writer to master the elements of literary craft. Will this, in every case, produce a great writer? No. Again, great writing depends on the individual writer's imagination. But until craft is mastered, imagination is a useless, largely inapplicable abstraction. Mastering craft gives the writer access to the fullness of his or her imagination, because it gives the writer the ability to deploy and apply it. Everyone can imagine a house. Only a carpenter can build one. And the wisest among them always keeps in mind the fact that he or she is building a place for others to live in, just as the well-trained writer never loses sight of the fact that it is the reader who will ultimately inhabit the story.

"No reader who doesn't actually experience," O'Connor reminds us, "who isn't made to feel the story is going to believe anything the fiction writer merely tells him. The first and most obvious characteristic of fiction is that it deals with reality through what can be seen, heard, smelt, tasted, and touched." This, in essence, is the fiction writer's first and only commandment, as well as the touchstone for the workshop admonition "show, don't tell." Showing a reader a character's actions and describing the sensory world that a character inhabits is the sole task and responsibility the writer bears. Showing offers the reader experience; telling supplies mere information.

But showing, not telling, can be overdone. The result is often anemic, banal work drained of excess or risk. Careful, technically correct, but completely dead stories. "Workshop fiction," to use the pejorative label attached to a narrow sampling of work produced by an extremely varied group of writers.

Is the Workshop guilty of spawning several generations of mediocre, monochromatic writers, as some critics charge? Or is this a simplistic cliché that ignores the strength, variety, and distinctiveness of work by Flannery O'Connor and Jane Smiley, Andre Dubus and T. C. Boyle, Joy Williams and Thom Jones? To paraphrase the cliché, those who can't do, teach, those who can't write, bitch. (Most literary writers, these days, do a little of both.)

This tendency of complaint occurs in Workshop from time to time, too, with "show, don't tell" often trying to force the work under consideration toward a consensual middle ground, to bleed it of the often annoying, idiosyncratic tics and flaws that give it juice. It's good at these times to be reminded—and someone in the room inevitably steps forward to do so, for compassion and wisdom is always in as great a supply among one's peers at the Workshop as anxiety, envy, and despair—that Wayne Booth's *Rhetoric of Fiction* pointed out that even when a writer is showing, he's telling. The writer decides what to show, how to show it, and how it will sound to a reader. In other words, the writer decides how his or her story will be told to his or her "ideal reader."

In workshop, one quickly finds that not everyone in the room is going to play this role. What moves or thrills one reader about your work numbs or nauseates another. So be it. You learn, just as you've learned patience, to be objective about your own work by training yourself to put yourself in the reader's place, by empathizing not only with your characters but with the reader who will inhabit the fictional house you build.

Your workshop mates are readers, very good and attentive readers, on whom you get to practice, and some prove tougher than others. "Your fellow apprentices," Barth attests, "will be sharp. As much of what happens in successful workshops happens outside them, among the apprentices, at all hours, as in their official meetings and conferences with the boss writer. The best thing they offer you is the finest audience any writer can have until his work is famous enough to attract wide professional critical attention."

Through your classmates, you learn to hear, if not necessarily heed, all criticisms. You learn objectivity, not creativity. Once you've surrendered all your previous illusions, this is what the Workshop finally teaches—objectivity. And it teaches it by teaching technique, because as Mark Schorer wrote, "Technique objectifies."

NOT DOING—THE RIGHT WAY

"I'VE GOT THE STORY but I don't have any technique," a student once told Flannery O'Connor. At its worst, technique appears to be nothing more than a highbrow term for formula. But a formula demands that you follow it faithfully; technique is studied so a full range of devices may be used by a writer to make a story tellable, artful, which in some cases includes breaking with conventions. Formula imposes limits on a writer; technique frees a writer to expand the methods of convention, should he or she choose to take that path. The only rule to observe when breaking convention is extremely simple. Do not purposely confuse the reader. Make clear the new method you're employing. If the reader cannot follow it, you've failed. If the reader can, you've done what Flaubert did—invent a new convention (in his case, modern point of view) for literature's future use.

"Technique is a word they all trot out," O'Connor wrote, lamenting the cart-before-the-horse approach to storytelling, which characterized her student's confusion about the act of discovery. For although technique can be studied, technique alone will never produce a story. What's more, one can never claim to have a story yet lack the technique for telling it. That's the same as saying I've written the story, now I just have to write the sentences. What O'Connor's student had was the *idea* of a story, not the story itself, which is inextricable from the "words on the page" used to tell it. And these words, just like Flaubert's innovations concerning omniscient point of view, are discovered solely in the act of writing.

"The only way, I think, to learn to write short stories," O'Connor said, "is to write them, and then try to discover what you have done. The time to think of technique is when you've actually got the story in front of you." Sound, unassailable advice. Also the last thing many apprentice writers want to hear, because getting the story in front of you is terrifying, painful, and in many cases nearly impossible. Technique, we naively hope, is a miracle cure, some kind of combination tranquilizer-antidepressant-pain reliever for our distressed literary condition. It isn't.

"Technique," according to Mark Schorer, "is the means by which the writer's experience, which is his subject matter, compels him to attend to it; technique is the only means he has of discovering, exploring, developing his subject, of conveying its meaning, and, finally, of evaluating it."

Without a masterful understanding of literary technique a writer is doomed never to fully communicate his or her story, its rendered experiences and their various meanings, to a reader. "The writer capable of the most exacting technical scrutiny of his subject matter," Schorer believed, "will produce works . . . which reverberate . . . with maximum meaning."

The problem for the fledgling writer is that "technical scrutiny" must be brought to bear on the raw, awkward, flawed, often embarrassing words one has placed on the page. Until he cultivates the patience to surrender it, the writer's ego remains overly involved with his work, a bit too protective of and attached to the products of his imagination. Essentially, he's asked to split himself, first by extinguishing his personality, as Eliot advised, in order to produce a story, then by turning around and applying an "exacting" standard of objective criticism to his own creation.

Consider how different and more excruciating this is than studying music. To learn how to play the piano, all you study is technique. You have the products of Bach's musical imagination to practice on. The writer has to practice on his or her own imagination. The equivalent is being told by your piano teacher after two lessons, "Okay, go home, compose a sonata, and we'll see what's wrong with it when you come back." You've heard a piano before. Why can't you write a sonata? With all the stories you've heard and told in your life, why can't you write a story?

The answer lies in the exact opposite of the equation laid out by O'Connor's student: I haven't got the story because I don't have any control of technique. If you can't count time and play in key, you can't produce music. The same goes for fiction—if you can't control point of view and narrative voice, you can't write a story.

In workshop, this seemingly genetic and nearly universal shortcoming announces itself with the regularity of trumpets in a Shakespeare play. Shifting point of view and betraying the consistency of the narrative voice in ways that confuse and undermine the reader's confidence are the most obvious flaws in a story up for discussion. Point of view controls the way actions in a story are perceived—what is seen and by whom. Narrative voice expresses the attitude of the speaker toward the actions depicted, and this attitude needs to be rendered credibly in order to seduce or charm a reader into suspending his or her disbelief in the artificiality of events. To be credible, a voice has to be seamless. If the narrator starts out sounding like a hayseed, then five pages later begins issuing pronouncements like a member of the British Parliament, you've got trouble. Fiction is built like that house of cards that Nabokov says must be turned into a palace of steel and glass. Consequently, once the narrative voice skids out of control, point of view begins to lose its focus, because the narrator's attitude determines how actions are seen and therefore rendered. If the narrator's voice is tentative, the point of view it speaks for no longer knows exactly where to look, and the story goes astray.

But abstract explanations like this take a writer only partway toward Not Doing. To know what not to do, the Workshop invokes the virtues and traditions of literature. It does not say, this is how you create narrative voice or conjure up a point of view. Instead, just as the fiction writer makes human emotions appear real by describing the concrete actions of characters, the Workshop turns the apprentice writer to works of literature in order to transform the abstract into the specific.

Studying literature, noting its technical graces, slows the writer down, makes one pay attention to his or her own work until, finally, one is capable of selecting the right word, the best phrase or sentence rhythm, the perfect action to illuminate character and move the story forward.

On the contrary, it is impossible to apply Lacan's "language is what hollows being into desire"—say what?—to writing fiction. And, if anyone in Workshop ever used the words "similarity is superinduced upon contiguity" to suggest a path toward revision, there'd be unbridled pummeling of the unwitting semiotician.

For the writer, literary theory not only is of no use but is detrimental to his progress and well-being. Once a writer starts believing that theory and not literature can be his guide through the labyrinth, he's doomed. His path always leads to literature, not theories about literature.

Even literary theoretician Terry Eagleton reaches this conclusion. After delineating the "analytical" method of inquiry into a literary text's "deep structures," a notion advanced by the imaginatively named group the Structuralists, which claims that the "content of the narrative is in its structure . . . its own internal relations, its modes of sense-making," an issue dealt with in Workshop by discussing whether a story's form properly suits and illuminates its content, its how matching its what, and by asking if a given story's "modes of sense-making" are clearly apparent to the reader; after asserting that "meaning was neither a private experience nor a divinely ordained occurrence [but] the product of certain shared systems of signification," a problem Workshop tackles by asking if a story has honored the pact of sharing its creation with a reader; after admitting that the "literary movement of modernism . . . brought structuralist and post-structuralist criticism to birth in the first place," then noting that theory's construction of a psychological school of criticism is based on the examination of how a story's "sub-text" reveals the "unconscious" intentions of—what, exactly? It can't be the author's intentions, since according to theory the author is dead. The "unconscious" intentions of language? Does language have an "unconscious"?; after all the dubious, self-defeating conundrums literary theory has foisted upon literature for the past half century, what does Eagleton propose to keep theory from "pressing its own implications too far" and thereby arguing "itself out of existence"? Rhetoric: "the received form of critical analysis all the way from ancient society to the eighteenth century, examined the way discourses are constructed in order to achieve certain effects."

"Rhetoric," he continues, "wanted to find out the most effective ways of pleading, persuading and debating, and rhetoricians studied such devices in other people's language in order to use them more productively in their own. It was, as we would say today," and as the Workshop has been saying for the past seventy years, "a creative as well as a critical activity."

The Iowa Writers' Workshop returned the study of literature and creative writing to a tradition that had served Western culture admirably from the time of Cicero up until the aberration called the cult of genius sprang into being during the Romantic period. The Workshop reconnected literary study to what Eagleton praises about classical rhetoric, its "grasping such practices as forms of . . . pleading, persuading, inciting" and examining "such devices in terms of concrete performance" in order to tell, as well as they could be told, the necessary stories of our age. To accomplish this, the Workshop's repeated No, its focus on what not to do because it isn't working, was always complemented by a suggestion of where the writer should look for guidance. To Faulkner for control of long sentences. To Dickens for deepening caricature into character. To Jane Austen for seamlessly blending cultural criticism with comedy. To all of literature for example, as well as for solace and faith.

The Workshop jettisoned genius and ignored literary theory because, like the centuries-old tradition of rhetoric, it believed, in the words of Paul Engle, that writing was a "form of activity inseparable from the wider social relations between writers and readers," and that the nurture and love of literature could "materially affect American culture."

The stories in the pages that follow attest to the perpetual summer, abundance, and variety of Iowa's achievement, proof of its lush resonance in American culture. And if the writer himself is subject to bone-cold dejection and loneliness during the winters of his writing life, he is nonetheless in every season wreathed by the continual flowering of his and her mates, with whom he shares lifelong solidarity. And this faith in one another, and in the endurance of literature, is enough to sustain each of us, writer and reader alike.

stories

1930s

FOR THE BEST history of the Iowa Writers' Workshop through the 1970s, readers should look for Steve Wilbur's detailed work, *The Iowa Writers' Workshop*, published by the University of Iowa Press. Robert Dana's lively companion volume, A *Community of Writers: Paul Engle and the Iowa Writers' Workshop*, which covers Paul Engle's years as director, was published in 1999 by the Iowa Press as well. It includes essays by Kurt Vonnegut, Gail Godwin, Bharati Mukherjee, Charles Wright, W. D. Snodgrass, Richard Stern, Marvin Bell, Robert Bly, and other Workshop faculty and graduates concerning their experiences at Iowa during Paul Engle's twenty-four-year tenure as director.

Both books agree that George Cook's 1896 "Verse Making" class and, later, Clark Fisher Ansley's course on the short story form led to Edwin Piper's "Poetics" class, which served as the prototype for Workshop. That is, Piper created a class in which students' works were discussed critically. This method mandated a return to the study of classical rhetoric, a belief that literary craft could be learned. Piper, therefore, is in many ways the founder of the Workshop. In 1922, Piper and University of Iowa dean Carl Seashore convinced the graduate faculty to award graduate degree credit for creative work, rare among universities nationwide.

An essay published in a 1998 issue of *The Chronicle of Higher Education* by then-president of the University of Iowa Mary Sue Coleman explained that Iowa was in the position to "go out on a limb in establishing the writer's workshop to fill an unmet need" in higher education and the arts because of its status as a state school, unlike the more prestigious private universities such as Harvard and Yale, which had different reputations at stake. Harvard did make a minor move in the direction of accepting creative writing. Wendell Barrett proposed it as a way to enrich the study of literature. But by taking the risk first and continuing to capitalize on it, as Coleman points out, Iowa's "creative writing program became the model for university-sponsored workshops at public and private institutions all over the country."

In part, Edwin Piper, a staunch "Regionalist," began to teach creative writing as a reaction to what he perceived as East Coast elitism, an attitude he shared to a degree with the New Critics, who saw a return to southern agrarian roots as an antidote to twentieth-century industrialization.

This direction changed in 1931 when Norman Foerster, director of the School of Letters, convinced the administration to grant students submitting a creative dissertation a Ph.D., further separating Iowa from any other university in the country. Foerster diminished the "Regional" focus of the emerging writing program. He advocated the study of literature as a means of aiding the development of the writer. His efforts, while not always welcomed, ultimately gave the Writers' Workshop the beginnings of its autonomy. By the end of the 1930s, the university course catalogue listed the creative writing class for the first time as "Writers' Workshop," taught by Wilbur Schramm, who later became the Workshop's first official director. Schramm's workshops were informal, with only a handful of students meeting at his house whenever anyone had a piece of work ready for discussion. Still, the Workshop tradition of tearing apart one another's work began early, with Schramm urging the wide reading of literature for guidance.

Paul Engle received a master's degree in Creative Writing from Iowa during the 1930s. Engle, who won the Yale Series of Younger Poets Award in 1932 and was one of the most influential poets of his time, would later go on to develop Foerster's ambitions for the Workshop. Indeed, founder of *Best American Short Stories* Edward J. O'Brien claimed that Engle set the path for the development of American literature for the middle of the century. O'Brien and Engle met in 1934, a year after Engle's landmark poem "America Remembers" appeared in *Poetry*. O'Brien told him that his poem expressed exactly what the American "short story has been doing to interpret American consciousness."

It's of little surprise, then, that Engle's Iowa Workshop and O'Brien's *Best American* anthology shared a similar vision for literature. *Midland*, a journal established in Iowa City in 1914, was noted by O'Brien in the very first introduction to *Best American Short Stories* in 1915 as containing "the most vital interpretation in fiction of our national life."

Like Engle and Wilbur Schramm, O'Brien worked selflessly on behalf of the American short story, which he felt had "developed as an art form to the point where it may fairly claim a sustained superiority, as different in kind as in quality from the tale or *conte* of other literatures." He proselytized against the slick commercial story, charging that "the tremendous advertising development of the American magazine has bound American literature in the chains of commercialism." Between 1915 and 1929, O'Brien noted that short story writers such as Sherwood Anderson and Ernest Hemingway revolted against the popular style by writing stories that shaped life "into the most beautiful and satisfying form, by skillful selection and arrangement of his material." Stories in which one feels "the striving of a nation to express itself, and thereby to come to a knowledge of its own character." And the change was not merely an aesthetic one but a political one, for the novels of Dreiser and, shortly afterward, Steinbeck and Richard Wright used literature as a form of protest against economic and racial injustices in American life.

By 1930, O'Brien believed that Boston and New York were no longer the "geographical centers of American literary life," Iowa City was. Articles, however, began to replace short stories in magazines with wide circulations. O'Brien's 1915 *Best American* anthology contains a ninety-eight-page list of titles from stories published that year alone. Fifteen years later, all of the stories published in the first issue of *Story* had been rejected by commercial outlets. O'Brien reprinted three of them in *Best American* 1931, believing that "America has found its most characteristic form of expression in the short story . . . The most faithful reflection we have of the American soul and American life."

Like Paul Engle, Wallace Stegner received his master's degree in Creative Writing from Iowa in the 1930s. He also believed deeply that a writer's work was linked to his sense of place. Stegner was born in Iowa, but his later work encompassed the American West, where he ultimately made his home. Resolutely "Regional" in the best sense of the word, that is, writing about the specifics of place in a manner that engaged the rest of the world, Stegner published an enormous body of work. He published six books in the 1930s alone, including *Remembering Laughter,* for which he won the Little, Brown Novelette Prize. In 1971 he won the Pulitzer Prize for his novel *Angle of Repose.*

"CHIP OFF THE OLD BLOCK" is a classic rite-of-passage story, originally published in the *Virginia Quarterly Review,* a sure signal that the so-called little magazines had begun publishing the best fiction in the United States. The story is set in Montana during the flu epidemic of 1918, a time when schoolhouses doubled as emergency hospitals and selling liquor was a family's only means of earning money. Its style is pure American realism, a style that would dominate much of the literature produced by writers who followed.

TOM GRIMES

WALLACE STEGNER

Chip Off the Old Block

SITTING ALONE LOOKING at the red eyes of the parlor heater, Chet thought how fast things happened. One day the flu hit. Two days after that his father left for Montana to get a load of whisky to sell for medicine. The next night he got back in the midst of a blizzard with his hands and feet frozen, bringing a sick homesteader he had picked up on the road; and now this morning all of them, the homesteader, his father, his mother, his brother Bruce, were loaded in a sled and hauled to the schoolhouse-hospital. It was scary how fast they all got it, even his father, who seldom got anything and was tougher than boiled owl. Everybody, he thought with some pride, but him. His mother's words as she left were a solemn burden on his mind. "You'll have to hold the fort, Chet. You'll have to be the man of the house." And his father, sweat on his face even in the cold, his frozen hands held tenderly in his lap, saying, "Better let the whisky alone. Put it away somewhere till we get back."

So he was holding the fort. He accepted the duty soberly. In the two hours since his family had left he had swept the floors, milked old Red and thrown down hay for her, brought in scuttles of lignite. And sitting now in the parlor he knew he was scared. He heard the walls tick and the floors creak. Every thirty seconds he looked up from his book, and finally he yawned, stretched, laid the book down, and took a stroll through the whole house, cellar to upstairs, as if for exercise. But his eyes were sharp, and he stepped back a little as he threw open the doors of bedrooms and closets. He whistled a little between his teeth and looked at the calendar in the hall to see what day it was. November 4, 1918.

A knock on the back door sent him running. It was the young man named Vickers who had taken his family away. He was after beds and blankets for the schoolhouse. Chet helped him knock the beds down and load them on the sled. He would sleep on the couch in the parlor; it was warmer there, anyway; no cold floors to worry about.

In the kitchen, making a list of things he had taken, Vickers saw the keg, the sacked cases of bottles, the pile of whisky-soaked straw sheaths from the bottles that had been broken on the trip. "Your dad doesn't want to sell any of that, does he?" he said.

Chet thought briefly of his father's injunction to put the stuff away. But gee, the old man had frozen his hands and feet and caught the flu getting it, and now when people came around asking. . . . "Sure," he said. "That's what he bought it for, flu medicine."

"What've you got?"

"Rye and bourbon," Chet said. "There's some Irish, but I think he brought that special for somebody." He rummaged among the sacks. "Four dollars a bottle, I think it is," he said, and looked at Vickers to see if that was too much. Vickers didn't blink. "Or is it four-fifty?" Chet said.

Vickers's face was expressionless. "Sure it isn't five? I wouldn't want to cheat you." He took out his wallet, and under his eyes Chet retreated. "I'll go look," he said. "I think there's a list."

He stood in the front hall for a minute or two before he came back. "Four-fifty," he said casually. "I thought probably it was."

Vickers counted out twenty-seven dollars. "Give me six rye," he said. With the sack in his hand he stood in the back door and looked at Chet and laughed. "What are you going to do with that extra three dollars?"

Chet felt his heart stop while he might have counted ten. His face began to burn. "What three dollars?"

"Never mind," Vickers said. "I was just ragging you. Got all you need to eat here?"

"I got crocks of milk," Chet said. He grinned at Vickers in relief, and Vickers grinned back. "There's bread Ma baked the other day, and spuds. If I need any meat I can go shoot a rabbit."

"Oh." Vickers's eyebrows went up. "You're a hunter, eh?"

"I shot rabbits all last fall for Mrs. Rieger," Chet said. "She's 'nemic and has to eat rabbits and prairie chickens and stuff. She lent me the shotgun and bought the shells."

"Mmm," Vickers said. "I guess you can take care of yourself. How old are you?"

"Twelve."

"That's old enough," said Vickers. "That's pretty old, in fact. Well, Mervin, if you need anything you call the school and I'll see that you get it."

"My name isn't Mervin," Chet said. "It's Chet."

"Okay," Vickers said. "Don't get careless with the fires."

"What do you think I am?" Chet said in scorn. He raised his hand stiffly as Vickers went out. A little tongue of triumph licked up in him. That three bucks would look all right, all right. Next time he'd know better than to change the price, too. He took the bills out of his pocket and counted them. Twenty-seven dollars was a lot of dough. He'd show Ma and Pa whether he could hold the fort or not.

But holding the fort was tiresome. By two o'clock he was bored stiff, and the floors were creaking again in the silence. Then he remembered suddenly that he was the boss of the place. He could go or come as he pleased, as long as the cow was milked and the house kept warm. He thought of the two traps he had set in muskrat holes under the river bank. The blizzard and the flu had made him forget to see to them. And he might take Pa's gun and do a little hunting.

"Well," he said in the middle of the parlor rug, "I guess I will."

For an hour and a half he prowled the river brush. Over on the path toward Heathcliff's he shot a snowshoe rabbit, and the second of his traps yielded a stiffly frozen muskrat. The weight of his game was a solid satisfaction as he came up the dugway swinging the rabbit by its feet, the muskrat by its plated tail.

Coming up past the barn, he looked over toward Van Dam's, then the other way, toward Chapman's, half hoping that someone might be out, and see him. He whistled loudly, sang a little into the cold afternoon air, but the desertion of the whole street, the unbroken fields of snow where ordinarily there would have been dozens of sled tracks and fox-and-goose paths, let a chill in upon his pride. He came up the back steps soberly and opened the door.

The muskrat's slippery tail slid out of his mitten and the frozen body thumped on the floor. Chet opened his mouth, shut it again, speechless with surprise and shock. Two men were in the kitchen. His eyes jumped from the one by the whisky keg to the other, sitting at the table drinking whisky from a cup. The one drinking he didn't know. The other was Louis Treat, a halfbreed who hung out down at the stable and sometimes worked a little for the Half-Diamond Bar. All Chet knew about him was that he could braid horsehair ropes and sing a lot of dirty songs.

"Aha!" said Louis Treat. He smiled at Chet and made a rubbing motion with his hands. "We 'ave stop to get warm. You 'ave been hunting?"

"Yuh," Chet said automatically. He stood where he was, his eyes swinging between the two men. The man at the table raised his eyebrows at Louis Treat.

"Ees nice rabbit there," Louis said. His bright black button eyes went over the boy. Chet lifted the rabbit and looked at the frozen beads of blood on the white fur. "Yuh," he said. He was thinking about what his father always said. You could trust an Indian, if he was your friend, and you could trust a white man sometimes, if money wasn't involved, and you could trust a Chink more than either, but you couldn't trust a halfbreed.

Louis's voice went on, caressingly. "You 'ave mushrat too, eh? You lak me to 'elp you peel thees mushrat?" His hand, dipping under the sheepskin and into his pants pocket, produced a long-bladed knife that jumped open with the pressure of his thumb on a button.

Chet dropped the rabbit and took off his mitts. "No thanks," he said. "I can peel him."

Shrugging, Louis put the knife away. He turned to thump the bung hard into the keg, and nodded at the other man, who rose. "Ees tam we go," Louis said. "We 'ave been told to breeng thees wisky to the 'ospital."

"Who told you?" Chet's insides grew tight, and his mind was setting like plaster of Paris. If Pa was here he'd scatter these thieves all the way to Chapman's. But Pa wasn't here. He watched Louis Treat. You could never trust a halfbreed.

"The doctor, O'Malley," Louis said. Keeping his eye on Chet, he jerked his head at the other man. "'Ere, you tak' the other end."

His companion, pulling up his sheepskin collar, stooped and took hold of the keg. Chet, with no blood in his face and no breath in his lungs, hesitated a split second and then jumped. Around the table, in the dining room door, he was out of their reach, and the shotgun was pointed straight at their chests. With his thumb he cocked both barrels, click, click.

Louis Treat swore. "Put down that gun!"

"No, sir!" Chet said. "I won't put it down till you drop that keg and get out of here!"

The two men looked at each other. Louis set his end gently back on the chair, and the other did the same. "We 'ave been sent," Louis said. "You do not understan' w'at I mean."

"I understand all right," Chet said. "If Doctor O'Malley had wanted that, he'd've sent Mr. Vickers for it this morning."

The second man ran his tongue over his teeth and spat on the floor. "Think he knows how to shoot that thing?"

Chet's chest expanded. The gun trembled so that he braced it against the frame of the door. "I shot that rabbit, didn't I?" he said.

The halfbreed's teeth were bared in a bitter grin. "You are a fool," he said.

"And you're a thief!" Chet said. He covered the two carefully as they backed out; and when they were down the steps he slammed and bolted the door. Then he raced for the front hall, made sure that door was locked, and peeked out the front window. The two were walking side by side up the irrigation ditch toward town, pulling an empty box sled. Louis was talking furiously with his hands.

Slowly and carefully Chet uncocked the gun. Ordinarily he would have unloaded, but not now, not with thieves like those around. He put the gun above the mantel, looked in the door of the stove, threw in a half-scuttle of lignite, went to the window again to see if he could still see the two men. Then he looked at his hands. They were shaking. So were his knees. He sat down suddenly on the couch, unable to stand.

FOR DAYS the only people he saw were those who came to buy whisky. They generally sat a while in the kitchen and talked about the flu and the war, but they weren't much company. Once Miss Landis, his schoolteacher, came apologetically and furtively with a two-quart fruit jar under her coat, and he charged her four dollars a quart for bulk rye out of the keg. His secret hoard of money mounted to eighty-five dollars, to a hundred and eight.

When there was none of that business (he had even forgotten by now that his father had told him not to meddle with it), he moped around the house, milked the cow, telephoned to the hospital to see how his folks were. One day his dad was pretty sick. Two days later he was better, but his mother had had a relapse because they were so short of beds they had had to put Brucie in with her. The milk crocks piled up in the cellarway, staying miraculously sweet, until he told the schoolhouse nurse over the phone about all the milk he had, and then Doctor O'Malley sent down old Gundar Moe to pick it up for the sick people.

Sometimes he stood on the porch on sunny, cold mornings and watched Lars Poulsen's sled go out along the road on the way to the graveyard, and the thought that maybe Mom or Bruce or Pa might die and be buried out there on the knoll by the sandhills made him swallow and go back inside where he couldn't see how deserted the street looked, and where he couldn't see the sled and the steaming gray horses move out toward the south bend of the river. He resolved to be a son his parents could be proud of, and sat down at the piano determined to learn a piece letter-perfect. But the dry silence of the house weighed on him; before long he would be lying with his forehead on the keyboard, his finger picking on one monotonous note. That way he could concentrate on how different it sounded with his head down, and forget to be afraid.

And at night, when he lay on the couch and stared into the sleepy red eyes of the heater, he heard noises that walked the house, and there were crosses in the lamp chimneys when he lighted them, and he knew that someone would die.

On the fifth day he sat down at the dining room table determined to write a book. In an old atlas he hunted up a promising locale. He found a tributary of the Amazon called the Tapajos, and firmly, his lips together in concentration, he wrote his title across the top of a school tablet: "The Curse of the Tapajos." All that afternoon he wrote enthusiastically. He created a tall, handsome young explorer and a halfbreed guide obscurely like Louis Treat. He plowed through steaming jungles, he wrestled pythons and other giant serpents which he spelled "boy constructors." All this time he was looking for the Lost City of Gold. And when the snakes got too thick even for his taste, and when he was beginning to wonder himself why the explorer didn't shoot the guide, who was constantly trying to poison the flour or stab his employer in his tent at midnight, he let the party come out on a broad pampa and see in the distance, crowning a golden hill, the lost city for which they searched. And then suddenly the explorer reeled and fell, mysteriously stricken, and the halfbreed guide, smiling with sinister satisfaction, disappeared quietly into the jungle. The curse of the Tapajos, which struck everyone who found that lost city, had struck again. But the young hero was not dead. . . .

Chet gnawed his pencil and stared across the room. It was going to be hard to figure out how his hero escaped. Maybe he was just stunned, not killed. Maybe a girl could find him there, and nurse him back to health. . . .

He rose, thinking, and wandered over to the window. A sled came across the irrigation ditch and pulled on over to Chance's house. Out of it got Mr. Chance and Mrs. Chance and Ed and Harvey Chance. They were well, then. People were starting to come home cured. He rushed to the telephone and called the hospital. No, the nurse said, his family weren't well yet; they wouldn't be home for three or four days at least. But they were all better. How was he doing? Did he need anything?

No, Chet said, he didn't need anything.

But at least he wasn't the only person on the street any more. That night after milking he took a syrup pail of milk to the Chances. They were all weak, all smiling. Mrs. Chance cried every time she spoke, and they were awfully grateful for the milk. He promised them, over their protests, that he would bring them some every day, and chop wood and haul water for them until they got really strong. Mr. Chance, who had the nickname of Dictionary because he strung off such jaw-breaking words, told him he was a benefactor and a Samaritan, and called upon his own sons to witness this neighborly kindness and be edified and enlarged. Chet went home in the dark, wondering if it might not be a good idea, later in his book somewhere, to have his explorer find a bunch of people, or maybe just a beautiful and ragged girl, kept in durance vile by some tribe of pygmies or spider men or something, and have him rescue them and confound their captors.

ON THE AFTERNOON OF THE EIGHTH DAY Chet sat in the kitchen at Chance's. His own house had got heavier and heavier to bear, and there wasn't much to eat there but milk and potatoes, and both stores were closed because of the flu. So he went a good deal to Chance's, doing their chores and talking about the hospital, and listening to Mr. Chance tell about the Death Ward where they put people who weren't going to get well. The Death Ward was the eighth-grade room, his own room, and he and Ed Chance speculated on what it would be like to go back to that room where so many people had died—Mrs. Rieger, and old Gypsy Davy from Poverty Flat, and John Chapman, and a lot of people. Mrs. Chance sat by the stove and when anyone looked at her or spoke to her she shook her head and smiled and the tears ran down. She didn't seem unhappy about anything; she just couldn't help crying.

Mr. Chance said over and over that there was certainly going to be a multitude of familiar faces missing after this thing was over. The town would never be the same. He wouldn't be surprised if the destitute and friendless were found in every home in town, adopted and cared for by friends. They might have to build an institution to house the derelict and the bereaved.

He pulled his sagging cheeks and said to Chet, "Mark my words, son, you are one of the fortunate. In that hospital I said to myself a dozen times, 'Those poor Mason boys are going to lose their father.' I lay there—myself in pain, mind you— and the first thing I'd hear some old and valued friend would be moved into the Death Ward. I thought your father was a goner when they moved him in."

Chet's throat was suddenly dry as dust. "Pa isn't in there!"

"Ira," said Mrs. Chance, and shook her head and smiled and wiped the tears away. "Now you've got the child all worked up."

"He isn't in there now," said Mr. Chance. "By the grace of the Almighty—" he bent his head and his lips moved, "he came out again. He's a hard man to kill. Hands and feet frozen, double pneumonia, and still he came out."

"Is he all right now?" Chet said.

"Convalescing," Mr. Chance said. "Convalescing beautifully." He raised a finger under Chet's nose. "Some people are just hard to kill. But on the other hand, you take a person like that George Valet. I hesitate to say before the young what went on in that ward. Shameful, even though the man was sick." His tongue ticked against his teeth, and his eyebrows raised at Chet. "They cleaned his bed six times a day," he said, and pressed his lips together. "It makes a man wonder about God's wisdom," he said. "A man like that, his morals are as loose as his bowels."

"Ira!" Mrs. Chance said.

"I would offer you a wager," Mr. Chance said. "I wager that a man as loose and discombobulated as that doesn't live through this epidemic."

"I wouldn't bet on a person's life that way," she said.

"Ma," Harvey called from the next room, where he was lying down. "What's all the noise about?"

They stopped talking and listened. The church bell was ringing madly. In a minute the bell in the firehouse joined it. The heavy bellow of a shotgun, both barrels, rolled over the snowflats between their street and the main part of town. A six-shooter went off, bang-bang-bang-bang-bang-bang, and there was the sound of distant yelling.

"Fire?" Mr. Chance said, stooping to the window.

"Here comes somebody," Ed said. The figure of a boy was streaking across the flat. Mr. Chance opened the door and shouted at him. The boy ran closer, yelling something unintelligible. It was Spot Orullian.

"What?" Mr. Chance yelled.

Spot cupped his hands to his mouth, standing in the road in front of Chet's as if unwilling to waste a moment's time. "War's over!" he shouted, and wheeled and was gone up the street toward Van Dam's.

Mr. Chance closed the door slowly. Mrs. Chance looked at him, and her lips jutted and trembled, her weak eyes ran over with tears, and she fell into his arms. The three boys, not quite sure how one acted when a war ended, but knowing it called for celebration, stood around uneasily. They shot furtive grins at one another, looked with furrowed brows at Mrs. Chance's shaking back.

"Now Uncle Joe can come home," Ed said. "That's what she's bawling about."

Chet bolted out the door, raced over to his own house, pulled the loaded shotgun from the mantel, and burst out into the yard again. He blew the lid off the silence in their end of town, and followed the shooting with a wild yell. Ed and Harvey, leaning out their windows, answered him, and the heavy boom-boom of a shotgun came from the downtown district.

Carrying the gun, Chet went back to Chance's. He felt grown up, a householder. The end of the war had to be celebrated; neighbors had to get together and raise Cain. He watched Mrs. Chance, still incoherent, rush to the calendar and put a circle around the date, November 11. "I don't ever want to forget what day it happened on," she said.

"Everyone in the world will remember this day," said Mr. Chance, solemnly, like a preacher. Chet looked at him, his mind clicking.

"Mr. Chance," he said, "would you like a drink, to celebrate?"

Mr. Chance looked startled. "What?"

"Pa's got some whisky. He'd throw a big party if he was home."

"I don't think we should," said Mrs. Chance dubiously. "Your father might . . ."

"Oh, Mama," Mr. Chance said, and laid his arm across her back like a log. "One bumper to honor the day. One leetle stirrup-cup to those boys of the Allies. Chester here is carrying on his father's tradition like a man." He bowed and shook Chet's hand formally. "We'd be delighted, sir," he said, and they all laughed

SOMEHOW, NOBODY knew just how, the party achieved proportions. Mr. Chance suggested, after one drink, that it would be pleasant to have a neighbor or two, snatched from the terrors of the plague, come and join in the thanksgiving; and Chet, full of hospitality, said sure, that would be a keen idea. So Mr. Chance called Jewel King, and when Jewel came he brought Chubby Klein with him, and a few minutes later three more came, knocked, looked in to see the gathering with cups in their hands, and came in with alacrity when Chet held the door wide. Within an hour there were eight men, three women, and the two Chance boys, besides Chet. Mr. Chance wouldn't let the boys have any whisky, but Chet, playing bartender, sneaked a cup into the dining room and all sipped it and smacked their lips.

"Hey, look, I'm drunk," Harvey said. He staggered, hiccoughed, caught himself, bowed low and apologized, staggered again. "Hic," he said. "I had a drop too much." The three laughed together secretly while loud voices went up in the kitchen.

"Gentlemen," Mr. Chance was saying, "I give you those heroic laddies in khaki who looked undaunted into the eyes of death and saved this ga-lorious empire from the rapacious Huns."

"Yay!" the others said, banging cups on the table. "Give her the other barrel, Dictionary."

"I crave your indulgence for a moment," Mr. Chance said. "For one leetle moment, while I imbibe a few swallows of this delectable amber fluid."

The noise went up and up. Chet went among them stiff with pride at having done all this, at being accepted here as host, at having men pat him on the back and shake his hand and tell him, "You're all right, kid, you're a chip off the old block. What's the word from the folks?" He guggled liquor out of the sloshing cask into a milk crock, and the men dipped largely and frequently. About four o'clock, two more families arrived and were welcomed with roars. People bulged the big kitchen; their laughter rattled the window frames. Occasionally Dictionary Chance rose to propose a toast to "those gems of purest ray serene, those unfailing companions on life's bitter pilgrimage, the ladies, God bless 'em!" Every so often he suggested that it might be an idea worth serious consideration that some liquid refreshments be decanted from the aperture in the receptacle.

The more liquid refreshments Chet decanted from the aperture in the receptacle, the louder and more eloquent Mr. Chance became. He dominated the kitchen like an evangelist. He swung and swayed and stamped, he led a rendition of "God Save the King," he thundered denunciations on the Beast of Berlin, he thrust a large fist into the lapels of new arrivals and demanded detailed news of the war's end. Nobody knew more than that it was over.

But Dictionary didn't forget to be grateful, either. At least five times during the afternoon he caught Chet up in a long arm and publicly blessed him. Once he rose and cleared his throat for silence. Chubby Klein and Jewel King booed and hissed, but he bore their insults with dignity. "Siddown!" they said. "Speech!" said others. Mr. Chance waved his hands abroad, begging for quiet. Finally they gave it to him, snickering.

"Ladies and gen'lemen," he said, "we have come together on this auspicious occasion . . ."

"What's suspicious about it?" Jewel King said.

". . . on this auspicious occasion, to do honor to our boys in Flanders' fields, to celebrate the passing of the dread incubus of Spanish influenza . . ."

"Siddown!" said Chubby Klein.

". . . and last, but not least, we are gathered here to honor our friendship with the owners of this good and hospitable house, Bo Mason and Sis, may their lives be long and strewn with flowers, and this noble scion of a noble stock, this tender youth who kept the home fires burning through shock and shell and who opened his house and his keg to us as his father would have done. Ladies and gen'lemen, the Right Honorable Chester Mason, may he live to bung many a barrel."

Embarrassed and squirming and unsure of what to do with so many faces laughing at him, so many mouths cheering him, Chet crowded into the dining room door and tried to act casual, tried to pretend he didn't feel proud and excited and a man among men. And while he stood there with the noise beating at him in raucous approbation, the back door opened and the utterly flabbergasted face of his father looked in.

There was a moment of complete silence. Voices dropped away to nothing, cups hung at lips. Then in a concerted rush they were helping Bo Mason in. He limped heavily on bandaged and slippered feet, his hands wrapped in gauze, his face drawn and hollow-eyed and noticeably thinner than it had been ten days ago. After him came Chet's mother, half-carrying Bruce, and staggering under his weight. Hands took Bruce away from her, sat him on the open oven door, and led her to a chair.

All three of them, hospital-pale, rested and looked around the room. And Chet's father did not look pleased.

"What the devil is this?" he said.

From his station in the doorway Chet squeaked, "The war's over!"

"I know the war's over, but what's this?" He jerked a bandaged hand at the uncomfortable ring of people. Chet swallowed and looked at Dictionary Chance.

Dictionary's suspended talents came back to him. He strode to lay a friendly hand on his host's back; he swung and shook his hostess's hand; he twinkled at the white-faced, big-eyed Bruce on the oven door.

"This, sir," he boomed, "is a welcoming committee of your friends and neighbors, met here to rejoice over your escape from the dread sickness which has swept to untimely death so many of our good friends, God rest their souls! On the invitation of your manly young son here we have been celebrating not only that emancipation, but the emancipation of the entire world from the dread plague of war." With the cup in his hand he bent and twinkled at Bo Mason. "How's it feel to get back, old hoss?"

Bo grunted. He looked across at his wife and laughed a short, choppy laugh. The way his eyes came around and rested on Chet made Chet stop breathing. But his father's voice was hearty enough when it came. "You got a snootful," he said. "Looks like you've all got a snootful."

"Sir," said Dictionary Chance, "I haven't had such a delightful snootful since the misguided government of this province suspended the God-given right of its free people to purchase and imbibe and ingest intoxicating beverages."

He drained his cup and set it on the table. "And now," he said, "it is clear that our hosts are not completely recovered in their strength. I suggest that we do whatever small jobs our ingenuity and gratitude can suggest, and silently steal away."

"Yeah," the others said. "Sure. Sure thing." They brought in the one bed from the sled and set it up, swooped together blankets and mattresses and turned them over to the women. Before the beds were made people began to leave. Dictionary Chance, voluble to the last, stopped to praise the excellent medicinal waters he had imbibed, and to say a word for Chet, before Mrs. Chance, with a quick pleading smile, led him away. The door had not even closed before Chet felt his father's cold eye on him.

"All right," his father said. "Will you please tell me why in the name of Christ you invited that God damned windbag and all the rest of those sponges over here to drink up my whisky?"

Chet stood sullenly in the door, boiling with sulky resentment. He had held the fort, milked the cow, kept the house, sold all that whisky for all it was worth, run Louis Treat and the other man out with a gun. Everybody else praised him, but you could depend on Pa to think more of that whisky the neighbors had drunk than of anything else. He wasn't going to explain or defend himself. If the old man was going to be that stingy, he could take a flying leap in the river.

"The war was over," he said. "I asked them over to celebrate."

His father's head wagged. He looked incredulous and at his wits' end. "You asked them over!" he said. "You said, 'Come right on over and drink up all the whisky my dad almost killed himself bringing in.' " He stuck his bandaged hands out. "Do you think I got these and damned near died in that hospital just to let a bunch of blotters . . . Why, God damn you," he said. "Leave the house for ten days, tell you exactly what to do, and by Jesus everything goes wrong. How long have they been here?"

"Since about two."

"How much did they drink?"

"I don't know. Three crocks full, I guess."

His father's head weaved back and forth, he looked at his wife and then at the ceiling. "Three crocks. At least a gallon, twelve dollars' worth. Oh Jesus Christ, if you had the sense of a piss-ant . . ."

Laboriously, swearing with the pain, he hobbled to the keg. When he put his hand down to shake it, his whole body stiffened.

"It's half empty!" he said. He swung on Chet, and Chet met his furious look. Now! his mind said. Now let him say I didn't hold the fort.

"I sold some," he said, and held his father's eyes for a minute before he marched out stiff-backed into the living room, dug the wad of bills from the vase on the mantel, and came back. He laid the money in his father's hand. "I sold a hundred and twenty-four dollars' worth," he said.

The muscles in his father's jaw moved. He glanced at Chet's mother, let the breath out hard through his nose. "So you've been selling whisky," he said. "I thought I told you to leave that alone?"

"People wanted it for medicine," Chet said. "Should I've let them die with the flu? They came here wanting to buy it and I sold it. I thought that was what it was for."

The triumph that had been growing in him ever since he went for the money was hot in his blood now. He saw the uncertainty in his father's face, and he almost beat down his father's eyes.

"I suppose," his father said finally, "you sold it for a dollar a bottle, or something."

"I sold it for plenty," Chet said. "Four-fifty for bottles and four for quarts out of the keg. That's more than you were going to get, because I heard you tell Ma."

His father sat down on the chair and fingered the bills, looking at him. "You didn't have any business selling anything," he said. "And then you overcharge people."

"Yeah!" Chet said, defying him now. "If it hadn't been for me there wouldn't 'ave been any to sell. Louis Treat and another man came and tried to steal that whole keg, and I run 'em out with a shotgun."

"What?" his mother said.

"I did!" Chet said. "I made 'em put it down and get out."

Standing in the doorway still facing his father, he felt the tears hot in his eyes and was furious at himself for crying. He hoped his father would try thrashing him. He just hoped he would. He wouldn't make a sound; he'd grit his teeth and show him whether he was man enough to stand it. . . . He looked at his father's gray expressionless face and shouted, "I wish I'd let them take it! I just wish I had!"

And suddenly his father was laughing. He reared back in the chair and threw back his head and roared, his bandaged hands held tenderly before him like helpless paws. He stopped, caught his breath, looked at Chet again, and shook with a deep internal rumbling. "Okay," he said. "Okay, kid. You're a man. I wouldn't take it away from you."

"Well, there's no need to laugh," Chet said. "I don't see anything to laugh about."

He watched his father twist in the chair and look at his mother. "Look at him," his father said. "By God, he'd eat me if I made a pass at him."

"Well, don't laugh!" Chet said. He turned and went into the living room, where he sat on the couch and looked at his hands the way he had when Louis Treat and the other man were walking up the ditch. His hands were trembling, the same way. But there was no need to laugh, any more than there was need to get sore over a little whisky given to the neighbors.

His mother came in and sat down beside him, laid a hand on his head. "Don't be mad at Pa," she said. "He didn't understand. He's proud of you. We all are."

"Yeah?" said Chet. "Why doesn't *he* come and tell me that?"

His mother's smile was gentle and a little amused. "Because he's ashamed of himself for losing his temper, I suppose," she said. "He never did know how to admit he was wrong."

Chet set his jaw and looked at the shotgun above the mantel. He guessed he had looked pretty tough himself when he had the drop on Louis Treat and his thieving friend. He stiffened his shoulders under his mother's arm. "Just let him start anything," he said. "Just let him try to get hard."

His mother's smile broadened, but he glowered at her. "And there's no need to laugh!" he said.

1940s

TODAY, WHEN TENURED PROFESSORS are seemingly so removed from the grit and tussle of the world beyond the university's walls, it is amazing to consider that the Workshop's first director, Wilbur Schramm, requested a leave of absence in 1942 to assist in the country's war effort. By all accounts a modest man dedicated to advancing the study of creative writing and to bringing practicing writers into the university in order to enrich university life, he emphasized studying the work of other writers in his workshops, as well as New Critical attention to language and close reading. When Schramm returned from the service, he officially turned over the direction of the Workshop to the hands of interim director Paul Engle, who would remain director for twenty-four years.

Engle transformed the Workshop into a unique, national literary center, largely through his belief that only publishing writers should teach workshop. His ambition won him praise as well as enemies. But, as he once said, "You do not create new programs without driving hard and if you drive hard you're going to irritate people. Quiet people don't offend." Engle clearly stated his vision of the Workshop in a volume of Workshop writing published under the title *Midland, an Anthology of Poetry and Prose* some years later. "We do not pretend to have produced the writers included in this book. Their talent was inevitably shaped by the genes rattling in the ancestral closets. We did give them a community in which to try out the quality of their gift."

Following Iowa's example, universities around the country soon began to include writers as faculty members. This movement of writers into the academy was, in part, the result of historical forces. By the early 1940s, the formerly well-paying market for short stories was in decline. The plotted, gimmicky story popularized by O'Henry lost favor in both the commercial and critical arenas. So-called little magazines and literary journals sprang onto the scene, publishing short stories as "Art" rather than entertainment, but they paid little, if at all, hastening the movement of writers into the academy. But the growth of programs nationwide was slow, with only a hand-ful—the program initiated at Stanford University by Wallace Stegner being the most notable—in existence by the end of the decade.

On February 24, 1941, Edward O'Brien died at age fifty-one while serving as an air-raid warden in England. Martha Foley, editor of *Story*, took over his editorship of *The Best American Short Stories*. Like O'Brien, she discovered that small magazines published the best stories, with the *New Yorker* also being noted for its increasingly distinguished fiction. She found that the war had actually increased readership. In 1946, more short stories were published in journals than ever before, a trend that, despite the poor and often nonexistent pay for them, continued throughout the decade, as did the style of "social realism" practiced by Steinbeck, Wright, the young Saul Bellow, Norman Mailer, and Nelson Algren. With the war and the Great Depression vivid memories, American writers continued to feel the need to produce politically engaged fiction, a trend that Algren would later claim creative writing programs stifled.

Foley recognized, as well, the effect of the GI Education bill. After the war, veterans enrolled at universities in record numbers, a phenomenon that accounted for the high percentage of men participating in the Workshop's early years. Among these young men was R. V. Cassill, himself an ex-GI, as well as the winner of an "Atlantic First" prize for one of his early short stories. His classmates included Flannery O'Connor, one of only three women in the Workshop in the late 1940s.

As different as the two are as writers, their work speaks to the vitality of form and artistry that Edward O'Brien envisioned as the supreme accomplishment of the emerging American short story. Cassill's story is a particularly acute study of literary reputation and yearning and, to my mind, as gorgeously written as *The Great Gatsby*. O'Connor offers her typically wicked reminders of the wages of virtue, as well as the downside of the puritanical streak that continues to run through the American character.

IN FACT AS I REMEMBER IT, there once was a poet and teacher of writing at the University of Iowa who had been a working cowboy in his earlier life, and who at the time he was my teacher had achieved a modest reputation as a Regionalist when that was still a barely decent thing to be. He had published at least two volumes of poetry that had been well reviewed at the time of their publication.

But the tide was running out on Regionalism in those years when I knew him, and he made up for its ebbing and his nonglamorous scholarship by a personal decency so heroic that it overshadowed possible scorn for his craft and literary themes. What he brought to his classes was a transcendent goodness so lofty that it soared over the ambitions he expected us to aspire to. I thought, when I thought of him later, as a man whose sufficient talent lay in this superlative vision of what literature might encompass. His name was Edwin Ford Piper. It is a name that, I suppose, has long disappeared from literary anthologies. In my story I have given him another name and a modestly resurrected renown. Alms and laurels for oblivion.

As I still picture him, he had a mane of pure white hair and a golden glitter to eyes that had been sharpened on western prairies. He was exquisitely tolerant of bullshit but he made you—how shall I say it?—ashamed to offer it in his class. When I learned to read Tolstoy I felt I knew who had taught me how.

But my story is not about the loftiness of my teacher, though his clear spirit informs it. It contains as well some bits of bone-chilling narrative I got from Florence Gould, who struggled with the poisonous young married couple in a class she taught at the University of Washington long ago, and from golden friends I had in classes I took from Piper and his peers, from ruthless competitors in universities here and there, and in a multitude of their kind I have invented in my novel *Clem Anderson* and from my own reflections from a long career.

I no longer know where I got the flashing old man's dance that ends the action here. All I know is that I stole it from some poet or other. Yeats? Thomas? I am only sure I stole it and it is mine. And what I stole from Florence Gould is mine. And what I stole from Mr. Piper is mine as well.

R. V. CASSILL

R . V . C A S S I L L

And in My Heart

THEY CAME ACROSS like a flood when the traffic light changed, the girls in sweaters with books shelved in their folded arms and the wind fiddling with their hair, the young men in shirtsleeves or field jackets, bareheaded or wearing canvas hats. Toward the time when the campanile bell would ring two o'clock they had loitered out as couples or little groups from restaurants and rooming houses until they jammed the corner opposite the campus with a nearly amorphous concentration of movement. Except for linked arms here and there and a few couples holding hands, the bodies in the crowd did not quite touch. Nevertheless, when the light turned green, they moved as a single mass and carried Orin Corrigan with them over to the diverging campus walks.

A girl in a plaid skirt shouldered into him, looked up with innocent, hard eyes. After she had reasoned that such an old man must be a professor, she said, "Par me." Then she trotted ahead of him as if she counted on pure hurry to bring her up with friends sooner or later.

Corrigan took the same walk as she and watched the distance between them increasing. He saw her fat little hips work comically under the plaid until she was screened from sight by a crossing flow of students. I wasn't really laughing at her, he thought, turning right to avoid the crowd—nor at any of their genitive fashions. He was laughing because to his eye all this had never changed.

Once again the drying elm leaves and the autumnal brassiness of the sky kept a silence for him over the babble of the students surging toward their first classes. Under the changeless sky their rhythm and tone seemed exactly what it had been when he first came along this walk in 1921. He was a student himself then, but had been no more a part of them than he was now. Then he was, if you please, a cowboy from western Nebraska who had never been farther from home than Fort Riley, where he served a short hitch in the cavalry. He had come to the university with a new black suit from Denver wrapped in paper at the bottom of his suitcase, wearing that same black suit nearly every day through his first three years. He had worn it on this very sidewalk, his hands hanging raw and big and awkward from the sleeves like the token burdens of his separation from the others. He was older than they, even then, almost thirty when he enrolled as a freshman here. He was also taller than most and had the habit of walking with his head thrown back a little—partly from shyness, partly to catch the air and the overhead sights, and partly because it had seemed a poetic stance.

His unaltered habit of alertness let him hear and see—no clearer after all these years of expectancy—the murmured harmony the unknown students made with such a day. The emotional part of his imagination transposed it to an entity crowded with wings and horns that blew the failing seasonal magic, the dignity of youth, and the dignity of their faithful ignorance as it clattered on under such a sky.

Well, well, well—he had caught this much of meaning before, many times. He had come to the university first because he caught—like a tall snowman catching snowballs in the face—many things which beat up his emotions and which he meant to write out as poetry. And when you came right down to it, he had stayed too long because he had never quite managed to find the verbal shapes for what he knew. There had been no failure of initial vision, he thought soberly, but a failure of language, a failure to convert. The passage of thirty-odd years had clarified and then accommodated that failure.

Quite a lot of years ago he had published two volumes of verse—*Ranger Ballads* and *Days West*. Nice things had been said about the books when they were new. For a little while in the late twenties he had been a figure on the national literary scene. He was one of the "younger poets" compared rather favorably with Sandburg, Masters, and Lindsay. That was fine—worth what it was worth. His wife had been proud of his position, though by the time he had married Gail, his little bit of fame was already fading into the past. To the end of her life Gail believed that he had "contributed something" to American poetry, and he was glad she thought so. But for him the illusion that his published work mattered went with everything else.

It was not in his nature to be bitter about his failure. The effort to write had carried him high enough to see life better than if he had not tried. If there were no words of his own for *all this*, there was, like an armory open to him, poetry to borrow for the expression of his reverence. He might have "gone farther," as some of his colleagues said, if he had not learned here so awfully much of the poetry on the library shelves. He thought what he had learned worth the price of ambition. He had got what he needed most.

For two steps he limped as the shock of remembered words met the shock of his straining senses. "And in my heart how deep, unending ache of love . . ." For every detail of it all, he thought—for these kids, the weather, the disastrous neoclassic buildings of the main campus, the postprandial mellowness of his bowels. Armed with verse he could confront the mystery of the day without a shadow of dread.

A workman on top of Sedley Hall threw down a handful of leaves from a choked rain gutter. They fell separating and flashing yellow from the height of the building. A few struck among the vines on the wall and then tumbled after the others like a shower of notes from stringed instruments. "Beauty is momentary in the mind . . . but in the flesh it is immortal." Stevens's paradox might be a game of wit for some of his younger colleagues. As for himself, he believed it. Leaves fell and his good young wife was dead and their beauty for having been was immortal. What had been was the unchangeable and everlasting.

In truth—through the truth of poetry—what *had been* was enough for a man and left no room for anguish. He had lived close to despair when Gail died two years before. She had so much wanted not to die and she had gone before he had taught her that neither of them quite needed to be what she had always wanted and sometimes imagined them to be. "A little too soon," he had thought in a terrible sacrilegious rebellion against her death.

But finally he knew better. In the very incompleteness of life was its immortality— a tricky and worthless enough immortality without poetry to illuminate it, he sup- posed. But there *was* poetry, and in it the whole story was told, finished, rounded to completeness. The true aspiration was not to alter or add to it, but to rise through emulation to the point at which it could be grasped. That was all he must slyly teach his students. He must nudge them on to accept gladly the loss of the world.

HIS BEGINNING CLASS in writing was waiting for him in the room directly above his office. He knew two of the boys from the spring semester of his Chaucer class. Good boys, and he had seen some—well, uh—*promising* verse that each of them had done. The others were all strangers to him. The leavings from Moore Tyburn's class, he supposed. He had not gone to registration this year, but it did not require bitterness for him to believe that most of these—provided they were really serious about their work—would have preferred to leap right into Tyburn's advanced class and probably would be there if Tyburn had accepted them.

The girl sitting next to the door had the library's ancient red copy of *Days West* on the arm of her chair where he could not help seeing it. She bit decisively at her nails as he walked past her to his chair.

"Now then," he said, swinging his chair to face them and crossing his long legs. "I want to tell you how glad I am to have you with me this semester. I'm a little surprised, though, on a day like this that you would come to class. Perhaps I'm a little disappointed. Independent spirits ought to spend a day like this inviting their souls and confounding academic conformities."

The nail biter giggled and nodded to show that she was going to be fast on the uptake for his humor.

"Bu-ut, since you have accepted the yoke, here we are in what I want to be a very, very informal circle. We're here because we want to learn what we can about writing. Naturally I include myself when I say that. The university says I am your teacher. But you know how universities are. They like to set up chains of command, like the army, while literature is maybe not even a republic but an anarchy . . ."

The boy to his left, the Jewish boy in a field jacket and suntan pants, was watching him cynically through the fingers on which he rested his face. Obviously he was thinking, What a lot of horsehockey. Clearly this boy was one of Tyburn's rejects, doomed to miss—and to resent missing—Tyburn's incisive explications. Noting the boy's disrespect for what he had said, Corrigan liked him at once.

But he went on evenly with his familiar banalities. ". . . only eleven of us altogether, and we want to speak with perfect frankness with each other about our work. We'll take turns reading our work aloud in class. I've been working on some verses that I'd like to expose. And I hope we'll all put aside any feeling that an honest criticism of what we write is, ah, an equivalent of an assault on anyone's chastity."

Again the nail biter giggled helpfully. From under his lids Corrigan glanced at the other three girls. Two of them were smiling with ordinary tolerance. The beautiful girl in the corner sat as though she had not heard—in fact, as though she were not listening to anything he said. Her face was as perfect and lustrous as china, and except for its excellent shapes seemed just as expressionless. Her pale hair was drawn back with a lavender ribbon so that her ears were exposed, and these, Corrigan saw, had an extraordinary translucence. Glass ears and glass eyes, he thought, wondering why she had come to his class. It was part of his belief that beautiful women never wrote much or well, nor wanted to.

". . . I have no lectures for you. Rather than ramble on like this through the period, I'd like to make a game of having each of you write a description of—well, of a tree. That sounds trivial for your talents, but it will serve for a beginning. Write about any tree you've seen or imagined. We don't want to admit that only God can make a tree. Everyone shall put forth his own leaves in this class. With hints from nature, of course." He waved his hands in a coaxing signal for them to get ready, set, and go.

He gave them a quarter of an hour, and when they were finished the papers were passed around the circle of chairs to him. He leafed quickly down through the pile, his eyes alert for something that might set them arguing. The top paper began, "My tree is a friend . . ." Oh, oh. From the nail biter, he guessed. Perhaps when she felt more at ease in the class she would do better.

"Here's something interesting," he said. He extracted the paper and held it up. "Whose prose?"

"Mine." The boy in the field jacket flipped up one finger from his chair arm to identify himself.

"Mr. Forest. Steve Forest," Corrigan read. "I'll read Mr. Forest's description of a tree to the class and the rest of you will be preparing to criticize it as I read. Now," he said, hitching his feet back under his chair, readying himself for the sport.

" 'The tree looked like a broken hand. Every branch had been cut by shrapnel. Some of the branches were ripped off clean, but most of them hung by fibers like tendons sticking through skin. The stripped trunk looked like a patient idiot who had been beaten a long time and doesn't understand why. There were ax marks on the trunk which were still bleeding a clotted sap. The ocean clouds behind it looked like scabs floating in a bucket of mucus.' " As he read the last simile, Corrigan let his voice rise up theatrically. "There!" he said. "There we have something to talk about. What do you think of this bit of writing . . . Miss Emery?" He had picked a name at random from the class roll.

The nail biter answered. "Why—why—*goodness!*" She had expressed herself so adequately that all of them laughed. "It doesn't sound like just a tree, I mean," she said, and the laugh went around again.

"Mr. Kelsey."

"Mmm. I liked it. It's kind of Wastelandish."

"Mr. Jost."

"I think it has its *own kind* of power. I think you *see* this. I think he gets you to sort of *know* what kind of tree it is he means."

"I don't *see* it," Miss Emery said, bold from her previous success. "Is it an elm or a maple? Ha. *What* kind?"

Corrigan saw the blaze of Forest's contempt leap toward the girl and diverted it by saying, "Mr. Forest, you might like to tell us—"

"I think *this girl* simply doesn't want to see it."

"I certainly don't," Miss Emery snapped. "There's nothing objective about it."

"Let's have another opinion," Corrigan said. He swung his glance around the circle and picked out the beautiful girl. He indicated that she was to speak.

"I . . . I . . . I don't feel well," she said. The class roared its delighted approval.

But the girl got up and raced for the door. She was barely past it when Forest jumped up and followed her out. The others watched with various shades of amusement and sympathy.

Corrigan dismissed them all soon afterward, diverting their thought from the little episode as well as he could. He anticipated the problem the girl might have in forcing herself to come back. Like an animal trainer quieting his beasts, he called up the tricks learned from many years of teaching to blur down and unfocus their curiosity. By the time they all left, he felt that he had been successful in his attempt.

But his own curiosity was caught on the spike of a single question—why it had been Forest who had followed her. Forest and the girl had been sitting on opposite sides of the room. He had caught no sign of familiarity between them, and, granting that Forest might be the kind of rambunctious boy who would try to shoot all the quail in the class, still following a girl when she is about to throw up is an unpromising approach. Maybe it was pure compassion or even guilt on Forest's part.

Half amused, he thought of Forest following the girl with remorse and saying to her, "I'm sorry I wrote that tree for you. Look, I'll write you another, with unspoiled green leaves and a little toy wind monkeying around in it . . ." He had liked Forest, and he rather hoped this was the way it might turn out.

As he dawdled in the classroom then, Forest came back. The boy seemed to want to say something, and Corrigan waited. Forest gathered up his books and crossed the room to gather those the girl had left.

"We must grant a certain *power* to your prose," Corrigan said gently. "Is the young lady all right? Or did she vanish? She seems a very ethereal creature. Not quite of this world."

"Of this world, all right," Forest said bitterly. "I told her not to come in this class. But I'll be damned if her being here is going to keep me from writing the way I please. And to hell with all the other bastards, too."

"Why—why—"

Corrigan saw the boy's brown eyes fixed on him with reckless begging. "Why, they all mean well," he assured Forest. "They may be sort of amateur in their standards, but they mean well. They—I take it you know this young lady?"

"My wife," Forest said, his beggarly eyes shifting now as if he could not meet even Corrigan's gentle gaze.

"Wife? I didn't see any Mrs. Forest on the roll," Corrigan said. "But then I miss things."

"Elaine Biddle," Forest said. "The two-day bride. We're not living together. She only came into this class because she's damn sure she's going to get at me. If I could've got in—"

Forest stopped with clumsy abruptness, but Corrigan finished the sentence for him. If Forest could have got in Tyburn's class, the wife, parasite, nemesis—what was she, then?—would have been kept out where she belonged by Tyburn's standards. Kept out of the realm of art where this boy was scrabbling for a foothold. But in Corrigan's catchall class, open to all comers, she was very much a presence to be reckoned with.

"I'll be glad to hear more about all this," Corrigan said encouragingly. "But I don't feel we can exclude her from the rolls—if that's the problem."

"It isn't that," Forest said. "It isn't that. It's so goddam much more than that."

"If I can help—"

"You can't help," Forest said. "Only I may drop your class, too. Nobody can help." Abruptly he turned and stalked out.

But he's taking her books to her, Corrigan noted. He sighed as he started back to his office. He felt a faint, undefinable disappointment at Forest's outburst. He liked the boy so well that he wished him beyond self-pity.

MOORE TYBURN WAS DOING the talking. It seemed that from his strategically placed easy chair in the corner of the Franklins' living room he had been talking for a very long time; his speech had the quality of a monologue that must have had its true beginning not only hours or days but years before this little gathering of professors and their wives had assembled in the house of the head of the English department.

He sat under a modish floor lamp, drinking from time to time from a glass of milk that the wife of Professor Peltus kept constantly refilled for him. He finished a story about Dylan Thomas and the old days "at the Horse" with a contemptuous, final remark about the degeneration of this tavern in the Village since Thomas's death. "No one goes there any more," he said.

"We were there just two weeks ago," Mrs. Peltus said, with a half-defiant, half-apologetic snicker. "Just to *see* it. It seemed to be quite full of tourists and phonies."

"Oh?" Tyburn asked her coldly, pondering her qualifications for distinguishing phonies from genuines.

This was Tyburn's first year on the faculty. He had lectured here at the university once during the past winter, had thereafter been considered as a possible colleague.

When it came to hiring him, the executive committee of the department had gone along enthusiastically with Corrigan's recommendation. "We need somebody who's in touch with the new things. A writer from New York, preferably," he had said. Among Tyburn's qualifications was the fact that he had been on the staff of a famous literary review and appeared ready, like some of its other editors, to move up to *Life* or *Time*. He was a real catch for the department. Their formula for accommodating him was that he was hired not so much to supplant as to extend the writing program that Corrigan had run for so long. But they had greeted him with lively expectations and no little awe.

Physically he was a fascinating little figure, with an aggressive, blue-stubbed chin that flashed metallically when he spoke. His slightly protruding eyes never met those of the person to whom he was talking but swung with quick anxiety to that person's face as soon as his gaze was distracted. His wide, curving brow was in constant perspiration this evening.

He repeatedly "denied intellectual responsibility" to this or that writer of national reputation and had several times referred knowingly to Trotsky as "the old man." An air of barely suppressed wrath charged nearly every one of his sentences. And these mannerisms of his speech exerted a hypnotic fascination on the listening faculty wives.

Corrigan sat there almost as rapt as they. For several years he had admired Tyburn's poetry and his critical articles on Joyce, Thomas, and Lowell. He was happy to see the young wizard in action, to note with sleepy irony the adroit corrections he was administering to Mrs. Peltus and the liberal Mrs. Thorne, whom Tyburn quickly exposed as "Stalinoid," denying her intellectual responsibility between two sips of milk.

But before long Corrigan began to sense his error in coming to sit at the young man's feet. (Figuratively at his feet; actually he was clear across the room, in shadow, being as quiet as an old man can who has taken enough good Scotch whiskey to scramble his senses.) In his earlier talks with Tyburn there had been a tacit fraternal ease, the complicity of two practitioners isolated, as Tyburn seemed to see it, among the mere merchants or middlemen of literature constituting the rest of the staff. But as this evening progressed Corrigan began to hear in the passion of Tyburn's monologue a probing scorn that he could only take as personally directed at him, whatever the others made of it.

"Our great curse at the *Review*," Tyburn was saying, "was that absolute legions of contributors failed to realize that Whitman is dead. The old beard is gone. For my money he's back at Paumanok where he started. And yet, though it's past mid-century, there are still these highly emotional sodbusters and sodbustresses who go on trying to extend the Whitman catalogue of American goodies, busters who feel that coming from west of Chicago is, in itself, qualification as a poet. You can't imagine how many man-hours the staff wastes reading poems in praise of Lake Michigan and Abraham Lincoln. It's perfectly true—so what?—that every American hamlet is a Spoon River. Go read the gravestones, feel deeply, send the results to the *Review* with—by all means—return postage included. Maybe it is Edgar Masters they don't know is dead.

"Maybe the new leisure is going to continue the explosion of yokel poets, but it's the duty of responsible local and state officials to head the stampede off, stamp it out wherever it shows its dowdy head. I've seriously weighed the possibility of putting poets on reservations like Indians and prohibiting the reading of Whitman and Masters in the same spirit that firewater is prohibited our red brethren. The sheer increment of defiled paper coming from the hinterland is enough in itself to delay the building of a literature. And Europe's gaining on us again. We've got to clear away the crud. Obliterate." For a moment he dropped his face into his spread hands as if to weep. Then he shook himself and hissed, "I do blame it on Masters more than poor old Whitman. If the sonofabitch were here I'd hit him in the face. *I'd hit him in the face.*" He struck his knee with his clenched fist. "Once I went to the trouble of finding out where Masters was buried, and I made the pilgrimage there to spit on his grave. Pork-barrel poetry is killing us."

Mrs. Peltus, her face aglow, poured him another glass of milk. "Masters was one of my favorite poets—*when I was in high school*," she confided naughtily.

In the center of the room Professor Peltus shuffled his feet and coughed. "That's very interesting. You would agree with James's remark in, I believe, *The Art of the Novel*, in which he says he sees no reason why the acceptance or rejection of a duke shouldn't be more interesting than, say, a lady with a cicatrice or, say, the adventures of Jeeter Lester's daughter. Not of course that James had read Caldwell. In merely using that as an illus—"

"People aren't talking so much about James now," Tyburn said ominously. "But exactly. The smell of horse dung does not automatically make it literature. But what a long time that theory rode in the saddle. Hey. You see I'm using the Regionalist lingo myself. Help. I'm drowning."

Belatedly sensing that the stage had been set for a debate between Tyburn and

Corrigan, Peltus said, "What do you think of that, Orin? Your interests have always been more or less regional. Not that Professor Corrigan as a poet *was* a Regionalist," he said with a castrated chuckle.

"I've read his books," Tyburn said sharply. He was not going to allow quarter.

"Bu-u-ut," Peltus said, oblivious, "he was something of a forerunner of the Regionalism that developed here—in the thirties. Never a part of it, but—"

"I think . . ." Orin Corrigan said slowly, setting his empty glass on the rug and pulling his legs under him—then, in a moment of terror, he did not know what he thought. There was an absence, as if the growing nausea and resentment with which he had been listening to Tyburn had brought him to the edge of a precipice and pushed him over. Recovering with a burst of anger as if adrenaline had been spilled into his bloodstream, he thought, This tormented little bastard has always from grade school up had to assert his superiority by running something else down, and doesn't even know he's doing it. He's got his little yellow teeth in the butt of something marching to power and he doesn't mean to let go. He'll hang on for the ride the way ten years ago he would have held onto Henry James and twenty years ago to Regionalism. And he's got enough teeth to hang on tight. More than enough. If you heard—*heard* what he said about Masters and still think he's a fit person to discuss things with, then nothing I can say or have ever said in the years you've been my students and been on the staff with me will make any difference.

He said, breaking with his thought as the thought had broken angrily with the darkness beyond the precipice of surrender, "Will you pass me—or, no, would you fill my glass, Mrs. Dillon? Scotch and water. Thank you. I think that Regionalism had its weaknesses."

Did they—did any of them—realize how baldly Tyburn's remarks about Masters had been meant as a thrust at him? Evidently not. And in a smeared moment of self-pity he stared at Tyburn and asked, silently, Why? Because he had written and published a few poor poems a long time ago? If they were so bad—and no doubt they were—then they might be allowed to die out gently, as such things always would. But he knew, intuitively and with a fear he could not wholly understand, that Tyburn did not mean to let them die quietly. They would have to be ridiculed and hounded from the minds of men. He did not, just then, hate Tyburn, but with despair he recognized Tyburn as a pattern of things to come. He would be the new power on the English staff here. His sharp tongue and his hate would mold these opinionless men and women—these Peltuses.

Blind among enemies, Orin Corrigan thought as he drank his Scotch and water down swiftly. Then the corrective intelligence in him changed this modestly so he thought, Only, I am the one that wrote *Sweet Grass Bend* and *Crazy Horse Is Dead*— not either *Lycidas* or *Paradise Lost*. That's not my line. I didn't write it, so it's not my line. Great Jesus, men who were not poets (practicing) could claim, in their anguish, the great things Milton said. But once you went in the ring, you had to fight there with your own.

"Now in your class in writing . . ." Tyburn said challengingly, sensing his advantage, meaning to pin the old man to the wall. His voice was exultant, triumphant as a steel rasp hitting pith.

"It hasn't been awfully successful," Corrigan said. "None of my students ever published much." He groped his way to his feet, nodding and smiling and thinking that he might have acquitted himself better if he had not had that last Scotch.

OUTSIDE THE MAUDLIN, red moon shone on the streets and through the frames of branches. There was an extravagance of longing and of inhuman loneliness in its color.

But don't write about that, Corrigan thought. He felt giddily drunk and tired and ashamed of both these things. Don't write about that moon, or the seventeen miles of grass that lie between Emerald and Dumont or the way young men used to ride it (before that war, before that Strange Thing, Phelps Putnam called it, when the talking rats of Europe came and carried us all off from what we were), singing and passing back and forth a bottle of corn whiskey on a night like this, or how one of those got killed the next day in a Regionalistic manner (by the brother of the girl he fooled. Who said they would marry in a month and a day?). Don't write about such things or some sonofabitch from New York will ridicule you for it sooner or later. Maybe he ought to pass that bit of wisdom on to his writing class.

I could go back and sock the little bastard, he thought, bumping against the wall of a building and recovering himself.

Without knowing how he had come there, he was downtown in the traffic of the little city that lived off the college. He saw the door of a bar which was as purely anonymous to him as any could possibly be. A platonic bar. He went inside and had two more drinks while his suppressed rage against Tyburn swung tormentingly against himself. It was no one else's strength but merely his own weakness that was hard to face. It was hard to endure the change of things where the best that you had known and done became, in the metamorphosis of time, the unmistakable sign of what you had missed. Some devilish spirit of justice impelled him to think that Tyburn must be right. What had been the truth was changed. Then it was but now it wasn't. . . .

Suddenly he realized with shame that he had slid off the seat of the booth and was sitting on the floor without strength to raise himself. The waiter was supporting him so that he would not fall flat.

"You got to watch that forty rod," the waiter said. "Work up on it more easy, Professor."

He knows me and I ought to know him, Corrigan thought. But as far as he could tell he had never seen the waiter before in his life. When the man helped him shakily to his feet, he managed a small laugh and said, "I'd appreciate it if you'd call me a cab."

Looking around now, as he had not when he came into the bar, he saw that two of the young men from his class, Forest and Kelsey, were watching him with a sort of skeptical compassion. He grimaced and waved to them before he waddled out. He did not think they had been laughing at him, but that made very little difference. They had seen. He had lost something to them that he could probably not afford to give up.

At the door of his apartment he thought miserably, If Gail were here the whole smeared evening could still be made all right and its misfortunes be given the quality of an ultimately joyful farce. I'd go reeling in to tell her how beautiful the night is, he thought, and that all the sonsofbitches in the world don't count. But she wasn't there and they did.

FOR THE FIRST TWO MONTHS of the fall semester, the beautiful girl, Elaine Biddle, handed in exactly nothing to Corrigan. He made no formal demands on any of his students for any particular volume of work, preferring to let them go at their own speed, concentrating his critical assistance on the best of what was brought to him. He hoped the encouragement and examination of excellence would do all that could be done to lead the stragglers.

But the Biddle girl—or Mrs. Forest, whichever might be the truer name for her—gave no sign that she ever meant to hand anything in. She came regularly to class and sat always in the same chair. Once she had found her place she sank into a beautiful remoteness which isolated her like a bell glass from the rest. It was not that she was utterly speechless or expressionless—when one of the other students had read aloud his production, a poem or a short story, and Corrigan called on her for comment, she would open her pink lips to deliver a brief cliché of praise. When the rest of the class laughed or grew excited in argument, an extremely faint smile or furrowing of her sleek brow indicated that she heard and was acknowledging from far away the concerns that the others met so frankly.

It was clear by now that Forest—her husband, in a legal sense at least—was a storm center of the class. When Miss Emery read a story of her own about the adventures of two girls on a bus, Forest announced immediately that it was "crap." Whereupon Miss Emery fled the classroom in tears and Forest tried to cover his real consternation over this result by an impassioned attack on all stories that had surprise endings. When Forest read his own work—he had read two stories thus far—Miss Emery got her own back by saying they were certainly very much like the stories of James Farrell, if *that* was what he had been aiming at. Scabs in a bucket of mucus, *indeed!*

Well, it certainly was what he was aiming at, Forest told her, only he meant to write a better prose than Farrell's. And the whole class—except his wife—slam-banged into an argument about realism, naturalism, and the happiness of most human beings.

She only watched from her china-blue eyes, as though she were looking in at the rest of them through the bars of a cage. She had no opinion to offer.

And finally Corrigan concluded that she was not in the class because she wanted to write—whatever her motive for being there might be. It was largely curiosity that moved him to keep her after class one day when the others had left.

"You haven't handed anything in to me yet, Miss Biddle," he said gently.

A quizzical expression showed on her face, as though he were giving her some odd bit of news. Then she nodded in agreement, but she said nothing.

"Well, when can I expect to see your work?" he prodded.

"You mean," she asked slowly, "that I'm supposed to write something?"

"That's the general purpose of this class," he said. As he watched her, trying to see through the mask of her withdrawal to the real person within, it suddenly occurred to him that maybe there wasn't any. This manner of hers might cover an incredible vacuity, an absolutely interstellar emptiness onto which most observers might project an image of themselves. As on the first day she had come to his class, he was struck by the inexplicable peculiarity of her beautiful head. Now, as then, her hair was held back by a lavender ribbon. She wore a lavender cashmere sweater on which he saw a pearl-rimmed sorority pin. She seemed to shrink inside the sleek, furry black coat that she had thrown over her shoulders.

"All right," she said faintly. "I'll write one." With the faint grimace of one who tries to remember something, she turned and left him.

The next morning he found her story on his desk when he came to his office. It was on ten faultlessly typed pages, the pages themselves conveying some of the quality he had sensed in her person—aloofness, a sort of nonpresence that still left a physical track to dissemble its lack of reality. And the story—the story was wonderfully, or horribly, more of the same. As he began to read it he had no sense of its quality. In terms of language it had none of the awkwardness or straining for effect that he was so familiar with in the attempts of his students.

On the other hand, he had the sense that it might have been written at top speed in this single, perfect draft, with no pauses at all for reflection and no conscious concern except for an awe-inspiring neatness. He was not sure that her story meant anything at all.

"It's not a realistic story," he ventured as an exploratory beginning on the afternoon when he called her in for a conference.

"No," she said. Her pretty head was inclined over the pages laid on his desk top, and it seemed to him that there was an unusual flush to her skin, as if she were afraid.

"But it's interesting," Corrigan said. "It *seems* interesting, though I have to admit I found it opaque. I read about the old woman and the girl and her doll, and I know that the old woman breaks the girl's doll. But I don't know what this all means, what I'm supposed to understand by these events."

He saw the coral-colored tongue touch the girl's lips, and she said in a small, thrilling voice, "My theme is the death of beauty."

The precise little sentence stung something in Corrigan's mind. His first—defensive—reaction was that such precision was comic. He was glad she had not declared herself with such patness in front of the class. He could imagine their nervous intolerant response. But as his mind repeated the silvery tone in which she had spoken he heard in it an unbearable candor—as if, he thought, a sibyl had spoken directly to him. It was at some deep level terrifying to admit what he had heard.

"Yaaaas," he said in his encouraging classroom voice, urging her to go on, to expand her explanation of this theme. But she sat as if she had told him all he needed to know.

He dropped his attention to the baffling pages. As he turned through them he began his own paraphrase, in the hope that his interpretation might unlock the frozen structure of it. "Yaaas, I see. The doll is the symbol of beauty, then. Something that the living little girl holds and loves in her naive childish belief that because it is beautiful to her it is also eternal—or we might say indestructible. Then when the old woman wantonly takes the doll from her and destroys it, the girl learns that beauty is transitory. That's the main line of the story, isn't it? *Now*, what does this discovery mean to the girl? What does she do with it, for the rest of her life?"

"Nothing."

He laughed at the abruptness of her answer—hearing in his own laughter the bray of insensitivity, but puzzled as to how else he might proceed. "I mean, suppose that in life someone perceives things as this little girl has. Now, as we go on living this perception somehow gets carried into our lives. How would it affect her relations with other people? What's the human consequence of this rather abstract perception? Does this girl go on through life making her protest against the death of beauty? Is that her problem? I don't mean you have to write all this down in the pages of your story. I'd like to help you think around it, to see if we can't bring its meaning more out in the open—"

Now Miss Biddle was shaking her head. "The girl doesn't protest. She's glad the doll is broken. Here . . ." She reached for the manuscript, opened it with precision and put a sharp fingernail on a line near the bottom of the page. "She laughs because the old woman does what she wants in breaking the doll. See?"

"Go on," Corrigan encouraged. He had read the line she indicated. It said the little girl laughed—but there was a total omission of motive for the laugh.

"That's all," Miss Biddle said. "She's glad it's broken." She swayed back from his desk and the manuscript into a ramrod stiffness in her chair. Her exquisitely painted lips were open just enough to show the glitter of her teeth. "If it's broken no one else can have it," she said slowly.

Again it seemed to Corrigan that he heard a sibylline finality and inclusiveness in her interpretation—if that was what it could be called. Beyond any psychological interpretation that might be made of either her story or her comprehension of its meaning there seemed to ring a metaphysical knowledge. It was as if she said that beauty might act on men but had no intention of rewarding them, that it did not intend itself for life, but was a mischief there.

She knew that? Slowly, and with a certain fatigued resignation, he assured himself that she *knew* nothing of the kind. Any attempt to question her in the words at his command would only baffle her, he believed, would break like ocean froth against the stone limits of her vocabulary. And yet it seemed to him that the knowledge was with her, and he felt something of the ancient terror that might impel a man to lay his hands on an immortal and hold on for an answer that he must have.

He brushed the manuscript aside decisively. "Well, it's *interesting* work," he said in ironic bafflement. "Now there's one other matter I've been a little curious about. Sometimes I've wondered *why* you were in my class. I've had a chance to discuss their intents and aspirations with other members of the class, but you and I have never talked much. Now just what—"

Her eyes blazed fiercely. "*He's* been complaining to you about me. He thinks I'm just here to spy on him. But he needs someone to look out for him. He's got to be careful." There was no doubt in Corrigan's mind that she was talking about her husband, but the emotional outburst was thus far as opaque and inscrutable to him as her manuscript had been.

"Now, now," he said, trying to placate her. "No one's complained to me. Maybe if you'd tell me a little more what this is all about, I could—"

"It's none of your business," she said in anguish so unmistakable that he was stung to the heart by it. "It's none of your business." She snatched her manuscript and dashed from the office. She left behind a faint odor of perfume and scented soap. Corrigan heard the sleet rattle on the window of his office. Outside he saw the black trees motionless in the icy downpour, and like a child terrified to learn that others, too, are lonely, he suffered from the ache of mystery she had left.

"SHE DIDN'T WRITE THAT, you know," Forest said. "She got scared when you asked her why she hadn't handed in anything and went to the sorority files and found something, copied it, and handed it in." He ended his charge with a low-toned but almost hysterical intensity. Corrigan saw that his hand was trembling.

He had been walking along the street when Forest called to him—from the door of the bar in which he had collapsed that night at the beginning of the fall. There was something very important that he needed to know, Forest said, inviting him into the bar for a drink. And as soon as they sat down he began an impassioned revelation of how his wife had cheated by handing in a story she had not composed herself.

"It was quite an extraordinary piece of work," Corrigan objected. He squinted into the fog of pipe smoke that he was laying between himself and the boy. Since his interview with Miss Biddle he had permitted his imagination to wind around the meaningless—or uninterpretable—elements of her story until they had closed into a coherent structure. Her offering had struck its needling roots into his thought and his thought had nourished it, until by now it had become more a story *about* the sibylline Miss Biddle than a product by her—or by someone else, if he were to credit her husband's information.

He did not want to credit it. The story of the child and doll, the old woman and Miss Biddle, was now, in its growing, his property. "It's an especially unusual piece for her to find in the sorority files. I thought they were more given to storing successful freshman essays than this sort of thing."

"Maybe they clip literary magazines from other colleges," Forest said. "They're resourceful. They'll do anything. I don't know where *they* got it, but I know where she got it, because she told me."

"And you're telling me," Corrigan muttered into the cloud of pipe smoke. With his usual moderation of tone he added, "I'd have preferred to find this out—if I found it out—by myself."

Forest nodded somberly, "So I'm an informer. I don't care. I've got to do things the only way I can. With her it's kill or be killed."

"Oh, now," Corrigan cautioned. "It can't be that desperate."

Forest spread his hands in suffering exasperation. "For me it is. If she'd give me a little time, then it might not be. A few years. I know if I'm going to make anything as a writer I'd better concentrate all I've got on it now. I'm not so strong that I can afford not to." He peered down in dismay at his quivering hand on the table top between them. "I think if I can have as much time as Dostoevsky, and nobody gets in my road, then I'll be as great as Dostoevsky, because I see what he's talking about. You know what I mean."

"Yes."

"But she doesn't want to give me any time. It's *now, now, now* with her. Like her getting in your class and pretending to be a writer. Ha. *That's* why I have to stoop to informing on her."

"Mmmmmm." Corrigan was not, by any means, sure that he understood what he was hearing. Hints of a pattern from Forest's rambling seemed to spread sensibly across his mind, but it was such a pattern as only the imagination can credit, and not the sort which could provide a credibility sufficient for action or even advice. "How did you happen to marry this—this virago?" he asked.

"I hashed at her sorority house last year," Forest said toughly. He took a savage gulping drink and then, while his eyes met Corrigan's with beggarly frankness, the left side of his mouth sagged as if it were being pulled down by a hook. "I fell in love with her, with *them*," he said, and with a resumption of his tough affectations went on. "That sorority was a heady brew for somebody who comes from PS 214. And the year before I'd been in Korea. No hero stuff. I was a clerk in Pusan. But it *was* Korea. And then you know how the girls smell when they come down for breakfast."

"I expect they must perfume themselves."

"Whether they bathe or not," Forest said, writhing with the memory of his temptation. "Every one of them smells like the big thing asleep upstairs."

"Thing?" Forest had made it sound like a hibernating female mastodon, drowsing in some gilded twilight where all mastodons are gray.

"The girl thing," Forest said impatiently. "The real thing. The most important of all. So you get to telling yourself if you could just get into one of them once it would be the moon. You'd have it. You get desperate enough you'd even marry one of them for it."

"Desperation indeed!" Corrigan said, but he was no more amused than impressed by this passion.

"Well, maybe it wasn't just as crude as that," Forest conceded. "Maybe I even loved her. I don't know anymore. I really don't know why I married her or why she married me. But I know that even if it was made in heaven, now—this year— wouldn't be the right time for it. Do you see? And she doesn't want anything any more except to ruin me."

"I doubt that. I really doubt it," Corrigan said. It was his public duty to doubt, and his private, poetic and illicit pleasure to believe that he was listening to the simple truth. On Forest's hints he was visualizing the girl not as an object of love but as Love herself, an emanation of intolerable perfumes from tabooed regions that Forest called "upstairs." An implacable spirit whose purposes were no more charitable than those of a dynamo or a forge.

And in the core of his being he could believe that Forest was the chosen victim of divinity pursuing its own ends, the crass youth who ignored all warnings of normalcy, who might have peeked on Diana herself and was now torn by his own hounds.

Against such belief, of course, his duty as a teacher stood foursquare. At the command of duty he must categorize the Forests as a fairly ordinary young couple agitated by the ordinary discords of those who marry in college. It was his duty to submit as a listener while they needed one, to let them use his ear as a poultice drawing out the poisonous extravagance a literary temperament would stir up from the commonplace.

"One of her tricks was to be at me every minute," Forest was saying. "Sexually. She may look cold. Before we were married I thought she would be," he confided, only refraining from the probable truth that he had hoped she might be. "But when I got a lousy bronchial condition I didn't feel like doing it, and even then she wouldn't leave me alone. Not that she liked it—"

Corrigan gestured for him to stop such revelations. Of course it was for Forest's own sake that he wanted him to desist. Nevertheless, his old nerves had tingled as if in the presence of a sacrilege. Superstitiously he felt that *She* was overhearing them and would be revenged.

"Now, now, now," he said in a cautionary tone. He increased the density of the smoke cloud into which they were peering so profanely. "Now we needn't transgress certain secrets."

"I don't give a damn about proprieties," Forest said. As if he had not already made that plain, and made plain that a blindness to the real nature of his antagonist was part of the means by which She was destroying him. "Christ, I've talked about it to other people—"

"And they all laughed," Corrigan said, laughing gently, feeling a superstitious shudder threaten his control, threaten to crescendo the laugh louder into an obscene hysteria. "She's a very attractive woman, and it's easy to see you wouldn't get much sympathy as long as she's pursuing you. No."

"They all laughed," Forest said. "Nobody else realizes what a bitch she is. Nobody can tell—like in class when I try to say something. She's there hanging on every word I say, so that I always mess it all up and sound *stupid*."

"She delivers you to your enemies," Corrigan mused. And it seemed to him that the other members of the class, who did not think of themselves as Forest's enemies, who in general admired him at least for his stubborn, headlong ferocity and probably for the glow of real promise they saw in his work (he the one they would most probably think of as an artist)—they were indeed the enemies of the biding, still-imperfect self that Forest staked everything on becoming.

"Perhaps because she loves you," Corrigan went on tentatively.

"I don't ask her for that," Forest said bitterly. "That's the last thing I'd ask her for."

"But more likely because you love her," Corrigan said, feeling with a certain relief that the clichés of verbal communication tempered and controlled the very paradoxes they might create. "You don't want her to see anything but the best. Yaaaas. It may be that I understand. I see it might be better if you weren't both in the same class."

"If she was only willing to *wait*," Forest said. As if the arrow flying at the heart could listen to the merely human cry that protests its flight. "See, I want to be generous with her—or anybody. I don't like what I'm doing to her. But before I could ever get quite set to give her something, she'd already asked for it and tried to get it."

"Well now, well now," Corrigan said. "I can't do a miracle for you. Alas. But now I wonder if I can't do something to relieve your situation. Let me try."

BECAUSE HE WOULD NOT and could not—given what he had glimpsed, being transformed thereby into a less than innocent bystander—expel Miss Biddle from his class for cheating, he chose another method of separating her and her husband. He went rather humbly to Moore Tyburn and asked him to take Forest into the advanced class.

"Why not?" Tyburn asked. His hurtling, insatiable appetite for fodder to hurl into the mill of literature had brought him past the point of setting standards for admission into his class. He would welcome new recruits.

"Actually this boy does pretty well," Corrigan said. "Most of his stuff has been fairly autobiographical, but melodramatic, accounts of his war experience in Korea. He hasn't much sense of organization, but if you'll read these things of his I've brought, I think you'll find a certain power."

"I don't need to read them," Tyburn said. "If you found merit in them, that's good enough for me. I'll be glad to get him. Sure, send him to my class. Do you want to handle the red tape of transferring him or shall I?"

Corrigan said, "There's possibly just one thing I ought to tell you, and that is you'll find Forest . . . fragile. No, that's not the word, but he's more advanced in his opinion of himself than his work will show. *He's* out ahead of his obvious limitations. He's the 'artist as a young man,' " he concluded awkwardly.

And admitting the awkwardness of his statement, he could not exactly blame Tyburn for laughing in response, "Oh. *That* bullshit. I've pretty well got my people over that so they look at the *work*. I've convinced them they're all Midwestern bourgeois anyway, who've been laved by the horn of plenty since the war, so there's no bloody use in them going around like the *poets maudits* or sobbing about themselves as if they came out of the *thirties.*"

Corrigan waved a big, soft, freckled hand as if to erase an error written on a blackboard. He said, "I don't mean that Forest is full of self-pity. It's hard to state, but he sees himself as—well, as he said to me, as an incomplete Dostoevsky." He put one sausage-sized finger at one end of Tyburn's desk and one at the opposite end and said, *"Here's* what he actually is and *here's* what he *knows* he is."

Tyburn nodded in smiling complicity, closing his eyes. One staff man to another. "I already had one of those," he said. "I beat that bullshit out of him and now he's doing some pretty fair things."

"Well," Corrigan said. "Maybe you can beat it out of Forest. There's another thing. He's having a lot of trouble with his wife and—"

"Who hasn't had?" Tyburn said gaily. "Anguish and agony. We all get it. There'd be nothing to write about if we didn't. Good," he said, like a colonel accepting a junior officer from another colonel. "I'll be glad to get your boy. Look, Corrigan, I was going to call you. You know Randolph Markwell is coming here Tuesday. We're going to have a few drinks with him and eat at the hotel before he goes up to Old Main for his lecture. I wondered if you'd go with me to his train to meet him. And I *also* wondered if you'd introduce him instead of me. Franklin thought I should introduce him, but I have the strong feeling that since we *made* him at the *Review*, it would be fresher all the way around if you or someone else from the outside sort of summed up his work for the audience."

THE DIRECT CONSEQUENCE of Corrigan's meddling was that Forest's wife quit his class. She came to him in a quite unexpected burst of passion. Her translucent ears glowed like pink neon from a suffusion of blood. (Was it from the cold, which by then had gripped the campus in a pre-Christmas chill, he wondered when she came into his office? It was not. It was from sheer female rage.)

"I know all about it," she said in a shrill, simple voice. "I know you listened to him and believed everything he said to you about me."

"Now, now," Corrigan said in a fumbling, pipe-stoking embarrassment. "You surely don't think I'd listen to anything too personal in nature. Or that he would divulge so much of your personal affairs as you seem to think." As he spoke he remembered Forest's telling how she would not leave him alone even when he had a bad cold—and her ice-absolute blue eyes seemed to be reading now the exact content of Forest's confidences to him. "He wanted to get into the advanced class. I felt it justified—oh, for a number of reasons. I have great hopes for your husband, Mrs. Forest."

"Don't you think he told me how he'd tricked you?" she said. "He's a lot more neurotic than you think. He's told me that you fell for a big old sob story he gave you."

Corrigan took the implications of this as calmly as he could. "You'll—both of you will—have to forgive me for not keeping your pace. I've never quite encountered a similar situation before. I wasn't aware that you and he were still in such close communication. Evidently I misjudged."

"Oh, he comes around to tell me when he thinks he's put something over on me," she said. Then in the exhaustion of her anger she said with a grave mellowness which in its commonplaceness might have been that of any girl, "I only try to do what I can to take care of him. I don't want him to hurt himself. He is a strange one. I knew that and Mother and Daddy knew it and everyone at the sorority house knew it. But everyone wanted to help him. If he could just accept anything. If he could just accept for me to be with him. At least I could keep him from killing himself. He's not such a genius as he thinks. But you encourage him."

"Do I?" Corrigan asked. Then, smiling and with half-closed eyes, he said, "I don't know that I do anything at all. You two seem to be using me for purposes I don't understand. I feel like the hall carpet. I sense a great deal of running back and forth over me."

Finally, more in sorrow than in anger, she announced that she would not be coming back to his class. Tacitly they both agreed there would be no point in her continuing now.

THE VISIT OF THE POET Randolph Markwell went off rather successfully. To begin with, his appearance brought the welcome necessity for Corrigan to read all three volumes of the young man's poetry, where he found, as he was prepared to do, an excellence and a power that moved him greatly. One night as he read late in his study at home, he let Markwell's book fall from his hands and smilingly remembered the evening at Franklin's when Tyburn had spoken of going to spit on Masters's grave. Yes, Corrigan thought, what these young fellows of Tyburn's and Markwell's generation had done justified all the fury they might feel toward their predecessors. "Drive your plow and your cart over the bones of the dead," he thought. *They* had obeyed Blake's injunction in these last twenty-five years, and if they had ridden over many things that had been precious to him (even Whitman, he thought, they had to grind into the earth to get their foothold), here, in this book he had been reading, was the warranty for their ruthlessness. It *was* better than the poetry produced by Masters's generation; at least it was alive now with that keening thrum of work that has matched its hour, while the verses of Sandburg, Masters, Robinson, Lindsay, Jeffers—even Frost—remained alive in another sense altogether, like memories of joy or honor outlived.

He had been reading Markwell's long poem on Orpheus and Eurydice, marveling at the rich progression of the structure—the first section, in which themes, rhythms, allusive names, hieratic words were strewn down with a profligacy approaching disorder, to be caught up again, expanded, connected with each other, inflected by their new place in the constellation of images, brought to an ironic halt, destroyed, and then resurrected in a final choral harmony where each held its properly subordinated place so that what was partly a narrative of the search through hell for the loved one moved not merely in a narrative line but on a broad, devastating front. There was something of Rilke's treatment of the myth in Markwell's poem—none of the good young ones since Eliot were ashamed of confiscating what they needed— but there was in the poem as a whole the honk and gibber of an emotion that exceeded the form. The hell where Eurydice was sought was real and no less mythic for being the contemporary scene and culture, Eurydice no less fabulous for being— as the literary gossips were well aware—the poet's first wife, now in an asylum in Massachusetts.

The poem lit up many darknesses, Corrigan thought, half-drowsing in his chair. It was in the glow of the poem, after all, that he had seen the propriety of hatred between a generation and its predecessors, a rigid necessity of rejection that was not without its beauty. And then—perhaps more important, perhaps less—there was a kind of morality in the very structuring of the anguish and separation that were the subject matter of the poem. If it did not, by its argument, justify God's ways to man, it did justify again his belief that art was not helpless before the sweep of time. It was strange how that knowledge satisfied a need primitive as hunger.

Of itself the story of Orpheus and Eurydice was unbearable. Not only the loss of the wife, but the mocking condition of the God—the *Thou shalt not look back* which demanded a faith that uncertain humanity could not bear. But the bargain was otherwise with art added. The loss was irreparable, but the looking back was not a hopeless glance into the void. Out of memory a song could be made, and the celebration of what had been defied the mockery of gods or things. She *was*, the poet said. I *loved*. And loss was not the void.

Why, I've moralized Mr. Markwell's very modern poem, Corrigan thought slyly, and I don't think he'd like it if he caught me pinning a tail like this on it.

But in the comfort of his study and his solitude, he did not care much what Markwell's response might be. The poem was his tonight, and he could dandle it on his knee and spoil it like a sentimental grandfather if he chose.

He looked out through the wide windows to where the street lights were shining on thick snow. He knew well enough that that denying whiteness was hell, and he knew with a sort of total clarity how sick with love he had been for his wife and others who were lost in it. I can watch them go without howling, he thought, because I can look back and know that if we go, we have been.

CAREFULLY WITHHOLDING THE PRIVATE REFLECTIONS that had come from reading Markwell, he shaped his other thoughts of that night into an introduction for Markwell's lecture in the Old Main auditorium. To which Markwell responded, as soon as he rose to speak, by saying, Goodness, he hadn't known there was *all that* in his l'il old poem about Orpheus and Eurydice—a tongue-in-cheek disclaimer which satisfied the entire, diverse audience of librarians, English faculty, graduate English students, writing students, and a scattering of out-of-towners who had driven in through a growing blizzard to get the Markwell word. It produced a yak, and, as a lecturer, Markwell was in business for yaks. His enthusiastic approach to modern poetry was of the golly, gee whiz, lookee how old Eliot juggles so many balls at the same time school. He was not going to be caught *solemn* by any quick throw rifled down the third-base line, he let it be known.

His talk was unflaggingly entertaining, Corrigan thought, and foolish. To which he had no objection at all. It seemed to him that anyone who had written *Orpheus and Eurydice* had every right to masquerade in public as a clown and a trifler. There was no safe audience for a poet to meet face to face. And yet he felt a qualm lest some of those he saw down there in the audience should think the stream of sparkling inanities from Markwell was the business of a poet. Loafing in his chair beside Markwell and screened from the room's attention by Markwell's pyrotechnics, Corrigan could watch the faces of his students lifted in the bright hypnotism of belief that the end of their efforts was to be, somewhere and sometime, as entertaining as Markwell was tonight. Of course, he supposed, it was part of the department's purpose in bringing "name writers" here to the campus to foster the illusion that a writer's career might come approximately to the same kind of success as that available to an actor or an automobile salesman. Given the hostile pressures of the world they would have to find their lives in, it was, perhaps, an illusion they deserved.

He saw Elaine Biddle in one of the front rows. She was watching Markwell's every move with a coldly carnivorous stare as if she meant to find, then and there, the secret of his success and appropriate it. At least so it seemed to Corrigan, sensing her ruthlessness, though he could hardly have said why she might want the secret. Surely not for her own use, unless she meant to make a career out of plagiarizing manners as well as manuscripts.

HE WAS STILL WONDERING about her motives for venturing out on such a cold night when he saw her at the reception for Markwell that Tyburn had arranged to follow the lecture. "I'm not asking any of the old goats like Peltus and Franklin," Tyburn had confided to him, marking him sheep with the same opportunistic recklessness that had marked him goat on another occasion. "I plan to lay in a little booze and give the writers on the campus—maybe some of the younger people from the art department—a chance to take down their hair with Mark. He'll like that." For this proposed intimacy, Tyburn had rented a private dining room above one of the town restaurants.

The room was filled, an hour after the lecture, with the happily drinking young sheep from the writing classes and faculty. A bar had been improvised at one side of the room. Opposite it, on a couch that seemed to date from pioneer days, Markwell continued to play his role of Poet as Success. Corrigan made no immediate effort to join the group around him, but paused on its outskirts long enough to hear that the topic was basketball and the university's prospects during the current season. He saw that Elaine Biddle had found a place beside Markwell on the couch and was watching his face with that unwavering intentness that a careless man might mistake for an interest in what he was saying.

At the bar Forest was haranguing Kelsey and Jost. He had not taken off his green GI coat. His face was red and sweating and he was drinking very fast. "No," he was saying as Corrigan came up to them, "no, that's not my point at all. I'm not saying Markwell is no good. I haven't read his stuff, so how could I say that?"

"If you haven't read his work . . ." Jost said, shrugging and laughing.

"I have read *some* of it," Forest insisted. "Not bad. He's got some good lines. What I'm talking about, for Christ's sake, is why he's doing the kind of thing he's doing and how he's got where he is. I mean, what's the good of writing that kind of thing anymore? So he does it very well. So he's learned *how* to do it very well and he knows all the tricks, and how to make it sound like it said something on three levels, and so maybe the quince is the emblem of love and happiness to the ancients *and* the symbol of European civilization. What difference does all that make? Who cares? Do you care?"

The rhetoric was addressed to Jost, who, more nimble socially than Forest, ducked it by stepping back to acknowledge Corrigan's arrival, at the same time passing the question to him as if it were a plate of cookies. Noting that Corrigan must have overheard the substance of Forest's question, he asked, laughing, "Do *you* care, Professor Corrigan?"

With Forest watching him from furious eyes (though he was laughing too), Corrigan considered the question with hmms and ahhhs until they had put a drink in his hand. Then he said, "Do I care about the symbols of European civilization? I hope I do."

The young men, Forest included, took his answer as a joke and respectfully ignored its feebleness.

"I don't care about them," Forest said. "I don't feel anything for them at all. They're a lot of junk jewelry as far as I'm concerned. One thing I have read of Markwell's is this long-winded pretentious business about Orpheus and Eurydice. No doubt it's a pretty story, but it's not important to us."

"Important as what?" Corrigan asked.

Forest seemed annoyed by the pedagogic demand for an illustration. "Well, as important as the things Dostoevsky wrote about, for example. Or the things that Lawrence wrote about. You see what I mean." His tone added the impatient postscript "If you seriously want to and aren't just wasting our time."

Corrigan said, "A colleague of mine consistently finds Shakespeare superior to all modern poets. Maybe that's not all there is to be said, though."

"I mean there isn't any point in second-rate work," Forest said. "Anything that there's something of it better than just clutters up—"

" 'Something of it better than . . .'?" Jost giggled. But Forest was above any mere sniping at his syntax. He was plainly in the grip of his vision, which happened, as it had with more than a few from the literary pantheon, to be a vision in which he did not distinguish between himself and greatness, between the plant that does not grow on mortal soil and the imperious need for recognition he felt within himself. At this point he plunged on to another incoherent fragment from his reflections. "You read about Van Gogh at the time he and some of the others, Impressionists, had a show of their paintings, and you can see Van Gogh standing in front of his, waiting for people to come and look at it. How embarrassing he'd be to everyone else who'd kind of stand back and say, 'My little daub doesn't amount to anything,' when Van Gogh knew his did and no one else could see it." It was shockingly clear— to Corrigan at least—that Forest was talking about himself, that he saw himself here, among this crowd of dilettantes and poseurs, as the lonely and furious Van Gogh.

And would it not be, Corrigan wondered, an impertinence to ask, Where is your work? Van Gogh, Rimbaud, Joyce, or any other of the furious egoists must indeed have seemed as intolerably vain as Forest now, but couldn't Forest realize that everyone else looked at that vanity through the justifying frame of hallowed works, while only he presumed to look at it nakedly and share it with no visible sign of justification? To feel oneself not only an artist but a great artist was a recklessness that approached insanity—and he could believe that was exactly what Forest felt of himself. He did not want to deny what Forest felt, but by his whole temperament and from the mellowing that age had given him, he wanted to interpose a *maybe* between Forest's reckless *I am* and the certain denial he would encounter if he exposed himself too far.

"I have the weakness of liking all art," he said, seriously wishing to take up Forest's argument. "For me the libraries and museums aren't big enough. I like whatever is done in the right spirit, and I don't always know how to put it in ranks— first, second, and so on." It seemed to him at that moment he knew what it was he had to teach Forest, if there were time and opportunity for it—the way to accept a scaling down from the vision to the accomplishment. He knew what it meant, and the boy needed to know, and there was the true valence of pedagogy. But as they were met here, he could not even find a way of assuring Forest. While he was composing a way to lure on Forest's argument, Forest's wife slipped between them and took her husband's arm.

"Come on over and talk to *him*," she said to Forest. "He said to bring you over."

"Go on," Corrigan urged. "It's not every day you have the opportunity." He was lightly disappointed by her intrusion at that moment, but ironically pleased, too, that she should be demonstrating her usefulness as a wife. So now he knew why she had braved the blizzard to come out tonight. The little pirate wanted Markwell for her husband—not his scalp or his money, but the Success of him, softened up and in a mood to talk to Forest as an equal. She knew, he thought, what kind of gifts were likely to touch this strange husband of hers, and if she could not offer him her physical charms directly, at least she knew how to use them in barter for something he wanted.

He had fallen into a banal, edgeless talk with Jost when he heard the shouting from the couch. It was Markwell's voice.

"Everyone's a writer," Markwell was shouting bitterly. "Paper's cheap, so you're a writer too." It was Forest at whom he was shouting, Forest planted on a chair in front of him, staring at the poet with the knowing smile of an inquisitor who has just exposed a phony. "Jesus Christ," Markwell shouted, "I know your type. The Village is full of them. Find them in every college, little sonofabitching pipsqueaks who have to bolster their ego by attacking someone. How I *pity* you. I didn't come here to be attacked. I thought I was among friends." He swung, as if desperately, toward Forest's wife, and, seeing in her eyes the sympathy of a mother cobra, twisted toward Tyburn as if Tyburn could exorcise these nightmare figures which had appeared to disturb his peace. "I'm leaving. Moore, I'm going back to my hotel. When's the first plane out of this goddam hick town? All I asked for was a reasonable amount of manners. Did I ask for anything more?" he demanded of the hushed group gathered around him.

"Take it easy, Mark," Tyburn advised. "Get him another drink, you. I don't know where this one crept in from," he told Markwell, pointing his elbow at Forest.

Then the voice of Forest's wife, piercing and memorable as the shriek of a seabird, cut its ice edge through the racket. "Well, it was stupid," she said. "Everything you said all evening was stupid. Did you think you were talking to a kindergarten?" she said to Markwell. She dragged at Forest's shoulder. "Come on, Steve," she said. "Let's go out of here."

As if he were intoxicated, or rapt in the continuation of the dialogue that Markwell had cut off, Forest, still smiling his fixed, catatonic smile, let her lead him from the room.

"My God," Corrigan said to Tyburn a while later. "What happened over there?" He held one hand over his eyes as if it were his own embarrassment he was hiding. "What brought on the fuss?"

"This kid attacked him," Tyburn said. "Mark was just talking about the Dodgers—perfectly innocent—and what's-his-name butted in and asked 'Who do you think you're talking to?' and Mark ignored that. But he butted in again with something about Mark sounding more like a traveling salesman than a poet. Wow. Where do you dig up characters like that? It's unbelievable. It was like some silly thing out of Dostoevsky. And then that girl with him, who'd been making big eyes at Mark, turned on him too. Christ, I don't want this to get back to New York. Now I'm going to have to get Mark good and drunk."

As he filled Markwell's glass again with shaking hands he demanded of Corrigan, "That's the boy you peddled to me, isn't it?" With a semi-tolerant laugh he accused, "You didn't tell me he was crazy."

"Ah, well now," Corrigan comforted, "the boy's just awkward. I don't suppose he meant to offend anyone."

"These bleeding little egos," Tyburn said. " 'Exterminate the brutes.' " There was a momentary flash of puzzlement across his face, a frightened wonder, as if some perversion of the optic nerves had given him a short glimpse of a chimera. But then he said, "*Otherwise* it's not a bad party. Mark's seen students before. He'll just have to lump it. But the kid must be a clinical case."

Corrigan bowed his head to this judgment.

IT MUST HAVE been that night when he caught the bug. When he left the party not long after Forest's bombshell, the snow was falling with soundless emphasis, as if it meant to finish things off here and now. It was falling on top of other snow and already had hidden the hubs of cars parked along the street. Under the street lights and the shop lights it glittered with a fluffy, malign purity, and its delicate texture muffled the sound of the few cars still passing on the street.

The air was not cold. After the wind that had blown all day had died, there was a sort of neutrality in the temperature. Corrigan was sweating under his overcoat as he came into the district where no tracks broke the snow along the sidewalk. He had to wade with high prancing steps for the last few blocks before he came to his apartment building. He was panting when he came onto the steps, which the janitor had shoveled clear.

Then as he stood there looking back on the formless white that was already filling in even his own tracks, it occurred to him that he did not want to go in. Some rollicking impulse to go flounder in the inundation of snow held him awhile, staring back. Childish, he thought. Then he thought, Children hear it—the siren appeal of the snow that dissolves away the familiar forms and outlines of things so they know the intimate attraction of nothingness. Like a memory older than any memory of love he knew how falling snow and the night posed the question, "Do you care?" and what drunken delight it was for the child to answer, "No." Nothing in life was quite so keen as that presexual thrill of abandonment back to nothingness, the white center.

He heard the temptress's voice, oddly like Elaine Biddle's, and he thought, No one else I know would guess what lasciviousness it will be to yield. And then, as if he needed a conventional reason for staying out, he thought, I won't go far, and it is beautiful. To watch it awhile longer can't hurt. But the legs of his trousers were damp above the tops of the four-buckle overshoes his wife had bought him. All right, not tonight, he thought sadly, and went in to the comfort of his apartment and the precaution of his cold pills.

NEVERTHELESS, IN SPITE OF CAUTION, he had caught the bug. His first sign of it was an extremely nasty and literary waking dream of Forest's wife, in which she took the double role of the child and old woman in her story. It was nasty in its gross sexuality, and it was literary in its fantastic resemblance to the hunting days in *Sir Gawain and the Green Knight* when the Green Knight's wife comes to Sir Gawain's bed. Mrs. Forest had been to Corrigan's bed in a wintry castle and he had accepted her—if that was the word for the ugly connections they had made—both as prepubescent child and dripping grandmother.

He woke with a heavy sense of self-repugnance, found that his eyes and all his muscles ached, as if from immense effort, and that his throat was painfully sore. Some strain of ancient Calvinism made him glad of the pain. It was a specific and merited punishment for having dreamed as he had—though at the same time, at a remoter level of awareness, he understood that the dream itself was a graver rebuke than the pain. He gargled and tried to stretch his muscles with some bending exercises. Finally he got himself in shape to go to his office long enough for conferences with Miss Emery and a doctoral candidate preparing a thesis on Chaucer.

By afternoon he had to admit that he needed medical attention. He took a cab to the dispensary at the university hospital, and there, after an examination, the doctor ordered him into the hospital "for a few days."

"Bronchial pneumonia," the doctor said. "I don't think it's going to be serious, but we want to keep an eye on you."

"Sounds as if the police were taking me in," Corrigan said, his little pleasantry reflecting a deep-lying guilty sense that it was not for his illness that he was being taken in but for the improper dream that had accompanied it.

"Yes, protective custody," the doctor agreed absently, already occupying himself with the formalities of ordering Corrigan's admission. "I'm not expecting anything serious to happen. But we have to think of your age."

The pain was still slight, and that afternoon began like a holiday for Corrigan. Lightly intoxicated with the fever, he submitted contentedly to the attentions of the orderlies helping him into bed. The neutral whiteness of the bed in which he lay seemed a wonderfully privileged substitute for the snow that had called to him the night before. This was like a child's pretense of dying.

He felt fine in the bed, he felt wonderful. He had needed, he told himself, this stage setting for his thought more than he needed medical attention. After submitting to having his temperature and pulse taken he let himself slide swiftly back into a rehash of his morning's dream. Let the doctor believe he had pneumonia, he knew he had caught the Forests—they were in his psychic stream like the cocci in his blood. When he was prepared to deal with them—lying flat on his back seemed the position of choice for doing so—then his blood would expel the hostile bugs quickly enough.

In the meantime he was close to enjoying the spectacle of his fight against the contagions. His hospitalization was like a warrant for digging back through the unconscious panorama of the dream to the conscious preparation for it. (Only enforced leisure could warrant the impracticality of such speculation. It could produce no valuable return.) Here he would speculate on the way his dream of Forest's wife had grown like a wild vine from his perfectly conscious interpretation of her story, the way that little stolen seed had gestated within his life as within a natural womb.

As he lay there looking out from his windows onto the white campus and the white hills beyond the edge of town, it seemed to him that he could see through arch beyond arch beyond arch and behold, almost diagrammatically, how the process of imagination worked. And it seemed to him, with an exuberance he had not felt since he was a young man, that he was about to begin a tremendous imaginative work. Little Miss Biddle had stolen a story, and that was a crude illustration of how the process worked. But he—well, he was going to steal Miss Biddle and her story, and the story of her stealing the story, and the story of his stealing, and . . . Contentedly he fell asleep.

WITHIN A FEW DAYS he saw how he had been tricked into this euphoria by his fever. *Something* strange was happening in his mental life, but it was not the beginning of a new phase of creativity. All over again he had to admit what he had long ago humbly concluded—that his ability to write had been exhausted. The lifelong accumulation of experience and insight from reading had been somehow tipped loose and was avalanching *as if* toward some point of concentration where it might be transformed into a work of his own. But it never quite arrived. Instead it seemed to exhaust itself in the fireworks of literary dreams about Forest's wife and—sometimes—Forest. He had tried imaginatively (using the same heavily equipped critical probes that he might have brought to a poem) to pierce their lives. And he had gone too far. He no longer had any defense against them. Whenever he slept he would find himself dreaming about them in one literary situation or another. They were everyone, from Popeye and Temple Drake to Dante and Beatrice, Gatsby and Daisy, Heathcliffe and Cathy, Paul Morel and Miriam, Raskolnikov and Sonia, Paolo and Francesca, Maggie and Jiggs. Sometimes he was involved in their relationship carnally, sometimes spiritually, but after a time these dreams became his chief source of discomfort. Then they began to frighten him as he recognized them not as promises of new insights but as signs of dissolution.

After a few days he complained of them to the doctor. "They're embarrassing," he said.

The doctor listened but was not greatly impressed. "They'll go away when we get your fever down. You're clear enough when you're awake, aren't you?"

Yes, Corrigan admitted, he was, but wakefulness had become increasingly boring. Now his days seemed to pass in an uneasy suspension between the boring winter whiteness that his consciousness perceived and the unholy medley of his dreams.

It was as if he had abandoned that familiar vantage point from which he could turn safely toward either reason or fantasy. He felt a great fragility in himself and a bitter impatience with it.

The upshot of it was that he stayed in the hospital longer than his doctor had expected. As the doctor had promised, the disease had taken no serious turn, but his convalescence was slow. After the fever ended, his horrid literary dreams disappeared, and that was a testimony to the doctor's acumen, but Corrigan believed they were still going on inside him, more and more identified with the secret processes of dissolution that his bout of disease had accentuated. It was a humiliation that his last spark of creativity had turned to ashes so quickly.

The Christmas vacation passed while he was still in the hospital and he remained as the first semester drew to an end. It was late in January when, one day, Tyburn came to call on him, bringing a bottle of whiskey and an issue of *Botteghe Oscure* in which some of Tyburn's poems had been published.

At first Corrigan thought irritably that the younger man had come simply because it was the season when promotions and salaries for the following year were about to be decided, and that Tyburn might be simply angling for his support and a good word to the head of the department. That support wasn't needed. This was Tyburn's time. He was on top. He could ride. His generation had secured their reputations, and the head of the department could count up the number of publications credited to Tyburn without any help from Corrigan. (The departmental secretary kept a chart of publications by members of the staff, a chart which had always reminded Corrigan of the stack of an aircraft carrier with its painted emblems of the kills to be credited to each pilot.) Tyburn would rise.

But evidently Tyburn knew that too, and something else was bothering him. In the little time since last fall he had passed from worrying about his security on the staff to a deeper concern. When he had drunk a couple of drinks from his present to Corrigan, he slapped the *Botteghe Oscure* against the bedside table and cried, "The poems I've got in here are *wonderful*. But as soon as I read them I tore up everything I've written since last fall. I've lost my ladder."

"That can happen," Corrigan said drily.

"You've been through it," Tyburn said. "You should have a perspective on it. You were doing wonderful stuff before you settled down to teaching. So tell me, is it worth it?"

"I don't know."

"I've got to decide. It's not going to hurt me to stay here another year, and Franklin knows the people at the Guggenheim foundation, so there's a good reason for staying next year at least. But I've got to make up my mind. I've got to decide whether what I can do for my students is more valuable than what I can do for myself."

"Well?"

"I don't know," Tyburn said somberly. "I can't get the score. Look, that kid you sent to my class. The nutty one. Forest. You were there the night he took off on Markwell. All right. It was a thing that happened, and I made up my mind that it wasn't a capital offense. So, I called the kid in and had a long talk with him and thought we had everything straightened out, really. It seems there was more to it than met the eye. Markwell had been pinching his wife, this girl Markwell had been pinching was his wife, and *that* is what riled him up to call Mark down. Which makes *sense*. Those things happen, and I've seen Mark in trouble before, but I didn't know it at the time. So Forest and I had this good talk and I thought we were seeing eye to eye. Then about a week ago the kid gave me part of a novel he's been working on."

He paused and shook his head ponderously and poured himself another drink.

"Did it show merit?" Corrigan asked.

"*None,*" Tyburn said briskly. "Or I shouldn't say none, but it wasn't good."

Corrigan nodded slowly. "I'm afraid that Forest, after all, is a mute inglorious Dostoevsky. The fascinating question is whether or not that is a contradiction in terms. If mute, then Dostoevsky?"

"He *thought* he'd put so much into it," Tyburn said. "He thought it was the history of all the anguish he's had with this nympho wife of his, and there are some moving touches—uh, *moving*—when he describes how she made insatiable demands on him while he was suffering from the common cold and a big dream sequence where he has her raped by a gang of hoodlums in Chicago, but it's pornography at best."

"Oh my," Corrigan said, clicking his tongue.

"But when I tried to tell him this—"

"You didn't," Corrigan gasped. He could feel the spastic twisting in his stomach now, fierce and undeniable and hot and passionate as belief itself. "You didn't tell him it was pornography?"

"What's the point in criticism if it isn't honest?" Tyburn said. "So I told him. So—"

Through the muffled, bombing bursts of his breath, Corrigan gasped, "He swung on you." He saw Tyburn's eyes round out in solemn saucers as he nodded.

"Thank God I didn't lose my head," Tyburn said. "I ran down to the departmental office and the secretary and I held the door on him while Peltus called the campus police to come and take him away."

"Hooooo-ooooo," Corrigan shouted, the breath exploding now from his cramped lungs, "Hooooo-oooooo, hah." Like a leaping trout he flung himself up, scattering bedclothes wildly as he turned in midair. When he landed, with his face half-buried in the pillow, he was sobbing with helpless laughter.

"Tell me again," he gasped. "How you-ooo-ooo held the door on him."

Happily—it might have gone otherwise—Tyburn began to laugh too. When he could control himself Corrigan sat up and grasped the whiskey bottle by the neck. Between fiery gulps he said, "Don't talk any more about leaving, Tyburn. Where else would you find it like this? Where else on earth?"

"It is pretty funny," Tyburn said.

When they had finished the bottle between them, Corrigan was shouting for the nurse, demanding his clothes, swearing that he was going home.

HE THOUGHT AFTER this that the Forests were through with him. Just as the embarrassing dreams vanished—or went underground—after the fever, the young people moved in the course of time beyond his purview. When the second semester began, he learned from gossiping with some members of his class that Forest had not registered. He had left the campus, and Corrigan's informants did not know where he had gone. And his wife? Oh, still around, still living at the sorority house where she had been all winter.

Corrigan saw her one evening when an unseasonable warmth had turned early March for a few days into May. He had taken a long walk in the afternoon and was coming home feeling hungry and fit. He had entered Fraternity Row a few blocks above the campus. The imitations of English country houses spread a theatrical setting down the street ahead of him, and into this setting, like a swan boat, came the largest and most chrome-laden convertible he had ever seen. Softly, swishingly, ponderously it glided to the curb a few dozen yards ahead of him and stopped. From a door wide and massy as a church portal, Elaine Biddle Forest descended. She was in a white evening dress and on her shoulders was mink.

At the instant of her descent a gold bar of sunlight flashed through the thicket of elms and fraternity plantings across the street to illuminate her almost to incandescence. As if she had been expecting it, she paused momentarily in the light and with mannequin grace, mannequin blankness wheeled slowly for all the world (or all the universe, Corrigan thought breathlessly) to see.

Then her equerry—tall, broad-shouldered, short of hair and clean of feature, dinner-jacketed and most evidently odorless as the stratosphere—leaped out behind her and with an athletic step led her up the front steps and into the fraternity.

That tableau was staged to mean something, Corrigan thought. No part of it was accidental—but where in the universe of accident was the origin of this theatrical purpose, and *whose* exactly was the discrimination that chose the details of costuming and light and arranged the tempo of this visionary scene so that fleeting as it was it should continue to vibrate like the persisting hum of a tuning fork? Mine, he thought with ironic arrogance. It was my little eye that saw it all. But whose eye was his? The wind blew acidly from the northwest as if to remind him that the false-spring blandness of the afternoon was an illusion made by powers who need not recognize his claims as a stockholder.

As the tuning-fork hum of beauty died out and he walked on toward his dinner he fell into a depression, as if it should be an automatic hangover from the exultation he had felt in the instant of seeing her. The depression moved through phases as distinct as spectrum bands. He felt a kind of groaning compassion for Forest that he had lost this girl, that he had let her beauty go by default into the hands of—of that Philistine, that embryonic hotel manager or corporation lawyer. It was one up again for the enemy. In this vein of thought the convertible, which had seemed a swan boat to his eye, became a vulgar bit of ostentation, a commercial virility symbol by whose authority (*in hoc signo*) the collectivized male should ravish away the Queen of Love herself. Not that Elaine Biddle was, in this discounting phase, worth likening to the Queen of Love in any way, shape or form. He had it from Tyburn's instructed epithet as well as hints that Forest had given him that the girl was a "nympho." Probably very little ravishing was required. But at the basest level she was valuable poetic property, and recruit writers should learn to cling to their beautiful women, just as recruit soldiers should learn to hang onto their weapons.

In the violet gloom of his depression he realized with a nauseated shock that it was not exactly for Forest's sake that he regretted the loss of Elaine Biddle to the others. Remembering those desperate dreams he had had of her while he was sick he admitted with savage frankness that in his decrepitude *he* was the desolated lover. It was his abandonment and jealousy he lamented now that she had been carried away by that gloomy chariot. He thought, raging, If I had it to do over again, all my life, I'm damned if I'd be a poet. I'd have her. Like a sign of the imminence of his death he felt a swift resentment against his dead wife—that good, warm, encouraging, wise, and loving companion, whose very goodness had tricked him away from the absolute abandonment to a single need which had been—he saw it now—required of him. Insanely, he hated her.

And then, of course, he neutralized the insane revelation with countervailing admonitions to himself. He had had a fit and was over it again, luckily, and able as he had almost always been to see things in proportion. He would go on to the end as himself—a limited man trying to make at least the holy counterfeit of salvation out of his very limitations. With his mouth he would not willingly or overtly deny the woman who had been so faithful and precious to him. But in his heart, in its despicable slime and fear . . .

To the end now, he supposed, that heart would be telling him that he did not care about the past with its measured successes and its limited failures. It was only the monstrous and chimerical future that he loved, the future in which he had so little stake, the true hell of exclusion from which no singer could bring back a credible image of love.

SHE CAME TO HIM within three days after this, arriving at his office so demurely and so dully earnest that he would not identify her with the girl he had seen getting out of the convertible.

She had brought a package for him. She wanted him to read the manuscript of her husband's novel.

"Well, but if he'd wanted me to read it . . ." Corrigan began protestingly. "Mr. Tyburn's already read it, I think, and discussed it with your husband."

"Read it," she pleaded. "I want to know for sure if it's any good or not." Her pale eyes looked more guileless than she could possibly be. She had laid the swollen bundle of manuscript between them on the desk and, while he had not yet picked it up, his wariness conceived it as a bait that he still had the chance of refusing.

"Why?"

"Because as far as he's concerned he's thrown it away," she said. "He wouldn't even take it with him when he left. He would have burned it if I'd let him."

"I heard he was gone. Where?"

With a frown and small shrug of repugnance she said, "Back to New York. His brother-in-law edits comic books. He's going to work for him, writing stories or dialogue or something like that."

"Too bad."

"He had such high ideals."

"Too bad," Corrigan said, "but this isn't the end of his life. I have the hunch we're going to hear a good deal from that young man before it's through."

She, with that air of not seeming to hear anything she did not want to—rather, of testing with her need whatever was said to her and accepting into the realm of her concern only the useful—said, "I want him to come back here. I want him to finish this book."

"Why? A good many times it's wiser to put aside something that's badly begun and make a fresh start. I think you want me to advise him—encourage him—to go on with this, and I suspect Mr. Tyburn may have discouraged him rather sharply.

But isn't it likely that I might have the same reservations about it that Mr. Tyburn had?"

She did not hear him. She merely waited for him to admit the folly of his evasiveness.

"Why?" he asked again, and because she did not answer he answered the question himself with a sign of resignation. "Because it's about you."

"It's about both of us," she said in a high, silvery voice. "And he doesn't need to think he can leave it like this. I know him. He won't ever do anything without me. He's got to understand that. He's got to face it."

It was no outward display of force that lent her speech its absolute certainty. She was not the kind to clench her lovely jaw or even to lean forward for emphasis. The certainty came rather from that tantalizing, centripetal glow of frailty toward which she expected force to flow as the normal pressure of air breaks in toward a vacuum.

"You mean *I've* got to face it," Corrigan joked oddly, picking up the manuscript and hefting it. "I'll read this. I want to read it. But I don't know if anything you want will come from my reading it. I couldn't possibly use it as a basis for intervening in your personal life—even supposing that I had means for doing so effectively. I feel that you've brought me this as if I were a lawyer and this was a document—"

"Just read it," she said. "You'll see."

ALL THROUGH THAT NIGHT he sat at home reading the story of the Forests. It was not the "true" story of what they were and how they had come, so strangely matched, together—for, as he had often admonished his class, truth requires form, and the intent to tell the truth is no guarantee that it will be uttered. After the glimpses and conjectures by which he had known the Forests during the past winter, here was only another glimpse and conjecture. The manuscript was— as Tyburn must have pointed out—formless to an extreme. Sometimes it was confessional in form and reduced painful scenes to comedy, and at other points it was so ponderously stylized and rhetorical that the tissue of dialogue and scene was squeezed to death by the language. It was a big manuscript, and it was tedious. As a literary effort it was quite unmistakably inferior to the Korean war stories that Forest had shown him (and Corrigan realized with a pang that this was the precious work going on behind the scenes, saved until it could be shown to Tyburn's more fastidious gaze, while the pieces on which Forest had staked less were being shown to him). If he were to answer as a responsible critic, he could only say that the work was a complete failure.

And yet as he read toward midnight he knew that there were images rising from the turgid brew and begging for completeness that were of more than ordinary power. Mangled giants struggling through a swamp, he thought, and it seemed to him that what the work needed—all that it needed, but that which a literary work must never need—was to be considered an amputated chunk of the reality which should have been its subject.

He read of the spring night in the sorority house when Steve Forest (called Sid Fleischer in the manuscript, with a transparency so futile that Corrigan ignored it) had been washing dishes alone in the kitchen. As the young man worked at the sink he suddenly began throwing pieces of china out through the open window beside him, at first fearfully and then, when no one appeared to stop him, in an increasing rhythm, hearing them tinkle in the lonely dark outside. If he had stopped to think he might have rationalized this gesture as an appropriately defiant resignation of his job as hasher at the house. But he was not even thinking of it as defiance yet—only as something he must do because he was young and it was spring.

Then he heard behind him, without having heard her footsteps as she came into the kitchen, the trusting, uninflected voice asking, "Why are you doing that?"

Not knowing yet and never to know, Corrigan thought, how she had heard the tinkle of destruction and had come down from her second-floor room because it was destruction she loved, needed, or chose. Because she would have recognized any splintering of windshield, crash of falling walls, smash of bottles as a call to which she must respond, faithfully hounddogging the sign of destruction because it would have been for her the sound of her prison door opening.

"That's a stupid question," he had answered. Frightened, Corrigan thought, because he had been caught, expressing his fright in aggression, ready to "walk out" then as always later with his thumb to his nose, but tolerating her there, waiting, because she had come down smelling of them, all her sisters, because in her person *they* all stood there obediently waiting to be snowed with any silly explanation he might make up.

Then under her nonaccusing stare Forest had panicked. He did not want to be fired for breaking dishes, but most of all he did not want to be fired for having done something that he could not explain with dignity to the housemother when she got around to firing him. So he had gone out into the back lawn of the sorority house and begun to gather the broken pieces of china up in his bare hands and carry them down the slope to the trash barrels. The girl, still in stocking feet as she had come downstairs, tried to help him and (with what meaning, purpose, cunning?) stepped on a shark-tooth fragment of a cup. She sat there with the faint light slanting down on her from the kitchen window above, holding her foot while they both watched the blood ooze out through the dirty nylon. She said tranquilly, "It doesn't hurt. I can't feel it."

This was the image of their recognition. Its felt load of significance was grossly disproportionate to the scene in which Forest laid her for the first time some weeks later. Perhaps the one moving statement about their mating in the basement smoking room of the sorority was the sentence, "She cried." Only that in twenty pages of prose that Forest might have memorized from the reading of spicy magazines during his lonely nights in Korea.

There was little enough to be made from Forest's report of the long-drawn-out conversations they had during the time they decided they were engaged. Except even then Forest seemed to have suspected—what never became more than a suspicion—that she wanted him because she believed that he was "lower" than she. Her father was a lumber dealer in a middle-sized Illinois town—Anglo-Saxon, Methodist, the owner of a Cadillac and a twelve-room house, member of the country club, father of two boys in the insurance game, and a Republican. It never occurred to his daughter that these attributes were not marks of superiority. It was merely that she did not want them. Forest was a Jew, a houseboy in her sorority, and—in his own admission to her—an artist. By these signs she recognized him as beneath her, and she wanted him.

Already by the time she had gone home to Illinois for the summer vacation the horrid comedy in which she pursued and he tried to evade had begun.

If it had not been for their separation, Forest might have escaped her. He went with a friend in a battered car to Oregon for the summer. He hocked everything and borrowed money from his parents, intending in his own phrase "to jump off a cliff and live." If he went too dangerously far in his self-abandonment he would "knock himself off. A nice cool bullet through the head didn't seem like such a bad idea sometimes." But in Portland he got mixed up with a crowd of painters at a beer party and had an affair with a coed from UCLA "whose equipment was phenomenal." He could, or would, or should have been content with her and have transferred to UCLA for the fall term if it had not been for the letters from Elaine in Illinois.

He quoted one of the letters. It was an utterly flat and dull account of a weekend in which she had swum three afternoons at the country club and danced three evenings with some boys her cousin knew at Northwestern. She had been bored by it all, she said.

But the point was that Forest didn't believe the letters.

Precisely because they were so void of content, he had believed in anguish that there was something glamorous going on that she was not telling him. The hot prairie nights, the band playing under the stars, the colored lanterns quivering like live things in the palpitation of the air—Forest could imagine this and in the grip of his imagination could not conceive that in such a setting there was nothing going on that he needed to know about.

But you should have believed her, Corrigan thought, involved like the ever-passionate hick who yells warnings from the theater balcony, the sympathetic freshman who wants to tell Othello not to believe Iago and doesn't give a wandering damn whether Shakespeare made a work of art or not. You had to believe that it was dull there because—well, because if you or I or anyone else following us could just hang on to the literal truth of things we'd save ourselves this awful bother of fiction, poetry, pursuit of phantoms.

In the moment of his excitement, something banged Corrigan's chest like a stocking filled with sand. Palpitations, he thought. He poured himself a large glass of whiskey for a cure. It was not late yet. Not midnight. He was going to see this manuscript *through* before he went to bed, he told himself.

The memorable image of Forest's wedding was the present given him by his wife's parents. Because he was a writer—he took no pains to hide this from them when he suddenly appeared in their Illinois town and, with Elaine, announced what was about to happen—they gave him a Webster's unabridged dictionary.

But aside from the presentation of this ambiguous symbol the bride's parents seemed to have acquitted themselves rather decently under the shock of the marriage. In his manuscript Forest took pains to mock their staid Republicanism, and he had "bit his lip" to keep from laughing at the marriage ceremony performed in the Methodist parsonage. But the sheer fact that they had permitted it to take place at all stood mutely to their credit, as well as the clumsy attempts of the parents to make him (the dark, exotic stranger come into town hitch-hiking and carrying only one cardboard suitcase) feel that now he must look to them for help "if things ever didn't go quite right."

Justifiably, Forest contrasted the price of the dictionary to that of the Packard Sixes which the family had given his wife's brothers on the occasions of *their* marriages. Truly it was as if good common sense had told them not to spend too much for a marriage that wouldn't last. But again they had acted decently against this wariness in loaning the newlyweds the family Cadillac to drive to Chicago for a honeymoon.

The honeymoon was a horror. On the one hand he expected her to bring to the marriage bed in a cheap Northside hotel that glamour which she had so tantalizingly left out of her letters, that glamour of the upstairs in the sorority house—to bring him *the others* with whom he had so hopefully identified her. And she had lain there in his arms a single, naked, demanding self—not even as "phenomenally equipped" as the girl he had left in Oregon. He was too close to her, suddenly, to see that she was beautiful.

On the other hand, as soon as their first hasty bout on the rented bed was finished and even before she had commanded in that unworldly voice, "Do it again," he had glimpsed the immensity of her demand on him, the motive that had overridden parental objections and sorority platitudes about love and marriage as if they didn't exist. It was, Corrigan sensed, the depth of nothingness in her which had on the one hand permitted Forest to see whatever his desire could paint in her and conversely established her need for him. She must have someone whose imagination, whose occupation with her, would give her the reality she did not feel. From that first night when she had stepped on the glass and reported that she felt nothing, she had recognized Forest as the fabricator of her reality. She had watched him read *pain* when he saw the blood flowing. And if he had, in the proof, turned out to be an insufficient artist to turn her nothingness into existence, at least he was the only artist she had ever known. And she was determined that he must suffice.

Her demand emerged as a metaphysical one, and to call its expression nymphomania was at best a clumsy metaphor. In the same way it was clear what her ultimate motive had been in requiring Corrigan to read the manuscript about her. On the paradoxical bed in Chicago the Forests had failed the test wherein illusions and the need to be created might have fused in reality. Deserted, and as if feeling herself fading back to the nothing she had been, she had called out one more time, and this time not to Forest, but through Forest's work to him, "See me. Make me real."

The cursed honeymoon had lasted just two days before Elaine drove the Cadillac south out of Chicago by herself. And there was only one happy memory of it which Forest, with "Dostoevskian" self-abasement, had put down. During an hour when his new wife was out of the room he rifled her suitcase. It was full of such splendid underwear as he had seen only in store windows and advertisements before—a foundation garment of orchid-colored silk, a black half-bra and panties, a cloud of white lace, and a crisscrossing of white elastic straps with gleaming buckles—all that modern heraldry of romance and woman cult suddenly, as he said, "his." Staring down into this treasury, Forest confessed, he felt the one moment of generous lust that he would know on the entire honeymoon. This, and not the dangerous void of the woman, was what he wanted. He had plunged his hands recklessly into the yielding stuff.

("... arms closing on wind, lips speaking a name which must be her name ..." Corrigan incorporated this fragment from Markwell's Orpheus poem to piece out the prose with which Forest had described the episode. But he sensed, in an uncontrolled impulse of compassion and humility, that he was being called on for a belief greater than his belief in poetry. He must not lament—and poetry was lamentation—on pain of losing her. *Do not look back. Believe she is with you.*)

The Forests, he read, had made another effort to live together when they came back to school at the beginning of the fall semester. They rented a tiny apartment, installed in it the cloth of gold of her underwear, and his Webster's unabridged dictionary, and within a very few days it had become untenable for the two of them together. ("It was like having a body in the house with him," Forest had written with unintentional comedy.) She wanted to cook for him, and he was used to cooking for himself, a much better cook than she. She wanted him to stay home in the evenings and read his work aloud to her. (Since he was already deeply involved with this present manuscript in which he had so many derogatory things to say about her—its composition seemed to have progressed like that of a journal—he felt trapped by her request, dreading at the same time that he might hurt her and that she was stifling his "honesty.") When he did read to her he had the feeling that she was not listening "critically." She seemed to bathe in the sound of his voice with no interest in its meaning. When he tried explaining to her that he wanted to be like Dostoevsky, she smiled a catlike smile of satisfaction with him, as though he were *announcing* to her that he already was Dostoevsky. This made him wild. Couldn't she understand how goddam lousy and imperfect his work was *now*, while he was learning his craft? To which she would reply maddeningly that she could understand that *too* and at the same time. In her oceanic emptiness she drowned his attempts to organize his life and his work logically. She cared nothing if he choked on his own inconsistencies as long as she could have him with her—"In there with her," he wrote, referring to the hated apartment.

(" 'You're trying to make a doll's house out of this,' Sid Fleischer yelled as he walked out. He was going downtown to get drunk. He was going to get damn good and drunk. Let her fester there in the festoons of the bourgeois respectability she had brought with her. He thought of how she would be in bed waiting for him when he got home. The covers would be pulled up to her eyes. Her catlike eyes would be watching him when he came in reeling drunk. She never seemed to sleep. If he woke during the night, she always seemed to be awake before him. Let her stay awake tonight. He was going to get drunk and he was not coming home.")

This must have been about the time I first saw them, Corrigan thought. He wondered with a sort of tense fascination if he would presently appear as a character. He thought not. He would have seemed too unimportant, too neutral, to Forest. (And now he felt a queer, repentant impulse to accept Forest's judgment in the matter.)

It's only now, this way, as a reader, that I can belong in the story at all, he thought. Then he thought, They need me. If I weren't here, what Forest thinks of himself and her would be true, and if it is, he's already lost her. Or what the world thought of them would be true. And if it were, Forest had never loved her at all. It *must not* be true that the boy was a spoiled piece of slag from the Age of the Wars, an egomaniacal piece of waste who had blundered into marriage with a nymphomaniac. But if I am not real in this story by reading it and holding it all in my heart, then whatever game we've all started to play when we play at writing is lost, he thought. He was very tired now from the effort to compose the Forest story, but for the most important of reasons he would not let himself quit and go to bed.

He read on into the dream sequence that Tyburn had mentioned to him and discovered what Tyburn, with his psychological insight, must have discerned—that it was a wish-fulfillment fantasy, in which the imagined rape of the wife was a hope of diverting her frightening attentions from himself. But it had another correlation, too, which opened out like an exploding fireworks bomb. Placed against it with a perhaps unconscious cunning was a passage describing her confession of her first sexual experiences. Forest had overcome her reluctance to speak of them by making love to her, and in the very tempest of their embrace had paused to whisper, "Tell me all about it"—delighting to learn that it had been "a fraternity man, a real Joe College" who had deflowered her after a homecoming game.

Voyeur too, Corrigan thought with a groan, recognizing the dream as a means by which Forest saw through his wife to the multiplicity of experience that could never be his. Voyeur . . . that term must be justly added to the long list of other truths about this—this *writer*.

Yet, conceding impatiently the depravity involved, he relived in an over-lapping revery his own recent glimpse of the girl. She was again in front of the fraternity house, descending once again from the swan boat with the twentieth-century trim. The sun struck her gold. She turned with a hungry smile toward the light. Then, between submission and rapture, took the arm of her escort to let Joe College lead her up the stairs and in through the secret door of the fraternity house to her destiny among the lives of strangers. As she disappeared—out of memory, out of conception—Corrigan felt his own lips shape to the begging question, "Tell me."

But the door was closed behind her. She had come to them—not reluctantly, but pleading to be made alive. They had lost her and this was the way the story ended.

He finished the last pages of the manuscript. There were no surprises left to come. He looked up at the mantelpiece clock. It was almost three now. Of what night? Of what reality? He was an old man fondly wishing—and not for the first time, of course—that experience could be as coherent as desire. Then would I have held her—held them—in my heart.

But time was again the clock's time, and the story would end there as it must end. "Arms closing on air . . ." and "lips that would kiss form prayers . . ." while "love that robbed us of immortal things" gave nothing, gave nothing that time could not take back.

How could the Forests' story—which was his, now—end in time except with Forest going off to forge in the smithy of the comic-book trade the uncreated conscience of his race? While little Biddle, Eurydice of the expensive underwear, dropped back into the social millpond from which she had so maladroitly and with such wasted expense tried to raise herself.

In time the story ended with time's ending, and there would be neither occasion nor need for him to say the one thing that mattered. Precisely there was the unavoidable terror—that he could never say to her with the imperial emphasis required to establish all it meant, "I saw you."

In defeat he rose from his chair and started toward the bedroom. Tomorrow he would return the manuscript to Biddle (half-regained, lost on the instant of discovery), and he would try to be socially kinder than Tyburn when he discussed its weakness and its merits.

It is a terrible thing to be kind when you want to love.

He would, out of kindness, refuse her any encouragement she could pass on to her errant husband. What could he say except that time would have its way with them and their stories, fictionalized or real; that on either side of its narrow course remains the same primitive wall of darkness that has rimmed it from the beginning?

We cannot speak the living truth to each other. That was *so*, he thought furiously. But must not be. In the middle of the living room he stopped, feeling all his limbs tremble.

Suddenly—involuntarily, he thought—he spun on the toe of his right foot, kicking his left heel in the air. His left foot crashed down on the hardwood and he whirled on it. Around and around the room he went in a dizzying circle. Beyond all reason (also beyond all wish to stop) he yielded to the necessity of the dance. Bones creaking and muscles twinging he rioted on his way, an old man refusing to die until he heard the Forests' story come out right and clear, dancing in the face of its tragic fragmentation, dancing because in the circumstances it was the common-sense thing to do.

FLANNERY O'CONNOR IN THE
WRITERS' WORKSHOP

MY FIRST IMPRESSION OF FLANNERY O'CONNOR was that she looked too young and too shy to be a writer. We were graduate students at the University of Iowa and members of Paul Engle's Writers' Workshop during the fall and spring semester of 1947 and 1948. On the opening day of class, Flannery was sitting alone in the front row, over against the wall. She was wearing what I was soon to think of as her "uniform" for that year: plain gray skirt and neatly ironed silkish blouse, nylon stockings and penny brown loafers. Her only makeup was a trace of lipstick. Elizabeth Hardwick once described her as "like some quiet, puritanical convent girl from the harsh provinces of Canada," and there was something of the convent about Flannery that day—a certain intentness in the slight girlish figure that set her apart from the rest of us. She seemed out of place in that room composed mostly of veterans returned from World War II. Flannery was only twenty-two years old then, but she could easily have passed for seventeen or eighteen.

I don't believe she was to change very much in the next seventeen years before her death. In the later photographs, showing her on the aluminum crutches that became a permanent part of her life, there remains that same schoolgirl freshness, a young gentleness in her face and expression. Only in the unsmiling eyes of the stern self-portrait is there evidence of the Flannery who wrote bloodcurdling fiction.

It was her isolation from the other "writers" in the class that first drew me to her, and soon that semester I moved to the empty seat beside her. We and one other girl, Clyde McCleod (her father had named her Clyde), were the only women in the Workshop that year. Most of the others, the former GIs, were tuned in to New Criticism theories, and many sensitive young writers got shot down by the heavy onslaught of their critical fire. Stories were dissected like so many literary specimens; few stood up under the minute probing. Many years later when Flannery was speaking to a writing class at Hollins College in Virginia, I'm sure she was remembering those Workshop sessions at Iowa when she said, "Every time a story of mine appears in a freshman anthology, I have a vision of it, with its little organs laid open, like a frog in a bottle."

Sometime late that first semester I learned that Flannery had received the M.F.A. degree the year before and that she had already published one story. "The Geranium," the title story in her M.F.A. thesis, had appeared in *Accent* in the summer of 1946. And "The Train," also from the thesis, was scheduled to come out in the *Sewanee Review* the next spring. Flannery was staying on at Iowa for another year because Paul Engle had gotten her a grant of money to live on while she worked on her first novel. The one person I had thought to look least like a writer on the opening day of Workshop had turned out to be the most promising writer there! From then on, I may have looked forward more to sitting beside Flannery than to the Workshop itself, which in those days was something like going to a good movie. Writers read their own stories, sitting at the front of the room.

Flannery never entered into the Workshop discussions. I heard that when she was first in the Workshop in 1945, before she had published anything, her stories had not been well received and she had not tried to defend them. The only comment I ever heard her make in class was the next spring. Andrew Lytle was in charge that semester during Paul Engle's absence from campus, and he asked her what she thought of the story we were discussing that day. By then, most of the students knew she was already a published writer; everyone in the room wanted to hear what she would say. In a perfectly deadpan voice, addressing herself to the general emptiness of the front of the room, came her laconic reply: "I'd say the description of the crocodile in there was real good." The irony of Flannery's statement lay in the fact that the crocodile was the best thing in the story, but it had absolutely no meaning in the texture of the story itself. She had said all there was to say—but she would never have offered that much if Mr. Lytle hadn't asked her.

I saw Flannery very little that fall except at the Monday afternoon Workshop sessions and occasionally on Sunday noon at the Mad Hatter Tea Room that used to be up over Bremer's Clothing Store, where I worked as salad girl. Flannery's boardinghouse didn't serve meals on Sunday, and so she came there. I can remember meeting her only twice on the campus or the street. Once she was going to the library to check out *Dead Souls*. She said Robie Macauley recommended that book as one every writer should read, "so I reckon I'd better do it." (Years later she was to say that she supposed Gogol was an influence.) And the other time she was coming out of Woolworths' Five and Ten Cent Store where she had bought one cake of Palmolive soap. (I've thought about that single purchase since then, and it seems to me it says something about the uncluttered life she always lived. I doubt if Flannery ever bought two of anything at one time, unless it was peacocks or swans or bantam chicks. Her room at Iowa, when I saw it that one time, expressed the same kind of monastic simplicity: the neatly made bed, the typewriter waiting on the desk. There was nothing extraneous in that room except for a box of vanilla wafers beside the typewriter. She nibbled on cookies while she wrote, she said, because she didn't smoke.)

My friendship with Flannery continued the next semester. I would have liked to have gone to the movies with her or had a Coke with her, but it simply didn't occur to me that things like that could ever be a part of her life. I did, however, begin to consider myself her closest friend on the campus. Her favorite place to go in Iowa City was out to the City Park. Once, I walked out there with her on an especially bleak February Sunday afternoon to look at the two sad and mangy bears, the raccoons, and the special foreign chickens they had. It seemed a particularly desultory thing to be doing, and I was puzzled at how completely absorbed and interested Flannery was that day looking at these things which I knew she'd looked at many times before. She was still working on the novel then, of course (which was to be *Wise Blood*), although she never talked about it, and I knew nothing at that time about the zoo and park scenes in that book until I read it a few years later. But, I also realize now, her fondness for the zoo went beyond the fact that she may have been getting "material" for her work. Years later, in letters to me, she was to recall the City Park as almost the only asset Iowa City had to offer. The flowing letter begins with a comment on Iowa City housing and is dated December 28, 1952. She wrote:

I remember those boarding houses in Iowa City very well and all the cold rooms I looked at. My landlady, Mrs. Guzeman (at 115 E. Bloomington Street), was not very fond of me because I stayed at home and required heat to be on—at least ON. It was never UP that I remember. When it was on you could smell it and I got to where I warmed up a little every time I smelled it. One of these days I would like to see Iowa City again, but only for the zoo where those game bantams were and the bears donated by the Iowa City Lions Club. I am raising peafowl myself. They are beautiful; and contrary and expensive but I justify the expense on the grounds that I don't smoke or drink liquor or chew tobacco or have any bad habits that cost money. . . . One of these days I hope they'll be all over the place. . . .

That spring in the Workshop I heard Flannery read for the first time. It was a chapter from the novel she was working on and had made into a short story for the occasion (although it turned out to be for all time, since no trace of it ever turned up in either of her novels). She called the story "The Woman on the Stairs," and it was under this title that it was published the following year in the August 1949 *Tomorrow*. Although the story has since been described as perhaps the most purely comic of any of her stories, the odyssey of Ruby Hill on the stairs, this woman "shaped nearly like a funeral urn," proclaims the sorry human state that underlies most of her characters who suppose that they are in control of life and are calling all the shots.

In many of the stories Flannery was to write later, she permits a moment of vision to descend on the main character—very like the Joycean epiphany—in which he may see himself clearly for the first time. The moment of insight, when her characters see themselves as sinning beings, comes from the working of grace for them. It is achieved through things that cannot be predicted. It is something mysterious that cannot be elucidated. Grace comes to the grandmother of "A Good Man Is Hard to Find" in her recognition of the Misfit as her own child. It comes to Mr. Head of "The Artificial Nigger" through the artificial nigger, and to Mrs. Turpin of "Revelation" in the pigpen. But it does not come to Ruby Hill as she sits at the top of the stairs looking "down into the dark hole, down to the very bottom where she had started up so long ago," for she hears only the leery echo of her own empty words. Ruby Hill then may be one of Flannery O'Connor's truly damned characters, and the story, although exemplifying elements of the purely comic, becomes tragical in the sense that the character is denied any glimpse of self-understanding, and therefore salvation. She sits at the top of the stairs literally full of nothing, feeling the roll in her stomach "as if it were not in her stomach. It was as if it were out somewhere in nothing, out nowhere, resting and waiting with plenty of time."

But few, if any, of us knew that afternoon in the Workshop when Flannery read this story that it was about original sin, that her vision embraced the early Christian concept of man's loss of innocence with rejection of his first parents from the Garden, that she really did believe in evil and damnation and redemption. We knew none of these things, and I, for one, did not even know that day—and not until several years later—that Flannery O'Connor was a Roman Catholic.

Why then were we so strangely moved by her reading that afternoon, which I suppose was the most memorable Monday the Workshop has ever had, before or since? As I remember her voice now, its slight Southern drawl enhancing the country idiom she was just beginning to perfect and was always to use, both in her characters' dialogue and as a kind of indirect discourse, and giving a humorous reinforcement to the irony in that story, I realize that her stories are always intensely oral in the highest sense of the storytelling art. It is a great loss that no recordings were made of Flannery reading her fiction. But, of course, her voice alone could not account for the feeling we had that afternoon that we were in the presence of a significant writer.

I think now it was because her lonely fiction magnifies the drab and the colorless, and we were stirred to a recognition of ourselves in the human predicament. Flannery considered herself a realist above all else. Her characters, no matter how freakish and bizarre they may seem on the surface, or how commonplace and white trashy— no matter how unsettling—speak home dark truths and, if anything, become almost too lifelike. As Ruby Hill climbs the dark steep stairs, fighting off the knowledge of her pregnancy, which she equates with death, so do we all in some lonely moment of our lives struggle with that old paradox that life begets death. We, too, live in the funeral "urns" of our bodies.

After Flannery finished reading the story, we sat there until Andrew Lytle gave meaning to our silence by saying Workshop was over for the day. For once, there was not going to be any critical dissecting. Flannery disappeared out the door to go back to her room upstairs at Mrs. Guzeman's. Most of the others took off for the Brown Derby on Dubuque Street, which was the writers' hangout that semester. The Workshop afternoon was over. That he had said nothing about Flannery's story was a tribute to her genius. But I and Clyde McCleod wanted there to be something more—some more tangible token of our admiration. We went around Iowa City on that late spring afternoon, walking into people's yards as if they were public domain, to gather arms full of flowering branches, taking only the most beautiful, and we carried them up to Flannery.

JEAN WYLDER

FLANNERY O'CONNOR

The Comforts of Home

THOMAS WITHDREW to the side of the window and with his head between the wall and the curtain he looked down on the driveway where the car had stopped. His mother and the little slut were getting out of it. His mother emerged slowly, stolid and awkward, and then the little slut's long slightly bowed legs slid out, the dress pulled above the knees. With a shriek of laughter she ran to meet the dog, who bounded, overjoyed, shaking with pleasure, to welcome her. Rage gathered throughout Thomas's large frame with a silent ominous intensity, like a mob assembling.

It was now up to him to pack a suitcase, go to the hotel, and stay there until the house should be cleared.

He did not know where a suitcase was, he disliked to pack, he needed his books, his typewriter was not portable, he was used to an electric blanket, he could not bear to eat in restaurants. His mother, with her daredevil charity, was about to wreck the peace of the house.

The back door slammed and the girl's laugh shot up from the kitchen, through the back hall, up the stairwell and into his room, making for him like a bolt of electricity. He jumped to the side and stood glaring about him. His words of the morning had been unequivocal: "If you bring that girl back into this house, I leave. You can choose—her or me."

She had made her choice. An intense pain gripped his throat. It was the first time in his thirty-five years . . . He felt a sudden burning moisture behind his eyes. Then he steadied himself, overcome by rage. On the contrary: she had not made any choice. She was counting on his attachment to his electric blanket. She would have to be shown.

The girl's laughter rang upward a second time and Thomas winced. He saw again her look of the night before. She had invaded his room. He had waked to find his door open and her in it. There was enough light from the hall to make her visible as she turned toward him. The face was like a comedienne's in a musical comedy—a pointed chin, wide apple cheeks and feline empty eyes. He had sprung out of his bed and snatched a straight chair and then he had backed her out the door, holding the chair in front of him like an animal trainer driving out a dangerous cat. He had driven her silently down the hall, pausing when he reached it to beat on his mother's door. The girl, with a gasp, turned and fled into the guest room.

In a moment his mother had opened her door and peered out apprehensively. Her face, greasy with whatever she put on it at night, was framed in pink rubber curlers. She looked down the hall where the girl had disappeared. Thomas stood before her, the chair still lifted in front of him as if he were about to quell another beast. "She tried to get in my room," he hissed, pushing in. "I woke up and she was trying to get in my room." He closed the door behind him and his voice rose in outrage. "I won't put up with this! I won't put up with it another day!"

His mother, backed by him to her bed, sat down on the edge of it. She had a heavy body on which sat a thin, mysteriously gaunt and incongruous head.

"I'm telling you for the last time," Thomas said, "I won't put up with this another day." There was an observable tendency in all of her actions. This was, with the best intentions in the world, to make a mockery of virtue, to pursue it with such a mindless intensity that everyone involved was made a fool of and virtue itself became ridiculous. "Not another day," he repeated.

His mother shook her head emphatically, her eyes still on the door.

Thomas put the chair on the floor in front of her and sat down on it. He leaned forward as if he were about to explain something to a defective child.

"That's just another way she's unfortunate," his mother said. "So awful, so awful. She told me the name of it but I forget what it is but it's something she can't help. Something she was born with. Thomas," she said and put her hand to her jaw, "suppose it were you?"

Exasperation blocked his windpipe. "Can't I make you see," he croaked, "that if she can't help herself you can't help her?"

His mother's eyes, intimate but untouchable, were the blue of great distances after sunset. "Nimpermaniac," she murmured.

"Nymphomaniac," he said fiercely. "She doesn't need to supply you with any fancy names. She's a moral moron. That's all you need to know. Born without the moral faculty—like somebody else would be born without a kidney or a leg. Do you understand?"

"I keep thinking it might be you," she said, her hand still on her jaw. "If it were you, how do you think I'd feel if nobody took you in? What if you were a nimpermaniac and not a brilliant smart person and you did what you couldn't help and . . ."

Thomas felt a deep unbearable loathing for himself as if he were turning slowly into the girl.

"What did she have on?" she asked abruptly, her eyes narrowing.

"Nothing!" he roared. "Now will you get her out of here!"

"How can I turn her out in the cold?" she said. "This morning she was threatening to kill herself again."

"Send her back to jail," Thomas said.

"I would not send *you* back to jail, Thomas," she said.

He got up and snatched the chair and fled the room while he was still able to control himself.

Thomas loved his mother. He loved her because it was his nature to do so, but there were times when he could not endure her love for him. There were times when it became nothing but pure idiot mystery and he sensed about him forces, invisible currents entirely out of his control. She proceeded always from the tritest of considerations—it was the *nice thing to do*—into the most foolhardy engagements with the devil, whom, of course, she never recognized.

The devil for Thomas was only a manner of speaking, but it was a manner appropriate to the situations his mother got into. Had she been in any degree intellectual, he could have proved to her from early Christian history that no excess of virtue is justified, that a moderation of good produces likewise a moderation in evil, that if Antony of Egypt had stayed at home and attended to his sister, no devils would have plagued him.

Thomas was not cynical and so far from being opposed to virtue, he saw it as the principle of order and the only thing that makes life bearable. His own life was made bearable by the fruits of his mother's saner virtues—by the well-regulated house she kept and the excellent meals she served. But when virtue got out of hand with her, as now, a sense of devils grew upon him, and these were not mental quirks in himself or the old lady, they were denizens with personalities, present though not visible, who might any moment be expected to shriek or rattle a pot.

The girl had landed in the county jail a month ago on a bad check charge and his mother had seen her picture in the paper. At the breakfast table she had gazed at it for a long time and then had passed it over the coffee pot to him. "Imagine," she said, "only nineteen years old and in that filthy jail. And she doesn't look like a bad girl."

Thomas glanced at the picture. It showed the face of a shrewd ragamuffin. He observed that the average age for criminality was steadily lowering.

"She looks like a wholesome girl," his mother said.

"Wholesome people don't pass bad checks," Thomas said.

"You don't know what you'd do in a pinch."

"I wouldn't pass a bad check," Thomas said.

"I think," his mother said, "I'll take her a little box of candy."

If then and there he had put his foot down, nothing else would have happened. His father, had he been living, would have put his foot down at that point. Taking a box of candy was her favorite nice thing to do. When anyone within her social station moved to town, she called and took a box of candy; when any of her friend's children had babies or won a scholarship, she called and took a box of candy; when an old person broke his hip, she was at his bedside with a box of candy. He had been amused at the idea of her taking a box of candy to the jail.

He stood now in his room with the girl's laugh rocketing away in his head and cursed his amusement.

When his mother returned from the visit to the jail, she had burst into his study without knocking and had collapsed full-length on his couch, lifting her small swollen feet up on the arm of it. After a moment, she recovered herself enough to sit up and put a newspaper under them. Then she fell back again. "We don't know how the other half lives," she said.

Thomas knew that though her conversation moved from cliché to cliché there were real experiences behind them. He was less sorry for the girl's being in jail than for his mother having to see her there. He would have spared her all unpleasant sights. "Well," he said and put away his journal, "you had better forget it now. The girl has ample reason to be in jail."

"You can't imagine what all she's been through," she said, sitting up again, "listen." The poor girl, Star, had been brought up by a stepmother with three children of her own, one an almost grown boy who had taken advantage of her in such dreadful ways that she had been forced to run away and find her real mother. Once found, her real mother had sent her to various boarding schools to get rid of her. At each of these she had been forced to run away by the presence of perverts and sadists so monstrous that their acts defied description. Thomas could tell that his mother had not been spared the details that she was sparing him. Now and again when she spoke vaguely, her voice shook and he could tell that she was remembering some horror that had been put to her graphically. He had hoped that in a few days the memory of all this would wear off, but it did not. The next day she returned to the jail with Kleenex and cold-cream and a few days later, she announced that she had consulted a lawyer.

It was at these times that Thomas truly mourned the death of his father though he had not been able to endure him in life. The old man would have had none of this foolishness. Untouched by useless compassion, he would (behind her back) have pulled the necessary strings with his crony, the sheriff, and the girl would have been packed off to the state penitentiary to serve her time. He had always been engaged in some enraged action until one morning when (with an angry glance at his wife as if she alone were responsible) he had dropped dead at the breakfast table. Thomas had inherited his father's reason without his ruthlessness and his mother's love of good without her tendency to pursue it. His plan for all practical action was to wait and see what developed.

The lawyer found that the story of the repeated atrocities was for the most part untrue, but when he explained to her that the girl was a psychopathic personality, not insane enough for the asylum, not criminal enough for the jail, not stable enough for society, Thomas's mother was more deeply affected than ever. The girl readily admitted that her story was untrue on account of her being a congenital liar; she lied, she said, because she was insecure. She had passed through the hands of several psychiatrists who had put the finishing touches to her education. She knew there was no hope for her. In the presence of such an affliction as this, his mother seemed bowed down by some painful mystery that nothing would make endurable but a redoubling of effort. To his annoyance, she appeared to look on *him* with compassion, as if her hazy charity no longer made distinctions.

A few days later she burst in and said that the lawyer had got the girl paroled—to her.

Thomas rose from his Morris chair, dropping the review he had been reading. His large bland face contracted in anticipated pain. "You are not," he said, "going to bring that girl here!"

"No, no," she said, "calm yourself, Thomas." She had managed with difficulty to get the girl a job in a pet shop in town and a place to board with a crotchety old lady of her acquaintance. People were not kind. They did not put themselves in the place of someone like Star who had everything against her.

Thomas sat down again and retrieved his review. He seemed just to have escaped some danger which he did not care to make clear to himself. "Nobody can tell you anything," he said, "but in a few days that girl will have left town, having got what she could out of you. You'll never hear from her again."

Two nights later he came home and opened the parlor door and was speared by a shrill depthless laugh. His mother and the girl sat close to the fireplace where the gas logs were lit. The girl gave the immediate impression of being physically crooked. Her hair was cut like a dog's or an elf's and she was dressed in the latest fashion. She was training on him a long familiar sparkling stare that turned after a second into an intimate grin.

"Thomas!" his mother said, her voice firm with the injunction not to bolt, "this is Star you've heard so much about. Star is going to have supper with us."

The girl called herself Star Drake. The lawyer had found that her real name was Sarah Ham.

Thomas neither moved nor spoke but hung in the door in what seemed a savage perplexity. Finally he said, "How do you do, Sarah," in a tone of such loathing that he was shocked at the sound of it. He reddened, feeling it beneath him to show contempt for any creature so pathetic. He advanced into the room, determined at least on a decent politeness and sat down heavily in a straight chair.

"Thomas writes history," his mother said with a threatening look at him. "He's president of the local Historical Society this year."

The girl leaned forward and gave Thomas an even more pointed attention. "Fabulous!" she said in a throaty voice.

"Right now Thomas is writing about the first settlers in this county," his mother said.

"Fabulous!" the girl repeated.

Thomas by an effort of will managed to look as if he were alone in the room.

"Say, you know who he looks like?" Star asked, her head on one side, taking him in at an angle.

"Oh, someone very distinguished!" his mother said archly.

"This cop I saw in the movie I went to last night," Star said.

"Star," his mother said, "I think you ought to be careful about the kind of movies you go to. I think you ought to see only the best ones. I don't think crime stories would be good for you."

"Oh this was a crime-does-not-pay," Star said, "and I swear this cop looked exactly like him. They were always putting something over on the guy. He would look like he couldn't stand it a minute longer or he would blow up. He was a riot. And not bad looking," she added with an appreciative leer at Thomas.

"Star," his mother said, "I think it would be grand if you developed a taste for music."

Thomas sighed. His mother rattled on and the girl, paying no attention to her, let her eyes play over him. The quality of her look was such that it might have been her hands, resting now on his knees, now on his neck. Her eyes had a mocking glitter and he knew that she was well aware he could not stand the sight of her. He needed nothing to tell him he was in the presence of the very stuff of corruption, but blameless corruption because there was no responsible faculty behind it. He was looking at the most unendurable form of innocence. Absently he asked himself what the attitude of God was to this, meaning if possible to adopt it.

His mother's behavior throughout the meal was so idiotic that he could barely stand to look at her and since he could less stand to look at Sarah Ham, he fixed on the sideboard across the room a continuous gaze of disapproval and disgust. Every remark of the girl's his mother met as if it deserved serious attention. She advanced several plans for the wholesome use of Star's spare time. Sarah Ham paid no more attention to this advice than if it came from a parrot. Once when Thomas inadvertently looked in her direction, she winked. As soon as he had swallowed the last spoonful of dessert, he rose and muttered, "I have to go, I have a meeting."

"Thomas," his mother said, "I want you to take Star home on your way. I don't want her riding in taxis by herself at night."

For a moment Thomas remained furiously silent. Then he turned and left the room. Presently he came back with a look of obscure determination on his face. The girl was ready, meekly waiting at the parlor door. She cast up at him a great look of admiration and confidence. Thomas did not offer his arm but she took it anyway and moved out of the house and down the steps, attached to what might have been a miraculously moving monument.

"Be good!" his mother called.

Sarah Ham snickered and poked him in the ribs.

While getting his coat he had decided that this would be his opportunity to tell the girl that unless she ceased to be a parasite on his mother, he would see to it, personally, that she was returned to jail. He would let her know that he understood what she was up to, that he was not an innocent and that there were certain things he would not put up with. At his desk, pen in hand, none was more articulate than

Thomas. As soon as he found himself shut into the car with Sarah Ham, terror seized his tongue.

She curled her feet up under her and said, "Alone at last," and giggled.

Thomas swerved the car away from the house and drove fast toward the gate. Once on the highway, he shot forward as if he were being pursued.

"Jesus!" Sarah Ham said, swinging her feet off the seat, "where's the fire?"

Thomas did not answer. In a few seconds he could feel her edging closer. She stretched, eased nearer, and finally hung her hand limply over his shoulder. "Tomsee doesn't like me," she said, "but I think he's fabulously cute."

Thomas covered the three and a half miles into town in a little over four minutes. The light at the first intersection was red but he ignored it. The old woman lived three blocks beyond. When the car screeched to a halt at the place, he jumped out and ran around to the girl's door and opened it. She did not move from the car and Thomas was obliged to wait. After a moment one leg emerged, then her small white crooked face appeared and stared up at him. There was something about the look of it that suggested blindness but it was the blindness of those who don't know that they cannot see. Thomas was curiously sickened. The empty eyes moved over him. "Nobody likes me," she said in a sullen tone. "What if you were me and I couldn't stand to ride you three miles?"

"My mother likes you," he muttered.

"Her!" the girl said. "She's just about seventy-five years behind the times!"

Breathlessly Thomas said, "If I find you bothering her again, I'll have you put back in jail." There was a dull force behind his voice though it came out barely above a whisper.

"You and who else?" she said and drew back in the car as if now she did not intend to get out at all. Thomas reached into it, blindly grasped the front of her coat, pulled her out by it and released her. Then he lunged back to the car and sped off. The other door was still hanging open and her laugh, bodiless but real, bounded up the street as if it were about to jump in the open side of the car and ride away with him. He reached over and slammed the door and then drove toward home, too angry to attend his meeting. He intended to make his mother well-aware of his displeasure. He intended to leave no doubt in her mind. The voice of his father rasped in his head.

Numbskull, the old man said, put your foot down now. Show her who's boss before she shows you.

But when Thomas reached home, his mother, wisely, had gone to bed.

THE NEXT MORNING he appeared at the breakfast table, his brow lowered and the thrust of his jaw indicating that he was in a dangerous humor. When he intended to be determined, Thomas began like a bull that, before charging, backs with his head lowered and paws the ground. "All right now listen," he began, yanking out his chair and sitting down, "I have something to say to you about that girl and I don't intend to say it but once." He drew breath. "She's nothing but a little slut. She makes fun of you behind your back. She means to get everything she can out of you and you are nothing to her."

His mother looked as if she too had spent a restless night. She did not dress in the morning but wore her bathrobe and a gray turban around her head, which gave her face a disconcerting omniscient look. He might have been breakfasting with a sibyl.

"You'll have to use canned cream this morning," she said, pouring his coffee. "I forgot the other."

"All right, did you hear me?" Thomas growled.

"I'm not deaf," his mother said and put the pot back on the trivet. "I know I'm nothing but an old bag of wind to her."

"Then why do you persist in this foolhardy . . ."

"Thomas," she said, and put her hand to the side of her face, "it might be . . ."

"It is not me!" Thomas said, grasping the table leg at his knee.

She continued to hold her face, shaking her head slightly. "Think of all you have," she began. "All the comforts of home. And morals, Thomas. No bad inclinations, nothing bad you were born with."

Thomas began to breathe like someone who feels the onset of asthma. "You are not logical," he said in a limp voice. "*He* would have put his foot down."

The old lady stiffened. "You," she said, "are not like him."

Thomas opened his mouth silently.

"However," his mother said, in a tone of such subtle accusation that she might have been taking back the compliment, "I won't invite her back again since you're so dead set against her."

"I am not set against her," Thomas said. "I am set against your making a fool of yourself."

As soon as he left the table and closed the door of his study on himself, his father took up a squatting position in his mind. The old man had had the countryman's ability to converse squatting, though he was no countryman but had been born and brought up in the city and only moved to a smaller place later to exploit his talents. With steady skill he had made them think him one of them. In the midst of a conversation on the courthouse lawn, he would squat and his two or three companions would squat with him with no break in the surface of the talk. By gesture he had lived his lie; he had never deigned to tell one.

Let her run over you, he said. You ain't like me. Not enough to be a man.

Thomas began vigorously to read and presently the image faded. The girl had caused a disturbance in the depths of his being, somewhere out of the reach of his power of analysis. He felt as if he had seen a tornado pass a hundred yards away and had an intimation that it would turn again and head directly for him. He did not get his mind firmly on his work until mid-morning.

Two nights later, his mother and he were sitting in the den after their supper, each reading a section of the evening paper, when the telephone began to ring with the brassy intensity of a fire alarm. Thomas reached for it. As soon as the receiver was in his hand, a shrill female voice screamed into the room, "Come get this girl! Come get her! Drunk! Drunk in my parlor and I won't have it! Lost her job and come back here drunk! I won't have it!"

His mother leapt up and snatched the receiver.

The ghost of Thomas's father rose before him. Call the sheriff, the old man prompted. "Call the sheriff," Thomas said in a loud voice. "Call the sheriff to go there and pick her up."

"We'll be right there," his mother was saying. "We'll come and get her right away. Tell her to get her things together."

"She ain't in no condition to get nothing together," the voice screamed. "You shouldn't have put something like her off on me! My house is respectable!"

"Tell her to call the sheriff," Thomas shouted.

His mother put the receiver down and looked at him. "I wouldn't turn a dog over to that man," she said.

Thomas sat in the chair with his arms folded and looked fixedly at the wall.

"Think of the poor girl, Thomas," his mother said, "with nothing. Nothing. And we have everything."

When they arrived, Sarah Ham was slumped spraddle-legged against the banister on the boarding house front-steps. Her tam was down on her forehead where the old woman had slammed it and her clothes were bulging out of her suitcase where the old woman had thrown them in. She was carrying on a drunken conversation with herself in a low personal tone. A streak of lipstick ran up one side of her face. She allowed herself to be guided by his mother to the car and put in the back seat without seeming to know who the rescuer was. "Nothing to talk to all day but a pack of goddamned parakeets," she said in a furious whisper.

Thomas, who had not got out of the car at all, or looked at her after the first revolted glance, said, "I'm telling you, once and for all, the place to take her is the jail."

His mother, sitting on the back seat, holding the girl's hand, did not answer.

"All right, take her to the hotel," he said.

"I cannot take a drunk girl to a hotel, Thomas," she said. "You know that."

"Then take her to a hospital."

"She doesn't need a jail or a hotel or a hospital," his mother said, "she needs a home."

"She does not need mine," Thomas said.

"Only for tonight, Thomas," the old lady sighed. "Only for tonight."

Since then eight days had passed. The little slut was established in the guest room. Every day his mother set out to find her a job and a place to board, and failed, for the old woman had broadcast a warning. Thomas kept to his room or the den. His home was to him home, workshop, church, as personal as the shell of a turtle and as necessary. He could not believe that it could be violated in this way. His flushed face had a constant look of stunned outrage.

As soon as the girl was up in the morning, her voice throbbed out in a blues song that would rise and waver, then plunge low with insinuations of passion about to be satisfied and Thomas, at his desk, would lunge up and begin frantically stuffling his ears with Kleenex. Each time he started from one room to another, one floor to another, she would be certain to appear. Each time he was halfway up or down the stairs, she would either meet him and pass, cringing coyly, or go up or down behind him, breathing small tragic spearmint-flavored sighs. She appeared to adore Thomas's repugnance to her and to draw it out of him every chance she got as if it added delectably to her martyrdom.

The old man—small, wasp-like, in his yellowed panama hat, his seersucker suit, his pink carefully soiled shirt, his small string tie—appeared to have taken up his station in Thomas's mind and from there, usually squatting, he shot out the same rasping suggestion every time the boy paused from his forced studies. Put your foot down. Go to see the sheriff.

The sheriff was another edition of Thomas's father except that he wore a checkered shirt and a Texas type hat and was ten years younger. He was as easily dishonest, and he had genuinely admired the old man. Thomas, like his mother, would have gone far out of his way to avoid his glassy pale blue gaze. He kept hoping for another solution, for a miracle.

With Sarah Ham in the house, meals were unbearable.

"Tomsee doesn't like me," she said the third or fourth night at the supper table and cast her pouting gaze across at the large rigid figure of Thomas, whose face was set with the look of a man trapped by insufferable odors. "He doesn't want me here. Nobody wants me anywhere."

"Thomas's name is Thomas," his mother interrupted. "Not Tomsee."

"I made Tomsee up," she said. "I think it's cute. He hates me."

"Thomas does not hate you," his mother said. "We are not the kind of people who hate," she added, as if this were an imperfection that had been bred out of them generations ago.

"Oh, I know when I'm not wanted," Sarah Ham continued. "They didn't even want me in jail. If I killed myself I wonder would God want me?"

"Try it and see," Thomas muttered.

The girl screamed with laughter. Then she stopped abruptly, her face puckered and she began to shake. "The best thing to do," she said, her teeth clattering, "is to kill myself. Then I'll be out of everybody's way. I'll go to hell and be out of God's way. And even the devil won't want me. He'll kick me out of hell, not even in hell . . ." she wailed.

Thomas rose, picked up his plate and knife and fork and carried them to the den to finish his supper. After that, he had not eaten another meal at the table but had had his mother serve him at his desk. At these meals, the old man was intensely present to him. He appeared to be tipping backwards in his chair, his thumbs beneath his galluses, while he said such things as, She never ran me away from my own table.

A few nights later, Sarah Ham slashed her wrists with a paring knife and had hysterics. From the den where he was closeted after supper, Thomas heard a shriek, then a series of screams, then his mother's scurrying footsteps through the house. He did not move. His first instant of hope that the girl had cut her throat faded as he realized she could not have done it and continue to scream the way she was doing. He returned to his journal and presently the screams subsided. In a moment his mother burst in with his coat and hat. "We have to take her to the hospital," she said. "She tried to do away with herself. I have a tourniquet on her arm. Oh Lord, Thomas," she said, "imagine being so low you'd do a thing like that!"

Thomas rose woodenly and put on his hat and coat. "We will take her to the hospital," he said, "and we will leave her there."

"And drive her to despair again?" the old lady cried. "Thomas!"

Standing in the center of his room now, realizing that he had reached the point where action was inevitable, that he must pack, that he must leave, that he must go, Thomas remained immovable.

His fury was directed not at the little slut but at his mother. Even though the doctor had found that she had barely damaged herself and had raised the girl's wrath by laughing at the tourniquet and putting only a streak of iodine on the cut, his mother could not get over the incident. Some new weight of sorrow seemed to have been thrown across her shoulders, and not only Thomas, but Sarah Ham was infuriated by this, for it appeared to be a general sorrow that would have found another object no matter what good fortune came to either of them. The experience of Sarah Ham had plunged the old lady into mourning for the world.

The morning after the attempted suicide, she had gone through the house and collected all the knives and scissors and locked them in a drawer. She emptied a bottle of rat poison down the toilet and took up the roach tablets from the kitchen floor. Then she came to Thomas's study and said in a whisper, "Where is that gun of his? I want you to lock it up."

"The gun is in my drawer," Thomas roared, "and I will not lock it up. If she shoots herself, so much the better!"

"Thomas," his mother said, "she'll hear you!"

"Let her hear me!" Thomas yelled. "Don't you know she has no intention of killing herself? Don't you know her kind never kill themselves? Don't you . . ."

His mother slipped out the door and closed it to silence him and Sarah Ham's laugh, quite close in the hall, came rattling into his room. "Tomsee'll find out. I'll kill myself and then he'll be sorry he wasn't nice to me. I'll use his own lil gun, his own lil ol' pearl-handled revol-lervuh!" she shouted and let out a loud tormented-sounding laugh in imitation of a movie monster.

Thomas ground his teeth. He pulled out his desk drawer and felt for the pistol. It was an inheritance from the old man, whose opinion it had been that every house should contain a loaded gun. He had discharged two bullets one night into the side of a prowler, but Thomas had never shot anything. He had no fear that the girl would use the gun on herself and he closed the drawer. Her kind clung tenaciously to life and were able to wrest some histrionic advantage from every moment.

Several ideas for getting rid of her had entered his head but each of these had been suggestions whose moral tone indicated that they had come from a mind akin to his father's, and Thomas had rejected them. He could not get the girl locked up again until she did something illegal. The old man would have been able with no qualms at all to get her drunk and send her out on the highway in his car, meanwhile notifying the highway patrol of her presence on the road, but Thomas considered this below his moral stature. Suggestions continued to come to him, each more outrageous than the last.

He had not the vaguest hope that the girl would get the gun and shoot herself, but that afternoon when he looked in the drawer, the gun was gone. His study locked from the inside, not the out. He cared nothing about the gun, but the thought of Sarah Ham's hands sliding among his papers infuriated him. Now even his study was contaminated. The only place left untouched by her was his bedroom.

That night she entered it.

In the morning at breakfast, he did not eat and did not sit down. He stood beside his chair and delivered his ultimatum while his mother sipped her coffee as if she were both alone in the room and in great pain. "I have stood this," he said, "for as long as I am able. Since I see plainly that you care nothing about me, about my peace or comfort or working conditions, I am about to take the only step open to me. I will give you one more day. If you bring the girl back into this house this afternoon, I leave. You can choose—her or me." He had more to say but at that point his voice cracked and he left.

At ten o'clock his mother and Sarah Ham left the house.

At four he heard the car wheels on the gravel and rushed to the window. As the car stopped, the dog stood up, alert, shaking.

He seemed unable to take the first step that would set him walking to the closet in the hall to look for the suitcase. He was like a man handed a knife and told to operate on himself if he wished to live. His huge hands clenched helplessly. His expression was a turmoil of indecision and outrage. His pale blue eyes seemed to sweat in his broiling face. He closed them for a moment and on the back of his lids, his father's image leered at him. Idiot! the old man hissed, idiot! The criminal slut stole your gun! See the sheriff! See the sheriff!

It was a moment before Thomas opened his eyes. He seemed newly stunned. He stood where he was for at least three minutes, then he turned slowly like a large vessel reversing its direction and faced the door. He stood there a moment longer, then he left, his face set to see the ordeal through.

He did not know where he would find the sheriff. The man made his own rules and kept his own hours. Thomas stopped first at the jail where his office was, but he was not in it. He went to the courthouse and was told by a clerk that the sheriff had gone to the barber shop across the street. "Yonder's the deppity," the clerk said and pointed out the window to the large figure of a man in a checkered shirt, who was leaning against the side of a police car, looking into space.

"It has to be the sheriff," Thomas said and left for the barber shop. As little as he wanted anything to do with the sheriff, he realized that the man was at least intelligent and not simply a mound of sweating flesh.

The barber said the sheriff had just left. Thomas started back to the courthouse and as he stepped on to the sidewalk from the street, he saw a lean, slightly stooped figure gesticulating angrily at the deputy.

Thomas approached with an aggressiveness brought on by nervous agitation. He stopped abruptly three feet away and said in an over-loud voice, "Can I have a word with you?" without adding the sheriff's name, which was Farebrother.

Farebrother turned his sharp creased face just enough to take Thomas in, and the deputy did likewise, but neither spoke. The sheriff removed a very small piece of cigarette from his lip and dropped it at his feet. "I told you what to do," he said to the deputy. Then he moved off with a slight nod that indicated Thomas could follow him if he wanted to see him. The deputy slunk around the front of the police car and got inside.

Farebrother, with Thomas following, headed across the courthouse square and stopped beneath a tree that shaded a quarter of the front lawn. He waited, leaning slightly forward, and lit another cigarette.

Thomas began to blurt out his business. As he had not had time to prepare his words, he was barely coherent. By repeating the same thing over several times, he managed at length to get out what he wanted to say. When he finished, the sheriff was still leaning slightly forward, at an angle to him, his eyes on nothing in particular. He remained that way without speaking.

Thomas began again, slower and in a lamer voice, and Farebrother let him continue for some time before he said, "We had her oncet." He then allowed himself a slow, creased, all-knowing, quarter smile.

"I had nothing to do with that," Thomas said. "That was my mother."

Farebrother squatted.

"She was trying to help the girl," Thomas said. "She didn't know she couldn't be helped."

"Bit off more than she could chew, I reckon," the voice below him mused.

"She has nothing to do with this," Thomas said. "She doesn't know I'm here. The girl is dangerous with that gun."

"*He,*" the sheriff said, "never let anything grow under his feet. Particularly nothing a woman planted."

"She might kill somebody with that gun," Thomas said weakly, looking down at the round top of the Texas type hat.

There was a long time of silence.

"Where's she got it?" Farebrother asked.

"I don't know. She sleeps in the guest room. It must be in there, in her suitcase probably," Thomas said.

Farebrother lapsed into silence again.

"You could come search the guest room," Thomas said in a strained voice. "I can go home and leave the latch off the front door and you can come in quietly and go upstairs and search her room."

Farebrother turned his head so that his eyes looked boldly at Thomas's knees. "You seem to know how it ought to be done," he said. "Want to swap jobs?"

Thomas said nothing because he could not think of anything to say, but he waited doggedly. Farebrother removed the cigarette butt from his lips and dropped it on the grass. Beyond him on the courthouse porch a group of loiterers who had been leaning at the left of the door moved over to the right where a patch of sunlight had settled. From one of the upper windows a crumpled piece of paper blew out and drifted down.

"I'll come along about six," Farebrother said. "Leave the latch off the door and keep out of my way—yourself and them two women too."

Thomas let out a rasping sound of relief meant to be "Thanks," and struck off across the grass like someone released. The phrase, "them two women," stuck like a burr in his brain—the subtlety of the insult to his mother hurting him more than any of Farebrother's references to his own incompetence. As he got into his car, his face suddenly flushed. Had he delivered his mother over to the sheriff—to be a butt for the man's tongue? Was he betraying her to get rid of the little slut? He saw at once that this was not the case. He was doing what he was doing for her own good, to rid her of a parasite that would ruin their peace. He started his car and drove quickly home but once he had turned in the driveway, he decided it would be better to park some distance from the house and go quietly in by the back door. He parked on the grass and on the grass walked in a circle toward the rear of the house. The sky was lined with mustard-colored streaks. The dog was asleep on the back door-mat. At the approach of his master's step, he opened one yellow eye, took him in, and closed it again.

Thomas let himself into the kitchen. It was empty and the house was quiet enough for him to be aware of the loud ticking of the kitchen clock. It was a quarter to six. He tiptoed hurriedly through the hall to the front door and took the latch off it. Then he stood for a moment listening. From behind the closed parlor door, he heard his mother snoring softly and presumed that she had gone to sleep while reading. On the other side of the hall, not three feet from his study, the little slut's black coat and red pocketbook were slung on a chair. He heard water running upstairs and decided she was taking a bath.

He went into his study and sat down at his desk to wait, noting with distaste that every few moments a tremor ran through him. He sat for a minute or two doing nothing. Then he picked up a pen and began to draw squares on the back of an envelope that lay before him. He looked at his watch. It was eleven minutes to six. After a moment he idly drew the center drawer of the desk out over his lap. For a moment he stared at the gun without recognition. Then he gave a yelp and leaped up. She had put it back!

Idiot! his father hissed, idiot! Go plant it in her pocketbook. Don't just stand there. Go plant it in her pocketbook!

Thomas stood staring at the drawer.

Moron! the old man fumed. Quick while there's time! Go plant it in her pocketbook.

Thomas did not move.

Imbecile! his father cried.

Thomas picked up the gun.

Make haste, the old man ordered.

Thomas started forward, holding the gun away from him. He opened the door and looked at the chair. The black coat and red pocketbook were lying on it almost within reach.

Hurry up, you fool, his father said.

From behind the parlor door the almost inaudible snores of his mother rose and fell. They seemed to mark an order of time that had nothing to do with the instants left to Thomas. There was no other sound.

Quick, you imbecile, before she wakes up, the old man said.

The snores stopped and Thomas heard the sofa springs groan. He grabbed the red pocketbook. It had a skin-like feel to his touch and as it opened, he caught an unmistakable odor of the girl. Wincing, he thrust in the gun and then drew back. His face burned an ugly dull red.

"What is Tomsee putting in my purse?" she called and her pleased laugh bounced down the staircase. Thomas whirled.

She was at the top of the stair, coming down in the manner of a fashion model, one bare leg and then the other thrusting out the front of her kimono in a definite rhythm. "Tomsee is being naughty," she said in a throaty voice. She reached the bottom and cast a possessive leer at Thomas whose face was now more gray than red. She reached out, pulled the bag open with her finger and peered at the gun.

His mother opened the parlor door and looked out.

"Tomsee put his pistol in my bag!" the girl shrieked.

"Ridiculous," his mother said, yawning. "What would Thomas want to put his pistol in your bag for?"

Thomas stood slightly hunched, his hands hanging helplessly at the wrists as if he had just pulled them up out of a pool of blood.

"I don't know what for," the girl said, "but he sure did it," and she proceeded to walk around Thomas, her hands on her hips, her neck thrust forward and her intimate grin fixed on him fiercely. All at once her expression seemed to open as the purse had opened when Thomas touched it. She stood with her head cocked on one side in an attitude of disbelief. "Oh boy," she said slowly, "is he a case."

At that instant Thomas damned not only the girl but the entire order of the universe that made her possible.

"Thomas wouldn't put a gun in your bag," his mother said. "Thomas is a gentleman."

The girl made a chortling noise. "You can see it in there," she said and pointed to the open purse.

You *found* it in her bag, you dimwit! the old man hissed.

"I found it in her bag!" Thomas shouted. "The dirty criminal slut stole my gun!"

His mother gasped at the sound of the other presence in his voice. The old lady's sybil-like face turned pale.

"Found it my eye!" Sarah Ham shrieked and started for the pocketbook, but Thomas, as if his arm were guided by his father, caught it first and snatched the gun. The girl in a frenzy lunged at Thomas's throat and would actually have caught him around the neck had not his mother thrown herself forward to protect her.

Fire! the old man yelled.

Thomas fired. The blast was like a sound meant to bring an end to evil in the world. Thomas heard it as a sound that would shatter the laughter of sluts until all shrieks were stilled and nothing was left to disturb the peace of perfect order.

The echo died away in waves. Before the last one had faded, Farebrother opened the door and put his head inside the hall. His nose wrinkled. His expression for some few seconds was that of a man unwilling to admit surprise. His eyes were clear as glass, reflecting the scene. The old lady lay on the floor between the girl and Thomas.

The sheriff's brain worked instantly like a calculating machine. He saw the facts as if they were already in print: the fellow had intended all along to kill his mother and pin it on the girl. But Farebrother had been too quick for him. They were not yet aware of his head in the door. As he scrutinized the scene, further insights were flashed to him. Over her body, the killer and the slut were about to collapse into each other's arms. The sheriff knew a nasty bit when he saw it. He was accustomed to enter upon scenes that were not as bad as he had hoped to find them, but this one met his expectations.

1950s

THE WORKSHOP BECAME A NATIONAL INSTITUTION during the 1950s. Graduates published in the best magazines and journals, novels and poetry selections were accepted, and a rotating faculty included Vance Bourjaily, John Berryman, Hortense Calisher, and Robert Lowell. The students were older, the program smaller than it is today, the classes held in temporary tin buildings known as "huts" erected near the Student Union.

As enrollment began to grow, Paul Engle split the workshops into Fiction and Poetry sections and, later, added a course in "Form and Theory" to better train students to study the "predominant techniques in the modern short story." Workshop meetings became more formal and regular. Then, as now, mimeographed copies of student stories would be distributed each week for Workshop discussion. Increasingly, this work made its way directly from Workshop to major magazines and quarterlies.

To close the decade, *Esquire* held a two-day symposium at Iowa. Fifteen hundred writers and critics attended to hear Norman Mailer and Ralph Ellison speak on "The Writer in a Mass Culture," and when the symposium concluded, *Esquire* editor-publisher Arnold Gingrich told *Writers Digest*, "[T]he academic centers are increasingly valuable breeding grounds for creative writing. And the most fertile of creative writing centers is Paul Engle's Writers' Workshop here in Iowa City."

On the national literary scene, *Best American* editor Martha Foley noted the increased sophistication of student writers and foresaw a rich period in American literature just ahead. Not that the U.S. government or commercial America was any help. In 1950, no "Department of Arts" existed in the United States, one of the few advanced nations in the world where this was the case. Forty years later, the National Endowment for the Arts teeters on the brink of extinction in the late '90s. Commercially, the 1951 *Best American* compilation included only a single story from "popular" magazines, and *Story* magazine ceased publication. For despite the growth of Iowa and the artistic grace of the new American short story, the publishers' mantra was the same then as now: "Love your stories, let me see your first novel." "Publishers have not found short story collections popular," Foley noted.

Stylistically, Foley found that "literary magazines seemed to be publishing a preponderance of stories concerning the main character's 'moment of realization,'" or epiphany. Yet, as epiphanies began to be mass-produced by young writers, the London *Economist* wrote, "Even before television, Americans had not acquired the habit of reading good books." Or buying them, either. A "women's" magazine analyzed the annual purchases of a family earning (in 1959) $200,000, only to discover that the entire household had spent a whopping $60 on books.

So, a strange process was under way as the '50s ended. American literature had begun to grow in stature and volume. The '50s saw the first National Book Award go to Nelson Algren, a great writer whose temperament simply didn't coincide with Workshop, as well as the emergence of Ralph Ellison, the blossoming career of future Nobel Prize winner Saul Bellow, and the arrival of soon-to-be Iowa faculty member Philip Roth. But with rare exceptions, the "literary writer" encountered an increasingly insular, and limited, audience, and the "moment of realization" story slowly began to replace the "social realist" style and political concerns of much American fiction. What allowed this development, in part, was the proliferation of creative writing programs around the country. An academic, or teachable, sort of story that could be successfully workshopped, and possibly published in a small literary journal, became for many writing students a viable goal. And not simply because it fulfilled a personal artistic ambition to write and be published, but because the expansion of creative writing programs began to produce jobs for teachers of creative writing. The widespread institutionalization of creative writing had begun.

Still, the vigor and variety of Iowa's expanding influence are admirably exemplified by the work of Bette Pesetsky, Richard Stern, and Thomas Williams. If Pesetsky and Stern manifest the comic exuberance of the Jewish-American literary tradition popularized by Bellow and Roth, Thomas Williams seems closer in spirit to Wallace Stegner's realism and concern for man finding his place in nature. In any event, by the close of the 1950s, Regionalism at Iowa was, like McCarthyism, history.

IF THERE'S A HOUSE specialty, in terms of my work, it's a story that packages material that would suffice for a novel into one-tenth novel-size.

In the seven or eight thousand words of "The Illegibility of This World," you have at least the illusion of knowing much of the narrator's life, especially as it bears on the discomfort growing within its vaunted and treasured comfort. Around his life are lives that are apparently far less secure—those of Deejay, Peter, Harry, even the "absent" Anne, the dead Kafka, and the dead Celan, whose poem supplies the story's title.

If there's a story model for "The Illegibility," it's Tolstoy's "Death of Ivan Ilyich." The models for the characters are, as usual, fusions of distorted reality and—I hope—undistorted imagination.

RICHARD STERN

TUGGED BY SUNLIGHT and the phone from a dream about populating the universe with sperm; a spaceship stocked with fertile cells unloading on empty planets with the blueprints of civilization; the humanization of the universe. "Yes?"

"Mista Biel. Deejay."

"Jeesus. What time is it?"

"Comin on nine, cep you put the clock back. Joo member to do that?"

Did I? "Yes." On the table, the knowing pine face of the clock, gold fingers at VII and X. "It's ten of seven."

"Rilly eight."

"How many times, Deejay?"

"Was finkin you wanted those leaves up."

"The leaves, yes, me, no."

"You doan want me to come over?"

"I should say 'No.' "

"No?"

"No, come on over."

"I be over haf'n hour." This could mean three hours or the next day, depending on whom he ran into or what; what bottle, that is.

"You don't need to ring. You've got the garage key."

"I need mawr bags."

Ellen wanted me to get rid of him. "Never darken our door again." I can't. We're the last people on the block for whom he can work. He botches most tool jobs. Still he can fetch, lift, carry, mow the lawn, pick up leaves, he's not stupid, he's honest, he's not always drunk; I like him. "I'll put some on the porch."

This weekend, between the World Series and Halloween, I'm alone. Ellen's in

Buffalo for our daughter Annie's thirty-sixth birthday. Friday, I drove her to Midway, then went downtown to my one-room office on Adams, checked the markets, bought a Kansas City municipal, faxed a letter to our insurance agent, sent copies of our living wills to our granddaughter—old enough now to be in on it, who knows, she might be the one to unplug the tubes—and walked five blocks to the Pub Club for the best hour of the day, lunch at the Round Table on the eleventh floor looking over the silver river and the blue bulge of the State of Illinois Building.

I've been a club member thirty-five years. It's more important than ever now that I've retired. I used to ridicule my Uncle Bert's life, a shuttle between the City Athletic Club and his rooms at the Hotel Warwick across the street. I thought that twenty-five-yard shuttle the icon of his narrowness and ignorance. Now my life resembles his. I arrive early enough—11:45—to insure a seat at the Round Table. (It's gauche to turn up earlier, but if you come as late as 11:50, the table's full and you take your chances with less congenial company.) The table doesn't have the best view, but I've had enough scenic views in my life. I hunger for the day's stories, for jokes, for the latest aches, grandkids, market tips, slants on the news.

We usually start with stories in the *Wall Street Journal,* the *Trib* and *The New York Times.* Royko's column gets big play from us. International, national, local news, the latest this or that. We've got fellows who follow science, books, the arts, we're all readers and TV watchers. Mondays we go over the Bears' game. We cover restaurants, travel, we're a worldly bunch. We know each other's formsheet, we have roles: I'm the left-winger; three or four of us are political neanderthals basically unhappy that Gorbachev has changed the old game. Two regulars have been Assistant Secretaries (one of State, one of Commerce) and one of us was on Reagan's Economic Council; we feel we're privy to inside dope. Anecdotes about politics in Washington and Chicago are one of our stocks-in-trade.

The talk I prefer is personal. Friday, we talked about fathers: time has cleared mine of wrong, translating his naiveté into honesty, his timidity into modesty. I told how he read the morning *Times,* so lost in it he flicked cigarette ash into his coffee and drank without blinking. No one laughed. I described his going down the elevator in his pajamas, forgetting his address in a taxi. I drew another blank: the Round Tablers know what's around our own corners. We've all had operations. Bill Trask's back curls with osteoporosis, Harlan Schneirman's lip from last year's stroke. Death bulletins are a regular, if unstressed, feature of our talk.

Of his father, Harry Binswanger says, "I shcarcely knew him." Though he's been in America more than forty years, German phonemes pass in and out of his speech. Till he retired, he was my dentist, a good one, though Dr. Werner, my dentist since, says my mouth was in poor shape when I came to him. Harry—it used to be Heinz—is large, clumsy, thick-fingered. I felt secure with the heft of his fingers around my jaw, though they may have handicapped the delicacy of his bridge and canal work. I've heard something of his history for twenty-five years, but there's always more to know. Nor do I mind listening to what's familiar. (I'd have to leave the Round Table if I did.) Harry's parents divorced when he was eight. He visited his father in Mainz every Christmas. "Muzzer sent him my presentss. He unwrappd zem, showed me vat zey vur, zen mailed zem back." Harry shook his head, a semaphore of passed anger. "He vass eggcentric, eggcitable, unshtable, couldn't make a liffing. Muzzer's fazzer said she deserfed vat she got, marrying 'a *hergelaufenen Juden*,' 'a Jew from God knows vere.' Fazzer had a farm near zuh Neckar Riffer. He bought turkeyss; zey drowned; he bought marigoldss—he luffed flowerss; zuh riffer flooded zem; he bought pigss; zey broke out of zuh penss. Grandpa said, 'Not even pigss vill stay viz him.' He became a portrait photographer, but vass no good viz children. He vanted a picture uff me on zuh riffer, crying. I vouldn't sit on zuh raft. He tied me zere, slapped my face: 'Now cry.' He put his photographss in—vat-do-you-say?—a cabinet viz a glass front. *Vitrine*. Tough kidss—Nazi toughss—broke it. He said, 'It's time to get out.' He vanted to go to Brassil. He'd been born in Bufovina, zuh Rumanianss lost his paperss. At zuh Emigration Office zey said, '*Für uns, bestehen sie gar nicht.*' 'For us, you don't exist.' He vuss schtuck. Somehow he made it srough zuh var. I saw him after, vonce. He lived in a basement room, zuh rest of zuh block vuss wrecked. Outside his vindow vur a few inches of dirt viz sree zinnias."

Driving back home along the lake by the Museum of Natural History, it struck me that Harry's in-and-out German accent was his mind's way of preserving that *hergelaufener* father of his, even as his stories turned him into comic relief.

ELLEN CALLED at eight o'clock. "How're you doing?"

"Fine. I warmed up the chicken. Delicious. How's Annie?"

She was fine, so were Chuck and little Anne, the Buffalo weather was being its notorious self; the plane was an hour late. "Take care, dear," she said. "I'll see you Monday."

"You'd better."

Though it was nice to be alone, a hue of freedom I hadn't noticed that I hadn't noticed. At the same time, the house felt loose around me, slightly spooky.

In my leather armchair, I read a new book about an escaped prisoner and stopped at a German phrase I didn't understand. (The second time today.) "*Die Unlesbarkeit dieser Welt.*" *The illegibility of this world.* The German pleased me, and I repeated the words till they felt at home on my tongue. Their author, a poet named Celan, was born—another coincidence—in Rumania. His mother was killed in a death camp—the phrase suddenly made sense—and, decades later, he drowned himself in the Seine.

There's a quiver in my pleasant self-sufficiency; but I am comfortable, snug, taken care of. (Because I've taken care?) Who knows, maybe Harry's father, in his basement, looking out at his zinnias, felt the same; having survived what so few had might have been his comfort. Harry himself had been sent to Amsterdam, and, like Anne Frank, hidden. After the war, unlike Anne, he'd gone to a Dutch school. Had

I forgotten, or never known, how he'd gotten to America, this man with whom I'd spent five or six hours a week for twenty-five years, whose hands had been in my mouth, to whom I'd paid thousands of dollars?

SATURDAY MORNING, I drove up to see my son, Peter. He'd moved again, the third time in five years. He gets bored with a neighborhood, seeks what he calls "action." A large, rangy boy—I shouldn't say boy, he's thirty-two—with lots of energy, he's chosen to be a salesman because he can't sit still. He sells polyvinyl traffic cones and is on the road three weeks a month. He doesn't much like the job, or any other he's had. The routines of money-making, the hierarchy of business authority, the cheerleading and critiques of salesmanship, the ups and downs of sales, go against his grain. And grain he has. As a boy, he was exceptionally gentle; in adolescence, he assumed a roughness which I felt contradicted his nature. He's still rough, argumentative, sarcastic, but now he mocks the roughness and regards it as a comic scurf he can remove at will. Deep down—whatever this means—is the gentle boy he was at five and six; very lovable.

A year after he graduated from the University of Illinois in Champaign he married a girl he met in a singles bar; a year later they divorced. He asked his mother and me why we hadn't stopped him from marrying. "Couldn't you see it was a mistake?"

His mother said she'd suspected it, but what could she do? I said, "I liked Louise."

Ten years and many girls later he's still unsettled. I ask him, "How long can you go on being Casanova?"

"Envious?"

"A little. Mostly worried. Not just about disease. This is a critical decade of your life. Squander it courting, you'll end up like the queen in *Alice in Wonderland,* just where you are."

"What's wrong with that?"

"I don't mind, but I think you do."

His new apartment is on the first floor of a redbrick six-flat on one of the thousand tree-lined, quiet streets which root Chicago in a domestic independence which gets it through bad times better than the other industrial cities around the Lakes: Cleveland, Detroit, Erie.

The front door is open, he's been watching for me. I follow him into a bright room with an old couch, an armchair, a stack of pictures leaning against the wall, boxes of books and dishes. There's a stereo, no TV. "I don't want to get addicted." His addiction is bars, music, girls, cigarettes. There are four rooms, all in more or less the same tumbled shape, though the kitchen has a built-in orderliness. "Nice," I say. "It's light, the rooms are a good size, it's a pretty street. How much're you paying, may I ask?"

"Five hundred."

"I should move down here myself."

"Too much action for you."

"Not that I can see. Except for the hurricane that hit your place."

"Come back in two weeks, it'll be immaculate. Ready to play?"

Now and then he consents to play tennis with me. I've been playing over half a century, and still get around pretty well. I know where the ball's coming and get it back. Peter has speed and power, and when he's playing well, doesn't give me any points, but I can frustrate him with tenacity and junk shots. Then he starts slamming balls out, or laughs so hard he misses them altogether. Now and then he gets angry—"*Hit* the goddamn ball"—but rarely, and I enjoy playing with him. Since I had a hernia operation a couple of years ago, the old sweetness of his boyhood comes through, and he's been easy on me. There's also some—I suppose classic—resentment. As we drive a few blocks to public courts on Montrose, he tells me what a lucky life I've led. "You retired early, you've had a good marriage, you've got a granddaughter, and except for that hernia, you haven't been sick; you still play tennis, you liked your job, you've got some dough, you haven't been hassled—"

"The demographics were in my favor. No baby boom."

"Right. I'm one of too many."

"I wasn't much of a boomer."

"Two's more than enough."

There's some sibling resentment, though he and Annie are good friends.

It's a bit chilly. I keep my windbreaker on, but play well, serve hard and hit good backhands. I run Peter around the court, which he needs. He sets up the game so he has to chase around. Life cramps him. He spends too much time in cars, writing reports, closed up in his apartment, in bars. On vacations he goes to national parks where he climbs or paddles white water. A few times he's gone to the Alps and the Pyrenees. But it's not enough for him.

Sometimes I feel that I stand in his way, a wordless—usually wordless—rebuke to his life. Then too I was off a lot on sales trips—neckwear, accessories—when he grew up; he missed me and I think he thinks I sacrificed him. The travel seemed more romantic to him than the chore it was. He thinks I've seen much more than I have, know much more than I do. I feel that he hardly knows me at all, which I don't mind. Should fathers and sons know each other? Or love each other? Well, I love him, though there are gaps of cold in all affection. Yet if the love isn't constant, it is recurrent. That should be enough for security, shouldn't it?

I win the set, 6–3. A rarity. We play another, and I don't win a game. I'm delighted. I always either try hard or appear to try hard, but it's been years since I've wanted to do better than Peter at anything. I want him to have what I've had and more. Above all, I want him to have—to want to have, and have—a child.

Back at his place, I clean up in the bathroom, he washes himself at the kitchen sink. He comes into the living room, the towel working over his wet body. I haven't seen him naked for years, and I'm a little shocked. He's very hairy, has a bit of a belly. This man, who as a boy looked like an angel, is into middle age. I look away.

I don't want to see him this way. There's a book open on the beaten couch, I move it and sit down. "What's this?" I ask. He's got on his jockey shorts. His legs are enormous, they should be running up and down basketball courts or hills.

"Kafka," he says.

"Never really read him. Good stuff?"

"Not exactly." He's buttoning a blue shirt. "You ought to read that one."

" 'Ought to'?"

"You'd understand me better."

"Maybe that's not a good idea. What's it about?"

"Read it. Take it home. But return it. I need it for my sessions."

"Your doctor's paid to understand you. All I have to do is love you."

He's put on blue jeans. "What's to love?"

"I'd better read it."

He's putting on white socks and sneakers. "How do you know it's me you love if you don't understand me?"

"That's too complicated. Do you have to understand *me* to love *me*?" As soon as I say this, I feel the discomfort of presumption. Maybe he doesn't love me. Love's too big a word anyway. It's used much too often. Morons in front of microphones hold out their arms to millions they never met and cry, "I love you." All they mean is, "How wonderful to be shining up here." I never talked about love with my wife or children, my parents didn't with me, and I'm grateful. Love was assumed. A million feelings were bunched up in it.

I'm against all domestic analysis, I'm against understanding. That word also means too much. You understand a request, a situation, but how do you understand a person? You reduce him, that's how. Do I understand myself? Does Harry Binswanger understand his father? In a way, yes, because he hardly knew him. That is, he turned his father into a little vaudeville act, a comic handle that lets him carry the hot pan around. Why did he remember "For us you don't exist"? Because of his own fright that his father didn't exist for him, except as some snapshots of intimidation and pathos. Not enough, he knows it's not enough. Peter and I have had thousands and thousands of moments with each other, many of them, maybe most of them, charged with something you can call love. But the word itself is just a convenience, a pigeonhole that can't really hold the complexity of it all.

His blue-shirted arms lie on the seamed, brown arms of the chair; he looks as big as Lincoln in the Memorial. He says, "I'm paying through the nose to find out if I'm capable of loving anyone."

That night, back in my armchair, I read the book. Had to force myself through it, though it's short, sixty or seventy pages, a story about a salesman, the support of his parents and sister, who wakes up one morning transformed into a huge bug. He can't go to work, they pound on his door, the chief clerk of the office comes to fetch him. (It's rather ridiculous.) Naturally he astounds, terrifies and disgusts his parents and the young sister who for a while takes care of him, bringing him the rancid leftovers he prefers to fresh food. In time he annoys them so much, they want him to die; when he does, they're released and happy.

Now what in God's name makes Peter think that this *Metamorphosis* story has anything to do with him? In the kitchen, I open a bottle of red wine, pour a third of it into a water glass, clip and light a cigar, and go back to my chair to think it out.

In the first place, Peter's never supported us. *Au contraire,* though in the last three years he's made a point of not taking money from me at Christmas and his birthday. Still, he knows I'm there, ready to help him. "I helped your sister when she and Chuck bought the house, and I want to help you when you're ready to buy." I wouldn't dream of his sharing, let alone taking, a check in a restaurant. All right, then, what's the similarity? Does he feel like a bug? Have his mother and I made him feel like a bug? Does he disgust us? Do we want him dead? Absurd. I sit puffing, sipping. Beyond this lamplit circle, it's dark. Here, it's warm, comfortable, charged with the warm pleasure of the wine, the special, bittersweet fullness of the smoke; yet my heart's hammering away. Clearly, Peter feels that he's inadequate, repulsive. What's askew in this boy of mine?

Or is he putting it on, dramatizing himself, using the author's own self-dramatics as his crutch? (But the author invented these things, and, I think, thought they were funny. There is something funny about it.)

I went to the desk and wrote a note.

Dear Peter,
     You're no bug, and I hope I'm not a bit like that pompous, cringing, bullying, self-righteous father. I don't see this story as a key to you. Maybe you can explain it to me. You can do it over the best lunch in Chicago, or in one of your bars. You choose.
                                        Love—if that's still a permissible word,
                                                                      Dad

I'm on my way upstairs to draw a bath when I wonder what the word actually means. *Metamorphosis.* I go down again, lift out the heavy—eight pounds, I once weighed it on the bathroom scale—first volume of the Compact Edition of the OED, for which we joined the Book of the Month Club about twenty years ago. I polish the big magnifying glass on my pants and read *Change of form,* from the Greek.

Upstairs, as I unbutton my shirt, I feel restless. I need a walk. I button up, put on a sweater, exchange my moccasins for the springy walking shoes Annie gave me last Christmas, and, downstairs, put on the black leather jacket young people on the street or in stores look at in surprised approval. (Sometimes they say something like "Niice.") I pat my pocket to make sure the key's there—I don't want to be stuck outside with Ellen in Buffalo. I hope she doesn't call when I'm out, getting the answering machine, worrying that I'm looped around a lamppost on the Outer Drive.

The relief of the air, the dark. There's moonlight after the early evening shower, the oak tree on the lawn has shed its last leaves, they're thick on the lawn, a sea of shapes. The branches are transformed by bareness, a predeath bareness. Lucky, in a great city, to live on a street that registers the seasons so clearly.

The cold air feels wonderful. The small lights of the small houses, the interrogative iron curl of the lampposts, the pools of moonlight on the metal skin of the cars; beautiful. I don't want to leave this. After my operation, I was so fatigued I didn't care about living or dying. Only the idea of leaving Ellen kept me going. Now I understand what I'd laughed at in the obit column this week, the eighty-nine-year-old mogul, William Paley, asking people why he had to die. I know life usually wears you down and you're ready to go. Not with him. Not with me.

A *Trib* piece said Paley was a rat, sold out everyone who loved or helped him, took credit for everything; in short, a perfect dead horse for newspaper whips. Is egomania what keeps you alive? Maybe for tycoons. I don't need an empire. Leaves are enough, the moon, the air.

I walk through the bank parking lot, I turn left on Dorchester. The maples are half-full of pumpkin-colored leaves. (Are the ones still there the Paleys?) Pumpkins are lit on porches. The confidence in these houses. Chairs, lamps, bookshelves, the purple flair of TVs.

I'm the only one on the street. No, up ahead, someone coming. Should I turn? No. Courage. A black man in a raincoat, eyeglassed; a fellow burgher. We should say "Good evening," the way they do in small towns, but we don't. We just pass each other, relieved. I round the brick six-flat on the corner. Back on my block a couple I know stands on their porch, white man, black woman. I don't know their names. I wave, she waves.

My block.

IN THE BATH, my body looks heavy, fattish, knees big, dingus floating in soapy foam. God, man's ugly. No wonder people write about metamorphosis. My body. Peter's. My body forming his, my mind—whatever that is—his. Chromosomes, genes, strings of sugar and protein generating versions of themselves which somehow become others. There's some of Uncle Bert in me. Is it why I live as he did? Transmission. This floating dingus rose to Ellen's innards and generated Annie, and later Peter. Annie's Anne has my stuff in her, and when she signals doctors to turn off my life, she turns her own spigot. Thought. Ghosts. Spooks. The world, so clear and snug, isn't. Metamorphosis. A rational man turns verminous. A rational country declares some citizens verminous and kills them.

I soap arms, armpits, the side where my scar begins, the left leg, the right, the crack, the ankles, the toes. Lovely. The mind lolls. What is a thought? Form without bulk. "For us, you don't exist." How could he not exist? He was there. But existence meant a paper, a name, a class. Citizen, father, uncle, niece, son, president. Tuesday's Election Day. Men and women run *to be,* to be entitled. I'll push a stylus through numbers on a card to make a governor, a senator. (Later, they could make or unmake me.) The father in *Metamorphosis* becomes a bank messenger, has a uniform with brass buttons and, like the doorman in that old film *The Last Laugh,* swells with pride. Fired, uniform taken away, the doorman shrivelled.

If I died here in the tub, Ellen would be a widow. She wouldn't know it till she came home. Knowing changed things. That's why you had to remember, especially those who did nothing memorable, had no children, planted no trees, wrote no books, carved no stones, left nothing but lines in old telephone directories, on stones in suburban cemeteries. Where is Bert buried?

What's the sense of remembering the unmemorable? Can't be helped, it's involuntary. Why hasn't evolution weeded it out? What does it have to do with survival? On our bedroom calendar, the November quotation (in blue letters beside the ironic, ethereal face of Albert Einstein) is: "What I value in life is quality rather than quantity, just as in Nature the overall principles represent a higher reality than does the single object." But isn't quality in the single object? What's worth more, the singular jerk, or the genetic dictionary which formed him?

"Don't foul your own nest." Uncle Bert.

That was what he told me forty-odd years ago. My parents and sister had taken off for a month, to Banff, Lake Louise, the Rockies, California. I was left in our apartment alone, very happy. I worked in the Paramount Films Sales Trainee Program on 43rd and Broadway. Weekends I went up with my cousin Andy—who had a car—to Quakerridge, my sister's club. I played tennis, swam, ate hamburgers and signed her name to the chits. One Saturday I saw Lynette Cloudaway lying by the pool. Two months before there'd been a feature spread about her in *Life,* an Arkansas girl who'd come to New York to be an actress. A photographer followed her around snapping pictures, at work, shopping, taking a bath, kissing her boyfriend goodnight. I'd fallen for her in *Life,* and here she was, in the flesh, by the pool. I could hardly speak. "May I sit here?"

"Sure." The smile I recognized, the throaty voice was new, devastating.

"I recognize you."

"It's me."

"What are you doing here?"

"I'm with Willy." The guy she kissed goodnight. "Not exactly 'with,' he's playing golf."

"Good. You can marry me."

"What name will I have?"

"Mrs. Larry Biel."

"Set the date."

We talked schools, jobs, where we lived, siblings, boy and girlfriends, movies, books, songs, the works. How confident Willy must be to leave this perfection by herself; he didn't deserve her. "Leave him."

"I haven't had my swim yet."

From the diving board, she jumped into the water. I paddled after her, dodging kids and dowagers. Beyond the flagstones, cigar smokers played bridge. On umbrellaed lounges, bodies toasted. Lawns, blue sky, the rich, Lynette; a Jewish Fitzgerald scene (the madness and cruelty evaporated).

Andy showed up. "Time to go."

To Lynette: "I better not miss my ride."

"You coming to the dance?"

"I will now. If I have to walk."

But I talked Andy into driving up again, white jacket and all.

Bare shouldered, breasts under lace, Lynette was in another gear of beauty. On the dance floor, I kissed her ear, her cheek, her mouth.

"We shouldn't do that."

"Why not?"

"I like it. And Willy would see."

"Let him," I mouthed. Tough guy, who'd melt at a leer.

"Let's not dance for a half hour or so."

"If you think so." Snootily. But before she went back to Willy I got her phone numbers.

Monday I called her office from mine. "Lunch?"

"Tomorrow."

We met at Toffenetti's, the glittery restaurant a block from the Paramount. I brought her the Viking Portable Fitzgerald, told her to read *Tender Is the Night*, and asked her to go out with me Saturday.

"I spend weekends with Willy."

Thursday night she called me at home where I was working off my passion for her by myself. "Willy's going fishing in the Adirondacks. I've got to get my shoes fixed on 82nd and Amsterdam. I could come by your place after if you like."

Would I like. I bought the first bottle of wine in my life, got whitefish and rye bread from Barney Greengrass, stacked records on the phonograph, and by noon was lathered out of my mind. When the bell rang, I nearly fainted. Again, she looked different, playful, subtle. How many selves was she? I trembled too much to kiss her, could hardly talk. I managed to unscrew the bottle and trot out the sandwiches. We listened to Bing Crosby sing "Moonlight becomes you, it goes with your hair, you certainly know the right thing to wear." I had to go to the bathroom. The phone rang.

"Shall I get it?"

"Yes." Proud to show whoever called what I had going here.

"It's your Uncle Bert. He wants you to call him back. He sounded funny."

"A laugh a minute. What's he want?"

"He didn't say. Better call'm."

I did.

"Larry," he said, "Don't foul your own nest."

Old sap. *Foul.* Even then I felt its comic pathos. Yet also sensed the stupid debris of something brought down in stone. "She's my friend Al's wife," I said. "We're just going out."

"All right, but you don't foul your own nest."

The condom I'd gotten from the bathroom was ready, and I was getting there when the phone rang again. I didn't answer but thought, "The bastard'll probably come up here." It was nervousness talking. Despite my reading, despite six months' fornicating with my first girl between rows of boxwood near the stadium at Chapel Hill, I knew nothing. (Six years after Lynette, a week before Annie's birth, I still believed children were born through the—enlarged—navel.)

Don't foul your own nest. You fouled it for me, you old jerk.

Wednesday, Lynette called my office. "I have something to show you." At lunch, she held out her hand with the diamond ring.

I never saw her again. In person.

Two years ago, *Life* published an anniversary issue, and there was Lynette as she'd been, mouth open, gawking at a Broadway street scene on her way to work. Ravishing, perfect, the girl of my life. Under the forty-year-old photograph was one of a crinkled granny: Lynette today. I tried to see the young Lynette in the old face; couldn't, not a molecule. A caption said that she and Will lived in Seattle near their grandchildren. I thought of writing her. But why? I didn't want this grandmother. I wanted, *still,* the girl who'd come to the apartment.

REMEMBERING ACTS ON you, not you on it.

Why remember Bert? That sterile neatness, that concupiscent propriety. Immaculate in his blue suit, white silk handkerchief in the lapel pocket, gold tie and collar pins tucking him into himself, black silk socks taut in black garters, black shoes and hair gleaming with different fluids. So clean. My mother, another acolyte of cleanliness, was, in womanliness, beyond that. You wouldn't say she was immaculate. There was flow to her, dress over breasts and rear.

Arms hooked, she and Bert strolled Fifth Avenue, mirrored paragons, proud to be with each other, going into Saks and Sulka's, Bert commandeering the service that was the chief source of his self-satisfaction. That and his Packard, his annuities, his neckties, his opinions, the blondes whose signed portraits—"To Bert with love, Jocelyn"—stood on his chiffereau.

I'm unfair. I'm repaying the resentment he felt for me as mother's baby. There was decency and generosity in him. I needed five thousand dollars to put down on a house—it would be fifty thousand today—and he gave it to me. Every winter, he sent Ellen and me a crate of grapefruit and oranges from Boca Raton. Isn't he in that generous gold fruit as much as in the Sulka ties and antique injunctions? (The last crate of it arrived a week after he keeled over in a Florida pool.)

AFTER DEEJAY'S CALL, I try and fail to crawl back into the dream, then put cold water on my face, pee, brush my teeth, and go down the L of carpeted staircase to the kitchen for my branflakes and muesli mix. I get out a pack of two-ply, thirty-gallon refuse bags, put them against a post on the porch, and bring in the Sunday *Tribune.*

Taking in the news with these flakes of dried grain is as close as I get to a sacrament. Today, election predictions and polls; Edgar and Hartigan in a dead heat, Simon ahead of Lynn Martin. Then Hussein, Bush and Desert Shield, features on the wives, mothers and children of reservists yanked from their cereal and *Tribunes.* Then the usual montage of misery, the shot, the burned, the flooded, the starved, the planet's daily moil served up as *digestif.* Even the prick of conscience about this serves my well-being.

I wash my blue breakfast bowl—always the same—go upstairs with the Entertainment and Book sections and, sitting on the john, shave with my Norelco's trinity of rotor blades. Then another sacrament: a television show I've watched for years, stories about small towns in crisis, the courage of the handicapped, musicians, photographers, all introduced fluently, over fluently, by a benign, wise roly-poly. The program's critics are literate and scornful, their taste is mine (or becomes mine). Is this the equivalent of a Victorian gentleman's hundred lines of Tennyson?

The doorbell. Deejay, holding the bags, leans against the porch post. He wears stiff black pants, a porkpie hat, a stained brown windbreaker. His small mahogany face is, as usual, intense. There's always something pressing him. "Mawnin." A lace of booze on his breath, a flash of gold molar.

"Morning, Deejay. What can I do for you?"

"That downspout near the back porch's rotted out. You gotta get you a new one, for winter. You member that ice piled up there last year."

"Is that the reason?"

"Sure it is. What you think it was?"

I go around with him to the back porch, he taps the spout, breaks off a rusted section. "Take a look a that."

"Doesn't look good."

"I can go git one, put it on tomorrow."

Ellen doesn't want him doing any more jobs that require tools—he puts hinges on upside down, he broke our mailbox, he screwed up a toilet, he painted windows shut—but she won't be home till late afternoon. "Fine. How much do you need?"

"Ten bucks, maybe twelve. I git you the receipt."

"I know." If there's a gene for honesty, he has it. "I'm gonna do some raking with you."

"You calls it." He's of two minds about this: it cuts down his work time, but he likes company. He lives alone, somewhere in the neighborhood, has a schoolteacher brother who looks down on him. I don't think he's ever been out of Chicago. Occasionally he takes the El looking for jobs. They've never worked out. A couple of months ago, he took a Quality Control course which "guaranteed a full-time job." He came by dressed in a grim tie, his windbreaker and porkpie, to borrow bus fare to the North Side. Two days later, he came by again asking if he could mow the lawn.

"What happened to the job?"

"I took that bus a hour, walked bout two miles, and this man at the plant says they doan have nothin' for me."

"I thought he told the school to send someone up."

"He said I should be bilinguial for the job."

"But you're not."

"I got a brother knows Russian, I can learn Spanish."

"It's not easy to learn a language. I've been trying to learn German since high school. Almost fifty years."

"My God, man, you old."

"And I still don't know it."

"I know some Nippon. Least I can unnerstan it, I can't talk it."

Sure, Greek and Hittite, too. Still, I was angry for him. "He should've given you the job. You went through the school."

"Maybe it's this secession."

That took me a second, but one language I've learned is Deejay. "A job's a job. He told the school he had one for a graduate."

Deejay made the old shrugging motions of human acceptance, but I was upset. That job was his, bilingual or not. Unless of course he'd started popping off about how he'd rearrange the plant, or what he'd told Mayor Daley or Brother Farrakhan about running Chicago. Anything could come out of him when he got going.

"I'll do the flower beds," I said. Ellen doesn't like him working there, claims he pulls out what she plants.

We rake away within yards of each other. I pick up a refuse bag to fill it. He says, "Lemme do that." I hold, he fills.

We rake in a sort of harmony. I like it, but wonder if he feels awkward. After all, I'm doing what he's paid to do, cutting into his space, his authority. Even his habits; if I hadn't been there, he'd've smoked a cigarette.

He calls over, "What you fink bout this Ayrab war?"

"Not a war yet."

"Boosh gonna get us in?"

"What do you think?"

"Somepin mean bout his mouf."

"I guess that means war." He doesn't answer that. "You been in the army, Deejay?"

"They wouldn't let me."

"Who wouldn't?"

"The army, who you fink?"

"Why not?"

"What they gonna do wiv me? Rakin' bullets? How bout you, you a vet?"

"Too young for World War II, married by Korea, too old for Vietnam."

"We bof lucky. Doan haveta shoot nobody. What you fink bout dis Hussein?"

"A tough guy. He's shot people."

"He sure has nice suits. A nice moostache too."

"You like that?"

"I like a good moostache."

"Hitler had a hell of a mustache."

Deejay breaks up at this. "You a card, Mista Biel. You oughta grow *you* a moostache. A nice white one. Look like a million dollars on you."

"I'm not old enough."

He breaks up again.

Enough. I go in the front door, then think of something. "All these years you've been coming by here, and it just struck me, I don't know your full name. Is Deejay a nickname?"

He leans on the rake and laughs, showing the gold molar and eight or nine discolored teeth. "Deejay's mah nishes. Daron James. That's the name."

"Your whole name, first and last?"

"First and last. Like Lawrence Biel. 'at's your name, ain't it?"

"That's it." For some reason, I come down the stairs and shake hands, as if, after all these years, we've finally been introduced.

DRIVING DOWNTOWN TUESDAY, I recover from the small dislocation of Ellen's return. Spend so many years with a person, seeing her again after even a brief absence is like seeing her in closeup. Many unnoticed things are noticed, lines in the face, white in the hair, a rawness in the voice, dents and discolorations in the body. The least strange person in the world is, for an hour or two, a stranger. Perplexing, a little frightening.

Then the indispensability of the familiar returns, feelings of reliance, confidence, the identity and accepted disparity of views. There are habits of self-restraint as well as self-expression. It's one package.

I enjoy the grace and ease with which Ellen unpacks; her reports on the trip. At supper it's mostly about Annie, Chuck and Anne. New problems, the resolution of old ones; the death of the big oak across the street; Chuck's worry about the recession—though a pharmacist should be almost recession-proof—the new Medicare regulations. "Are things better with Bostorf?" This is Chuck's assistant, who Annie thinks is swindling him.

"He's still trouble. At least, Annie's worry about him is troublesome."

We've been worried about Chuck and Annie. They express their difficulties with each other obliquely; Bostorf is one of the targets of this indirection. "And Anne?" We worry a lot about the dangers to which so decent, open and, we believe, innocent a girl can fall into in an American high school. For someone as much concerned as I am about the future of my seed, my fear about Anne's fall into womanhood—the antique phrase that comes to me—is puzzling.

I tell her about Peter, omitting *Metamorphosis*.

While we're stacking the plates in the dishwasher, the phone rings. "Mista Biel?"

"Deejay. Didn't you get the money?"

"I got it, but I need another twenny."

It's the second time this month that he's called up to ask for more than we'd agreed. Ellen doesn't like this at all. "It's a bad month for me. Lots of bills."

"How bout ten?"

"You really need it?"

"Would I be askin?"

"Sorry."

"Spose I come roun now."

"How about tomorrow?"

"Tomorrow I doan need it."

He must be buying all the liquor tonight. "I'll leave it under the mat."

"Twenny?"

"Ten."

"You a hard man."

"That's right."

"Least you stick wimme."

And you wimme, you poor bastard.

SOME AFTERNOONS ARE HARD. After the Round Table, I play cards, or billiards, or read the magazines, then walk back to the office and check the market close. I get going at 3:30, before the rush hour, and am home by 4:15. We eat at 6:00 in front of the MacNeil-Lehrer Report, then watch one of the scandal programs, people abusing, deceiving, molesting, kidnapping, killing; the human works. Then we read, watch programs, occasionally go out, or have friends in for bridge; then bath and bed. Beside Ellen's familiar warmth and fragrance, I go to sleep. Sometimes feelings bunch and we're active; afterwards, we express gratitude to each other.

I don't sleep as I used to, and often go to the guest room to read till my eyes tire. I'm conscious of aches in the balls of my hands, my feet, my chest. Sometimes I fear these aches. After all, how much longer is there?

I've been a bystander, done nothing memorable. I've had no real trouble, have lasted six-and-a-half decades, raised—whatever that means—what will live after me, and live in my paid-up house with someone I love. I'm lucky. Still, now and then, it comes to me that I don't understand anything. As if the world's speaking a language I can't follow. Fear gets so loud, I can't sleep. Once in a while, I go back to our room and hold on to Ellen. Sometimes this helps—like finding a dictionary— but sometimes it doesn't.

A MAN AFTER A fish has got to equip himself with rod and reel, with backing and line and leader, with wet flies and dry flies, a vest bemedaled with zingers and hemostats and split shot, and he should also carry, shoved into the pocket of his shirt, a couple of onion sandwiches. Onion sandwiches? That's what Nick Adams ate for lunch up on the Big Two-Hearted River. And so really the crazy omnium-gatherum of tackle of any man after a fish includes, if he's a writer, more than a little Hemingway in it, a little Hem he must acknowledge and then get rid of, as Thomas Williams does in "The Fisherman Who Got Away." Hemingway's main strength was a genius for optimism; even in a burned-over world that blackens the grasshoppers he finds a stretch of river that flows clean and clear from the old remembered world, a stretch of river that rewards his hope; and once he arrives he knows not to go any farther, that there will be "plenty of days coming when he could fish the swamp."

Williams tells a darker story, bleaker because it's partly a comedy. The main character, Richard Adgate, had "never jumped into new things, dangerous things; he'd crept in, somehow, slowly and cautiously, and got to the danger all the same." The grand, exact moment, the exalted life, clarified and perhaps arrived at by acute vision, never comes for Richard. He is not Nick Adams. Instead, "unprepared was his motto." His fishing is clumsy. He goes too far. He gets encoiled in his own flyline. He doubts his skill, his timing, his entire life. Along the way, there are small beauties, in Richard's world, in Williams's writing. A fish on the line is described as "a heartbeat, a small spasm of opinion." In the end Richard lands the great fish anyway, the fish of a lifetime. And Williams comes to his fish not through skills born of Hemingway's pride and hope, instead finding his catch somewhere beyond there, in a smaller, darker world of private comedy and even more private reconciliation.

CHARLES D'AMBROSIO

THOMAS WILLIAMS

The Fisherman Who Got Away

RICHARD ADGATE was at Romeo LaVigne's fishing camp on Baie Felicité, Lake Chibougamau, Quebec, with two friends. They were three Americans of middle age, husbands away from their wives and families.

His wife had been unhappy about his coming on this trip, but he'd been working hard, and how often had he ever done anything like go off fishing for a week? He'd asked her this with a defensive stridency she'd of course detected. She, the woman he'd lived with for more than a quarter of a century. He could feel what she felt. She couldn't understand why on earth he'd ever want to escape her, who considered herself fair-minded and good to him. That he wanted to go away with two friends—pretty good friends—why? The children were grown and gone now, and she could easily have come, but she hadn't been asked. How would he like not being asked?

And so it was like that, not something he thought about every minute, but there was an edge, an incompleteness, that made him just slightly oversurprised when on the broad lake a series of ponderous golden boulders as big as houses suddenly appeared beneath his keel when he thought he was in deep water. He didn't want to look down, to have the other world rise up like that to within an arm's reach.

He'd gone out by himself this afternoon in one of Romeo LaVigne's rental boats, a seventeen-foot aluminum square-ended canoe with a rock in the bow for ballast, and a four-horse Evinrude motor. Pete Wallner's boat was a little crowded with three in it, and Joe Porter was getting a divorce and needed conversation, reassurance, or whatever; that was no good with three, either. It seemed unfishermanlike, Joe's constant preoccupation with his problem. Or perhaps it was that a real getting away, a forever getting away, was antithetical to the furlough of a fishing trip. "She" was the word constantly on Joe's lips. "She." Her name was Lois, but it was always "she," and in spite of the immediate unpleasantness, Joe was about to be free of her after all the years. There was a perverse sort of envy in his listeners, too, and Richard could only wonder what it would be like if there were no "she" to make him return, no tether of loyalty and pity and partnership.

In any case, here he was, Richard Adgate, a man no better and no worse in his frailties than other men, he thought, forty-nine years old and quite alone in the suffering of his wife's disapprobation. Her name, empowered by the years, was Nora.

He'd been trolling around a small island a mile or two from Romeo LaVigne's rather shabby log cabins, the only man-caused things in sight except for the Indian camp a couple of hundred yards away from the cabins—log frames with bright red and blue plastic tarps over them. Pete, who had a Lowrance sonar, had told him that the depth dropped to forty feet about fifty yards out from the island, and then to ninety feet ten to twenty yards farther out, so he trolled a medium silver Mooselook Wobbler on lead-core line, with about six colors out, hoping to find that small plateau and not get hung up too often.

The July day was blue, clouds forming always to the southwest, growing, looking dark but not amounting to a rainstorm. The little island was covered by the narrow spruce, virgin spruce less than a foot in diameter, that was the dominant tree everywhere, and so thick you couldn't push your way through them. There were a few birch and a few aspen. Mountain ash was a bush this far north. So far he'd seen a scruffy-looking red fox, a beaver, a sharp-tailed grouse with five or six chicks (the first he'd ever seen), a vole, ravens, unidentified ducks, a killdeer. This was the boreal forest, chilled and stunted most of the year by the polar winds. But in July the air was mild. The lake was warm on the surface, but a foot down it was forty degrees, and the lake trout (*grise* to the French) were not very deep.

After a while, no fish taking the silver wobbler, he reeled in, shut off the idling motor, and let the mild wind and little waves tilt him and move him slowly to the northeast, toward a distant, spruce-black shore.

He got his map from his pack and opened it along its folds to where he was, feeling the familiar small shock caused by a map's ideal, formulated authority, its precision reflecting the wide, moving actuality of the lake and the distant, oddly shaped hills. Magnetic north was nearly twenty degrees west of true north here, a knife-sharpening angle. He balanced on his spine in the delicately balanced canoe, above the depths of another inhabited world.

Some of the hills were steep as stairs, cut flat on top; others were rounded like normal hills. None were more than a few hundred feet high, according to his map, yet they had an uninhabited authority and bulk. In a certain light, like the mild sunlight of this afternoon, a superficial glance made this lake any of the lakes at home, before he noticed that there were no houses, no roads. From certain places outside the bay a buff-colored mine building could be seen, miles to the south, a narrow tower at least a hundred feet high, though it was difficult to tell at such a distance. On the way in they'd driven through the modern mining and lumbering town of Chibougamau, an island itself of neat houses and stores, familiar gas stations, municipal buildings and even parks, an outpost set in the forest that ran north to tundra and Hudson Bay. Of course, the winter here would be like iron, and seem to last forever; no wonder the little town seemed so defensively maintained and civilized. Even Romeo La Vigne, old *voyageur* that he was, and a friend of the Cree, moved back into town when winter came.

To the east, according to his map, was a narrow northward extension of the lake, a passage five or six miles long which opened into a large bay with many islands, where a good-sized river entered, with the symbol for rapids. Lake trout were fine, beautiful fish, but most of his life he'd been a brook trout fisherman, and only occasionally a troller. For him the fish most familiar to his hand, least alien to touch, was the squaretail, the brookie, here called speckled trout or *moucheté*.

There were supposed to be large brook trout in the rivers hereabouts, especially in rapids. But up that long passage, into a place where no one else would be, miles away from anyone—did he really want to go there? Wouldn't those islands loom strangely, and the bottom rise up to startle him? The far bay had a name, Baie Borne; and the river, Rivière Tâche—he didn't know what they meant in French.

Along with his rods and tackle box he had, in his pack, a sandwich, some chocolate, two bottles of Laurentide Ale, and all of the usual outdoors stuff, such as a compass, Band-Aids, nylon line, aspirin, binoculars, safety pins, toilet paper, bug stuff—things gathered over the years. He didn't consider himself fussy or over-cautious in these matters. When he went out in a boat he wore a life vest, and when it might rain he wore a broad-brimmed felt hat and took along raingear. It was stupid to suffer the lack of any little thing. On his belt he wore his sheath knife and a pair of Sargent wire-cutter pliers.

He was drifting toward the entrance to the northern passage. He had a full three-gallon tank of gas. Why not go there? Because he was here in northern Quebec in some ridiculous way without permission, and because, for all his years and his knowledge of the water and the woods, there was still within him a small child afraid of the deep and the dark.

In his life he'd never jumped into new things, dangerous things; he'd crept in, somehow, slowly and cautiously, and got to the danger all the same. Not that there could be a real danger here, unless a storm came up, and even then he'd be in no mortal danger. He could always run to shore and wait it out, no matter how long the storm lasted. Even if his motor conked out, broken beyond his ability to fix it, he had a paddle. It would be only time that he could lose. So his friends might worry about him—so what? But it did worry him that they might worry—a small threat of anxiety, a small twinge of that psychic nausea. It all seemed so demeaning he decided he would have to go to the strange bay and the river. He liked to be alone. He did. He was always saying that he did. He started the motor and swung northeast, looking for the passage. Of course, he might go in, and he might not.

The entrance to the passage toward Baie Borne was narrow, full of boulders and with a definite current. He could see that the passage beyond widened and deepened quickly, however, so he throttled down and just made headway as he left the broad lake. He thought of those who explored caves—spelunkers (where did that word come from?) who sometimes crawled into holes so narrow they'd have to bet upon a larger space ahead because they couldn't crawl out backwards. A cowardly thought on a bluebird day. But he got through without touching and went on, at least for now, with dark hills rising on each side.

He didn't know how deep the water might be, but since he edged into this passage at trolling speed he let out the silver wobbler, its long leader, and a couple of colors. One swath on the western hills had been logged, and the greener brush was a wash of light. On top, some birches had been left, their tall trunks against the sky like African trees—a view of Kenya that slowly passed. A small bay opened on his left, and, yes, the map was disconcertingly true again. As he passed the bay's entrance it silently let him by, its farther regions secret, not caring, set for eternity. A heavy cloud to the north, moving away, made his pathway dark.

His rod quivered—a snag or a hit. A fish, he knew as he picked it up, because it moved a little to the side, undulant, like a heartbeat, a small spasm of opinion. He shut off the motor and checked the star drag as he reeled, feeling the caught thing, the line alive between them. A pull from below answered the question of size; it was small, probably a lake trout. It came up against all of its will, no match for his eight-pound leader, the silver three-pronged hook in its flesh somewhere. He would see it soon.

The fish was dark and narrow—a small pike about fourteen inches, hardly a keeper. The brown eyes in the slanted skull saw him. The way to grab a large pike, he'd been told, was to put your thumb and middle finger into its eye sockets, squashing the eyes into the skull: this was supposed to stop their thrashing. He reached down and grabbed this one behind its head, the smooth body a muscle, and forced the tines of the hook down and out, a fragment of white cartilage, broken by a barb, flowing half-loose. His too-strong hands let the small pike go back down. As he let it go he felt a little magnanimous, slightly closer to the vision all fishermen would like to have of themselves someday—a distinguished older man with well-patched waders and a split-bamboo rod, Yeats's fisherman, a "wise and simple man," the paragon of dignified age who is usually observed in the middle distance as he performs each ceremonial fishing rite with understated skill. He always catches a fine brown trout and of course releases it, his sparse gray hackle glowing in the falling light, a tiny hatch, like reversed snow, haloing his old felt hat. Oh, yes, the classic fisherman, his aesthetics honed to the finest moral patina. With age was supposed to come wisdom that was not detachment, mastery that was not boredom, experience that never bred despair.

His canoe moved steadily north through the dark water. He hoped the northern cloud would soon pass and the water would turn a less forbidding blue again. Was he really going to go all the way to the river and its indicated rapids, or not? Looking back, he saw the entrance from the lake had disappeared behind God knew how many hills. That the larger bay and its many islands would come up, inevitably, on map and in real distance, had some of the quality of the sudden boulders that had appeared beneath him in the broad lake.

The motor plugged on smoothly; the long bow moved ahead exactly where he had it go. He might troll, but decided not to because of apprehension about what he might catch. No, not apprehension but because to catch something here might delay him too much. He would catch a Silkie, a monster half fish, half woman, both natures writhing with hatred as they died. He could see in the deep the golden scales on the thighs, the fishbelly-pale shoulders, the inward-turning teeth of a pike. If he trolled he would be mixing exploration, which was perhaps neutral with the gods, with the intent to do harm.

He leaned forward and hefted the gas tank; of course it was still heavy. He could go ten times the map distance with that much gas, and he knew it. If he were at home he would be safe, though deprived of the opportunity to make this lovely, lonely choice. Of course, his wife was home right now, her unhappiness a distant and unsettling power.

Rivière Tâche must be a mile or so farther, with rapids at its mouth, and in some wonderment at his deliberate progress he steered on toward it. Rocks here and there caused tan blushes near the surface of the water, between deep places where to look down was to see, hopefully, nothing but the dark water-gray of depth.

Baie Borne: perhaps *borne* was a cognate—". . . from which no traveler returns." A border? Another land? Across its wide blue he moved, now over sand with patches of weeds here and there, water lilies of some kind with floating round leaves, and then into the positive current from the river. The spruce came nearer on each side, and ahead were rocks and some white water. The southeast wind was at his back, so he shut off the motor, the wind holding him against the current, and got his fly rod out of its tube. In his reel was a sinking line, an old leader, and a tippet he was too lazy or impatient to change. He was always nervous as he strung the leader through the eyelets, but he got the line correctly strung and chose for a fly a medium-sized Gray Ghost. His fingers trembled as he tied his knot and clipped off the tag end. The water was five or six feet deep, the rocks below darker, denser-looking than the boulders out in the bay. His canoe turned in the wind and current, and he tilted the motor up before casting. He would begin here and then go up toward the frothings of white water.

After the first cast, which was only a half-decent cast, in fact a lousy cast, with the leader dropping in a messy coil not ten yards away, he began to strip in his line, worrying only about getting a knot in his leader and not at all about a fish. But the line jerked out straight and his supple pole bent. "My God!" he said. "It's a fish!" He wasn't ready at all, and there was a sense of wrong, of bad timing, as though he'd rather not have a strong fish on just yet, after such a stupid mess of a cast. But the fish was there, whatever it was. He should have changed the tippet; surely more than three pounds had already stretched it out. His nerves went down to the invisible tippet as he let out line, let it out and recovered it. Careful, now! The fish ran up-current, then held for a moment before running down along the far bank, not quite to a snag angled into the water—a complicated dead spruce. He just managed to decrease by tender force the radius of the fish's run down that bank. Then it stopped, and he kept what he hoped was a permissible pressure on it, and then just a little bit more, but he couldn't move it. He was afraid of the sudden emptiness of no connection. "Don't happen," he said. "Don't happen."

He didn't know what kind of fish it was, only that it was big and strong. If it was a brook trout it would be the biggest one he'd ever seen, he was sure of it, a salmon-sized brook trout. It might be a pike, or a large walleye, or a lake whitefish—what else was there here? With one hand he freed his boat net from the paddle: presumptuous to think of netting a fish he couldn't even move. But then the fish came in a little, maybe just a foot or so; the canoe was moving, so it was impossible to tell. But the fish didn't like that, and pulled so hard, so suddenly, he knew the tippet had to break, and for a moment thought it had, a hollow moment, but the fish had come toward him, and now it veered away upstream, the line cutting the surface. He must keep the fish from winding the leader around a rock—just to the limit of what he could do with a three-pound tippet, which was probably good for at least five pounds, except that it was old, so God knew what strength it had. He mustn't get used to its holding.

He had to see this fish. He wanted to own it, to have it. What a will it had, what strength! But the long minutes with his rod quivering, line in and out in desperation, might be too worrying for him. He'd deliberately put himself into a situation in which he felt anxiety. Why had he done that?

Beneath the water the cold muscles fought for life against this fragile extension of his touch. How sickening it must be to be pulled by the invisible—like having a fit, epilepsy, a brain spasm. What did the fish think pulled him so hard, and what part of him said no? He must know the fly itself was too small to have such power; everything he'd ever hunted and eaten told him that, but some force wanted to haul him away from the dark rocks to the ceiling of his world and out of it. Everything smaller than he that moved in his world was food, yet now this small thing he'd tried to eat was overpowering him, little by little, with a constant pressure that felt like death. What else must he know in his neurons, in his lateral canals, and in all the circuits of his perfect body, when he'd lived a life of caution, too, hunter and hunted both?

The wild thing deep in the current was so tenuously bound to him by his skill and desire. . . . By what skill? He was a nervous wreck, trembling and sighing. His line looped at his feet, a coil of it encircling the shank of the paddle. If the fish ran now it would be all over, so he held the rod high and reached down to free the line. The bunched collar of his jacket pushed his hat forward, and because he hadn't thought to fasten the chin strap a gust blew his hat overboard. He reached for it and nearly shipped water, came upright again, and noticed that his tackle box, weighted by the open tray, had dumped lures and eyelets and split shot and all kinds of necessary little objects into the bilge. His hat floated away; the coil of line was still around the paddle. He saw but didn't feel on his line the fish as it came to the surface of the water in a quick, inturning swirl. It was black on its back, deep in the body, spotted, with a flash of orange at the fins; every memory, every known subtlety of shape and behavior, said trout, said eight to ten pounds, the fish of his life that would make this moment, for better or for worse, forever a brilliant window of memory.

He did clear the line from the paddle, and miraculously the fish was still on. He hauled in line as the fish came straight at him. He'd meant to get a multiplying reel and make it left-handed, so he could reel all this line in—why hadn't he done that? Why hadn't he done that long ago, as Ray Bergman had suggested in his book? The stripped line slopped half in and half out of the boat, some of it among his spilled lures so that he'd probably have a bloody Christmas tree of ornaments on it when it came up again.

Something shoved him hard in the back—a mean, hurtful sort of shove; the canoe had drifted into the bank, and it was a dead spruce stub that wanted to push him onto his face. The fish moved upstream again, well out from the bank, thank God. If he could just get hold of the paddle, or even that nasty stub, and push himself away from the bank. He couldn't see why the fish was still on. It could just run away if it wanted—take out his line and all his backing and easily snap the tippet. Of course, the next thing the wise and skillful fisherman would do would be to capsize the boat.

Where was his hat? Over by a sandbar, beached by the wind. He could get it later, if there was going to be a later. His arms seemed to be pushing as well as pulling— pushing against his tendency to pull too hard—and were getting tired. He must keep the fish working against the pitifully small pressure he dared use. He knew he was never going to possess this fish, because it was too good, too beautiful, for the stupid, incompetent likes of Richard Adgate.

For a long time the fish hung into the current. He managed to reach the paddle and to push away from the hostile bank—at least for the moment, though the canoe turned perversely in the current and wind as if it, too, had an opinion about the outcome.

He had time to think that he was not enjoying any of this. His hopes were ridiculous; whatever gods of luck there were had chosen him for their sport.

Yet the fish fought for its life, and did Richard Adgate want to kill to have? He *had* to kill in order to have—a soft hesitation immediately gone banished as too stupid to consider. Just a sickish little echo of a feeling was left, and what did it matter anyway? If only he hadn't been so impatient, and had put on a new leader, maybe six to eight pounds; this was no little midsummer trout brook in New Hampshire. What all this showed was a major flaw in his character, the story of his life. *Unprepared* was his motto.

But the fish stayed on. The wind had been coming up, blowing the canoe up into the current, but at least near the center of the river. Though he'd been turning and turning, he began to see a pattern in the fish's runs; it liked a certain oval area of water and never went to either bank or to the dead spruce. Maybe bigger monsters lurked there and kept it away, although what of its own element might frighten a fish this large he didn't want to think about. Maybe the fish was as stupid as he was, but you didn't get that large by being stupid.

Time passed, and passed, his arms aching, his nervousness institutionalized, or solidified, a sort of seismic temblor in the seat of pain. He had a vaguely hopeful theory that the longer he kept the fish from its fish-business, the weaker it would have to become. Sure, just think of salmonids as weaklings.

He found himself guiding, turning, touching the living fish but thinking of other things. He wondered if he would ever be brave enough to camp out alone here, say on one of the small islands in this bay, alone in the dark night. Could he endure the blackness of that night, the silence of it, when even in broad daylight he was unnerved by the strange coves of a small bay seen in passing?

A rose-white slab glinted over there on the surface—a large fish rolled, and it was his fish, on its side for a moment, its tail giving a tired-looking scull or two before it sank down again. Then there were a few pulls, weaker shakes of the head, weak though irritated: what *is* this thing pulling on me all the time? And he thought all at once that he might actually bring the fish to the side of the canoe. Maybe. It had been on more than half an hour, now, probably because of his caution, or his cowardice.

The fish came, slowly. When it first saw the canoe, it ran, but not far, and he gently snubbed its run and turned it again. If he startled it too much it would simply run away from him, because it was not really as weak as it seemed. Nothing was as it seemed. With the rod in his left hand, the line snubbed with his fingers, he sneakily got the big boat net handy, then went back to his gentle urging, turning, and soon the fish was next to the canoe. With desperate strength he took the net and scooped it up and into the canoe amidst all the spilled and tangled gear and line and who cared what? He was on his knees, his hands over the net and his fish. What teeth it had! It was a brook trout all right, but changed by size into something oceanic, jaws like forearms, gill covers like saucers.

The Gray Ghost was deep in its tongue, the tippet not even in existence any longer. His metal stringer was in the mess in the bottom of the boat, and he clipped one hanger through the trout's lower jaw and another around a thwart into the chain—of course he would never trust it in the water. As if it understood, the trout wrestled itself out of his grasp, into the air, then came down thrashing on the mess of lures, eyelets, spoons, net, line, sinkers, flies, reel-grease tubes, spinners, hooks, split rings—all the picky little toys and trinkets a fisherman collects.

And it was all right. He could sit back, drift where he would, and look at the sky, which he did for a while. Then he paddled over to the sandbar and retrieved his hat, his good old felt Digger hat that had protected him from so many storms. Good old hat!

He took his De-liar from his fly-fishing vest and measured the fish: twenty-eight inches, eight and a half pounds. The beautiful great fish trembled, dying as it must, as it must. And with that flicker of sadness, "as cold and passionate as the dawn," the world changed for him. It was seven o'clock on this subarctic afternoon, a crisp southeast wind raising a few whitecaps on Baie Borne, the bluest of waters. He pulled the canoe up on the sand and carefully cleaned everything up, put everything away, sponged out all water and slime, made everything shipshape and Bristol fashion.

On his way back through the long passage he headed into the wind, his bow pounding across the larger waves, a Laurentide Ale in his hand. There lay the trout, monstrous, outsized, beyond dreaming of. Who cared that it was nothing he deserved, that because of his clownish errors he should have lost it six times? The knowledge of his fear and awkwardness would only heighten memory. All the rest of his life he would see the pure and desolate bay and the pulse of incoming river, its turbulence meeting the blue water. The black density of the spruce, on island and hill, grew vividly into the past.

But what if he'd lost this fish? Would the shadows fall across these hills in tones of lead? Maybe, but the great fish hadn't got away. That alternate fate was past and gone, as were so many alternates, large and small, to the course of his own life. No matter now; he was brought back, for better or for worse, along a line as sure and fragile as his own.

THE OFFSPRING of a union between two disparate souls carries such weight—all those ancestral traits seeking dominance and the very air scented with immigrant passions. In the drawer under the best linen tablecloth with its folds dutifully yellowing as expected were three photographs with their studio origins stamped on the back in case you wished to order more. Celebratory photographs and traditional in size, two were taken at the weddings of cousins, and one was from the Golden Anniversary party of my paternal grandparents. I had to stare at the pictures for a moment before I noticed the woman who had squeezed herself in the back row of each of these family-crowded and commercially posed pictures. She smiles fiercely and stares right at the camera. In the wedding photograph taken in the 1940s she wears a large hat rather ridiculously perched on the back of her head—and thus almost detracts from the bride who sits in a circle of satin. These photographs cover a period of almost twenty years, and the woman grows older yet remains quite recognizable. Who was she? My mother had no idea. Perhaps the smiling face belonged to a relative from the other side—whatever side that was. I went then to the aunts, those archival keepers of secrets, who traveled en masse. They looked one to another and shook their heads. No, they didn't know who that woman was. I decide then that the smiles shown by that unidentified woman seemed less free than the smiles of those around her. That, of course, might not be true. I might be inventing that. Someone suggested that she could be a caterer's assistant playing a joke. Most unlikely that each family used the same caterer. Did I know who the woman was? a cousin asked me. No, I didn't. You see, I wasn't present at any of those family parties—so forced to imagine the woman's identity, I endowed her with that most fearful of burdens—I made her an offspring.

BETTE PESETSKY

BETTE PESETSKY

Offspring of the First Generation

ONE DAY IT CAME TO ME that I was neither adopted nor the illegitimate daughter of the King of Rumania and Magda Lupescu. Everything, of course, has run downhill since then.

I have noticed that many people do not like me. As a result of analysis, a flood of repressed memories has run ashore. My analyst did not like me. I made an early decision to have two or three children, certain that when they grew up they would be of my blood and therefore would desire my company. I was wrong.

Lachman, my lover, pushes past the beaded curtain and walks into the kitchen. He is portly and dignified even in pajamas. In profile, he resembles the Swiss bankers and French magistrates whose grainy pictures are sometimes seen in newspapers.

"Why in hell don't you take these beads down? They grab at you like a centipede," he says.

"I mean to," I say. I am deferential. The beads are the last reminder of my daughter.

"How pale you are," Lachman says. He touches my forehead. "Do you work too hard at the store?"

"Work at a store? Don't you know anything about me?"

"Well," he says and sits down. "You used to work at a store."

Lachman will be leaving me soon. He will have the choice of many women. Already weeks go by between his visits.

"It's been a long time," Lachman says. "What's the news?"

I clear my throat. "Harriet's husband left her. There are five children in the house. It is an unthinkable thing. There is an Eldorado in the driveway. The house is heavy with furniture. Willa Hoomes comes three times a week to clean the house. Morty

Goldfarb's wife left him. They had three boys. Morty Jr., Titus, and Pender. Morty is a good man. He hopes one day to live on a farm."

"I've been thinking," Lachman says, "of trying California."

"Yes," I reply. I got over it before he even said it.

I HAVE AUNTS, uncles, many cousins. Their houses are filled with inheritances of hallmarked silver, translucent china, Kerman carpets. These abundant *landsleit* have gatherings, parties. I am seldom asked to join them. But I go, anyway.

I call someone and say, "See you on Sunday."

"At Duvey's?"

"Yes," I say. "At Duvey's." This is how I discover where they gather to eat themselves silly.

Also useful is a large calendar to mark anniversaries, birthdays. This way I can also project weddings and graduations. Thus, I went to the wedding of Lueta and Talsman, ignoring the fact that their invitation to me went astray. I had to check with the three catering halls acceptable to the family in order to determine time and place.

I am not cheap. I send good gifts. For Lueta, I purchased a gold wine cup for ceremonial occasions. Gold objects are always twenty-four carat. The china I supply is neither cut-rate nor seconds. If the gift is cash, I think only in three figures.

I stand reasonably in the middle range of fashion. I cannot be pointed out in family pictures as strange. I appear in many photographs, slipping quickly into the last row before the shutter is snapped. In my family album, I have just pasted the latest picture. Lueta is a lovely bride in an old-fashioned wedding dress that belonged to her great-aunt. In my blue taffeta dress, I am third from the left in the row behind the bride's family.

My conduct is always decorous. No one will be embarrassed. I inquire about the state of your health and your family's. I remember to avoid the divorces, the other women, the wayward children, the failing of once-thriving businesses.

Yet I remain the one pushed from the pack. Alert to the instinctive lack of sympathy to be found in my species, I keep my grievances and despair to myself. My husband, who fell in front of a D train, died just before the divorce papers were filed. The funeral was a disgrace. The young woman at the graveside, who I observed was my cousin Sylvie, was in truth the woman my husband had planned to run off with.

Martin, my son of the five-hundred-dollar suits, has sources of money to tear out my heart. Leslie, who has married twice, lives somewhere in the West. Her mail is unforwardable. Noam, my youngest son, is twenty-four and lives with me. We survive on the proceeds of my late husband's insurance wisely invested in utilities. Also, I have an income as a political pamphleteer. I can turn out the text of a pamphlet in four to eight hours. "Your Philosophy Is Mine" is my motto.

Noam was married to Abigail. She locked him out of their apartment after shouting abuse at him. She charged him with impotence, sodomy, lechery, and other vile behavior. He took his two suitcases and came home. "Leave me alone, Ma," he said, and walked down the hall to the spare bedroom.

I have known hard times, unpleasantness, fear. All of this I am unable to share. I do not for a moment accept isolation as the legitimate leitmotif of my life. Against the early signs of my shunning, I daily checked myself in the mirror. How do they know that I am not to be liked? Chosen last? I worked hard to be smart and pretty. I washed dishes for my mother, ran errands for my father, gave up the biggest piece for everybody.

One day Noam leaves his bedroom. "What is it?" he shouts. "I care. I am not unkind. They hate me for the right answer. They applaud my errors."

"Your blood is too good for transfusions," I say.

I want to help Noam. I have always been a follower of honorable causes. I worked in favor of peace. I am a registered voter. I contribute to the support of an Asian child.

Theories change. So I am investigating the possibility of analysis for Noam. The cost is robbery. The time deducted from life enormous. Noam will have forgotten his youth. And I know that if the smell of the litter is not on you, it is hopeless. Is there no cure for being disliked?

My parents did not enjoy my presence. On my wedding day, they whispered in the corner that I was pregnant, that the marriage was forced. During the ceremony, they stood like stones.

Young, pale Jonathan swayed beneath the canopy. Within a year, he was unfaithful—in less time than that, loathsome. His body could have fouled mine with disease.

Noam says, "Abigail grew to despise me. I was a good husband, generous, kind, ardent. You are nothing, she said to me. Never in a thousand years should I have married you."

I have shelves, drawers, boxes full of outlines and lists. They are useful in my work. One list is headed "Desirable Traits." I made this list when I was a schoolgirl. On the left side of the paper are the names of ten of the most popular girls I knew. Opposite each name are the qualities of personality that I surmised inspired admiration. Which traits didn't I possess? I had them all. Moreover, I was idealistic, honest, truthful. I observed that other children cheated at games, were lazy, practiced masturbation, lied.

How did I fail Noam? Was it something I didn't do when he was a child? But he never gave me any trouble. Whereas Martin was delinquent, truant, a scholastic failure. Leslie traded on her prettiness. I read to Noam. I cooked his meals, mended his clothes. Was it a button I maybe missed?

The note I slip under Noam's door says, "Return to work. Don't give up the ship."

Noam writes me a reply.

"I was a member of the management team. Responsibility was delegated to me, and I complied. I did not have my own secretary. I dictated onto an IBM belt in my portable hand-held unit. This belt then went to the typing pool. The work came back to me in large brown inter-office envelopes. Often, two or three days went by when no one spoke to me. At first, I was not concerned. The work was enough to fill the time. After a month or so, I noticed that I ate lunch alone. I tried all the nearby coffee shops. I saw only strangers. If I joined a group, they did not make me welcome. Their conversations dealt with matters I did not understand, and they would not explain."

AT PARTIES, I join a group and cannot be removed. I have this skill for appropriate comments, witticisms, anecdotes. When someone gives a party, I volunteer to help the hostess. "Let me," I say, and reach for a bowl. I will serve, wash up, run to the store for whatever you forgot. When the party's over, I'm the first to say, "I'll drive you home. No need to call for a taxi."

Once I gave Ethel Lee twenty-five dollars in exchange for an invitation to her sixteenth birthday party. Was this the gift? It was not. The gift was a sterling silver, heart-shaped pin.

The city fills with dirty rain. There are filthy puddles everywhere. My head aches with the falling barometer. Two leaves have dropped from my geranium plant. My body is swollen and poisoned.

My work schedule lags, I am so busy thinking about Noam. How can I help him? Although we do not speak when we pass in the hallway, I know it is from me that he expects deliverance. If I can help him, then he will love me forever, and forever we will celebrate holidays together.

I have heard that the old man upstairs has committed suicide. He used barbiturates to do it. He was a cartographer. We had been neighbors for years. But we never spoke. Sometimes, I would remark about the state of the weather. But the cartographer did not reply. His son and daughter-in-law came from Queens and carried his body away. If I die, there is a card I keep in my wallet. I have willed my organs. My underwear is clean.

Noam does not join me in the living room in the evenings. But his presence in the apartment is felt. I believe he weeps. The door to his room is locked. "Let me in," I beg.

Noam says one day, "I can't take it any more. I once had friends. People sometimes sought me out. I had Abigail. Mother!"

"Join a club," I tell him. "Write letters. Keep active."

I recopy the list of Desirable Traits into a single column minus the names of the girls. I push the list under Noam's door. "I cannot afford to support you!" I call through the door.

Noam takes a job.

"Try to be friendly," I tell him. "Dress neatly. Be confident. Check yourself in the mirror."

I drain my experiences. I try to find examples for Noam. Between the ages of eleven and seventeen, only three persons voluntarily spoke to me. Still, I moved in the world. I avoided eccentricities of behavior. My grades were good. I have had terrible quarrels. Martin and Leslie have yelled at me, denying our ties of blood. My late husband often threatened me. "I shall reveal you to the world," he would say. "Hateful! Despicable!" People have shouted at me. I have been the target of unjust accusations. But look at me now, a guest.

It's only a question of vision.

NOAM HAS BEGUN to perk up. I leave his dinner warming in the oven while I retreat to my room. I have many assignments. The work goes well.

"I am being transferred to another city," Noam says. "It will be good for me." I agree, kiss his cheek, help him pack. I give him a check. The sum astonishes him. Also me.

"Send a letter," I implore. "Keep in touch."

He leaves me standing on the doorstep.

Noam writes that he has married. We did not have a real wedding, he says. Just a simple little ceremony.

Yet in my heart I know that her parents were there, weeping and toasting the blissful couple. I would have seen for myself if someone had invited me.

1960s

IN THE '60S, Iowa's reputation began to go mainstream. *Mademoiselle* ran a long, laudatory profile of the program which noted that "sixty novels have been published in the last twenty-five years by former students of the Workshop." *Writers' Digest* and *Look* ran pieces on the Workshop. Random House published *Midland: Twenty-five Years of Fiction and Poetry Selected from the Writing Workshops of the State University of Iowa*, edited by Paul Engle, with assistance from Henri Colette and Donald Justice. In his introduction to the volume, Engle again made his case for teaching creative writing at universities. His message was obviously received, as programs, of which only a handful existed in 1959, proliferated at institutions around the country, many of them founded and staffed by Iowa graduates.

None captured the nation's attention like Iowa. Not all portraits, however, were flattering. Philip Roth wrote disparagingly about his experiences there for *Esquire* in 1962. He was not critical of the Workshop, but of Iowa City itself, claiming that it suffered from a "vacancy of imagination" as far as architecture was concerned (true), was a difficult place to buy a drink (no longer true by a long shot), and served some of the least inspired food on the planet (still pretty close to absolutely true). These cultural drawbacks did nothing to stifle the Workshop's literary production. In fact, it could be argued that the awful food and weather, as well as the total absence of distractions, encouraged creativity as a means of psychic survival. Write, or be bored to death. So many chose the former path that Rust Hills, *Esquire*'s esteemed fiction editor, wrote in 1963 that one-third of the total number of writers who appeared on *Esquire*'s list of "everyone of any serious consequence" in the literary world were former Iowa students and faculty members.

Despite, and partly because of, these accolades, political battles developed between the English Department and the Workshop. A member of the literature faculty summed up the condescension many directed toward the Workshop. "The scholars feel that writing doesn't involve so much effort and precision as straight scholarship does." According to this logic, Shakespeare's work pales in comparison to the task of footnoting it. Engle, never one to shy away from a good fight, responded bluntly. "They know perfectly well that the brightest people we get are writers. The most brilliant scholars will go to Harvard and places like that, but where can the writers go except here and Stanford?"

Bharati Mukherjee has often told the story of her father asking a dinner guest at his Calcutta home where in the United States to send his daughter to study writing. The guest answered, Paul Engle. Delighted to be applying to an individual and not an institution, Bharati's father immediately wrote Engle a personal note asking him to take care of his daughter, but addressed it to Paul Engle, Ames, Iowa. Despite listing the wrong city, the letter was delivered, signaling the Workshop and Engle's growing fame. As the '60s progressed, Joy Williams and Gail Godwin arrived, bringing to the Workshop for the first time a strong, varied body of women writers.

Engle tired of academic battles, though, by the mid-1960s. He resigned as director to begin the International Writing Program, which to this day brings writers from around the world to Iowa City each year. George Starbuck ably directed the Workshop through the end of the decade, while American culture at large and the politicians stewarding it continued to abandon literature. At a 1962 U.S. Senate Hearing on budget requests, Senator John McClellan provided a vision of the chances for an enduring, national agency to support the arts when he said, "I don't think that a book of short stories or fiction is going to be of any great value or produce results." *Harper's*, which had once published as many as eight stories per issue, cut this total to one. The *Atlantic Monthly* dramatically reduced the space it allotted to fiction. And in 1969, the *Saturday Evening Post*, which had published Bellow, Algren, Roth, Nobel laureate I. B. Singer, and Arthur Miller, closed its doors, lamenting its readership's lack of interest in good fiction.

Due, somewhat, to this trend, as well as to the continuing institutionalization of creative writing, some writers turned to "metafiction," fiction about fiction, stories about the act of writing. Blessedly, it was a short-lived epoch, a temporary throwback to the head games of High Modernism and the Romantic artist's self-deification. The best of this fiction retained a political edge that can be found in the work of Kurt Vonnegut, as well as Norman Mailer's blending of fact and fiction in a style dubbed "The New Journalism." Overall, the strength of American fiction continued to flourish in a variety of styles and forms. As seen here, the late Andre Dubus's Chekhovian realism differs from the sly, realistic surface of Raymond Carver's sometimes parable-like episodes of almost Kafkan strangeness. Walter Tevis carries on Nelson Algren's concern for the marginal element of society. Clark Blaise and Bharati Mukherjee bring worldy perspectives to their stories of immigrants and outsiders. Joy Williams seems to have invented an apocalyptic style all her own, while William Kittredge keeps alive a vision of the West that Wallace Stegner would have lauded. And Iowa's teacher-writer relationships demonstrate the surprising influence that vastly different aesthetics can nonetheless have on one another. Kurt Vonnegut, for example, mentored both Gail Godwin and, despite his Dickensian leanings, John Irving, a Workshop graduate so famous he has had his own vodka ad. (You can read one of his short stories in his ad for Absolut, published in the fall of 1998.)

As the '60s closed, literature, for virtually the last time in the twentieth century, made an impact that, as Paul Engle said, "materially affected American culture." Writers were at the forefront of marches on the Pentagon and the antiwar movement. Workshop alumnus Robert Lowell locked arms with Norman Mailer as they approached the Capitol. Kurt Vonnegut wrote *Slaughterhouse-Five*. Major American writers voiced ideas about how to change the world, and their work inspired a generation of readers to an activism that created the kind of "results" Senator McClellan never imagined, or perhaps feared. It is a legacy of moral vitality that the Workshop, for all its occasional isolation and seeming careerism, still champions on behalf of literature.

IN THE EARLY 1950s, Walter Tevis worked in a Kentucky poolroom while going to college. Here he mingled with the people whom he later wrote about in several short stories, practicing his stroke, you might say, before writing *The Hustler*.

Poolrooms in those days had bad reputations that were often well earned. Traveling gamblers, known as crossroaders, went to poolrooms to learn who and where the action was. Gambling was not limited to pool, but included dice, poker, darts, and gin rummy. The old-time poolrooms were dimly lit, heavy with smoke, and rarely cleaned beyond a weekly mopping of the floor. They usually served burgers and fries and soda pop. Each place had its hierarchy of players, and every big-time gambler operated out of his home club. Nicknames were common among gamblers due to the transience of the occupation.

That world is pretty much gone now. Pool has become popular among the middle class, and some fancy rooms are open in the cities. Casinos are proliferating on rivers and reservations. Most states have lotteries. When gambling emerged from the shadows, the poolroom lost its place in the culture, and professional pool players had fewer places to work. The quality of the game has since declined.

Walter Tevis could not have foreseen this when he wrote the following short story. He merely wrote about the world he knew. He didn't know that in making his art, he was also preserving a rich piece of American heritage.

The antagonist in this story is called Louisville Fats. Two years later, Tevis used a similar character in his classic novel *The Hustler*, but he changed the name to Minnesota Fats. Following publication of *The Hustler* and the subsequent movie, a well-known pool player changed his name to Minnesota Fats.

In this way, Tevis not only preserved American heritage, he changed it.

CHRIS OFFUTT

WALTER TEVIS

The Hustler

THEY TOOK SAM OUT of the office, through the long passageway, and up to the big metal doors. The doors opened slowly, and they stepped out.

The sunlight was exquisite; warm on Sam's face. The air was clear and still. A few birds were circling in the sky. There was a gravel path, a road, and then, grass. Sam drew a deep breath. He could see as far as the horizon.

A guard drove up in a gray station wagon. He opened the door and Sam got in, whistling softly to himself. They drove off, down the gravel path. Sam did not turn around to look at the prison walls; he kept his eyes on the grass that stretched ahead of them, and on the road through the grass.

When the guard stopped to let him off in Richmond he said, "A word of advice, Willis."

"Advice?" Sam smiled at the guard.

"That's right. You got a habit of getting in trouble, Willis. That's why they didn't parole you, made you serve full time, because of that habit."

"That's what the man told me," Sam said. "So?"

"So stay out of poolrooms. You're smart. You can earn a living."

Sam started climbing out of the station wagon. "Sure," he said. He got out, slammed the door, and the guard drove away.

It was still early and the town was nearly empty. Sam walked around, up and down different streets, for about an hour, looking at houses and stores, smiling at the people he saw, whistling or humming little tunes to himself.

In his right hand he was carrying his little round tubular leather case, carrying it by the brass handle on the side. It was about thirty inches long, the case; and about as big around as a man's forearm.

At ten o'clock he went to the bank and drew out the $600 he had deposited there under the name of George Graves. Only it was $680, it had gathered that much interest.

Then he went to a clothing store and bought a sporty tan coat, a pair of brown slacks, brown suede shoes, and a bright green sport shirt. In the store's dressing room he put the new outfit on, leaving the prison-issued suit and shoes on the floor. Then he bought two extra sets of underwear and socks, paid, and left.

About a block up the street there was a clean-looking beauty parlor. He walked in and told the lady who seemed to be in charge, "I'm an actor. I have to play a part in Chicago tonight that requires red hair." He smiled at her. "Can you fix me up?"

The lady was all efficiency. "Certainly," she said. "If you'll just step back to a booth we'll pick out a shade."

A half hour later he was a redhead. In two hours he was on board a plane for Chicago with a little less than $600 in his pocket and one piece of luggage. He still had the underwear and socks in a paper sack.

In Chicago he took a fourteen-dollar-a-night room in the best hotel he could find. The room was big, and pleasant. It looked and smelled clean.

He sat down on the side of the bed and opened his little leather case at the top. The two-piece billiard cue inside was intact. He took it out and screwed the brass joint together, pleased that it still fit perfectly. Then he checked the butt for tightness. The weight was still firm and solid. The tip was good, its shape had held up; and the cue's balance and stroke seemed easy, familiar; almost as though he still played with it every day.

He checked himself in the mirror. They had done a perfect job on his hair; and its brightness against the green and brown of his new clothes gave him the sporty, racetrack sort of look he had always avoided before. His once ruddy complexion was very pale. Not a pool player in town should be able to recognize him: he could hardly recognize himself.

If all went well he would be out of Chicago for good in a few days; and no one would know for a long time that Big Sam Willis had even played there. Six years on a manslaughter charge could have its advantages.

In the morning he had to walk around town for a while before he found a poolroom of the kind he wanted. It was a few blocks off the Loop, small; and from the outside it seemed to be fairly clean and quiet.

Inside, there was a short order and beer counter up front. In back there were four tables; Sam could see them through the door in the partition that separated the lunchroom from the poolroom proper. There was no one in the place except for the tall, blond boy behind the counter.

Sam asked the boy if he could practice.

"Sure." The boy's voice was friendly. "But it'll cost you a dollar an hour."

"Fair enough." He gave the boy a five-dollar bill. "Let me know when this is used up."

The boy raised his eyebrows and took the money.

In the back room Sam selected the best twenty-ounce cue he could find in the wall rack, one with an ivory point and a tight butt, chalked the tip, and broke the rack of balls on what seemed to be the best of the four tables.

He tried to break safe, a straight pool break, where you drive the two bottom corner balls to the cushions and back into the stack where they came from, making the cue ball go two rails and return to the top of the table, killing itself on the cushion. The break didn't work, however; the rack of balls spread wide, five of them came out into the table, and the cue ball stopped in the middle. It would have left an opponent wide open for a big run. Sam shuddered.

He pocketed the fifteen balls, missing only once—a long shot that had to be cut thin into a far corner—and he felt better, making balls. He had little confidence on the hard ones, he was awkward; but he still knew the game, he knew how to break up little clusters of balls on one shot so that he could pocket them on the next. He knew how to play position with very little English on the cue, by shooting "natural" shots, and letting the speed of the cue ball do the work. He could still figure the spread, plan out his shots in advance from the positions of the balls on the table, and he knew what to shoot at first.

He kept shooting for about three hours. Several times other players came in and played for a while, but none of them paid any attention to him, and none of them stayed long.

The place was empty again and Sam was practicing cutting balls down the rail, working on his cue ball and on his speed, when he looked up and saw the boy who ran the place coming back. He was carrying a plate with a hamburger in one hand and two bottles of beer in the other.

"Hungry?" He set the sandwich down on the arm of a chair. "Or thirsty, maybe?"

Sam looked at his watch. It was 1:30. "Come to think of it," he said, "I am." He went to the chair, picked up the hamburger, and sat down.

"Have a beer," the boy said, affably. Sam took it and drank from the bottle. It tasted delicious.

"What do I owe you?" he said, and took a bite out of the hamburger.

"The burger's thirty cents," the boy said. "The beer's on the house."

"Thanks," Sam said, chewing. "How do I rate?"

"You're a good customer," the boy said. "Easy on the equipment, cash in advance, and I don't even have to rack the balls for you."

"Thanks." Sam was silent for a minute, eating.

The boy was drinking the other beer. Abruptly, he set the bottle down. "You on the hustle?" he said.

"Do I look like a hustler?"

"You practice like one."

Sam sipped his beer quietly for a minute, looking over the top of the bottle, once, at the boy. Then he said, "I might be looking around." He set the empty bottle down on the wooden chair arm. "I'll be back tomorrow; we can talk about it then. There might be something in it for you. If you help me out."

"Sure, mister," the boy said. "You pretty good?"

"I think so," Sam said. Then when the boy got up to leave he added, "Don't try to finger me for anybody. It won't do you any good."

"I won't." The boy went back up front.

Sam practiced, working mainly on his stroke and his position, for three more hours. When he finished his arm was sore and his feet were tired; but he felt better. His stroke was beginning to work for him, he was getting smooth, making balls regularly, playing good position. Once, when he was running balls continuously, racking fourteen and one, he ran seventeen without missing.

The next morning after a long night's rest, he was even better. He ran more than ninety balls one time, missing, finally, on a difficult rail shot.

The boy came back at one o'clock bringing a ham sandwich this time and two beers. "Here you go," he said. "Time to take a break."

Sam thanked him, laid his cue stick on the table, and sat down.

"My name's Barney," the boy said.

"George Graves." Sam held out his hand, and the boy shook it. "Just," he smiled inwardly at the thought, "call me Red."

"You *are* good," Barney said. "I watched you a couple of times."

"I know." Sam took a drink from the beer bottle. "I'm looking for a straight pool game."

"I figured that, Mister Graves. You won't find one here, though. Up at Bennington's they play straight pool."

Sam had heard of Bennington's. They said it was a hustler's room, a big money place.

"You know who plays pool there, Barney?" he said.

"Sure. Bill Peyton, he plays there. And Shufala Kid, Louisville Fats, Johnny Vargas, Henry Keller, a little guy they call 'The Policeman' . . ."

Henry Keller was the only familiar name; Sam had played him once, in Atlantic City, maybe fourteen years ago. But that had been even before the big days of Sam's reputation, before he had got so good that he had to trick hustlers into playing him. That was a long time ago. And then there was the red hair; he ought to be able to get by.

"Which one's got money," he asked, "and plays straight pool?"

"Well," Barney looked doubtful, "I think Louisville Fats carries a big roll. He's one of the old Prohibition boys; they say he keeps an army of hoods working for him. He plays straights. But he's good. And he doesn't like being hustled."

It looked good; but dangerous. Hustlers didn't take it very well to find out a man was using a phony name so he could get a game. Sam remembered the time someone had told Bernie James who he had been playing and Bernie had got pretty rough about it. But this time it was different; he had been out of circulation six years, and he had never played in Chicago before.

"This Fats. Does he bet big?"

"Yep, he bets big. Big as you want." Barney smiled. "But I tell you he's mighty good."

"Rack the balls," Sam said, and smiled back. "I'll show you something."

Barney racked. Sam broke them wide open and started running. He went through the rack, then another, another, and another. Barney was counting the balls, racking them for him each time. When he got to eighty Sam said, "Now I'll bank a few." He banked seven, knocking them off the rails, across and into the pockets. When he missed the eight he said, "What do you think?"

"You'll do," Barney said. He laughed. "Fats is good; but you might take him."

"I'll take him," Sam said. "You lead me to him. Tomorrow night you get somebody to work for you. We're going up to Bennington's."

"Fair enough, Mister Graves," Barney said. He was grinning. "We'll have a beer on that."

At Bennington's you took an elevator to the floor you wanted; billiards on the first, pocket pool on the second, snooker and private games on the third. It was an old-fashioned setup, high ceilings, big, shaded incandescent lights, overstuffed leather chairs.

Sam spent the morning on the second floor, trying to get the feel of the tables. They were different from Barney's, with softer cushions and tighter cloths, and it was a little hard to get used to them; but after about two hours he felt as though he had them pretty well, and he left. No one had paid any attention to him.

After lunch he inspected his hair in the restaurant's bathroom mirror; it was still as red as ever and hadn't yet begun to grow out. He felt good. Just a little nervous, but good.

Barney was waiting for him at the little poolroom. They took a cab up to Bennington's.

Louisville Fats must have weighed 300 pounds. His face seemed to be bloated around the eyes like the face of an Eskimo, so that he was always squinting. His arms, hanging from the short sleeves of his white silk shirt, were pink and doughlike. Sam noticed his hands; they were soft-looking, white and delicate. He wore three rings, one with a diamond. He had on dark green, wide suspenders.

When Barney introduced him, Fats said, "How are you, George?" but didn't offer his hand. Sam noticed that his eyes, almost buried beneath the face, seemed to shift from side to side, so that he seemed not really to be looking at anything.

"I'm fine," Sam said. Then after a pause, "I've heard a lot about you."

"I got a reputation?" Fats' voice was flat, disinterested. "Then I must be pretty good maybe?"

"I suppose so," Sam said, trying to watch the eyes.

"You a good pool player, George?" The eyes flickered, scanning Sam's face.

"Fair. I like playing. Straight pool."

Oh," Fats grinned, abruptly, coldly. "That's my game too, George." He slapped Barney on the back. The boy pulled away, slightly, from him. "You pick good, Barney. He plays my game. You can finger for me, sometime, if you want."

"Sure," Barney said. He looked nervous.

"One thing," Fats was still grinning. "You play for money, George? I mean, you gamble?"

"When the bet's right."

"What you think is a right bet, George?"

"Fifty dollars."

Fats grinned even more broadly; but his eyes still kept shifting. "Now that's close, George," he said. "You play for a hundred and we play a few."

"Fair enough," Sam said, as calmly as he could.

"Let's go upstairs. It's quieter."

"Fine. I'll take my boy if you don't mind. He can rack the balls."

Fats looked at Barney. "You level with that rack, Barney? I mean, you rack the balls tight for Fats?"

"Sure," Barney said, "I wouldn't try to cross you up."

"You know better than that, Barney. OK."

They walked up the back stairs to the third floor. There was a small, bare-walled room, well lighted, with chairs lined up against the walls. The chairs were high ones, the type used for watching pool games. There was no one else in the room.

They uncovered the table, and Barney racked the balls. Sam lost the toss and broke, making it safe, but not too safe. He undershot, purposely, and left the cue ball almost a foot away from the end rail.

They played around, shooting safe for a while. Then Fats pulled a hard one off the edge of the rack, ran thirty-five and played him safe. Sam jockeyed with him, figuring to lose for a while, only wanting the money to hold out until he had the table down pat, until he had the other man's game figured, until he was ready to raise the bet.

He lost three in a row before he won one. He wasn't playing his best game; but that meant little, since Fats was probably pulling his punches too, trying to take him for as much as possible. After he won his first game he let himself go a little and made a few tricky ones. Once he knifed a ball thin into the side pocket and went two cushions for a breakup; but Fats didn't even seem to notice.

Neither of them tried to run more than forty at a turn. It would have looked like a game between only fair players, except that neither of them missed very often. In a tight spot they didn't try anything fancy, just shot a safe and let the other man figure it out. Sam played safe on some shots he was sure he could make; he didn't want to show his hand. Not yet. They kept playing and, after a while, Sam started winning more often.

After about three hours he was five games ahead, and shooting better all the time. Then, when he won still another game, Sam said, "You're losing money, Fats. Maybe we should quit." He looked at Barney and winked. Barney gave him a puzzled, worried look.

"Quit? You think we should quit?" Fats took a big silk handkerchief from his side pocket and wiped his face. "How much money you won, George?" he said.

"That last makes six hundred." He felt, suddenly, a little tense. It was coming. The big push.

"Suppose we play for six hundred, George." He put the handkerchief back in his pocket. "Then we see who quits."

"Fine." He felt really nervous now, but he knew he would get over it. Nervousness didn't count. At 600 a game he would be in clover and in San Francisco in two days. If he didn't lose.

Barney racked the balls and Sam broke. He took the break slowly, putting to use his practice of three days, and his experience of twenty-seven years. The balls broke perfectly, reracking the original triangle, and the cue ball skidded to a stop right on the end cushion.

"You shoot pretty good," Fats said, looking at the safe table that Sam had left him. But he played safe, barely tipping the cue ball off one of the balls down at the foot of the table and returning back to the end rail.

Sam tried to return the safe by repeating the same thing; but the cue ball caught the object ball to thick and he brought out a shot, a long one, for Fats. Fats stepped up, shot the ball in played position, and ran out the rest of the rack. Then he ran out another rack and Sam sat down to watch; there was nothing he could do now. Fats ran seventy-eight points and then, seeing a difficult shot, played him safe.

He had been afraid that something like that might happen. He tried to fight his way out of the game, but couldn't seem to get into the clear long enough for a good run. Fats beat him badly—125 to 30—and he had to give back the $600 from his pocket. It hurt.

What hurt even worse was that he knew he had less than 600 left of his own money.

"Now we see who quits." Fats stuffed the money in his hip pocket. "You want to play for another six hundred?"

"I'm still holding my stick," Sam said. He tried not to think about that "army of hoods" that Barney had told him about.

He stepped up to the table and broke. His hand shook a little; but the break was a perfect one. In the middle of the game Fats missed an easy shot, leaving Sam a dead setup. Sam ran fifty-three and out. He won. It was as easy as that. He was 600 ahead again, and feeling better.

Then something unlucky happened. Downstairs they must have closed up because six men came up during the next game and sat around the table. Five of them Sam had never seen, but one of them was Henry Keller. Henry was drunk now, evidently, and he didn't seem to be paying much attention to what was going on; but Sam didn't like it. He didn't like Keller, and he didn't like having a man who knew who he was around him. It was too much like that other time. That time in Richmond when Bernie James had come after him with a bottle. That fight had cost him six years. He didn't like it. It was getting time to wind things up here, time to be cutting out. If he could win two more games quick, he would have enough to set him up hustling on the West Coast. And on the West Coast there weren't any

Henry Kellers who knew that Big Sam Willis was once the best straight-pool shot in the game.

After Sam had won the game by a close score Fats looked at his fingernails and said, "George, you're a hustler. You shoot better straight than anybody in Chicago shoots. Except me."

This was the time, the time to make it quick and neat, the time to push as hard as he could. He caught his breath, held steady, and said, "You've got it wrong, Fats. I'm better than you are. I'll play you for all of it. The whole twelve hundred."

It was very quiet in the room. Then Fats said, "George, I like that kind of talk." He started chalking his cue. "We play twelve hundred."

Barney racked the balls and Fats broke them. They both played safe, very safe, back and forth, keeping the cue ball on the rail, not leaving a shot for the other man. It was nerve-racking. Over and over.

Then he missed. Missed the edge of the rack, coming at it from an outside angle. His cue ball bounced off the rail and into the rack of balls, spreading them wide, leaving Fats at least five shots. Sam didn't sit down. He just stood and watched Fats come up and start his run. He ran the balls, broke on the fifteenth, and ran another rack. Twenty-eight points. And he was just getting started. He had his rack break set up perfectly for the next shot.

Then, as Fats began chalking up, preparing to shoot, Henry Keller stood up from his seat and pointed his finger at Sam.

He was drunk; but he spoke clearly, and loudly. "You're Big Sam Willis," he said. "You're the World's Champion." He sat back in his chair, heavily. "You got red hair, but you're Big Sam." He sat silent, half slumped in the big chair for a moment, his eyes glassy, and red at the corners. "There's nobody beats Big Sam, Fats. Nobody *never*."

The room was quiet for what seemed to be a very long while. Sam noticed how thick the tobacco smoke had become in the air; motionless, it was like a heavy brown mist, and over the table it was like a cloud. The faces of the men in the chairs were impassive; all of them, except Henry, watching him.

Fats turned to him. For once his eyes were not shifting from side to side. He looked Sam in the face and said, in a voice that was flat and almost a whisper, "You Big Sam Willis, George?"

"That's right, Fats."

"You must be pretty smart, Sam," Fats said, "to play a trick like that. To make a sucker out of me."

"Maybe." His chest and stomach felt very tight. It was like when Bernie James had caught him at the same game, except without the red hair. Bernie hadn't said anything, though; he had just picked up a bottle.

But, then, Bernie James was dead now. Sam wondered, momentarily, if Fats had ever heard about that.

Suddenly Fats split the silence, laughing. The sound of his laughing filled the room, he threw his head back and laughed; and the men in the chairs looked at him, astonished, hearing the laughter. "Big Sam," he said, "you're a hustler. You put on a great act; and fool me good. A great act." He slapped Sam on the back. "I think the joke's on me."

It was hard to believe. But Fats could afford the money, and Sam knew that Fats knew who would be the best, if it came to muscle. And there was no certainty whose side the other men were on.

Fats shot, ran a few more balls, and then missed.

When Sam stepped up to shoot he said, "Go ahead, Big Sam, and shoot your best. You don't have to act now. I'm quitting you anyway after this one."

The funny thing was that Sam had been shooting his best for the past five or six games—or thought he had—but when he stepped up to the table this time he was different. Maybe it was Fats or Keller, something made him feel as he hadn't felt for a long time. It was like being the old Big Sam, back before he had quit playing the tournaments and exhibitions, the Big Sam who could run 125 when he was hot and the money was up. His stroke was smooth, steady, accurate, like a balanced, precision instrument moving on well-oiled bearings. He shot easily, calmly, clicking the shots off in his mind and then pocketing them on the table, watching everything on the green, forgetting himself, forgetting even the money, just dropping the balls into the pockets, one after another.

He did it. He ran the game. One hundred and twenty-five points, 125 shots without missing. When he finished Fats took $1200 from his still-big roll and counted it out, slowly, to him. He said, "You're the best I've ever seen, Big Sam." Then he covered the table with the oilcloth cover.

After Sam had dropped Barney off he had the cab take him by his hotel and let him off at a little all-night lunchroom. He ordered bacon and eggs over light, and talked with the waitress while she fried them. The place seemed strange, gay almost; his nerves felt electric and there was a pleasant fuzziness in his head, a dim, insistent ringing sound coming from far off. He tried to think for a moment; tried to think whether he should go to the airport now without even going back to the hotel now that he had made out so well, had made out better, even, than he had planned to be able to do in a week. But there was the waitress and then the food; and when he put a quarter in the jukebox he couldn't hear the ringing in his ears anymore. This was no time for plane trips; it was a time for talk and music, time for the sense of triumph, the sense of being alive and having money again, and then time for sleep. He was in a chromium and plastic booth in the lunchroom and he leaned back against the padded plastic backrest and felt an abrupt, deep, gratifying sense of fatigue, loosening his muscles and killing, finally, the tension that had ridden him like a fury for the past three days. There would be plane flights enough tomorrow. Now, he needed rest. It was a long way to San Francisco.

The bed at his hotel was impeccably made; the pale blue spread seemed drum-tight, but soft and round at the edges and corners. He didn't even take off his shoes.

When he awoke, he awoke suddenly. The skin at the back of his neck was itching, sticky with sweat from where the collar of his shirt had been pressed, tight, against it. His mouth was dry and his feet felt swollen, stuffed, in his shoes. The room was as quiet as death. Outside the window a car's tires groaned gently, rounding a corner, then were still.

He pulled the chain on the lamp by the bed and the light came on. Squinting, he stood up, and realized that his legs were aching. The room seemed too big, too bright. He stumbled into the bathroom and threw handsfull of cold water on his face and neck. Then he dried off with a towel and looked in the mirror. Startled, he let go of the towel momentarily; the red hair had caught him off guard; and with the eyes now swollen, the lips pale, it was not his face at all. He finished drying quickly, ran his comb through his hair, straightened out his shirt and slacks hurriedly. The startling strangeness of his own face had crystallized the dim, half-conscious feeling that something was wrong. The hotel room, himself, Chicago; they were all wrong. He should not be here, not now; he should be on the West Coast, in San Francisco.

He looked at his watch. Four o'clock. He had slept three hours. He did not feel tired, not now, although his bones ached and there was sand under his eyelids. He could sleep, if he had to, on the plane. But the important thing, now, was getting on the plane, clearing out, moving West. He had slept with his cue, in its case, on the bed. He took it and left the room.

The lobby, too, seemed too bright and too empty. But when he had paid his bill and gone out to the street the relative darkness seemed worse. He began to walk down the street hastily, looking for a cabstand. His own footsteps echoed around him as he walked. There seemed to be no cabs anywhere on the street. He began walking faster. The back of his neck was sweating again. It was a very hot night; the air felt heavy against his skin. There were no cabs.

And then, when he heard the slow, dense hum of a heavy car moving down the street in his direction, heard it from several blocks away and turned his head to see it and to see that there was no cab light on it, he knew—abruptly and lucidly, as some men at some certain times know these things—what was happening.

He began to run; but he did not know where to run. He turned a corner while he was still two blocks ahead of the car and when he could feel its lights, palpably, on the back of his neck, and tried to hide in a doorway, flattening himself out against the door. Then, when he saw the lights of the car as it began its turn around the corner he realized that the doorway was too shallow, that the lights would pick him out. Something in him wanted to scream. He pushed himself from his place, stumbled down the street, visualizing in his mind a place, some sort of a place between buildings where he could hide completely and where the car could never follow him. But the buildings were all together, with no space at all between them; and when he saw that this was so he also saw at the same instant that the car lights were flooding him. And then he heard the car stop. There was nothing more to do. He turned around and looked at the car, blinking.

Two men had got out of the backseat; there were two more in front. He could see none of their faces, but was relieved that he could not, could not see the one face that would be bloated like an Eskimo's and with eyes like slits.

The men were holding the door open for him.

"Well," he said. "Hello, boys," and climbed into the backseat. His little leather case was still in his right hand. He gripped it tightly. It was all he had.

"DID YOU HEAR THAT?" Ray said. We were crossing a street in San Francisco. "That's the last Christmas he'll spoil for us." Ray's eyes were gleaming. "That's what she said." He pointed to a woman who had been standing behind us while we waited for the light.

Ray Carver paid more attention to the ways people around him actually spoke and acted than anyone else I've ever known. Ray was a natural mimic, and after a party, in the days when he was drinking, he would recite, and act out with gestures, whole strings of talk he'd overheard. He reworked these moments in his stories. As a result, often, like this one, his stories and poems came from something that had happened to him.

Ray's attentiveness, I think, wasn't entirely the result of loving gossip, although he surely did. It also came naturally from his fascination with ordinary life, what we say and how we act toward one another, and how we indirectly reveal ourselves, and the consequences, which run off in such unplanned ways, and are oftentimes simultaneously funny and heartbreaking. Ray's fundamental project, I think, involved urging us to try a shot of empathy, some compassion—put yourself in my shoes, try my isolation, my blindness, my fearfulness, my anger—we're all in the same sinking boat, let's see if we can't understand and forgive one another.

WILLIAM KITTREDGE

RAYMOND CARVER

Put Yourself in My Shoes

THE TELEPHONE RANG while he was running the vacuum cleaner. He had worked his way through the apartment and was doing the living room, using the nozzle attachment to get at the cat hairs between the cushions. He stopped and listened and then switched off the vacuum. He went to answer the telephone.

"Hello," he said. "Myers here."

"Myers," she said. "How are you? What are you doing?"

"Nothing," he said. "Hello, Paula."

"There's an office party this afternoon," she said. "You're invited. Dick invited you."

"I don't think I can come," Myers said.

"Dick just this minute said get that old man of yours on the phone. Get him down here for a drink. Get him out of his ivory tower and back into the real world for a while. Dick's funny when he's drinking. Myers?"

"I heard you," Myers said.

Myers used to work for Dick. Dick always talked of going to Paris to write a novel, and when Myers had quit to write a novel, Dick had said he would watch for Myers' name on the best-seller list.

"I can't come now," Myers said.

"We found out some horrible news this morning," Paula continued, as if she had not heard him. "You remember Larry Gudinas. He was still here when you came to work. He helped out on science books for a while, and then they put him in the field, and then they canned him? We heard this morning he committed suicide. He shot himself in the mouth. Can you imagine? Myers?"

"I heard you," Myers said. He tried to remember Larry Gudinas and recalled a tall, stooped man with wire-frame glasses, bright ties, and a receding hairline. He could imagine the jolt, the head snapping back. "Jesus," Myers said. "Well, I'm sorry to hear that."

"Come down to the office, honey, all right?" Paula said. "Everybody is just talking and having some drinks and listening to Christmas music. Come down," she said.

Myers could hear it all at the other end of the line. "I don't want to come down," he said. "Paula?" A few snowflakes drifted past the window as he watched. He rubbed his fingers across the glass and then began to write his name on the glass as he waited.

"What? I heard," she said. "All right," Paula said. "Well, then, why don't we meet at Voyles for a drink? Myers?"

"Okay," he said. "Voyles. All right."

"Everybody here will be disappointed you didn't come," she said. "Dick especially. Dick admires you, you know. He does. He's told me so. He admires your nerve. He said if he had your nerve he would have quit years ago. Dick said it takes nerve to do what you did. Myers?"

"I'm right here," Myers said. "I think I can get my car started. If I can't start it, I'll call you back."

"All right," she said. "I'll see you at Voyles. I'll leave here in five minutes if I don't hear from you."

"Say hello to Dick for me," Myers said.

"I will," Paula said. "He's talking about you."

Myers put the vacuum cleaner away. He walked down the two flights and went to his car, which was in the last stall and covered with snow. He got in, worked the pedal a number of times, and tried the starter. It turned over. He kept the pedal down.

AS HE DROVE, he looked at the people who hurried along the sidewalks with shopping bags. He glanced at the gray sky, filled with flakes, and at the tall buildings with snow in the crevices and on the window ledges. He tried to see everything, save it for later. He was between stories, and he felt despicable. He found Voyles, a small bar on a corner next to a men's clothing store. He parked in back and went inside. He sat at the bar for a time and then carried a drink over to a little table near the door.

When Paula came in she said, "Merry Christmas," and he got up and gave her a kiss on the cheek. He held a chair for her.

He said, "Scotch?"

"Scotch," she said, then "Scotch over ice" to the girl who came for her order.

Paula picked up his drink and drained the glass.

"I'll have another one, too," Myers said to the girl. "I don't like this place," he said after the girl had moved away.

"What's wrong with this place?" Paula said. "We always come here."

"I just don't like it," he said. "Let's have a drink and then go someplace else."

"Whatever you want," she said.

The girl arrived with the drinks. Myers paid her, and he and Paula touched glasses.

Myers stared at her.

"Dick says hello," she said.

Myers nodded.

Paula sipped her drink. "How was your day today?"

Myers shrugged.

"What'd you do?" she said.

"Nothing," he said. "I vacuumed."

She touched his hand. "Everybody said to tell you hi."

They finished their drinks.

"I have an idea," she said. "Why don't we stop and visit the Morgans for a few minutes. We've never met them, for God's sake, and they've been back for months. We could just drop by and say hello, we're the Myerses. Besides, they sent us a card. They asked us to stop by during the holidays. They *invited* us. I don't want to go home," she finally said and fished in her purse for a cigarette.

Myers recalled setting the furnace and turning out all the lights before he had left. And then he thought of the snow drifting past the window.

"What about that insulting letter they sent telling us they heard we were keeping a cat in the house?" he said.

"They've forgotten about that by now," she said. "That wasn't anything serious, anyway. Oh, let's do it, Myers! Let's go by."

"We should call first if we're going to do anything like that," he said.

"No," she said. "That's part of it. Let's not call. Let's just go knock on the door and say hello, we used to live here. All right? Myers?"

"I think we should call first," he said.

"It's the holidays," she said, getting up from her chair. "Come on, baby."

She took his arm and they went out into the snow. She suggested they take her car and pick up his car later. He opened the door for her and then went around to the passenger's side.

SOMETHING TOOK HIM when he saw the lighted windows, saw snow on the roof, saw the station wagon in the driveway. The curtains were open and Christmas-tree lights blinked at them from the window.

They got out of the car. He held her elbow as they stepped over a pile of snow and started up the walk to the front porch. They had gone a few steps when a large bushy dog hurtled around the corner of the garage and headed straight for Myers.

"Oh, God," he said, hunching, stepping back, bringing his hands up. He slipped on the walk, his coat flapped, and he fell onto the frozen grass with the dread certainty that the dog would go for his throat. The dog growled once and then began to sniff Myers' coat.

Paula picked up a handful of snow and threw it at the dog. The porch light came on, the door opened, and a man called, "Buzzy!" Myers got to his feet and brushed himself off.

"What's going on?" the man in the doorway said. "Who is it? Buzzy, come here, fellow. Come here!"

"We're the Myerses," Paula said. "We came to wish you a Merry Christmas."

"The Myerses?" the man in the doorway said. "Get out! Get in the garage, Buzzy. Get, get! It's the Myerses," the man said to the woman who stood behind him trying to look past his shoulder.

"The Myerses," she said. "Well, ask them in, ask them in, for heaven's sake." She stepped onto the porch and said, "Come in, please, it's freezing. I'm Hilda Morgan and this is Edgar. We're happy to meet you. Please come in."

They all shook hands quickly on the front porch. Myers and Paula stepped inside and Edgar Morgan shut the door.

"Let me have your coats. Take off your coats," Edgar Morgan said. "You're all right?" he said to Myers, observing him closely, and Myers nodded. "I knew that dog was crazy, but he's never pulled anything like this. I saw it. I was looking out the window when it happened."

This remark seemed odd to Myers, and he looked at the man. Edgar Morgan was in his forties, nearly bald, and was dressed in slacks and a sweater and was wearing leather slippers.

"His name is Buzzy," Hilda Morgan announced and made a face. "It's Edgar's dog. I can't have an animal in the house myself, but Edgar bought this dog and promised to keep him outside."

"He sleeps in the garage," Edgar Morgan said. "He begs to come in the house, but we can't allow it, you know." Morgan chuckled. "But sit down, sit down, if you can find a place with this clutter. Hilda, dear, move some of those things off the couch so Mr. and Mrs. Myers can sit down."

Hilda Morgan cleared the couch of packages, wrapping paper, scissors, a box of ribbons, bows. She put everything on the floor.

Myers noticed Morgan staring at him again, not smiling now.

Paula said, "Myers, there's something in your hair, dearest."

Myers put a hand up to the back of his head and found a twig and put it in his pocket.

"That dog," Morgan said and chuckled again. "We were just having a hot drink and wrapping some last-minute gifts. Will you join us in a cup of holiday cheer? What would you like?"

"Anything is fine," Paula said.

"Anything," Myers said. "We wouldn't have interrupted."

"Nonsense," Morgan said. "We've been ... very curious about the Myerses. You'll have a hot drink, sir?"

"That's fine," Myers said.

"Mrs. Myers?" Morgan said.

Paula nodded.

"Two hot drinks coming up," Morgan said. "Dear, I think we're ready too, aren't we?" he said to his wife. "This is certainly an occasion."

He took her cup and went out to the kitchen. Myers heard the cupboard door bang and heard a muffled word that sounded like a curse. Myers blinked. He looked at Hilda Morgan, who was settling herself into a chair at the end of the couch.

"Sit down over here, you two," Hilda Morgan said. She patted the arm of the couch. "Over here, by the fire. We'll have Mr. Morgan build it up again when he returns." They sat. Hilda Morgan clasped her hands in her lap and leaned forward slightly, examining Myers' face.

The living room was as he remembered it, except that on the wall behind Hilda Morgan's chair he saw three small framed prints. In one print a man in a vest and frock coat was tipping his hat to two ladies who held parasols. All this was happening on a broad concourse with horses and carriages.

"How was Germany?" Paula said. She sat on the edge of the cushion and held her purse on her knees.

"We loved Germany," Edgar Morgan said, coming in from the kitchen with a tray and four large cups. Myers recognized the cups.

"Have you been to Germany, Mrs. Myers?" Morgan asked.

"We want to go," Paula said. "Don't we, Myers? Maybe next year, next summer. Or else the year after. As soon as we can afford it. Maybe as soon as Myers sells something. Myers writes."

"I should think a trip to Europe would be very beneficial to a writer," Edgar Morgan said. He put the cups into coasters. "Please help yourselves." He sat down in a chair across from his wife and gazed at Myers. "You said in your letter you were taking off work to write."

"That's true," Myers said and sipped his drink.

"He writes something almost every day," Paula said.

"Is that a fact?" Morgan said. "That's impressive. What did you write today, may I ask?"

"Nothing," Myers said.

"It's the holidays," Paula said.

"You must be proud of him, Mrs. Myers," Hilda Morgan said.

"I am," Paula said.

"I'm happy for you," Hilda Morgan said.

"I heard something the other day that might interest you," Edgar Morgan said. He took out some tobacco and began to fill a pipe. Myers lighted a cigarette and looked around for an ashtray, then dropped the match behind the couch.

"It's a horrible story, really. But maybe you could use it, Mr. Myers." Morgan struck a flame and drew on the pipe. "Grist for the mill, you know, and all that," Morgan said and laughed and shook the match. "This fellow was about my age or so. He was a colleague for a couple of years. We knew each other a little, and we had good friends in common. Then he moved out, accepted a position at the university down the way. Well, you know how these things go sometimes—the fellow had an affair with one of his students."

Mrs. Morgan made a disapproving noise with her tongue. She reached down for a small package that was wrapped in green paper and began to affix a red bow to the paper.

"According to all accounts, it was a torrid affair that lasted for some months," Morgan continued. "Right up until a short time ago, in fact. A week ago, to be exact. On that day—it was in the evening—he announced to his wife—they'd been married for twenty years—he announced to his wife that he wanted a divorce. You can imagine how the fool woman took it, coming out of the blue like that, so to speak. There was quite a row. The whole family got into it. She ordered him out of the house then and there. But just as the fellow was leaving, his son threw a can of tomato soup at him and hit him in the forehead. It caused a concussion that sent the man to the hospital. His condition is quite serious."

Morgan drew on his pipe and gazed at Myers.

"I'VE NEVER HEARD such a story," Mrs. Morgan said. "Edgar, that's disgusting."

"Horrible," Paula said.

Myers grinned.

"Now *there's* a tale for you, Mr. Myers," Morgan said, catching the grin and narrowing his eyes. "Think of the story you'd have if you could get inside that man's head."

"Or her head," Mrs. Morgan said. "The wife's. Think of *her* story. To be betrayed in such fashion after twenty years. Think how she must feel."

"But imagine what the poor *boy* must be going through," Paula said. "Imagine, having almost killed his father."

"Yes, that's all true," Morgan said. "But here's something I don't think any of you has thought about. Think about *this* for a moment. Mr. Myers, are you listening? Tell me what you think of this. Put yourself in the shoes of that eighteen-year-old coed who fell in love with a married man. Think about *her* for a moment, and then you see the possibilities for your story."

Morgan nodded and leaned back in the chair with a satisfied expression.

"I'm afraid I don't have any sympathy for her," Mrs. Morgan said. "I can imagine the sort she is. We all know what she's like, that kind preys on older men. I don't have any sympathy for him, either—the man, the chaser, no, I don't. I'm afraid my sympathies in this case are entirely with the wife and son."

"It would take a Tolstoy to tell it and tell it *right*," Morgan said. "No less than a Tolstoy. Mr. Myers, the water is still hot."

"Time to go," Myers said.

He stood up and threw his cigarette into the fire.

"Stay," Mrs. Morgan said. "We haven't gotten acquainted yet. You don't know how we have . . . speculated about you. Now that we're together at last, stay a little while. It's such a pleasant surprise."

"We appreciated the card and your note," Paula said.

"The card?" Mrs. Morgan said.

Myers sat down.

"We decided not to mail any cards this year," Paula said. "I didn't get around to it when I should have, and it seemed futile to do it at the last minute."

"You'll have another one, Mrs. Myers?" Morgan said, standing in front of her now with his hand on her cup. "You'll set an example for your husband."

"It *was* good," Paula said. "It warms you."

"Right," Morgan said. "It warms you. That's right. Dear, did you hear Mrs. Myers? It warms you. That's very good. Mr. Myers?" Morgan said and waited. "You'll join us?"

"All right," Myers said and let Morgan take the cup.

The dog began to whine and scratch at the door.

"That dog. I don't know what's gotten into that dog," Morgan said. He went to the kitchen and this time Myers distinctly heard Morgan curse as he slammed the kettle onto a burner.

MRS. MORGAN BEGAN to hum. She picked up a half-wrapped package, cut a piece of tape, and began sealing the paper.

Myers lighted a cigarette. He dropped the match in his coaster. He looked at his watch.

Mrs. Morgan raised her head. "I believe I hear singing," she said. She listened. She rose from her chair and went to the front window. "It *is* singing. Edgar!" she called.

Myers and Paula went to the window.

"I haven't seen carolers in years," Mrs. Morgan said.

"What is it?" Morgan said. He had the tray and cups. "What is it? What's wrong?"

"Nothing's wrong, dear. It's carolers. There they are over there, across the street," Mrs. Morgan said.

"Mrs. Myers," Morgan said, extending the tray. "Mr. Myers. Dear."

"Thank you," Paula said.

"*Muchas gracias,*" Myers said.

Morgan put the tray down and came back to the window with his cup. Young people were gathered on the walk in front of the house across the street, boys and girls with an older, taller boy who wore a muffler and a topcoat. Myers could see the faces at the window across the way—the Ardreys—and when the carolers had finished, Jack Ardrey came to the door and gave something to the older boy. The group moved on down the walk, flashlights bobbing, and stopped in front of another house.

"They won't come here," Mrs. Morgan said after a time.

"What? Why won't they come here?" Morgan said and turned to his wife. "What a goddamned silly thing to say! Why won't they come here?"

"I just know they won't," Mrs. Morgan said.

"And I say they will," Morgan said. "Mrs. Myers, are those carolers going to come here or not? What do you think? Will they return to bless this house? We'll leave it up to you."

Paula pressed closer to the window. But the carolers were far down the street now. She did not answer.

"Well, now that all the excitement is over," Morgan said and went over to his chair. He sat down, frowned, and began to fill his pipe.

Myers and Paula went back to the couch. Mrs. Morgan moved away from the window at last. She sat down. She smiled and gazed into her cup. Then she put the cup down and began to weep.

Morgan gave his handkerchief to his wife. He looked at Myers. Presently Morgan began to drum on the arm of his chair. Myers moved his feet. Paula looked into her purse for a cigarette. "See what you've caused?" Morgan said as he stared at something on the carpet near Myers' shoes.

Myers gathered himself to stand.

"Edgar, get them another drink," Mrs. Morgan said as she dabbed at her eyes. She used the handkerchief on her nose. "I want them to hear about Mrs. Attenborough. Mr. Myers writes. I think he might appreciate this. We'll wait until you come back before we begin the story."

MORGAN COLLECTED THE cups. He carried them into the kitchen. Myers heard dishes clatter, cupboard doors bang. Mrs. Morgan looked at Myers and smiled faintly.

"We have to go," Myers said. "We have to go. Paula, get your coat."

"No, no, we insist, Mr. Myers," Mrs. Morgan said. "We want you to hear about Mrs. Attenborough, poor Mrs. Attenborough. You might appreciate this story, too, Mrs. Myers. This is your chance to see how your husband's mind goes to work on raw material."

Morgan came back and passed out the hot drinks. He sat down quickly.

"Tell them about Mrs. Attenborough, dear," Mrs. Morgan said.

"That dog almost tore my leg off," Myers said and was at once surprised at his words. He put his cup down.

"Oh, come, it wasn't that bad," Morgan said. "I saw it."

"You know writers," Mrs. Morgan said to Paula. "They like to exaggerate."

"The power of the pen and all that," Morgan said.

"That's it," Mrs. Morgan said. "Bend your pen into a plowshare, Mr. Myers."

"We'll let Mrs. Morgan tell the story of Mrs. Attenborough," Morgan said, ignoring Myers, who stood up at that moment. "Mrs. Morgan was intimately connected with the affair. I've already told you of the fellow who was knocked for a loop by a can of soup." Morgan chuckled. "We'll let Mrs. Morgan tell this one."

"You tell it, dear. And Mr. Myers, you listen closely," Mrs. Morgan said.

"We have to go," Myers said. "Paula, let's go."

"Talk about honesty," Mrs. Morgan said.

"Let's talk about it," Myers said. Then he said, "Paula, are you coming?"

"I want you to hear this story," Morgan said, raising his voice. "You will insult Mrs. Morgan, you will insult us both, if you don't listen to this story." Morgan clenched his pipe.

"Myers, please," Paula said anxiously. "I want to hear it. Then we'll go. Myers? Please, honey, sit down for another minute."

Myers looked at her. She moved her fingers, as if signaling him. He hesitated, and then he sat next to her.

Mrs. Morgan began. "One afternoon in Munich, Edgar and I went to the Dortmunder Museum. There was a *Baubaus* exhibit that fall, and Edgar said the heck with it, let's take a day off—he was doing his research, you see—the heck with it, let's take a day off. We caught a tram and rode across Munich to the museum. We spent several hours viewing the exhibit and revisiting some of the galleries to pay homage to a few of our favorites amongst the old masters. Just as we were to leave, I stepped into the ladies' room. I left my purse. In the purse was Edgar's monthly check from home that had come the day before and a hundred and twenty dollars cash that I was going to deposit along with the check. I also had my identification cards in the purse. I did not miss my purse until we arrived home. Edgar immediately telephoned the museum authorities. But while he was talking I saw a taxi out front. A well-dressed woman with white hair got out. She was a stout woman and she was carrying two purses. I called for Edgar and went to the door. The woman introduced herself as Mrs. Attenborough, gave me my purse, and explained that she too had visited the museum that afternoon and while in the ladies' room had noticed a purse in the trash can. She of course had opened the purse in an effort to trace the owner. There were the identification cards and such giving our local address. She immediately left the museum and took a taxi in order to deliver the purse herself. Edgar's check was there, but the money, the one hundred twenty dollars, was gone. Nevertheless, I was grateful the other things were intact. It was nearly four o'clock and we asked the woman to stay for tea. She sat down, and after a little while she began to tell us about herself. She had been born and reared in Australia, had married young, had had three children, all sons, been widowed, and still lived in Australia with two of her sons. They raised sheep and had more than twenty thousand acres of land for the sheep to run in, and many drovers and shearers and such who worked for them at certain times of the year. When she came to our home in Munich, she was then on her way to Australia from England, where she had been to visit her youngest son, who was a barrister. She was returning to Australia when we met her," Mrs. Morgan said. "She was seeing some of the world in the process. She had many places yet to visit on her itinerary."

"Come to the point, dear," Morgan said.

"Yes. Here is what happened, then. Mr. Myers, I'll go right to the climax, as you writers say. Suddenly, after we had had a very pleasant conversation for an hour, after this woman had told about herself and her adventurous life Down Under, she stood up to go. As she started to pass me her cup, her mouth flew open, the cup dropped, and she fell across our couch and died. Died. Right in our living room. It was the most shocking moment in our lives."

Morgan nodded solemnly.

"God," Paula said.

"Fate sent her to die on the couch in our living room in Germany," Mrs. Morgan said.

Myers began to laugh. "Fate . . . sent . . . her . . . to . . . die . . . in . . . your . . . living . . . room?" he said between gasps.

"Is that funny, sir?" Morgan said. "Do you find that amusing?"

Myers nodded. He kept laughing. He wiped his eyes on his shirt sleeve. "I'm really sorry," he said. "I can't help it. That line *'Fate sent her to die on the couch in our living room in Germany.'* I'm sorry. Then what happened?" he managed to say. "I'd like to know what happened then."

"Mr. Myers, we didn't know what to do," Mrs. Morgan said. "The shock was terrible. Edgar felt for her pulse, but there was no sign of life. And she had begun to change color. Her face and hands were turning *gray*. Edgar went to the phone to call someone. Then he said, 'Open her purse, see if you can find where she's staying.' All the time averting my eyes from the poor thing there on the couch, I took up her purse. Imagine my complete surprise and bewilderment, my utter bewilderment, when the first thing I saw inside was my hundred twenty dollars, still fastened with the paper clip. I was never so astonished."

"And disappointed," Morgan said. "Don't forget that. It was a keen disappointment."

Myers giggled.

"If you were a real writer, as you say you are, Mr. Myers, you would not laugh," Morgan said as he got to his feet. "You would not dare laugh! You would try to understand. You would plumb the depths of that poor soul's heart and try to understand. But you are no writer, sir!"

Myers kept on giggling.

Morgan slammed his fist on the coffee table and the cups rattled in the coasters. "The real story lies right here, in this house, this very living room, and it's time it was told! The real story is *here*, Mr. Myers," Morgan said. He walked up and down over the brilliant wrapping paper that had unrolled and now lay spread across the carpet. He stopped to glare at Myers, who was holding his forehead and shaking with laughter.

"Consider *this* for a possibility, Mr. Myers!" Morgan screamed. *Consider!* A friend—let's call him Mr. X—is friends with . . . with Mr. and Mrs. Y, *as well as* Mr. and Mrs. Z. Mr. and Mrs. Y and Mr. and Mrs. Z. do not know each other, unfortunately. I say *unfortunately* because if they *had* known each other this story would not exist because it would never have taken place. Now, Mr. X learns that Mr. and Mrs. Y are going to Germany for a year and need someone to occupy their house during the time they are gone. Mr. and Mrs. Z are looking for suitable accommodations, and Mr. X tells them he knows of just the place. But before Mr. X can put Mr. and Mrs. Z in touch with Mr. and Mrs. Y, the Ys have to leave sooner than expected. Mr. X, being a friend, is left to rent the house at his discretion to anyone, including Mr. and Mrs. Y—I mean Z. Now, Mr. and Mrs. . . . . Z move into the house and bring a cat with them that Mr. and Mrs. Y hear about later in a letter from Mr. X. Mr. and Mrs. Z bring a cat into the house *even though* the terms of the lease have expressly forbidden cats or other animals in the house because of Mrs. Y's asthma. The *real* story, Mr. Myers, lies in the situation I've just described. Mr. and Mrs. Z—I mean Mr. and Mrs. Y's moving into the Zs' house, *invading* the Zs' house, if the truth is to be told. Sleeping in the Zs' bed is one thing, but unlocking the Zs' private closet and using their linen, vandalizing the things found there, that was against the spirit and letter of the lease. And this *same* couple, the *Zs,* opened boxes of kitchen utensils marked 'Don't Open.' And broke dishes when it was spelled out, *spelled out* in that same lease, that they were not to use the owners', the Zs' *personal,* I emphasize *personal,* possessions."

Morgan's lips were white. He continued to walk up and down on the paper, stopping every now and then to look at Myers and emit little puffing noises from his lips.

"And the bathroom things, dear—don't forget the bathroom things," Mrs. Morgan said. "It's bad enough using the Zs' blankets and sheets, but when they also get into their *bathroom* things and go through the little private things stored in the *attic,* a line has to be drawn."

"That's the *real* story, Mr. Myers," Morgan said. He tried to fill his pipe. His hands trembled and tobacco spilled onto the carpet. "That's the real story that is waiting to be written."

"And it doesn't need Tolstoy to tell it," Mrs. Morgan said.

"It doesn't need Tolstoy," Morgan said.

MYERS LAUGHED. HE and Paula got up from the couch at the same time and moved toward the door. "Good night," Myers said merrily.

Morgan was behind him. "If you were a real writer, sir, you would put that story into words and not pussyfoot around with it, either."

Myers just laughed. He touched the doorknob.

"One other thing," Morgan said. "I didn't intend to bring this up, but in light of your behavior here tonight, I want to tell you that I'm missing my two-volume set of 'Jazz at the Philharmonic.' Those records are of great sentimental value. I bought them in 1955. And now I insist you tell me what happened to them!"

"In all fairness, Edgar," Mrs. Morgan said as she helped Paula on with her coat, "after you took inventory of the records, you admitted you couldn't recall the last time you had seen those records."

"But I am sure of it now," Morgan said. "I am positive I saw those records just before we left, and now, now I'd like this *writer* to tell me exactly what he knows of their whereabouts. Mr. Myers?"

But Myers was already outdoors, and, taking his wife by the hand, he hurried her down the walk to the car. They surprised Buzzy. The dog yelped in what seemed fear and then jumped to the side.

"I insist on *knowing!*" Morgan called. "I am waiting, sir!"

Myers got Paula into the car and started the engine. He looked again at the couple on the porch. Mrs. Morgan waved, and then she and Edgar Morgan went back inside and shut the door.

Myers pulled away from the curb.

"Those people are crazy," Paula said.

Myers patted her hand.

"They were scary," she said.

He did not answer. Her voice seemed to come to him from a great distance. He kept driving. Snow rushed at the windshield. He was silent and watched the road. He was at the very end of a story.

THE STORY "SAINTS" was published in *Threepenny Review* (Berkeley) in 1984, and then reprinted in Bharati's first collection of stories, *Darkness* (Viking-Penguin Canada), a year later. Those were desperate times in our family; we'd left Canada in 1979, worked three years in upstate New York (the setting for this story), quit, and returned to Iowa City without jobs, only the memories of our having met and married in Iowa City twenty years before. Bharati had not written in nearly seven years, the victim of racism in Canada, and feared she would never write again. Our older son was a senior in high school, our younger just a ninth grader. We promised him we'd stay in Iowa and eke out a living until he graduated.

One day, our friend and mentor Bernard Malamud sent his new book of *Collected Stories*. Bharati sat down to read it and suddenly saw that his characters were hers, his themes were hers. Russian and Jewish or Lower East Side, or Indian and upscale; they were all heroes of self-transformation, whether or not the outer world viewed them as whole or half, funny or frightening. On another cold Iowa morning she got a phone call from Atlanta inviting her for a term of writer-in-residence at Emory University. A moment of pure grace; she'd not applied for it or even suspected she was known. She began writing stories as soon as she arrived in her faculty apartment, and couldn't stop; ten of the twelve stories of *Darkness* were written in a period of three months.

Much of the background to this story is rooted in our sons' experiences and perspectives: the chess and debate teams filled with various Asian-Americans, the Vietnamese closest friend, the operatic outbursts of love and hate and the process of Americanization being played out in shopping malls and trailer parks, in rock music and pizza joints, the mutual fascination and repugnance between new America and the old that has since become Bharati's signature, patented material (see *The Middleman, Jasmine, The Holder of the World,* and *Leave It to Me*).

It all started here, in this story. Shawn Patel embodies confusion: he is an all-seeing, all-knowing saint. He suffers his mother's pain and his father's twisted ambition. He is disturbed and headed for trouble, but whatever the diagnosis, he is shockingly sane in an insane world.

CLARK BLAISE

Saints

"AND ONE MORE THING," Mom says. "Your father can't take you this August."

I can tell from the way she fusses with the placemats that she is interested in my reaction. The placemats are made of pinkish linen and I can see a couple of ironing marks, like shiny little arches. Wayne is coming for dinner. Wayne Latta is her new friend. It's the first time she's having him over with others, but that's not why she's nervous.

"That's okay," I tell her. "Tran and I have plans for the summer."

Mom rolls up the spray-starched napkins and knots them until they look like nesting birds on each dinner plate. "It isn't that he's really busy," she says. She gives me one of her I-know-you're-hurting, son, looks. "I don't see why he can't take you. He says he has a conference to go to in Hong Kong at the end of July, so he might as well do China in August."

"It's okay. Really," I say. It's true, I am okay. At fifteen I'm too old to be a pawn between them, and too young to get caught in problems of my own. I'm in a state of grace. I want to get to my room in this state of grace before it disintegrates, and start a new game of "Geopolitique 1990" on the Apple II-Plus Dad gave me last Christmas.

"Can you get the flower holders, Shawn?" Mom asks.

I take a wide, flat cardboard box out of the buffet.

She lifts eight tiny glass holders out of the box, and lines them up in the center of the table. She hasn't used them since things starting going bad between Dad and her. When things blew up, they sold the big house in New Jersey and Mom and I moved to this college town in upstate New York. Mom works in the Admissions Office. Wayne calls it a college for rich bitches who were too dumb to get into Bennington or Barnard.

"Get me a pitcher of water and the flowers," Mom says.

In a dented aluminum pot in the kitchen sink, eight yellow rosebuds are soaking up water. Granules of sugar are whitish and still sludgy in the bottom of the pot. Mom's a believer; she's read somewhere that sugar in lukewarm water keeps cut flowers fresh. I move the pot to one side and fill a quart-sized measuring cup with lukewarm water. I know her routines.

It's going to be an anxious evening for Mom. She's set out extra goblets for spritzers on a tray lined with paper towels. Index cards typed up with recipes for dips and sauces are stacked on the windowsill. She shouldn't do sauces, nothing that requires last-minute frying and stirring. She's the flustery type, and she's only setting herself up for failure.

"What happened to the water, Shawn?"

It's a Pizza Hut night for me, definitely. I know what she's going through with Wayne. He's not at all like Dad, the good Dr. Manny Patel, who soothes crazies at Creedmore all day. Nights he's a playboy and slum landlord, Mom says.

Mom says, "Your father will call you tomorrow, he said. He wants to talk to you himself. He wants to know what you want this Christmas."

This is only the first Thursday in November. Dad's planning ahead is a joke with us. Foresight is what got him out of Delhi to New York. "Could I have become a psychiatrist and a near-millionaire if I hadn't planned well ahead?" Dad used to tell Mom in the medium-bad days.

Mom thinks making a million is a vicious, selfish aim. But Dad's really very generous. He sends money to relatives and to Indian orphanages. He's generous but practical. He says he doesn't want to send me stuff—cashmere sweaters and Ultra-suede jackets, the stuff he likes—that'll end up in basement cedar closets.

"I'll be late tomorrow," I remind Mom. "Fridays I have my chess club."

Actually, Tran and I and a bunch of other guys from the chess club play four afternoons a week. Thursdays we don't play because Tran has Debate Workshop.

"You know what I want, Mom. You can tell him."

I ask for computer games, video cassettes, nothing major. So twice a year Dad sends big checks. Dad's real generous with me. It makes him feel the big benefactor, Mom says, whenever a check comes in the mail. But that's only because things went really bad two years ago. They sent me away to boarding school, but they still couldn't work things out between them.

At five, Wayne comes into our driveway in his blue Toyota pickup. The wheels squeal and rock in the deep, snowy ruts. Wayne has a cord of firewood in the back of the truck. Mom paid him for the firewood yesterday and for the time he put in picking up the cord from some French guy in Ballston Spa. Wayne's a writer; meantime he works as a janitor in the college. A "mopologist" is what he calls himself. It's so corny, but every time Wayne uses that word, Mom gives him a tinkly, supportive laugh. Janitors are more caring than shrinks, the laugh seems to say.

We hear Wayne on the back porch, cursing as he drops an armload of logs. For all his muscles, he's a clumsy man. But then Mom could never have gotten Dad to carry the logs himself. Dad would have had them delivered or done without them.

Mom takes five-dollar bills out of the buffet drawer and counts out thirty dollars. "For the wine, would you give it to him? I couldn't do a production all by myself on a weeknight."

"Why do a production at all?"

She stiffens. "I'm not ashamed of Wayne," she says. "Wayne is who he is."

Wayne finally comes into the dining room. I slip him the money; it's more than he expected. "I got some beer too, Mila." Mom's name is Camille but he calls her Mila. That's a hard thing to get used to. He drops my rucksack on the floor, turns the chair around and straddles it. There are five other chairs around the table and two folding chairs brought up from the basement for tonight. Under Wayne's muscular thighs, the dining room chair looks rickety, absurdly elegant. Red longjohns show through the knee rips of his blue jeans. He keeps his red knit cap on. But he's not as tough as he looks. He keeps the cap on because he's sensitive about his bald, baby-pink head.

"Hey, Shawn," he says to me. "Still baking the competition?"

It's Wayne's usual joke about my playing competitive chess. Our school team has T-shirts that we paid for by working the concession stands on basketball nights last winter. Tran plays varsity first board, I play third. Now we need chess cheerleaders, Wayne kids me. "*Hey, hey, push that pawn! Dee-fense, dee-fense, King's Indian dee-fense!*" Wayne isn't a bad sort, not for around here. Last year we went for trout out on the Battenkill. The day with Wayne wasn't bad, given our complicated situation. I went back to the creek with Tran a week later, but it was different. Tran's idea of fishing is throwing a net across the river, tossing in a stick of dynamite, then pulling it up.

"You'll like Milos and Verna," Mom tells Wayne. "They're both painters in the Art Department. From Yugoslavia, but I think they're hoping to stay in the States."

From the soft, nervous look she's giving Wayne, I know it isn't the Yugoslavs she's thinking of right at the moment. Wayne grabs her throat in his thick hairy hands. She lifts her face. Then she glances at me in a quick guilty way as if she's already given away too much.

I know about feelings. I've got a secret life, too.

"D'you have enough for a pizza?" Mom asks me. She's moved away from Wayne. Yeah, I have enough.

FROM THE PIZZA HUT, Tran and I go back to Tran's place. Tran's sixteen and he owns a noisy used Plymouth. It's two-tone, white and aquamarine. I like the colors. Tran's a genuine boatperson. When he was younger, the English teacher made him tell the class about having to hide from pirates and having to chew on raw fish just to stay alive. Women on his boat hid any valuable stuff they had in their vaginas. "That's enough, Tran, thank you," the teacher said. Now he never mentions his cruise to America.

We skid to a stop inside the Indian Lookout Point Trailer Park where he lives with his mother in a flash of aqua. The lights are on in Tran's mobile home. Tran's mother's muddy Chevy and his stepfather's Dodge Ram are angle-parked. Tran's real father got left behind in Saigon.

"I don't know," Tran says. He doesn't cut the engine. We sit in the warm, dark car. "Maybe we ought to go on to your place. He never gets home this early."

It's minus ten outside, maybe worse with the windchill factor. I open the car door softly. The carlight on Tran's face makes his face look ochre-dingy, mottled with pimples.

"Mom's entertaining tonight," I warn him. The snow is slippery cold under my Adidas. I pick my way through icy patches to the trailer, and look in a little front window.

Tran's mom is at the kitchen sink, washing a glass. She's still wearing her wool coat and plaid scarf. Her face has an odd puffy quiver. There are no signs of physical violence, but someone's sure been hurt. Tran's stepfather (he didn't, and can't, adopt Tran until some agency can locate Tran's real father and get his consent) is sitting hunched forward in a rocker, and drinking Miller Lite.

Like Tran, I've learned to discount homey scenes.

"That's okay," Tran says. He's calling out from the car. His sad face is in the opened window. "Your place is bigger."

It makes sense, but I can't move away from his little window.

"I can show you a move that'll bake Sato," he says. "I mean really bake his ass."

We both hate Sato but Sato isn't smart enough to wince under our hate or even smart enough to know when his ass has really been baked.

"Okay." There's that new killer chess move, and a new Peter Gabriel for us to listen to. Tran's chess rating is just under 1900. Farelli's is higher, but Farelli is more than arrogant. He's so arrogant he dropped off the team. He goes down to Manhattan instead and hustles games in Times Square or in the chess clubs. Tran's a little guilty about playing first board; he knows he owes it to Farelli's vanity. The difference between Farelli and Tran is about the same as between Tran and me. Farelli wants to charge the club four-fifty an hour for tutoring. He's the only real American in the club. The rest of us have names like Sato, Chin, Duoc, Cho and Prasad. My name's Patel, Shawn Patel. Mom took back her maiden name, Belliveau, when we moved out of Upper Montclair. We're supposed to be out of Dad's reach here, except for checks.

A WEEK AFTER Mom's dinner party, Tran and I are coming out of an arcade on Upper Broadway Street when we see Wayne walking our way. Upper Broadway's short and squat. The storefronts have shallow doorways you can't hide in. Wayne is with the Yugoslav woman, the painter who doesn't intend to go back to her country. They aren't holding hands or anything, they aren't even touching shoulders, but I can tell they want to do things. The Yugoslav has both her hands in the pockets of her duffle coat. A toggle at her throat is missing and the loop has nothing to weigh it down. The Yugoslav has red cheeks. With her red cheeks, her button nose and her long, loose hair, she looks very young. Maybe it's a trick of afternoon light or of European makeup, but she looks too young to be a friend of Mom's.

Wayne wants to hug her. I can tell from the way he arches his upper body inside his coat. He wants to sneak his hand into her pocket, pull out her fist, swing hands on Upper Broadway and be stared at by everyone.

I pull Tran back inside the arcade.

"I got to get to Houston," Tran says. We're playing "Joust," his favorite game, but his slight body is twisted in misery.

"It'll work out," I tell him. Wanting to go to Houston has to do with his mother and stepfather. Things always go bad between parents. "You can't leave in the middle of the semester. It doesn't make sense."

"What does?"

Tran has an older brother in Houston, in engineering school. Tran thinks his mother will come up with the bus fare south. She works at Grand Union, and weekends she waitresses. "My luck's got to change," he says.

Luck has nothing to do with anything, I want to say. You're out of the clutch of pirates now. No safe hiding places.

Wayne and his painter make us spend too many tokens on this Joust machine.

MOM'S IN THE EATING NOOK of the kitchen, reading a book on English gardens when I come in the back door. She's wearing a long skirt made of quilted fabric and a matching jacket. The quilting makes her look fat, and ridiculous.

She catches my grin. "It's warm, don't knock it," she says of her skirt. These upstate houses are drafty. Then she pulls her feet up under her and wriggles her raised knees gracelessly under the long skirt. "And I love the color on me."

I bleed. Mom should have had a daughter. Two women could have consoled each other. I can only think of Wayne, how even now he's slipping the loops over Serbian toggles. It's a complicated feeling. I bleed because I'm disloyal.

"Your father's sent a present by UPS," she says. She doesn't look up from the illustration of a formal garden of a lord. A garden with a stiff, bristly hedged maze to excite desire and contain it. "I put the package on your desk upstairs. It looks like a book."

She means to say, Dad's presents are always impersonal.

Actually it's two books that Dad has sent me this time. The thick, heavy one is an art book, reproductions of Moghul paintings that Dad loves. Even India was once an empire-building nation. The other is a thin book with bad binding put out by a religious printing house in Madras. The little book is about a Hindu saint who had visions. Dad has sent me a book about visions.

May this book bring you as much happiness as it did me when I was your age," Dad's inscription reads. Then a p.s. "The saint died of throat cancer and was briefly treated by your great-uncle, the cancer specialist in Calcutta."

Forty pages into the book, the saint describes a vision. "I see the Divine Mother in all things." He sees Her in ants, dogs, flowers, the latrine bowls in the temple. He keeps falling into trances as he goes for walks or as he says his prayers. In this perfect state, sometimes the saint kicks his disciples. He eats garbage thrown out by temple cooks for cows and pariah dogs.

"Did I kick you?" the saint asks when he comes out of his trance. "Kick, kick," beg the disciples as they push each other to get near enough for a saintly touch.

My father, healer of derangements, slum landlord with income properties on two continents, believer of visions, pleasure-taker where none seems present, is a mystery.

Downstairs Mom is dialing Wayne's number. In the whir of the telephone dial, I read the new rhythms of her agony. Wayne will not answer his phone tonight. Wayne is in bed with his naked Yugoslav.

It's my turn to call. I slip my bony finger into the dial's fingerholes. "Want to ball?" I whisper into the mouthpiece. My throat is raspy from the fullness of desire.

"What?" It's a girlish voice at the other end. "What did you say?"

The girl giggles. "You dumb pervert." She leaves it to me to hang up first.

THE NEXT NIGHT, a Friday night, Tran and I come down from my room to get Mountain Dew out of the fridge. Mom and Wayne are making out in the kitchen. He has her jammed up against the eating nook's wall. There are Indian paintings on that wall. She kept the paintings and gave Dad the statues and framed batiks. Wayne holds Mom's head against dusty glass, behind which an emperor in Moghul battledress is leading his army out of the capital. Wayne's got his knee high up Mom's quilted skirt. The knee presses in, hard. I see love's monstrous force bloat her face. Wayne has her head in his grasp. Her orange hair tufts out between his knuckles, and its orange mist covers the bygone emperor and his soldiers.

Tran's used to living in small, usurped spaces. He drops a shy, civil little cough, and right away Wayne lets go of Mom's hair. But his knee is still raised, still pressing into her skirt.

"Get outta here, guys," he says. He looks pleased, he sounds good-natured. "You got better things to do. Go push your pawns."

"Tell her about the painter," I say. My voice is even, not emotional.

"What're you talking about? What's the matter with you?"

Tran says, "Let's get the soda, Shawn." He picks up the six-pack and two glasses and pushes me toward the stairwell.

Upstairs, Tran and I take turns dialling the town's other insomniacs. "Do you have soft breasts?" I ask. I really want to know. "Yes," one of them confesses. "Very soft and very white and I'm so lonely tonight. Do you want to touch?"

Tran reads aloud an episode from the life of the Hindu saint. Reaching the state of perfection while strolling along the Ganges one day, the saint fell and broke his arm. The saint had been thinking of his love for the young boy followers who lived in the temple. He had been thinking of his love for them—love as for a sweetheart, he says—when he slipped into a trance and stumbled. Love and pain: in the saint's mind there is no separation.

Tran makes the last of our calls for the night. "You bitch," he says as he shakes his thin body in a parody of undulation. To me he says, "Mother won't come through with the bus fare to Houston."

Tonight Tran wants to sleep over in my room. Tomorrow we'll find a way to raise the bus fare.

I want to tell him things, to console him. Bad luck and good luck even out over a lifetime. Cancer can ravage an ecstatic saint. Things pass. I don't remember Dad in any intimate way except that he embarrassed me when he came to pick me up from my old boarding school. The overstated black Mercedes, the hugging and kissing in such a foreign way.

A LITTLE BEFORE MIDNIGHT, Tran's moan startles me awake. He must be dreaming of fathers, pirates, saints and Houston. For me the worst isn't dreams. It's having to get out of the house at night and walk around. At midnight I float like a ghost through other people's gardens. I peer into other boys' bedrooms, I become somebody else's son.

Tonight I'm more restless than other nights. I look for an Indian name in the phone book. The directory in our upstate town is thin; it caves against my eager arms. The first name I spot is Batliwalla. Meaning perhaps bottlewalla, a dealer in bottles in the ancestral long-ago. Batliwalla, Jamshed S., M.D.

I dress in the dark for a night of cold roaming. It'll be a night of walking in a state of perfect grace. For disguise, I choose Mom's red cloth coat from the hall cupboard and her large red wool beret into which she has stuck a pheasant feather. She keeps five more feathers, like a bouquet, in a candy jar. The feathers are from Wayne the hunter. Wayne's promised to put a pheasant on our table for Thanksgiving dinner. I can taste its hard, stringy birdflesh and pellets of buckshot.

Like the Hindu saint, I walk my world in boots and a trance. But in this upstate town the only body of water is an icy creek, not the Ganges.

The Batliwallas have no curtains on their back windows. I look into a back bedroom that glows from a bedside lamp. A kid in pajamas is sitting up in bed, a book in his hands. He's a little kid, a junior high kid, or maybe a studious dwarf. The dwarfkid rocks back and forth under his bedclothes. He seems to be learning something, maybe a poem, by heart. He's the conqueror of alien syllables. His fleshy, brown lips purse and pout ferociously. His tiny head in its helmet of glossy black hair bumps, bumps, bumps the bed's white vinyl headboard. The dwarfkid's eyes are screwed tightly shut, and his long eyelashes look like tiny troughs for ghosts to drink out of. Wanting good grades, the dwarfkid studies into the night. He rocks, he shouts, he bumps his head. I can't hear the words, but I want to reach out to a fellow saint.

When I get home, the back porch is dark but the kitchen light is on. I sit on the stack of firewood and look in. I'm not cold, or sleepy. Wayne and Mom are fighting in the kitchen, literally slugging each other. I had Wayne figured wrong. He isn't the sly operator after all. He's opened up my Mom's upper lip. It's blood Mom is washing off.

"Get out," Mom screams at him. This time I can make out all the words. I feel like a god, overseeing lives.

The faucet is running as it had done the day there were yellow rosebuds in a kitchen pot. Steam from the hot, running water frizzes Mom's hair. She looks old. "Get out of my house."

"I'm getting out," Wayne says. But he doesn't leave. First he lights a cigarette, something Mom doesn't permit. Then he flops down on one of the two kitchen stools, props his workboots on the other and starts to adjust the laces. "I wouldn't stay if you begged me."

"Get out, out!" Mom's still screaming as I turn my house key in the lock. She might as well know it all. "Do me a favor, get out. Lace your goddamn boots in your goddamn truck. Please get out."

I move through the bright kitchen into the dark dining room, and wait for the lovers to finish.

In a while Wayne leaves. He doesn't slam the door. He doesn't toss the key on the floor. The pickup's low beams dance on frozen bushes.

"My god, Shawn!" Mom has switched on a wall light in the dining room. She's staring at me, she's really looking at me. Finally. "My god, what have you done to your face, poor baby."

Her fingers scrape at the muck on my face, the cheekblush, lipstick, eyeshadow. Her bruised mouth is on my hair. I can feel her warm, wet sobs, but I don't hurt. I am in a trance in the middle of a November night. I can't hurt for me, for Dad, I can't hurt for anyone in the world. I feel so strong, so much a potentate in battle-dress.

How wondrous to be a visionary. If I were to touch someone now, I'd be touching god.

"DUNKELBLAU" ("DEEP BLUE") was written in Atlanta a few months after Clark's mother died in Winnipeg of Alzheimer's disease. In her case, a whole shelf of history had been silenced, except for the stories she'd told Clark and our sons; the world of frontier western Canada and prewar Germany, of Montreal and the Deep South. Clark's portrait is not strictly autobiographical, but it does capture the spirit of skeptical progressiveness that was my mother-in-law. It would be like her to chase boys away from harming gypsies. She would appreciate the romance and artistry of gypsy life. She would also keep an eye on her valuables.

Like many an only child of irreconcilably mismatched parents, Willi (as does Clark) seeks solace in art and in the artful: the disappearance of color-tabs in margarine, blueing in the wash, little men in the radio. The outer world was a fantasy as well: the trolley cars, the museum and library, the paintings, Pittsburgh and its allegorical verticality of steel mills and the gilded age.

The working title of this story had been "1945," when Clark was five. It was as far back as he could remember, and he mentioned that the story had come to him in surges, like touching a live wire. His father's Packard rounding the corner, the blackened collars, the constant dyeing and tinting, all the promise and grittiness of wartime Pittsburgh, and the clash between the optimistic, salesman father and the tragically inclined, artist mother. This was the best of years, the beginning of a glorious future; it was the bleakest of years, confirmation of man's bestiality. The gypsies of course tip the scales; we know where the writer stands.

Nevertheless, it ends on a positive note: the new year, 1946, and with it, symbolically, a second birth.

BHARATI MUKHERJEE

CLARK BLAISE

Dunkelblau

WILLI NADEAU HAS LAIN abed since birth, dumb and apparently unreachable, his bones as fragile as rods of hollow glass. He sleeps on pillows, his crib is padded. He is four. His mother is forty-two and has lost her only family. The boy, the lump, is all she lives for. Two succeeding pregnancies have ended in the seventh month. She remembers a burning, the heavy settling, and knows she is carrying another death. A brother is still-born and a sister, lumpish as Willi, survives three months. Willi lives—if that's the word—because he is the first, before she developed anti-bodies to his father. His parents are profoundly incompatible.

In 1944, Army research synthesizes a thyroid extract. The pills are tiny, mottled brown. Two weeks after giving him the medicine, his mother feels his neck twitch as she sponges him in the kitchen sink. A week later, he kicks, and in a moment as dramatic in his family as Helen Keller at the water-pump, he starts singing the words and music of "Don't Fence Me In." He justifies all her faith in keeping him at home, in reading the medical journals and pestering doctors, the four years of talking to him in both her languages, reading to him, hanging maps and showing pictures.

Like many a genius before him, though he is nearly five, he speaks in complete sentences before taking his first step. He demands his dozen glasses of cold milk a day be served in a heated bunny mug. He is a willful, confident child, his mother's image. He likes the feel of heat on his lips, the icy cold going down. Each glass has to have a spoonful of molasses or of Horlick's Malted Milk, unstirred, at the bottom. No flecks of cream can show. The nightly slabs of liver or other organ meats, pur-chased on special rations, are shaped into states or countries, predetermined by Willi and his mother from prior consultation. She starts taking him to Carnegie Library and Museum as soon as he can walk.

He memorizes the Pittsburgh trolley-numbering system. The Holy Roman Emperors, the Popes, the Kings of England. He memorizes everything, his brain is ruthlessly absorptive, a sponge, like his bones and muscles. Toy-sized yellow and red trolleys pass across a forested valley outside his bedroom window. He is still unsteady on his feet in the winter of 1945 when they take their Number Ten trolley down to Liberty Avenue and then one of the Seventies out to Oakland to the Library and Museum.

His first memories are of the Library, the smell of old books, the low chairs and tables of the children's room, and of staring into the adult reading room—no children allowed—while his mother checks the carts of new arrivals. The adult room is a cave of wonders, where steam rises from the piled-up coats and scarves. The six-storeyed ceiling, the polished wood and the corridors of books overhead absorb the coughs and page-shufflings of the white-haired men and women who sit around the tables. That is the world that awaits him—admission to the adult room, permission to sit under those long-necked lamps that hang from the rafters six floors up to nearly graze the tabletops, flooding the tables with a rich yellow light under bright green shades. It is a world worth waiting for, like the dark blue volumes of *My Book House*, which his mother reads from every night and which are laid out above his bed, mint green to marine blue, a band of promise to take him from infancy to adolescence.

The main hall that connects the Library with the Museum is lined with paintings that his mother holds him up to see. Murky oils, Pittsburgh scenes from the Gilded Age, opera-goers alighting from horse-drawn cabs in the gaslit snows of Grant Street, children riding their high-wheeled bicycles down Centre Avenue. He feels the stab of every passing, irretrievable image. He can look in those faces of 1870, at the girls with their hands in fur muffs and their collars up, their eyes glittering and cheeks round and pink and full of life, and know exactly what his mother is thinking, because she is always thinking it: even these happy children are all gone, as dead as the snows and horses and all but the finest buildings, gone forever.

And there are darker Pittsburgh landscapes, with the orange glow of hellish pits fanning through the falling snow, the play of fires lighting the genteel ridges high above. Pittsburgh, with its blackened skies and acrid fumes, its intimate verticality of heaven and hell, forces allegory on all who live there. "So simplistic," she says, drawing his finger so close to the canvas that the guards stand and snap their fingers. Columned mansions on gaslit streets, perched above the unbanked fires, the bright pouring of molten streams of steel by sooty, sweating men far below. Heaven and Hell on the Monongahela. On their trolley rides, high on the sides of smoke-blackened buildings, he sees faded signs in lettering he can't read but knows is old. That the signs have accidentally survived but mean nothing fills him with dread and wonder, and he asks if the companies are still there, *Isidor Ash, Iron-Monger*. Those three-and four-digit telephone numbers, do they still work, who do you get if you call, an imprisoned voice? Where do they all go?

He thinks of Hans von Kaltenborn and Gabriel Heatter and all the singers as being inside the radio. He presses his forehead against the back of the radio, inhaling the hot electric thrill of music from faraway cities, watching for miniature Jack Bennys and Edgar Bergens. "Be very quiet, and quick, they'll run if they see you," his mother says. In 1945, his father calls all the men on the street over to study the first sketches of the 1946 Ford, with headlights in the fenders and no running boards. When the war is finally over he promises to junk their '38 Packard for one of these streamlined babies.

Nineteen forty-five means the children gather at the top of the dead-end street to intercept their fathers as they turn in, to be swept to their driveways like young footmen standing on the running boards and clinging to the mirrors and spotlights. The loudest kids live across the street. They're the three sons of the football coach at Duquesne. In the winter, he sleds with his father, held tight in his lap while two of the coach's sons stand on a toboggan and pass them, arguing about the war. We'll win because the Russians are on our side and Russians are eight feet tall.

In the winter, his mother piles up old papers and boards around the edge of their five-by-five porch off the kitchen and floods it in order to teach him ice-skating. She ties a pillow around him and lets him walk around the edges of the porch. His feet and ankles are undefined, like pillows. Coming down hard on an ankle, a hip, an arm, can crack a bone. But his father is Canadian and his parents met there and they skated and skied together before he was born. Knowing how to skate makes him a better son. It is important to his father and to his doctor for him to pass for normal as soon as possible.

They live on a crowded street at the edge of a heavily wooded valley that surrounds a tributary of the Allegheny River. In the winter, his father and the football coach ski down a path they have cleared to the rocks and boulders that mark the stream-bed. He's older than the coach, but a better skier and skater. "What a beautiful animal your father is," his mother says, watching him from the porch. On clear winter days, a rarity in Pittsburgh in those years, he can see through the blackened branches to the top of the Gulf Building and red lights on Mt. Washington. Willi transplants all his mother's night-time readings of Robin Hood into those woods. It is Sherwood Forest. Pittsburgh is Nottingham. The deer and bear and Merry Men are all out there, somewhere.

In the spring, when the ice is a morning's whitened blister over the concrete, the porch becomes his mother's studio. The buds have not yet opened, yet she arranges her paints and papers on the card table and carries out a chair to do her watercolors. She puts Mozart records on to play and keeps the kitchen door open so she can hear.

She brought her paints and bundles of drawings from Europe. Everything else is lost. Her brushes burst with colors that never drip. It reminds the boy of Disney cartoons, when a full paintbrush washes over the screen, creating the world as it touches down. That's how her paintings grow. Her colors seem especially intense, and have German names which never have satisfactory equivalents in English. He doesn't know they're enemy words; he thinks of them as irreplaceable tablets of pure color. He laughs at *dunkelblau*, a funny word that becomes a code between them.

Sometimes a fat man is Herr Dunkelblau. The last volumes of *My Book House* where the stories require too much explaining, are deep blue, dunkelblau. Other times she lies in bed behind closed window shades, holding her head with a dunkelblau. The opposite of dark, *dunkel*, he knows is *hell*, light.

"Watercolor must come down like rain," she says. "It should come quick like a shower and make everything shine, like rain. But it should not touch everything, not like oils." Oils sound old and dutiful, like the museum.

"A paintstorm," he says.

She sets him up with his paper and brushes and Woolworth's paints though he sometimes sneaks a swipe of her colors, thick and gripping as mud on his brush. Every few minutes she has to blow soot off her paper. When her German paints are gone, she'll quit painting.

She's a woman of Old World habits. Mondays and Fridays she does the wash. Because of the soot she has to take down all the white curtains, beat the rugs and bedspreads, take off the slipcovers and scrub the white shirts whose collars come back each day so black they look dipped in ink. Tuesdays are dyeing days, mixing the boxes of Rit that line the window ledge over the washtubs, to bring lime green to a Pittsburgh winter, or dunkelblau to a hot summer. Thursdays she makes the soap. Antiseptic odors fill the house, making his eyes run. Orange cakes of fresh soap are cut into shapes of states and countries. The shirts and sheets sink into the hot tub where she adds broken cakes of soap, and he adds the drops of blueing, and loses himself in the smoky trail of its dispersion. Such excitement for a child, catching the world in one of its paradoxes: adding stains to make clothes whiter. He can watch it spread forever, like watching cigarette smoke rise from his mother's ashtray or from the stubs his father burns down to nothingness, the smoke going straight up then suddenly hitting an invisible barrier and spreading out. On cleaning days, he's allowed to play in the coal bin, reading the old marks and dates of deliveries from before he was born, and throw his clothes in at the last minute, standing against the cold enamel of the washing tub as the islands of his shirt and pants and under-wear resist, then drown.

Wednesdays she does the shopping, which means an afternoon of baking breads and an evening of stirring the bright orange color tabs into the margarine. It's another low-grade art experience, like the blueing, with the added pleasure of being able to eat some of the results, melted over a bowl of Puffed Rice.

IN THE LATE SUMMER of 1945, the war in Europe is over and the spirit on the radio is always upbeat. The arrival of troop ships is announced and train schedules from New York or Los Angeles tell Pittsburghers where to meet their boys. His mother listens for news of Europe, but there's never enough. Nineteen forty-five is a year to gladden everyone but her. "Just because you're German and you lost?" he asks her once, remembering the taunt of the coach's sons, and she runs from the room. He asks her who the best singer is—Bing Crosby, she says—and the funniest person—Bob Hope, she guesses, though they both prefer Jack Benny—and the prettiest woman—she couldn't say, ladies don't know who's pretty that way, but maybe he could ask his father—so, okay, the handsomest man—Van Johnson, they say—but the men she thinks are handsomer aren't around anymore.

Nineteen forty-five is the happiest year in his father's life and in the lives of the men on their street, whose jobs will all be getting bigger. There'll be houses to buy and new businesses to open and of course new cars, especially new cars. They're all thinking of leaving Pittsburgh. The Depression mentality is over, they've won the war, they're Number One in the world. But everything about 1945 makes his mother sadder, especially everyone's happiness. She shows him pictures of old men and women and children in striped pajamas. "So now we know that men are hideous beasts," she says. "What kind of world is this?" Nineteen forty-five is the saddest year in existence. His father says it's like a sickness, her questions. You're crazy, he says. We'll all be rich if she'll just shut up and give him a chance.

She's busier than ever on the afternoons when the housework and shopping are done, painting the full, dark green summer of August, 1945. The atom bomb ends the war with Japan. He watches the woods and asks her if that isn't a bit of smoke rising through the trees, coming from the bottom of the woods, along the riverbank.

His father's winter ski-run offers a sightline through the woods if he goes between their house and Hutchisons' and stretches out on his stomach and peers down it as far as he can. He sees nothing at first, just the collapse of the vanishing point into a thicket of trees, but then he sees something: men, and maybe a horse. Horses in the woods! The woods are uninhabited, vast and practically virgin timber. When he shouts "Men!" and "Horses!" his mother says, "Oh, God!" and puts her brush in a glass of clean water.

They go out the front of the house, to the top of the street. They walk down a block, turn and come to another dead-end street much like theirs, but poorer. The houses are low and wooden, more like sheds or garages. Their house is brick. Dogs and chickens run over the yards. Where the street abuts on a different part of the woods, a rutted path eases down into the dark. From there, they can see what the forest has given birth to: many men and some children, and two horses pulling a wagon.

"Gypsies!" she whispers.

Already the women on the street are chasing down their dogs and loose chickens. They stand at the top of the trail and shout at the wagoneers in words he can't understand. "It's Polish," his mother says. "They're warning them not to come too close." Children come out of the houses, carrying utensils and beating them with spoons.

"Stay close," she says.

They wait for the wagon to mount the hill. The wagon is fat, ready to split, decked out in bells and leather straps with metal pots hanging from the corners. The men wear black hats with silver disks around the brims. There are no women. There are boys with long curly hair under their hats and men with open shirts and blackened

arms beating spoons against the pots making a kind of chant. Street dogs are howling. The gypsies stop the noise just in front of the line of Polish women, and the
boys lower the cart's back gate to expose a stone wheel operated by an old, white-
haired man. The man wears an earring, something the boy has never seen, and it
frightens him.

She wants him to watch. She holds him up, as she does in front of the paintings
at the Library. And then she walks the length of the wagon with him, peering inside.
"You should see and not be frightened," she says. The gypsies don't seem to care.
The gypsy children follow them, laughing, and pull at his mother's skirt.

"Stop it!" she commands. "You're very ill-behaved."

They pull again.

"Brats! *Bengeln!*"

They giggle louder. *"Unverschämt!"*

When she speaks harshly like that, she's usually very angry and usually the person
she's angry with, his father, does not understand. Bad behavior is the only thing
that gets her angry. Other things make her sad. Finally one of the men inside the
wagon barks out a command and the children back off.

"Come to my street when you finish," she says, pointing over the row of low,
unpainted houses. "I have some things." The Polish women are now lined up with
knives and scissors and some large cooking pots.

In one of the dark blue *Book Houses* there's a picture of a gypsy man holding a
white horse in the moonlight, calling under a girl's window. For Willi, gypsies are
a people out of the dream world of pictures and legends, and this is the first time
he's seen something from his books come alive. In his light green world of *Book
House* the pictures are all of talking animals. Later on they become magicians in tall
caps decorated with stars and moons, then knights on horseback, Crusaders, and
explorers. He's not given up the notion that their woods contain Robin Hood and
his men, and now that it's given birth to gypsies, he takes heart again.

They hurry back to their house and his mother empties all the kitchen drawers
and takes out the pots and pans and cake dishes, everything metal that is scratched
or dented or has grown dull. She bundles them in a sheet and lays them on the
front lawn. Then she grabs her drawing pad and some pencils and starts sketching
from the front of the house. It's the first time she's sketched the street and not the
woods. The beauty, she says, is all in the back.

In the front are houses just like theirs, and an open lot across the street where
the larger boys play football and fathers play catch with their sons. He can't play—
any shock can still shatter his bones. The opposite side of the street is much higher
than theirs, even the empty lot is higher than the roof of their house. He can stand
on the grass and see over his house and over the woods all the way to the Gulf
Building. In other summers the sons of the football coach batted tennis balls and
scuffed-up golf balls into high arcs over his house and the Hutchisons' into the trees
and valley beyond.

Before the gypsies turn the corner, with the distant banging of the pots and clanging of the bells, and then the sharp cracking of the horsewhip, his mother has sketched in the roof lines, the trees, and the open lot. She's gotten the big tricycles in the driveways and one parked car.

"Gypsies! Lock your houses, take in your children, mind your dogs!" women on the street yell out, but soon enough they stand in their driveways clutching their knives and cooking pots. His mother pulls the covering sheet off her pile of metal utensils and tells a man everything needs polishing and sharpening and smoothing out, and she doesn't care how long it takes. By the time they're finished, she's gotten their picture, every detail in place with her pencils and charcoal: the horses, the children in their hats chasing dogs, all the clutter the wagon contains. She keeps sharpening her pencils against a block of sandpaper. She ignores the children who watch over her shoulder. Normally she stops anything she's drawing in order to demonstrate. When they leave, her arms are shaking, her hair is sticking to her forehead.

Later, when she sprays fixative, she says she hasn't worked so hard since her days at art school. She adds the drawing to her oldest sketches, those of German cathedral doors and Egyptian pottery and Nefertiti's head from the Berlin Museum, and country scenes of cows and horses and farmers bundling hay.

"A drawing should show everything," she says, and that's what she likes about the gypsies; they are art, frightening and fascinating, their wagons are beautiful because they totally express the lives they lead.

"The war was fought over people like them," she says. "And people like us."

But the gypsies don't go away. Smoke from their encampment drifts up from the riverside, settles in a blue haze with the rest of Pittsburgh's smog. Through the early fall they're a familiar sight on the streets, and gradually the girls and women appear too, dressed in bandannas and wide colorful skirts. They come to the front doors, bold as you please, the neighbors say, offering to do housework and tell fortunes, selling eggs and strange-smelling flowers so strong they can drug you in the night. His mother draws the line at letting gypsies in the house. She doubts the wide skirts are purely a fashion statement.

AS THE LEAVES TURN and drop they can see through to the encampment. There are four wagons and several cooking fires. His mother sketches it all, the ghostly outlines of the wagons through the tracery of branches, the horses, the pen for animals rumored but unseen—bears, panthers, half-tamed wolves. It's a curious relationship she has with gypsies, to admire but not to trust, to adore as subjects while wishing they'd leave. The boy wants them gone. They excite his mother and make her strange. The gypsies are closer than he'd thought possible. He can hear them at night.

The assault begins with the coach's sons. They throw crushed limestones from the open lot across the street. They bat stones and golf balls, they use slingshots and their well-trained arms. They sneak down the slope and throw from the Nadeaus'

side of the street, even from the corridor between their house and the Hutchisons',
until his mother chases them off. From the sharp whinny of the horses, the barking
and the occasional echo of stones on wood or metal, he knows the stones are striking
home.

In early November the gypsies leave. "West Virginia," people say, a proper place
for gypsies. Winter comes and the snows. His father and the coach are back on their
ski run and the boy is strong enough to skate across the flooded porch. His father's
plans are to leave Sears and go south, now that the country is back to normal. No
more Carnegie Library, no more streetcar numbers to memorize and maybe he'll
never get a card for the adult reading room. When his father mentions the word
"south" his mother shudders and leaves the room.

BEING EUROPEAN, she doesn't believe in baby-sitters. She doesn't leave him until
he is strong enough to walk on his own and be careful with appliances. On New
Year's Eve they're invited to a party next door at Hutch and Marge's, friends of his
father, a gregarious man. It's a cold, snowless night and he's allowed to sleep in the
living room on the sofa with the radio on to see if he can stay awake for 1946. His
mother promises she'll come over and wake him.

The Christmas tree is up, the electric train circles the wrinkled sheet city of snowy
hills. When he wakes up with only the tree lights on, the radio is humming but not
playing music and he thinks he must have slept through everything. Nineteen forty-
five is the first year of his consciousness, the year of his true birth, and now it is
over. It has died, and he is born. The worst year in history, his mother says. The
best, his father counters. He gets up and looks next door to Hutch and Marge's
where a light is on and it looks close enough to run to, barefoot in his pajamas.

The door is open and the vestibule is jammed with fur coats. The air inside is
hot and thick with smoke and forced, loud laughter. His father and the coach are
the oldest men in the room, and the loudest and happiest. Theirs is a young street
of mainly childless couples ready now to start their families. The women are getting
pregnant, there's a sharp bite of sexuality in the air, lives are going places but still
on hold, the country is going places, big places, but hasn't quite gotten over its
wartime gloom and pinchpenny habits. Those are the attitudes he hears and takes
as truth. He sides with his father in the arguments because his father's a great one
for looking ahead, on the bright side, to the future. The aluminum Train of Tomorrow is barreling down the tracks, taking them all to a chrome-plated, streamlined, lightweight future and cities like Pittsburgh with their dirty bricks and labor
problems are in the way of progress. If you're in the way, better clear out. A damned
shame some people just can't get in the spirit.

"And you think the south is progress?" his mother demands.

His father is singing, with his back to the fireplace. Not French songs, the way
they usually ask him to at parties, but Bing Crosby songs. Around the mirror over
the mantel, Hutch and Marge have pasted all their Christmas cards. Their tree is

bigger than the Nadeaus', and the lights blink and some other candles bubble. Everyone is outlined in blue and red and faint ghostly yellow. All the women except his mother are blondes, with big round coral earrings and bright lipstick that stains their cigarettes. Some still wear little hats with their veils half pulled down.

He stands in the hallway, leaning against a fur coat, peering around the edge. They're singing the New Year's Song his mother taught him, and they're blowing on paper trumpets and strapping on little cone-shaped hats. His mother stands at the far end of the living room, by the kitchen door where the light is strongest. *I don't feel like celebrating,* she declared earlier and his father had left on his own, shouting, *You can't ruin it for me,* but she went anyway, a few minutes later. He peels off his pajamas and wraps himself in her fur coat. No one notices him. Her head is down and her hands hold the sides of her face, pressing down her veil. She seems to be rocking back and forth. Someone has set a lime-green party hat on top of her black pillbox with the single pheasant feather.

They're counting backwards. When the numbers get smaller, the noise increases and he's shouting with everyone, trailing the heavy coat, "It's 1946! It's 1946!" running naked into the living room like the Baby New Year with the sash. A few women hug him and squeeze him tight in their unsteadiness. His father looks around to see how he's gotten there—he has Marge and another woman on his arms—and all the men are going around collecting kisses.

"For God's sake, Liesl—" his father calls and she drops to her knees with her arms open as he pushes his way to her through a jitterbugging dance floor. It seems to take hours. She rolls up her veil to touch her eyes with a paper napkin.

Her fur coat falls from his shoulders as she lifts him. He rubs his cheek against the rough and the fine mesh of her veil, feels her cool satin dress against his naked body, and they dance. It seems the whirling will go on forever, even as the music dies out, then the laughter, and he and his mother dance their way out the door, shivering, across the icy grass to home.

AS A STUDENT in the 1960s at the Workshop, Andre Dubus studied with Richard Yates. Like his mentor, Dubus is a master of contemporary realism, a title confirmed by his receipt of a MacArthur Foundation "Genius" Fellowship for his extraordinary body of work.

"Falling in Love" enlarges Dubus's exploration of the core subjects of his work—the relationship between men and women, and the need for religious faith. "I need a philosophy to go out there with," the story's main character Ted tells his friend. In a secular world increasingly given over to the rejection of absolutes, Dubus's work draws its fierce beauty from his vivid portrayals of the sacrifices that are sometimes necessary in order to sustain, and honor, one's beliefs.

Andre Dubus died several weeks after welcoming this introduction to his story. He is missed; his work endures.

TOM GRIMES

TED BRIGGS CAME BACK from the war seven years before it ended, and in spring
two years after it ended he met Susan Dorsey at a cast party after a play's final
performance, on a Sunday night, in a small town north of Boston. He did not want
to go to the play or to the party, but he was drinking with Nick. They started late
Sunday afternoon at the bar of a Boston steak house. In the bar's long mirror they
watched women. Nick said: "Come with me. My sister likes it."

"She's directing it."

"She's hard to please."

"What's the play?"

"I forget. Some Frenchman. You'd know the name." Ted looked at him. "It
sounds like another word. Which isn't the point. The party is the point. These theater
people didn't need the sexual revolution."

"I don't have to see a play to get laid."

"Why are you pissed off? You act benighted. You're always reading something;
you go to plays." Nick motioned to the bartender, then waved his hand at the hostess
standing near the front door; when she looked at him, he signaled with his first two
fingers in a V and pointed to the tables behind them. Ted looked at his fingers and
said: "It's that."

Nick lowered his hand to the bar and said: "It's what?"

"The peace sign. I was at a party once, with artists. People asked about my leg.
I told them. They were polite."

"Polite."

"It was an effort."

"For them."

"Yes."

"Hey, we're lawyers. They'll hate both of us."

Ted looked at Nick's dark and eager face and said: "We can't let our work keep us home, can we?"

"Men like us."

"Men like us."

TED BRIGGS was a tall man with a big chest and strong arms and a thick brown mustache, and Susan Dorsey liked his face when she saw him walk into the party, into the large and crowded living room in an apartment she had walked to from the theater where she had worked so well that now, drinking gin and tonic, she felt larger than the room. She did not show this to anyone. She acted small, modest. She was twenty-two and had been acting with passion for seven years, and she knew that she could show her elation only to someone with whom she was intimate. To anyone else it would look like bravado. Her work was a frightening risk, and during the run of the play she had become Lucile as fully as she could, and she knew that what she felt now was less pride than gratitude. She also knew this fullness would leave her, perhaps in three days, and then for a while she would feel arid and lost. But now she drank and moved among people to the man with a drink in his left hand, his right hand resting on a cane, his biceps filling the short sleeves of his green shirt. Beside him was a shorter and older man with dark skin and black curls over his brow. She stopped in front of them and said her name, and knew from their eyes that they had not seen her in the play. Nick's last name was Kakonis. Ted leaned his cane against his leg and shook her hand. She looked at his eyes and said: "Did you like the play?"

"We just got here," Nick said, and Ted said: "What was it?"

"*The Rehearsal.* By Jean Anouilh."

"*That* Frenchman," Nick said.

"I like his plays," Ted said. "Were you in it?"

"I was Lucile."

"We got lost," Ted said.

THEY GOT LOST in vodka, in wine with their steaks, in cognac; then Nick drove them out of the city and north. Once they had to piss and Nick left the highway and stopped on a country road, and they stood beside the car, pissing on grass. Then he drove on the highway again; they talked about work and women, and time was not important. They were leaving the city and going to the cast party. If the play started on time, the curtain had opened while they were driving out of Boston. When they reached the town and found the theater, they were an hour and five minutes late; they drank coffee at a café and, through its window, watched the theater's entrance across the brick street. When people came out, Ted and Nick went to the theater, and in the lobby, among moving people, Nick found his sister, a large woman in a black dress; her face was wide and beautiful, and she said to Nick: "Asshole."

Then she hugged him and shook Ted's hand. Her name was Cindy. They walked on brick sidewalks to the apartment of the stage manager, who taught drama at a college. The air was cool and Ted could smell the ocean; he felt sober and knew he was not. Outside the apartment, an old two-story house, he heard voices and a saxophone solo. They climbed to the second floor and Cindy introduced them to people standing near the door, and left them. Ted and Nick went to the long table holding liquor and an ice chest and poured scotch into plastic glasses. They stood with their backs to a window and Ted looked at a young red-haired woman in a beige dress walking toward him, looking at his eyes, and smiling. He exhaled and for a moment did not breathe.

Then she was there, looking at him still; her eyes were green; she looked at Nick and said: "Susan Dorsey," and gave him her hand. Ted leaned his cane against his leg and took her hand. For the rest of the party he stayed with her, except to go to the bathroom; to go to the table and pour their drinks, stirring hers with the knife he used to cut the lime; to go to Nick and say "Excuse me" to the woman Nick was with; to turn Nick away from her and say in his ear: "Does this town have a train station?"

Nick put his arm around Ted and squeezed.

"You don't need one," he said. "She lives in Boston."

"How do you know?"

"Cindy told me. I might be heading a bit farther north. How do I look?"

"You look great."

AT ONE O'CLOCK Susan finished her gin and tonic, and when Ted took her glass, she said: "I'll have a Coke."

She was afraid of dying young. She had talent and everything was ahead of her and she was afraid it would be taken away. This fear came to her in images of death in a car, in a plane. There was no music now, and people had been speaking quietly since eleven, when the stage manager asked them to remember his neighbors. She watched Ted walking toward her, her glass and his in the palm of his left hand. A shell from a mortar had exploded and flung him off the earth and he had fallen back to it, alive. She wanted to be naked, holding him naked. She took the Coke from his hand and said: "I need an hour. I don't want to drive drunk."

"Are you?"

"It's hard to tell, after working."

Her car was small, and when they got in, he pushed his seat back to make room for his leg; its knee did not bend. She pushed her seat back and turned to him and held him and kissed him. She liked the strength in his arms hugging her. She started the car and left the seat where it was; only the upper half of her foot was on the gas pedal. She drove out of the town and through wooded country and toward the highway, then said: "You have very sad eyes."

"Not now."

"Even when they twinkle. You wanted to be a corpsman."

"It wasn't what you think. I joined the Navy to get it over with, on a ship. Before I got through boot camp, I felt like a cop-out. Then I asked to be a corpsman and to go with the Marines. A lot of times at Khe Sanh, I wished I had just joined the Marines."

"So you could shoot back?"

"Something like that. Were you good in the play?"

Yes filled her, and she closed her lips against it and reached into her purse on the floor, her arm pressing his leg; then she put her hand on the wheel again and looked at the tree-shadowed road and said: "I forgot to buy cigarettes."

"From a squirrel?"

He lit one of his Lucky Strikes and gave it to her and she drew on it and inhaled and held it, but the smoke did not touch what filled her. She blew it out the window and said: "I was great in the play."

AFTER HE CAME home from the war, making love was easy. He had joined the Navy after his freshman year at Boston College, because his mind could no longer contain the arguments and discussions he had had with friends, most of them boys, and with himself since he was sixteen years old. One morning he woke with a hangover and an instinct he followed to the Navy recruiting office. When he came home from the war and eight months in the Navy hospital in Philadelphia, kept there by infections, he returned to Boston College and lived in the dormitory. He had made love in high school and college before the war, but the first time with each girl had surprised him. After the war he was not surprised anymore. He knew that if a girl would come to his room or invite him to hers or go on a date with him, off the campus, walking in Boston, she would make love. There were some girls who did not want to know him because he had been in the war and his cane was like a uniform. Few of them said anything, but he saw it in their eyes. He felt pain and fury but kept silent.

There were boys like that, too, and men who were his teachers, people he wanted to hit. In his room he punched a medium bag and worked with weights. Sometimes, drunk in bed with a girl, he talked about this until he wept. No girl could comfort him, because the source of his tears was not himself. It was for the men he knew in the war, the ones he bandaged, the ones he saved, the ones he could not save; and for the men who were there for thirteen months and were not touched by bullets, mortars, artillery. "They're not abstractions in somebody else's mind," he said one night to a girl; and, holding her, he said aloud some of their names; for him they were clearly in the dark room; but not for her. Then looking at her face, he saw himself in the war, bandaging and bandaging and bandaging, and he stopped crying. He said: "How the fuck would you like to be hated because you did a good job, without getting killed?" This one soothed him; she said she'd want to kill somebody.

Now he was twenty-eight and it was still easy; it could be counted on; he only had to invite a woman to go someplace, for a drink, or dinner. The women decided quickly and usually he could see it in their eyes within the first hour of the date. If they felt desire and affection, they made love. Susan would, too. They were on the highway now and he looked at her profile. He was drunk and in love. Nearly always he felt he was in love on his first night with a woman. It happened quickly, as they drank and talked and glanced at menus. It lasted for months, weeks, sometimes days. He touched Susan's cheek and said: "Maybe I should court you. Bring you flowers. Hold your hand in movies. Take you to restaurants, and on picnics. Kiss you good night at your door."

"You've got about twenty minutes. Maybe twenty-five."

LYING BESIDE HIM, using the ashtray he held on his chest, she wanted to feel what she was feeling, had wanted to for a long time, this rush of love, pulling her up the three flights of stairs to her small apartment, into the bathroom for the diaphragm she had used often this year with different men, but now her heart was full, as it had not been for over a year, and she was not certain whether it was love that filled her or so wonderfully being Lucile and ending that work with this strong man with sad eyes and a bad knee and a history she could feel in his kiss. When they made love, she could feel the war in him, could feel him ascending from what he had seen, what he had done; from being blown up. Her heart knew she was in love. She said: "I like you a lot."

"But what?"

"Nothing. Am I going to see you again?"

"Has that happened to you?"

"Of course it has. I'm easy. So are you."

"You'll see me a lot. Let's have dinner tonight. French—for the play."

"That you missed."

"We weren't lost. We drank too much. We talked too much."

"And you both got lucky."

"I think I got more than lucky."

"You did. I wish you had seen me."

"So do I. I'll see the next one, every night."

"It's at the Charles Playhouse. We start rehearsals in two weeks." He moved the ashtray to the bedside table and she put her hand on his chest and looked at his eyes. "After that I'm going to New York. Last month I got an agent."

"Good. It's where you should be."

"Yes. I want all of it: movies too."

"New York is just a shuttle away."

"I hope more than one."

She kissed him; she held him.

HE ATE LUNCH with Nick. They wore suits and ties. He had slept for two hours, waked at seven to Susan's clock radio, turned it off before she woke, phoned for a cab he waited for on the sidewalk, gone to his apartment to shower and shave and dress, and then walked to his office. At nine o'clock he was at his desk. Nick came forty minutes later, and stopped at Ted's door to smile, shrug, say: "Lunch?"

At lunch Nick ordered a Bloody Mary, and said: "I hate Monday hangovers. You don't have one."

Ted was drinking iced tea.

"No. I was drunk when we left the party. But I didn't drink again and I was awake till five. By then I was sober."

"We drank."

"I don't drink for a hangover anyway. I cure it with a workout. Susan's going to New York."

"Permanently?"

"Nothing's permanent. She's an actress."

"New York's not far."

"Hollywood is."

"How do you know she's that good?"

"A hunch."

"What happened?"

"I spent the night with her."

"But what happened? Two weeks ago you said you wanted a girlfriend you saw on weekends. You may even have said *some* weekends. Even if she gets Hollywood, they take her out of thousands of pretty young actresses, that sounds like a weekend to me."

"I want her to get Hollywood; I want her to get Broadway. And I want her."

He was with her every night and, before her rehearsals started, they met for lunch and drank martinis and he was out of his office for two hours. On weekends he made picnic lunches and drove with her to the ocean. The water was cold, but the sun was warm and they wore sweatshirts and sat on the beach. At night they ate in restaurants and they made love and slept in her apartment or his. When she started rehearsals, she did not have time for lunch, and all day as he worked, he waited to see her. "I'm easy," she had said, and when he imagined her living in New York, working as a waitress, rehearsing with men, he could not bear it. He knew she loved him and he believed she wanted to be faithful to him; but she was beautiful and a hedonist and there would be men trying to make love with her, and she would feel something for some of them. Without telling her, he tried to give her license, tried to imagine a situation he could accept: if she were drunk one night in New York and it happened only that night.

But it would not be one night with one man. By now he had seen her in the new play. She played the youngest sister, Beth, in a large family gathered at the mother's home while the mother died. Beth was the one who had not moved away; had stayed in the small town and lived near her mother, and cared for her when she was sick, as she had cared for her father. The others lived far away and were very busy and usually drunk. Beth was twenty-nine and Ted believed the playwright had given her age and her not having a lover more importance than they deserved, as though she were Laura in *The Glass Menagerie*; but Susan made Beth erotic and lonely and brave, and you knew she would have a lover, in time, when she was ready, when she chose to; and Ted knew that, unless Susan was very unlucky, she would work in New York and in Hollywood. So it would not be one night drunk with one man; Susan was going on the road for the rest of her life.

She had a toothbrush now in his apartment, a robe, a nightgown, a novel she was reading. Two weeks before the play closed, she had a yard sale, let go of her apartment, and moved into his. It was large and from its living room he could see the Charles River. When the play closed, his pain began; but he was excited, too, about weeknights and weekends in New York, and about Susan acting there. And he believed she had greatness in her, and he wanted to see it. On a Friday afternoon near sunset, they stood at his windows, looking at the river and Cambridge. She said: "I have to do something before I go to New York. I'm six weeks pregnant."

He looked at her eyes, and knew that what was falling inside him would not stop falling till it broke. He said: "No."

"No what? I'm not pregnant? Did you think you were shooting blanks?"

"No, don't do it."

"I'm twenty-two years old, I'm going to New York, and you want me to have a fucking baby?"

The falling thing in him hit and broke and he trembled and said: "Not a fucking baby. Our baby, Susan. Our baby."

He had to look away from the death of everything he saw in her eyes.

SHE LOOKED at the river. Since seeing her doctor in the middle of the afternoon, she had felt very unlucky and as sad as she had ever been; now Ted was begging her to marry him. No one had ever asked her to marry, or even mentioned it, and Ted was begging for it. Finally she looked at him. She said: "It has nothing to do with marriage. I can't even think about marriage. I don't want a baby. Why can't you understand that?"

"Then have it, and give it to me."

"Have it? *You* have it."

"Seven and a half months. That's all I'm asking."

"You think it's numbers? A fucking calendar? You want me to go through all of that so you can have a baby? Go find somebody else to breed with."

"I did. Now you want to kill it."

"I don't *want* to kill anything. What I want is not to be pregnant. What I want is never to have fucked you."

"Well you did. Now it's time for some sacrifice. Okay? Maybe pain, too. And what's new about *those*. For just seven and a half months. Of your life you think is so fucking significant."

She raised her hand to slap his face, his glare, his voice, but she did not; all the bad luck and sadness she had felt till she told him filled her, and his face enclosed her with it, and she felt alone in a way she had never felt alone before. She did not want to be alive. Then she was crying and with her raised hand she covered her eyes. He touched her arms and she recoiled, stepped back, wiped her tears, and opened her eyes.

"You don't know anything," she said. "You think I could have a baby and not love it? Are you that stupid? I can't love a baby. Not now. I thought I could love you. That was enough."

"You don't love anyone."

"Yes I do. And I didn't mean I wished I had never fucked you. But I won't fuck you again. War hero with your cane. *Sacrifice. Pain.* Don't *ever* think I don't know about those. Don't *ever* think you're the only one in pain. Do something for me. Leave. I'm going to Cindy's. I don't want you here while I pack. Lurking around and crying and asking me to change my life. Okay? Just leave. Go drink someplace. You're good at that."

She wanted something different. She could not imagine what it was: some transformation, of Ted, of herself, of time. He said: "You're good at evicting."

He walked out, and she phoned Cindy and said: "Cindy?" then sobbed.

Soon she was in New York, but for a long time a desert was inside her; it was huge and dry and there was nothing in it. Someday she would get an intrauterine device, but not now; maybe later in the summer, or in the fall. First she needed work to flood that dry sand.

ON A SUMMER EVENING Ted went to dinner with Nick, then to Fenway Park to watch the Red Sox play the Orioles; it was a very good game, well pitched and intense, and till the Red Sox lost in the ninth, with the tying run on third and the winning run on second, Ted's sorrow was not deep; was only a familiar distraction like his knee, which kept his leg in the aisle. He had drunk martinis with Nick before dinner and wine with dinner and they drank beer during the game. Then Nick walked with Ted to his apartment and they rode the elevator upstairs. Ted poured two snifters of cognac and held their stems in his left hand and took them to the living room, where Nick stood, looking out the open windows. Ted said: "That's where she was, the last time I saw her. We were looking at the river."

He felt alert, but his left knee bent now and then, on its own, and he knew he was drunk. When he drank a lot, he drank standing: his right knee was useless as a signal, but the left one warned him. The sounds of car engines rose from the street, and faint voices of people walking. Nick said: "What's it been? A month?"

"Five weeks tonight."

Ted raised the snifter and breathed the sharpness of the cognac, tasting it before he drank; then he drank. He looked over the glass rim at Nick, drank again and looked at light reflected on the dark river, looked across it at the lights of Cambridge. He said: "Then she went to the abattoir. 'The old men are all dead. It is the young men who say yes or no. . . . The little children are freezing to death. . . .'" He knew Nick was watching him, but he could not feel Nick watching; he felt the lucidity and eloquence of grief let out of its cage by drinking. "'I want to have time to look for my children and see how many I can find. Maybe I shall find them among the dead. . . . I am tired; my heart is sick and sad. From where the sun now stands I will fight no more forever.'"

Closing his eyes, he saw Susan's face, felt that if he opened them quickly, but at the right moment out of all the night's moments, her face would be in front of him; she would be standing here. Nick said: "That was good. Chief Joseph."

Ted opened his eyes and said: "I used to know the whole thing." He looked away from the river, at Nick, and said loudly: "You know what I say, Nick? From where the sun now stands I will ejaculate no more forever in the body of a woman who will kill our child," and saying it, and saying it loudly, released all the grief, as something he felt he could see, touch, in the air before his face, and now he felt only rage, and the strength and conviction it brings; it filled him, and his arms and cognac and cane rose with it, his mouth opened to cry out with it; he saw Nick and the windows, but he did not see them; then it was gone, as the flame of a candle is blown out, and the gentle breath that dispelled it was a woman's. She was many women; she was any woman whose eyes, whose touch, whose voice, whose lips would draw him again, and he closed his mouth and lowered his arms, lowered his head. He looked at Nick's brown loafers, feeling only helpless now; and ashamed, knowing what a woman could do to him, knowing she could do it because he wanted her to. Then Nick's hand was on the back of his neck, squeezing, and Nick said: "You've got to start dating again. This time get one on the pill."

Ted looked at him, tossed his cane onto the couch, and held Nick's arm. He said: "The pill isn't a philosophy. I need a philosophy to go out there with. You know? I can't just go out there with a cock, and a heart. Maybe I need a wife."

"Wives are good. I'd like a wife. I'm two baseball seasons from forty. Do you know at the turn of the century, in America, the average man lived forty-seven years? For women, it was forty-six. Maybe a wife is what you need."

"I need a vacation."

"You've been on one for five weeks."

"Not from women. From women, too. I mean two weeks someplace. Mexico. Alone. I don't speak Spanish. I can order from a menu. But I won't understand the rest. I'll be alone. I need to think, Nick. All I've been doing is feeling. Find a village near an airport. Something in the mountains. Bring some books, have one drink before dinner, maybe a beer while I eat. Hole up, walk around; be silent. Look the demon in the eye."

Nick rubbed his neck and said: "Drink bottled water. Peel the fruit. Don't shit your brains out."

"If I did, all you'd see in the bowl is water."

"Stop that. It's just something that happened. And leave the demon here. You've looked at it enough."

"No. I haven't looked at it. I've fucked it. Now I'm going to look at it; talk to it."

Holding Nick's arm, he closed his eyes and pressed the back of his neck into Nick's hand.

THE FIRST STORY I submitted to Workshop was single-spaced. I thought it looked more published that way. R. V. Cassill wrote on it, *"Double space, you!"* I think that was about it for that one. I loved being at Iowa. We met in old Quonset huts on the river. It was very cold in the winter and in the spring we were half mad with the heat. I was nineteen, I felt a mature twelve. I could only talk to people for about twenty seconds and then I had to excuse myself. There was only one other woman in the class. I can only remember that tuna fish reminded one of her characters of sex. The other writers were the big boys, Jim Whitehead, Andre Dubus, Ted Weesner, Mark Costello, Jim Crumley. They were all married with babies. They were all brilliant and serious and dashing. Ray Carver was in the poetry workshops. I knew him through his wife Mary Ann with whom I worked at some Country Club restaurant. I was fired when I was found eating fruit cup at a time when I was apparently not supposed to be eating fruit cup. My two Workshop years were wonderful. It was all literature and writing and marveling about what could be done. Those years made me long to be a real writer.

JOY WILLIAMS

HE WAS NINE. "Nine," his father would say, "there's an age for you. When I was nine . . ." and so on.

His father's name was Walter and he was a mechanic at a Chevrolet garage in Tallahassee. He had a seventeen-year-old brother named Walter, Jr., and he was Tommy. The boys had no mother, she had been killed in a car wreck a while before.

It had not been her fault.

The mother had taken care of houses that people rented on the river. She cleaned them and managed them for the owners. Just before she died, there had been this one house and the toilet got stopped up. I told the plumber, Tommy's mother told them, that I wanted to know just what was in that toilet because I didn't trust those tenants. I knew there was something deliberate there, not normal. I said, you tell me what you find there and when he called back he said well you wanted to know what I found there and it was fat meat and paper towels.

She had been very excited about what the plumber had told her. Tommy worried that his mother had still been thinking about this when she died—that she had been driving along, still marveling about it—fat meat and paper towels!—and that then she had been struck, and died.

She had slowed for an emergency vehicle with its lights flashing which was tearing through an intersection and a truck had crashed into her from behind. The emergency vehicle had a destination but there hadn't been an emergency at the time. It was supposed to be stationed at the stock-car races and it was late. The races—the first of the season—were just about to begin at the time of the wreck. Walter, Jr., was sitting in the old bleachers with a girl, waiting for the start, and the announcer had just called for the drivers to fire up their engines. There had been an immense roar in the sunny, dusty field, and a great cloud of insects had flown up from the rotting wood of the bleachers. The girl beside Walter, Jr., had screamed and spilled her Coke all over him. There had been thousands of the insects which were long, red, flying ants of some sort with transparent wings.

Tommy had not seen the alarming eruption of insects. He had been home, putting together a little car from a kit and painting it with silver paint.

Tommy liked rope. Sometimes he ate dirt. Fog thrilled him. He was small for his age, a weedy child. He wore blue jeans with deeply rolled cuffs for growth, although he grew slowly. Weeks often went by when he did not grow. He wore white, rather formal shirts.

The house they lived in on the river was a two-story house with a big porch, surrounded by trees. There was a panel in the ceiling which gave access to a particularly troublesome water pipe. The pipe would leak whenever it felt like it but not all the time. Apparently it had been placed by the builders at such an angle that it could neither be replaced nor repaired. Walter had placed a bucket in the crawl space between Tommy's ceiling and the floor above to catch water, and this he emptied every few weeks. Tommy believed that some living thing existed up there which needed water as all living things do, some quiet, listening, watching thing that shared his room with him. At the same time, he knew there was nothing there. Walter would throw the water from the bucket into the yard. It was important to Tommy that he always be there to see the bucket being brought down, emptied, then replaced.

In the house, with other photographs, was a photograph of Tommy and his mother taken when he was six. It had been taken on the bank of the river, the same river the rest of them still lived on, but not the same place. This place had been further upstream. Tommy was holding a fish by the tail. His mother was fat and had black hair and she was smiling at him and he was looking at the fish. He was holding the fish upside down and it was not very large but it was large enough to keep apparently. Tommy had been told that he had caught the fish and that his mother had fried it up just for him in a pan with butter and salt and that he had eaten it, but Tommy could remember none of this. What he remembered was that he had found the fish, which was not true.

Tommy loved his mother but he didn't miss her. He didn't like his father, Walter, much, and never had. He liked Walter, Jr.

Walter, Jr., had a mustache and his own Chevy truck. He liked to ride around at night with his friends and sometimes he would take Tommy on these rides. The big boys would drink beer and holler at people in Ford trucks and, in general, carry on as they tore along the river roads. Once, Tommy saw a fox and once they all saw a naked woman in a lighted window. The headlights swept past all kinds of things. One night, one of the boys pointed at a mailbox.

"See that mailbox. That's a three-hundred-dollar mailbox."

"Mailbox can't be three hundred dollars," one of the other boys screamed.

"I seen it advertised. It's totally indestructible. Door can't be pulled off. Ya hit it with a ball bat or a two-by-four, it just busts up the wood, don't hurt the box. Toss an M-80 in there, won't hurt the box."

"What's an M-80?" Tommy asked.

The big boys looked at him.

"He don't know what an M-80 is," one of them said.

Walter, Jr., stopped the truck and backed it up. They all got out and stared at the mailbox. "What kind of mail you think these people get anyway?" Walter, Jr., said.

The boys pushed at the box and peered inside. "It's just asking for it, isn't it," one of the boys said. They laughed and shrugged, and one of them pissed on it. Then they got back in the truck and drove away.

Walter, Jr., had girlfriends too. For a time, his girl was Audrey, only Audrey. Audrey had thick hair and very white, smooth skin and Tommy thought she was beautiful. Together, he thought, she and his brother were like young gods who made the world after many trials and tests, accomplishing everything only through wonders, only through self-transformations. In reality, the two were quite an ordinary couple. If anything, Audrey was peculiar looking, even ugly.

"If you marry my brother, I'll be your brother-in-law," Tommy told her.

"Ha," she said.

"Why don't you like me?" He adored her, he knew she had some power over him.

"Who wants to know?"

"Me. I want to know. Tommy."

"Who's that?" And she would laugh, twist him over, hang him upside down by the knees so he swung like a monkey, dump him on his feet again, and give him a stale stick of gum.

Then Walter, Jr., began going out with other girls.

"He dropped me," Audrey told Tommy, "just like that."

It was the end of the summer that his mother had died at the start of. Her clothes still hung in the closet. Her shoes were there too, lined up. It was the shoes that looked as though they most expected her return. Audrey came over every day and she and Tommy would sit on the porch of the house on the river in two springy steel chairs painted piggy pink. Audrey told him,

"You can't trust anybody,"

and

"Don't agree to anything."

When Walter, Jr., walked by, he never glanced at her. It was as though Audrey wasn't there. He would walk by whistling, his hair dark and crispy, his stomach flat as a board. He wore sunglasses, even though the summer had been far from bright. It had been cool and damp. The water in the river was yellow with the rains.

"Does your dad miss the Mom?" Audrey asked Tommy.

"Uh-huh."

"Who misses her the most?"

"I don't know," Tommy said. "Dad, I think."

"That's right," Audrey said. "That's what true love is. Wanting something that's missing."

She brought him presents. She gave him a big book about icebergs with colored pictures. He knew she had stolen it. They looked at the book together and Audrey read parts of it aloud.

"Icebergs were discovered by monks," Audrey said. "That's not exactly what it says here, but I'm trying to make it easier for you. Icebergs were discovered by monks who thought they were floating crystal castles." She pointed toward the river. "Squeeze your eyes up and look at the river. It looks like a cloud lying on the ground instead, see?"

He squeezed up his eyes. He could not see it.

"I like clouds," he said.

"Clouds aren't as pretty as they used to be," Audrey said. "That's a known fact."

Tommy looked back at the book. It was a big book, with nothing but pictures of icebergs or so it seemed. How could she have stolen it? She turned the pages back and forth, not turning them in any order that he could see.

"Later explorers came and discovered the sea cow," she read. "The sea cows munched seaweed in the shallows of the Bering Strait. They were colossal and dim-witted, their skin was like the bark of ancient oaks. Discovered in 1741, they were extinct by 1768."

"I don't know what extinct is," Tommy said.

"Seventeen sixty-eight was the eighteenth century. Then there was the nineteenth century and we are in the twentieth century. This is the century of destruction. The earth's been around for 4.6 billion years and it may take only fifty more years to kill it."

He thought for a while. "I'll be fifty-nine," he said. "You'll be sixty-five."

"We don't want to be around when the earth gets killed," Audrey said.

She went into the kitchen and helped herself to two popsicles from the freezer. They ate them quickly, their lips and tongues turned red.

"Do you want me to give you a kiss?" Audrey said.

He opened his mouth.

"Look," she said. "You don't drool when you kiss and you don't spit either. How'd you learn such a thing?"

"I didn't," he said.

"Never mind," she said. "We don't ever have to kiss. We're the last generation."

Walter drank more than he had when the boys' mother was alive. Still, he made them supper every night when he came home from work. He set the table, poured the milk.

"Well, men," he would say, "here we are." He would begin to cry. "I'm sorry, men," he'd say.

The sun would be setting in a mottled sky over the wet woods and the light would linger in a smeared radiance for awhile.

Tommy would scarcely be able to sleep at night, waiting for the morning to come and go so it would be the afternoon and he would be with Audrey, rocking in the metal chairs.

"The last generation has got certain responsibilities," Audrey said, "though you might think we wouldn't. We should know nothing and want nothing and be nothing, but at the same time we should want everything and know everything and be everything."

Upstairs, in his room, Walter, Jr., was lifting weights. They could hear him breathing, gasping.

Audrey's strange, smooth face looked blank. It looked empty.

"Did you love my brother?" Tommy asked. "Do you still love him?"

"Certainly not," Audrey said. "We were just passing friends."

"My father says we are all passing guests of God."

"He says that kind of thing because the Mom left so quick." She snapped her fingers.

Tommy was holding tight to the curved metal arms of the chair. He put his hands up to his face and sniffed them. He had had dreams of putting his hands in Audrey's hair, hiding them there, up to his wrists. Her hair was the color of gingerbread.

"Love isn't what you think anyway," Audrey said.

"I don't," Tommy said.

"Love is ruthless. I'm reading a book for English class, *Wuthering Heights*. Everything's in that book, but mostly it's about the ruthlessness of love."

"Tell me the whole book," Tommy said.

"Emily Brontë wrote *Wuthering Heights*. I'll tell you a story about her."

He picked at a scab on his knee.

"Emily Brontë had a bulldog named Keeper that she loved. His only bad habit was sleeping on the beds. The housekeeper complained about this and Emily said that if she ever found him sleeping on the clean white beds again, she would beat him. So Emily found him one evening sleeping on a clean white bed and she dragged him off and pushed him in a corner and beat him with her fists. She punished him until his eyes were swelled up and he was bloody and half blind, and after she punished him, she nursed him back to health."

Tommy rocked on his chair, watching Audrey. He stopped picking. The scab didn't want to come off.

"She had a harsh life," Audrey said, "but she was fair."

"Did she tell him later that she was sorry?" Tommy asked.

"No. Absolutely not."

"Did Keeper forgive her?"

"Dogs aren't human. They can't forgive."

"I've never had a dog," Tommy said.

"I had a dog when I was little. She was a golden retriever. She looked exactly like all golden retrievers. Her size was the same, the color of her fur, and her large, sad eyes. Her behavior was the same. She was devoted, expectant, and yet resigned. Do you see what I mean? But I liked her a lot. She was special to me. When she died, I wanted them to bury her under my window, but you know what they said to me? They said, 'The best place to bury a dog is in your heart.' "

She looked at him until he finally said, "That's right."

"That's a crock," she said. "A crock of you know what. Don't agree to so much stuff. You've got to watch out."

"All right," he said, and shook his head.

Sometimes, Audrey visited him at school. He told her when his recess was and she would walk over to the playground and talk with him through the playground's chain-link fence. Once she brought a girlfriend with her. Her name was Flan and she wore large clothes, a long, wide skirt and a big sweater with little animals running in rows. There were only parts of the little animals where the body of the sweater met the sleeves and collar.

"Isn't he cute," Flan said. "He's like a little doll, like, isn't he."

"Now don't go and scare him," Audrey said.

Flan had a cold. She held little wadded tissues to her mouth and eyes. The tissues were blue and pink and green and she would dab at her face with them and push them back in her pockets but one spilled out and fluttered in the weeds beside the schoolyard fence. It would not blow away but stay fluttering there.

"I ain't scaring him. Where'd you get all them moles around your neck?" she said to Tommy.

"What do you mean, where'd he get them," Audrey said. "He didn't get them from anywhere."

"Don't you worry about them moles?" the girl persisted.

"Naw," Tommy said.

"You're a brave little guy, aren't you," Flan said. "There's other stuff, I know. I'm not saying it's all moles." She tugged at the front of the frightful sweater. "Audrey gave me this sweater. She stole it. You know how she steals things and after awhile she puts them back? But I like this so it's not going to get put back."

Tommy gazed unhappily at the sweater and then at Audrey.

"Sometimes putting stuff back is the best part," Audrey said. "Sometimes it isn't."

"Audrey can steal anything," Flan said.

"Can she steal a house?" Tommy asked.

"He's so *cute*," Flan shrieked.

"I gotta go in," Tommy said. Behind him, in the schoolyard, the children were playing a peculiar game. Running, crouching, calling, there didn't seem to be any rules. He trotted toward them and heard Flan say, "He's a cute little guy, isn't he."

Tommy never saw Flan again and he was glad of that. He asked Audrey if Flan was in the last generation.

"Yes," Audrey said. "She sure is."

"Is my brother in the last generation too?"

"Technically he is, of course," Audrey said. "But he's not really. He has too much stuff."

"I have stuff," Tommy said. He had his little cars. "You've given me stuff."

"But you don't have possessions because what I gave you I stole. Anyway, you'll stop caring about that soon. You'll forget all about it but Walter, Jr., really likes possessions and he likes to think about what he's going to do. He has his truck and his barbells and those shirts with the pearl buttons."

"He wants a pair of lizard boots for his birthday," Tommy said.

"Isn't that pathetic," Audrey said.

Every night, Walter would come home from work, scrub down his hands and arms, set the table, pour the milk. The boys sat on either side of him. The chair where their mother used to sit looked out at the yard, at a woodpile there.

"Men," Walter began, "when I was your age, I didn't know . . ." He shook his head and drank his whiskey, his eyes filling with tears.

He had been forgetting to empty the bucket in the space above Tommy's room. A pale stain had spread upon the ceiling. Tommy showed it to Audrey.

"That's nice," she said, "the shape, all dappled brown and yellow like that, but it doesn't tell you anything really. It's just part of the doomed reality all around us." She climbed up and brought the bucket down.

"A monk would take this water and walk into the desert and pour it over a dry and broken stick there," she said. "That's why people become monks, because they get sick of being around doomed reality all the time."

"Let's be monks," he said.

"Monks love solitude," Audrey said. "They love solitude more than anything. When monks started out, long, long ago, they were waiting for the end of time."

"But the end of time didn't happen, did it?" Tommy asked.

"It was too soon then. They didn't know what we know today."

She wore silver sandals. Once she had broken a strap on the sandal and Tommy had fixed it with his Hot Stuff Instant Glue.

"Someday we could have a little boy just like you," she said, "And we'd call him Tommy Two."

But he was not fond of this idea. He was afraid that it would come out of him somehow, this Tommy Two, that he would make it and be ashamed. So, together, they dismissed the notion.

One day, Walter, Jr., said to him, "Look, Audrey shouldn't be hanging around here all the time. She's weird. She's no mommy, believe me."

"I don't need a mommy," Tommy said.

"She's mad at me and she's trying to get back at me through you. She's just practicing on you. You don't want to be practiced on, do you? She's just a very unhappy person."

"I'm unhappy," Tommy said.

"You need to get out and play some games. Soccer, maybe."

"Why?" Tommy said. "I don't like Daddy."

"You're just trying that out," Walter, Jr., said. "You like him well enough."

"Audrey and me are the last generation and you're not," Tommy said.

"What are you talking about?"

"You should be but you're not. Nothing can be done about it."

"Let's drive around in the truck," Walter, Jr., said.

Tommy still enjoyed riding around in the truck. They passed by the houses their mother had cleaned. They looked all right. Someone else was cleaning them now.

"You don't look good," Walter, Jr., said. "You're too pale. You mope around all the time."

Inside the truck, the needle of the black compass on the dashboard trembled. The compass box was filled with what seemed like water. Maybe it was water. Tommy was looking at everything carefully, but trying not to think about it. Audrey was teaching him how to do this. He remembered at some point to turn toward his brother and smile, and this made his brother feel better, it was clear.

The winter nights were cool. Audrey and Tommy still sat in their chairs at dusk on the porch but now they wrapped themselves in blankets.

"Walter, Jr., is dating a lot anymore," Audrey said. "It's nice we have these evenings to ourselves but we should take little trips, you know? I have a lot to show you. Have you ever been to the TV tower north of town?"

The father, Walter, was already in bed. He worked and drank and slept. He had saved the fragments of soap his wife had left behind in the shower. He had wrapped them in tissue paper and placed them in a drawer. But he was sleeping in the middle of the bed these nights, hardly aware of it.

"No," Tommy said. "Is it in the woods?"

"It's a lot taller than the woods and it's not far away from here. It's called Tall Timbers. It's right smack in the middle of birds' migration routes. Thousands of birds run into it every year, all kinds of them. We can go out there and look at the birds."

Tommy was puzzled. "Are the birds dead?"

"Yes," she said. "In an eleven-year period, thirty thousand birds of a hundred and seventy species have been found at the base of the tower."

"Why don't they move it?"

"They don't do things like that," Audrey said. "It would never occur to them."

He did not want to see the birds around the tower. "Let's go," he said.

"We'll go in the spring. That's when the birds change latitudes. That's when they move from one place to another. There's a little tiny warbler bird that used to live around here in the spring, but people haven't seen it for years. They haven't found it at the base of any of the TV towers. They used to find it there, that's how they knew it wasn't extinct."

"Monks used to live on top of tall towers," Tommy said, for she had told him this. "If a monk stayed up there, he could keep the birds away, he could wave his arms around or something so they wouldn't hit."

"Monks live in a cool, crystalline half-darkness of the mind and heart," Audrey said. "They couldn't be bothered with that."

They rocked in their chairs on the porch. The porch had been painted a succession of colors. Where the chairs had scraped the wood there was light green, dark green, blue, red. Bugs crawled around the lights.

"If I got sick, would you stay with me?" Tommy asked.

"I'm not sure. It would depend."

"My mommy would have stayed."

"Well you never know," Audrey said. "You got to realize mommies get tired. They're willing to let things go sometimes. They get to thinking and they're off."

"Do you have a mommy?" he asked cautiously.

"Technically I do," Audrey said, "but she's gone as your mommy actually. Before something's gone, it had to have been there right? Even so, I don't feel any rancor about her. It's important not to feel rancor."

"I don't feel rancor," Tommy said.

Then one afternoon, Walter came home from his work at the garage and it was as though he had woken from a strange sleep. He didn't appear startled by his awakening. His days and nights of grief came to an end really with no harder shock than that of a boat's keel grounding upon a river's shore. He stopped drinking and weeping. He put his wife's things in cardboard boxes and stored the boxes. In fact, he stored them in the space above Tommy's room.

"Why's that girl here all the time?" Walter asked. "She's not still Walter, Jr.'s girlfriend, is she?"

He said, "She shouldn't be here all the time."

"Audrey's my friend," Tommy said.

"She's not a nice girl. She's too old to be your friend."

"Then I'm too young to be your friend."

"No, honey, you're my son."

"I don't like you," Tommy said.

"You love me but you don't like me, is that it?" Walter was thinner and cleaner. He spoke cheerfully.

Tommy considered this. He shook his head.

At school, at the edge of the playground, Audrey talked through the chain-link fence to Tommy.

"You know that pretty swamp close by? It's full of fish, all different kinds. You know how they know?"

He didn't.

"They poison little patches of it. They put out nets and then they drop the poison in. It settles in the gills of the fish and suffocates them. The fish pop up to the surface and then they drag them out and classify and weigh and measure each one."

"Who?" Tommy said.

"They do it a couple times a year to see if there's as many different kinds and as many as before. That's how they count things. That's their attitude. They act as though they care about stuff, but they don't. They're just pretending."

Tommy told her that his father didn't want her to come over to the house, that he wasn't supposed to talk to her any more.

"The Dad's back is he," Audrey said. "What it is is that he thinks he can start over. That's pathetic."

"What are we going to do?" Tommy said.

"You shouldn't listen to him," Audrey said. "Why are you listening to him? We're the last generation, there's something else we're listening to."

They were silent for awhile, listening. The other children had gone inside.

"What is it?" Tommy asked.

"You'll recognize it when you hear it. Something will happen, something unusual for which we were always prepared. The Dad's life has already taken a turn for the worse, it's obvious. It's like he's a stranger now, walking down the wrong road. Do you see what I mean? I could put it another way."

"Put it another way," Tommy said.

"It's his life that's like the stranger, standing real still. A stranger standing along-side a dark road, waiting for him to pass."

It appeared his father was able to keep Audrey away. Tommy wouldn't have thought it was possible. He knew his father was powerless, but Audrey wasn't coming around. His father moved through the house in his dark, oiled boots, fixing things. He painted the kitchen, restacked the woodpile. He replaced the pipe above the ceiling in Tommy's room. It had long been accepted that this could not be done, but now it was done, it did not leak, there was no need for the bucket. The bucket was used now to take ashes from the woodstove. Walter, Jr., had a job in the gym he worked out in. He had long, hard muscles, a distracted air. He worried about girls, about money. He wanted an apartment of his own, in town.

Tommy lived alone with his father. "Talk to me, son," Walter said. "I love you."

Tommy said nothing. His father disgusted him a little. He was like a tree walking, strange but not believable. He was trying to start over. It was pathetic.

Tommy only saw Audrey on schooldays, at recess. He waited by the fence for her in the vitreous, intractable light of the southern afternoon.

"I had a boy tell me once my nipples were like bowls of Wheaties," Audrey said.

"When," Tommy said. "No."

"That's a simile. Similes are a crock. There's no more time for similes. There used to be that kind of time, but no more. You shouldn't see what you're seeing thinking it looks like something else. They haven't left us with much but the things that are left should be seen as they are."

Some days she did not come by. Then he would see her waiting at the fence, or she would appear suddenly, while he was waiting there. But then days passed, more days than there had been before. Days with Walter saying,

"We need each other, son. We're not over this yet. We have to help each other. I need your help."

It was suppertime. They were sitting at a table over the last of a meal Walter had put together.

"I want Audrey back," Tommy said.

"Audrey?" Walter looked surprised. "Walter, Jr., heard about what happened to Audrey. She made her bed as they say, now she's got to lie in it." He looked at Tommy, then dismayed, looked away.

"Who wants you," Tommy said. "Nobody."

Walter rubbed his head with his hands. He looked around the room, at some milk on the floor that Tommy had spilled. The house was empty except for them. There were no animals around, nothing. It was all beyond what was possible, he knew.

In the night, Tommy heard his father moving around, bumping into things, moaning. A glass fell. He heard it breaking for what seemed a long time. The air in the house felt close, sour. He pushed open his bedroom window and felt the air fluttering warmly against his skin. Down along the river, the water popped and smacked against the muddy bank. It was close to the season when he and Audrey could go to the tower where all the birds were. He could feel it in the air. Audrey would come for him from wherever she was, from wherever they had made her go, and they would go to the tower and find the little warbler bird. Then they would know that it still existed because they had found it dead there. He and Audrey would be the ones who would find it. They were the last generation, the ones who would see everything for the last time. That's what the last generation does.

I WROTE THIS STORY in the spring of 1966—or rather I re-wrote it. Halfway through the writing I realized I was turning inside-out a chapter of a novel I'd written while at law school. The chapter was sentimental and false. By switching from third person to first person I myself moved to a distance from which I could see what was really going on but still leave the narrator with a blind side. Vance Bourjaily and Kurt Vonnegut were encouraging. I sent it out, got three rejection letters, shelved it. I didn't want to be distracted from a second novel I'd started. When that novel got turned down my wife discovered she was pregnant. I decided to send out some stories. Vance said to try William Maxwell at *The New Yorker*. He bought it. I'd also sent out a nonfiction piece to *Sports Illustrated*, and that was accepted. A muse (or her agent) said, "So. You write two novels, you get to publish two stories. That's the deal, kid." I sent another story to Mr. Maxwell and he bought that, too. A muse with a sense of humor. I moved to Rhode Island with wife and child and didn't sell another word for two years. But the muse did arrange that I had very good luck fishing . . .

JOHN CASEY

JOHN CASEY

A More Complete Cross-Section

WHEN I FIRST HEARD that I was to go on active duty in the Army—specifically at Fort Knox, Kentucky—I welcomed the news. I regarded the ensuing six months' military service as an opportunity to see a more complete cross-section of my fellow man.

I was cheated at first. There were only surfaces. The people circled me like the moon the earth, always presenting the same face, keeping the dark side hidden.

Moreover, the shock of being suddenly piled together in Fort Knox distorted even the surface appearances; I saw them as though through a prismatic kaleidoscope, their true colors and shapes scattered. No one was in his natural setting. I don't know why I had expected at least some of the people to be at home, but I could see that they were not—just by the way they fingered their stiff fatigue uniforms and ran their hands fitfully over their shaved heads. One man fainted when they clipped off his hair. That was interesting, but he disappeared from the reception center. There was only the prevailing fabric of the Army that held steady. That, however, was somewhat more richly textured than I had imagined. When I arrived at Fort Knox, the commanding general's name was Wonder. General Wonder. There were a number of coincidences of name, all of them equally hauntingly unperceived. The master sergeant who lectured us on military courtesy, company formations, and the meaning of bugle calls was named Roland. The supply sergeant who came to supervise us while we dyed our brown government-issue boots with black government-issue dye was named Glissen. If we had been asked to paint white roses red, I could not have been more delighted.

The first week of basic training we continued to be rushed about. There was always a great flurry, but our roles were so undemanding and passive that it was soothing. I did note that we had an apparently authentic sergeant. He was small and thin, with a rather unpleasant, fair—almost hairless—face. "My name is McQueen," he said, underlining his name tag with the chewed end of his cigar. "My first name is Sergeant." He walked down the front row, looking up into our faces, and stopped in front of the boy next to me. "Ellridge," he said, reading the name tag in front of his nose.

"Yes, sir," Ellridge said.

"Don't call me 'sir.' I earn my money."

"All right." Ellridge was a Southerner with a soft agreeable voice.

McQueen spun on his heel and whistled. I turned to look at Ellridge while the sergeant's back was turned. His thin neck drooped forward as he watched Mc-Queen with puzzlement. McQueen, facing him again, reached out. I rolled my eyes to watch. His fingers grasped the middle button of Ellridge's fatigue shirt. The button was unbuttoned. In the sergeant's belt buckle I could see the reflection of Ellridge's left hand as it moved. I turned and saw him cover the top of his own left thigh with it.

"You're pretty sloppy, Ellridge. Do you really want that button?"

Ellridge smiled nervously.

McQueen ripped it off. "You'd better sew it on, then," he said.

"I could have just buttoned it," Ellridge said.

McQueen stared at him. Then his eyes lighted on Ellridge's left hand. "What's your hand doing there, Ellridge? You going to play with yourself?"

There was general laughter. Ellridge looked at me with dismay, and I looked curiously at McQueen.

He stared back at me. "What're you staring at, troop? You want to get in on it too?"

There was more laughter.

"You better get your eyes front!" he said, grunting the last word so that it had a rather attractive nasal resonance.

But he also disappeared. The first sergeant told me that he had been flown to Walter Reed Hospital on compassionate leave to be with his Korean stepdaughter while she had an eye operation.

First Sergeant Plisetsky was a large man. His chest was at least fifty inches around, as were his waist and hips. He invited me to his office at Company HQ. He told me McQueen was gone and that there was no one in charge of my barracks. He invited me to sit down.

"I see you smoke cigars," he said, pointing to the large flat tin in my breast pocket. I offered him one. He took the tin and said with benevolence, "Have one yourself." We puffed in silence. "You didn't get these at the PX," he said, handing me back the package.

"No," I answered.

"Very fine," he said, "very fine. I like cigars. Kipling liked cigars. I like Kipling too."

"Yes," I said.

"So you used to wrestle up at college," he said, tapping my 201 file with his finger. "Fine sport. That why you dropped R.O.T.C.?"

"In a way."

"I understand," he said. "It's all right."

He reached in a drawer of his desk and pulled out a navy-blue brassard with three chevrons on it and handed it to me. "This is just field stripes," he said. "No pay." He paused and then added with satisfaction, "But that won't bother you."

I pinned the brassard on with the safety pins hanging from the worn felt.

He sighed. "I used to be first sergeant for a training company of clerk-typists. They used to play bridge. You don't play bridge, do you? I thought we could get up a foursome. I often spend the night here," he said, pointing to the cot behind him. "I'm a bachelor."

"No," I said.

"The best bridge player I ever met was a Harvard man too. Big fellow, dark hair. But that was some years back. You wouldn't know him."

We smoked awhile.

"You won't have to stand guard, or do any KP," he said. "But try to stop the fighting. They're lonely, they're nervous, they're"—he stopped to knock a cigar ash into the saucer of his coffee cup—"pent up. We used to run. Even my clerk-typists used to run. If they run, they just go to bed. But we can't run anymore while it's warm. A boy died of heat stroke running up a hill. More likely it was a weak heart. Not in our regiment, but still we can't run. So try to control the horseplay in the barracks. I'll stop by before the evening meal and tell them you're the platoon guide. As far as they're concerned, you're just like a sergeant." He started to sigh again but yawned. "It's not so bad. Not so bad as they all say. I do my job. You do your job. We all do a job. You'll all be gone soon."

I WENT SLIGHTLY and pleasantly mad during the next three weeks. The sun shone through the dust in such a mysterious way that I could not believe what we were all doing. I had looked forward to the time in the Army as one of disembodied observation, but I found I still couldn't see the people as I had hoped. It was arranged that we rarely talked, but I also couldn't see them because the sun only seemed to shine on things. I saw the black high gloss on the rows of boot tips melt into dullness under the sun. I saw sweat spreading across the softened fibers of fatigue shirts, squeezed out from under the suspenders of the pack harness. I saw hands groping with pieces of rifle. Interminably. And I was dazzled by looking at my shiny thumbnail through the bores of all their rifles. When I looked down the spirals, I had no idea how far away the other end was. I could feel my left hand around the barrel, and I could see my right thumbnail flicking the sunlight at my eye—but sometimes so close it was only the distance through a keyhole, sometimes so far that my stomach lunged up to my chest. Pleasurably, I think. It was a beautiful sight—the glistening foreshortened rifling—and I was often hypnotized.

The roads we walked on were sometimes soft. The asphalt gave off colorless heat waves reminiscent of the beams in the rifle barrel, but the road itself was velvet, velvet gray as it climbed the hill ahead of us toward the sun.

I was a half ghost when the sun went down. I could not tell the men from shadows then. There was nothing to do. It seemed a profanation of the place to read. I could hear voices calling to each other. "Him? He don't care. Just as long as your shit don't smell." There were also many small radios that tissue-papered a song— "Come-a come-a come-a come-a to me"—while steam poured out of the shower room, through the latrine (bearing with it the smell of mentholated shaving cream), and out the double screen doors in the flank of the barracks.

Every night my bunkmate—Demry McGlaughlin was his name—asked me softly, "Is anything wrong, man?"

"No," I said. It startled me every time.

What was wrong was—perhaps was—that I knew I made up so much of each day and yet I felt the shadow of all their minds pass over it. I did not know whether they were drawn into my imagination or whether I was drawn into seeing what they saw. Whichever it was, it was a great strain. To be sure, when they slept I was released. As soon as they closed their eyes, I felt the bloat of my authority subside. I was alone, and I saw only what concerned me. I alone saw the moon shine on the white foot powder on the floor, as soft as flour on a pantry table. I saw the moon-light—on the pronged silver knob of the drinking fountain, gleaming hard at a great distance from my open eye. In the morning I felt good. I used to sing as I bloused my fatigue pants. Once someone said behind my back, "What's he singing about— all the crap he's gonna give us?"

I said out loud without turning, "I don't think you've thought very carefully about what you said. The chair gives you leave to reconsider."

Usually I ignored who said what. There were so few freedoms for them that I thought they should at least have the freedom of speech. The only way they could be sure of it was by my perfect impartiality, and perfect impartiality is ignorance.

Demry chuckled. He was the only one in the barracks appreciably bigger than I.

I favored him. Otherwise I was fair. I favored him not because he was the biggest, nor because he was a Negro, but because he was the first to emerge. I saw him speaking to me and heard him, both at once.

In general, my reaction to the swell of voices within the barracks was like the sort of puzzlement one has watching a flock of birds, hearing them call to each other but being unable to associate a particular call with a particular bird. As a conse-quence I could never address anyone by name unless he was wearing a clean name tag and happened to be standing within reading distance and facing me. However, on several occasions I called the roll at assembly entirely from memory. But I knew Demry. Demry was like a large crow flapping along from tree to tree in plain sight, cawing down at me, sometimes companionably, sometimes derisively, but always clearly. That may have been because he seemed to be humoring me. He laughed quite a lot.

What I said fell heavily on the others. I sometimes would say whatever I was thinking and it dismayed them, especially since the first sergeant often appeared to tell them that he stood behind whatever *I* told them. Thus, a number of lyric and scientific observations became curiously embedded in my impersonation of a sergeant, the whole batch of which was repeatedly stamped with approval by the first sergeant. I could also say "InspickSHUNNN . . . HARums!" Click. Click. Clickety-click. "You min *will* do that again and you min *will* do it ERRIGHT!" as well as some other things along that line.

But those were only the ornaments and accidents of my efforts; the substance was plain and just. Their hours in the barracks were arranged on concentric cardboard wheels that I set each morning after breakfast. In the field the first sergeant's voice reached us all on every main question. I believed no one had reason to complain.

Yet there was fighting. The first time it was two very small people. Demry held one and I the other. We put them under the shower. The second time it was somewhat larger people, but after a blow had been struck on each side someone saw a plump nurse from the dental clinic walking slowly past the barracks. The crowd rushed to line the roads. The two men fighting became puzzled, and then alarmed. They left off fighting. One man—not one of the two—went on sick call with a swollen knee. He had been pushed down the wooden steps on the way out.

Sometimes things happened quickly. But mostly time was quicker. The usual day would be half gone before anything of substance came along. We moved very slowly from point to point—both while walking and while learning our rudiments. There was a special stillness about the faces and postures of all the people in the company— gathered outside the mess hall, inside a classroom, on the roadside—that gave me the feeling that they had been told they were being used as models for a laborious and richly detailed mural painting. Even when we were marching it seemed so— especially in the woods when a bird or a squirrel would appear and disappear at a natural speed. There was so much time passing that I could watch the sun's shadow move from one side of a nose to the other. But sometimes things happened quickly. One late afternoon we left the company formation, trooped through the barracks, and were seated outside cleaning rifles before the dust had settled on the assembly area, a hundred yards away, visible from the wooden steps of our side porch. A few people stayed inside, but most of the platoon, stripped to their white T-shirts, were gathered on the ground in groups of three or four, their dog tags clanking gently as they slowly moved their forearms about, pulling apart their rifles with the peaceful rhythm of sheep tugging at clumps of grass. I went inside to drink at the water fountain. Demry was sitting on his bunk. I heard Ellridge ask him for the bore cleaner. Demry ignored him. He asked again. Demry said, "You'll get it. You'll get it. Just get off my back, boy."

Ellridge giggled loudly. I was surprised.

"Something funny?" Demry said. "You think that's funny? You go on and *tell* me what's funny, boy."

Ellridge said, "Oh, *you* know." His eyelids drooped almost languidly. But when he looked up again his eyes were wide, his mouth parted, and his cheeks sucked in with fear. I began to see the point about "boy." It was astonishing how quickly they had come to the point, without a word of elaboration, without having anything else in common. Even so, I would have thought Demry was being overly subtle, but I could see Ellridge's response of coyness and panic. And there *is* something about ineptness—ineptness at daring as well as ineptness at flight—that arouses loathing and aggression.

"You better say something, boy," Demry said.

Ellridge looked over at me and gave another nervous laugh. "I don't have to talk to you," he said to Demry.

There were ten men in from the steps before Ellridge finished answering. They loved a fight. They probably smelled it when he opened his mouth the first time. We hadn't had a real fight for a week. Demry got up and moved toward Ellridge. The men moved closer until they were packed tight in a ring. They knew I was behind them and that I was supposed to break it up. More men came in and squeezed around.

It was disgusting how terrified Ellridge looked. I was surprised when he began to move his mouth again and said, with great effort, "I don't have to talk to you." It was like a turtle laying eggs—a quick nervous convulsion for each word, the eyes blinking slowly, out of phase with the movements of his mouth.

Ellridge backed up, but then he laughed again. The laugh was out of control and dragged up an ugly whimper at the end. He hiccuped. It would have been funny except for Demry's bulk leaning forward. Ellridge's hands flew out to steady himself. One hand against the wall, the other against the rifle rack.

Demry said, "I'm gonna make you quit laughing, boy."

One of the men in the front row called out, "He's not gonna fight him—he's gonna rape him!"

Attacked by their laughter, Ellridge pulled an M-1 from the rack. For an instant I was afraid he might have smuggled a cartridge back from the range, but he came to a kind of high port arms and said, "Don't you come near me—I'll split your head." He waggled the butt of the rifle. Demry grabbed an end of the iron locking bar and pulled it out of the last slot, from which it had been jutting askew. It trailed by his foot for an instant. He seemed to swing it lightly, but the rifle jumped two feet in the air. Ellridge jumped back into the corner as it fell. There was a notch in the side of the stock in front of the trigger housing. I'd hate to think it was the sight of damage to government property that moved me, but it was then that I pushed aside the people in front of me. I called to Demry. He turned.

"He's a good deal smaller than you are," I said. "You could break him into pieces. You know that. But we couldn't put him back together, you know. . . ."

Demry looked at me meditatively.

"Do you want him to apologize?" I asked.

"No," he said, and handed me the locking bar. He walked back to his bunk, sat down, and held the barrel of his rifle up to his eye, pointing the other end at the window as though he were looking at the sky with a telescope.

"Get out," I said to the others. They really were terrible bloodsuckers sometimes.

"Not you," I said, somewhat unnecessarily, to Ellridge, who was still standing in the corner. The others sluggishly passed out the double door. Ellridge put the rifle back and followed me out the front door. We went around to the furnace-room side of the barracks. I leaned against the side of the building, wondering for a moment what people thought of Ellridge where he came from. Did life there go on in such simple harmony that it didn't matter what they thought—that whatever he was was all that anyone hoped for him? Leave him to his same old tune. Or were people there distressed at weakness too? He should at least try to turn out all right. He stood facing me. When I finally spoke, he suddenly checked the buttons to the flaps of his shirt pockets.

I said, "It might seem unfair to you but I wish you would stay away from McGlaughlin. Don't talk to him. Don't get in his way. In fact, don't even put yourself next to him in formation."

"It was the colored boy started it."

"His name is McGlaughlin," I said. "And who started it doesn't matter. This is just to maintain the peace—like the United States keeping Chiang Kai-shek from overrunning China."

But that was just part of my old tune. He didn't listen to it.

"They said it would be a lot worse," he said softly. "Back home they said that."

"It's not so bad, then," I concluded hopefully. "And it should get better for all of us. It's not so long now."

I ALSO DEFENDED THEM. One night, long after lights out, a newly assigned member of the company cadre intruded. At that time he held the rank of specialist fourth class. When I woke up, he was shining a flashlight on a pile of foot powder on the floor and demanding that it be swept up.

I got out of bed and went over. Ellridge was sleepily refusing to get up, and the specialist, whose name was Shoemaker, brayed at him more and more noisily.

"Jesus, Ellridge, why is it always you?" I said. "Never mind, never mind. . . ."

"You get back in the rack," Shoemaker said, shining the light in my eyes.

I put my hand over the lens, saying, "Don't shine the light in my eyes."

"Don't get lively, Bonzo. You're in the Army now. You touch me and they'll lock you up."

"You're making an awful lot of noise. Why don't you step outside and discuss sweeping the floor in the morning?"

"Who the hell are you?" he asked.

"He's the sergeant," Ellridge said.

"The hell he is," Shoemaker replied.

"I have field stripes, I think they're called."

"Field rank don't mean diddly, Bonzo."

"Doesn't," I said. "But I think it does."

"You come with me," Shoemaker insisted. "You come with me and you'll find out what's what." I turned to get my clothes. "You just come as you are. You won't get frostbite."

I ignored him. He turned back to Ellridge. "That better be off the floor when I get back."

He followed me down to my end of the barracks and, while I dressed, took the lid off the trash barrel. "This place is a pigsty," he said, peering in. He shone his light on Demry in the lower bunk. "You go dump this in the dumpster." Demry rolled over. I pulled my boots on without lacing them and went out the side door. Shoemaker followed me; he didn't want me to get to Sergeant Plisetsky first. Yet when we got to the HQ he didn't want to be the one to wake him. He invited me to. I declined.

"They're going to crucify you," he said. He put his flashlight down on the desk sharply. Then he pulled open a drawer and dropped it in. Sergeant Plisetsky rolled onto his back, crossed his forearms on his stomach like flippers, and exhaled at length. He looked very comfortable. Shoemaker opened a drawer very quietly. He took up a pencil and, looking up at my name tag several times, wrote my name down on a note pad.

"I've got your name," he said, tapping it with his forefinger.

"Well done!" I said.

"I've had about enough out of you, Bonzo. Now get out. Get out of here before I put my boot so far up your ass you won't be able to tell shit from Shinola."

I put my finger to my lips and nodded toward the sleeping First Sergeant.

Shoemaker contrived a number of small inconveniences immediately after that. I think he held up some mail for a while. For example, my weekly tin of Danish cigars was late, and a little stale. But, without becoming threatened directly, he was cured of being a bother at night.

IT SUDDENLY TURNED COLD two days before we went on our bivouac. I liked the feel of the ground turning hard. I'd never been so constantly exposed to the countryside during a change of season. In the same cubic yard of air that was warm one afternoon you could see your breath the next. The C.O.'s jeep took a wrong turn when wheel ruts in what had been simply a damp intersection became as intransigent as railroad switches. The leaves on the ground were no longer soft and colored but shriveled up, in plain brown rigor mortis. Dull as wrapping paper. It was the evergreens that grew darker and richer. And the stars grew brighter, especially as the moon waned.

We pitched our tents in rows on top of a ridge. The iron tent pegs were the only ones that went in successfully. There was a good deal of muttering when I asked those with iron pegs to share them with those with wooden ones, so they could at least start their holes. It was as though the cold withered their small patches of generosity as it had the leaves. Of course, most of them were sick too. When the weather changed, First Sergeant Plisetsky had us run, and the sweat chilled on them when they would lie down during the breaks.

The first night on bivouac it was our platoon's chore to post a sentry every two hours of the night. Demry drew two to four and Ellridge four to six—the last two watches. As we sat outside our tent smoking, Demry didn't seem to mind either the cold or his assignment. From the ridge we could see the blinking light on top of the hospital, the tallest building in Fort Knox. It was seven miles away. We could hear the firing from the artillery range in between the gusts of wind, but we couldn't see the flashes.

"There's a shooting star," he said.

"Maybe it was a flare," I said. "Or an airplane landing."

"No. It was a shooting star. I know shooting stars all right." He lay back. "Just look at those stars. There must be thousands of them. Hundreds of miles away."

I laughed.

"What's so funny?"

"To begin with, there're not thousands of them but millions. More likely billions. And they're not hundreds of miles away. Most of them are so far they have to be measured in light-years. A light-year is the distance that light travels in a year."

"Where'd they teach you that? At college?"

"No. I don't know. I learned it here and there. Like the names of birds . . ."

"Uh-huh," he said.

"Or the names of football teams."

"You know all that too. That's real good."

I said nothing.

"You still didn't tell me what's the funny part," he said.

I answered hastily, "Look—if I had asked, 'Who's Joe Louis?' or—or anyone. Elvis Presley. You would have found that funny."

"Uh-huh. I bet you know all about Joe Louis, though. I don't think I could tell you a thing about Joe Louis. We *all* know about Joe Louis."

Again I said nothing, although I thought how unfair it was that each slip of my tongue should have been misinterpreted just enough to keep the chance to explain slightly beyond my reach. It also occurred to me that he was deliberately taking advantage of my inexperience in a worse way than I had unwittingly offended his.

We went to sleep without saying anything else. At two o'clock the sentry reached between the buttons on the front flaps and shook my foot. "McGlaughlin, you're on," he said, and left. I made a note of that. The sentry was supposed to wait until his relief was on his feet and clearly awake. But then, he might have been afraid of Demry. Or he might have waked me on purpose. I tried not to think that. Having only recently overcome my inability to see these people, I didn't want to swing to the other extreme of paranoia.

I shook Demry's shoulder. He sat up. I could hear his head scraping the top of the tent.

"What time is it?" he asked.

"Two. You're on guard duty."

"Two o'clock in the morning?" he said.

"Yes."

"Two o'clock in the morning."

"That's right."

"Man, that's my bedtime." He lay down again.

"Someone's got to be on guard."

"I'll just guard everything right here."

"Come on, Demry," I said, laughing.

"You go on and laugh," he said. "I'm staying right here. It's cold out there."

"Someone's got to be on guard duty."

"You're someone. You may have forgot that."

"Look, Demry. You know as well as I do that the only way this whole thing can work is if everyone takes his turn. You have to have turns. That's the only way discipline can be imposed and still be fair."

He sat up again. "You're very big on discipline, man. And you know why? It's because you don't really live here. You don't live here at all. You get out of here and you go home. You know, home. That place where they send you magazines from. And those little cigars. *That's* right—you got it—home. Where you live. But get this—I live here. I am here and you are not." I could hear his rapid breathing as he paused. "So as long as I'm *here*, I'm not going to get sick or go crazy over your rules. You have it nice and easy, right? And if I sleep right alongside you a little of that is going to rub off. So we're just going to skip walking around out there. . . ." He lay down. I didn't say anything. "I'll tell you," he continued. "You may know a hell of a lot of things, but one thing you do *not* know is how to get *me* out *there*."

I got out from under my blankets and knelt on top of them. I thought awhile. "Would you stand guard for me?" I asked.

He exhaled with his teeth closed. "I'm not going to talk all night, man." He turned over. "O.K. I'll tell you," he said in a more moderate way. "If it was me, I'd roll over and not give a damn. If I was you, I'd say, 'Demry baby, have yourself a good sleep!'"

"O.K.," I said, and put my clothes on. "I'll do it for you," I said, and unbuttoned the flaps, crawled out with my rifle and boots, and pulled my field jacket with the chevrons on it through the hole behind me as though it were a soul leaving a body.

The stars were very bright. It really did look as though they might be not so far away—even as though it were the wind that was fanning them into a fiercer glow. I wondered if Demry thought that stars were cold.

I walked in zigzags down the bare slope to the nearest pine trees and waited. It finally occurred to me that no matter what happened while I was in the Army, I would not really be changed—not the way I was by school or college. I was no longer being formed. All I could have from now on were sensations, which would be absorbed and digested by the way I already was. I cast my thoughts back to where my real life was going on. Where it was being considered, planned, felt. Where it was carefully creeping forward. When I would catch up with it. Way stations, rungs, nests, and resting places. Here I was a swallow flying through a long barn. A swallow among bats.

Yet I was still a little deranged. The pine trees were very clear to me. I went and touched them, their straight needles and their unknotted trunks, not as cold as I thought they would be, or as cold as I was.

I walked back up to the rows of tents. I didn't hear the wind, I was so used to it. The startling noise was the coughing. From one tent at a time it came—no particular sequence to it, no set interval. As the time passed, it seemed to me I was tending one large beast that was making its noises into the night.

At ten past four I looked at my watch. I went to wake Ellridge. They had only three buttons on their front flaps. I unhooked the loop and pulled it up. The buttons came out of the worn holes. Ellridge was sitting in the back, his knees to his chest, his blanket pulled around his shoulders. He looked like a monkey crouched in an outside cage in wintertime. He hadn't taken his boots off. How unfair it is, I thought, to add my order to the Army's. They suffer enough. I was about to put the flap down again when Ellridge spoke. "I'm not asleep," he said.

"O.K. On your feet." I said it by instinct.

He came out with his blanket around his shoulders. "How come McGlaughlin isn't on guard?"

"Look—I'm tired. It's my bedtime. Enough of this chitchat. Get your field jacket on and start walking around."

"I thought you didn't have to do any of this guard."

He was exultant in a strange way, his eyes wide open and his mouth emitting little explosions—"ha! ah! oh!"—as though he had caught me doing something surprisingly daring and bad. He sucked in his breath, partly meaningfully and partly because he discovered how cold it was.

"You were covering up. You were covering up so he could stay wrapped up. That's right. The middle of the night. Then you came to get me up so you can crawl back in there. So you can crawl back into your hole alongside that—I didn't say it. I didn't say it, but I'll say it if you make me. If you make me stand out here with you crawling in there. But I will say it—oh, God, I will."

"Ellridge, will you get your rifle and stop gibbering."

"Oh, no. No, I won't! I thought you was somebody pretty good, you know that? I thought you was all right. I thought you was something special, but Lord, you're a sorry thing. You're a nigger-lover! Nothing else at all! That's all you do is just care for that nigger. That's all you do is love him. Is love him and kiss him . . ."

"I can't begin to tell you how stupid you are, Ellridge."

He looked at the sky, as though he could see the wind in it. Then he tucked his nose under the edge of his blanket and began to cry.

"O.K., Ellridge. Get back inside."

He stood there. I took him by the shoulders and turned him toward the tent. "Wait," he said.

We waited until he stopped crying. Then he stooped down and crawled back into the tent. I pulled the loop of the flap down over the peg and left while he was doing up the buttons.

I wanted to go down to the pine trees again, but I stayed by the tents. I wasn't tempted either to call Ellridge or to go into my tent and sleep. I couldn't face either of them. I was tempted to go lie down among the pine trees, but instead I tried to resist the wind. I tried to imagine that it was blowing right through me—so cleanly and so fast that it didn't hurt. That worked for a while. Then I couldn't keep imagining well enough, and I began to endure every minute, looking at my watch too often.

During the breaks the next day I had to lie down. I didn't seem to be sweating very much, so I thought it would be all right. Each time I lay down I thought of how when we got back for the night I would gather blanketfuls of pine needles to put under me, and even around me.

We stayed out late. And even though I knew I would be warmer with the pine needles, I didn't get them. I crawled into the tent and lay down. Demry went to sleep. I was about to fall asleep too when I felt a hand on my foot. I sat up expectantly, but no one said, "McGlaughlin, you're on." There was no one there. I lay awake alternately shivering and burning, trying to command my body to be calm. It is possible, but I couldn't bring myself to the right pitch to do it.

First Sergeant Plisetsky noticed that I wasn't myself the next day, and sent me on sick call. I was grateful. Everyone else was jealous. Demry thought I was lucky too. I had given in to so much by then that I even complained to him—explaining in a collapsed way that I had stood two watches.

"Well, you'll get to make it all up now," he said. There was something in his tone that I couldn't decipher. I thought he still considered me lucky, although I hoped he meant it encouragingly. They didn't take people into the infirmary with less than a hundred and one.

I got out of the hospital in only three days, but the company had already returned to the barracks, a day ahead of schedule. Shoemaker had been put in charge of the fourth platoon in my absence. He came up to me while I was sitting on my bunk cleaning my rifle. He had brand-new sergeant's stripes sewn on his fatigues. The distinction is between field rank and acting rank. Acting rank you may sew on.

"Did you have a nice rest?" he said, simpering. "We missed you. Yes, all of the boys really missed you, Bonzo."

"It was great," I said. "The nurses all loved me."

Demry laughed.

"Ooh, I don't know what we can do about that," Shoemaker said. "But I'll tell all the boys to try real hard and see if they can't just *like* you a whole lot."

Demry laughed again. So did the other people sitting around. And, seeing all of them, so did Acting Sergeant Shoemaker. Sitting in my upper bunk, I felt as though I were in a canoe floating down a river of inane chortling noise. I picked up the separated stock of my rifle and began to make paddling motions. Pausing for a moment, I let the stock trail as though I were steering. "My God, Celia," I said to Shoemaker. "Will these jungle noises never cease?"

Shoemaker stopped laughing, and gradually so did everyone else."

"I don't get you, Bonzo. You trying to be funny?"

"Yes," I said. I was sick of the lot of them. While Shoemaker pondered his rejoinder, I added, "Did you have something specific for me to do or were you just wasting time?"

"O.K., O.K.," he said. "Why don't you go on down to the mess hall and make yourself useful. Tell the mess sergeant I sent you."

It was a relief to get out of the barracks. I would gladly have volunteered for KP for the remaining eight days of basic. Among other things there was a feeling of grand accomplishment hovering about which I didn't like. It was self-indulgent. And it was false—the whole training period had been pretty much of a disappointment, in fact. We hadn't had any really stiff marches. There hadn't been any bayonet drill. Target shooting was mildly pleasurable, but there had been no more than two weeks of that—not enough time for real improvement. For what they might have been worth by way of aesthetic incentive, the formal aspects of the military remained unelaborated. Even the scenery was drab now that the illuminations of fall were over. A shoddy damp grayness penetrated everywhere, without the threat of a storm. All that was really happening here was time passing, steadily and unprofitably. But— and this was what excited them—certifiably.

Only eight days. And then fifteen days' leave at home before I was reassigned to a more reasonable environment. I gladly peeled potatoes in a corner of the kitchen. With any kind of solitary chore I could make the time trickle more nimbly. In every spiral shaving I cut loose I saw artful progress, as though I were freeing my own spirit from the crust of living in that place. By the time I splashed the last potato in the vat I felt miles away and much more at peace.

Calm is most regularly induced to enter the physical world by a series of ornamentations; it doesn't matter whether it is nature or oneself that executes them, so long as there is a stretch of repetitive exertion from a single source. Waves before the wind. The footfalls of a runner spinning the world beneath him. Paddle swirls in the wake of a canoe. Or curlicues of potato skin, as unbroken as the phrases sliding out from under the bowing hand of a cellist.

These repetitions are felt by our bodies, the deft, hardworking, and unsuspecting bundles in which we are enmeshed. Unsuspecting because it is by their efforts, the spasms of nerves and muscles that *we* command into rhythm, that they are calmed. And the calm rends them—plucks their fibers apart so that the spirit escapes to a dominant position. That is contentment, I suppose, and most people happen on it only by chance.

Since the complete exercise takes concentration as well as a certain amount of cunning, I was still exhilarated at my accomplished change in fortune as I served supper. This state of well-being even lasted until bedtime, although I knew that sleep would undo it. The Duc de Saint-Simon disliked the shock of a new day so much (I presume because his spirit was again stuck down in his body) that he would not leave his bed until his valet said to him, "Get up, get up, Monsieur le Duc, you have great things to do today!" How different Acting Sergeant Shoemaker's first words would be I did not care to imagine.

I waited until the latrine was empty and the lights were out in the squad bay before I went in to shave. I disliked rushing in the morning. As I stepped out of the latrine a blanket was thrown over my head. There was a great deal of shoving, and the noise of feet scraping on the floor. I was hit in the middle of the forehead. I gathered that a number of them were trying to beat me through the blanket, and they might have really done it had they used their fists, but, as I saw later, they were using the handles from the push brooms. There wasn't enough room to wield them effectively, and I heard a yelp when somebody holding the blanket over me was hit. I couldn't recognize their voices. In fact, they could have done without the bother of the blanket altogether—I doubt if I would have recognized their faces. After I recovered from the surprise, it took me very little time to break loose. I think I may have rammed one person into the drinking fountain. But as I was about to get rid of the blanket they gathered again and pushed me through the side door so swiftly that I fell heavily down the wooden steps. By the time I was on my feet again and clear of the blanket, they had scuttled back to their beds. I shook myself and padded back up the steps. I could have found them, I suppose, by their heavy breathing. The push broom handles—three of them—lay on the floor. I saw, too, that the blanket they had used was from my bed, so I had to go outdoors again to retrieve it. I folded it in half and shook the dust out of it. My hands were beginning to stiffen. They had received the few well-aimed strokes that had followed the initial one to my forehead.

I wanted to find it absurd, but my body took it as a humiliation. My forehead felt wet, although it wasn't bleeding. My hips hurt too, from the fall. But most of all, my stiff hands trembled, not in the fingers but from the wrist and elbow. I wanted to find the people absurd, but my fluttering arms and damp bruises took them seriously.

"Demry," I said, "where were you?"

He rolled onto his back to face me. "You're very big on waking me up, man. Last time I saw you, you were waking me up."

"You weren't scared, were you, Demry?"

"I was sleeping, man."

"You don't feel bad about it, do you?" I said.

"They didn't do you no real harm, did they?"

"No," I said. "But I hope you don't feel bad."

"Not me," he said. "I was catching up on my sleep."

I said, "Give me a boost up, would you, Demry? I'm somewhat stiff."

He thought about that awhile. But he was essentially a helpful fellow—even kind. He got out of bed and gave me a shove up as I clambered onto the upper bunk.

I lay on my side. I knew they were there. They had reached me, and it was I that was scuttling away. They had reached my state of mind—not with their blows but with their intentions. I was protected by my own strength, by the shortness of time, even by rules and laws—I had nothing to fear physically. But I had to scuttle away, because they tore apart the pleasant distance at which I lived.

All together they made a spirit that was opaque and probably at odds with itself, but very large and probing. The irony of it was that had I been small and weak, there would have been no need for them to gather. The irony of it was also that I had been fair. But irony would not work to keep the distance. They all at once came closer to me until what had been wandering creatures on my lawn became hands and faces pressed against the windows. All the time I'd thought I could cry "Whoosh!" and they would remove themselves like a carpet of pigeons from a park sidewalk. I had been taught, of course, to treat them better; I knew that fairness was not just a tactical consideration. What I had been taught and its manifestations, however, did not interest them; what did was my real state of mind. I think their final outburst was almost more curiosity than resentment. They probably wanted to see too.

Shoemaker came down the stairs from the cadre room, where he now lived. He shone his flashlight here and there about the room.

"All right, I want quiet," he said. The beam lighted on Ellridge kneeling on his lower bunk, his hands clutching the hollow bars that supported the upper.

"Aren't you going to get them?" Ellridge said to me.

"Shut up, Ellridge. You're on KP tomorrow," Shoemaker said. He shone the light on my face and approached. "Was it you, Bonzo?"

"Put out the light," I said.

"Was it you, Bonzo?"

I reached out and grabbed his throat. "Put out the light," I said. He did. "Be reasonable," I continued, shaking him just a little, "or I'll throttle you." I didn't mean it. He meant very little one way or the other. I let him go.

He retreated to the stairs and turned his light on, pointing it down. "You're on KP too, Bonzo."

I was glad that I hadn't hurt him. "All right," I said. That was reasonable of him.

I lay awake during the night. The moon was waxing again, and shining on the knob of the drinking fountain, but the air was still turbulent between the drinking fountain and me. Even though they slept, the turbulence stayed on. I didn't recognize those same cubic yards of air. Common pasturage during the day, they now kept on that way through the night. What had been mine now coincided with what was theirs at every corner. It was as though their gathered spirit could leave indelible traces.

The next day I was entirely present. They looked curiously at me as I served the meals—at the spot on my forehead, although they knew better than I where it came from. I was entirely present, as though they had thrown a blanket of my own skin over me and pulled it tight all the way to the ground.

"A SORROWFUL WOMAN" was written in its earliest form at the Iowa Writers' Workshop where I was a student in the late 1960s. The idea had lurked in my psyche for years—a woman who'd had enough and gave everything in the end but herself. My first draft had *dreams* in it. As the woman withdrew from her family, the dreams got more violent. In her final dream they die—bashed against the rocks, their little boat shattered. She is their boat. My teacher Robert Coover loved this story and we sent it to Gordon Lish, fiction editor at *Esquire*. He wanted to publish it—if I would let him excise the dreams . . . "make her more inscrutable." I (reluctantly) agreed. As my punishment, I have seen this story anthologized and anthologized, and my students and teachers have written to ask me: what is the meaning of her inscrutable act? Perhaps Lish was right. I don't know and never will. I failed to keep a copy of the first draft so I can't reread it and judge.

The potion, by the way, that her doctor-husband gave her really exists, and it is brown. I was briefly married to a doctor-husband who gave me the same bedtime potion to speed me into unconsciousness. I will not give the ingredients.

GAIL GODWIN

ONE WINTER EVENING she looked at them: the husband durable, receptive, gentle; the child a tender golden three. The sight of them made her so sad and sick she did not want to see them ever again.

She told the husband these thoughts. He was attuned to her; he understood such things. He said he understood. What would she like him to do? "If you could put the boy to bed and read him the story about the monkey who ate too many bananas, I would be grateful." "Of course," he said. "Why, that's a pleasure." And he sent her off to bed.

The next night it happened again. Putting the warm dishes away in the cupboard, she turned and saw the child's gray eyes approving her movements. In the next room was the man, his chin sunk in the open collar of his favorite wool shirt. He was dozing after her good supper. The shirt was the gray of the child's trusting gaze. She began yelping without tears, retching in between. The man woke in alarm and carried her in his arms to bed. The boy followed them up the stairs, saying, "It's all right, Mommy," but this made her scream. "Mommy is sick," the father said, "go and wait for me in your room."

The husband undressed her, abandoning her only long enough to root beneath the eiderdown for her flannel gown. She stood naked except for her bra, which hung by one strap down the side of her body; she had not the impetus to shrug it off. "If only there were instant sleep," she said, hiccuping, and the husband bundled her into the gown and went out and came back with a sleeping draught guaranteed swift. She was to drink a little glass of cognac followed by a big glass of dark liquid and afterward there was just time to say, "Thank you and could you get him a clean pair of pajamas out of the laundry, it came back today."

The next day was Sunday and the husband brought her breakfast in bed and let her sleep until it grew dark again. He took the child for a walk, and when they returned, red-cheeked and boisterous, the father made supper. She heard them laughing in the kitchen. He brought her up a tray of buttered toast, celery sticks, and black bean soup. "I am the luckiest woman," she said, crying real tears. "Nonsense," he said. "You need a rest from us," and went to prepare the sleeping draught, find the child's pajamas, select the story for the night.

She got up on Monday and moved about the house till noon. The boy, delighted to have her back, pretended he was a vicious tiger and followed her from room to room, growling and scratching. Whenever she came close, he would growl and scratch at her. One of his sharp little claws ripped her flesh, just above the wrist, and together they paused to watch a thin red line materialize on the inside of her pale arm and spill over in little beads. "Go away," she said. She got herself upstairs and locked the door. She called the husband's office and said, "I've locked myself away from him. I'm afraid." The husband told her in his richest voice to lie down, take it easy, and he was already on the phone to call one of the baby-sitters they often employed. Shortly after, she heard the girl let herself in, heard the girl coaxing the frightened child to come and play.

After supper several nights later, she hit the child. She had known she was going to do it when the father would see. "I'm sorry," she said, collapsing on the floor. The weeping child had run to hide. "What has happened to me? I'm not myself anymore." The man picked her tenderly from the floor and looked at her with much concern. "Would it help if we got, you know, a girl in? We could fix the room downstairs. I want you to feel freer," he said, understanding these things. "We have the money for a girl. I want you to think about it."

And now the sleeping draught was a nightly thing; she did not have to ask. He went down to the kitchen to mix it; he set it nightly beside her bed. The little glass and the big one, amber and deep rich brown, the flannel gown and the eiderdown.

The man put out the word and found the perfect girl. She was young, dynamic, and not pretty. "Don't bother with the room, I'll fix it up myself." Laughing, she employed her thousand energies. She painted the room white, fed the child lunch, read edifying books, raced the boy to the mailbox, hung her own watercolors on the fresh-painted walls, made spinach soufflé, cleaned a spot from the mother's coat, made them all laugh, danced in stocking feet to music in the white room after reading the child to sleep. She knitted dresses for herself and played chess with the husband. She washed and set the mother's soft ash-blond hair and gave her neck rubs, offered to.

The woman now spent her winter afternoons in the big bedroom. She made a fire in the hearth and put on slacks and an old sweater she had loved at school, and sat in the big chair and stared out the window at snow-ridden branches, or went away into long novels about other people moving through other winters.

The girl brought the child in twice a day, once in the late afternoon when he would tell of his day, all of it tumbling out quickly because there was not much time, and before he went to bed. Often now, the man took his wife to dinner. He made a courtship ceremony of it, inviting her beforehand so she could get used to the idea. They dressed and were beautiful together again and went out into the frosty night. Over candlelight he would say, "I think you are better, you know." "Perhaps I am," she would murmur. "You look . . . like a cloistered queen," he said once, his voice breaking curiously.

One afternoon the girl brought the child into the bedroom. "We've been out playing in the park. He found something he wants to give you, a surprise." The little boy approached her, smiling mysteriously. He placed his cupped hands in hers and left a live dry thing that spat brown juice in her palm and leapt away. She screamed and wrung her hands to be rid of the brown juice. "Oh, it was only a grasshopper," said the girl. Nimbly she crept to the edge of a curtain, did a quick knee bend, and reclaimed the creature, led the boy competently from the room.

"The girl upsets me," said the woman to her husband. He sat frowning on the side of the bed he had not entered for so long. "I'm sorry, but there it is." The husband stroked his creased brow and said he was sorry, too. He really did not know what they would do without that treasure of a girl. "Why don't you stay here with me in bed," the woman said.

Next morning she fired the girl, who cried and said, "I loved the little boy, what will become of him now?" But the mother turned away her face and the girl took down the watercolors from the walls, sheathed the records she had danced to, and went away.

"I don't know what we'll do. It's all my fault, I know. I'm such a burden, I know that."

"Let me think. I'll think of something." (Still understanding these things.)

"I know you will. You always do," she said.

With great care he rearranged his life. He got up hours early, did the shopping, cooked the breakfast, took the boy to nursery school. "We will manage," he said, "until you're better, however long that is." He did his work, collected the boy from the school, came home and made the supper, washed the dishes, got the child to bed. He managed everything. One evening, just as she was on the verge of swallowing her draught, there was a timid knock on her door. The little boy came in wearing his pajamas. "Daddy has fallen asleep on my bed and I can't get in. There's not room."

Very sedately she left her bed and went to the child's room. Things were much changed. Books were rearranged, toys. He'd done some new drawings. She came as a visitor to her son's room, wakened the father, and helped him to bed. "Ah, he shouldn't have bothered you," said the man, leaning on his wife. "I've told him not to." He dropped into his own bed and fell asleep with a moan. Meticulously she undressed him. She folded and hung his clothes. She covered his body with the bedclothes. She flicked off the light that shone in his face.

The next day she moved her things into the girl's white room. She put her hairbrush on the dresser; she put a note pad and pen beside the bed. She stocked the little room with cigarettes, books, bread, and cheese. She didn't need much.

At first the husband was dismayed. But he was receptive to her needs. He understood these things. "Perhaps the best thing is for you to follow it through," he said. "I want to be big enough to contain whatever you must do."

All day long she stayed in the white room. She was a young queen, a virgin in a tower; she was the previous inhabitant, the girl with all the energies. She tried these personalities on like costumes, then discarded them. The room had a new view of streets she'd never seen that way before. The sun hit the room in late afternoon, and she took to brushing her hair in the sun. One day she decided to write a poem. "Perhaps a sonnet." She took up her pen and pad and began working from words that had lately lain in her mind. She had choices for the sonnet, ABAB or ABBA for a start. She pondered these possibilities until she tottered into a larger choice: she did not have to write a sonnet. Her poem could be six, eight, ten, thirteen lines, it could be any number of lines, and it did not even have to rhyme.

She put down the pen on top of the pad.

In the evenings, very briefly, she saw the two of them. They knocked on her door, a big knock and a little, and she would call "Come in," and the husband would smile though he looked a bit tired, yet somehow this tiredness suited him. He would put her sleeping draught on the bedside table and say, "The boy and I have done all right today," and the child would kiss her. One night she tasted for the first time the power of his baby spit.

"I don't think I can see him anymore," she whispered sadly to the man. And the husband turned away, but recovered admirably and said, "Of course, I see."

So the husband came alone. "I have explained to the boy," he said. "And we are doing fine. We are managing." He squeezed his wife's pale arm and put the two glasses on her table. After he had gone, she sat looking at the arm.

"I'M AFRAID it's come to that," she said next time. "Just push the notes under the door; I'll read them. And don't forget to leave the draught outside."

The man sat for a long time with his head in his hands. Then he rose and went away from her. She heard him in the kitchen where he mixed the draught in batches now to last a week at a time, storing it in a corner of the cupboard. She heard him come back, leave the big glass and the little one outside on the floor.

Outside her window, the snow was melting from the branches, there were more people on the streets. She brushed her hair a lot and seldom read anymore. She sat in her window and brushed her hair for hours, and saw a boy fall off his new bicycle again and again, a dog chasing a squirrel, an old woman peek slyly over her shoulder and then extract a parcel from a garbage can.

In the evening she read the notes they slipped under her door. The child could not write, so he drew and sometimes painted his. The notes were painstaking at first, the man and boy offering the final strength of their day to her. But sometimes, when they seemed to have had a bad day, there were only hurried scrawls.

One night, when the husband's note had been extremely short, loving but short, and there had been nothing from the boy, she stole out of her room as she often did to get more supplies, but crept upstairs instead and stood outside their doors, listening to the regular breathing of the man and boy asleep. She hurried back to her room and drank the draught.

She woke earlier now. It was spring, there were birds. She listened for sounds of the man and the boy eating breakfast; she listened for the roar of the motor when they drove away. One beautiful noon, she went out to look at her kitchen in the daylight. Things were changed. He had bought some new dishtowels. Had the old ones worn out? The canisters seemed closer to the sink. She inspected the cupboard and saw new things among the old. She got out flour, yeast, salt, milk (he bought a different brand of butter), and baked a loaf of bread and left it cooling on the table.

The force of the two joyful notes slipped under her door that evening pressed her into the corner of the little room; she had hardly space to breathe. As soon as possible, she drank the draught.

Now the days were too short. She was always busy. She woke with the first bird. Worked till the sun set. No time for hair-brushing. Her fingers raced the hours.

Finally, in the nick of time, it was finished one late afternoon. Her veins pumped and her forehead sparkled. She went to the kitchen cupboard, took what was hers, closed herself into the little white room, and brushed her hair for a while.

The man and boy came home and found: five loaves of warm bread, a roast stuffed turkey, a glazed ham, three pies of different fillings, eight molds of the boy's favorite custard, two weeks' supply of fresh-laundered sheets and shirts and towels, two hand-knitted sweaters (both of the same gray color), a sheath of marvelous watercolor beasts accompanied by mad and fanciful stories nobody could ever make up again, and a tablet full of love sonnets addressed to the man. The house was redolent of renewal and spring. The man ran to the little room, could not contain himself to knock, flung back the door.

"Look, Mommy is sleeping," said the boy. "She's tired from doing all our things again." He dawdled in a stream of the last sun for that day and watched his father tenderly roll back her eyelids, lay his ear softly to her breast, test the delicate bones of her wrist. The father put down his face into her fresh-washed hair.

"Can we eat the turkey for supper?" the boy asked.

WHAT I SAW, in my mind's eye, was two young men in boxing shorts, battering at one another in the gloom of the old Klamath Falls Armory, where my grandfather took me to see "the fights" when I was a boy. The image seemed emblematic of the life I'd grown up in, and loved, and yearned to escape.

I started writing in the mid-1960s, and vowed that I would never give it up, but I had no idea how a story should be structured. I'd never heard of "recognitions." I bought texts and read and underlined, but not to much avail. They made sense in the abstract but weren't any help as I tried to figure out what should happen in my stories. So I was thrown back on trying to intuit what my people would do. There wasn't any way to think it through. The events had to be felt, response by response, draft after draft. I began "Thirty-four Seasons of Winter" when I was still living on the ranch in southeastern Oregon and rewrote it endlessly, like a puppy worrying a rag doll. But not until Iowa City, taking workshops from Dick Yates, did I realize that this was the way stories, at least for me, were always going to figure themselves out. With Dick Yates's help, this story got as finished as it's going to get.

WILLIAM KITTREDGE

WILLIAM KITTREDGE

Thirty-Four Seasons of Winter

BEN ALTON REMEMBERED years in terms of winter. Summers all ran together, each like the last, heat and baled hay and dust. "That was '59," he'd say. "The year I wintered in California." He'd be remembering manure-slick alleys of a feedlot outside Manteca, a flat horizon and constant rain.

Or flood years. "March of '64, when the levees went." Or open winters. "We fed cattle the whole of February in our shirt-sleeves. For Old Man Swarthout." And then he'd be sad. "One week Art helped. We was done every day by noon and drunk by three." Sad because Art was his step-brother and dead, and because there'd been nothing but hate between them when Art was killed.

Ben and Art fought only once, when they were thirteen. Ben's father, Corrie Alton, moved in with Art's old lady on her dry-land place in the hills north of Davanero, and the boys bunked together in a back room. The house was surrounded by a fenced dirt yard where turkeys picked, shaded by three withering peach trees; and the room they shared was furnished with two steel-frame cots and a row of nails where they hung what extra clothing they owned. The first night, while the old people were drinking in town, the boys fought. Ben took a flattened nose and chipped tooth against one of the cot frames and was satisfied and didn't try again.

The next year Art's mother sold the place for money to drink on, and when that was gone Ben's old man pulled out, heading for Shafter, down out of Bakersfield, going to see friends and work a season in the spuds. Corrie never came back or sent word, so the next spring the boys took a job setting siphons for an onion farmer, doing the muddy and exhausting work of one man, supporting themselves and Art's mother. She died the spring they were seventeen; and Art began to talk about getting out of town, fighting in the ring, being somebody.

So he ran every night, and during the day he and Ben stacked alfalfa bales, always making their thousand a day, twenty bucks apiece, and then in the fall Art went to Portland and worked out in a gym each afternoon, learning to fight, and spent his evenings swimming at the YMCA or watching movies. Early in the winter he began to get some fights; and for at least the first year he didn't lose. People began to know his name in places like Salem and Yakima and Klamath Falls.

HE FOUGHT AT HOME only once, a January night in the Peterson barn on the edge of town, snow falling steadily. The barn warmed slowly, losing its odor of harness leather and rotting hay; and under the circle of lights which illuminated the fighters in a blue glare, country people smoked and bet and drank. Circling a sweating and tiring Mexican boy, Art tapped his gloves and brushed back his thin blond hair with a quick forearm, sure and quiet. Then he moved under an overhand right, ducking in a quick new way he must have learned in Portland; and then he was inside, forcing, and flat on his feet, grunting as he followed each short chop with his body. The Mexican backed against one of the rough juniper posts supporting the ring, covered his face, gloves fumbling together as he began sinking and twisting, knees folding; and it ended with the Mexican sprawled and cut beneath one eye, bleeding from the nose, and Art in his corner, breathing easily while he flexed and shook his arms as if he weren't loose yet. Art spit the white mouthpiece onto the wet, gray canvas and ducked away under the ropes.

That night, Ben sat in the top row of the little grandstand and watched two men drag the other fighter out of the ring and attempt to revive him by pouring water over his head. Ben hugged his knees and watched the crowd settle and heard the silence while everybody watched. Finally the Mexican boy shook his head and sat up, and the crowd moved in a great sigh.

THE NEXT SUMMER Art showed up with Clara, brought her back with him from a string of fights in California. It was an August afternoon, dead hot in the valley hayfields, and dust rose in long spirals from the field ahead where five balers were circling slowly, eating windrows of loose hay and leaving endless and uniform strings of bales. Ben was working the stack, unloading trucks, sweating through his pants every day before noon, shirtless and peeling.

The lemon-colored Buick convertible came across the stubble, bouncing and wheeling hard, just ahead of its own dust, and stopped twenty or thirty yards from the stack. Art jumped out holding a can of beer over his head. The girl stood beside the convertible in the dusty alfalfa stubble and squinted into the glaring light, moist and sleepy-looking. She was maybe twenty, and her sleeveless white blouse was wrinkled from sleeping in the car and sweat-gray beneath the arms. But she was blond and tan and direct in the one-hundred-degree heat of the afternoon. "Ain't she something?" Art said. "She's a kind of prize I brought home." He laughed and slapped her on the butt.

"Hello, Ben," she said. "Art told me about you." They drank a can of beer, iced and metallic tasting, and Art talked about the fighting in California, Fresno, and Tracy, and while he talked he ran his fingers slowly up and down Clara's bare arm. Ben crouched in the shade of the convertible with his beer and tried not to watch the girl. That night he lay awake and thought about her, and everything about that meeting seemed too large and real, like some memory of childhood.

Anyway, she was living and traveling with Art. Then the fall he was twenty-five, fighting in Seattle, Art broke his right hand in a way that couldn't be fixed and married Clara and came home to live, driving a logging truck in the summer and drinking in the bars and drawing his unemployment through the winters, letting Clara work as a barmaid when they were broke. The years got away until one afternoon in a tavern called The Tarpaper Shack, when Ben and Art were thirty-one. Art was sitting with a girl named Marie, and when Ben came in and wandered over to the booth she surprised him by being quiet and nice, with brown eyes and dark hair, not the kind Art ran with on his drunks; and by the end of the summer Marie and Ben were engaged.

WHICH CAUSED NO TROUBLE until Christmas. The stores were open late, but the streets with their decorations were deserted, looking like a carnival at four in the morning, lighted and ready to tear down and move.

"You gonna marry that pig?" Art said. Art was drunk. The barkeeper, a woman called Virgie, was leaning on the counter.

"I guess I am," Ben said. "But don't sweat it." Then he noticed Virgie looking past them to the far corner of the vaulted room. A worn row of booths ran there, beyond the lighted shuffleboard table and bowling machine. Above the last booth he saw the shadowed back of Clara's head. Just the yellow hair and yet certainly her. Art was grinning.

"You see her," he said talking to Ben. "She's got a problem. She ain't getting any."

Ben finished the beer and eased the glass back to the wooden counter, wishing he could leave, wanting no more of their trouble. Clara was leaning back, eyes closed and the table in front of her empty except for her clasped hands. She didn't move or look as he approached.

"Hello, Clara," he said. And when she opened her eyes it was the same, like herons over the valley swamps, white against green. Even tired she looked good. "All right if I sit?" he asked. "You want a beer?"

She sipped from his, taking the glass without speaking, touching his hand with her hand, then smiling and licking the froth from her lips. "Okay," she said, and he ordered another glass and sat down beside her.

"How you been?" he said. "All right?"

"You know," she said, looking sideways at him, never glancing toward Art. "You got a pretty good idea how I been." Then she smiled. "I hear you're getting married."

"Just because you're tied up," he said, and she grinned again, more like her old self now. "I mean it," he said. "Guess I ought to tell you once."

"Don't," she said. "For Christ sake. Not with that bastard over there laughing." She drank a little more of the beer. "I mean it," she said, after a moment. "Leave me alone."

Ben picked up his empty glass and walked toward the bar, turning the glass in his hand and feeling how it fit his grasp. He stood looking at the back of Art's head, the thin hair, fine and blond; and then he wrapped the glass in his fist and smashed it into the hollow of Art's neck, shattering the glass and driving Art's face into the counter. Then he ran, crashing out the door and onto the sidewalk.

His hand was cut and bleeding. He picked glass from his palm and wrapped his hand in his handkerchief as he walked, looking in the store windows, bright and lighted for Christmas.

Clara left for Sacramento that night, lived there with her father, worked in a factory southeast of town, making airplane parts and taking care of the old man, not coming back until he died. Sometimes Ben wondered if she would have come back anyway, even if the old man hadn't died. Maybe she'd just been waiting for Art to come after her. And then one day on the street he asked, "You and Art going back together?" just hoping he could get her to talk awhile.

"I guess not," she said. "That's what he told me."

"I'm sorry," Ben said. And he was.

"I came back because I wanted," she said. "Guess I lived here too long."

THAT SPRING BEN AND MARIE WERE MARRIED and began living out of town, on a place her father owned; and the next fall his father was killed, crushed under a hillside combine in Washington, just north of Walla Walla, drunk and asleep at the leveling wheel, dead when they dug him out. And then the summer Art and Ben turned thirty-four Marie got pregnant and that winter Art was killed, shot in the back of the head by a girl named Steffanie Rudd, a thin red-haired girl just out of high school and, so people said, knocked up a little. Art was on the end stool in The Tarpaper Shack, his usual place, when the girl entered quietly and shot before anyone noticed. He was dead when he hit the floor, face destroyed, blood splattered over the mirror and glasses behind the bar. And all the time music he'd punched was playing on the jukebox. *Trailer for sale or rent*; and, *I can't stop loving you*; and, *Time to bum again*; and *That's what you get for loving me:* Roger Miller, Ray Charles, Waylon Jennings.

BEN AWAKENED THE NIGHT of the shooting and heard Marie on the phone, felt her shake him awake in the dim light of the bedroom. She seemed enormously frightened and continued to shake him, as if to awaken herself. She was eight months pregnant.

"He's dead." She spoke softly, seeming terrified, as if some idea she feared had been at last confirmed. "He never had a chance," she said.

"He had plenty." Ben sat up and put his arm around her, forced from his shock.

"They never gave him anything." She bent over and began to cry.

Later, it nearly morning, after coffee and cigarettes, when Marie gave up and went to bed, Ben sat alone at the kitchen table. "Afraid of everything," Art had said. "That's how they are. Every stinking one."

Ben saw Art drunk and talking like he was ready for anything, actually involved with nothing except for a string of girls like the one who shot him. And then, somehow, the idea of Art and Marie got hold of Ben. It came from the way she had cried and carried on about Art. There was something wrong. Sitting there at the table, feeling the knowledge seep around his defenses, Ben knew what it was. He got up from the chair.

She was in the bedroom, curled under the blankets, crying softly. "What is it?" he asked. "There's something going on." She didn't open her eyes, but the crying seemed to slow a little. Ben waited, standing beside the bed, looking down, all the time wondering, as he became more sure, if it had happened in this bed, and all the time knowing it made no difference where it happened. And it was her fault. Not any fault of Art's. Art was what he was. She could have stopped him. Ben's hands felt strange, as if there was something to be done he couldn't recognize. He asked again, hearing his voice harsh and strained. "What is it? Marie?"

She didn't answer. He forced her onto her back and held her there, waiting for her to open her eyes while she struggled silently, twisting her upper body against his grip. His fingers sank into her shoulder and his wrist trembled. They remained like that, forcing against each other. Then she relaxed and opened her eyes. "What is it?" he asked again. "It was something between you and Art, wasn't it?"

Her eyes were changed, shielded. She shook her head. "No," she said. "No."

"He was screwing you, wasn't he? Is it his kid?"

"It was a long time ago," she said.

"My ass." He let go of her shoulder. "That's why you're so tore up. Because you ain't getting any more from him." He walked around the bed, unable for some reason, because of what he was left with, to ask her if it happened here, in this bed. "Isn't that right?" he said. "How come you married me? He turn you down?"

"Because I was afraid of him. I didn't want him. He was just fooling. I wanted you, not him."

Ben slapped her, and she curled quickly again, her hands pressed to her mouth, crying, shoulders hunching. He made her face him. "You ain't getting away," he said. "So I was a nice tame dog, and you took me."

"You'll hurt the baby."

"His goddamned baby!"

"It all broke off when I met you," she said. "He told me to go ahead, that you'd be good to me." It had surprised him when they met that she was with Art, but somehow he'd never until now gotten the idea they had anything going on. "It was only a few times after I knew you," she said. "He begged me."

"So I got stuck with the leavings." He cursed her again, at the same time listening to at least a little of what she said. "He begged me." That was sad. Remembering Art those last years, after he came home to stay, Ben believed her.

"So he dumped you off onto me," Ben said. "I wish I could thank him."

"It wasn't like that. He loved you. He said for me to marry you and be happy."

"So you did. And I was stupid enough to go for it."

"He was a little boy. It was fun, but he was a little boy."

"I'm happy," Ben said, "things worked out so nice for you." She shook her head and didn't answer. Ben wondered what he should do. It was as if he had never been married, had been right in always imagining his life as single. He'd watched his friends settle, seen their kids start to grow up, and it had seemed those were things he was not entitled to, that he was going to grow old in a habit of taverns, rented rooms, separate from the married world. And now he was still there, outside. And she'd kept it all a secret. "You stinking pig," he said slowly.

"Ben, it was a long time ago. Ben."

He was tired and his work was waiting. Maybe it was a long time ago and maybe it wasn't. He left her there crying while he dressed to go out and feed her father's cattle.

In the afternoon she had the house picked up and a meal waiting. She watched while he ate, but they didn't talk. He asked if she wanted to go to the funeral, and she said no and that was all. When he was drinking his coffee, calm now, and so tired his chest ached, he started thinking about Clara. He wondered if she'd known. Wouldn't have made any difference, he thought. Not after everything else.

THREE DAYS LATER, heading for the burial, he was alone and hunched against the wheel, driving through new snow that softly drifted across the highway. His fingers were numb, the broken cracks in the rough calluses ingrained with black. A tire chain ticked a fender, but he kept going. He'd gone out at daylight to feed, a mandatory job that had to be done every day of winter, regardless of other obligations. The rust-streaked Chevrolet swayed on the rutted ice beneath the snow. The steady and lumbering gait of the team he fed with, two massive frost-coated Belgian geldings, the creaking oceanic motion of the hay wagon, was still with him, more real than this.

The Derrick County cemetery was just below the road, almost five miles short of town. They were going to bury Art in the area reserved for charity burials, away from the lanes of Lombardy poplars and old-time lilacs. By dark the grave would be covered with snow. Ben parked and got out, and went over to look down in the hole. Far away in town, the bells of the Catholic church were faintly tolling. Ben stood a moment, then started back toward the car. He sat in the front seat with his hands cupped in his crotch, warming them. After a time, he backed slowly out of the graveyard.

Davanero was on the east side of the valley, scattered houses hung with ice, windows sealed against wind by tacked-on plastic sheeting. The still smoke of house fires rose straight up. Ben drove between lots heaped with snow-covered junk, past shacks with open, hanging doors where drifters lived in summer, into the center of town. The stores were open and a few people moved toward the coffee shops. He felt cut away from everything, as if this were an island in the center of winter.

The OPEN sign hung in the front window of The Tarpaper Shack. Ben wondered if Clara was tending bar and if she intended to go to the funeral. He parked and walked slowly through the snow to the door. The church bells were louder, close and direct now. Inside, the tavern was dark and barnlike, empty except for Clara, who was washing glasses in a metal sink. Ben went to the far end, where Art always sat, and eased onto a stool. "I'd take a shot," he said. "A double. Take one yourself."

"I'm closing up," she said. "So there's no use hanging around." She stayed at the sink and continued to wash the glasses.

"You going to the funeral?" Ben said.

"I'm closing up." Her hands were still in the water. "I guess you need a drink," she said. "Go lock the door."

She was sitting in one of the booths when he got back. "You ain't going to the funeral?" he asked again.

"What good is that?"

"I guess you feel pretty bad."

"I guess." She drank quietly. "I would have took anything off him. Any damned thing. And that stupid bitch kills him. I would have given anything for his kid."

Ben finished his whiskey, and Clara took his glass and went for some more. "To hell with their goddamned funeral," he said.

Clara played some music on the juke box, slow country stuff; and they danced staggering against the stools and the shuffleboard table, holding each other. She pushed him away after a few songs. "If you ain't one hell of a dancer," she said. "Art was a pretty dancer." She sat down in the booth and put an arm on the table and then lay her head alongside it, facing the wall. "Goddamn," she said. "I could cry. I ain't cried since I was a little girl," she said. "Not since then. Not since I was a little girl."

Ben wandered around the barroom, carrying his drink. He called his wife on the telephone. "You bet your sweet ass I'm drunk," he shouted when she answered, then hung up.

"Ain't you some hero," Clara said. She drank what whiskey was left in her glass. "You're nothing," she said. "Absolutely nothing."

Outside, the bells had stopped. Nothing. That was what he felt like. Nothing. Like his hands were without strength to steer the car. He sat awhile in the front seat, then drove to the jail, a gray brick building with heavy wire mesh over the windows.

The deputy, a small bald man in a gray uniform, sat behind a desk in the center of the main room, coffee cup beside him. He smiled when he saw Ben, but he didn't say anything.

"How's chances of seeing that girl?" Ben asked. He didn't know why he'd come. It was just some idea that because she'd hated Art enough to kill him, because of that, maybe she understood and could tell him, Ben, why he wasn't nothing. He knew, even while he spoke, that it was a stupid, drunk idea.

"Okay," the deputy said, after a minute. "Come on. I guess you got a right."

THEY WENT THROUGH two locked doors, back into a large cinder-block room without any windows. Light came from a long fluorescent tube overhead. Two cells were separated by steel bars six inches apart. The room was warm. The girl was sitting on a cot in the left-hand cell, legs crossed, with red hair straight down over her shoulders and wearing a wrinkled blue smock without pockets. She was looking at her hands, which were folded in her lap. "What now?" she said when she looked up. Her voice was surprisingly loud.

"Ben wanted to see you," the deputy said.

"Like a zoo, ain't it." The girl grinned and raised and lowered her shoulders.

"AND YOU'RE NOT one bit sorry?" Ben said. "Just a little bit sorry for what you did?"

"Not one bit," the girl said. "I've had plenty of time to think about that. I'm not. I'm happy. I feel good."

"He wasn't no bad man," Ben said. "Not really. He never really was."

"He sure as hell wasn't Winston Churchill. He never even *tried* to make me happy." She put her hands in her lap.

"I don't see it," Ben said. "No way I can see you're right. He wasn't that bad."

"The thing I liked about him," she said, "was that he was old enough. He was like you. He was old enough to do anything. He could have been nice if he'd wanted."

The deputy laughed.

"I felt so bad before," the girl said, "killing him was easy. The only thing I feel bad about is that I never got down into him and made him crawl around. That's the only thing. I'm sorry about that, but that's all."

"He didn't owe you nothing," Ben said.

The girl looked at the deputy. "Make him leave," she said.

BEN DROVE SLOWLY home in the falling snow. He could only see blurred outlines of the trees on either side of the lane that led to his house. He parked the car, kicked the snow from his boots, and went inside the house. Marie was in the bedroom, sleeping. The dim room was gray and cold, the bed a rumpled island. Marie was on her back, her stomach a mound beneath the blankets. Her mouth gaped a little.

After he got out of his clothes, Ben sat on the edge of the bed. Marie sighed in her sleep and moved a little, but she didn't waken. Ben reached to touch her shoulder and then stopped. Her eyelids flickered open. "Come on," she said. "Get under the covers."

"In a minute," Ben said. He went back out to the kitchen and smoked a cigarette. Then he went back into the bedroom and crawled in beside her and put his hand on her belly, hoping to feel the baby move. He remembered a warm, shirt-sleeve day in February, working with Art, hurrying while they fed a final load of bales to the cattle that trailed behind, eager to get to town, noon sun glaring off wind-glazed fields of snow.

1970s

JOHN LEGGETT BEGAN his seventeen-year tenure as director of the Workshop in 1970. By this time, the Workshop had become an institution, its alumni winning every major literary prize given, its rotating faculty composed each year of writers of national distinction, such as John Cheever and John Irving.

Iowa's success bred dozens of imitators. Where there were only a half dozen M.F.A.-granting creative writing programs in the country before, by the end of the 1970s there were well in excess of a hundred. This success conjured up the inevitable backlash. I have already addressed Nelson Algren's attack on the Workshop, and in fairness to Algren, whose work and spirit I've long admired, I suspect that his bitterness toward Iowa may have been connected to his trials as a writer. During the McCarthy witch-hunts of the 1950s, he was denied a passport to visit his lover Simone de Beauvoir because of his leftist politics. At the same time, Doubleday, fearing any taint of Communist sympathy, refused to publish Algren's excellent book-length essay, *Nonconformity: Writing on Writing*, which went unreleased until 1996, some fifteen years after his death as an isolated, and sadly forgotten, American writer. I dwell on Algren's plight because his resentment of Iowa's "quietism" has some merit. What began as a bold fight on behalf of creative writing and the artistic imagination in the 1920s had become, half a century later, an industry that perhaps had done too good a job of encouraging democratic accessibility to the writing life.

For detractors who see no good in them, the proliferation of creative writing programs bred exactly what Algren loathed—politically unengaged, stylistically timid, and above all, contextually narrow, bourgeois subject matter. The standard workshop product is often the sincere first-person narrator story about his or her dysfunctional family, capped by a maturation-inducing epiphany. (I'm guilty of writing one myself. We all start somewhere.) These stories can be quite affecting. Who can't empathize with a helpless adolescent?

But the Workshop's increasing prestige drew an increasingly mainstream student body, young people often straight out of college, rather than Korean War vets or construction workers. Since writers, especially insecure apprentice writers, relentlessly seek approval, that longed-for state of validation, there's a dangerous tendency to "write for workshop," to produce work that seems to have the greatest chance of receiving the workshop's approbation. Since the majority of the average writing workshop's student body is mid-twenties, white, and middle class, stories based on experiences in that world tend to dominate. This trend virtually supplanted politically engaged fiction in the '70s. As Abraham Rothenberg wrote to Martha Foley while compiling the 1972 *Best American* anthology, "There are more stories about children and old people and the cruelties inflicted on them than I care to read and most of them not very good." Foley also found that the "social consciousness that inflamed Dickens . . . and the 'proletariat' writers of the thirties has been replaced by ethnicity . . . [T]he other extreme seems to have disappeared as well . . . I have read no good stories about the rich in a long time."

The diminished social canvas and moral power of much workshop student writing poses a valid concern. Taken in tandem with the cornucopia of literary journals that publish hundreds of mediocre stories annually, the workshop phenomenon at large could be said to have fulfilled Truman Capote's quip about Kerouac, "That's not writing, it's typing."

But the phenomenon has also provided a hidden boon for literature, one not often credited to the Workshop. Jane Smiley once noted that creative writing workshops do not necessarily make students better writers, but in every case they make them better *readers*. Readers more attuned to the rhetoric employed by a story's narrator and language's relation to truth, evasion, and prejudice. As I write this in the shadow of the 1990s core witch-hunt text, *The Starr Report,* a document that conflates the Constitution of the United States with a Harlequin romance, teaching readers to distinguish between an *objective* narrator and an *unreliable* one amounts to a political act, one that the study of creative writing offers American culture in the service of liberty.

At the aesthetic level, the Workshop method has improved the study of literature. Frank Kermode, one of the twentieth century's greatest literary critics, argued in his memoir *Not Entitled* that "people who have actually written Petrarchan sonnets, villanelles, sestinas, ballades, and so forth, whatever the merit of their performances, actually understand more about poetry than people who haven't." After encountering students who had studied creative writing before enrolling in his literature courses, Kermode admitted, "this is where the study of literature ought to begin"— with creative writing.

Iowa, having the deepest roots of any program in the country, has been able to carry on without any loss of artistic vitality and variety, as the work of this decade's writers attests. From Thom Jones's deft skewering of capitalism's "let the market rule" mania and Stuart Dybek's fablelike love story which shares kinship with the hyperreal tales of Hawthorne, to James Alan McPherson and Allan Gurganus's sublime and loving examinations of worlds now swept up into the myth of our racial past, the '60s experiments with fabulism and metafiction, as well as the political activism of the times, seem to inform the sensibilities of these '70s writers. Ron Hansen and Richard Bausch each deploy a superb control of craft to reimagine the events often encountered in mainstream fiction until they combine high comedy with genuine, unexpected, and gracefully effortless pathos, just as Jayne Anne Phillips and Jane Smiley use realistic surfaces to capture the slippery, difficult-to-articulate emotional worlds that lurk just beneath the clean, well-lighted places their characters inhabit. And Denis Johnson has circumvented the exhaustion of the Joycean form by creating a character, Fuckhead, who's generally so stoned and oblivious that his epiphanies actually become anti-epiphanies. When Fuckhead and his wife wander out into "a town flooded with white, buoyant stones" produced by a passing hailstorm, he distills no *rational* meaning from his ecstatic vision, only the *feeling* that "Birth should have been like that." Johnson discards the neat closure offered by epiphanic endings in favor of an ecstasy, or wonder, bordering on the irrational. Yet, amazingly, Fuckhead's feelings remain crystal clear to the mind of the objective reader.

I WAS LIVING in Iowa City rewriting a Hollywood script when the story "Mouses" came to me. I hadn't written a short story for quite a while and began to wonder if I ever would again. The story I had done prior to "Mouses" was "A Midnight Clear," something that I must have put through thirty drafts. Agony. Nothing much was coming through. Certainly the story-a-month pace of earlier times was over, and as soon as I consigned myself to a career of script rewrites, "Mouses" came to me— one of those rare gifts. It practically wrote itself.

I grew up in Aurora, Illinois, across the street from a dairy where a field was kept from the days when milk wagons were drawn by horses. In fact, I remember the horses, used to ride them. The owner of the dairy was a kindly man and let the horses live their lives out in pleasant retirement there in the field. The kids in my neighborhood played football and baseball in the field. It was a long and narrow strip of land, fenced with white plank boards and surrounded by oak and elm trees. Very bucolic. The perfect retirement home for a hardworking dairy horse. Anyhow, a dairy will have rats. Big ones. I don't think I'm alone in my fear of them. They can do something like 16 mph in a sprint.

One day I remember my brother-in-law, Roger, a tough guy, an ironworker, was out in the garage working on his dragster. It was night and my family was inside playing hearts. I came out to get beer out of the spare refrigerator when a rat popped up in the garage. I didn't think Roger saw it because he made no move whatever, whereas my hair stood on end like instant Don King. It practically caught on fire. Roger picked up a hammer that was at hand, and in a sudden move hammered the rat stone-cold dead. Without taking his eyes off the dragster, he grabbed the dead rat and tossed it into the garbage can before me, the way you see a kid in school slam-dunk a milk carton into a wastebasket. Roger was that way; I was used to it and went back into the house and resumed the card game. A couple hours went by and I made a foray back into the garage to dump pizza cartons. When I lifted the lid of the garbage can, there was the dead rat, bigger than I remembered and I was horrified anew. The memory buried itself deeply within an integument of my brain. Remember those wood-burning kits you got for Christmas? That's what the smell of that memory getting burned into my brain smelled like.

Years go by. I'm in Iowa City. I finished the first draft of my script rewrite, FedExed it to L.A., and received a call from a furious producer who called it the worst piece of crap he had ever seen and demanded that I fly to L.A. for a script conference. I got a first-class plane trip to L.A., spent a night in a suite the size of a large apartment, had a four-minute meeting with the producer (a meeting that could have been easily handled on the phone), then returned to Iowa City. It had been hot and I was sleeping on a mattress I dragged into the basement. Something rodential had been eating my various cereals, and I stashed them in a new place but lay in bed nights thinking of Roger's rat. One morning I felt something like a bug on the top of my foot. I kicked and a tiny mouse flopped on my chest. I got instant Don King hair again. I fled the room like a frightened rabbit. Like a Merrytoons' elephant with a phobia for mice. Hopped in the Saab and drove to the Thriftway where I bought mousetraps. By the next morning I had three victims and the mouse invasion was over.

Three other real-life episodes completed the raw material of my story:

1. A friend was fired from his job as an engineer. For more than two years now he calls me and goes into long raps about what it means to be a "No-Job" in America.
2. The second real incident, the one that occurred at the Greek restaurant, is also a true story. It happened to a friend of mine in Seattle. He wasn't arrested but three waiters chased him more than seven blocks total.
3. The line, "If it works on a chicken, then you know it's gotta work on me." Frank Conroy delivered that line to me one day in front of the Prairie Lights Bookstore in Iowa City. We had just had something to eat at the Mill. I can't remember the exact context of the speech overall, but Frank and I often talked about diabetes and used to discuss various schemes whereby we could continue to smoke cigarettes, mitigating their toxic properties with vitamin E, folic acid, and things of this sort. Frank had an even better line. When his doctor told him to quit smoking his retort was this: "Motherfucker, I would rather die." Frank did quit however.

The voice I used in "Mouses" was similar to the voice I used in "Pickpocket," which appeared in my second collection, *Cold Snap*. The first-person voice often appears to be Easy City but it's far from that. Still, "Mouses" was one of the easiest stories I have ever written. My agent sent it to the *New Yorker* and they ran it almost immediately. Unfortunately that was in the summertime and in a thin issue at that. Magazines pile up unread in summers. Or so goes the rumor. In any case, "Mouses" pushed me into that critical mass territory when I knew I was close to having enough stories for another collection. I began writing them again, easily. There was no "I Want to Live!" No "The Pugilist at Rest," no "Cold Snap" even, but I felt that the stories for *Sonny Liston Was a Friend of Mine* were pretty good overall. Most have either been anthologized or have received honorable mentions in top anthologies. "Mouses," for instance, was an honorable mention in *Best American,* '98. All in all I was happy; the only thing that troubled me was the novella at the end of the book, "You Cheated, You Lied." I started working on my novel again. The proofs to the collection came, and as soon as I returned them I came up with one of my absolute favorite stories to date, too late of course for the collection. Like by two days. I would have liked to have been able to pull that novella and use the last story but it was too late. That story appeared in the December 1998 *Playboy,* and if I live long enough, will appear in the collection subsequent to the publication of my novel.

"Mouses" was my own personal favorite story in this latest collection. It's a story about alienation and, sadly enough, how things are in a high-tech society, hassled, rushed, stressed out, etc. When Anson is fired and becomes mired into "No-jobdom," he gets close to rock bottom. A new job, a few new friends, and he reforms and becomes once again a productive member of society. It's not much of a message, but I wrote it because I know it's going on, that that's how things are now.

Very little makes me laugh. Comics on TV, etc. Nothing. When people try to do routines for me, I often say to them, "Look, I'm sure you're pretty funny and all that, but don't waste your time doing impressions because I won't laugh, you'll get depressed, and it just isn't worth it. Do them elsewhere." I would tell this to Chris Rock, Eddie Murphy, Richard Pryor. But "Mouses" is funny. I know that I wrote it and should be more humble, but who among you didn't think it was piss-in-your-pants funny? Who didn't get a couple of chuckles? Huh? I rest my case.

THOM JONES

THOM JONES

Mouses

RODENTS INFILTRATED my place at the first hard frost of the fall. I had a minor premonition that this would happen, and then, lo, it happened. For a couple of days it was in the back of my mind, in the twilight area where minor worries flourish—no big alarm bell rang, because most of the stuff you worry about never comes to pass. But then came the evidence, the irrefutable fact that not only did said perpetrators (previously unknown to me) claw and chew through a box of Wheat Thins, they defecated at the scene of the crime, leaving sizable pellets behind. Apparently "Don't shit where you eat" isn't in the rodent codebook. Hygiene is not a big concern with them. At first, I was in a state of denial. My place is sealed as tight as a drum. How could they get in? Also, I was thinking, I don't need this now. I really *do not* need this. I was facing problems at work. There were rumors of a cutback at the plant. In spite of my seniority—I've been an engineer for ten years—I knew I was high on the shit list. I'm a convenient target. Why? Because I'm very short in stature. Five feet nothing. And I have a slight spinal deformity—a hump. No matter what goes wrong at that hellhole, I get blamed. "Anson, the midget, did it." A computer goes down, blueprints get lost, milk sours in the lunchroom refrigerator: "The midget did it!"

So at first I buried my head in the sand. I had woken up late that day, no morning coffee, and my feet had barely hit the floor when I saw the chewed-to-shit Wheat Thins box. What a sight! It looked as if a wolverine had gone through it. There I was, standing in my pajamas in a state of complete disbelief. This was no time to conduct a full-scale pest investigation. I was late for work.

That night in bed, when fears are greatly magnified, not only was I worried about my suck-ass job, I began to think that the intruder might be a big black rat with an appetite for human flesh. Jurassic. The Wheat Thins box looked like it had been blasted by a shotgun and, as I said, the waste pellets were mighty big. For all I knew there could be a whole pack of vermin running around my place bearing disease and pestilence. Off a ship from Africa or something. Can you get rabies from *proximity*? That's what I was thinking. About 3 A.M. a miasma of moldy rodential air came wafting into my bedroom. I hadn't noticed *that* before. Somewhere, unseen, these vermin were stirring about, revved up into a state of high activity, giving off odoriferous secretions.

The next morning I was up early to see what dirty work had occurred during the night. I entered the kitchen with a heavy brogan shoe in my hand, and it was just as I thought: they had been at it again. Bolder than ever! I had thrown out the contaminated food, and closed the cupboard tight, but—hey!—no problem: the culprits had gone to the breadbox! Its lid was ajar, a good inch and a half. Had I closed it? You'd think you'd remember a pertinent detail like that, especially if you're in a batten-down-the-hatches frame of mind. And what if I *had* closed the breadbox? This rodent must be very strong. This rodent might very well be a rat—a rat that bench-pressed No. 3 vegetable cans and probably played tackle for the local ratball team. Black Bart, the Norway power rat. Fangola from Borneo.

On no sleep, work that morning was an ongoing hell. I had to sneak out to my car at lunch and catch a nap, but I woke up three hours later not in the least refreshed: it wasn't a nap, it was a damn coma. The boss called me in: "Yeah yeah, ying ying, ya ya, where in the *hell* have you been?" Put the fear of God in me. I stayed late working on the annual report, which made no sense to me anymore. I was just sitting there, "pretending," which is a lot harder than actually working. You could chop logs all day, stack thirty cords of wood, and not get as tired. When the boss bagged out, I waited five minutes and then left. My back was killing me. The hump veers toward my left shoulder. It was all hot and knotted up like an angry fist. Just complete agony.

I stopped at the supermarket for some Advil and asked a stocker where the mousetraps were. Evidently, there'd been a run on rodent traps. "Cold weather," he said.

I said, "You haven't been selling *rat* traps?"

"Rat traps, yeah, sold a few," he said, pointing them out. They were huge rectangular slabs of pinewood with monstrous springs and rectangular clap bars made of heavy-gauge metal. Big enough to snag a Shetland pony.

"Whoa, man!" I said. "I hope I don't need one of those."

"Where do you live?" he asked me, and I told him the neighborhood and he said no doubt my problem was mice. Rats don't frequent upscale places, he said. They go for the shitholes where people leave garbage around. He couldn't guarantee it but he was ninety percent sure. Then he left me alone in the aisle to inspect the merchandise. I chided myself for being melodramatic. No rats, just some mice. And others were having the same problem. I was reassured. I was fortunate to be able to get any traps at all. There were only five left and I bought all five.

I thought of using poison, going for complete and certain eradication, but I wanted to see the corpses. Your mouse poisoner is like a bomber pilot flying miles above a war zone—the bloodless battle. That's cool, but sometimes you hear of poisoned mice dying in parts of the house that are inaccessible to the homeowner and giving off a horrible smell. People start yanking off drywall panels to get to the smelly things, knocking down chimneys, tearing up the foundation.

Vacor, for instance, a rodenticide that looks like cornmeal, destroys the beta cells of the pancreas, causing instant diabetes, followed by chest pain, impaired intellect, coma, and finally death. A diabetic mouse with severe hyperglycemia will develop an incredible thirst and head outside to look for water—you don't have to tear your house apart tracking down odors. Strychnine is another possibility. An overdose of strychnine destroys the nerves and causes convulsions. The sick rodent cannot bear noise or bright light. It dies a prolonged, agonizing death of utter torment. That kind of mouse wouldn't opt for the hustle and bustle of the outdoors. That's a hide-in-the-drywall mouse.

All in all, the trap is more humane. But I was so angry at the inconvenience I had been through—disturbed sleep, fright, the loss of snack foods—that the thought of a mouse writhing in pain out in a field somewhere did not bother my conscience in the slightest. The opposite was the case. It gave me satisfaction. Die, suckah!

I SET THREE of the traps in the kitchen using peanut butter as bait. I put another in the bedroom and one behind the living-room couch. That night, moments after I turned off the lights, I heard one of the kitchen traps go off. *Wap!* Man, I almost hit the ceiling. I wasn't sure if I heard a shriek or not. It all happened so fast. In the blink of an eye, an execution.

I'm embarrassed to admit that I was a little afraid to confront the consequences. But what could I do? I picked up my heavy shoe and went out. The victim was a gray mouse with broad, powerful shoulders, prickly chin whiskers, red beady eyes, and a short stumpy tail. Its mouth was open, exposing a crimson tongue and sharp yellow teeth. Ahggh! The trap had snapped its neck. I picked up the trap and quickly tossed it in the garbage. How that mouse had so totally destroyed the Wheat Thins was beyond me, but such are the mysteries of life. There, I'm thinking. Done! Half an hour later I was sawing logs.

In the morning I got up and went to the kitchen to make coffee and I saw another mouse, this one still alive, with one paw caught in a trap. It was trying to drag-ass out of there. I got my work gloves out of the garage and picked up the trap, the mouse hanging down from it, wriggling. I put the mouse in a coffee can, and then—I don't know what made me do it, maybe because Christmas was coming—I punched some holes in it for air. The mouse's foot was smashed, but otherwise it was OK. I set the can in the garage and went off to work.

I was tired again, with moderate-to-severe hunch pains. Except for short-lived bursts of activity when my boss passed by with a scowl on his repugnant face, all I could do was sit at my desk and "pretend" all day. Even though I'd got some sleep, I was thrashed, body and soul.

When I got home I threw some wood shavings into an old aquarium and put the mouse in there. If it was in pain, I couldn't tell. I gave it a little dish of water and some cornflakes. The thing was this: I couldn't stand having an invisible invader prowling around in my house at will, but with the animal caged and me in full control, I could tolerate it. I mean the mouse was just trying to get by like the rest of us. I named him Al.

After a few days, Al's foot turned black and fell off. He wouldn't eat for a while. I think he had a fever. A close call with death. I put out some whole-wheat bread with peanut butter on it. He loved that. He was going to weather the crisis. He started to gain weight. I found a hamster wheel at a garage sale and the guy just gave it to me to get rid of it.

That's when Al began his rehab therapy. Without his foot, he got by hobbling, but his whole left shoulder was weak. On the wheel, he struggled and became disoriented. To encourage him, I put his favorite treat, a Hershey's chocolate square, in a little box in front of the wheel. Stick and carrot. Pretty soon Al was running his ass and lost all the weight from his peanut-butter days of convalescence. With treats to motivate him, he'd put in five hours a night on the wheel. One night, just as I was getting him his Hershey's square, he hopped into my palm and let me hand-feed him. It was a momentous transition. Suddenly this little wild animal was on the road to domestication. He trusted me. I felt like I was in tune with the universe. But not for long.

THE NEXT DAY at work, the boss stuck his ugly face inches from my own. "You're terminated, Anson. Clean out your desk! You have one hour."

The heartless bastard. I'd known it was coming, but I was devastated just the same. He couldn't wait until after Christmas. I immediately drove to the unemployment office. Filled out the forms. Stood around and waited. Geez, what a seedy stink-ass joint.

If you're an engineer, a job in these times is the hardest thing in the world to find. There are thousands of engineers.

I put together a résumé and scanned the want ads. There was nothing. One of the no-jobs at the unemployment office told me that nobody hires during the Christmas season, so just chill out.

At night I watched TV. It was me and Al, with him crawling up my arm and on top of my head and whatnot. Once in a while out slipped a mouse pellet but what are you going to do? Al is my friend, so it was no biggie. I wondered if he missed his life in the wild. I wondered if he was bored. If I let him go in the spring, with no foot, what would happen?

One night after a futile and discouraging day of handing out résumés, I popped over to the pet shop and bought a companion for Al. A pet mouse cost a dollar and eighty-nine cents. I got a female and named her Angela. I put her in with Al and they sniffed each other out for a bit, but when I turned my back they started fighting. Angela was kicking ass. She bit the piss out of Al and he was left bleeding all over, especially from his stub. I broke up the fight, stuck her in the coffee can, and put her in the dark garage for punishment. Then I put hydrogen peroxide on Al's wounds. If it wasn't for the incredible cardiovascular reserve he'd built up running the wheel, I think she would have killed him.

I took to hand-feeding Al again—I had to—and he eventually came around. He seemed to like the mouse chow I got him. I figure that animals have body wisdom and will eat the right thing if you provide it for them. Pretty soon Al was on the wheel again, and we were watching TV together at night, and everything was just hunky. He padded around on my scalp with his three little paws, up and down my arm, with no fear at all. It was like we'd been pals in some previous lifetime. Bosom buddies.

I fashioned a divider panel for the aquarium and took Angela out of the punishment can. But I was still hating her. I gave her nothing but peanut butter. I denied her access to the exercise wheel. And in a couple of weeks she was a disgusting tub of lard. Meanwhile, Al, on his good diet, exercise regime, and nightly entertainment, was the very picture of health. Angela was practically eating her body weight in peanut butter every day. She ballooned up. I started weighing her on a postal scale, and one time she bit me. She didn't break the skin, but after the infraction it was three more days in the punishment can.

BY NOW I HAD BEEN TO EVERY FUCKING ENGINEERING FIRM in the city. Nobody was hiring. If you're a senior engineer, forget it. They hire a guy out of college, pay him a substandard salary, and get him to do the work of ten people. I reformulated my résumé and started looking for a job as a technician.

Angela was still eating peanut butter by the tablespoon. One day I came home and she was lying on her back with four feet in the air, stiff. Heart attack. In just six weeks' time. I enjoy peanut butter myself. I had been carrying peanut-butter sandwiches in my briefcase as I canvassed the city looking for work. I switched to lowfat turkey. It costs a fortune and, hungerwise, it doesn't satisfy, but I got to thinking of all the stuff I had eaten in my life, the whole pile of it. In peanut butter alone, there would be a warehouse. Cigarettes? Truck trailers full. After what I'd seen happen to Angela in six weeks, I felt lucky to be alive. I squared my diet away.

I got some Just for Men and colored my hair jet-black. I began to figure that my age was another handicap. But then one of the no-jobs at unemployment asked me if I'd lost my mind. "Anson, you look like Bela Lugosi!" Another said, "Man, that's a dye job you can spot a mile away." Some skaters on the street asked me if I was the singer Roy Orbison. Maybe they said this because I was wearing a pair of shades, or maybe they were just dicking with me. I said, "No, man, I'm Junior fuckin' Walker."

When I got home and checked myself out in the mirror, I saw that the no-jobs were right about my hair. It was too dark and it made my skin look pale. It was almost green. I looked like an undertaker. Plus, I'd lost weight, and my clothes were too big. Overnight, I had metamorphosed from a Stage One no-job to a Stage Three. Up all night with pain, I finally dropped off and didn't get up till four in the afternoon. Too late to go out. I didn't shave. I was thinking, What's the point of looking? They don't want to hire you. Capitalism sucks. The big companies just want to get rich. I got to hating everybody.

I DROVE OVER to the pet store and bought two dozen mice and a separate wire cage for each. You read stuff in medical reports about how a certain drug or vitamin did something in some study but it will be five years before the general public can get it. Or you read that something has produced miraculous results in chickens but they haven't tried it on humans yet. I'm the kind that figures, hell, if it works on a chicken it's going to work on everybody. I mean, if some guy spots mold on bread and turns it into penicillin, why not me? If I can't get a job, maybe I'll just go out and win the Nobel Prize.

I put the mice on a variety of diets and subjected them to various stresses. I kept a control group and fed its members the same mouse chow I fed Al. Other mice—eating a diet similar to my own, drinking a proportionate amount of coffee, and keeping the same hours—were dead in five weeks. Challenge, a momentary adaptation to stress, then exhaustion and death. I accepted the results with equanimity. I knew what was in the cards for me; once again I had evidence. Maybe I was lucky to have been canned. What I needed now was a plan: I wasn't going to be a victim anymore.

At 3 A.M. I took off my white lab coat, washed my hands, and called up my ex-boss. *Brrringgg! Ding-a-ling! Brrringgg!* When he answered, I hung up! Ah, ha, ha, shit! I then had a snack and about twenty minutes later—just when he'd fallen back to sleep—I called again. Ha, ha, ha, fuck! I pictured him lying there seething.

I put another batch of mice on a regime mimicking my old schedule, but I fortified their diets with vitamins. They died in just *under* five weeks, confirming something I always suspected: vitamins, especially the kind that have a strong smell, not only make you feel bad but can hasten your demise! The result held even for the mice that had the antioxidants cocktail: flavonoids, soy, red-wine extract, beta carotene, etc.

To some mice I gave huge amounts of coffee. Coffee mice became very aggressive and would often bite me. For each attempted bite, it was no coffee and three days in a punishment can. It skewed the validity of the experiments, but I already suspected the ultimate outcome. They say coffee is pretty much harmless, but after studying a coffee mouse's brains at autopsy I calculated otherwise. Shrunken thymus glands, a swelling in the cranial cavity, and a shriveling of the adrenal glands. They could run the most complicated labyrinths I constructed, but they were burning it at both ends.

ONE NIGHT I called my ex-boss and he fucking *made* me. He said he got Caller I.D. and knew it was me on the line. He threatened to turn me in to the police. I didn't say boo, man, I just hung up. I worried until dawn. I could hear my heart thumping in my chest. Was what I'd done a jailable offense? So much for the job recommendation.

And then, lo, one of my hundreds of résumés bore fruit! I got a call from a large electronics firm, went in, and took some grueling tests involving math, calculus, even physics. I was interrogated by a panel of hard-ass guys with starched white shirts and stern faces. At the conclusion, they said I was one of fifteen people being considered. Two hundred applicants had already been rejected. They told me that employees were subject to random drug tests. They said they would do a background check. Then they'd call me.

THE HARDIEST OF MY MICE turned out to be the swimmers and walkers. The walkers were put on exercise wheels equipped with speed governors and forced to march at a 9 mph pace eight hours a day. Along the bottoms of their cages were metal grids wired to give them an electric shock if they decided to hop off the wheel and shirk their duty. A few rebelled, but the rebellion was dealt with easily: I merely dialed up the electricity. This made me realize the folly of my so-called punishment cans. A nice dark spot in a quiet room was not "punishment." True punishment, such as that reserved for recidivist biters, now took place in a proper punishment room with hot bright lights and severe jolts of electricity. A yoga mouse that I happened to take a dislike to, a little Hare Krishna crybaby who couldn't handle the 9 mph pace, died after thirty-four hours of continuous exercise. The shock burns on its feet, tail, and stomach were secondary to cardiac arrest. Hey! I'm sorry, but it's survival of the fittest. My tests demonstrated that a reasonable amount of hard physical labor each day produced health and contentment. Bodies are made for work, not idleness.

MAN, WHAT ELSE could go wrong? I was standing on a corner, minding my own business, and this no-job I knew, a Stage Three, came along and offered to buy me dinner at a Greek restaurant. I said sure, thinking some windfall had come his way. We did a fair amount of drinking and then had this big meal, several courses, with rounds of ouzo for the house. Then he got nervous for some reason. When he reached the register, some drastic thought passed through his brain like a dark cloud.

He said to me, "Have you got any money?" I told him I had about sixty cents, and he stood there for a moment. He looked up, down, over his shoulder. Suddenly he yelled "Run!" and bolted. I was standing flat-footed. A couple of waiters took off after him. So did the cook, with a fifteen-inch blade. What a shocker! Too late, I ran the other way, and the older waiters started after me. Six long blocks they chased me. The no-job got away. Me, I was arrested. The police handcuffed me, shoved me into a patrol car, and whipped me off to the precinct station with their lights flashing. I spent the weekend in jail and finally arranged bond on Monday morning. To cap things off, when I got home I found Al in his aquarium with his three feet in the air, stone dead. I won't lie to you. It was very upsetting. I burst into tears. The lady living above me heard my raking sobs and knocked on the door to see if I was OK.

HANNIBAL WAS A WELL-EXERCISED GLADIATOR MOUSE. He had a piebald coat, white and tan. I fed him a diet of meat, vegetables, and grain. I gave him testosterone injections from ground-up mouse testicles. He got little boils at the injection sites, but he also became supermuscular. Hannibal won the first annual Gladiator Mouse Championship, killing in succession two swimmers, two walkers, a coffee mouse, and the remaining population of yoga mice—seventeen victims in all. I just kept throwing them in, one after another, getting more and more excited by the ferociousness of the battle. I felt like Caligula. Oh, man! It was too much.

Hannibal's capacity for work and his resistance to the usual stressors, including the punishment sessions, exceeded that of any of my previous specimens. His entire torso was pure muscle. The discipline he showed on the wheel, in the maze, in the pool, or defending his life in the gladiator pit, his appetite for work, and his willingness to meet any challenge made him my most interesting success. I knew I was on to something huge if only there was some way to dampen his murderous impulses, his relentless aggression, and his compulsive sexuality. To be able to harness all that drive and latent productivity. What a challenge!

I was able to farm more testosterone, and I injected it into female mice. The results were dramatic—similar to those which had occurred with Hannibal. But the female supermice, with a natural supply of estrogen, were more tractable. I was at a crossroads in my research. Was this the answer? A female named Cynthia defeated Hannibal in a tooth-and-nail gladiator bout. Yet she stopped short of killing the former champion. I removed his battered body from the little arena and administered adrenaline to his wounds, and then Hannibal bit me on the quick of my fingernail. Yeowza! What happened next was a blur. I slammed Hannibal against the wall like Randy Johnson hurling a 98 mph fastball. He bounced off and started scrambling around on the floor. I gave chase and stomped him to death in my stocking feet. What an ingrate! And after all I'd done for him.

A few weeks later I was at the university veterinary school, checking out some books on mouse anatomy, when it seemed to me that people were purposefully avoiding me. It went beyond the normal thing you get from being little. Was my fly open? Did I have something in my nose? As I walked up to the checkout desk, I smelled B.O. I put two and two together and realized that the B.O. was coming from me. I tested my breath by licking the back of my wrist and smelling it. It was awful. How far had I sunk? I had a brief panic attack outside and quickly made for home. After I'd had a long bath, the episode passed off.

With the help of the textbooks, I started harvesting other mouse hormones, even though the organ systems were often so tiny I felt I was performing microsurgery. It was also frustrating. The boils Cynthia developed from growth-hormone injections turned into large hard lumps that eventually proved fatal: upon autopsy, I discovered that these were tumors. Cynthia's liver nourished tumors as well. One by one, all my female supermice developed the same symptoms. Another dead end.

I never got the call from the firm that interviewed me. A month had passed, so, taking the bull by the horns, I called the firm and said that I had enjoyed our meeting and would be grateful for a job. I knew it was too late, and it made me angry. Just because I'm five feet tall! I hinted at the possibility of a discrimination suit. A vice president got on the line and told me that my size had nothing to do with it. They were impressed by my qualifications. I had the job in the bag, but my former boss had given me a poor recommendation: he said I made harassing phone calls at three in the morning. The man said I could have even skated on that charge, but he'd noticed an item in the police blotter involving an incident at a Greek restaurant. I was so shaken by this disclosure that I said it must have been someone else with the same name as mine. A transparent lie. Despondent, I went out and bought two six-packs of beer. The next day I couldn't get out of bed. Nor on the following. I got a violent, three-day hangover and vowed never to drink again.

Court. Oh, God! The very thought of it. I went over to the restaurant and offered full restitution. Nothing doing, they said. I tried to explain what had happened but they made furious Greek gestures at me—God knows what they meant. They said, "See you in court, haffa pint! Broke-a-back. Shorty pants!"

Well, wait a minute, I said. It was the other guy's fault. I gave them the whole story. They said, Tell us who the other guy is and we'll drop the charge. Actually, I don't know the guy. I mean I "know" him, but he told so many lies I don't know if up is down with him. At one point he told me he was an actor and had been engaged to Catherine Deneuve. He was a smoothie, and handsome—I half believed him.

I threw myself on the mercy of the court and got reamed with a two-hundred-and-fifty-dollar fine, court costs, six months probation, and a hundred hours of community service. Plus, now I've got a record. Also, I got hit for a hundred and fourteen in unpaid traffic tickets.

After court I lost interest in the mice and fell into a deep, Stage Five no-job depression. The Nobel Prize? Screw it. I went to a clinic and got a prescription for antidepressants and anti-anxiety drugs. On them, all I wanted to do was sleep. Twenty hours? No problem. It was a pleasant escape. After years of insomnia, I was in heaven.

But the medicine made me fat. Bloat weight. I gained back all that I'd lost. Pretty soon I couldn't get into the clothes that had once been hanging on me. I got a huge gut, a pair of thighs like twin water heaters, and a fat ass that stuck out like a clown's. I'd never thought that I could sink this low. I resorted to wearing sweatpants.

I started setting my alarm clock for late-afternoon appointments and even then I missed about half of them. I wondered how I would ever reassimilate myself into the mainstream of American life. I felt so low and so bad I didn't want to talk to anybody. The landlord came by: people were complaining about a smell. I didn't want him to see my mouse lab. The way things were going it would have been a federal bust—Dr. Mengele Nabbed at Last! I told the landlord I was taking care of a pair of hamsters for a friend, don't worry, I'll deal with the smell. He said, "Man, Anson, you gained weight." Well, no shit, Sherlock!

I cleaned out the mouse cages, replacing the soiled sawdust with fresh cedar shavings. Then it occurred to me to put the mice on this antidepressant that was kicking my ass so bad. Whenever I tried to get off it, I got this full-body pulsar buzz, and everything began to vibrate until I took another pill. I calibrated doses and started medicating the mice. Within three hours all of them were out. Dead? I couldn't tell. But it turned out no, they weren't dead—they were in comas. I wondered if that's what I looked like at night. One slept for two days and didn't change positions: frozen in one posture. I put another on the punishment wheel, and it was oblivious to the shocks. Blue sparks were popping off its paws and it ignored them.

I mentioned earlier that most of the bad stuff you worry about never comes to pass. But sometimes, I was now discovering, it does. You fall into a kind of Bermuda Triangle of hard-ass reality. How long was this going to go on? I asked myself. I finally managed to get off the drugs by taking smaller and smaller doses. And slowly the bloat weight came off. I phoned for an interview for a technician's job at a factory less than a mile from my building, and I was hired that very day. I couldn't believe it. The job was a piece of cake, too. I went in and read the paper and drank coffee for an hour before anyone got ambitious. There were numerous breaks and good camaraderie all the way around. Even so, it was hard to get through a day. I didn't have the stamina. Coming back from Stage Five was tough business. In the annals of no-jobdom, it's rare. Almost unheard of. I had pulled off a big one.

Pretty soon some of the design engineers were hanging out with me, asking my advice on projects and so on. One thing led to another, and I was promoted to senior engineer and making a third more than I got at the last place. It was easy duty, this job. I got into the work and—zing!—the time just flew. I never had a job I *liked* before. I didn't think such a thing existed.

THE MICE, as they died off, I buried in little toilet-paper tubes. They have a life expectancy of three years. I didn't replace them. Ashes to ashes, dust to dust. What I did was pretty unconscionable. Absolute power, as they say. I'm not proud of my behavior. I had been living without checks and balances. The crap I pulled makes me think of what the space invaders will do to us if they conquer the world. Make slaves of us, eat us, flay us alive and torture us, do every kind of sinister thing in the book. There's a dark side to intelligent beings, an irrational craving for war, personal defilement, and reckless destruction, even if we know better. So if aliens are out there and they do come down I don't expect good things. Aliens aren't out there flying around on errands of mercy or benevolence. To them, we're just so much protein. We're calories. When the space invaders take over, it's the end of the human era. Before that happens, I want to get in a few good times—travel to Ireland, learn how to dance, take tuba lessons, who knows. Happiness is like the gold in the Yukon mines, found only now and then, as it were, by the caprices of chance. It comes rarely in chunks or boulders but most often in the tiniest of grains. I'm a free-floater now, happy to take what little comes my way. A grain here, a grain there. What more can you ask for?

MY DAUGHTER, RACHEL, is visiting me here during her vacation from college. Yesterday one of her friends, Venice Monogan, came by to see Rachel. Venice is now entering her third year at Princeton and has plans to enter the business world. Rachel herself wants to be a writer. She has already begun planning how she will spend her junior year abroad; either in Ghana or in Italy. I told both girls that the world they live in now is radically different from the world in which I and Alfreda Monogan, Venice's mother, grew up. They would not be able to understand it.

I grew up under complete segregation in Savannah, Georgia. I attended a black college in Atlanta, armed with only a change of underwear, one suit, and a National Defense Student Loan. It was expected that I would work my way through college, as a waiter or as a janitor. But it happened that in the fall of 1961, while I was getting a haircut in the dorm room of a man named Dewey, his roommate came in, just off "the road." His name was Ira Kemp, and he talked about all the money he had made, and the sights he had seen, "running" as a dining car waiter between Chicago and Seattle on the Great Northern Railroad. I asked him if I could apply for such a job. He gave me the name of a man named James Hall, who was the assistant superintendent in charge of hiring dining car waiters for the summer. I wrote to Mr. Hall, and he responded. He told me that he planned to visit Atlanta in order to hire college boys for the summer months, when the line was most busy. To make this short, I was hired, along with a number of other young men, and in late May we took trains from Atlanta to Chicago and then on to St. Paul.

That first train trip proved to be my introduction to the larger world. The train out of Atlanta was segregated, so all black people sat in the "black" coach. We could not use the snack car or the dining room. But after midnight, at Chattanooga, Tennessee, a black man with a food cart got on the train at our car to sell snacks to the black people. He whispered, "This is the Mason-Dixon line. Y'all don't have to sit in this car anymore. You can go up to the white cars." Well, nobody moved. This is what segregation does to the human spirit. It makes you think of freedom as a potential crime. When we got to Chicago, those of us going on to St. Paul had to transfer to the Great Northern. Aboard that train the entire car was suddenly white. I think that mine was the only black face. I am saying here that a very slow psychological explosion began to take place as I realized that I would have to learn how to make my way in a world totally different from the world in which I had grown up. I was eighteen at that time. When we got to St. Paul, I was hungry. I walked into the depot restaurant, sat down next to a white female and her child, and ordered a hamburger and a glass of milk. I kept waiting for someone, even a policeman, to order me out of the place. This was the extent of the psychological damage that had been done to me.

The larger world opened up more when, after being trained as a waiter, I began to make "runs." I began to learn from the other waiters, through their stories and comments, that a whole world of folklore had been created by many generations of dining car waiters. In point of fact, in those days of segregation the dining car waiters and the Pullman porters were the aristocrats of the black group. They traveled widely, knew about first-class styles, conversed with upper-class people. They abstracted the styles they encountered and brought them back into the black community. What most fascinated me about them were the "moves" they had evolved in order to ensure that six waiters and five cooks (black waiters, white cooks) would be able to cooperate in a very tight dining car space. Have you ever watched a stewardess on an airline going through demonstrating for the passengers the nature of the safety equipment aboard the flight? Their moves are "dancelike." I have often thought, while watching them, that they shared with the dining car waiters a dance-like efficiency. A signal like, "Move your booty, Judy" or "Skin your dick" was a warning from another waiter, carrying a loaded tray, to "swing" out of his way. But best of all were the stories they would tell around the lunch table or around the dining table or in the crew car at night. They would tell stories about the texture of the lives they had led and about the great waiters of the past, the "waiter's waiter."

I know now that all these waiters were trying to pass on their memories of a dying way of life. I know now that I was able to get the job in the first place because the Great Northern needed to avoid hiring permanent people who would expect pensions from the company. Instead, they hired college boys for the summer months, boys who would not remain in St. Paul and who would not get involved in union agitation against the company. The expansion of the airlines, the beginnings of Amtrak, the development of interstate highway systems—had begun to make the Great Railroads extinct. There was a sense of impending tragedy among the waiters, and years later, when I wrote this story, I made up a character named Doc Craft as a symbol of the best that they were. The "waiter's waiter."

JAMES ALAN MCPHERSON

JAMES ALAN MCPHERSON

A Solo Song: For Doc

SO YOU WANT TO KNOW THIS BUSINESS, youngblood: So you want to be a Waiter's Waiter? The Commissary gives you a book with all the rules and tells you to learn them. And you do, and think that is all there is to it. A big, thick black book. Poor youngblood.

Look at me. *I* am a Waiter's Waiter. I know all the moves, all the pretty, fine moves that big book will never teach you. *I* built this railroad with my moves; and so did Sheik Beasley and Uncle T. Boone and Danny Jackson, and so did Doc Craft. That book they made you learn came from our moves and from our heads. There was a time when six of us, big men, danced at the same time in that little Pantry without touching and shouted orders to the sweating paddies in the kitchen. There was a time when they *had* to respect us because our sweat and our moves supported them. We knew the service and the paddies, even the green dishwashers, knew that we did and didn't give us the crap they pull on you.

Do you know how to sneak a Blackplate to a nasty cracker? Do you know how to rub asses with five other men in the Pantry getting their orders together and still know that you are a man, just like them? Do you know how to bullshit while you work and keep the paddies in their places with your bullshit? Do you know how to breathe down the back of an old lady's dress to hustle a bigger tip?

No. You are summer stuff, youngblood. I am old, my moves are not so good anymore, but I know this business. The Commissary hires you for the summer because they don't want to let anyone get as old as me on them. I'm sixty-three, but they can't fire me: I'm in the Union. They can't lay me off for fucking up: I know this business too well. And so they hire you, youngblood, for the summer when the tourists come, and in September you go away with some tips in your pocket to buy pussy and they wait all winter for me to die. I *am* dying, youngblood, and so is this business. Both of us will die together. There'll always be summer stuff like you, but the big men, the big trains, are dying every day and everybody can see it. And nobody but us who are dying with them gives a damn.

Look at the big picture at the end of the car, youngblood. That's the man who built this road. He's in your history books. He's probably in that big black bible you read. He was a great man. He hated people. He didn't want to feed them but the government said he had to. He didn't want to hire me, but he needed me to feed the people. I know this, youngblood, and that is why that book is written for you and that is why I have never read it. That is why you get nervous and jump up to polish the pepper and salt shakers when the word comes down the line that an inspector is getting on at the next stop. That is why you warm the toast covers for every cheap old lady who wants to get coffee and toast and good service for sixty-five cents and a dime tip. You know that he needs you only for the summer and that hundreds of youngbloods like you want to work this summer to buy that pussy in Chicago and Portland and Seattle. The man uses you, but he doesn't need you. But me he needs for the winter, when you are gone, and to teach you something in the summer about this business you can't get from that big black book. He needs me and he knows it and I know it. That is why I am sitting here when there are tables to be cleaned and linen to be changed and silver to be washed and polished. He needs me to die. That is why I am taking my time. I know it. And I will take his service with me when I die, just like the Sheik did and like Percy Fields did, and like Doc.

Who are they? Why do I keep talking about them? Let me think about it. I guess it is because they were the last of the Old School, like me. We made this road. We got a million miles of walking up and down these cars under our feet. Doc Craft was the Old School, like me. He was a Waiter's Waiter. He danced down these aisles with us and swung his tray with the roll of the train, never spilling in all his trips a single cup of coffee. He could carry his tray on two fingers, or on one and a half if he wanted, and he knew all the tricks about hustling tips there are to know. He could work anybody. The girls at the Northland in Chicago knew Doc, and the girls at the Haverville in Seattle, and the girls at the Step-Inn in Portland and all the girls in Winnipeg knew Doc Craft.

But wait. It is just 1:30 and the first call for dinner is not until 5:00. You want to kill some time; you want to hear about the Old School and how it was in my day. If you look in that black book you would see that you should be polishing silver now. Look out the window; this is North Dakota, this is Jerry's territory. Jerry, the Unexpected Inspector. Shouldn't you polish the shakers or clean out the Pantry or squeeze oranges, or maybe change the linen on the tables? Jerry Ewald is sly. The train may stop in the middle of this wheatfield and Jerry may get on. He lives by that book. He knows where to look for dirt and mistakes. Jerry Ewald, the Unexpected Inspector. He knows where to look; he knows how to get you. He got Doc.

Now you want to know about him, about the Old School. You have even put aside your book of rules. But see how you keep your finger in the pages as if the book was more important than what I tell you. That's a bad move, and it tells on you. You will be a waiter. But you will never be a Waiter's Waiter. The Old School died with Doc, and the very last of it is dying with me. What happened to Doc? Take your finger out of the pages, youngblood, and I will tell you about a kind of life these rails will never carry again.

When your father was a boy playing with himself behind the barn, Doc was already a man and knew what the thing was for. But he got tired of using it when he wasn't much older than you, and he set his mind on making money. He had no skills. He was black. He got hungry. On Christmas Day in 1916, the story goes, he wandered into the Chicago stockyards and over to a dining car waiting to be connected up to the main train for the Chicago-to-San Francisco run. He looked up through the kitchen door at the chef storing supplies for the kitchen and said: "I'm hungry."

"What do you want *me* to do about it?" the Swede chef said.

"I'll work," said Doc.

That Swede was Chips Magnusson, fresh off the boat and lucky to be working himself. He did not know yet that he should save all extra work for other Swedes fresh off the boat. He later learned this by living. But at that time he considered a moment, bit into one of the fresh apples stocked for apple pie, chewed considerably, spit out the seeds and then waved the black on board the train. "You can eat all you want," he told Doc. "But you work all I tell you."

He put Doc to rolling dough for the apple pies and the train began rolling for Doc. It never stopped. He fell in love with the feel of the wheels under his feet clicking against the track and he got the rhythm of the wheels in him and learned, like all of us, how to roll with them and move with them. After that first trip Doc was never at home on the ground. He worked everything in the kitchen from putting out dough to second cook, in six years. And then, when the Commissary saw that he was good and would soon be going for one of the chef's spots they saved for the Swedes, they put him out of the kitchen and told him to learn this waiter business; and told him to learn how to bullshit on the other side of the Pantry. He was almost thirty, youngblood, when he crossed over to the black side of the Pantry. I wasn't there when he made his first trip as a waiter, but from what they tell me of that trip I know that he was broke in by good men. Pantryman was Sheik Beasley, who stayed high all the time and let the waiters steal anything they wanted as long as they didn't bother his reefers. Danny Jackson, who was black and knew Shakespeare before the world said he could work with it, was second man. Len Dickey was third. Reverend Hendricks was fourth, and Uncle T. Boone, who even in those early days could not straighten his back, ran fifth. Doc started in as sixth waiter, the "mule." They pulled some shit on him at first because they didn't want somebody fresh out of a paddy kitchen on the crew. They messed with his orders, stole his plates, picked up his tips on the sly, and made him do all the dirty work. But when they saw that he could take the shit without getting hot and when they saw that he was set on being a waiter, even though he was older than most of them, they settled down and began to teach him this business and all the words and moves and slickness that made it a good business.

His real name was Leroy Johnson, I think, but when Danny Jackson saw how cool and neat he was in his moves, and how he handled the plates, he began to call him "the Doctor." Then the Sheik, coming down from his high one day after missing the lunch and dinner service, saw how Doc had taken over his station and collected fat tips from his tables by telling the passengers that the Sheik had had to get off back along the line because of a heart attack. The Sheik liked that because he saw that Doc understood crackers and how they liked nothing better than knowing that a nigger had died on the job, giving them service. The Sheik was impressed. And he was not an easy man to impress because he knew too much about life and had to stay high most of the time. And when Doc would not split the tips with him, the Sheik got mad at first and called Doc a barrel of motherfuckers and some other words you would not recognize. But he was impressed. And later that night, in the crew car when the others were gambling and drinking and bullshitting about the women they had working the corners for them, the Sheik came over to Doc's bunk and said: "You're a crafty motherfucker."

"Yeah?" says Doc.

"Yeah," says the Sheik, who did not say much. "You're a crafty motherfucker but I like you." Then he got into the first waiter's bunk and lit up again. But Reverend Hendricks, who always read his Bible before going to sleep and who always listened to anything the Sheik said because he knew the Sheik only said something when it was important, heard what was said and remembered it. After he put his Bible back in his locker, he walked over to Doc's bunk and looked down at him. "Mister Doctor Craft," the Reverend said. "Youngblood Doctor Craft."

"Yeah?" says Doc.

"Yeah," says Reverend Hendricks. "That's who you are."

And that's who he was from then on.

II

I CAME TO THE ROAD away from the war. This was after '41, when people at home were looking for Japs under their beds every night. I did not want to fight because there was no money in it and I didn't want to go overseas to work in a kitchen. The big war was on and a lot of soldiers crossed the country to get to it, and as long as a black man fed them on trains he did not have to go to that war. I could have got a job in a Chicago factory, but there was more money on the road and it was safer. And after a while it got into your blood so that you couldn't leave it for anything. The road got into my blood the way it got into everybody's; the way going to the war got in the blood of redneck farm boys and the crazy Polacks from Chicago. It was all right for them to go to the war. They were young and stupid. And they died that way. I played it smart. I was almost thirty-five and I didn't want to go. But I took *them* and fed them and gave them good times on their way to the war, and for that I did not have to go. The soldiers had plenty of money and were afraid not to spend it all before they got to the ships on the Coast. And we gave them ways to spend it on the trains.

Now in those days there was plenty of money going around and everybody stole from everybody. The kitchen stole food from the company and the company knew it and wouldn't pay good wages. There were no rules in those days; there was no black book to go by and nobody said what you couldn't eat or steal. The paddy cooks used to toss boxes of steaks off the train in the Chicago yards for people at the restaurants there who paid them, cash. These were the days when ordinary people had to have red stamps or blue stamps to get powdered eggs and white lard to mix with red powder to make their own butter.

The stewards stole from the company and from the waiters; the waiters stole from the stewards and the company and from each other. I stole. Doc stole. Even Reverend Hendricks put his Bible far back in his locker and stole with us. You didn't want a man on your crew who didn't steal. He made it bad for everybody. And if the steward saw that he was a dummy and would never get to stealing, he wrote him up for something and got him off the crew so as not to slow down the rest of us. We had a redneck cracker steward from Alabama by the name of Casper who used to say: "*Jesus Christ!* I ain't got time to hate you niggers. I'm making so much money." He used to keep all his cash at home under his bed in a cardboard box because he was afraid to put it in the bank.

Doc and Sheik Beasley and me were on the same crew together all during the war. Even in those days, as young as we were, we knew how to be Old Heads. We organized for the soldiers. We had to wear skullcaps all the time because the crackers said our hair was poison and didn't want any of it to fall in their food. The Sheik didn't mind wearing one. He kept reefers in his and used to sell them to the soldiers for double what he paid for them in Chicago and three times what he paid the Chinamen in Seattle. That's why we called him the Sheik. After every meal the Sheik would get in the linen closet and light up. Sometimes he wouldn't come out for days. Nobody gave a damn, though; we were all too busy stealing and working. And there was more for us to get as long as he didn't come out.

Doc used to sell bootlegged booze to the soldiers; that was his speciality. He had redcaps in the Chicago stations telling the soldiers who to ask for on the train. He was an open operator and had to give the steward a cut, but he still made a pile of money. That's why that old cracker always kept us together on his crew. We were the three best moneymakers he ever had. That's something you should learn, young-blood. They can't love you for being you. They only love you if you make money for them. All that talk these days about integration and brotherhood, that's a lot of bullshit. The man will love you as long as he can make money with you. I made money. And old Casper had to love me in the open although I knew he called me a nigger at home when he had put that money in his big cardboard box. I know he loved me on the road in the wartime because I used to bring in the biggest moneymakers. I used to handle the girls.

Look out that window. See all that grass and wheat? Look at that big farm boy cutting it. Look at that burnt cracker on that tractor. He probably has a wife who married him because she didn't know what else to do. Back during wartime the girls in this part of the country knew what to do. They got on the trains at night.

You can look out that window all day and run around all the stations when we stop, but you'll never see a black man in any of these towns. You know why, young-blood? These farmers hate you. They still remember when their girls came out of these towns and got on the trains at night. They've been running black men and dark Indians out of these towns for years. They hate anything dark that's not that way because of the sun. Right now there are big farm girls with hair under their arms on the corners in San Francisco, Chicago, Seattle and Minneapolis who got started on these cars back during wartime. The farmers still remember that and they hate you and me for it. But it wasn't for me they got on. Nobody wants a stiff, smelly farm girl when there are sporting women to be got for a dollar in the cities. It was for the soldiers they got on. It was just business to me. But they hate you and me anyway.

I got off in one of these towns once, a long time after the war, just to get a drink while the train changed engines. Everybody looked at me and by the time I got to a bar there were ten people on my trail. I was drinking a fast one when the sheriff came in the bar.

"What are you doing here?" he asks me.

"Just getting a shot," I say.

He spit on the floor. "How long you plan to be here?"

"I don't know," I say, just to be nasty.

"There ain't no jobs here," he says.

"I wasn't looking," I say.

"We don't want you here."

"I don't give a good goddamn," I say.

He pulled his gun on me. "All right, coon, back on the train," he says.

"Wait a minute," I tell him. "Let me finish my drink."

He knocked my glass over with his gun. "You're finished *now*," he says. "Pull your ass out of here *now!*"

I didn't argue.

I was the night man. After dinner it was my job to pull the cloths off the tables and put paddings on. Then I cut out the lights and locked both doors. There was a big farm girl from Minot named Hilda who could take on eight or ten soldiers in one night, white soldiers. These white boys don't know how to last. I would stand by the door and when the soldiers came back from the club car they would pay me and I would let them in. Some of the girls could make as much as one hundred dollars in one night. And I always made twice as much. Soldiers don't care what they do with their money. They just have to spend it.

We never bothered with the girls ourselves. It was just business as far as we were concerned. But there was one dummy we had with us once, a boy from the South named Willie Joe something who handled the dice. He was really hot for one of these farm girls. He used to buy her good whiskey and he hated to see her go in the car at night to wait for the soldiers. He was a real dummy. One time I heard her tell him: "It's all right. They can have my body. I know I'm black inside. *Jesus*, I'm so black inside I wisht I was black all over!"

And this dummy Willie Joe said: "Baby, *don't you ever change!*"

I knew we had to get rid of him before he started trouble. So we had the steward bump him off the crew as soon as we could find a good man to handle the gambling. That old redneck Casper was glad to do it. He saw what was going on.

But you want to hear about Doc, you say, so you can get back to your reading. What can I tell you? The road got into his blood? He liked being a waiter? You won't understand this, but he did. There were no Civil Rights or marches or riots for something better in those days. In those days a man found something he liked to do and liked it from then on because he couldn't help himself. What did he like about the road? He liked what I liked: the money, owning the car, running it, telling the soldiers what to do, hustling a bigger tip from some old maid by looking under her dress and laughing at her, having all the girls at the Haverville Hotel waiting for us to come in for stopover, the power we had to beat them up or lay them if we wanted. He liked running free and not being married to some bitch who would spend his money when he was out of town or give it to some stud. He liked getting drunk with the boys up at Andy's, setting up the house and then passing out from drinking too much, knowing that the boys would get him home.

I ran with that one crew all during wartime and they, Doc, the Sheik and Reverend Hendricks, had taken me under their wings. *I* was still a youngblood then, and Doc liked me a lot. But he never said that much to me; he was not a talker. The Sheik had taught him the value of silence in things that really matter. We roomed together in Chicago at Mrs. Wright's place in those days. Mrs. Wright didn't allow women in the rooms and Doc liked that, because after being out for a week and after stopping over in those hotels along the way, you get tired of women and bullshit and need your privacy. We weren't like you. We didn't need a woman every time we got hard. We knew when we had to have it and when we didn't. And we didn't spend all our money on it, either. You youngbloods think the way to get a woman is to let her see how you handle your money. That's stupid. The way to get a women is to let her see how you handle other women. But you'll never believe that until it's too late to do you any good.

Doc knew how to handle women. I can remember a time in a Winnipeg hotel how he ran a bitch out of his room because he had had enough of it and did not need her anymore. I was in the next room and heard everything.

"Come on, Doc," the bitch said. "Come on honey, let's do it one more time."

"Hell no," Doc said. "I'm tired and I don't want to anymore."

"How can you say you're tired?" the bitch said. "How can you say you're tired when you didn't go but two times?"

"I'm tired of it," Doc said, "because I'm tired of you. And I'm tired of you because

I'm tired of it and bitches like you in all the towns I been in. You drain a man. And I know if I beat you, you'll still come back when I hit you again. *That's* why I'm tired. I'm tired of having things around I don't care about."

"What *do* you care about, Doc?" the bitch said.

"I don't know," Doc said. "I guess I care about moving and being somewhere else when I want to be. I guess I care about going out, and coming in to wait for the time to go out again."

"You crazy, Doc," the bitch said.

"Yeah?" Doc said. "I guess I'm crazy all right."

Later that bitch knocked on my door and I did it for her because she was just a bitch and I knew Doc wouldn't want her again. I don't think he ever wanted a bitch again. I never saw him with one after that time. He was just a little over fifty then and could have still done whatever he wanted with women.

The war ended. The farm boys who got back from the war did not spend money on their way home. They did not want to spend any money on women, and the girls did not get on at night anymore. Some of them went into the cities and turned pro. Some of them stayed in the towns and married the farm boys who got back from the war. Things changed on the road. The Commissary started putting that book of rules together and told us to stop stealing. They were losing money on passengers now because of the airplanes and they began to really tighten up and started sending inspectors down along the line to check on us. They started sending in spotters, too. One of them caught that redneck Casper writing out a check for two dollars less than he had charged the spotter. The Commissary got him in on the rug for it. I wasn't there, but they told me he said to the General Superintendent: "Why are you getting on me, a white man, for a lousy son-of-a-bitching two bucks? There's niggers out there been stealing for *years!*"

"Who?" the General Superintendent asked.

And Casper couldn't say anything because he had that cardboard box full of money still under his bed and knew he would have to tell how he got it if any of us was brought in. So he said nothing.

"Who?" the General Superintendent asked him again.

"Why, all them nigger waiters steal, *everybody knows that!*"

"And the cooks, what about them?" the Superintendent said.

"They're white," said Casper.

They never got the story out of him and he was fired. He used the money to open a restaurant someplace in Indiana and I heard later that he started a branch of the Klan in his town. One day he showed up at the station and told Doc, Reverend Hendricks and me: "I'll see you boys get *yours.* Damn if I'm takin' the rap for you niggers."

We just laughed in his face because we knew he could do nothing to us through the Commissary. But just to be safe we stopped stealing so much. But they did get the Sheik, though. One day an inspector got on in the mountains just outside of Whitefish and grabbed him right out of that linen closet. The Sheik had been smoking in there all day and he was high and laughing when they pulled him off the train.

That was the year we got in the Union. The crackers and Swedes finally let us in after we paid off. We really stopped stealing and got organized and there wasn't a damn thing the company could do about it, although it tried like hell to buy us out. And to get back at us, they put their heads together and began to make up that big book of rules you keep your finger in. Still, *we* knew the service and they had to write the book the way we gave the service and at first there was nothing for the Old School men to learn. We got seniority through the Union, and as long as we gave the service and didn't steal, they couldn't touch us. So they began changing the rules, and sending us notes about the service. Little changes at first, like how the initials on the doily should always face the customer, and how the silver should be taken off the tables between meals. But we were getting old and set in our old service, and it got harder and harder learning all those little changes. And we had to learn new stuff all the time because there was no telling when an inspector would get on and catch us giving bad service. It was hard as hell. It was hard because we knew that the company was out to break up the Old School. The Sheik was gone, and we knew that Reverend Hendricks or Uncle T. or Danny Jackson would go soon because they stood for the Old School, just like the Sheik. But what bothered us most was knowing that they would go for Doc first, before anyone else, because he loved the road so much.

Doc was over sixty-five then and had taken to drinking hard when we were off. But he never touched a drop when we were on the road. I used to wonder whether he drank because being a Waiter's Waiter was getting hard or because he had to do something until his next trip. I could never figure it. When we had our layovers he would spend all his time in Andy's, setting up the house. He had no wife, no relatives, not even a hobby. He just drank. Pretty soon the slicksters at Andy's got to using him for a good thing. They commenced putting the touch on him because they saw he was getting old and knew he didn't have far to go, and they would never have to pay him back. Those of us who were close to him tried to pull his coat, but it didn't help. He didn't talk about himself much, he didn't talk much about anything that wasn't related to the road; but when I tried to hip him once about the hustlers and how they were closing in on him, he just took another shot and said:

"I don't need no money. Nobody's jiving me. I'm jiving them. You know I can still pull in a hundred in tips in one trip. I *know* this business."

"Yeah, I know, Doc," I said. "But how many more trips can you make before you have to stop?"

"I ain't never gonna stop. Trips are all I know and I'll be making them as long as these trains haul people."

"That's just it," I said. "They don't *want* to haul people anymore. The planes do that. The big roads want freight now. Look how they hire youngbloods just for the busy seasons just so they won't get any seniority in the winter. Look how all the Old School waiters are dropping out. They got the Sheik, Percy Fields just lucked up and died before they got to *him,* they almost got Reverend Hendricks. Even *Uncle T.* is going to retire! And they'll get us too."

"Not me," said Doc. "I know my moves. This old fox can still dance with a tray and handle four tables at the same time. I can still bait a queer and make the old ladies tip big. There's no waiter better than me and I know it."

"Sure, Doc," I said. "I know it too. But please save your money. Don't be a dummy. There'll come a day when you just can't get up to go out and they'll put you on the ground for good."

Doc looked at me like he had been shot. "Who taught you the moves when you were just a raggedy-ass waiter?"

"You did, Doc," I said.

"Who's always the first man down in the yard at train-time?" He threw down another shot. "Who's there sitting in the car every tenth morning while you other old heads are still at home pulling on your longjohns?"

I couldn't say anything. He was right and we both knew it.

"I have to go out," he told me. "Going out is my whole life. I wait for that tenth morning. I ain't never missed a trip and I don't mean to."

What could I say to him, youngblood? What can I say to you? He had to go out, not for the money; it was in his blood. You have to go out too, but it's for the money you go. You hate going out and you love coming in. He loved going out and he hated coming in. Would *you* listen if I told you to stop spending your money on pussy in Chicago? Would he listen if I told him to save *his* money? To stop setting up the bar at Andy's? No. Old men are just as bad as young men when it comes to money. They can't think. They always try to buy what they should have for free. And what they buy, after they have it, is nothing.

They called Doc into the Commissary and the doctors told him he had lumbago and a bad heart and was weak from drinking too much, and they wanted him to get down for his own good. He wouldn't do it. Tesdale, the General Superintendent, called him in and told him that he had enough years in the service to pull down a big pension and that the company would pay for a retirement party for him, since he was the oldest waiter working, and invite all the Old School waiters to see him off, if he would come down. Doc said no. He knew that the Union had to back him. He knew that he could ride as long as he made the trains on time and as long as he knew the service. And he knew that he could not leave the road.

The company called in its lawyers to go over the Union contract. I wasn't there, but Len Dickey was in on the meeting because of his office in the Union. He told me about it later. Those fat company lawyers took the contract apart and went through all their books. They took the seniority clause apart word by word, trying to figure a way to get at Doc. But they had written it airtight back in the days when the company *needed* waiters, and there was nothing in it about compulsory retirement. Not a word. The paddies in the Union must have figured that waiters didn't *need* a new contract when they let us in, and they had let us come in under the old one thinking that all waiters would die on the job, or drink themselves to death when they were still young, or die from buying too much pussy, or just quit when they had put in enough time to draw a pension. But *nothing* in the whole contract could help them get rid of Doc Craft. They were swearing, they were working so hard. And all the time Tesdale, the General Superintendent, was calling them sons-of-bitches for not earning their money. But there was nothing the company lawyers could do but turn the pages of their big books and sweat and promise Tesdale that they would find some way if he gave them more time.

The word went out from the Commissary: "Get Doc." The stewards got it from the assistant superintendents: "Get Doc." Since they could not get him to retire, they were determined to catch him giving bad service. He had more seniority than most other waiters, so they couldn't bump him off our crew. In fact, all the waiters with more seniority than Doc were on the crew with him. There were four of us from the Old School: me, Doc, Uncle T. Boone, and Danny Jackson. Reverend Hendricks wasn't running regular anymore; he was spending all his Sundays preaching in his Church on the South Side because he knew what was coming and wanted to have something steady going for him in Chicago when his time came. Fifth and sixth men on that crew were two hardheads who had read the book. The steward was Crouse, and he really didn't want to put the screws to Doc but he couldn't help himself. Everybody wants to work. So Crouse started in to riding Doc, sometimes about moving too fast, sometimes about not moving fast enough. I was on the crew, I saw it all. Crouse would seat four singles at the same table, on Doc's station, and Doc had to take care of all four different orders at the same time. He was seventy-three, but that didn't stop him, knowing this business the way he did. It just slowed him down some. But Crouse got on him even for that and would chew him out in front of the passengers, hoping that he'd start cursing and bother the passengers so that they would complain to the company. It never worked, though. Doc just played it cool. He'd look into Crouse's eyes and know what was going on. And then he'd lay on his good service, the only service he knew, and the passengers would see how good he was with all that age on his back and they would get mad at the steward, and leave Doc a bigger tip when they left.

The Commissary sent out spotters to catch him giving bad service. These were pale-white little men in glasses who never looked you in the eye, but who always felt the plate to see if it was warm. And there were the old maids, who like that kind of work, who would order shrimp or crabmeat cocktails or celery and olive plates because they knew how the rules said these things had to be made. And when they came, when Doc brought them out, they would look to see if the oyster fork was stuck into the thing, and look out the window a long time.

"Ain't no use trying to fight it," Uncle T. Boone told Doc in the crew car one night, "the black waiter is *doomed.* Look at all the good restaurants, the class restaurants in Chicago. *You* can't work in them. Them white waiters got those jobs sewed up fine."

"I can be a waiter anywhere," says Doc. "I know the business and I like it and I can do it anywhere."

"The black waiter is doomed," Uncle T. says again. "The whites is taking over the service in the good places. And when they run you off of here, you won't have no place to go."

"They won't run me off of here," says Doc. "As long as I give the right service they can't touch me."

"You're a goddamn *fool!*" says Uncle T. "You're a nigger and you ain't got no rights except what the Union says you have. And that ain't worth a damn because when the Commissary finally gets you, those niggers won't lift a finger to help you."

"Leave off him," I say to Boone. "If anybody ought to be put off it's you. You ain't had your back straight for thirty years. You even make the crackers sick the way you keep bowing and folding your hands and saying, 'Thank you, Mr. Boss.' Fifty years ago that would of got you a bigger tip," I say, "but now it ain't worth a shit. And every time you do it the crackers hate you. And every time I see you serving with that skullcap on *I* hate you. The Union said we didn't have to wear them *eighteen years ago!* Why can't you take it off?"

Boone just sat on his bunk with his skullcap in his lap, leaning against his big belly. He knew I was telling the truth and he knew he wouldn't change. But he said: "That's the trouble with the Negro waiter today. He ain't got no humility. And as long as he don't have humility, he keeps losing the good jobs."

Doc had climbed into the first waiter's bunk in his longjohns and I got in the second waiter's bunk under him and lay there. I could hear him breathing. It had a hard sound. He wasn't well and all of us knew it.

"Doc?" I said in the dark.

"Yeah?"

"Don't mind Boone, Doc. He's a dead man. He just don't know it."

"We all are," Doc said.

"Not you," I said.

"What's the use? He's right. They'll get me in the end."

"But they ain't done it yet."

"They'll get me. And they know it and I know it. I can even see it in old Crouse's eyes. He knows they're gonna get me."

"Why don't you get a woman?"

He was quiet. "What can I do with a woman now, that I ain't already done too much?"

I thought for a while. "If you're on the ground, being with one might not make it so bad."

"I hate women," he said.

"You ever try fishing?"

"No."

"You want to?"

"No," he said.

"You can't keep *drinking.*"

He did not answer.

"Maybe you could work in town. In the Commissary."

I could hear the big wheels rolling and clicking along the tracks and I knew by the smooth way we were moving that we were almost out of the Dakota flatlands. Doc wasn't talking. "Would you like that?" I thought he was asleep. "Doc, would you like that?"

"Hell no," he said.

"You have to try *something!*"

He was quiet again. "I know," he finally said.

III

JERRY EWALD, THE UNEXPECTED Inspector, got on in Winachee that next day after lunch and we knew that he had the word from the Commissary. He was cool about it: he laughed with the steward and the waiters about the old days and his hard gray eyes and shining glasses kept looking over our faces as if to see if we knew why he had got on. The two hardheads were in the crew car stealing a nap on company time. Jerry noticed this and could have caught them, but he was after bigger game. We all knew that, and we kept talking to him about the days of the big trains and looking at his white hair and not into the eyes behind his glasses because we knew what was there. Jerry sat down on the first waiter's station and said to Crouse: "Now I'll have some lunch. Steward, let the headwaiter bring me a menu."

Crouse stood next to the table where Jerry sat, and looked at Doc, who had been waiting between the tables with his tray under his arm. The way the rules say. Crouse looked sad because he knew what was coming. Then Jerry looked directly at Doc and said: "Headwaiter Doctor Craft, bring me a menu."

Doc said nothing and he did not smile. He brought the menu. Danny Jackson and I moved back into the hall to watch. There was nothing we could do to help Doc and we knew it. He was the Waiter's Waiter, out there by himself, hustling the biggest tip he would ever get in his life. Or losing it.

"Goddamn," Danny said to me. "Now let's sit on the ground and talk about how *kings* are gonna get fucked."

"Maybe not," I said. But I did not believe it myself because Jerry is the kind of man who lies in bed all night, scheming. I knew he had a plan.

Doc passed us on his way to the kitchen for water and I wanted to say something to him. But what was the use? He brought the water to Jerry. Jerry looked him in the eye. "Now, Headwaiter," he said. "I'll have a bowl of onion soup, a cold roast beef sandwich on white, rare, and a glass of iced tea."

"Write it down," said Doc. He was playing it right. He knew that the new rules had stopped waiters from taking verbal orders.

"Don't be so professional, Doc," Jerry said. "It's me, one of the *boys.*"

"You have to write it out," said Doc, "it's in the black book."

Jerry clicked his pen and wrote the order out on the check. And handed it to Doc. Uncle T. followed Doc back into the Pantry.

"He's gonna get you, Doc," Uncle T. said. "I knew it all along. You know why? The Negro waiter ain't got no more humility."

"Shut the fuck up, Boone!" I told him.

"You'll see," Boone went on. "You'll see I'm right. There ain't a thing Doc can do about it, either. We're gonna lose all the good jobs."

We watched Jerry at the table. He saw us watching and smiled with his gray eyes. Then he poured some of the water from the glass on the linen cloth and picked up the silver sugar bowl and placed it right on the wet spot. Doc was still in the Pantry. Jerry turned the silver sugar bowl around and around on the linen. He pressed down on it some as he turned. But when he picked it up again, there was no dark ring on the wet cloth. We had polished the silver early that morning, according to the book, and there was not a dirty piece of silver to be found in the whole car. Jerry was drinking the rest of the water when Doc brought out the polished silver soup tureen, underlined with a doily and a breakfast plate, with a shining soup bowl underlined with a doily and a breakfast plate, and a bread-and-butter plate with six crackers; not four or five or seven, but six, the number the Commissary had written in the black book. He swung down the aisle of the car between the two rows of white tables and you could not help but be proud of the way he moved with the roll of the train and the way that tray was like a part of his arm. It was good service. He placed everything neat, with all company initials showing, right where things should go.

"Shall I serve up the soup?" he asked Jerry.

"Please," said Jerry.

Doc handled that silver soup ladle like one of those Chicago Jew tailors handles a needle. He ladled up three good-sized spoonfuls from the tureen and then laid the wet spoon on an extra bread-and-butter plate on the side of the table, so he would not stain the cloth. Then he put a napkin over the wet spot Jerry had made and changed the ashtray for a prayer-card because every good waiter knows that nobody wants to eat a good meal looking at an ashtray.

"You know about the spoon plate, I see," Jerry said to Doc.

"I'm a waiter," said Doc. "I know."

"You're a damn good waiter," said Jerry.

Doc looked Jerry square in the eye. "I know," he said slowly.

Jerry ate a little of the soup and opened all six of the cracker packages. Then he stopped eating and began to look out the window. We were passing through his territory, Washington State, the country he loved because he was the only company inspector in the state and knew that once we got through Montana he would be the only man the waiters feared. He smiled and then waved for Doc to bring out the roast beef sandwich.

But Doc was into his service now and cleared the table completely. Then he got the silver crumb knife from the Pantry and gathered all the cracker crumbs, even the ones Jerry had managed to get in between the salt and pepper shakers.

"You want the tea with your sandwich, or later?" he asked Jerry.

"Now is fine," said Jerry, smiling.

"You're going good," I said to Doc when he passed us on his way to the Pantry. "He can't touch you or nothing."

He did not say anything.

Uncle T. Boone looked at Doc like he wanted to say something too, but he just frowned and shuffled out to stand next to Jerry. You could see that Jerry hated him. But Jerry knew how to smile at everybody, and so he smiled at Uncle T. while Uncle T. bent over the table with his hands together like he was praying, and moved his head up and bowed it down.

Doc brought out the roast beef, proper service. The crock of mustard was on a breakfast plate, underlined with a doily, initials facing Jerry. The lid was on the mustard and it was clean, like it says in the book, and the little silver service spoon was clean and polished on a bread-and-butter plate. He set it down. And then he served the tea. You think you know the service, youngblood, all of you do. But you don't. Anybody can serve, but not everybody can become a part of the service. When Doc poured that pot of hot tea into that glass of crushed ice, it was like he was pouring it through his own fingers; it was like he and the tray and the pot and the glass and all of it was the same body. It was a beautiful move. It was fine service. The iced tea glass sat in a shell dish, and the iced tea spoon lay straight in front of Jerry. The lemon wedge Doc put in a shell dish half-full of crushed ice with an oyster fork stuck into its skin. Not in the meat, mind you, but squarely under the skin of that lemon, and the whole thing lay in a pretty curve on top of that crushed ice.

Doc stood back and waited. Jerry had been watching his service and was impressed. He mixed the sugar in his glass and sipped. Danny Jackson and I were down the aisle in the hall. Uncle T. stood behind Jerry, bending over, his arms folded, waiting. And Doc stood next to the table, his tray under his arm looking straight ahead and calm because he had given good service and knew it. Jerry sipped again.

"Good tea," he said. "Very good tea."

Doc was silent.

Jerry took the lemon wedge off the oyster fork and squeezed it into the glass, and stirred, and sipped again. "*Very* good," he said. Then he drained the glass. Doc reached over to pick it up for more ice but Jerry kept his hand on the glass. "Very good service, Doc," he said. "But you served the lemon wrong."

Everybody was quiet. Uncle T. folded his hands in the praying position.

"How's that?" said Doc.

"The service was wrong," Jerry said. He was not smiling now.

"How could it be? I been giving that same service for years, right down to the crushed ice for the lemon wedge."

"That's just it, Doc," Jerry said. "The lemon wedge. You served it wrong."

"Yeah?" said Doc.

"Yes," said Jerry, his jaws tight. "Haven't you seen the new rule?"

Doc's face went loose. He knew now that they had got him.

"Haven't you *seen* it?" Jerry asked again.

Doc shook his head.

Jerry smiled that hard, gray smile of his, the kind of smile that says: "I have always been the boss and I am smiling this way because I know it and can afford to give you something." "Steward Crouse," he said. "Steward Crouse, go get the black bible for the headwaiter."

Crouse looked beaten too. He was sixty-three and waiting for his pension. He got the bible.

Jerry took it and turned directly to the very last page. He knew where to look. "Now, Headwaiter," he said, "*listen* to this." And he read aloud: "Memorandum Number 22416. From: Douglass A. Tesdale, General Superintendent of Dining Cars. To: Waiters, Stewards, Chefs of Dining Cars. Attention: As of 7/9/65 the proper service for iced tea will be (a) Fresh brewed tea in teapot, poured over crushed ice at table; iced tea glass set in shell dish (b) Additional ice to be immediately available upon request after first glass of tea (c) Fresh lemon wedge will be served on bread-and-butter plate, no doily, with tines of oyster fork stuck into *meat* of lemon." Jerry paused.

"Now you know, Headwaiter," he said.

"Yeah," said Doc.

"But why didn't you know before?"

No answer.

"This notice came out last week."

"I didn't check the book yet," said Doc.

"But that's a rule. Always check the book before each trip. *You* know that, Head-waiter."

"Yeah," said Doc.

"Then that's *two* rules you missed."

Doc was quiet.

"Two rules you didn't read," Jerry said. "You're slowing down, Doc."

"I know," Doc mumbled.

"You want some time off to rest?"

Again Doc said nothing.

"I think you need some time on the ground to rest up, don't you?"

Doc put his tray on the table and sat down in the seat across from Jerry. This was the first time we had ever seen a waiter sit down with a customer, even an inspector. Uncle T., behind Jerry's back, began waving his hands, trying to tell Doc to get up. Doc did not look at him.

"You *are* tired, aren't you?" said Jerry.

"I'm just resting my feet," Doc said.

"Get up, Headwaiter," Jerry said. "You'll have plenty of time to do that. I'm writing you up."

But Doc did not move and just continued to sit there. And all Danny and I could do was watch him from the back of the car. For the first time I saw that his hair was almost gone and his legs were skinny in the baggy white uniform. I don't think

Jerry expected Doc to move. I don't think he really cared. But then Uncle T. moved around the table and stood next to Doc, trying to apologize for him to Jerry with his eyes and bowed head. Doc looked at Uncle T. and then got up and went back to the crew car. He left his tray on the table. It stayed there all that evening because none of us, not even Crouse or Jerry or Uncle T., would touch it. And Jerry didn't try to make any of us take it back to the Pantry. He understood at least that much. The steward closed down Doc's tables during dinner service, all three settings of it. And Jerry got off the train someplace along the way, quiet, like he had got on.

After closing down the car we went back to the crew quarters and Doc was lying on his bunk with his hands behind his head and his eyes open. He looked old. No one knew what to say until Boone went over to his bunk and said: "I feel bad for you, Doc, but all of us are gonna get it in the end. The railroad waiter is *doomed*."

Doc did not even notice Boone.

"I could of told you about the lemon but he would of got you on something else. It wasn't no use. Any of it."

"Shut the fuck up, Boone!" Danny said. "The one thing that really hurts is that a crawling son-of-a-bitch like you will be riding when all the good men are gone. Dummies like you and these two hardheads will be working your asses off reading that damn bible and never know a goddamn thing about being a waiter. *That* hurts like a *motherfucker!*"

"It ain't my fault if the colored waiter is doomed," said Boone. "It's your fault for letting go your humility and letting the whites take over the good jobs."

Danny grabbed the skullcap off Boone's head and took it into the bathroom and flushed it down the toilet. In a minute it was half a mile away and soaked in old piss on the tracks. Boone did not try to fight, he just sat on his bunk and mumbled. He had other skullcaps. No one said anything to Doc, because that's the way real men show that they care. You don't talk. Talking makes it worse.

IV

WHAT ELSE IS THERE to tell you, youngblood? They made him retire. He didn't try to fight it. He was beaten and he knew it; not by the service, but by a book. *That book,* that *bible* you keep your finger stuck in. That's not a good way for a man to go. He should die in service. He should die doing the things he likes. But not by a book.

All of us Old School men will be beaten by it. Danny Jackson is gone now, and Reverend Hendricks put in for his pension and took up preaching, full-time. But Uncle T. Boone is still riding. They'll get *me* some soon enough, with that book. But it will never get you because you'll never be a waiter, or at least a Waiter's Waiter. You read too much.

Doc got a good pension and he took it directly to Andy's. And none of the boys who knew about it knew how to refuse a drink on Doc. But none of us knew how to drink with him knowing that we would be going out again in a few days, and he was on the ground. So a lot of us, even the drunks and hustlers who usually hang around Andy's, avoided him whenever we could. There was nothing to talk about anymore.

He died five months after he was put on the ground. He was seventy-three and it was winter. He froze to death wandering around the Chicago yards early one morning. He had been drunk, and was still steaming when the yard crew found him. Only the few of us left in the Old School know what he was doing there.

I am sixty-three now. And I haven't decided if I should take my pension when they ask me to go or continue to ride. I *want* to keep riding, but I know that if I do, Jerry Ewald or Harry Silk or Jack Tate will get me one of these days. I could get down if I wanted: I have a hobby and I am too old to get drunk by myself. I couldn't drink with you, youngblood. We have nothing to talk about. And after a while you would get mad at me for talking anyway, and keeping you from your pussy. You are tired already. I can see it in your eyes and in the way you play with the pages of your rule book.

I know it. And I wonder why I should keep talking to you when you could never see what I see or understand what I understand or know the real difference between my school and yours. I wonder why I have kept talking this long when all the time I have seen that you can hardly wait to hit the city to get off this thing and spend your money. You have a good story. But you will never remember it. Because all this time you have had pussy in your mind, and your fingers in the pages of that black bible.

IF IT WAS POSSIBLE to excavate a story the way a city can be excavated, then underneath "Paper Lantern" would be found the ruins of a prose poem. The title of the prose poem was "The Prose Poem." It had nothing to do with paper lanterns, time travel, or drives through Iowa. It was about—what else?—writing prose poems. I think of the prose poem as a form that lends itself to taking chances, as an especially good arena for working out nonnarrative strategies for telling a story, as a form that adapts well to the experimental. So there was a laboratory in "The Prose Poem."

I once spent a winter night drinking with a poet who was known at that time for his prose poems. His drink of choice was apricot brandy. It was a bitterly cold night and we were driving around in an old orange VW bug convertible of mine. The top was up but it really didn't make much difference. Extremes of weather have a way of obliterating intellectual concerns. Rather than discussing prose poems, our conversation as I remember it was variations on, "Jeez, it's cold!" "Goddamn it's cold." Etc.

So it was winter in "The Prose Poem." I left the apricot brandy out of it as it's syrupy, noxious stuff. Maybe the apricot brandy got replaced by the tea in the Chinese restaurant. The restaurant was modeled in part on a Chinese laundry on Waverly Place downstairs from where W. S. Merwin once had a great apartment that he was kind enough to share. The back kitchen windows of the apartment overlooked the roof of the Village Vanguard. Somehow this is all connected on a level of feeling that even the most scrupulous excavation could never unearth.

I couldn't get "The Prose Poem" to work to my satisfaction (or that of the few people who saw it) and at some point—sour grapes?—I remembered that I'd long claimed to distrust the subgenre of poems about poetry, anyway. Too many seem predictably pious to me, and narcissistic in the Rilke wanna-be way that is also responsible for the infestation of angels in American verse. Maybe that's why the lab caught on fire in "The Prose Poem."

Although I'd messed around with it for years, I'm glad "The Prose Poem" failed. By then, I probably knew too much about it, whereas the story—"Paper Lantern"— that somehow evolved from it, is something I know very little about; it still seems mysterious to me, which is how I intend to leave it.

STUART DYBEK

STUART DYBEK

Paper Lantern

WE WERE WORKING late on the time machine in the little makeshift lab upstairs. The moon was stuck like the whorl of a frozen fingerprint to the skylight. In the back alley, the breaths left behind by yowling toms converged into a fog slinking out along the streets. Try as we might, our measurements were repeatedly off. In one direction, we'd reached the border at which clairvoyants stand gazing into the future, and in the other we'd gone backward to the zone where the present turns ghostly with memory and yet resists quite becoming the past. We'd been advancing and retreating by smaller and smaller degrees until it had come to seem as if we were measuring the immeasurable. Of course, what we really needed was some new vocabulary of measurement. It was time for a break.

Down the broken escalator, out the blue-lit lobby past the shuttered newsstand, through the frosty fog, hungry as strays we walk, still wearing our lab coats, to the Chinese restaurant around the corner.

IT'S A RESTAURANT that used to be a Chinese laundry. When customers would come for their freshly laundered bundles, the cooking—wafting from the owner's back kitchen through the warm haze of laundry steam—smelled so good that the customers began asking if they could buy something to eat as well. And so the restaurant was born. It was a carryout place at first, but they've since wedged in a few tables. None of us can read Chinese, so we can't be sure, but since the proprietors never bothered to change the sign, presumably the Chinese characters still say it's a Chinese laundry. Anyway, that's how the people in the neighborhood refer to it— the Chinese Laundry, as in "Man, I had a sublime meal at the Chinese Laundry last night." Although they haven't changed the sign, the proprietors have added a large, red-ribbed paper lantern—their only nod to decor—that spreads its opaque glow across the steamy window.

We sit at one of the five Formica tables—our favorite, beside the window—and the waitress immediately brings the menu and tea. Really, in a way, this is the best part: the ruddy glow of the paper lantern like heat on our faces, the tiny enameled teacups warming our hands, the hot tea scalding our hunger, and the surprising, welcoming heft of the menu, hand-printed in Chinese characters, with what must be very approximate explanations in English of some of the dishes, also hand-printed, in the black ink of calligraphers. Each time we come here the menu has grown longer. Once a dish has been offered, it is never deleted, and now the menu is pages and pages long, so long that we'll never read through it all, never live long enough, perhaps, to sample all the food in just this one tucked-away, neighborhood Chinese restaurant. The pages are unnumbered, and we can never remember where we left off reading the last time we were here. Was it the chrysanthemum pot, served traditionally in autumn when the flowers are in full bloom, or the almond jelly with lichees and loquats?

"A poet wrote this menu," Tinker says between sips of tea.

"Yes, but if there's a poet in the house, then why doesn't this place have a real name—something like the Red Lantern—instead of merely being called the Chinese Laundry by default?" the Professor replies, wiping the steam from his glasses with a paper napkin from the dispenser on the table.

"I sort of like the Chinese Laundry, myself. It's got a solid, working-class ring. Red Lantern is a cliché—precious chinoiserie," Tinker argues.

They never agree.

"Say, you two, I thought we were here to devour aesthetics, not debate them."

Here, there's nothing of heaven or earth that can't be consumed, nothing they haven't found a way to turn into a delicacy: pine-nut porridge, cassia-blossom buns, fish-fragrance-sauced pigeon, swallow's-nest soup (a soup indigenous to the shore of the South China Sea; nests of predigested seaweed from the beaks of swifts, the gelatinous material hardened to form a small, translucent cup). Sea-urchin roe, pickled jellyfish, tripe with ginger and peppercorns, five-fragrance grouper cheeks, cloud ears, spun-sugar apple, ginkgo nuts and golden needles (which are the buds of lilies), purple seaweed, bitter melon . . .

Nothing of heaven and earth that cannot be combined, transmuted; no borders, in a wok, that can't be crossed. It's instructive. One can't help nourishing the imagination as well as the body.

We order, knowing we won't finish all they'll bring, and that no matter how carefully we ponder our choices, we'll be served instead whatever the cook has made today.

AFTER SUPPER, sharing segments of a blood orange and sipping tea, we ceremoniously crack open our fortune cookies and read aloud our fortunes as if consulting the I Ching.

"*Sorrow is born of excessive joy.*"

"Try another."

"*Poverty is the common fate of scholars.*"

"Does that sound like a fortune to you?" Tinker asks.

"I certainly hope not," the Professor says.

"*When a finger points to the moon, the imbecile looks at the finger.*"

"What kind of fortunes are these? These aren't fortune cookies, these are proverb cookies," Tinker says.

"*In the Year of the Rat you will be lucky in love.*"

"Now that's more like it."

"What year is this?"

"The Year of the Dragon, according to the placemat."

"*Fuel alone will not light a fire.*"

"Say, did anyone turn off the Bunsen burner when we left?"

The mention of the lab makes us signal for the check. It's time we headed back. A new theory was brewing there when we left, and now, our enthusiasm rekindled, we return in the snow—it has begun to snow—through thick, crumbling flakes mixed with wafting cinders that would pass for snowflakes except for the way the wind is fanning their edges to sparks. A night of white flakes and streaming orange cinders, strange and beautiful until we turn the corner and stare up at our laboratory.

Flames occupy the top floor of the building. Smoke billows out of the skylight, from which the sooty moon has retreated. On the floor below, through radiant, buckling windows, we can see the mannequins from the dressmaker's showroom. Naked, wigs on fire, they appear to gyrate lewdly before they topple. On the next floor down, in the instrument repair shop, accordions wheeze in the smoke, violins seethe like green kindling, and the saxophones dissolve into a lava of molten brass cascading over a window ledge. While on the ground floor, in the display window, the animals in the taxidermist's shop have begun to hiss and snap as if fire had returned them to life in the wild.

We stare helplessly, still clutching the carryout containers of the food we were unable to finish from the blissfully innocent meal we sat sharing while our apparatus, our theories, our formulas, and years of research—all that people refer to as their "work"—were bursting into flame. Along empty, echoing streets, sirens are screaming like victims.

Already a crowd has gathered.

"Look at that seedy old mother go up," a white kid in dreadlocks says to his girlfriend, who looks like a runaway waif. She answers, "Cool!"

And I remember how, in what now seems another life, I watched fires as a kid— sometimes fires that a gang of us, calling ourselves the Matchheads, had set.

I remember how, later, in another time, if not another life, I once snapped a photograph of a woman I was with as she watched a fire blaze out of control along a river in Chicago. She was still married then. Her husband, whom I'd never met, was in a veteran's hospital—clinically depressed after the war in Vietnam. At least, that's what she told me about him. Thinking back, I sometimes wonder if she even had a husband. She had come to Chicago with me for a fling—her word. I thought at the time that we were just "fooling around"—also her words, words we both used in place of others, like "fucking" or "making love" or "adultery." It was more comfortable, and safer, for me to think of things between us as fooling around, but when I offhandedly mentioned that to her she became furious, and instead of fooling around we spent our weekend in Chicago arguing, and ended up having a terrible time. It was a Sunday afternoon in early autumn, probably in the Year of the Rat, and we were sullenly driving out of the city. Along the north branch of the river, a factory was burning. I pulled over and parked, dug a camera out of my duffle, and we walked to a bridge to watch the fire.

BUT IT'S NOT the fire itself that I remember, even though the blaze ultimately spread across the city sky like a dusk that rose from the earth rather than descended. The fire, as I recall it, is merely a backdrop compressed within the boundaries of the photograph I took of her. She has just looked away from the blaze, toward the camera. Her elbows lean against the peeling gray railing of the bridge. She's wearing the black silk blouse that she bought at a secondhand shop on Clark Street the day before. Looking for clothes from the past in secondhand stores was an obsession of hers—"going junking," she called it. A silver Navajo bracelet has slid up her arm over a black silk sleeve. How thin her wrists appear. There's a ring whose gem I know is a moonstone on the index finger of her left hand, and a tarnished silver band around her thumb. She was left-handed, and it pleased her that I was too, as if we both belonged to the same minority group. Her long hair is a shade of auburn all the more intense for the angle of late-afternoon sunlight. She doesn't look sullen or angry so much as fierce. Although later, studying her face in the photo, I'll come to see that beneath her expression there's a look less recognizable and more desperate: not loneliness, exactly, but *aloneness*—a look I'd seen cross her face more than once but wouldn't have thought to identify if the photo hadn't caught it. Behind her, ominous gray smoke plumes out of a sprawling old brick factory with the soon-to-be scorched white lettering of GUTTMAN & CO. TANNERS visible along the side of the building.

Driving back to Iowa in the dark, I'll think that she's asleep, as exhausted as I am from our strained weekend; then she'll break the miles of silence between us to tell me that disappointing though it was, the trip was worth it if only for the two of us on the bridge, watching the fire together. She loved being part of the excitement, she'll say, loved the spontaneous way we swerved over and parked in order to take advantage of the spectacle—a conflagration the length of a city block, reflected over the greasy water, and a red fireboat, neat as a toy, sirening up the river, spouting white geysers while the flames roared back.

Interstate 80 shoots before us in the length of our racing headlight beams. We're on a stretch between towns, surrounded by flat black fields, and the candlepower of the occasional distant farmhouse is insufficient to illuminate the enormous horizon lurking in the dark like the drop-off at the edge of the planet. In the speeding car, her voice sounds disembodied, the voice of a shadow, barely above a whisper, yet it's clear, as if the cover of night and the hypnotic momentum of the road have freed her to reveal secrets. There seemed to be so many secrets about her.

She tells me that as the number of strangers attracted by the fire swelled into a crowd, she could feel a secret current connecting the two of us, like the current that passed between us in bed the first time we made love, when we came at the same moment, as if taken by surprise. It happened only that once.

"Do you remember how, after that, I cried?" she asks.

"Yes."

"You were trying to console me. I know you thought I was feeling terribly guilty, but I was crying because the way we fit together seemed suddenly so familiar, as if there were some old bond between us. I felt flooded with relief, as if I'd been missing you for a long time without quite realizing it, as if you'd returned to me after I thought I'd never see you again. I didn't say any of that, because it sounds like some kind of channeling crap. Anyway, today the same feeling came over me on the bridge, and I was afraid I might start crying again, except this time what would be making me cry was the thought that if we *were* lovers from past lives who had waited lifetimes for the present to bring us back together, then how sad it was to waste the present the way we did this weekend."

I keep my eyes on the road, not daring to glance at her, or even to answer, for fear of interrupting the intimate, almost compulsive way she seems to be speaking.

"I had this sudden awareness," she continues, "of how the moments of our lives go out of existence before we're conscious of having lived them. It's only a relatively few moments that we get to keep and carry with us for the rest of our lives. Those moments *are* our lives. Or maybe it's more like those moments are the dots and what we call our lives are the lines we draw between them, connecting them into imaginary pictures of ourselves. You know? Like those mythical pictures of constellations traced between stars. I remember how, as a kid, I actually expected to be able to look up and see Pegasus spread out against the night, and when I couldn't it seemed like a trick had been played on me, like a fraud. I thought, Hey, if this is all there is to it, then I could reconnect the stars in any shape I wanted. I could create the Ken and Barbie constellations . . . I'm rambling . . ."

"I'm following you, go on."

She moves closer to me.

"I realized we can never predict when those few special moments will occur," she says. "How if we hadn't met, I wouldn't be standing on a bridge watching a fire, and how there are certain people, not that many, who enter one's life with the power to make those moments happen. Maybe that's what falling in love means—the power to create for each other the moments by which we define ourselves. And there you were, right on cue, taking my picture. I had an impulse to open my blouse, to take off my clothes and pose naked for you. I wanted you. I wanted—not to 'fool around.' I wanted to fuck you like there's no tomorrow against the railing of the bridge. I've been thinking about that ever since, this whole drive back."

I turn to look at her, but she says, "No . . . don't look . . . Keep driving . . . Shhh, don't talk . . . I'm sealing your lips."

I can hear the rustle behind me as she raises her skirt, and a faint smack of moistness, and then, kneeling on the seat, she extends her hand and outlines my lips with her slick fingertips.

I can smell her scent; the car seems filled with it. I can feel the heat of her body radiating beside me, before she slides back along the seat until she's braced against the car door. I can hear each slight adjustment of her body, the rustle of fabric against her skin, the elastic sound of her panties rolled past her hips, the faintly wet, possibly imaginary tick her fingertips are making.

"Oh, baby," she sighs.

I've slowed down to fifty-five, and as semis pull into the passing lane and rumble by us, their headlights sweep through the car and I catch glimpses of her as if she'd been imprinted by lightning on my peripheral vision—disheveled, her skirt hiked over her slender legs, the fingers of her left hand disappearing into the V of her rolled-down underpants.

"You can watch, if you promise to keep one eye on the road," she says, and turns on the radio as if flicking on a nightlight that coats her bare legs with its viridescence.

What was playing? The volume was so low I barely heard. A violin from some improperly tuned-in university station, fading in and out until it disappeared into static—banished, perhaps, to those phantom frequencies where Bix Beiderbecke still blew on his cornet. We were almost to Davenport, on the river, the town where Beiderbecke was born, and one station or another there always seemed to be playing his music, as if the syncopated licks of Roaring Twenties jazz, which had burned Bix up so quickly, still resonated over the prairie like his ghost.

"You can't cross I-80 between Iowa and Illinois without going through the Beiderbecke Belt," I had told her when we picked up a station broadcasting a Bix tribute on our way into Chicago. She had never heard of Bix until then and wasn't paying him much attention until the DJ quoted a remark by Eddie Condon, an old Chicago guitarist, that "Bix's sound came out like a girl saying yes." That was only three days ago, and now we are returning, somehow changed from that couple who set out for a fling.

We cross the Beiderbecke Belt back into Iowa, and as we drive past the Davenport exits, the nearly deserted highway is illuminated like an empty ballpark by the bluish overhead lights. Her eyes closed with concentration, she hardly notices as a semi, outlined in red clearance lights, almost sideswipes us. The car shudders in the backdraft as the truck pulls away, its horn bellowing.

"One eye on the road," she cautions.

"That wasn't my fault."

We watch its taillights disappear, and then we're alone in the highway dark again, traveling along my favorite stretch, where in the summer the fields are planted with sunflowers as well as corn and you have to be on the alert for pheasants bolting across the road.

"Baby, take it out," she whispers.

The desire to touch her is growing unbearable, and yet I don't want to stop—don't want the drive to end.

"I'm waiting for you," she says. "I'm right on the edge just waiting for you."

We're barely doing forty when we pass what looks like the same semi, trimmed in red clearance lights, parked along the shoulder. I'm watching her while trying to keep an eye on the road, so I don't notice the truck pulling back onto the highway behind us or its headlights in the rearview mirror, gaining on us fast, until its high beams flash on, streaming through the car with a near-blinding intensity. I steady the wheel, waiting for the whump of the trailer's vacuum as it hurtles by, but the truck stays right on our rear bumper, its enormous radiator grille looming through the rear window and its headlights reflecting off our mirrors and windshield with a glare that makes us squint. Caught in the high beams, her hair flares like a halo about to burst into flame. She's brushed her skirt down over her legs and looks a little wild.

"What's his problem? Is he stoned on uppers or something?" she shouts over the rumble of his engine, and then he hits his horn, obliterating her voice with a diesel blast.

I stomp on the gas. We're in the right lane, and since he refuses to pass, I signal and pull into the outside lane to let him go by, but he merely switches lanes too, hanging on our tail the entire time. The speedometer jitters over ninety, but he stays right behind us, his high beams pinning us like spotlights, his horn bellowing.

"Is he crazy?" she shouts.

I know what's happening. After he came close to sideswiping us outside Davenport, he must have gone on driving down the empty highway with the image of her illuminated by those bluish lights preying on his mind. Maybe he's divorced and lonely, maybe his wife is cheating on him—something's gone terribly wrong for him, and whatever it is, seeing her exposed like that has revealed his own life as a sorry thing, and that realization has turned to meanness and anger.

There's an exit a mile off, and he sees it too and swings his rig back to the inside lane to try and cut me off, but with the pedal to the floor I beat him to the right-hand lane, and I keep it floored, although I know I can't manage a turnoff at this speed. He knows that too and stays close behind, ignoring my right-turn signal, laying on his horn as if to warn me not to try slowing down for this exit, that there's no way of stopping sixty thousand pounds of tractor-trailer doing over ninety.

But just before we hit the exit I swerve back into the outside lane, and for a moment he pulls even with us, staying on the inside as we race past the exit so as to keep it blocked. That's when I yell to her, "Hang on!" and pump the brakes, and we screech along the outside lane, fishtailing and burning rubber, while the truck goes barreling by, its air brakes whooshing. The car skids onto the gravel shoulder, kicking up a cloud of dust, smoky in the headlights, but it's never really out of control, and by the time the semi lurches to a stop, I have the car in reverse, veering back to the exit, hoping no one else is speeding toward us down I-80.

It's the Plainview exit, and I gun into a turn, north onto an empty two-lane, racing toward someplace named Long Grove. I keep checking the mirror for his headlights, but the highway behind us stays dark, and finally she says, "Baby, slow down."

The radio is still playing static, and I turn it off.

"Christ!" she says. "At first I thought he was just your everyday flaming asshole, but he was a genuine psychopath."

"A real lunatic, all right," I agree.

"You think he was just waiting there for us in his truck?" she asks. "That's so spooky, especially when you think he's still out there driving west. It makes you wonder how many other guys are out there, driving with their heads full of craziness and rage."

It's a vision of the road at night that I can almost see: men, not necessarily vicious—some just numb or desperately lonely—driving to the whining companionship of country music, their headlights too scattered and isolated for anyone to realize that they're all part of a convoy. We're a part of it too.

"I was thinking, Oh, no, I can't die now, like this," she says. "It would be too sexually frustrating—like death was the ultimate tease."

"You know what I was afraid of," I tell her. "Dying with my trousers open."

She laughs and continues laughing until there's a hysterical edge to it.

"I think that truck driver was jealous of you. He knows you're a lucky guy tonight," she gasps, winded, and kicks off her sandal in order to slide a bare foot along my leg. "Here we are together, still alive."

I bring her foot to my mouth and kiss it, clasping her leg where it's thinnest, as if my hand were an ankle bracelet, then slide my hand beneath her skirt, along her thigh to the edge of her panties, a crease of surprising heat, from which my finger comes away slick.

"I told you," she moans. "A lucky guy."

I turn onto the next country road. It's unmarked, not that it matters. I know that out here, sooner or later, it will cross a gravel road, and when it does I turn onto the gravel, and after a while turn again at the intersection of a dirt road that winds into fields of an increasingly deeper darkness, fragrant with the rich Iowa earth and resonating with insect choirs amassed for one last Sanctus. I'm not even sure what direction we're traveling in any longer, let alone where we're going, but when my high beams catch a big turtle crossing the road I feel we've arrived. The car rolls to a stop on a narrow plank bridge spanning a culvert. The bridge—not much longer than our car—is veiled on either side by overhanging trees, cottonwoods probably, and flanked by cattails as high as the drying stalks of corn in the acres we've been passing. The turtle, his snapper's jaw unmistakable in the lights, looks mossy and ancient, and we watch him complete his trek across the road and disappear into the reeds before I flick off the headlights. Sitting silently in the dark, we listen to the crinkle of the cooling engine, and to the peepers we've disturbed starting up again from beneath the bridge. When we quietly step out of the car, we can hear frogs plopping into the water. "Look at the stars," she whispers.

"If Pegasus was up there," I say, "you'd see him from here."

"Do you have any idea where we are?" she asks.

"Nope. Totally lost. We can find our way back when it's light."

"The backseat of a car at night, on a country road—adultery has a disconcerting way of turning adults back into teenagers."

We make love, then manage to doze off for a while in the backseat, wrapped together in a checkered tablecloth we'd used once on a picnic, which I still had folded in the trunk.

IN THE PALE early light I shoot the rest of the film on the roll: a close-up of her, framed in part by the line of the checkered tablecloth, which she's wearing like a shawl around her bare shoulders, and another, closer still, of her face framed by her tangled auburn hair, and out the open window behind her, velvety cattails blurred in the shallow depth of field. A picture of her posing naked outside the car in sunlight that streams through countless rents in the veil of the cottonwoods. A picture of her kneeling on the muddy planks of the little bridge, her hazel eyes glancing up at the camera, her mouth, still a yard from my body, already shaped as if I've stepped to her across that distance.

What's missing is the shot I never snapped—the one the trucker tried to steal, which drove him over whatever edge he was balanced on, and which perhaps still has him riding highways, searching each passing car from the perch of his cab for that glimpse he won't get again—her hair disheveled, her body braced against the car door, eyes squeezed closed, lips twisted, skirt hiked up, pelvis rising to her hand.

Years after, she called me out of nowhere. "Do you still have those photos of me?" she asked.

"No," I told her, "I burned them."

"Good," she said, sounding pleased—not relieved so much as flattered—"I just suddenly wondered." Then she hung up.

But I lied. I'd kept them all these years, along with a few letters—part of a bundle of personal papers in a manila envelope that I moved with me from place to place.

I had them hidden away in the back of a file cabinet in the laboratory, although certainly they had no business being there. Now what I'd told her was true: they were fueling the flames.

OUTLINED IN FIRELIGHT, the kid in dreadlocks kisses the waif. His hand glides over the back of her fringed jacket of dirty white buckskin and settles on the torn seat of her faded jeans. She stands on tiptoe on the tops of his gym shoes and hooks her fingers through the empty belt loops of his jeans so that their crotches are aligned. When he boosts her closer and grinds against her she says, "Wow!" and giggles. "I felt it move."

"Fires get me horny," he says.

The roof around the skylight implodes, sending a funnel of sparks into the whirl of snow, and the crowd *ahs* collectively as the beakers in the laboratory pop and flare.

Gapers have continued to arrive down side streets, appearing out of the snowfall as if drawn by a great bonfire signaling some secret rite: gangbangers in their jackets engraved with symbols, gorgeous transvestites from Wharf Street, stevedores and young sailors, their fresh tattoos contracting in the cold. The homeless, layered in overcoats, burlap tied around their feet, have abandoned their burning ashcans in order to gather here, just as the shivering, scantily clad hookers have abandoned their neon corners; as the Guatemalan dishwashers have abandoned their scalding suds; as a baker, his face and hair the ghostly white of flour, has abandoned his oven.

Open hydrants gush into the gutters; the street is seamed with deflated hoses, but the firemen stand as if paired off with the hookers—as if for a moment they've become voyeurs like everyone else, transfixed as the brick walls of our lab blaze suddenly lucent, suspended on a cushion of smoke, and the red-hot skeleton of the time machine begins to radiate from the inside out. A rosy light plays off the up-turned faces of the crowd like the glow of an enormous red lantern—a paper lantern that once seemed fragile, almost delicate, but now obliterates the very time and space it once illuminated. A paper lantern raging out of control with nothing but itself left to consume.

"*Brrrr.*" The Professor shivers, wiping his fogged glasses as if to clear away the opaque gleam reflecting off their lenses.

"Goddamn cold, all right," Tinker mutters, stamping his feet.

For once they agree.

The wind gusts, fanning the bitter chill of night even as it fans the flames, and instinctively we all edge closer to the fire.

"WORK" IS A SKETCHY RENDERING of vaguely recollected scenes from a misspent youth. If I remember right, I wrote the opening and the barroom scenes, and then a long time later set down the events of the day the nameless protagonist spends with Wayne along the Iowa River. Shortly after that I lost any conception of what I was trying to do, and so I stopped trying to do it and just abandoned the project. Except for a little cutting, the piece was never revised.

DENIS JOHNSON

DENIS JOHNSON

Work

I HAD BEEN STAYING AT THE HOLIDAY INN with my girlfriend, honestly the most beautiful woman I'd ever known, for three days under a phony name, shooting heroin. We made love in the bed, ate steaks at the restaurant, shot up in the john, puked, cried, accused one another, begged of one another, forgave, promised, and carried one another to heaven.

But there was a fight. I stood outside the motel hitchhiking, dressed up in a hurry, shirtless under my jacket, with the wind crying through my earring. A bus came. I climbed aboard and sat on the plastic seat while the things of our city turned in the windows like the images in a slot machine.

Once, as we stood arguing at a streetcorner, I punched her in the stomach. She doubled over and broke down crying. A car full of young college men stopped beside us.

"She's feeling sick," I told them.

"Bullshit," one of them said. "You elbowed her right in the *gut*."

"He did, he did, he did," she said, weeping.

I don't remember what I said to them. I remember loneliness crushing first my lungs, then my heart, then my balls. They put her in the car with them and drove away.

But she came back.

This morning, after the fight, after sitting on the bus for several blocks with a thoughtless, red mind, I jumped down and walked into the Vine.

The Vine was still and cold. Wayne was the only customer. His hands were shaking. He couldn't lift his glass.

I put my left hand on Wayne's shoulder, and with my right, opiated and steady, I brought his shot of bourbon to his lips.

"How would you feel about making some money?" he asked me.

"I was just going to go over here in the corner and nod out," I informed him.

"I decided," he said, "in my mind, to make some money."

"So what?" I said.

"Come with me," he begged.

"You mean you need a ride."

"I have the tools," he said. "All we need is that sorry-ass car of yours to get around in."

WE FOUND my sixty-dollar Chevrolet, the finest and best thing I ever bought, considering the price, in the streets near my apartment. I liked that car. It was the kind of thing you could bang into a phone pole with and nothing would happen at all.

Wayne cradled his burlap sack of tools in his lap as we drove out of town to where the fields bunched up into hills and then dipped down toward a cool river mothered by benevolent clouds.

All the houses on the riverbank—a dozen or so—were abandoned. The same company, you could tell, had built them all, and then painted them four different colors. The windows in the lower stories were empty of glass. We passed alongside them and I saw that the ground floors of these buildings were covered with silt. Sometime back a flood had run over the banks, cancelling everything. But now the river was flat and slow. Willows stroked the waters with their hair.

"Are we doing a burglary?" I asked Wayne.

"You can't burgulate a forgotten, empty house," he said, horrified at my stupidity. I didn't say anything.

"This is a salvage job," he said. "Pull up to that one, right about there."

The house we parked in front of just had a terrible feeling about it. I knocked.

"Don't do that," Wayne said. "It's stupid."

Inside, our feet kicked up the silt the river had left here. The watermark wandered the walls of the downstairs about three feet above the floor. Straight, stiff grass lay all over the place in bunches, as if someone had stretched them there to dry.

Wayne used a pry bar, and I had a shiny hammer with a blue rubber grip. We put the pry points in the seams of the wall and started tearing away the Sheetrock. It came loose with a noise like old men coughing. Whenever we exposed some of the wiring in its white plastic jacket, we ripped it free of its connections, pulled it out, and bunched it up. That's what we were after. We intended to sell the copper wire for scrap.

By the time we were on the second floor, I could see we were going to make some money. But I was getting tired. I dropped the hammer, went to the bathroom. I was sweaty and thirsty. But of course the water didn't work.

I went back to Wayne, standing in one of two small empty bedrooms, and started dancing around and pounding the walls, breaking through the Sheetrock and making a giant racket, until the hammer got stuck. Wayne ignored this misbehavior.

I was catching my breath.

I asked him, "Who owned these houses, do you think?"

He stopped doing anything. "This is my house."

"It is?"

"It was."

He gave the wire a long, smooth yank, a gesture full of the serenity of hatred, popping its staples and freeing it into the room.

We balled up big gobs of wire in the center of each room, working for over an hour. I boosted Wayne through the trapdoor into the attic, and he pulled me up after him, both of us sweating and our pores leaking the poisons of drink, which smelled like old citrus peelings, and we made a mound of white-jacketed wire in the top of his former home, pulling it up out of the floor.

I felt weak. I had to vomit in the corner—just a thimbleful of grey bile. "All this work," I complained, "is fucking with my high. Can't you figure out some easier way of making a dollar?"

Wayne went to the window. He rapped it several times with his pry bar, each time harder, until it was loudly destroyed. We threw the stuff out there onto the mud-flattened meadow that came right up below us from the river.

It was quiet in this strange neighborhood along the bank except for the steady breeze in the young leaves. But now we heard a boat coming upstream. The sound curlicued through the riverside saplings like a bee, and in a minute a flat-nosed sports boat cut up the middle of the river going thirty or forty, at least.

This boat was pulling behind itself a tremendous triangular kite on a rope. From the kite, up in the air a hundred feet or so, a woman was suspended, belted in somehow, I would have guessed. She had long red hair. She was delicate and white, and naked except for her beautiful hair. I don't know what she was thinking as she floated past these ruins.

"What's she doing?" was all I could say, though we could see that she was flying.

"Now, that is a beautiful sight," Wayne said.

ON THE WAY to town, Wayne asked me to make a long detour onto the Old Highway. He had me pull up to a lopsided farmhouse set on a hill of grass.

"I'm not going in but for two seconds," he said. "You want to come in?"

"Who's here?" I said.

"Come and see," he told me.

It didn't seem anyone was home when we climbed the porch and he knocked. But he didn't knock again, and after a full three minutes a woman opened the door, a slender redhead in a dress printed with small blossoms. She didn't smile. "Hi," was all she said to us.

"Can we come in?" Wayne asked.

"Let me come onto the porch," she said, and walked past us to stand looking out over the fields.

I waited at the other end of the porch, leaning against the rail, and didn't listen. I don't know what they said to one another. She walked down the steps, and Wayne followed. He stood hugging himself and talking down at the earth. The wind lifted and dropped her long red hair. She was about forty, with a bloodless, waterlogged beauty. I guessed Wayne was the storm that had stranded her here.

In a minute he said to me, "Come on." He got in the driver's seat and started the car—you didn't need a key to start it.

I came down the steps and got in beside him. He looked at her through the windshield. She hadn't gone back inside yet, or done anything at all.

"That's my wife," he told me, as if it wasn't obvious.

I turned around in the seat and studied Wayne's wife as we drove off.

What word can be uttered about those fields? She stood in the middle of them as on a high mountain, with her red hair pulled out sideways by the wind, around her the green and gray plains pressed down flat, and all the grasses of Iowa whistling one note.

I knew who she was.

"That was her, wasn't it?" I said.

Wayne was speechless.

There was no doubt in my mind. She was the woman we'd seen flying over the river. As nearly as I could tell, I'd wandered into some sort of dream that Wayne was having about his wife, and his house. But I didn't say anything more about it.

Because, after all, in small ways, it was turning out to be one of the best days of my life, whether it was somebody else's dream or not. We turned in the scrap wire for twenty-eight dollars—each—at a salvage yard near the gleaming tracks at the edge of town, and went back to the Vine.

Who should be pouring drinks there but a young woman whose name I can't remember. But I remember the way she poured. It was like doubling your money. She wasn't going to make her employers rich. Needless to say, she was revered among us.

"I'm buying," I said.

"No way in hell," Wayne said.

"Come on."

"It is," Wayne said, "my sacrifice."

Sacrifice? Where had he gotten a word like sacrifice? Certainly I had never heard of it.

I'd seen Wayne look across the poker table in a bar and accuse—I do not exaggerate—the biggest, blackest man in Iowa of cheating, accuse him for no other reason than that he, Wayne, was a bit irked by the run of the cards. That was my idea of sacrifice, tossing yourself away, discarding your body. The black man stood up and circled the neck of a beer bottle with his fingers. He was taller than anyone who had ever entered that barroom.

"Step outside," Wayne said.

And the man said, "This ain't school."

"What the goddamn fucking piss-hell," Wayne said, "is that suppose to mean?"

"I ain't stepping outside like you do at school. Make your try right here and now."

"This ain't a place for our kind of business," Wayne said, "not inside here with women and children and dogs and cripples."

"Shit," the man said. "You're just drunk."

"I don't care," Wayne said. "To me you don't make no more noise than a fart in a paper bag."

The huge, murderous man said nothing.

"I'm going to sit down now," Wayne said, "and I'm going to play my game, and fuck you."

The man shook his head. He sat down too. This was an amazing thing. By reaching out one hand and taking hold of it for two or three seconds, he could have popped Wayne's head like an egg.

And then came one of those moments. I remember living through one when I was eighteen and spending the afternoon in bed with my first wife, before we were married. Our naked bodies started glowing, and the air turned such a strange color I thought my life must be leaving me, and with every young fiber and cell I wanted to hold on to it for another breath. A clattering sound was tearing up my head as I staggered upright and opened the door on a vision I will never see again: Where are my women now, with their sweet wet words and ways, and the miraculous balls of hail popping in a green translucence in the yards?

We put on our clothes, she and I, and walked out into a town flooded ankle-deep with white, buoyant stones. Birth should have been like that.

That moment in the bar, after the fight was narrowly averted, was like the green silence after the hailstorm. Somebody was buying a round of drinks. The cards were scattered on the table, face up, face down, and they seemed to foretell that whatever we did to one another would be washed away by liquor or explained away by sad songs.

Wayne was a part of all that.

The Vine was like a railroad club car that had somehow run itself off the tracks into a swamp of time where it awaited the blows of the wrecking ball. And the blows really were coming. Because of Urban Renewal, they were tearing up and throwing away the whole downtown.

And here we were, this afternoon, with nearly thirty dollars each, and our favorite, our very favorite, person tending bar. I wish I could remember her name, but I remember only her grace and her generosity.

All the really good times happened when Wayne was around. But this afternoon, somehow, was the best of all those times. We had money. We were grimy and tired. Usually we felt guilty and frightened, because there was something wrong with us, and we didn't know what it was; but today we had the feeling of men who had worked.

The Vine had no jukebox, but a real stereo continually playing tunes of alcoholic self-pity and sentimental divorce. "Nurse," I sobbed. She poured doubles like an angel, right up to the lip of a cocktail glass, no measuring. "You have a lovely pitching arm." You had to go down to them like a hummingbird over a blossom. I saw her much later, not too many years ago, and when I smiled she seemed to believe I was making advances. But it was only that I remembered. I'll never forget you. Your husband will beat you with an extension cord and the bus will pull away leaving you standing there in tears, but you were my mother.

SHORTLY AFTER LEAVING the University of Iowa in 1974, I headed back through town on my way to New York City and stayed the night with T. Coraghessan Boyle and his wife, Karen. Tom was continuing on for his Ph.D. in English at Iowa and, as I remember it, had just heard that *Esquire* would publish his wonderful short story "Heart of a Champion," about a Lassie who surrenders to her animal lusts, kid in the well or no. We found ourselves talking about dogs not only for that reason but also because he'd just gotten a blue-eyed Akita that he'd seen in a pet shop window. "It was," T. told me, "love at first sight."

In the fall I was back in Nebraska, writing a still-unpublished novel at night, working by day as a painter and handyman for a brother-in-law who owned an office building in Columbus, and living in a lonely house on a lake just outside town. I felt like a guy on the lam, and I imagined how it would be to be a hood hiding from the law in similar surroundings with only a husky for company. I imagined it would finally be as awful as all his previous relationships had been.

I wrote "His Dog" in just a few nights, then, as is my habit with stories, put it away in my desk for a long time, only rewriting it in 1978 when I was at Stanford on a Wallace Stegner Fellowship and desperately needed something, however odd, to submit to the workshop. A friend there knew the fiction editor at *The Ark River Review* and so that's where I sent it. While I have sympathy for those who find "His Dog" weird and unsettling, I think of it as a comedy and still chuckle to myself as I read it.

RON HANSEN

His Dog

THIS WAS WHEN he first saw her. This was the job where he picked up four hundred dollars. He lifted the collar on his coat and stared into the window reflection of a liquor store across the street and of a fat man in a white shirt turning out the lights in the beer coolers.

The man in the street looked down. The window was the front of a pet shop. In a wicker basket puppies nuzzled and climbed one another in sleep. One of them was loose, prowling. The man tapped the glass with his finger and her ears perked. She had blue eyes. He put on a gruesome rubber mask. The puppy backed away, then yapped and jumped at the glass.

Shh! he said, smiling.

He saw the liquor-store owner begin to pull the iron grate across the high windows.

He crossed the street.

$403.45.

IN SEPTEMBER, in a park, he saw a boy with the same husky straining at a leash. She was much bigger now, almost grown. The boy dawdled and the pup leaned.

Hey, the man whispered.

The pup turned her head.

Remember?

HE PICKED BONE and gristle and choice bits off the plates in the kitchen of the café. The cook was giving him a weird look. He walked up a dark alley with a plastic bag warm and sticky under his arm. He bumped a garbage can and caught its lid. He peered over a hedge and grinned. He ripped the bag and threw it into the yard and watched the young dog snatch up the meat and jerk it back and drop it to the grass. She carried the bone away and sat there in shadow. He saw her eyes sparkle. She kept staring as he left.

HE SAT against the chain-link fence. His fingers twisted her fur. Occasionally she licked his chin through the mesh.

It's a crazy way of making a living, he said. Most of the time I just get by. Plus, you're alone all the time.

An autumn wind scattered alley leaves. He lifted the collar of his coat.

He said, I dreamt about you last night.

He said, This is my favorite time of year.

I've been thinking about retiring, he said. How would that be?

HE TAPPED the dollar bills together and wrapped them with rubber bands. He spoke through the rubber mask: And now your change.

The clerk stared at him, his arms at his sides.

Just get out one of those paper sacks and scoop in all the coins.

The clerk raised his hands and suddenly lurched for the gun. There was an explosion. The clerk flew back against a tin rack of cigarettes. He looked down at his bleeding chest. He slowly slid to the floor. He sat.

Goddamn it, the man said. He left the change. Smoke stayed under the light.

DEW SOAKED his knees as he unclipped the chain from her collar. She shook her head and shoulders and watched him walk out the gate. He turned and stood there, stooped and unsure. She tilted her head, glanced at the house. He slapped his thigh softly and she dashed to him and knocked him over with her paws.

Hey! he said. Careful.

He cuddled her and struggled to his feet. He turned happy, tottering circles, his eyes brimming. He rubbed his cheek in her fur. You and me, he whispered. You and me.

SHE WAS SKITTISH on his bed. He'd roll with the covers and she'd bolt to the floor. He'd drop his arm over her neck and she'd lie there as though her head were caught in a fence. In the morning she balanced on his chest and gazed out the motel window, barking at semi trailer trucks.

AS HE DROVE the jeep he scratched his dog's ears. The dog smiled and lifted her nose, so he spidered down the white patch of fur all the way to her chest. Then he looked in the rearview mirror and his hand went to the glove compartment. He put on the rubber mask. He slowed. A family in a station wagon tried to pass him. He looked at them. They dropped back. He cruised for a while and they slipped up on his left again. The children were wide-eyed, the man and woman laughing.

He glowered in his mask. The man floored his car and the children turned in their seats, staring until they vanished over the hill.

He looked at his dog with victory. She panted.

HE CRANKED DOWN the right window and his dog poked her head out. Her nose squirmed in the air.

We're on the lam. Ever hear that word before? It means we're hiding from the cops.

She bit at leaves and branches that slapped against the door. He chuckled. He patted her rump.

I could watch you for hours, you know that?

HE SET THE BRAKE and opened the jeep's door. His dog clambered over him and ran among the pine trees and across a moist, shady yard to the cabin. She sniffed at the door frame, hopped weeds to the back, came out prancing. She wandered to the lake, waded in to her belly, and lapped at the clear water. She walked out heavily and shook, spraying him. He sat on the bank and smoked a cigarette. When his dog came up and licked his face, he petted her so hard her eyes bulged.

HE SPLIT LOGS, nailed up shutters, patched the hull of the rowboat, skimmed stones. She stayed with him.

He found an aluminum bowl and poured in brown pellets. He unwrapped a package of meat and sliced raw liver into the meal. He called his dog. When she chewed at her food, the bowl rang.

He pushed himself back from the table and crossed his stocking feet over the arm of the other chair. He lit a cigarette and stared out at the night. Cigarette smoke splashed off the window. He petted her.

You know what?

Her ears perked forward.

This is exactly how I thought it would be.

HE PRIED A tin box, shook an envelope, stuffed it in his coat pocket. He looked through a stamp collection and sighed with puzzlement. He moved on to another room. He dumped a jewelry chest, stirred things with his finger, dropped a pair of earrings and a necklace in his pocket. He smashed the head of a piggy bank, shook it on the bed, picked out the quarters and dimes. The coins clinked in his pocket as he walked down the stairs.

Coming out of the lake house, he saw that his dog, the blue-eyed husky, had a rabbit in her mouth. He buried it and wiped the blood from his hands with a handkerchief. He wouldn't speak to her.

HE JERKED CUPBOARD DOORS, banged pans on the stove burners, looked out the cabin window all through the meal. Finally she came to him and rested her head in his lap. He cradled it and played with her ears and tipped her nose up so that her eyes fixed on his.

What's the deal with that rabbit? What's got into you, anyway?

HIS DOG was far ahead of him. There were noises in the distant woods, of tearing leaves and snapping twigs. It sounded like food frying, like talk. He picked up his pace and called to her. He caught his ankle in tangling vines. He shouted her name. The weeds rustled and his dog bounded through, her black fur thorny and snatched with brambles. She circled him and he thumped her side with his hand. He leaned against a tree, rubbed his brow, and looked through the bare upper branches at the sun. He kneaded the muscles of his arms. I'm so afraid I'm going to lose you.

SHE SHOOK the earrings off every time he clipped them on. The necklace was probably snagged on a stump somewhere.

HE FED the fire and knelt there, staring at his dog. She raised one eyebrow, then the other, and her tail beat against the chair. He broke a piece of kindling and tossed it to a corner. His dog chased the piece, bit it gingerly, flipped it in her mouth. He threw the stick again and his dog ran after it, paws rattling on the floor. They played like that for a while, then he picked up a hot stick from the fire and threw it. A wisp of smoke streamed after it. His dog stood there.

Well, get it.

His dog sat and looked around the room, smiling.

He glared, then stood, feeling his knees.

Good girl.

HE SAT at the table with his coffee and focused on the calendar tacked to the wall. Then he washed out his cup, put on a coat, and stuffed a gun in his pocket. He stood at the open door and patted his thigh. His dog cocked her head, then slowly walked past him to the jeep.

He followed. We gotta eat, he said.

THEY DROVE to a hardware store. He put on his mask and pointed his finger at his dog.

I don't want a sound out of you. I want you to stay put.

His mask quaked when he spoke. His dog's eyes darted and she settled on the floor. He sat there, looking out the windshield, then he opened the door. His dog smoothed her whiskers with her tongue and panted. He scraped his shoes on the wooden steps and walked inside. A bell chimed and he said something.

She smelled the litter basket and the space beneath the seat. She rolled a road flare back and forth, then far under the springs, out of reach.

He opened the door and climbed in, huffing. He angrily turned the ignition and lifted to readjust the gun in his coat pocket. He still had the mask on. He put the jeep in gear and aggressively rubbed his knuckles into her skull.

Hungry? he asked.

THAT NIGHT he crouched by the lake and watched a brief flurry of snowflakes speck the water and dissolve. He trudged back to the cabin and tried the door, but it was locked.

What is this?

He cupped his eyes and peered through the window. His dog lay by the orange fire, repeatedly licking her paw.

He tried the door again and it swung free. His dog looked at him.

THE OAR TIPS cut into the water and moved, stirring small whirlpools. The green lake was shiny with calm. He slouched back against the prow and zipped his mackinaw up to the collar. He could only see boat houses, boatless docks, woods of blurry red and gold, and over them a gunmetal sky. It looked as though it might snow again. He was alone on the lake, absolutely. He smiled for a moment and slowly rowed back to the cabin.

He thought, I should've brought a radio.

HIS DOG SAT patiently on the sand bank of the lake, her tail wagging, a bird of some sort clamped in her jaws.

What've you got? Huh?

He beached the boat, scraping it on rocks. His boots splashed in the water at the shore. He tamped the anchor into silt. He climbed tiredly to his dog.

Give me that.

He tapped her chin and she let the quail roll into his hand. He stroked the beak with his thumb and the head waggled. She danced around him and jumped. He held her by the collar, threw the bird to the fringe of the forest, wiped his hands on his pants. He knelt next to his dog and cupped her chin in his hand.

Don't you *ever* do that again!

She tried to pull away. He swatted her nose and she flinched. He was about to speak again when she jerked her head and slinked off. He gripped her collar and yanked her around.

Let's get something straight once and for all. That's the kind of thing I won't tolerate. That's the kind of thing that could ruin whatever we've got going here.

He walked slowly back to the cabin. She wouldn't heel. She crossed in and out of the forest.

You bitch! he shouted.

His boots rasped in gravel. His eyes were warm with tears. Bitch.

By evening she was gone.

HE THREW WOOD on the fire. He kicked a chair around. He slumped against the door.

IT BEGAN TO SNOW in earnest and he went to bed early.

He thought he heard a scratching at the door. He couldn't read the time on his watch. He stayed in bed and listened for the sound. He heard a whimper.

There was a faint pink glow from the fireplace. The door opened heavily with snow packed against it. He stood outside, shivering in his slippers and pajamas. The snow slanted in from the lake and, when the wind died, made the slightest crackle in the trees, like someone way out there was wadding cellophane. He walked around the cabin, sloughing through drifts, and saw nothing.

THE SNOW JEWELED in the sunlight. There were two sets of powdered prints around the cabin. He looked at them, a cigarette in his mouth, rubbing the sleeves of his flannel shirt.

I could've done that, he thought. I could've walked around the place twice. I was sleepy.

Then he sagged a bit and pressed his eyes with his thumb knuckles. He turned to go back inside when he heard a bark.

His dog plunged happily through the drifts.

He ran to her and waded and fell. He laughed and they rolled together and she ate big chunks of snow. She sneezed. He sprawled in the snow and smiled and playfully cuffed her head. His dog licked his face. He clutched the fur at her neck.

Baby Baby Baby.

SHE WOKE to a hammering at the door. The latch rattled like a broken toy. His dog sat there, her ears alert and her head cocked, like the dog peering at the Victrola.

A deep voice said, I'll huff and I'll puff and I'll blow your house down.

His dog whined, then yelped, and walked from side to side.

The door burst open and he stood there in his mackinaw and rubber mask.

Scare ya?

She greeted him and happily pushed her paws into his stomach. Her tongue dangled from her grin.

Look what I got.

He brought a transistor radio from behind his back and clicked it on. Then he picked up her paws and waltzed her to the music while she nipped at his fingers. He let her down and she rolled to her back, barking once. He knelt beside her and took off the mask. He touched sweat from his lip.

That was my last job, he said. I'm retired now. This time it's for real.

SHE STOOD over him on all fours in bed. His hands were behind his head. He gazed at the rafters as he talked.

I don't know. I guess women are all right, but they're demanding. They always want to make you something you're not. They're critical of how you act. I don't need that.

She nudged his chin and he smiled.

I need you.

HE DUSTED the windowsills and the mantelpiece. He shoveled the fireplace ashes onto a spread of newspapers. Dog hairs collected everywhere and blew away from his broom. He shook his head with annoyance. He washed the dishes and straightened up his room, and he came out carrying a large, gilt-framed mirror.

He set the mirror against the wall and turned the chair around to face it. His dog walked to him, her nails clicking on the floor. She sat at his feet.

He pointed to the mirror. See what I found?

In the mirror he was sitting in the chair in khaki pants and green rubber boots, his legs crossed at the ankles. He was wearing a Pendleton shirt and his hands rested heavily in his lap. Light slanted in from the window.

I wish I had a camera.

He glanced down and squeezed the flesh of his belly. I'm getting fat.

He could see in the mirror that his dog's head was tilted up at him. She dropped her chin on his knee.

Look at us, he said.

HIS FOOD TASTED BAD and he was out of cigarettes. He sat in a stuffed chair all day and watched his dog. Her teeth nitched at her paw. She groomed her tail. She splattered water when she drank from her pan. When he called, she didn't come.

He dealt solitaire and listened to the radio. Once he got up and squashed an insect that was loggily crawling the floor. His dog got up and sniffed it.

He put on his coat, loaded the magazine of his gun, and locked the cabin door from the outside. He waded through snow to the center of the clearing. He saw his dog barking at the cabin window, her paws on the sill, her breath fogging the glass. He carefully lowered the gun on each of the nearer trees. Bark exploded off with each shot. His dog dropped from the window.

He shoved the gun back into the pocket of his coat and filled his lungs with cold air and smiled agreeably. He stamped his boots on the porch step and saw that the door had somehow been unlocked. He went inside and saw his dog sitting primly by the chair. He slammed the door but it didn't close.

SHE SCRATCHED at her neck with a hind leg. It turned the leather collar, jangling the tags.

He grumpily paced the cabin.

Ching ching ching, he said. He bent to her level and said it louder. Ching ching ching ching ching!

His dog regarded him angrily.

SHE WOULD CHEW a swatch of hair, then lick it, then chew again.

The coffee in his tin cup was cold. He pushed it across the table, turned on the radio, and watched her teeth burrow higher. He watched for quite a while, then banged his cup. Why are you always eating at yourself?

She looked at him and returned to her thigh.

He went to the kitchen, rinsed his cup, and poured himself more coffee.

You never used to do that.

He saw new flakes of snow tap against the window.

I *hate* that sound.

HE KEPT WAKING in the middle of the night to see her there beside him on the comforter. She would be silent, observing him, stars of light in her eyes. He would resist touching her and shift to his side.

HIS DOG WAS off somewhere. He stumbled through the forest, blowing on his fingers. His gun was cold under his belt. He heard his dog growl and wrestle with something. He ran ploddingly through snow, his breath surging, the gun outstretched in both hands. He reached a clearing and saw his dog near a fallen deer, sniffing the red stains in the snow.

Quit that! he shouted. He rocked from side to side, stamping his boots. Quit that quit that quit that!

She stared at him, then trotted ahead, blithely sniffing at snow-laden ferns. She snapped at yellow weeds and dug through snow to the ground.

He ran a few steps and kicked her, knocking her into a tree. She yelped and shied from him and limped ahead, looking over her shoulder with suspicion.

HE WAS AWAKE all night. In the outer room she was growling.

Shut up, for God's sake.

She growled the way she did sometimes when he came too near her food. He threw the covers aside and stood next to the bedroom door. Shut up!

He opened the door and she raised her pitch. She glared at him.

Quiet!

Her nose wrinkled and her teeth showed.

He closed the door and leaned against it.

AT DAWN she still made the noise, but it was hoarse and dry, like bricks rubbed together. He dressed and went out to her. Her head was on her paws. She growled and lifted her eyebrows and glared at him.

What's the matter, girl? he said soothingly.

Then he reached for her and she grabbed his hand in her jaws. She jerked and shook his arm painfully. He slapped at her but she held. He kicked at her and fell. He yanked a drawer and the lamp table tipped. His gun clattered onto the floor.

She let him go.

The skin was badly torn. He pressed it with his handkerchief. I guess that does it, doesn't it? You and me are finished.

He let his hand bleed under the cold water of the kitchen tap. He couldn't move his fingers. He came out of the kitchen with the bite wrapped.

I mean, do you think I could live with that? Huh?

She looked at him mistrustfully.

HE THREW HIS THINGS in the back of the jeep, brushed off snow, and started it. His dog leapt at the jeep windows, scratching the paint, then barked at the caking tires. He put the gun on the seat beside him, and the rubber mask over it. In his rearview mirror he could see her chasing him.

He could brake and throw the jeep into reverse. There'd be a bump and a screech from her. She'd lie in his tracks, shaking with agony. He could then back up over her. The jeep would raise and lower.

He did not do that. But he drove away thinking nothing was too awful for her. She deserved the worst.

HE SWERVED his jeep to the front of a small grocery store. He shut off the engine. He rested his forehead on the steering wheel for a minute, then put on his rubber mask.

His dog slept on the bed in the cabin.

I WROTE THIS STORY during my student days at Iowa. A women's restaurant—Grace and Ruby's—had opened in town, a sort of women's club with a nominal membership fee, a place where women could gather without having to deal with men. The idea fascinated me. There were long-established men's clubs round the world (think of Bertie Wooster and where he'd be without them)—so why not a women's club? I took the idea of a pathologically fascinated man and ran with it. Legend has it that I myself, like the narrator of the story, dressed in drag and entered the inner sanctum. The legend is untrue (I had a confederate do my snooping for me: a bona fide member of the opposite sex, with real hair and real breasts and all the rest). Legend further has it that John Irving, who was then in the midst of writing *Garp*, was also fascinated by the idea of men in drag vis-à-vis the feminist movement. That legend seems to have been substantiated, at least in the pages of that funny and tender novel.

Now, there is more to the history of this story: it became locally controversial. The patrons of Grace and Ruby's read the story in print—or some of them did, or perhaps one of them—and felt that I was attacking them or feminism or their right to privacy, or some such thing. That was not my intention. My intention, as is the guiding purpose in most of my stories, was to explore an idea. Unfortunately, the story was not published in *Harper's* or *Esquire,* which had previously published stories of mine—I tried it on them, but they wouldn't bite. No, gasp!, *Penthouse* accepted it. In those years, the combined income of my wife and me, both students, was circa $5,000. I was happy to publish the story wherever I could and to receive actual money for it.

Now that the dust has cleared (cleared, settled, and turned into sedimentary rock,

I would think), an unbiased reader will find, I hope, a certain storytelling joy in this story, the fun of running with an idea to see where it will go. It is not a malicious story. It does not seek to devastate feminism (tweak it maybe, I'll admit to that), but in a twisted sort of way, to celebrate it.

T. CORAGHESSAN BOYLE

T. CORAGHESSAN BOYLE

A Women's Restaurant

. . . the monomaniac incarnation of all those malicious
agencies which some deep men feel eating in them, till
they are left living on with half a heart and half a lung.
—MELVILLE, Moby Dick

IT IS A WOMEN'S RESTAURANT. Men are not permitted. Women go there to be in the company of other women, to sit in the tasteful rooms beneath the ancient revolving fans and the cool green of spilling plants, to cross or uncross their legs as they like, to chat, sip liqueurs, eat. At the door, the first time they enter, they are asked to donate twenty-five cents and they are issued a lifetime membership card. Thus the women's restaurant has the legal appearance of a private club, and its proprietors, Grace and Rubie, avoid running afoul of the antidiscrimination laws. A women's restaurant. What goes on there, precisely, no man knows. I am a man. I am burning to find out.

This I do know: they drink wine. I have been out back, at night, walking my dog, and I have seen the discarded bottles: chablis, liebfraumilch, claret, mountain burgundy, Bristol Cream. They eat well too. The garbage is rich with dark exotic coffee grounds and spiced teas, the heads of sole, leaves of artichoke, shells of oyster. There is correspondence in the trash as well. Business things for the most part, but once there was a letter from Grace's mother in Moscow, Iowa. Some of the women smoke cigars. Others—perhaps the same ones—drive motorcycles. I watched two of them stutter up on a Triumph 750. In leathers. They walked like meatpackers, heavy, shoulders back, hips tight. Up the steps of the front porch, through the curtained double doors, and in. The doors closed like eyes in mascara.

There is more. Grace, for instance. I know Grace. She is tall, six three or four I would guess, thin and slightly stooped, her shoulders rounded like a question mark. Midthirties. Not married. She walks her square-headed cat on a leash, an advocate of women's rights. Rubie I have spoken with. If Grace is austere, a cactus tall and thorny, Rubie is lush, a spreading peony. She is a dancer. Five feet tall, ninety pounds, twenty-four years old. Facts. She told me one afternoon, months ago, in a bar. I was sitting at a table, alone, reading, a glass of beer sizzling in the sunlight through the window. Her arms and shoulders were bare, the thin straps of her dancer's tights, blue jeans. She was twirling, on point, between groups of people, her laughter like a honky-tonk piano. She came up from behind, ran her finger along the length of my nose, called it elegant. Her own nose was a pug nose. We talked, she struck poses, spoke of her body and the rigors of dancing, showed me the hard muscle of her arms. The sun slanted through the high windows and lit her hair. She did not ask about my life, about the book I was reading, about how I make a living. She did not sit down. When she swept away in a series of glissades, her arms poised, I ordered another beer. She wouldn't know me on the street.

THE WOMEN'S RESTAURANT fronts a street that must have been a main thoroughfare fifty years ago. It comprises the whole of an old mansion, newly painted and shuttered. There is a fence, a gate, a tree, a patch of lawn. Gargoyles. The mayor may once have lived there. On either side blocks of two-story brick buildings stretch to the street corners like ridges of glacial detritus. Apartments above, storefronts below: a used clothing store, an organic merchant, a candle shop. Across the street, incongruous, is a bar that features a picture window and topless dancers. From behind this window, washed in shadow, I reconnoiter the women's restaurant.

I have watched women of every stripe pass through those curtained front doors: washerwomen, schoolmarms, gymnasts, waitresses, Avon ladies, Scout leaders, meter maids, grandmothers, great-grandmothers, spinsters, widows, dikes, gay divorcées, the fat, the lean, the wrinkled, the bald, the sagging, the firm, women in uniform, women in scarves and bib overalls, women in stockings, skirts, and furs, the towering Grace, the flowing Rubie, a nun, a girl with a plastic leg—and yes, even the topless dancers. There is something disturbing about this gathering of women, this classless convocation, this gynecomorphous melting pot. I think of Lysistrata, Gertrude Stein, Carry Nation.

My eyes and ears are open. Still, what I have come to know of Grace & Rubie's is what any interested observer might know. I hunger for an initiate's knowledge.

II

I HAVE MY FIRST attempt to crack the women's restaurant.

The attempt was repulsed.

I was sitting at the picture window of the topless bar, chain-drinking tequila and tonic, watching the front porch of Grace & Rubie's, the bloom of potted flowers, the promise of the curtained doors, and women, schools of them, electric with color, slamming car doors, dismounting from bicycles, motorcycles, trotting up the steps, in and out, tropical fish behind a spotted pane of glass. The sun was drifting toward the horizon, dipping behind the twin chimneys, spooning honey over the roof, the soft light blurring edges and corners, smoothing back the sneers of the gargoyles. It was then that I spotted Rubie. Her walk fluid and unperturbed as a drifting skater. There was another girl with her, an oriental girl. Black hair like a coat. I watched the door gape and then swallow them. Then I stood, put some money in my pocket, left some on the table, and stepped out into the street.

It was warm. The tree was budding. The sun had dropped a notch and the house flooded the street with shadow. I swam toward it, blood beating quick, stopped at the gate to look both ways, pushed through and mounted the steps. Then made my first mistake. I knocked. Knocked. Who knocks at the door of a restaurant? No one answered. I could hear music through the door. Electric jazz. I peered through the oval windows set in the door and saw that the curtains were very thick indeed. I felt uneasy. Knocked again.

After an interval Grace opened the door. Her expression was puzzled. "Yes?" she said.

I was looking beyond her, feeling the pulse of the music, aware of a certain indistinct movement in the background, concentrating on the colors, plants, polished woodwork. Underwater. Chagall.

"Can I help you?"

"Yes, you can," I said. "I'd like—ah—a cup of coffee for starters, and I'd like to see the menu. And your wine list."

"I'm very sorry," Grace said. "But this is a women's restaurant."

III

A WOMEN'S RESTAURANT. The concept inflames me. There are times, at home, fish poached, pots scrubbed, my mind gone blank, when suddenly it begins to rise in my consciousness, a sunken log heaving to the surface. A women's restaurant. The injustice of it, the snobbery, the savory dark mothering mystery: what do they *do* in there?

I picture them, Rubie, Grace, the oriental girl, the nun, the girl with one leg, all of them—picture them sipping, slouching, dandling sandals from their great toes (a mental peep beneath the skirts). I see them dropping the coils of their hair, unfastening their brassieres, rubbing the makeup from their faces. They are soft, heavy, glowing with muliebrity. The pregnant ones remove their tentish blouses, pinching shoes, slacks, underwear, and begin a slow primitive shuffle to the African beat of the drums and the cold moon music of the electric piano. The others watch, chanting, an arcane language, a formula, locked in a rhythm and a mystery that soar grinning above all things male, dark and fertile as the earth.

Or perhaps they're shooting pool in the paneled back room, cigars smoking, brandy in snifters, eyes intense, their breasts pulled toward the earth, the slick cue sticks easing through the dark arches of their fingers, stuffed birds on the walls, the glossy balls clacking, riding down the black pockets like burrowing things darting for holes in the ground . . .

IV

LAST NIGHT THERE was a fog, milk in an atomizer. The streets steamed. Turner, I thought. Fellini. Jack the Ripper. The dog led me to the fence outside the women's restaurant, where he paused to sniff and balance on three legs. The house was a bank of shadow, dark in a negligee of moonlit mist. Fascinating, enigmatic, compelling as a white whale. Grace's VW hunched at the curb behind me, the moon sat over the peaked roof cold as a stone, my finger was on the gate. The gate was latched. I walked on, then walked back. Tied the dog to one of the pickets, reached through to unlatch the gate, and stepped into the front yard at Grace & Rubie's for the second time.

This time I did not knock.

Instead I slipped up to a window and peered through a crack in the curtains. It was black as the inside of a closet. On an impulse I tried the window. It was locked. At that moment a car turned into the street, tires chirping, engine revving, the headlights like hounds of heaven. Rubie's Fiat.

I lost my head. Ran for the gate, tripped, scrambled back toward the house, frantic, ashamed, mortified. Trapped. The car hissed to a stop, the engine sang a hysterical chorus, the headlights died. I heard voices, the swat of car doors. Keys rattling. I crouched. Then crept into the shrubbery beneath the porch. Out by the fence the dog began to whimper.

Heels. Muffled voices. Then Rubie: "Awww, a puppy. And what's he doing out here, huh?" This apparently addressed to the dog, whose whimpering cut a new octave. I could hear his tail slapping the fence. Then a man's voice, impatient. The gate creaked, slapped shut. Footsteps came up the walk. Stopped at the porch. Rubie giggled. Then there was silence. My hand was bleeding. I was stretched out prone, staring at the ground. They were kissing. "Hey," said Rubie, soft as fur, "I like your nose—did I tell you that?"

"How about letting me in tonight," he whispered. "Just this once."

Silence again. The rustle of clothing. I could have reached out and shined their shoes. The dog whimpered.

"The poor pup," Rubie breathed.

"Come on," the guy said. I hated him.

And then, so low I could barely catch it, like a sleeping breath or the hum of a moth's wing: "Okay." Okay? I was outraged. This faceless cicisbeo, this panting lover, schmuck, male—this shithead was going to walk into Grace & Rubie's just like that? A kiss and a promise? I wanted to shout out, call the police, stop this unthinkable sacrilege.

Rubie's key turned in the lock. I could hear the shithead's anticipatory breathing.

A wave of disillusion deadened me. And then suddenly the porch light was blazing, bright as a cafeteria. I shrank. Grace's voice was angry. "What is this?" she hissed. I held my breath.

"Look—" said Rubie.

"No men allowed," said Grace. "None. Ever. Not now, not tomorrow—you know how I feel about this sort of thing."

"—Look, I pay rent here too—"

I could hear the shithead shuffling his feet on the dry planks of the porch. Then Grace: "I'm sorry. You'll have to leave." In the shadows, the ground damp, my hand bleeding, I began to smile.

The door slammed. Someone had gone in. Then I heard Grace's voice swelling to hurricane pitch, and Rubie raging back at her like a typhoon. Inside. Muffled by the double doors, oval windows, thick taffeta curtains. The shithead's feet continued to shuffle on the porch. A moment ticked by, the voices storming inside, and then the light cut out. Dead. Black. Night.

My ears followed the solitary footsteps down the walk, through the gate and into the street.

V

I SHADOWED RUBIE for eight blocks this morning. There were packages in her arms. Her walk was the walk of a slow-haunching beast. As she passed the dark windows of the shops she turned to watch her reflection, gliding, flashing in the sun, her bare arms, clogs, the tips of her painted toenails peeping from beneath the wide-bottomed jeans. Her hair loose, undulating across her back like a wheatfield in the wind. She stopped under the candy-striped pole outside Red's Barber Shop.

I crossed the street, sat on a bench and opened a book. Then I saw Grace: slouching, wide-striding, awkward. Her sharp nose, the bulb of frizzed hair. She walked up to Rubie, unsmiling. They exchanged cheek-pecks and stepped into the barbershop.

When they emerged I dropped my book: Rubie was desecrated. Her head shaven, the wild lanks of hair hacked to stubble. Charlie Manson, I thought. Auschwitz. Nuns and neophytes. Grace was smiling. Rubie's ears stuck out from her head, the color of butchered chicken. Her neck and temples were white as flour, blue-veined and vulnerable. I was appalled.

They walked quickly, stiffly, Rubie hurrying to match Grace's long strides. Grace a sunflower, Rubie a stripped dandelion. I followed them to the women's restaurant. Rubie did not turn to glance at her reflection in the shop windows.

VI

I HAVE MADE my second attempt to crack the women's restaurant.

The attempt was repulsed.

This time I was not drunk: I was angry. Rubie's desecration had been rankling me all day. While I could approve of Grace's firmness with the faceless cicisbeo, I could not countenance her severity toward Rubie. She is like a stroke of winter, I thought, folding up Rubie's petals, traumatizing her roots. An early frost, a blight. But then I am neither poet nor psychologist. My metaphors are primitive, my actions impulsive.

I kicked the gate open, stamped up the front steps, twisted the doorknob and stepped into the women's restaurant. My intentions were not clear. I thought vaguely of rescuing Rubie, of entering that bastion of womanhood, of sex and mystery and rigor, and of walking out with her on my arm. But I was stunned. Frozen. Suddenly, and after all those weeks, I had done it. I was inside.

The entrance hall was narrow and dark, candlelit, overheated, the walls shaggy with fern and wandering Jew. Music throbbed like blood. I felt squeezed, pinched, confined, Buster Crabbe in the shrinking room. My heart left me. I was slouching. Ahead, at the far end of the hallway, a large room flowered in darkness and lights glowed red. Drum, drum, drum, the music like footsteps. That dim and deep central chamber drawing me; a women's restaurant, a women's restaurant: the phrase chanted in my head.

And then the door opened behind me. I turned. Two of the biker girls stepped through the doorway, crowding the hall. One of them was wearing a studded denim jacket, the collar turned up. Both were tall. Short-haired. Their shoulders congested the narrow hallway. I wheeled and started for the darkened room ahead. But stopped in midstride. Grace was there, a tray in her hand, her face looking freshly slapped. "You!" she hissed. The tray fell, glasses shattered, I was grabbed from behind. Rabbit-punched. One of the biker girls began emitting fierce gasping oriental sounds as her white fists and sneakered feet lashed out at me. I went down, thought I saw Rubie standing behind Grace, a soft flush of alarm suffusing her cheeks. A rhythm developed. The biker girls kicked, I huddled. Then they had me by belt and collar, the door was flung open and they rocked me, one, two, three, the bum's rush, down the front steps and onto the walk. The door slammed.

I lay there for a moment, hurting. Then I became aware of the clack of heels on the pavement. A woman was coming up the walk: skirt, stockings, platforms. She hesitated when she saw me there. And then, a look of disgust creasing her makeup, she stepped over me as if she were stepping over a worm or a fat greasy slug washed up in a storm. Her perfume was devastating.

VII

I HAVE BEEN meditating on the essential differences between men and women, isolating distinguishing traits. The meditation began with points of dissimilarity. Women, I reasoned, do not have beards, while they do have breasts. And yet I have seen women with beards and men with breasts—in fact, I came to realize, all men have breasts. Nipples too. Ah, but women have long hair, I thought. Narrow shoulders, expansive hips. Five toes on each foot. Pairs of eyes, legs, arms, ears. But ditto men. They are soft, yielding, dainty, their sensibilities refined—they like shopping. I ran through all the stereotypes, dismissed them one after another. There was only one distinguishing sexual characteristic, I concluded. A hole. A hole as dark and strange, as fascinating and forbidding, as that interdicted entrance to Grace & Rubie's. Birth and motherhood, I thought. The maw of mystery.

I have also been perusing a letter from Rubie, addressed to a person named Jack. The letter is a reconstruction of thirty-two fragments unearthed in the trash behind the women's restaurant. "I miss you and I love you, Jack," the letter said in part, "but I cannot continue seeing you. My responsibilities are here. Yes I remember the night on the beach, the night in the park, the night at the cabin, the night on the train, the night in Saint Patrick's Cathedral—memories I will always cherish. But it's over. I am here. A gulf separates us. I owe it to Grace. Take care of yourself and your knockout nose. Love, R." The letter disturbs me. In the same way that the women's restaurant disturbs me. Secrets, stifling secrets. I want admission to them all.

VIII

THE GIRL IN THE department store asked me what size my wife took. I hesitated. "She's a big one," I said. "About the same size as me." The girl helped me pick out a pink polyester pantsuit, matching brassiere, tall-girl panty hose. Before leaving the store I also visited the ladies' shoe department and the cosmetic counter. At the cosmetic counter I read from a list: glosser, blusher, hi-lighter, eyeshadow (crème, cake and stick), mascara, eyeliner, translucent powder, nail polish (frosted pink), spike eyelashes, luscious tangerine lipstick, tweezers, a bottle of My Sin and the current issue of *Be Beautiful*. At the shoe department I asked for Queen Size.

IX

AFTER TWO WEEKS of laying foundation, brushing on, rubbing in, tissuing off, my face was passable. Crude, yes—like the slick masks of the topless dancers—but passable nonetheless. And my hair, set in rollers and combed out in a shoulder-length flip, struck close on the heels of fashion. I was no beauty, but neither was I a dog.

I eased through the gate, sashayed up the walk, getting into the rhythm of it. Bracelets chimed at my wrists, rings shot light from my fingers. Up the steps, through the front door and into that claustrophobic hallway. My movement fluid, silky, the T-strap flats gliding under my feet like wind on water. I was onstage, opening night, and fired for the performance. But then I had a shock. One of the biker girls slouched at the end of the hallway lighting a cigar. I tossed my chin and strutted by. Our shoulders brushed. She grinned. "Hi," she breathed. I stepped past her, and into the forbidden room.

It was dark. Candlelit. There were tables, booths, sofas and lounge chairs. Plants, hangings, carpets, woodwork. Women. I held back. Then felt a hand on my elbow. It was the biker. "Can I buy you a drink?" she said.

I shook my head, wondering what to do with my voice. Falsetto? A husky whisper?

"Come on," she said. "Get loose. You're new here, right—you need somebody to show you around." She pinched my elbow and ushered me to a booth across the room—wooden benches like church pews. I slid in, she eased down beside me. I could feel her thigh against mine. "Listen," I said, opting for the husky whisper, "I'd really rather be alone—"

Suddenly Rubie was standing over us. "Would you like something?" she said.

The biker ordered a Jack Daniel's on the rocks. I wanted a beer, asked for a sunrise. "Menu?" said Rubie. She was wearing a leather apron, and she seemed slimmer, her shoulders rounded. Whipped, I thought. Her ears protruded and her brushcut bristled. She looked like a Cub Scout. An Oliver Twist.

"Please," I said, huskily.

She looked at me. "Is this your first time?"

I nodded.

She dug something—a lavender card—from an apron pocket. "This is our membership card. It's twenty-five cents for a lifetime membership. Shall I put it on the bill?"

I nodded. And followed her with my eyes as she padded off.

The biker turned to me. "Ann Jenks," she said, holding out her hand.

I froze. A name, a name, a name. This part I hadn't considered. I pretended to study the menu. The biker's hand hung in the air. "Ann Jenks," she repeated.

"Valerie," I whispered, and nearly shook hands. Instead I held out two fingers, ladylike. She pinched them, rubbed her thumb over the knuckles and looked into my eyes.

Then Rubie appeared with our drinks. "Cheers," said Ann Jenks. I downed the libation like honey and water.

AN HOUR AND A HALF LATER I was two sheets to the wind and getting cocky. Here I was, embosomed in the very nave, the very omphalos of furtive femininity—a prize patron of the women's restaurant, a member, privy to its innermost secrets. I sipped at my drink, taking it all in. There they were—women—chewing, drinking, digesting, chatting, giggling, crossing and uncrossing their legs. Shoes off, feet up. Smoking cigarettes, flashing silverware, tapping time to the music. Women among women. I bathed in their soft chatter, birdsong, the laughter like falling coils of hair. I lit a cigarette, and grinned. No more fairybook-hero thoughts of rescuing Rubie— oh no, this was paradise.

Below the table, in the dark, Ann Jenks's fingertips massaged my knee.

I studied her face as she talked (she was droning on about awakened consciousness, liberation from the mores of straight society, feminist terrorism). Her cheekbones were set high and cratered the cheeks below, the hair lay flat across her crown and rushed straight back over her ears, like duck's wings. Her eyes were black, the mouth small and raw. I snubbed out the cigarette, slipped my hand under the jacket and squeezed her breast. Then I put my tongue in her mouth.

"Hey," she said, "want to go?"

I asked her to get me one more drink. When she got up I slid out and looked for the restroom. It was a minor emergency: six tequila sunrises and a carafe of dinner wine tearing at my vitals. I fought an impulse to squeeze my organ.

There were plants everywhere. And behind the plants, women. I passed the oriental girl and two housewives/divorcées in a booth, a nun on a divan, a white-haired woman and her daughter. Then I spotted the one-legged girl, bump and grind, passing through a door adjacent to the kitchen. I followed.

The restroom was pink, carpeted: imitation marble countertops, floodlit mirrors, three stalls. Grace was emerging from the middle one as I stepped through the door. She smiled at me. I smiled back, sweetly, my bladder aflame. Then rushed into the stall, fought down the side zipper, tore at the silky panties, and forgot to sit down. I pissed, long and hard. Drunk. Studying the graffiti—women's graffiti. I laughed, flushed, turned to leave. But there was a problem: a head suspended over the door to the stall. Angry eyes. The towering Grace.

I shrugged my shoulders and held out my palms. Grace's face was the face of an Aztec executioner. This time there would be no quarter. I felt sick. And then suddenly my shoulder hit the door like a wrecker's ball, Grace sat in the sink, and the one-legged girl began gibbering from the adjoining compartment. Out the door and into the kitchen, rushing down an aisle lined with ovens, the stink of cooking food, scraps, greased-over plates, a screen door at the far end, slipping in the T-straps, my brassiere working round, Grace's murderous rasping shriek at my back, STOP HIM! STOP HIM!, and Rubie, pixie Rubie, sack of garbage in her hand at the door.

Time stopped. I looked into Rubie's eyes, imploring, my breath cut in gasps, five feet from her. She let the garbage fall. Then dropped her head and right shoulder, and hit my knees like a linebacker. I went down. My face in coffee grounds and eggshells. Rubie's white white arms shackles on my legs and on my will.

X

I HAVE PENETRATED the women's restaurant, yes, but in actuality it was little more than a rape. There was no sympathy, I did not belong: why kid myself? True, I do have a lifetime membership card, and I was—for a few hours at any rate—an unexceptional patron of the women's restaurant. But that's not enough. I am not satisfied. The obsession grows in me, pregnant, swelling, insatiable with the first taste of fulfillment. Before I am through I will drink it to satiety. I have plans.

Currently, however, I am unable to make bail. Criminal trespass (Rubie testified that I was there to rob them, which, in its way is true I suppose), and assault (Grace showed the bruises on her shins and voice box where the stall door had hit her). Probation I figure. A fine perhaps. Maybe even psychiatric evaluation.

The police have been uncooperative, antagonistic even. Malicious jokes, pranks, taunts, their sweating red faces fastened to the bars night and day. There has even been brutality. Oddly enough—perhaps as a reaction to their jibes—I have come to feel secure in these clothes. I was offered shirt, pants, socks, shoes, and I refused them. Of course, these things are getting somewhat gritty, my makeup is a fright, and my hair has lost its curl. And yet I defy them.

In drag. I like the sound of it. I like the feel. And, as I say, I have plans. The next time I walk through those curtained doors at Grace & Rubie's there will be no dissimulation. I will stroll in and I will belong, an initiate, and I will sit back and absorb the mystery of it, feed on honeydew and drink the milk of paradise. There are surgeons who can assure it.

After all, it is a women's restaurant.

I BEGAN COMPOSING it with just the two voices on the telephone—the daughter informing her father that she was getting married. In the first hour, it came to me that she was marrying someone much older than she was, and that the call was to inform her father that she was pregnant. I worked with this as the central trouble through several sessions, over a period of about four days, and it wasn't until I discovered that the father has news of his own to tell, that his own marriage is dissolving, that the true matter of the story emerged, and then over the following week or so, I put all that in. At one point, it ended with Ballinger's wife saying, "Who knows, maybe they'll be happy for a time. Weren't we, Jack? Weren't we?" But finally I understood what was bothering me about that: it sounded a little too like John O'Hara, and so I went through it one more time, and added the mostly expository lines at the end, to give it the resonance I was after. In doing so, I discovered the second conversation between father and daughter—which, for me, makes the story what it is.

The whole experience made me very happy. It took about two weeks to write, which is a bit faster than I am usually able to write them, though there are the rare occasions when they come faster—I wrote my story "Wedlock" in the space of an afternoon, and part of the following morning.

I like to read "Aren't You Happy for Me?" aloud, and Symphony Space has a marvelous recording of actor Steve Lang reading the story at one of their "Selected Shorts" evenings. He brought the house down and I was in the audience, with Karen and actor-director Bob Balaban. Balaban was putting the finishing touches on the film he'd adapted from my novel "The Last Good Time." Lang read the story so well that I was laughing, and I knew the whole damn thing almost by heart, having written it so many times. It is a good story for reading to an audience; I especially like the quiet that comes at the end, after all the laughs. My new book of stories, *Someone to Watch over Me,* contains a story called "Not Quite Final" that is about these same people.

RICHARD BAUSCH

"WILLIAM COOMBS, WITH TWO O'S ," Melanie Ballinger told her father over long distance. "Pronounced just like the thing you comb your hair with. Say it."

Ballinger repeated the name.

"Say the whole name."

"I've got it, sweetheart. Why am I saying it?"

"Dad, I'm bringing him home with me. We're getting *married*."

For a moment, he couldn't speak.

"Dad? Did you hear me?"

"I'm here," he said.

"Well?"

Again, he couldn't say anything.

"Dad?"

"Yes," he said. "That's—that's some news."

"That's all you can say?"

"Well, I mean—Melanie—this is sort of quick, isn't it?" he said.

"Not that quick. How long did you and Mom wait?"

"I don't remember. Are you measuring yourself by that?"

"You waited six months, and you do too remember. And this is five months. And we're not measuring anything. William and I have known each other longer than five months, but we've been together—you know, as a couple—five months. And I'm almost twenty-three, which is two years older than Mom was. And don't tell me it was different when *you* guys did it."

"No," he heard himself say. "It's pretty much the same, I imagine."

"Well?" she said.

"Well," Ballinger said. "I'm—I'm very happy for you."

"You don't sound happy."

"I'm happy. I can't wait to meet him."

"Really? Promise? You're not just saying that?"

"It's good news, darling. I mean I'm surprised, of course. It'll take a little getting used to. The—the suddenness of it and everything. I mean, your mother and I didn't even know you were seeing anyone. But no, I'm—I'm glad. I can't wait to meet the young man."

"Well, and now there's something *else* you have to know."

"I'm ready," John Ballinger said. He was standing in the kitchen of the house she hadn't seen yet, and outside the window his wife, Mary, was weeding in the garden, wearing a red scarf and a white muslin blouse and jeans, looking young— looking, even, happy, though for a long while there had been between them, in fact, very little happiness.

"Well, this one's kind of hard," his daughter said over the thousand miles of wire. "Maybe we should talk about it later."

"No, I'm sure I can take whatever it is," he said.

The truth was that he had news of his own to tell. Almost a week ago, he and Mary had agreed on a separation. Some time for them both to sort things out. They had decided not to say anything about it to Melanie until she arrived. But now Melanie had said that she was bringing someone with her.

She was hemming and hawing on the other end of the line: "I don't know, see, Daddy, I—God. I can't find the way to say it, really."

He waited. She was in Chicago, where they had sent her to school more than four years ago, and where after her graduation she had stayed, having landed a job with an independent newspaper in the city. In March, Ballinger and Mary had moved to this small house in the middle of Charlottesville, hoping that a change of scene might help things. It hadn't; they were falling apart after all these years.

"Dad," Melanie said, sounding helpless.

"Honey, I'm listening."

"Okay, look," she said. "Will you promise you won't react?"

"How can I promise a thing like that, Melanie?"

"You're going to react, then. I wish you could just promise me you wouldn't."

"Darling," he said, "I've got something to tell you, too. Promise me *you* won't react."

She said "Promise" in that way the young have of being absolutely certain what their feelings will be in some future circumstance.

"So," he said. "Now, tell me whatever it is." And a thought struck through him like a shock. "Melanie, you're not—you're not pregnant, are you?"

She said, "How did you *know*?"

He felt something sharp move under his heart. "Oh, Lord. Seriously?"

"Jeez," she said. "Wow. That's really amazing."

"You're—*pregnant*."

"Right. My God. You're positively clairvoyant, Dad."

"I really don't think it's a matter of any clairvoyance, Melanie, from the way you were talking. Are you—is it sure?"

"Of course it's sure. But—well, that isn't the really hard thing. Maybe I should just wait."

"Wait," he said. "Wait for what?"

"Until you get used to everything else."

He said nothing. She was fretting on the other end, sighing and starting to speak and then stopping herself.

"I don't know," she said finally, and abruptly he thought she was talking to someone in the room with her.

"Honey, do you want me to put your mother on?"

"No, Daddy. I wanted to talk to you about this first. I think we should get this over with."

"Get this over with? Melanie, what're we talking about here? Maybe I should put your mother on." He thought he might try a joke. "After all," he added, "I've never been pregnant."

"It's not about being pregnant. You *guessed* that."

He held the phone tight against his ear. Through the window, he saw his wife stand and stretch, massaging the small of her back with one gloved hand. *Oh, Mary.*

"Are you ready?" his daughter said.

"Wait," he said. "Wait a minute. Should I be sitting down? I'm sitting down." He pulled a chair from the table and settled into it. He could hear her breathing on the other end of the line, or perhaps it was the static wind he so often heard when talking on these new phones. "Okay," he said, feeling his throat begin to close. "Tell me."

"William's somewhat older than I am," she said. "There." She sounded as though she might hyperventilate.

He left a pause. "That's it?"

"Well, it's how much."

"Okay."

She seemed to be trying to collect herself. She breathed, paused. "This is even tougher than I thought it was going to be."

"You mean you're going to tell me something harder than the fact that you're pregnant?"

She was silent.

"Melanie?"

"I didn't expect you to be this way about it," she said.

"Honey, please just tell me the rest of it."

"Well, what did you mean by that, anyway?"

"Melanie, *you said* this would be hard."

Silence.

"Tell me, sweetie. Please?"

"I'm going to." She took a breath. "Dad, William's sixty—he's—he's sixty—sixty-three years old."

Ballinger stood. Out in the garden his wife had got to her knees again, pulling crabgrass out of the bed of tulips. It was a sunny near-twilight, and all along the shady street people were working in their little orderly spaces of grass and flowers.

"Did you hear me, Daddy? It's perfectly all right, too, because he's really a *young* sixty-three, and *very* strong and healthy, and look at George Burns."

"George Burns," Ballinger said. "George—George Burns? Melanie, I don't understand."

"Come on, Daddy, stop it."

"No, what're you telling me?" His mind was blank.

"I said William is sixty-three."

"William who?"

"Dad. My fiancé."

"Wait, Melanie. You're saying your fiancé, the man you're going to marry, *he's* sixty-three?"

"A young sixty-three," she said.

"Melanie. Sixty-three?"

"Dad."

"You didn't say six feet three?"

She was silent.

"Melanie?"

"Yes."

"Honey, this is a joke, right? You're playing a joke on me."

"It is not a—it's not that. God," she said. "I don't believe this."

"You don't believe—" he began. "You don't believe—"

"Dad," she said. "I told you—" Again, she seemed to be talking to someone else in the room with her. Her voice trailed off.

"Melanie," he said. "Talk into the phone."

"I know it's hard," she told him. "I know it's asking you to take a lot in."

"Well, no," Ballinger said, feeling something shift inside, a quickening in his blood. "It's—it's a little more than that, Melanie, isn't it? I mean it's not a weather report, for God's sake."

"I should've known," she said.

"Forgive me for it," he said, "but I have to ask you something."

"It's all right, Daddy," she said as though reciting it for him. "I know what I'm doing. I'm not really rushing into anything—"

He interrupted her. "Well, good God, somebody rushed into something, right?"

"Daddy."

"Is that what you call *him*? No, *I'm* Daddy. You have to call him *Grand*daddy."

"That is *not* funny," she said.

"I wasn't being funny, Melanie. And anyway, that wasn't my question." He took a breath. "Please forgive this, but I have to know."

"There's nothing you really *have* to know, Daddy. I'm an adult. I'm telling you out of family courtesy."

"I understand that. Family courtesy exactly. Exactly, Melanie, that's a good phrase. Would you please tell me, out of family courtesy, if the baby is his."

"Yes." Her voice was small now, coming from a long way off.

"I am sorry for the question, but I have to put all this together. I mean you're asking me to take in a whole lot here, you know?"

"I said I understood how you feel."

"I don't think so. I don't think you quite understand how I feel."

"All right," she said. "I don't understand how you feel. But I think I knew how you'd react."

For a few seconds, there was just the low, sea sound of long distance.

"Melanie, have you done any of the math on this?"

"I should've bet money," she said in the tone of a person who has been proven right about something.

"Well, but Jesus," Ballinger said. "I mean he's older than *I* am, kid. He's—he's a *lot* older than I am." The number of years seemed to dawn on him as he spoke; it filled him with a strange, heart-shaking heat. "Honey, nineteen years. When he was my age, I was only two years older than you are now."

"I don't see what that has to do with anything," she said.

"Melanie, I'll be forty-five *all the way* in December. I'm a *young* forty-four."

"I know when your birthday is, Dad."

"Well, good God, this guy's nineteen years older than your own father."

She said, "I've grasped the numbers. Maybe you should go ahead and put Mom on."

"Melanie, you couldn't pick somebody a little closer to my age? Some snot-nosed forty-year-old?"

"Stop it," she said. "Please, Daddy. I know what I'm doing."

"Do you know how old he's going to be when your baby is ten? Do you? Have you given that any thought at all?"

She was silent.

He said, "How many children are you hoping to have?"

"I'm not thinking about that. Any of that. This is now, and I don't care about anything else."

He sat down in his kitchen and tried to think of something else to say. Outside the window, his wife, with no notion of what she was about to be hit with, looked through the patterns of shade in the blinds and, seeing him, waved. It was friendly, and even so, all their difficulty was in it. Ballinger waved back. "Melanie," he said, "do you mind telling me just where you happened to meet William? I mean how do you meet a person forty years older than you are? Was there a senior citizen–student mixer at the college?"

"Stop it, Daddy."

"No, I really want to know. If I'd just picked this up and read it in the newspaper,

I think I'd want to know. I'd probably call the newspaper and see what I could find out."

"Put Mom on," she said.

"Just tell me how you met. You can do that, can't you?"

"Jesus Christ," she said, then paused.

Ballinger waited.

"He's a teacher, like you and Mom, only college. He was my literature teacher. He's a professor of literature. He knows everything that was ever written, and he's the most brilliant man I've ever known. You have no idea how fascinating it is to talk with him."

"Yes, and I guess you understand that over the years that's what you're going to be doing a *lot* of with him, Melanie. A lot of talking."

"I am carrying the proof that disproves *you*," she said.

He couldn't resist saying, "Did *he* teach you to talk like that?"

"I'm gonna hang up."

"You promised you'd listen to something *I* had to tell *you*."

"Okay," she said crisply. "I'm listening."

He could imagine her tapping the toe of one foot on the floor: the impatience of someone awaiting an explanation. He thought a moment. "He's a professor?"

"That's not what you wanted to tell me."

"But you said he's a professor."

"Yes, I said that."

"Don't be mad at me, Melanie. Give me a few minutes to get used to the idea. Jesus. Is he a professor emeritus?"

"If that means distinguished, yes. But I know what you're—"

"No, Melanie. It means *retired*. You went to college."

She said nothing.

"I'm sorry. But for God's sake, it's a legitimate question."

"It's a stupid, mean-spirited thing to ask." He could tell from her voice that she was fighting back tears.

"Is he there with you now?"

"Yes," she said, sniffling.

"Oh, Jesus Christ."

"Daddy, why are you being this way?"

"Do you think maybe we could've had this talk alone? What's he, listening on the other line?"

"No."

"Well, thank God for that."

"I'm going to hang up now."

"No, please don't hang up. Please let's just be calm and talk about this. We have some things to talk about here."

She sniffled, blew her nose. Someone held the phone for her. There was a muffled something in the line, and then she was there again. "Go ahead," she said.

"Is he still in the room with you?"

"Yes." Her voice was defiant.

"Where?"

"Oh, for God's sake," she said.

"I'm sorry, I feel the need to know. Is he sitting down?"

"I *want* him here, Daddy. We both want to be here," she said.

"And he's going to marry you."

"Yes," she said impatiently.

"Do you think I could talk to him?"

She said something he couldn't hear, and then there were several seconds of some sort of discussion, in whispers. Finally she said, "Do you promise not to yell at him?"

"Melanie, he wants me to promise not to *yell* at him?"

"Will you promise?"

"Good God."

"Promise," she said. "Or I'll hang up."

"All right. I promise. I promise not to yell at him."

There was another small scuffing sound, and a man's voice came through the line. "Hello, sir." It was, as far as Ballinger could tell, an ordinary voice, slightly lower than baritone. He thought of cigarettes. "I realize this is a difficult—"

"Do you smoke?" Ballinger interrupted him.

"No, sir."

"All right. Go on."

"Well, I want you to know I understand how you feel."

"Melanie says she does, too," Ballinger said. "I mean I'm certain you both *think* you do."

"It was my idea that Melanie call you about this."

"Oh, really. That speaks well of you. You probably knew I'd find this a little difficult to absorb and that's why you waited until Melanie was pregnant, for Christ's sake."

The other man gave forth a small sigh of exasperation.

"So you're a professor of literature."

"Yes, sir."

"Oh, you needn't 'sir' me. After all, I mean I *am* the goddam kid here."

"There's no need for sarcasm, sir."

"Oh, I wasn't being sarcastic. That was a literal statement of this situation that obtains right here as we're speaking. And, really, Mr. . . . It's Coombs, right?"

"Yes, sir."

"Coombs, like the thing you comb your hair with."

The other man was quiet.

"Just how long do you think it'll take me to get used to this? You think you might get into your seventies before I get used to this? And how long do you think it'll take my wife who's twenty-one years younger than you are to get used to this?"

Silence.

"You're too old for my *wife,* for Christ's sake."

Nothing.

"What's your first name again?"

The other man spoke through another sigh. "Perhaps we should just ring off."

"Ring off. Jesus. Ring off? Did you actually say 'ring off'? What're you, a goddam limey or something?"

"I am an American. I fought in Korea."

"Not World War One?"

The other man did not answer.

"How many other marriages have you had?" Ballinger asked him.

"That's a valid question. I'm glad you—"

"Thank you for the scholarly observation, *sir*. But I'm not sitting in a class. How many did you say?"

"If you'd give me a chance, I'd tell you."

Ballinger said nothing.

"Two, sir. I've had two marriages."

"Divorces?"

"I have been widowed twice."

"And—oh, I get it. You're trying to make sure that that never happens to you again."

"This is not going well at all, and I'm afraid I—I—" The other man stammered, then stopped.

"How did you expect it to go?" Ballinger demanded.

"Cruelty is not what I'd expected. I'll tell you that."

"You thought I'd be glad my daughter is going to be getting social security before I do."

The other was silent.

"Do you have any other children?" Ballinger asked.

"Yes, I happen to have three." There was a stiffness, an overweening tone, in the voice now.

"And how old are they, if I might ask."

"Yes, you may."

Ballinger waited. His wife walked in from outside, carrying some cuttings. She poured water in a glass vase and stood at the counter arranging the flowers, her back to him. The other man had stopped talking. "I'm sorry," Ballinger said. "My wife just walked in here and I didn't catch what you said. Could you just tell me if any of them are anywhere near my daughter's age?"

"I told you, my youngest boy is thirty-eight."

"And you realize that if *he* wanted to marry my daughter I'd be upset, the age difference there being what it is." Ballinger's wife moved to his side, drying her hands on a paper towel, her face full of puzzlement and worry.

"I told you, Mr. Ballinger, that I understood how you feel. The point is, we have a pregnant woman here and we both love her."

"No," Ballinger said. "That's not the point. The point is that you, sir, are not much more than a goddam statutory rapist. That's the point." His wife took his shoulder. He looked at her and shook his head.

"What?" she whispered. "Is Melanie all right?"

"Well, this isn't accomplishing anything," the voice on the other end of the line was saying.

"Just a minute," Ballinger said. "Let me ask you something else. Really now. What's the policy at that goddam university concerning teachers screwing their students?"

"Oh, my God," his wife said as the voice on the line huffed and seemed to gargle.

"I'm serious," Ballinger said.

"Melanie was not my student when we became involved."

"Is that what you call it? Involved?"

"Let me talk to Melanie," Ballinger's wife said.

"Listen," he told her. "Be quiet."

Melanie was back on the line. "Daddy? Daddy?"

"I'm here," Ballinger said, holding the phone from his wife's attempt to take it from him.

"Daddy, we're getting married and there's nothing you can do about it. Do you understand?"

"Melanie," he said, and it seemed that from somewhere far inside himself he heard that he had begun shouting at her. "Jee-zus good Christ. Your fiancé was almost *my* age *now* the day you were *born*. What the hell, kid. Are you crazy? Are you out of your mind?"

His wife was actually pushing against him to take the phone, and so he gave it to her. And stood there while she tried to talk.

"Melanie," she said. "Honey, listen—"

"Hang up," Ballinger said. "Christ. Hang it up."

"Please. Will you go in the other room and let me talk to her?"

"Tell her I've got friends. All these nice men in their forties. She can marry any one of my friends—they're babies. Forties—cradle fodder. Jesus, any one of them. Tell her."

"Jack, stop it." Then she put the phone against her chest. "Did you tell her anything about us?"

He paused. "That—no."

She turned from him. "Melanie, honey. What is this? Tell me, please."

He left her there, walked through the living room to the hall and back around to the kitchen. He was all nervous energy, crazy with it, pacing. Mary stood very still, listening, nodding slightly, holding the phone tight with both hands, her shoulders hunched as if she were out in cold weather.

"Mary," he said.

Nothing.

He went into their bedroom and closed the door. The light coming through the windows was soft gold, and the room was deepening with shadows. He moved to the bed and sat down, and in a moment he noticed that he had begun a low sort of murmuring. He took a breath and tried to be still. From the other room, his wife's voice came to him. "Yes, I quite agree with you. But I'm just unable to put this . . ."

The voice trailed off. He waited. A few minutes later, she came to the door and knocked on it lightly, then opened it and looked in.

"What," he said.

"They're serious." She stood there in the doorway.

"Come here," he said.

She stepped to his side and eased herself down, and he moved to accommodate her. He put his arm around her, and then, because it was awkward, clearly an embarrassment to her, took it away. Neither of them could speak for a time. Everything they had been through during the course of deciding about each other seemed concentrated now. Ballinger breathed his wife's presence, the odor of earth and flowers, the outdoors.

"God," she said. "I'm positively numb. I don't know what to think."

"Let's have another baby," he said suddenly. "Melanie's baby will need a younger aunt or uncle."

Mary sighed a little forlorn laugh, then was silent.

"Did you tell her about us?" he asked.

"No," she said. "I didn't get the chance. And I don't know that I could have."

"I don't suppose it's going to matter much to her."

"Oh, don't say that. You can't mean that."

The telephone on the bedstand rang, and startled them both. He reached for it, held the handset toward her.

"Hello," she said. Then: "Oh. Hi. Yes, well, here." She gave it back to him.

"Hello," he said.

Melanie's voice, tearful and angry: "You had something you said you had to tell *me*." She sobbed, then coughed. "Well?"

"It was nothing, honey. I don't even remember—"

"Well, I want you to know I would've been better than you were, Daddy, no matter how hard it was. I would've kept myself from reacting."

"Yes," he said. "I'm sure you would have."

"I'm going to hang up. And I guess I'll let you know later if we're coming at all. If it wasn't for Mom, we wouldn't be."

"We'll talk," he told her. "We'll work on it. Honey, you both have to give us a little time."

"There's nothing to work on as far as William and I are concerned."

"Of course there are things to work on. Every marriage—" His voice had caught. He took a breath. "In every marriage there are things to work on."

"I know what I know," she said.

"Well," said Ballinger. "That's—that's as it should be at your age, darling."

"Goodbye," she said. "I can't say any more."

"I understand," Ballinger said. When the line clicked, he held the handset in his lap for a moment. Mary was sitting there at his side, perfectly still.

"Well," he said. "I couldn't tell her." He put the handset back in its cradle. "God. A sixty-three-year-old son-in-law."

"It's happened before." She put her hand on his shoulder, then took it away. "I'm so frightened for her. But she says it's what she wants."

"Hell, Mary. You know what this is. The son of a bitch was her goddam teacher."

"Listen to you—what are you saying about her? Listen to what you're saying about her. That's our daughter you're talking about. You might at least try to give her the credit of assuming that she's aware of what she's doing."

They said nothing for a few moments.

"Who knows," Ballinger's wife said. "Maybe they'll be happy for a time."

He'd heard the note of sorrow in her voice, and thought he knew what she was thinking; then he was certain that he knew. He sat there remembering, like Mary, their early happiness, that ease and simplicity, and briefly he was in another house, other rooms, and he saw the toddler that Melanie had been, trailing through slanting light in a brown hallway, draped in gowns she had fashioned from her mother's clothes. He did not know why that particular image should have come to him out of the flow of years, but for a fierce minute it was uncannily near him in the breathing silence; it went over him like a palpable something on his skin, then was gone. The ache which remained stopped him for a moment. He looked at his wife, but she had averted her eyes, her hands running absently over the faded denim cloth of her lap. Finally she stood. "Well," she sighed, going away. "Work to do."

"Mary?" he said, low; but she hadn't heard him. She was already out the doorway and into the hall, moving toward the kitchen. He reached over and turned the lamp on by the bed, and then lay down. It was so quiet here. Dark was coming to the windows. On the wall there were pictures; shadows, shapes, silently clamoring for his gaze. He shut his eyes, listened to the small sounds she made in the kitchen, arranging her flowers, running the tap. *Mary*, he had said. But he could not imagine what he might have found to say if his voice had reached her.

WINTER: MENTOR

I rewrite to be reread.
—ANDRÉ GIDE

"EFFICIENCY APARTMENT"—rented long-distance—turned out to mean a room. The small back kitchen of a Victorian subdivided against itself—one of those overly porched behemoths banished to the disreputable end of Iowa Avenue. The bath, I shared. My single window offered me a marshy backyard self-planted with privets, cedars, and other unlovable (and therefore tenacious) weed trees.

I painted the room matte white. It was so small, I remember I finished the job in thirty-five minutes. So, I did another three drafts. As a writer, I was already humble about starting over. I was then twenty-four with a twenty-six-inch waist. I am now fifty-one and have no further comment.

MANY RENTAL HOMES and chambers later, that austere cell still accompanies me. It yet recalls van Gogh's "Room at Arles." A chair, a bed, a window, table. (And on it, my Hermes portable manual typewriter the exact green of Howard Johnson's pistachio ice cream.)

Every artist—beseiged by telephone and wage earning, by unexpected parenthood and all-too-predictable divorce—every artist whose growth has been stunted by a notice from the IRS beginning, "Please explain why our records show you paid no taxes for the following five years . . . ," every artist dreams of blissful imprisonment. They give you a cell, they keep it reasonably warm, they slip a couple so-so meals through that slot under the door. Then they just leave you the hell alone, to work.

Winter in Iowa remembers like that. The room was white, so was the typing paper, and, God knows, the landscape had been planned in the frozen-food department. I was a Southern boy, and even by mid-November, the door-shaking force of Winter seemed something coming in from a horror movie.

Looking back, I know I partied. I know I taught a class of cocky blondish undergrads. I know I fell in love twice (roughly a 4 and a 7 on the Richter scale). But what looms in memory like some iceberg met at night at sea is Winter and the poverty that stuck me in a room so small. Winter edited me. I put my desk beside that window and all the white out there bullied and classicized my prose, my calves. Compared to snow, black ink soon seemed green as a line from Marvell, no, greener—green as the bitter green that inspired that sweet true line by Marvell. I was left grateful for my body heat, my granny's quilt, my sexual partners' heat(s) and quilts. I learned to shop two-weeks' worth; I horded, and my lair came to seem a pretty respectable bachelor wolverine's den. Instead of going to the library, I reread my battered undergrad Balzac, Dickens, and Chekhov especially. By mid-February, I'd be waked by screaming wind. Then I'd get to lie there, fingers laced behind my head, arms then beautiful, feeling glad for Indoors and the coming morning's work.

Iowa snow never seemed to know that snow, once down, can melt. Come dawn, my window's icicles looked exiled, Siberian in their brutality. By noon, they glimmered molten, a Venetian delicate mouth-blownness.

My particular prison cell was blessed with the visiting hours of true friends. The cell was supplemented by backpack forays to a good brick library, by a few genius teachers (John Cheever, Stanley Elkin), and by a hardscrabble Midwestern culture—expectation of chores' daily handwork. Winter was my secret grant. An affair with a closet case.

On finishing a story at 11:30 P.M., I could ride my bike—ice conditions permitting—to Robert's house or Joanne's or Dick's. And I would wait, biting my nails in the front room as they read the work at their own desks, their young children sleeping nearby; then they stepped back out and told me. The truth in love. ("Your opening is almost as good as that opening you did once so ideally it almost seems pure luck now. But this one sags some in the middle, loses energy, I don't know about the mother-in-law, and then the thing certainly does end, but, as with certain second-tier State Fairs' firework displays, it ends about four times. Choose. Otherwise it's, like, perfect.") Let's celebrate. How about a snort of brandy before you try biking home? (Hint, hint.) These friends admitted that my prose did reveal I had been reading, what? Agee film criticism? Borges fables? and maybe a little too much oblique Henry Green dialogue; but I'd mainly paid back all my borrowings. And congratulations, and what say to that one shot of firewater? One only, to assure that my bike wouldn't skid on black ice, as I pedaled home through this blizzard's three-below. It was life and death for us. (How to get Character A out of bed, onto the toilet, and busy at the toaster in less than two textured paragraphs?) It was always either talking about Literature very late at night until it made so much sense over so much beer it later made no sense at all; or else trying to handmake some (literature) the very next morning.

We treated each other and each other's fiction with a loving seriousness that proved (to others than ourselves) how much it meant. Many waiting eager readers seemed implied. Already we were looking out for them. Gazing back from this age, our having found those many readers surprises me none at all. Our assuming them so early is what thrills me. We knew.

Because we really had nothing else, did we? Nothing past these rented rooms (sixty bucks a month), the borrowed books, the old "Literature" we read and the new literature that we, in every particle of our DNA, hoped to become then leave behind. We had our hope, our long, long winter, and each other.

In no room have I ever managed more ecstatic pressings against the edge of all I might yet know. As prairie winter tried again to get in here, some force of my own spirit sought its daily prison break. In no room have I ever bluffed and foxed myself beyond the icy checkpoints of my own limitations. But how? How?

With coffee enough, with afternoon classes, it was a morning rush as hot and irrational as that long drippy season was logical, on schedule, and bone-breakingly wicked in its chill. The wind cut unbroken off the Great Plains, rattling my single window that soon felt the only porthole on this drifting clapboard prison barge. Oh, blissful imprisonment.

The time remembers as a Geological Age, one precisely as eventful for me as that scrubby working-class backyard, which stayed polar, blank, molar, narcoleptic. That yard soon resembled those hundreds then thousands of manually typed pages piling up in view of it. The yard was also written—faint mortal black lines (branches, fence wire, clothesline posts) printed on the inexhaustible salacious purity of White. And that whole visible hibernating world cried out to us, "Cut me. Paste me back right. Simplify then know then sing me!"

And we did. I know I have tried. And still do, daily.

My friends from then still are, my friends. I am so proud of their work. Even now, they are my darling early readers. I'm tempted to rattle through the famous and almost-famous and not-yet-famous names, but that'd be cheap, unfair to who we were before anybody knew us but each other. We were so young that when the phone rang, it was always somebody you wanted to talk to!

We learned to work from how hard we saw each other working in plain sight. We didn't know yet how *not* to seem to want it. We came of age in a lucky time, just before faith in Shortcuts made Labor—terrible, poor-person's, manual, winter, tuber-grubbing, peasant labor—so embarrassing. We learned our truest gifts as artists from what, in our own work, best lit and warmed each other.

During that endless season of freezes and refreezings, sidewalks were barely visible through the lenses of so much water serially tortured, water hardened and released then rehardened then rereleased, like the clarifying drafts of our own layered chipped-away salt-burned and finally reburnished stories. Winter made our work as hard as ice. Clear as that. And, oh, as infinitely revisable.

Our truest alma mater?

Each other's fond regard. And "The Iowa Winter's Workshop."

ALLAN GURGANUS

ALLAN GURGANUS

Blessed Assurance:
A Moral Tale

In memory of James Zito
and for Grace Paley

I SOLD FUNERAL INSURANCE to North Carolina black people. I myself am not black. Like everybody else who was alive fifty-nine years ago, I was so young then, you know? I still feel bad about what went on. My wife says: telling somebody might help. Here lately, worry over this takes a percentage of my sleep right off the top.—So I'm telling you, okay?

See, I only did it to put myself through college. I knew it wasn't right. But my parents worked the swing shift at the cotton mill. We went through everything they earned before they earned it. I grew up in one of those employee row houses. Our place stood near the cotton loading ramp. Our shrubs were always tagged with fluff blown off stacked bales. My room's window screens looked flannel as my kiddie pajamas. Mornings, the view might show six white windblown hunks, big as cakes. You didn't understand you'd steadily breathed such fibers—not till, like Dad, you started coughing at age forty and died at fifty-one.—I had to earn everything myself. First I tried peddling the *Book of Knowledge*. Seemed like a good thing to sell. I attended every single training session. This sharp salesman showed us how to let the "T" volume fall open at the Taj Mahal. Our company had spent a little extra on that full-page picture. In a living room the size of a shipping crate, I stood before my seated parents. I practiced. They nodded. I still remember, "One flick of the finger takes us from 'Rome' to . . . 'Rockets'!" Before I hiked off with my wares, Mom would pack a bag lunch, then wave from our fuzzy porch, "Jerry? Say 'Please' and 'Thank you very much.' They like that."

OTHER SALESKIDS OWNED CARS. I had to walk from house to house lugging my sample kit: twenty-six letters' worth of knowledge gets heavy pretty fast. My arms and back grew stronger but my spirits sort of caved in. Our sales manager assigned me to the Mill district—he claimed I had inside ties. The only thing worse than facing strangers door-to-door is finding people you knew there.

Grinning, they'd ask me in. Mill employees opened their iceboxes, brought me good things. I chattered my whole memorized routine. Neighbors acted proud of me. But I felt like a circus dog and some stuffy teacher, mixed. Like a crook. When I finished, my hosts sighed, said this book set sure sounded great. Then they admitted what we'd all known all along: they just couldn't afford it. I'd spent forty minutes ignoring this. They looked troubled as I backed out, smiling. "Hey," I called. "It's copacetic, really. You'll save for the down payment. You'll get *Knowledge* on time— it'll mean more to you." Then I knocked at the next door. I stood praying for an empty house.

One day I came trudging over the Mill's suspension bridge—the weight of world knowledge was giving me a hernia. My third week of no sales. One middle-class kid had already won a trip to Mexico. "This boy's going places," our sales manager said. "Whereas Jerry's going home and napping every afternoon, right, Jer?" I threw my whole kit in the river. The case flew open. Out volumes shot: "Cat" through "Graph." "Uterine" through "Xanadu." All human learning (illustrated) lay sogged and ruined on the rocks below. And I loved it. I stayed to watch the current wash every book over the dam that ran the cotton mill that made the cloth that fattened accounts of the owners who'd kept my parents broke and wheezy forty years. Bye bye, *Knowledge*. I couldn't afford it.

(IN HERE, I tried selling a vegetable shredder. "Make a rose out of a radish and in no time." This is all I'll say about those two weeks of bloody fingertips and living off my demonstration salads.)

HERE COMES FUNERAL INSURANCE. Okay, I answered an ad. The head honcho says, "Son, I'm not promising you the moon." I loved him for that. He was so sad you had to trust him. On his desk, a photo of one pale disappointed-looking wife. There were six pictures of two kids shown being sweet but runty at three different ages in three different ways. I felt for the guy.

He kept his shoes propped on a dented desk. A bronze plaque there spelled *Windlass Insurance for Funerary Eventualities, Cleveland.* My new boss flashed me a nonpersonal salesman wink; he offered me a snort of whiskey from his pint bottle. I said No. I was under legal age. With Sam's legs crossed, with his eyes roaming the ceiling's waterstains, he rocked back and told. Admitting everything, his voice grew both more pained and more upbeat.

"Black people come from Africa. No news, right? But all Africans are big on funerals. It's how your dying tribe-people announce the respect they deserve in their next life, see? *I'm* not buying into this, understand—just laying out why a person who's got no dinner will cough up fifty cents to three bucks per Saturday for a flashy coffin and last party.

"Now, times, you might get to feeling—nice boy like you, college material—like maybe you're stealing from them. You take *that* attitude, you'll wind up like . . . like me. No, you've got to accept how another type of person believes. Especially when there's such a profit in it. And remember, Our Founder was a black man. Richest colored family in Ohio, I'm told. Plus, for all we know, they could be right, Jerry. If there *is* the so-called next world, they'll turn up in it, brass bands to announce them. And us poor white guys who sold them the tickets, we'll be deep-fat-frying underneath forever. That'd sure get a person's attention, wouldn't it? Coming to in Hell? For being Bad here?

"What I'm saying: You've got to work it out for yourself, and quick. Here's your premium book. Take plenty of change. Four bits to three bucks per week might sound like nothing to a crackerjack like you. But, with most of Colored Town paying, it adds up. And, Jerry, they *do* get it back when they break the bank. Soon as some next-of-kin comes in here with a legal death certificate, I pay off like clockwork. So, yeah, it's honest . . . I see that look on your face. Only thing, buddy, if they miss two weeks running, they forfeit. They lose the present policy and any other Windlass ones they've paid up. I don't care if they've put in thousands, and several of your older clients will have: if they let one, then two (count them) two big Saturdays roll by, their pile becomes the company's.

"You getting this? See, that's the catch. I warned them during my own feistier collecting days, I'd go, 'Hey, no remuneral, no funeral. No bucks, no box.' They'd laugh but they got my meaning. Your client misses two back-to-back Saturdays, it's hello potter's field. Could be worse. I mean, *they* won't be around to suffer through it.

"And listen. Jer. No exceptions to our two-week rule, none. Because, Jerry, they'll beg you. Hold firm. Way I see it, anybody who can't come up with fifty cents a week on this plane, they don't deserve the four-star treatment in the next, you know?—No, I lied. That's *not* the way I see it. The way I see it is: I wish I hadn't washed out of dental school. The Organic Chemistry, Jerry. The goddamn Organic Chemistry, I had a sick feeling about it from the first. Like a drink? That's right, you said No. So here's your book, names, addresses, amounts paid to date. See—our clients they've got nothing else—they're hoping for a better shot next go-round. Your middle-class black people wouldn't touch funeral insurance with somebody else's ten-foot pole.

"Jerry, I recommend a early start on Saturday. They mostly get paid Friday night. They've mostly spent every penny by Sunday morning. And, son, they *want* to pay.

So, do everybody a favor, especially yourself, grab it while it's in their hot hands. And if you need leverage, mention . . . you know."

"What?" I had to ask. "Please."

"It. A beaverboard box held together with thumbtacks. No flowers but what the neighbors pick. Not a single whitewalled Packard graveside. One attention-getter is—saying their hearse'll be from the City Sanitation Department. Face it: we've got a heartless business going here. And, Jer? the minute they smell heart on you, you're down the toilet, Jerry. They'll let Number One week slide by. Then here goes Numero Dou, and they'll start blaming you. And you'll believe them. Next they'll try and bribe you—homebrewed liquor, catfish, anything. I had one woman promise me her daughter. Girl couldn't have been older than twelve. I'm a family man, Jerry. But these people are fighting for their souls in the next life—you can understand, it matters to them. They'll do anything, anything, if you won't squeal and cut them off from their picture of heaven. But Jerry?—cut them off.

"The minute I got promoted from door-to-door, I swore I'd tell each new collector the whole rancid truth. You just got it straight-up, kiddo. Now head on out there. They'll love your argyle sweater vest—new, is it? Me, I plan to sit right here and get legless drunk. Hearing the deal spelled out again, it breaks me fourteen ways, it does. When I think of what a decent dental practice can net per year for a hard-working guy, when I remember certain pet clients who almost got the full treatment on the next plane, but . . . hey, this I'm giving you is a pep talk mostly. This is our business here. It's the food in our mouths.—Go, Jerry, go."

MY TERRITORY was a town of shacks. With dogs at every one. Dogs trained to attack Whitie. I, apparently, was Whitie. I bought a used car on credit. Had no choice. I couldn't walk for all the hounds—spotty small ones, ribby yellow lion-sized things—each underfed, many dingy—all taking it extra personally. Under my new J. C. Penney slacks, I soon wore three pair of woolen knee socks. I hoped the layers might soften my share of nips. I sprinted from my black Nash up onto a rickety front porch. I knocked, panting, whipping out the book. One very old woman seemed to peek from every door. Toothless, blue-black, her shy grin looked mischievous, a small head wrapped in the brightest kerchief. At some doorways, her hands might be coated with flour. At others she held a broom or some white man's half-ironed white business shirt. She wore male work boots four sizes too large, the toes curled up like elf shoes. Sometimes she smoked a pipe (this was in the Forties). Her long skirt dragged the floor, pulling along string, dustballs. She asked, "What they want now. You ain't the one from before—you a young one, ain't you?" and she chuckled at me. I smiled and swallowed.

I mentioned her upcoming funeral, its expenses, the weekly installment due today. Overdressed for my job, I admitted working my way through college. This had melted hearts among my parents' Milltown friends. But in this zone called Baby Africa, it didn't help.

"Working through a what? Well, child, we all gots to get through something, seem like."

Some customers asked if I owned the Funeral Home. Others asked if my daddy did. I tried explaining the concept of insurance. I failed. For one thing, my clients called it Surrance or Assurance or The Assurance. I gently corrected them. One woman frowned. "That what I *say*. . . . 'Assurance.' " These old ladies seemed to be banking on a last sure thing. Assurance meant heavenly pin money. Shouldn't it have tipped them off? Buying certainty from a confused, fresh-faced kid, nineteen, and about as poor as them?

"Fine morning," I kept grinning even in a downpour.

"Who you supposed to be?" Some giggled, pointing at my snappy-dresser's getup, then toward a pack of mongrels waiting, patrolling the mud yard. In the seam of a half-opened door, my clients' eyes would narrow. "Oh, is you . . . the Assurance?" It was our password and secret.

"So they tell me, ma'am." I smiled hard. "Yep, looks like we've got ourselves another winner of a Saturday morning going here, hunh?"

The insured snorted, then eased me into a dark room I didn't want to know about.

"Seem like it always Saturday," my customer mumbled and shook her head. I followed her in. It was my duty to.

THE SAME STOOPED old lady led me through sixty-five overheated homes. Even mid-July, a fire burned in the grate. White picket fencing was stacked, neat, her kindling. In bare wooden rooms hot as the tropics, rooms with shades drawn, a kerosene lamp helped. Some rooms were poor and filthy, some poor and tidy, but each held this ancient woman surrounded by two dozen grandkids. Children sometimes hid when I knocked but, slow, once I was inside, they seeped from behind doors, wiggled out from under beds. Their bellies looked swollen due to lacks. They swarmed around their grannie, tugged at her long skirts, begged for treats she didn't own and couldn't buy.

The roadsides of my route bristled with zinnias, with sunflowers thirteen feet high. To my eyes, these bright jagged hedges looked African. They seemed cut by a hand-crank can opener out of tin. When I later learned that our white ladies' Garden Club had done the planting, I couldn't believe it. I always figured the seeds of these plants had crossed the ocean in warm hands of slaves chained deep inside ships.

I BOUGHT NEW CLOTHES, trusting these might spiff up my errand. But Saturday after Saturday stayed the same blur: me kicking at my dog escort, me admiring the stiff flowers running defense along dirt roads, me knocking on the door, me sporting my brush-cut hairdo and mail-order bow tie, me grinning out my winning wasted good manners on people manners couldn't save.

It only made me smile the wider. My mouth stayed full of spit.

The door moaned open two inches. Heat, escaping like a sound, pretty much wilted me. Older children squinted in a stripe of daylight. Behind the largest kids and not much taller, easing onto tiptoes, the funeral's guest of honor, her face weather-beaten/permanent as any turtle's. She cupped a hand over her eyes. Sun hurt her. From so shadowy a hut the sun itself must've seemed just another big blond Caucasian visitor, come to collect.

"Oh, it you. It the boy back for Assurance." I got squired indoors then. I didn't want this. Into shacks, lean-tos, Quonset huts, through the smell of frying fat, toward backrooms of Mom and Pop grocery stores (mostly only Moms present). Through shanties, former stables, leaky bungalows no bigger than my parents' company dive. In I went—ducking under low doorways—in against my better judgment. The nervier farmed-out grandkids and great-grandkids touched my pale hands ("They *hot*!"). Others trailed me, stroking my new shirt: our latest miracle fabric, rayon ("It *look* squeaky"). I let myself be led as kids commented, "Ain't he pink?" For a Whitie, I was sure a shy Whitie. Did they believe I couldn't understand our mother tongue? Did they think that, even understanding, I wouldn't care how others saw me?— Downtown I'd overheard redneck white men speak loud about some passing black girl of real beauty. "Roy, is that the most purple dress you ever seen in your life, boy? My, but that'd be a fine little purple dress to take home late tonight, hunh, Roy?"

Now I stood in a dark hall and listened as children discussed Assurance's hair color, his two-tone shoes and rosy size. Trapped, I did what any embarrassed nineteen-year-old would do: grinned till the ears hurt. I pretended not to hear. It was what the beauty in the purple dress had done. It was all I could think of.

My customers feared me. I tried acting regular, I said Please and Thank you very much. But, given our setup, I couldn't be just regular. Fact is, from the start, this job scared me so bad. I couldn't afford to quit it yet. But, boy, I tell you I was already counting the Saturdays.

WINDLASS FUNERARY EVENTUALITIES INC. had been founded in Cleveland some ninety years before. It seemed that several of my collectees had been paying since the outfit's opening day. Behind some names, four completed policies'd piled up. I found amazing shameful dollar totals.

One month into the job, nobody knew my name. I'd stayed "Assurance." And my clients still looked pretty much alike to me. Maybe it sounds bad but, hey, they *were* alike. Me: their Saturday white boy. Them: all one old black woman. People started having names when I deciphered the last collector's rotten handwriting. One morning, it yielded like a busted code. Then the ladies began standing out from one another. Oh, man, I couldn't believe some of the tallies!

"Vesta Lotte Battle, 14 Sunflower Street—commenced payment on policy #1, Mar. 2, 1912, four policies complete, collected to date: $4,360.50."

DURING A MAJOR RAINSTORM, my old Nash had its first blowout. My parents had never owned a car. I didn't know how to change a flat. When I bought the used sedan, I'd been feeling cocky, grown, too vain to ask the salesman for instructions, please. Everybody else knew. I figured ownership itself would teach a guy. After all, new babies don't get lessons in breathing—it's something you pick up—on-the-job experience.

So this particular Saturday morning I'm trying to collect during what seems the start of a respectable hurricane. I'm tooling along Sunflower when here comes a bad bad thumping. My Nash gimps, then tilts. I was near Mrs. Battle's house but hardly knew her then. This early in my coin-collecting days, she still seemed like all the others.—The good old days.

Out loud, hoping to sound like an expert, I said, "I believe your problem is in the front-right-tire area, Jerry." "No lie," the live-in cynic answered. I climbed out, immediately kicking at the curs. Blinded by driving wet, dogs still lunged my way. Some now hid under the chassis where—safe and dry—they snapped at soggy passing argyle ankles. I took an umbrella from the trunk, lost it to wind, watched it disappear over a hedge of sunflowers whipping every whichaway. "So," I said, already drenched. I unclamped the spare and a trusty jack. Now what?

I should mention being watched. Four dozen black faces lined up on many porches, faces interested in weather, willing to look at anything and now all aimed—neutral—my way. I should admit: I don't think Mr. Laurel and Mr. Hardy could've filled an hour with more stupid accidents than I managed in this downpour. The car fell off its jack three times. People on porches didn't laugh outright, no, it was a deeper kind of pleasure. They fairly shivered with it and I couldn't blame them. I noticed how one of my clients, an obese widow, had huffed up onto an iron milk crate. She hoped for a clearer view of my misfortune above her peonies the wind kept scalping.

I knew that if I walked up to any of the dry people on their cozy porches and asked for help, I'd get help. That was the deal. But I couldn't ask. I was too young a man, too car-proud to admit being broken down on a street of walkers who mostly owed me money. So I just kept at it, on my hands and knees. I settled in mud—flat on my back under the Nash—trying to hold off attacking dogs by swinging a tire iron badly needed elsewhere. Once I struggled to my feet again, my own umbrella swooped back over sunflowers and hit me in the neck. I'm still not sure somebody didn't throw it. Spectators now lifted their babies. Old people in wheelchairs were being rolled out to see. I'd turned the color of the mud, then the color of the tires and was standing here considering sobbing.

"Get out the way, you." A husky voice spoke loud enough to outlive the gale. I looked behind me at this dark old woman, scarecrow thin, hands pressed on hips, acting furious with me. She'd been watching from a porch and was not amused. She seemed to hate incompetence and the pleasure my incompetence was giving to her neighbors. Seven blinking kids, black and white, surrounded her. They also seemed to be clucking, disgusted, shaking their heads. "Don't want any favors," said I. "Just show me how." Kids snatched my tire iron and lug wrench. Kids jerked the spare away from me like planning to roll the thing off and put it up for adoption after years of my mistreating it. Children worked around me like trained elves, the old woman snapping orders, pointing to a porch where I should go wait. Kids had just slipped the flat into my trunk when I noticed the spare already locked in place. I studied this through slanting blue water. Dogs, tails wagging, now sniffed at kids, forgetting me. "How can I thank you?" I hollered over the squall, wondering if I should offer money, all while following my helpers. Then I was going up some porch steps. I worried for this old woman, soaked at her age. But she ordered, "Get out them soggy clothes, you." Everybody else disappeared into the house. I was handed laundered flour sacks. I saw I should use these as towels. Kids brought me a stained silk maroon dressing robe—antique, some hand-me-down. I changed, in one corner of a small front room. It was stacked with consignment ironing. I dared not strip on the much-watched front porch. Next, hot tea appeared. Then we were all settled on this strange woman's porch, we were dry. We all sat sipping similar green tea from cups, no two alike. Everybody was silent. We could watch the rain let up or continue, it didn't much matter now. My car out there looked clean and new. My clothes had been spread to dry in the kitchen's open oven. Sitting in this borrowed robe, I smelled like an old house.

To be here with this group of helpful strangers—kids lined like a choir, plus the old woman—to see how all the neighbors on their porches, especially the fat one next door, now gaped, not at the car, but over here at our congregation staring straight out, sipping warm tea on this cool blue day, well, I felt rescued. It was a strange pleasure of the sort that makes you shudder at the time. When rain slacked some, I dashed inside, dressed fast and, half-apologizing, backed off her porch with an overload of talky etiquette that makes me cringe now to recall. Soon as I got in my car, I grabbed the premium book, checked her address, found the name, Vesta Lotte Battle.

The next Saturday I turned up to collect her regular fifty cents, nobody mentioned lending me a hand. Of course, with me being such a kid (one whose sin was and is the Sin of Pride), I never brought up my clumsiness, their help. No. Just let it pass. Soon everybody forgot this favor. Everybody but me.

FROM THEN ON, forever, 14 Sunflower Street was *Vesta Lotte Battle, $4,360.50.* This woman now looked quite specific while passing me ten hand-temperature nickels at a time. I wanted to tell her, "Look, ma'am, it's going on 1950. For the amount you've laid by, you could hire Duke Ellington's orchestra. You might get your own parade, the Goodyear blimp. Maybe even Mrs. Roosevelt."

Like other homes on my list, Vesta L. Battle's had its fair share of religious pictures; some were decaled onto varnished conch shells. But here I started noticing the unlikenesses. Mrs. Battle's place was furnished with fine if ruined furniture. Possible leftovers from some great plantation house. Her andirons were life-sized bronze greyhounds. The huge horsehair loveseat had a back of pretty jigsaw curves, but one cinder block and many bricks held up its crippled end. Vesta Lotte Battle was the first of my insured to start looking different from all others. I never forgot her. Times, I still try.

SHE ALWAYS WORE A USED AMETHYST NECKLACE—four of its six stones missing. Early in our acquaintance, I boldly asked her age. She shrugged. "Courthouse burned. Someplace uphill of ninety some, I reckon." She had cataracts. These meant that her whole head gleamed with the same flat blue-gray color. Like a concord grape's—that beautiful powdery blue you only find on the freshest ones. Greeting me, she stood so straight. But her face hung loose off its moorings, drooping free of her like more unpressed hired-out laundry, needing work. She always aimed her front toward my voice, not me. She seemed to pay me too much attention. Only slowly did I understand how blind she was.

Her house milled with stray kids, poor whites mixed with darker Sunflower neighbors. First time I visited after my flat tire, fifteen kids were making taffy in her kitchen. They wore whole gloves of pale sticky stuff. They kept saying "Yukk" and "Oogh." Two, happy with strands slacked between them, did a little dance. They backed apart—then, palms forward, rushed each other.

Mrs. Battle led me into this taffy workshop. "Look, you all, it the Boy come for Assurance." Her voice crackled, seeming even less stay-press than her shriveled face. Mrs. Battle's tone sounded smoked, flaky and layered, like the pane of isinglass I noticed glowing in her kitchen stove. She'd left off ironing a white shirt. It rested, arms drooping from a board, flattened by a set of irons she heated on her wood stove. To hold the sprinkling water, she used a Coke bottle plugged with a red celluloid-and-cork nozzle bought at Kress's for ten cents. Momma had the same one. The old woman now offered me hot tea. I nodded, wondering how much she earned per shirt. Candy makers cleared counter space for her.

I worried: accepting tea might be my first client-collector mistake. I hadn't asked for her tire help, either. Sam warned me: "Take nothing from anybody." But a person can't consider every kindness a form of bribe, can a person? Maybe I was a night-school Business Major, but I wasn't *always* counting. "Tea sounds great, ma'am." I watched her—slowed, so old—go through the ritual. Her hands knew everything's whereabouts. This lady, I told myself, trying to keep things logical, she's in too far to ever back out of her Insurance now. She can't live much longer, can she? Vesta Lotte Battle had entered that oldness beyond plain old age. She'd hit the part where you dry out, you've become a kind of living mummy sketch of who you were. They've stopped checking your meter. You've gone from Rocket back to Rome. Everything you could lose, you have. Lost.

Only stubborn habits keep you moving. Like this making tea. I watched her hands. They went right to each decanter, no nonsense, no waste. She'd started paying for her funeral decades before I got myself born. All those slow years, all these quick-arriving Saturdays.

She handed me a sky-blue teacup, then scuffed deeper into her narrow home, searching for my fifty cents. Should I follow a client into her bedroom or wait out on her porch? I figured: any place but the yard. Sixteen dogs were waiting in the yard.—Now, as ever in these small houses, I felt huge and I was. Sparrow-sized black ladies kept handing their coins up to me. In a tiny wizened hand, one quarter can look almost saucer-sized and made of mirror.

"You children so rude," the old voice hollered back. "Give Assurance some eats."

Kids surrounded me, their clownish mouths caked with sugar, egg whites. "Every kindness is a form of graft," I heard Sam's voice. But smiled. Kids held their hands up toward me. Candy *was* their hands, taffy wrapping to the wrists. One dark girl took my teacup, set it down then touched my hand. Over and under my ruddy right paw, she pressed her hands, mittened in white goo. I laughed, it felt odd, but good. I made a face. Kids hooted. I saw they'd been waiting. "How do it taste?" a cracked voice asked behind me. I really jumped. Vesta Lotte Battle made a sharp gasping sound I later guessed to be a laugh. I smiled, held one finger to my mouth, nibbled my knuckle, "Mmm. Thank you. It's taffy all right."

"We knows that," the dark girl stepped forward, ready to give me a teasing shove. Fearing for my new cardigan, I hopped back fast. They all roared. I laughed too. Somehow I didn't mind. I knew I looked ridiculous to them.

They showed me the pleasure in the joke—the joke of me, I mean. Then things felt easier. "More," I said, "please, I want more." Up hands shot. I faked munching on ten kids' extended palms, I grazed along fingers. Then everybody seemed satisfied, even bored. They went back to work. "*Now* can I wash?" I turned toward my client. My client was Mrs. Vesta Lotte Battle. By then I surely knew her name. She nodded, pointed me to her sink. It had no faucets, just a well you pumped. I pumped. I scrubbed hard, taffy still under my fingernails.

My hostess had returned to seeking her money, my money. I waited in the front room. This was taking forever. I heard two drawers open, a jar got shaken, some furniture was moved. Then, posture spoiled, Vesta Lotte Battle came creaking back toward me. She was bent nearly end-to-end, shrimp-wise. Her white hair grew in mossy coin-sized lumps under the headcloth. Both her hands were lifted, cupping nickels, pennies, and the one dime laid—proud—on top.

Every toasty coin she dropped into my big clean college hand, I counted aloud for her and with some cheer. Seemed the least I could do. But the brighter I sounded the worse I felt. Older children stopped to watch this payoff. I felt ashamed. "It's no popularity contest," Sam had advised me.

Since 1912, Vesta Lotte Battle had paid. While employed as a housemaid uphill, her weekly dues ran dollars higher. Now she had four completed policies, all ripe for forfeit if she missed just two current payments. She was in to Eventualities to the tune of nearly five thousand bucks. And on this particular taffy-making Saturday, she turned up twenty-one cents short. "Uh oh," I said. It was all I could think of.

"Let's see here. You had the twenty-nine but you're missing the twenty-one, correct? Look, just this time, all right, Mrs. Battle? We'll see you next week for the full amount, okay? But falling behind and all, it's just not copacetic."

"Copper-who?"

"It's just not . . . smart. No tardiness again, all right? All right."

"One thing," her voice sounded even smokier. "I ain't no 'Mrs.'"

"Fine. So, we'll see you for the makeup payment next week same time same station, okay? Okay. But, please, have it, Mrs. Battle."

Her shoulders lifted then dropped one at a time. She said, "Vesta Lotte Battle tries." It was a statement, not a promise—she made me know this.

Again she stood so straight, the clouded eyes aimed right at me. Her dignity was perfect. Right from the first, her poise just totally slayed me. It seemed some law of nature. Then she closed her unpainted door on me. Doing so, she proved: the rented hut, the tea I'd sipped, the candy nibbled, this houseful of borrowed kids, the life itself . . . insured or not—all these, she proved, were hers, not mine.

"After while, crocodile," I spoke to the door's pine planking, windblown silver as a coin. People were just starting to say, "See you later, alligator." Locally I was one of the first. I considered myself something of a pacesetter.

PART OF MY WINDLASS INSURANCE EARNINGS paid night-school tuition. The rest meant grocery or doctor money for my folks. I made A's in my classes, but breathing was getting lots harder for Dad. I bought him this expensive humidifier. We got him inhalers and sprays, anything.

The folks sometimes asked about my route, they called it. They remembered my paperboy years. To them, this job seemed easy as peddling *Herald Travelers* off a bike. I couldn't explain the terrible difference. You stop delivering somebody's morning paper, they go and buy one at the store. For Assurance, my clients couldn't turn to anybody but me. I never told my parents what this job really meant. My folks fretted enough. Just recently, an old friend sent me a snapshot of them dressed for church and sitting on our porch. She is in his lap and laughing, and they're both much handsomer than I'd let them be in memory. He wears a high white collar and has long good hands, and except for the cheap porch furniture, these two people might be Lord and Lady Somebody, larking it up for a reporter. Their good looks, recognized this late, only make me sadder. They could've done *any*thing.

When I was fifteen, I presented Dad a Christmas subscription to *Life* magazine. It continued ever after, best thing I ever gave him. He wore his bifocals only once a week when sitting down with the new issue. You'd think he had just received the Dead Sea Scrolls by mail for a first scholarly look-see. He turned pages one by one from the top corner. "They've got pretty much everything in here," he'd say. And if I lumbered in from work, Mom would hush me, smiling with strange pride. "Let's be a little quiet. He's reading."

THE FIRST TIME one of my customers, a retired bricklayer, fell behind payment-wise, I said something semi-stern, and he wept at me, then dropped onto arthritic knees. He pressed his wet face against my creased chinos.

"Please," I pulled him back up. "Don't *do* this to yourself. Nothing's worth this." I'd started seeing that these old folks were paying me for more than fancy burials. They were shelling out for the right to go on living for another week.

I should add how the last ingredient of my Saturdays was—along with old ladies (like Mrs. Battle herself) and many grandkids in hand-me-downs and cornrow braids (like Mrs. B's clan)—about a million Jesuses.

Every ashtray, each souvenir candy dish, the baby rattles, all hand fans (compliments of the three leading black funeral parlors), spoon rests, pillow covers, and, once, a whole couch—showed pastel pictures of a mild-looking soap-faced shepherd. He wore clean, pressed 100% cotton-looking robes. He had the sugar-water stare of a bad actress dolled up to play some fairy godmother. In Kress's frames, he held several sheep and one crook. I figured, maybe he gave my clients hope; whatever helped them, I was for that. But I worried: candle-white himself, he was shown clutching multicolored kids. From lithos and oleographs, he knocked on castle doors, he lifted lanterns, he carried blond infants over rickety footbridges. Promises, promises. He always turned up, central, in each rental box. Sometimes alongside His picture, I'd find one of President Roosevelt, a cleaner-shaven and plumper gent but still looking like some Jesus second-cousin, worthy.

I waited, half on clients' porches, partly in their front rooms, not wanting to seem too interested, hoping not to seem jaded either. I counted front rooms' Jesuses. I pretended not to notice my clients fishing fifty cents to three bucks out of nut-brown face powder or from behind clocks, from underneath the tubular legs of heavy beds where people who'd been sired and born, later died. Out coins came, wedged between the heel and sole of a work shoe. Quarters were egged into daylight from deep private panels of mended bras worn by my insured. Right in front of me, slack bodices got plundered. Old ladies didn't seem to mind my seeing where they squirreled their cash. (Maybe they knew I'd get it anyway?)

Their most regular hiding spots, of course, were Jesus places. Coins got taped behind tea-towel resurrections, tucked back of window-sized calendars that showed Christ walking the waters, sandaled footprints denting foamy whitecaps. I felt sea-sick, waiting for my money, waiting.

Already I'd started picturing my own hands putting all of Vesta Lotte Battle's redeemed funds—a chef's salad worth of crisp green—into her outstretched leather palms, bony hands that, so glad, trembled.

But instead it was me back at her orderly shanty, smiling, "Now, you see, you've fallen three weeks behind. We can't have this, ma'am. Really. *Three*."

She'd brought me tea in a mended bone-china cup with goldfish handpainted on it. The saucer (whole) was a different pattern but yellow bone-china too. I kept standing. So did she. Her French mantel clock, marble gilt and stopped years ago, showed a bronze blindfolded woman holding up a scale. All Mrs. B's furniture was missing limbs or spines or cushions—bricks and broomsticks were busy being everything's crutch—but the room looked beautiful anyhow. Especially if you squinted some. Vesta Battle had spent her life working for the owners of the cotton mill. It showed in how she handled the tea things, how she asked, "You wanting one lump or two, Assurance?"

"I was *saying*, 'You're three weeks overdue.' No sugar. One—maybe one—thank you, but listen, Mrs. Battle. Seriously. You've paid in so much. I just can't have you lose it. You let the latest policy go, they'll grab all your others. You signed, you agreed to this. I mean I've already absorbed that first twenty-one cents from a month back. Okay. I'll let that slide—I wasn't exactly overjoyed about advancing you that but I did. Since then I've paid your last three weeks my own self. Look, I'm poor too or else I wouldn't keep this job, believe me.—Now, maybe that dollar seventy-one doesn't sound like much to you . . . (no, I'm sorry, of course it's a lot to you or else you'd have paid. I see that). But, think, here I am, already lying to my boss. I'm paying out of my own pocket. And for your funeral, ma'am. I'd rather give you food money any day. Let's reason together, all right? It can't go on, can it. Are you even listening? I mean this. Can you hear me?"

Reserved, blue-brown, old the way trees are, she settled, hunched across from me and stated facts. Her eldest daughter, living in Detroit, usually mailed checks home. The last postal money order was five weeks overdue. Mrs. Battle admitted to worrying: maybe something bad had happened. Plus, she'd never much liked her daughter's man. He fought with the line boss at Ford. He hit Pearl way too much. Didn't seem much hope of finding what'd gone wrong.

"Now we're getting somewhere!" I said. "We can *do* something now, see? Action's always best. Just *phone* her."

No telephone here and no number in Detroit. Besides, Vesta Lotte Battle said she didn't trust phones, never planned to touch one; if lightning hit a wire any place between Detroit and here, the shock rode wires into your ear or mouth. Phones were still too new.

"Oh," I said. "Well then *write* her, for God's sake." My advice was growing loud. Kids peeked out of the kitchen then went back to chattering. I smiled noplace. Mrs. Battle sat studying her palm's worn lines.

"Look," I said. "Do you have her address, Pearl's? Let me jot it down. I'll write the letter myself. You mind? My eyes are better than yours." She went for it but had no paper in the place, none that wasn't either a Bible page or some form of printed Jesus. I'd started feeling ill at the sight of Him, meek and mild Saturday-to-Saturday from home to home. FDR seemed lots likelier to offer my clients a fair shake and a moment's assurance. I tore a back page from my ledger. I copied the Detroit address. Mrs. B didn't offer me a stamp or envelope. Okay, I had my own. That same Saturday

I mailed the letter. My tone tried balancing the businesslike with a tenderer jokey type of human lightness. Even at my age now, I still feel superstitious about mailing certain things. Back then, too. Before dropping Pearl's letter into the slot, I remember kissing all four corners of it—for luck. I waited and hoped.

INSURANCE WAS JUST ONE OF MY THREE PART-TIME JOBS. Mrs. Battle was only one of my insurance customers. Like her, others'd stopped seeming all that much alike now. That was just it: the more vivid each dark person became, the blanker, blander, and whiter I felt. A plug of stray cotton: cake-sized. Again I knocked at buckled doors, once more I answered challenges from inside: "It's Assurance. Open up. Hi. Just Assurance back again, ma'am." I'd stopped pointing out the difference between in- and as-surance. They only let me in if I spoke our word.

My ninth week on the job, all clients permanently broke down into themselves. There was the one missing two fingers, the one who always tried to give me geranium clippings for my mom, the plump one in the bed, the pretty young one in the wicker wheelchair, the old one in her metal wheelchair who wore a cowgirl hat, the one with the wig, the one who told the same three easy riddles each week, the one, the one . . .

My rounds sure felt easier when people had the decency to stay blended. Now I started worrying over payer and nonpayers too. You know how it is, once a crowd splits into separate faces, nothing can ever mash them back into that first safe shape.

I was now reading books on ways to cultivate a positive manner, how to make strangers sort of do what you wanted. I learned many innocent jokes by heart. I grinned even more, I switched to plainer clothes—black and white—trying to prove I wasn't all that flush myself. I shook the hands of bashful kids at all my Saturday homes. I taught these kids to holler—when I closed their front door—"After while, crocodile." Somehow it sounded joyless. I perspired a lot. It was a scorching September. You can't imagine the heat in some of my clients' homes.

Once, a drunk husband, wanting the surance money for his booze, tried to take it back. His wife helped fight him off me. "Run," she shouted my way. Pounding on her man's shoulders, wedging herself between him and my getaway, she sobbed at his chest, "No! It for our funeral, baby. Don't you hurt one flower on us two's funeral. Do, baby, and you done seen the last of me."

(I ASKED MYSELF: If life insurance is you betting on your own death—how much worse is the funeral kind?)

MRS. BATTLE OWED. A lot now. Owed me a lot. So did four others. By Christmas she was in to me for the most, to the tune of six dollars and some already. I'm sorry but during the Forties, to a kid in my bracket, six dollars meant something. I was getting in over my head. I knew it, but couldn't seem to stop. I considered whining to Sam. But that would mean ratting on several of my older clients. The ones who'd paid the most over time, they had the most to lose. I felt I should protect her, especially. Mrs. Battle. I don't know why exactly. Maybe because she never explained, never thanked me. She wouldn't consider apologizing. A real aristocrat. Visiting her was like going to see some fine old Duchess in a book. At other homes I refused dandelion wine (in gallon jugs), five free wire-wheeled tires, one lewd offer from this old man in a kimono!, two dozen wonderful-smelling home-cured hams. I only accepted Mrs. Battle's conversation and her green China tea. These soon seemed drudgery's one dividend. I looked forward to her face at the door. We still waited for Pearl's answer to my letters, we looked forward to Pearl's checks. Some Saturdays I'd save Mrs. B's house for last, like a reward, my commission.

Sam had tipped me off. "Once they smell heart on you, kid, you're lost." I wondered how heart would smell to a half-blind old woman. Like beef? Or bread. Or beer? Maybe vanilla extract. How?

ONE WINDY SATURDAY, walking through Mrs. Battle's yard, I heard a creaking in her roadside sunflowers—I found a signboard hid among the leaves. The wooden plaque was teapot-shaped, two feet across. It'd been enameled pink, then painted over with many black crack-marks and the words "Can Fix."

I wondered, What literate person had written those two words for her? Some child maybe. When I asked about the sign, she pointed to a red table set at the back of her kitchen. It was propped with glue pots, masking tape, brushes and—at the center—a little scaffolding of toothpicks, twigs, and Popsicle sticks. Some miniature ship seemed under construction but, holding my account book against my chest, I bent nearer and saw a fine old soup tureen. The thing looked imprisoned in its own splint. Hundreds of fissures had recently spoiled it, but each was now caked with white powdery stuff like a denture cream. Mrs. Battle, again startling me at how close she'd got so silently, explained: the porcelain paste, once dried and set, would wipe off with solvent. Someday, good as new. On the tureen's side, an old woodland view was daubed, done fast but with great skill. Mrs. B had set little support brads into its bowed porcelain. She'd hid metal clips right in the painted landscape; one paralleled a brown tree trunk. The brad's blue metal looked just like the tree's own shadow. You couldn't separate VLB's mending from the little ideal glade itself. I saw the beauty of the *fixed* tureen clearer than I would've noticed it, whole.

"It *looks* copa . . . terrif, really," I said, standing. "But will it ever hold soup again?"

"What good'd it be otherwise, Assurance? Ain't this *for* the soup?"

She seemed to consider mending a parlor game, said she'd learned it in a henhouse-workshop. A lady missionary, returned from China, taught local black girls this skill in the 18 and 70s. Final exam: You personally chose one hen's egg and jumped on it, then you personally rebuilt it so it looked unbroken to the picky naked eye. Excellent training for the world.

As I sat having tea with Mrs. B, an overdressed white lady appeared, apologizing for "having barged in." She handed over the dust of a ruined teacup. How ruined? It was in one of her husband's letter-sized business envelopes!

"Ooh my my," Mrs. B laughed dry but deep. "Somebody must've fell on this with both they boots." "Yes," the woman smiled my way. "I'm married to a man who doesn't, shall we say? have the lightest touch on earth?—What would we do without her?" and nodded to our mutual friend who ignored this. I did too.

Mrs. Battle sat shaking the envelope. Listening to crumbled porcelain rattle, her face went dreamy as somebody eavesdropping on a conch shell's pulse. "One big mess," she said with relish. "Yes, well"—the customer turned to leave—"I admit as how this may finally be beyond even your skills, my dear. Even so, do have a go at it. Otherwise, I fear Mother's service for twenty-four is totally useless. You'll try? Good day, young man." She nodded, maybe wondering if I'd brought VLB *my* busted fingerbowls. (Fat chance.) The lady stared like asking why a sternly dressed young gent should be here sipping tea midafternoon. But I saw she didn't disapprove a bit. If anything her glance seemed jealous of VLB. So, we understood each other. Every Saturday for weeks after, I asked to see the progress of Mrs. Fancy Schmantsy's cup.

First there were heaps of grit—then handle grit, side grit, bottom grit. Soon it became separate Wedgwood blue and white nuggets. Shaping from the bottom up, a roundness started showing—at its lower edges—the calm little sandals of pic-nicking gods and goddesses. I'd sometimes find Mrs. B using a magnifying glass big as Mr. Sherlock Holmes's. She'd hold the cup not just near but practically against her face—pressed over her best eye the way you mash beefsteak there to prevent swelling. She had so little eyesight left, she seemed to feel this last amount might squeeze out as a bonding glue. Once, I planned to surprise her and I stole up from behind. I heard her whisper into the cup's hollow like down some microphone, "Captain Wedgwood? Coming back to you senses? I setting up a meeting between you and Marse Earle Grey late next week. Won't be long now."

Uneasy, I tiptoed back out, lunged in again. "Assurance!"

The more relaxed I felt with her, the harder my job got. Friday night before collection mornings, I started having regular bad dreams. I saw myself turning roses into radishes. I kept shoving people off a high bridge. Mrs. Battle had fallen further and further behind. Three long-distance calls finally got me the Employment Office of the Ford Motor Co., Detroit. I asked after one Pearl Battle. They found four on their payroll; what was my Pearl's middle name? I didn't know but, wait, yes I did. "Vesta—either Pearl Vesta or Vesta Pearl. After six minutes of crackling long-distance time (me paying, naturally, me sweating bullets), they came back, No Vesta Pearl or the other. "Did I say Vesta? Must be slipping. I meant 'Lotte' Pearl Battle or else 'Pearl Lotte' Battle. Hello?" The line was dead. Not sure why, I went out and got drunk for the first time ever and, knee-walking smashed, considered driving to Michigan to find my favorite's favorite daughter.

One evening, pitifully sober, headed home after my last Saturday collection (some nights it took till ten), I motored along Summit Avenue, our town's richest white street. Boys I'd known at high school were out playing basketball. They were my age, lawyers' and dentists' sons home for Christmas break, back from freshman year at Duke, Carolina, Princeton. One goal was mounted over the big home's back door, another hung above its three-car garage. This morning when I rode by, bound for Baby Africa, the same guys had been playing.—Now parked nearby, I slunk low in my car, headlights doused, my windows down. I sat listening to their ball pinging in that clean trusty way basketballs do. It was so dark you wondered how players could see the goal but you still heard the swish of the net, point, point. Guys horsed around; one yodeled, "Glad I back in de land ob cotton, your feet stink and mine is rotten, look away . . ." They called each other butter-fingers, cross-eyed, air-brain. I just sat. Lamps were being lit inside the three-storied house. Then the mother of the place turned on a back-porch light and appeared carrying sandwiches and bottled sodas on a silver tray. She left this and—without a word—slipped indoors. All day these guys'd been here doing this.

I rolled up my window. I envied them but pitied them but mostly envied them. I drove off, slower than usual. I felt like crying. I wouldn't let myself. It seemed a luxury people like me couldn't afford.

I VISITED my night school's tuition office. I asked for a payment extension. Six weeks only. It wouldn't happen again. I blamed family problems. That seemed true. I was paying Dad's extra medical bills, paying for household food, plus funding the upcoming funerals of four black strangers, along with one ninety-some-year-old near-stranger. ("If they'd just hurry up and keel over while I'm supporting them, they'd all get the red-carpet treatment.")

I lied for them. I paid. And this stupid generosity made me feel ashamed, not good like it's supposed to. I told myself, "You're just too weak to give her up. No Princeton pre-law ballplayer would be such a sap. You're helping losers, clod, because you are one."

THE WEDGWOOD CUP, week to week, healed like a stupid perfect little garden vegetable on her second kitchen table. Then one day it was gone. I missed it. Back it went to its home set, and another white person's porcelain disaster took its place. I wondered what Mrs. B charged these country clubbers. Not enough, I guessed. She needed a manager.

Payment-wise, she had slipped further behind, no word from Pearl. I wondered if she'd made Pearl up. I knew better and felt ashamed, but even so . . . And yet, grouchy as I felt, I still sort of leaned toward having my tea with her. The kids at VLB's place usually behaved and often seemed funny, noisy in a good way. I decided not to mention how much Vesta Lotte Battle owed, not till the end of today's visit. That'd spare us both some embarrassment. While driving to her place, I'd mapped out my speech and tactics. But once arrived, there was something about her emptied necklace, the brocade bolsters sewn shut with clear fishing line. There was something about how the children at her house tried cleaning up after themselves and looked out for each other and her. Some Saturdays when she called me "Boy Assurance," I believed her. I wanted to. I called her "Vesta Lotte Battle" to her face and in my head. The name started sounding classic and someway fertile. But, hey, eventually, I *had* to bring it up—I mean the money.

"Look, did Pearl let you know yet? I told her to write you here."

Mrs. B sat rocking somebody else's sick baby. Seven older kids—all quiet, groggy-acting, maybe with fevers?—rested in sweet lost heaps around the room. My client hadn't answered me.

"Well? Are you planning to speak? I'm sorry but I'm getting cross here. I am. And who can blame me? It's January already. No word from Detroit?"

The blue-black head wagged sideways.

"Mrs. Battle, with all due respect, I earn about two dollars and eighty cents per Saturday doing this. A lot of it's going to you. I've cut off some of the others. You not. But it's plain. I can't keep this up much longer, right? I mean I've carried you—week by week, I have. It hurts me but I can't . . . much longer."

"You ain't got to."

Rocking the borrowed baby, she just looked at me. She said this. The thing was, she meant it. Maybe that's what always made me feel so bad. If I did drop her from the rolls, she wouldn't hold it against me. That was the absolute killer.

"Well, I know I don't *have* to. Not by law, I don't."

I stood before her chair, hoping she might at least offer me some tea. "But, Mrs. B, you'd lose your life savings. And that's taken you your whole life to save up, right, ma'am?"

She sat rocking, eyes aimed past me.

She seemed so unlike the others, unlike any person I've met since. How can I explain it to you? I want to. My other clients often faked long hunts for coins they knew weren't there. (Try and imagine the agony of standing before a wheelchair where an old lady in a cowgirl hat is going through every pocket of her housedress ten times while you wait, looking hopeful—trying to.) Clients would hide inside their homes. I'd peek through a window and notice six adults and two children lying face-up on the floor. Caught, they'd grin, then all fake napping. "Hi. I see you," I'd say.

"Please." You would not believe the hassles, sob stories, and runarounds I got each Saturday.

It's why I loved coming here. Mrs. Battle never blamed me for inventing the rigged setup. If all five of her policies got revoked, I knew she wouldn't fault me. (She hadn't even blamed me when I chose to take her payments on myself.) Today I understood, it was, from the start, my own doing, not hers.

Odd: standing before her chair, furious at our situation—meaning furious at *her*—I found myself wondering how Mrs. B must have looked when she was, say, my age. By now she had nothing left but this unexplainable . . . power, I'll call it. (Where do such put-upon people *learn* such pride?) Was it something time had done to her? Did it come because she knew so much, or did she understand very little but in a deep deep way? I have never bought the stuff about all old people being wise. You don't get Wisdom with your first Social Security check. I mean, here I am, near the brink of sixty and still waiting for the old light bulb to snap on overhead. That day, I saw: nothing was left her but a raw, quiet sureness. Mostly blind, stripped down to vitals, she could now take anything that came. Ninety-some, she'd finally got fairly limber. She could dodge it all. She could even take losing everything on my account. For that reason, I just would not permit it. No.

There was something about the old woman—I'm not sure that I can explain it or, if I do, that you'll believe me. Mrs. Battle had some kind of stature or something. I mean, aren't there people—maybe Churchill or Roosevelt maybe—who're lit up with a cranky kind of genius that everybody, even their own enemies, respects? True, I'd never seen Vesta Lotte Battle *do* all that much. She never saved the Free World or anything like that. Yeah, she once gave me shelter during a downpour, she mended collectors' item china practically for free, she let neighbor kids hang out at her house and make candy. She knew how to change a tire. So what? Most days she just sat in this rocker, rocking, looking out at a view on noplace. It galled me, standing here, waiting: I thought, almost envious, why should it be *one old black woman?* Aren't I crazy to consider that she knows this much? I must be insane to feel so much because of her. I must be making this up.

Still, right along, I was positive about it. I still am. That's why I'm bothering to tell this. Her? she knew. It was less anything she did or said, more who she was, I guess. She'd never seen the ocean, a hundred and ten miles from Falls. And yet, you just felt her life. Felt it go right into your own. You were helpless. Instantly you couldn't separate. You walked into the room and it was like that stove of hers burning when I met her in July. Her life stayed closer to the skin than most people's.

PART OF WHAT I'm saying is: It seemed unbelievable that such a woman couldn't come up with fifty cents a week.

SHE NOW ASKED would I go make our tea? Today she had a lapful. I did. I found I knew where she stored everything. I noted a ruined gravy boat, trying to regroup itself inside her toothpick bracings. For a second, putting water on to boil, I closed my eyes, imagining blindness—imagining *her* blindness. I admired how she managed to fake vision. She really looked right at you. Odd I'd never noticed any food in her kitchen, nothing but sugar and cream for my tea, nothing past candy makings for her kids. Did she live on tea, on whatever nourishment seeped into her mended cup from all the glue that held the thing together?

I brought Mrs. B her own best one-of-a-kind cup, laurel and nasturtiums painted around it. I was pouring tea as she started talking about slave days. Uh oh. I saw her start relaxing back back into being blind. She finally trusted me enough to let me see she couldn't see. "This is a trick!" something told me. I knew I shouldn't listen. I imagined Sam scolding me, "Jesus, kid, you just ask for trouble, you know that? Rule Numero Uno is: always think of your assigned list as the group. Group life, ever heard of it? Then everything'll go down easy as Jack Daniel's. But when you start slipping, start thinking, 'There's this man and that woman,' then they'll really nail you, son. They know this, they plan it." I shouldn't pay attention. History'd only make me feel worse, her history would. And yet here she was, cradling the kid in one arm, using her free hand to hold a teacup to her mouth. (*It* now seemed blind too). Between sips, she slowly told. (What was I going to do? mash my hand over her three-toothed mouth? What, was I going to run away or what?) Despising my own politeness, I settled cross-legged on plank flooring beside her busy rocker; the brocade and cinder-block chaise was too far off. OK, but I'd just fake listening.

She'd been born the property of our local mill-owning family. She said she'd got freed while still a child. The day after Sherman marched through our county, burning things, freed slaves killed all the plantation's livestock. The old groom cut the throats of two white Arabian horses he'd curried and exercised daily. Then, knife in hand, he stood over them, crying, "What *else* do I got?" She remembered everybody's dancing by torchlight in the Quarter. Ex-slaves raided their mistress's closets, wore all her gowns. Some of the funny little boys dressed up, tripping on hems. Freed slaves held a Harvest Ball in April, a candlelight party like ones that'd lit the big house before the War. That first night of freedom, three older men asked Vesta Lotte to marry them. Freed, she now felt free to say No three times running. She was eight.

Vesta Lotte, old, rocked on, telling me of huge forest fires that Sherman's troops had set. She'd watched our town's first cotton mill burn. She rambled, saying, "Then, right after it surrendered . . ."

I'd heard other older black people say "After It Surrendered." They seemed to speak about some octopus "it" that'd once had ahold of them. They never said "after Lee surrendered"—just this "It." I wanted to explain to my beloved client— Maybe General Lee did finally bow out in '65, but it, old it, had not surrendered yet. It still held her, still had us all.

Down here, I studied her men's work boots, the stick-thin black ankles. On she rocked. Her dignity irked me. I'd paid Eventualities Mrs. B's last nine dollars and fifty cents. *I* should be in the position of control here, right? But, just by holding still, by aiming her cataracts straight out toward the roadside's browned sunflowers (were they blurs to her? were they even visible?) she put me through these hoops of bad feelings, gave me moral insomnia.—In my night-school philosophy course, our teacher had read one line from an Eastern religious book: "Seventy-five righteous men carry the world." Considering what I imagined soon doing to Mrs. B, I muttered under my breath, "Today . . . marked down to seventy-four."

"*Why?*" I asked her now, interrupting. I got up onto my knees beside her chair, I set my cup down. I felt tempted to place my butch-waxed head into her lap beside the sick child panting there. "Why *funerals?*" Rude as it sounded, I couldn't help asking. How could anybody so smart sink all her money into last rites? What—I half-hollered—did she imagine for herself after death? Hunh?—The morticians' perks would get her into the next world; okay—then what? How did she picture this Heaven?

I wondered, did Saturday coins seem installments on some future boat fare? Did VLB think of her own afterlife as a long-awaited china mending, or maybe as Old Africa itself? Waiting for her answer, I imagined a jungle shore of flowers seen from some rocking boat: Home. I sat straighter, readying myself for her answer. Since I was bankrolling this voyage, I felt I had a right to hear. Pumping her for news of after-death kind of thrilled me. I figured, "Hey, if anybody knows the score, it's Vesta Lotte Battle here." I was nineteen. I admired her. She owed me.

I almost thought of her as mine.

I KEPT STILL, poised on my knees beside an active rocking chair. This was happening one quiet January Saturday on a side street in Falls, NC's worst possible neighborhood. The only steady noise: squabbles among the large black-owned dogs moping near my Nash, peeing on its whitewalls, waiting to chase me. "Roses," Mrs. Battle answered, husky, without hesitation. "Dozens. Roses. Thousands maybe."

(Somehow I'd pictured her paradise blooming shields, zinnias, spears, sunflowers. The beauty of roses seemed patented as Whitie's.) "So," I rushed her. "Roses for starters. What else?"

Time passed as youngsters curled into deeper napping. The baby in Mrs. B's lap made suckling noises, dreaming.

"And plane tickets for all my grown children so's they can come on back down here for it. Around-trips, too. A lined red casket be nice. Oh, and some big white town cars . . . I wouldn't mind." Hearing this, I felt sickened some, and slowed. I understood: For her, the funeral itself was a kind of heaven. She hadn't dared picture anything more glamorous than a decent middle-class send-off. "And marble markers with two rock lambs on top, or, if they out of lambs, maybe a couple baby angels'd do." Bobbing back and forth, clucking at the sick child, Mrs. Battle kept mulling over her list of funeral needs. She stared out a bright window and finally shrugged. In a voice too resigned to sound bitter, she said nowhere, "I ain't asking much."

I wondered aloud how many children would be heading south. "I mean 'eventually' of course." (I've always been more tactful than was needed, a disease.)

"Nineteen. Plus them ones what they lives with or be married to. It mount up."

I nodded. You had to admit: the transportation costs alone could really set a person back.

We just kept still for twenty minutes more. First I felt real gloomy, and next, slow, I got extra mad. Not at her now. But for her. For us. Resting by her creaking rocker, sipping lukewarm tea, it struck me: Vesta Lotte Battle's former owners still mostly owned my own broken-down wheezing parents. I wanted to kill somebody then, to go kill the people put in charge of us all.

"Okay." I finally stood, stiff, feeling old myself. I cleared her tea things, brushed at the seat of my pressed pants. "Okay," I sounded huffy, wronged. "But I warn you I'm only good for one more week. I know you understand how much I think of you. But, look, I've carried you, I've covered for you. I'm doing this fast-and-loose bookkeeping so my boss won't nab you. Finally, even for people like us, there are limits, you know. You know?" She gave me one dry shoulder-heave. The dark voice went, "I reckon you'll do what you wants." (Sam had told me, "There's always one that gets you. Really gets you." Odd, the worse I am at describing the power of Vesta Lotte Battle, the surer I am of it, the deeper I still feel it—right up under the rib cage.)

That very week I sent a telegram to Detroit: "Mother's funeral in jeopardy STOP of default STOP act quickly please STOP a friend STOP." I promised myself this'd have to be the final Christian act for soft-headed non-pre-law really un-Princeton Jerry. My sleep was suffering, gone spotty and shallow. I did well in my night-school business courses. I aced Philosophy but started feeling sneaky about my unnatural straight A average. For somebody nineteen, somebody American and intending to be self-made, I was growing pretty cynical pretty early. Funerary Eventualities had started eating me alive. On a night-school pop quiz, one question asked, "Define 'Business Ethics.' " I wrote, " 'Business Ethics' is a contradiction in terms."

Then I erased this.

So I'd pass.

LIFE DID AN ARTICLE about the heir to the Funerary fortune. Dad saved it for me. "You think this magazine is just pictures but they cover most everything, Jerry, what've I been telling you?" The heir, a Shaker Heights resident, was shown wearing his bathing suit. A coffee-and-cream-toned gent, he looked plump and sleek as a neutered seal. He was a millionaire many times over, his daughter sang opera, he'd been photographed beside his Olympic swimming pool. It was shaped like a clock—diving boards at the 12 and 6! Well, that helped me be firm. This week was it.

I rushed off to knock at Vesta Lotte Battle's door. I'd brought along a jar of my mother's excellent blackberry jam. I hoped this might sweeten and sort of humanize my bad news. I'd prepared a little speech. It incorporated a quote from Plato—one memorized for my *Book of Knowledge* spiel.

I planned to tell Mrs. B: her dignity seemed so safe, really, so beyond me or anybody, it was something that Time had given her and nobody could take away. This royal quality of hers consoled me and, in my remarks, I planned to mention it as praiseworthy. I'd add: since she seemed so secure about her long life, why this worry over burial? Why sweat the small stuff? I would point out necessary facts. Superstition seemed to me Vesta Lotte Battle's single fault. Maybe my nineteen-year-old perspective would finally help the woman see her life more clearly? Maybe it'd help her mind this less—being cut off and so forth.

I pushed open her door. No one had answered. There she stood, poking her own rocking chair idly to and fro. She'd been waiting for me. She'd sent her usual kids home. I grinned. I held out her jar of world-class jam. I'd bought a nice plaid ribbon, I'd tied it around the lid. "I'm afraid," I started, "I'm afraid this'll have to be your last free week. I believe we both knew this'd have to happen, right? From the day we met, even with our getting to be friendly and all, we've basically known it, right?"

"Word come," she fixed her ruined eyes on me, she offered me one yellow bit of paper. "Pearl dead."

Then Mrs. Battle pretended to reread her telegram. She was holding the thing upside down. She was holding the goddamn thing upside down. "No," I said. "You made it up. No."

I rushed over and flopped into her rocker. I clutched the jam against my chest, arms crossed over it, head down, chair bobbling back and forth, panting like my one job was to guard this gift I'd brought, this bribe. "No," my eyes wouldn't focus right. "A trick," I said, "I mean: a trick on both of us."

I heard Mrs. B step nearer, she touched my shoulder, trying to cheer me. Then her right hand crooked under my arm, she coached me into standing. Her palms pressed the small of my back, leading me toward her overheated kitchen for our usual tea. Her head came no higher than my elbow.

I stood beside her scrubbed oak table. I set down the jam, then leaned here, my hands flat, my full weight tilted forward. On her mending table, somebody's gold-rimmed fruit bowl dangerous in three hundred pieces.

I listened as, blind, efficient, she filled the teapot at her pump, doing everything so well. I kept staring at the scoured tabletop, saying, "What are we going to do here? Pearl was our only hope. Now I bet we're going to lose it. Help me, Mrs. Battle. Help me think this out for us. Really. Oh boy, what are we going to do here? God, what are we going to *do* with you?"

A dry brown hand pushed one mended apple-green cup into my vision, a scrap of steam, a perfect cup of tea.

"SOMETHING'S WRONG," Sam said. "Black circles creeping under your eyes. You're not taking this to heart? You *are* keeping the old heart well out of this, right, Jer?"

" 'Heart'?" I looked up, trying to grin. "What's a . . . 'heart'? I never heard of one of those. 'Heart'? What, is it something like a flashlight?"

" 'Flashlight'! Got to remember that." He showed me his kids' new school photos: the girl wore thick white hair ribbons that made her thin hair look transparent. Sam kissed her picture. "And this boy of mine's going to set the world on fire. You watch." Sam needed my opinion about a paint color—he planned improving his office here in maybe two or three years' time. Nursing the bourbon bottle, he said he only drank during *our* appointments. He didn't know, something about me got him. Sam asked how *I'd* done in organic chem? I sat looking at this man, he might've been speaking Latin, his face looked orange, solid orange to me.

Now I see I was in the middle of something like what's known today as a mini-breakdown. Then we called it the blues. We called it Having Black Circles Under Your Eyes for a While. The Whiteboy-with-Blackness-Under-His-BabyBlues-Blues. (And the whiter the person is, the more deadly his case can be. Cotton starts out white but if you breathe white cotton for years enough, it gives you something called Brown Lung. You figure it.)

Here I'll hurry what happened next. Sometimes you rush stories because you don't have sufficient info. In this case, a person's maybe got too much. You know those memo pads with "While You Were Out . . ." printed at the top, yellow pages maybe four inches by four? Well, inside my tweed windbreaker's breast pocket, I'd recently placed just such a piece of paper. Names were written on it in my own admirable forward-tilting Palmer script. I'd arrived at Sam's office building early. While waiting in the weedy park across the street, I chose a sunny bench. Bored, working from memory, I copied nine offenders' names (plus their dollar amounts in arrears). To the cent, I knew. I wrote just to soothe myself, I told myself. I've always been big into lists.

How carefully I inscribed each name. Lovingly almost. One example, I traced ridges like gutters over the TT in the middle of one name. I extended those crossbars to shelter the whole name LoTTe. That list, now hidden in my jacket pocket, crackled when I fidgeted, talking to Sam. The square of yellow paper burned me like a mustard plaster.

Everybody's superstitious. About money especially. "If I clear this figure by March, I'll give X amount to charity, really." "Like it or not, I'll only eat what's in the house till we go out and splurge on Friday." The folkways of the wallet. Pretty strange. Consider our nervous computerized stock market: It still uses a bull and a bear to explain itself to itself. Animals? Now? See, it's homemade magic. Where money comes in, we're all primitives. And, like that, I'd carefully copied a list so I'd *prevent* myself from saying out loud any name on that list. Got it? Logic, it's not—heartfelt, it is.

See, even as I made those two T's spread like a porch roof and guardian umbrella over the name beneath, I was giving myself one teentsy loophole. If, and only if, Sam smelled this list on me, if he asked for it point-blank, then and only then might I consider maybe possibly letting him just peek at it perhaps. And for one sec.

It's just, I'd been so silent for so long. Nine old people felt they owed me their lives. Once Sam read the thing, I knew I'd feel better, I'd find the stamina to sustain

Group Life a little longer.—I was, after all, legally responsible to Sam here and if a person's boss actually *orders* that person to hand over an inventory of backsliding wrongdoers, well . . .

What can I say? I was nineteen years old. I'd been buying my own clothes since I was eleven. Other guys my age and half as smart, a tenth as driven, were already off at college, lounging around, sleeping in till 11:30 A.M.

Early March, Sam's office overheated, but I couldn't take my jacket off because the list was in it. He'd see. Paper crackled if I didn't sit real still. Fiduciary voodoo.

MY WIFE SAYS: for somebody like me, somebody with a strong head for facts, it's even more important to empty out that head from time to time. So I am, okay? Clearing the books.

"BUDDY? SOMETHING'S OFF, RIGHT? College material like you, and with bags down to here. I'm seeing a wear-and-tear beyond the normal wear of raking in their coins come Saturday. Know what Sam here's starting to think? Somebody's holding out on you, kid. You definitely got moochers. More'n one, too. Your face gives it away. You're too young to know how to hide stuff yet. In time, you'll get that right— but now your kisser is like neon practically, going bloink blink blank. And this particular neon tells Sam, says 'Sam? Certain moneys are coming directly out of young Jerry's personal bone marrow.' You got parasites, Jer. It shows. Draining you.

"You're shielding them but who's looking after *you*? Your folks? Naw, you're on your own. *I'm* here for you. You were handsome when I hired you. *Now* look. Your pantcuffs are frayed, the boy can't even sit up straight.—Jerry, who you covering for? Let me help, son. I swear it won't get past this desk. You know their names, you maybe even wrote names down. Yeah—probably got those tucked somewheres on your person. Look, kid, trust me here. You want Sam to step around his desk, ease you against that wall and frisk you, Jer? You're a good-looking kid, Jerry, but not that good. Spare us both. Pass your uncle the names. I'll need the exact dollar amount each leech has sucked out of my favorite. Jerry? Tell your Uncle Sam."

Tears stood in my boss's eyes. That's when I knew I had to let him save me. Yellow is such a beautiful positive color, isn't it? *While You Were Out . . .*

I SLEPT SO WELL THAT NIGHT! Why lie about it? I dropped off saying things like "Figures don't lie." It was a sleep too deep to let one single dream come tax it— just blackness so pure I woke up sweaty, half-panting. Getting true rest seemed the most exerting thing I'd done in months. One room away, Dad coughed, Mom promised him it'd be all right, she pounded his back, Dad thanked her, he said it'd passed, he choked again.

THE FRIDAY AFTER, I was driving toward the night-school business office to make my overdue payment. I'd got certain bonuses and could again fund my education. I still collected for Windlass but now avoided the two hundred block of Sunflower Street. I called on that block's paying clients only after dark. It was a gusty March afternoon, dust devils spun along the roadside. Winds rocked even the biggest trees. One wad of cotton, large as a hassock, came tumbling down the center line, rolled up onto my car hood and snagged one windshield wiper. I braked, cussed, got out to yank it off and—two hundred yards away in Baby Africa's clay cemetery—saw a funeral in progress.

Women were hunched under shawls, men held hats against their chests. Everybody, fighting wind, kept faces turned down and aside. They all looked ashamed and—in my present state—this at once attracted me. An old woman stood surrounded by kids. "It's Pearl's," I said. "They're burying Pearl." My voice broke, but, understand I am not asking for credit. Fact is, I slunk back into my Nash, flipped down both sun visors, prepared to roar off. Then unexpectedly my car was pulling over, I was out in the air, was walking toward a familiar group. Like so much I did back then, I hadn't planned to.

I remember dry weeds snapping under my new loafers. I waited off to one side, hands joined before me. I was the only white person present.

Two weeks back, I made four phone calls to the Detroit morgue; I'd helped get Pearl's body shipped home in a railroad ice-car. The trip had taken her eleven days. Pearl's coffin was splintery pine. You could see black nail ends bent crooked under half-moon hammer dents. Must be the crate they packed her home in. Somebody'd tried painting out stenciled instructions: THIS SIDE UP. KEEP REFRIGERATED AT ALL TIMES. Near the coffin's tapering foot end, a Maxwell House can rested on the ground. It was stuffed with dried hydrangea blooms big as human heads. Alongside the jagged grave, a pile of earth waited. Wind kept flicking dirt off that and onto the mourners. Everybody stood with eyes closed, less in prayer than to protect themselves from the menace of flung grit. (I wondered why this didn't usually happen. I'd only been to two funerals but remembered that the undertakers usually spread a grass-green ground cloth over such waiting dirt to hide it, and protect the living.)

People lined up looking into the coffin a last time. I'd never seen an open coffin at the graveyard. But, having strolled over here, I felt I couldn't hold back. When I joined the line, Mrs. B's neighbor kids saw me. They suddenly closed ranks around her. Only then did she turn in my general direction. Her neck lengthened, the blue-gray head twisting my way. I knew she couldn't see me at this distance but both VLB's arms lifted from her sides, wavering noplace. She seemed to be hearing a sound or maybe scented me standing here. I felt so honored I got weak.

The woman in the box was over seventy, she wore a mostly emptied amethyst necklace. On her chest a gold pin-watch read FORD MOTORS, a perfect attendance prize. Her age shocked me. I'd always pictured Pearl as just a bit older than me. I now saw: that would've made Vesta Lotte Battle a mother at seventy-three or so.

In the makeshift coffin, Pearl's head had shifted to one side, she faced pine planks like a person choosing to look punished, refusing even a last chance at formality.

The coffin was then closed, boys nailed it shut. Nails kept doubling over and this looked so ugly it grieved me. Strong young boys lowered Pearl's crate by ropes. Mourners themselves started heaping in the dirt. Garden spades and shovels seemed brought from home, no professional gravedigger waited in sight.

The girl who'd once pressed my hand between her candied palms now led Mrs. B away, detouring to avoid me. I walked over anyway. I was helpless not to. My mouth and lips felt novocained (I later realized I'd been mercilessly biting them without noticing). I felt foolish and exposed here, *rude*. But I still needed something from the old lady. *My* old lady, I still thought of her, but knew I had no right.

She must have seen a pink blur fumble nearer. VLB resisted ten children who tried dragging her past me. When she stopped, kids eased back, but their chins stayed lifted, hands knotting into fists. I didn't blame them. I knew how I must look out here. They'd taught me. I kept swallowing to keep from smiling. I gulped down a beefy-yeasty-copperpenny taste that turned out to be blood.

Mrs. Battle—grieving like this, far from her familiar house—seemed disoriented. Her skin had lost its grapey luster; she now looked floured in fine ash—her eyes' fronts too. Daylight showed a face composed entirely of cracks depending on splits and folds; her hands stayed out in front of her, long fingers opening and closing, combing air. She groped my way, lightly, almost fondly. Plain daylight showed her to be so tiny, malnourished maybe. Sun made her look just like . . . a blind person! Completely blind. Somehow she seemed less dignified out here and less unique. I have to say: it made things easier on me just then.—I'm telling you everything. That's our deal.

She faltered quite close, finally touching my sleeve, but jerking back like from a shock. "Ah," her voice recognized me. "You, Assurance?"

"Yes ma'am." I studied my new shoes.

"You did come. I knew it. I done told them. And we thanks you. Pearl'd be glad.—Look, not to worry bout all that other, hear? We doing just fine. Fact is, been missing you more than we miss it, Assurance. You steadily helped me to find my Pearl, get her on back here. Don't go fretting none, child, you tried.—You gone be fine. I'm gone be fine."

Then she turned and moved away from me supported by neighbor kids' spindly arms and legs.

I waited till everybody left. The wind got worse. I stood at Pearl's grave. Handprints and shoe marks had packed the earth. Wind had tipped the coffee can. Water made mud of the grave's foot end. I squatted and crammed hydrangeas back into their tin and set it upright. Last year's hydrangeas had dried brown but still showed most of their strong first blue. You know the color of hydrangeas—that heavenly blue so raw it comes close to seeming in bad taste.

I drove out into the country and passed a rural mailbox I'd always admired and meant to check on. I did that now for no good reason. It was a life-sized Uncle Sam enameled red, white, and blue—meat-pink for his face and hands. The eyes were rhinestone buttons salvaged off some woman's coat. His vest buttons were dimes glued on and varnished. While I stood looking, the proud owner stepped out of a tractor shed, then headed over to tell me how he'd got the idea and to accept my compliments. I panicked, saw myself as one of those guys, like Dad, who'll jaw for forty minutes with complete strangers over nothing. I hopped back into my Nash and squalled away.

I drove to Lucas' All-Round Store, needing staples for my folks. Mom loved angel food cake. With a little teasing encouragement from me, she could sit at our kitchen table and pull off a bit of white fluff at a time till she'd eaten it, whole. The embarrassment was part of her joy. "I *ate* that? *I* ate it?" And somehow she never gained. So I got her a big Merita angel cake and, for Dad, the giant economy size of Vick's Vapo Rub. (On his worst coughing nights, he sometimes dipped one finger in and swallowed gobs of it till I had to leave the room.)

HERE RECENTLY, DREDGING all this up, I've decided: if a person's emotional life were only rational—if it just "came out" like algebra does—then none of us would ever need good listeners or psychiatrists, would we? We'd do nicely with our accountants. We'd bring our man a whole year of receipts, evidence, and pain. We'd spend two hours together in a nice office and, at the end, our hired guy could just poke the *Tally* button and we, his client, would feel clean again and solid, solvent. Nice work if you can get it.

After Pearl's burial, I dropped off my folks' supplies, explaining I was headed for our Public Library to hit the books. Instead—pretending I didn't know what I was up to—I drove along Sunflower, switched off my ignition and headlights, coasted to a halt three houses down from Mrs. Battle's.

I sat screened by dried sunflower stalks rustling in the breeze, I looked toward her kerosene-lit home. I heard kids in there talking loud, once a wave of laughing broke. Her narrow body, half-doubled, crisscrossed the room from ironing board to stove and back, for tea, for hotter irons. I knew hers was just a little bent black nail of a body, but she threw such large blue shadows. I slumped out here feeling like a spy or a spurned lover, like some hick planning a stepladder elopement. I knew if I walked up and knocked at her screen door, she'd greet me, "Look children, our Boy Assurance's back." Kids might act snooty but she'd go make me tea in a mended cup so fine you could hold it up and—even against a kerosene lantern's glow—read imprinted on the bottom, its maker's name.

I watched her shack, pretending to guard it. Dumb thoughts: What if it caught fire? Then I'd carry her out, lug all the kids to safety. I was big: I could, I could carry most of them at once.

Why was I waiting? Did I hope she'd sense me here and suddenly pop up like when my tire blew? Maybe I could take her for a car ride tonight, go find her and the kids ice cream someplace. On me, of course. Maybe have two cords of firewood sent? I soon disgusted myself and drove home. I stayed up extra late, studying. Days, I didn't get much time for schoolwork. I think I told you I was working a couple other jobs. Managing a soda fountain and, after hours, cleaning two laundromats for this hermit bachelor who owned much of Falls while spending absolutely nothing. Plus I had the four night-school courses a week.

Working late that night, I heard Dad hacking in a new way, more shrill, yappier. I stood up from the card table that was my desk. I eased along our short hall and waited outside my folks' room. The cough came again. Only, it was my mother coughing. Her case had never seemed as bad as his. Whenever Momma got to hacking, she always laughed, claiming it was just a kind of sympathy vote for *his* shortwindedness. They'd worked cleaning the same looming machines for thirty-some years. What made me believe she'd found a purer air supply than his? Did I think Justice made things easier for the ladies? I leaned there in our dark hallway—beaverboard paneling bowed under my weight. I'd always understood that Dad, after thirty-seven years, had pulled enough fiber into his plugged lungs so you could maybe weave a long-sleeve shirt from it. But Mom? That night, I started knowing she'd inhaled enough to make one lacy deadly blouse. I stood here listening, though this just meant asking for more trouble. It seemed to me then: Staying alive is learning to make meals out of setbacks. Eating them, eating them up.

SO IT'S SIX WEEKS after the Detroit police wired us news of Pearl's death, two weeks after Pearl's burial and I'm driving Sunflower, still collecting. I'm half past Vesta Lotte Battle's clean shanty when I see this fresh white wreath nailed to her front door. Poor Pearl, I thought. Lined along VLB's weathered porch, a dozen children, black white brown, all wearing play clothes, all sitting very still. They're eating the usual pale taffy but, today, kids gobble it like taking some group poison.

Then, slow, two blocks and a thousand sunflowers later, I understand: my favorite, the old lady herself, is dead.

I drove on, forgetting waiting clients—I speeded right through town, hands choking the wheel. It felt like some hypodermic had just wedged under my breastbone, sucking. What'd been leached out was my breath's continuing interest in itself, breath know-how. Your wind has to be ambitious minute to minute—has to have a renewable *interest* in continuing. Installments.

The roadway was turning yellow from the edges inward when I finally pulled over, parked in the open countryside. A meadowlark balanced on a cattail gone to seed. And all at once I remembered. How. To breathe. The gratitude. I sat in the Nash gasping like a diver who's just found—by accident—the top, his life again.

THIS MUCH WAS clear: I had to do something—for the dead Mrs. B, for my living folks, my customers, for everybody else—meaning myself. OK. Right there in the car, I decided to attend one. A funeral, a black funeral. I needed to see an ideal one. I discovered: Mrs. Battle's had been held two days before. Nobody'd let me know.

I checked Monday morning's *Herald Traveler* for a likely name and church. I called in sick to my laundromat-cleaning and soda-jerk jobs. I'd never done that before. The church I picked was just off Sunflower Street. I had to drive right past the Battle home. A staked 'FOR RENT' sign was already pounded into her front yard. Browned sunflowers had been cleared, the hanging enameled teapot was gone. I hoped Vesta Lotte Battle's kids had claimed the thing before some realtor removed it as an eyesore. Riding by, I grumbled: real-estate agents sure didn't waste any time, the bloodsuckers. I kept trying to forget my parents' new caliber of rattling. They now seemed to alternate the need to breathe—him then her, her then him—like taking turns, sex-wise, waiting for each other's pleasure.

Nothing reminds you of how fragile it all is—nothing like living with two mild and often funny people who, if offered any riches on earth, would choose to get one deep single breath again.

To myself, aloud, after passing her shack, I said, "Vesta Lotte Battle, Vesta Lotte Battle. Pray for Us Left Here." I am no believer . . . still, you never know. I'm a percentage player. Besides, I missed her more than seemed quite rational or possible. I was just nineteen but already knew that Mrs. Battle was only starting up for me.

When you suddenly hear news of a friend's death, you sometimes want to call up one particular person who'll listen and help you through the worst first brunt of it. And so you're rushing to the home of the single person who might really help you get through this when, en route, of course, you find: the only one you want to be with now, she's the one who died.

MY '39 NASH coasted still before a ramshackle church. Off Sunflower, on Atlantic Avenue, the Afro-Baptist Free Will Full-Gospel Church appeared bandaged in three kinds of tar-paper brick. Its roof showed crude dribbled asphalt mending. Set on the highest peak, one unpainted steeple tilted. The place looked home-crafted as some three-tiered dollhouse, doghouse, or outhouse. Even in early April, church windowboxes spilled great purple clouds of petunias. From one box, a sunflower had sprouted. Though it looked totally out of place—a windblown seed—though it'd already lifted a few feet high, straining toward the rusty gutters, it'd been allowed to live.

Parked in one low Hollywoodish line, hired white limos gleamed with sunlight, hurt your eyes. An empty hearse bloomed big ostrich plumes and small American flags from either silver fender. Black morticians loitered in white suits and dark glasses. The undertakers smoked, polished their cars, stood in proud jumpy groups.

They acted like Secret Service guys outside a civic building where some bigwig official is appearing. They waited, smug and antsy, for their boss: Today's highest-paying black body in Falls, NC.

Turns out I was one of three whites in a large loud congregation. I kept straightening my black tie. Elders welcomed me with great ceremony and graciousness that made me feel even more a worm, a spy. Why was I here? Respect. Paying respects, paying. Came time to view the corpse. Almost immediately it happened, people filed toward the box. All the people on my row stood. Somebody nudged me from the left. I rose, not quite meaning it. Like in drill formation, we marched toward the knotty-pine altar and a coffin propped over velvet-draped sawhorses.

This happened on a Monday. Somehow, my premium book and a few rolls of quarters had been stored in my car's glove compartment, left there from Saturday rounds. I didn't want to leave them outside: this neighborhood was dicey (being the neighborhood where I collected). I'd brought the things in with me and now took them toward somebody's open coffin. The insurance ledger was imitation black alligator, hinged so it flipped open like a paperboy's record book. It bulged now in my jacket pocket. I took it out and held it, hoping it'd appear to be some prayerbook maybe. Sweating like I was, I nearly dropped the slippery thing, then grabbed it, gulping. Imagine my list of names toppling into the box with this stiffening stranger.

SHE LOOKED to be about thirty-eight. All in lilac, a cocktail dress. Pinkish feathers curled around her head like some nightclub's idea of a halo. Her coffin was lined in white glove leather, the sides were plugged with gleaming chrome buttons; it was framed in oiled walnut—the thing smelled just like a brand-new Cadillac convertible. Giddy, for a moment, I wanted to climb in. I don't know why. I hadn't eaten much that day. Since Mrs. Battle died on me without a proper good-bye, I'd started feeling really tired, like I'd forgot to do something important.

The stranger's chest was massed with purple orchids. Flowers picked up the exact color of her dress. I wondered if the orchids might be painted. But, no, I could see that they were real. Huge curling bugle-nosed orchids seemed to crouch there on her breastbone—beautiful but someway wicked—like they were guarding her while feeding on the body. Above her luxurious coffin, along the empty choir loft's edge, dozens, maybe hundreds, of Easter lilies. Tin collection plates hid behind flowerpots. The lilies washed Afro-Baptist with so sweet a smell it burned your sinuses and eyes.

Stepping back toward my seat, I heard quarters jingling, one roll unpeeling in my pocket. I winced. Trying to tamp the sound, I grinned.

Soon as we settled, the huge choir swooped in. Lined up like a jury, they nearly outnumbered us mourners. Openmouthed, they arrived singing something called "Blessed Assurance." The scary appropriateness of this (for me, I mean) changed and deepened verse to verse. It went from seeming a wild coincidence to feeling almost expected, natural. I sat telling myself certain mumbo-jumbo things like: "You have chosen the right place. Today is the day you were intended to be here." I didn't really know what all this meant. I still don't.

Many small children belted out the hymn from behind spiky white lilies. Some of the kids might've been among Mrs. Battle's household regulars but I wasn't sure. (When a boy is nineteen, little kids all look alike for a while.) Over flowers you could see the dark cloudy hair of tallest children, heads tipping side to side as mouths moved:

> Blessed Assurance, Jesus is mine!
> Oh, what a foretaste of glory di-vine!
> Heir of salvation, purchase of God,
> Born of His Spirit, washed in His Blood.
> —This is my story, this is my song,
> Praising my Savior all the day long.

When human voices' pure pure sound rushed out carrying such words, I felt drunk, half-faint. I'd settled near the back. I could only bear to watch my own pale hands. I studied wrists' yellow hair shining in daylight. I thought odd things, "Strange, how no American coin is gold-colored." I looked at my long fingers' freckled backs, I turned over wet pink palms. These hands seemed to belong to one plump and silly boy. But my eyes, staring down on hands from what felt like a great and sickening height seemed the eyes of an old man, one teetering at some cliff's brink, a tired old person considering jumping.

Music swayed the choir that sang it. Each hymn swung singers toward a wilder kind of seasick. The people were one thing, their singing was another but, combined, these jumped past making an equal third. Everything seemed swollen past proportion, quantum. Some choir members turned in place—hard for me to watch, impossible to ignore—they spun around and around, white sleeves flaring like cheap wings. The choir loft was stairstepped in rows. At any moment three or four singers would be whirling, self-contained, white robes cheerfully slapping robes of those beside them.

AT FOOTBALL GAMES when your team is winning, everybody in your bleachers starts leaning side to side and shouting one thing—it was like that now. This was a funeral but the peppy choir still considered us the winning side.

I disagreed. I fought the row's rock and sway. I considered leaving. I felt out of my depth here. But I knew that, in climbing over six weeping strangers singing in my pew, I'd have to say, "Excuse me. So sorry. Thank you, oops, pardon." I couldn't bear to let manners make a fool of me again. Not here. Instead I fought this tilting. Everybody moved but me. I now turned into some blond Princeton boy, chilly with a vengeance. Soon the volume grew. They sure were working on me. Everyone nearby sang in three-part harmony—sang like conservatory grads—so skilled, their diction glassy, right. Soon it seemed the church building itself was tipping, a screened box that pans for gold, searching for some glint among the mud. It kept rocking us, helpless as pebbles shifting in the sieve—it kept us rattling back and forth, almost auditioning.

Everyone but me. Straight-backed, massive. I refused. No way. Bumped from either side, I muttered at the woman beside me. Cheerful behind her tears, she yelled, "Tell it, bro!" She was just encouraging me. I explained how a person could sure use a little more room here. She nodded. My complaints just swelled the hymn. Everybody took me for a singer. Glum, feeling semi-hateful, I got coached by "Blessed Assurance." On it rolled. First I hummed along just to be polite. (With me it's a disease.)

Jostled from left and right, I tested a chanting note here, a word there. A person almost had to. Pretty soon, though you still fought it (for the sake of principle), you did sort of catch on, you soon nearly liked it. But, wait, no. I stiffened my spine, wanting to prove something. What? Maybe to keep things controlled on behalf of these wild emotional people noisemaking around me. *Some*body had to stay in charge, right? It was a favor that you paid others who'd lost it. There were rules.

I asked myself what she'd advise me—what Vesta Lotte Battle'd say? ("Hey, you, un-hitch a inch. What you keeping back? You hiding something, boy?")—I soon joined somewhat in. I trusted her. I wanted to do well. Maybe I was overly conscientious at it—but, hey, after all, Whitie does what Whitie can!

My shoulders soon felt safe between others' rolling massaging shoulders holding mine up from either side. I wanted to blend in for once. I hated being the go-getter all alone out front. I longed to seem the same as everybody else.

Maybe too quick for safety, I felt enclosed, half-pardoned. I felt explained. All this was what I'd been so homesick for, and without ever having lived it!

Soon you were pretty much loving it. I was. It felt like dancing sitting down. Like fainting with your eyes open. Like singing in the shower but with others singing in their showers nearby, others who, like you, didn't sound so hot on their own, but pooled became an angel choir that exhales, not carbon dioxide, but perfect pitch. I felt like telling everybody why I'd come, like singing why.

Our group stopped in one ragged rush. I was loud—alone—amazingly off-key for a long long second. Nobody blamed me or much noticed as I sucked air, swallowed "Fool!," curled my toes. Others were now standing one by one. Fanning themselves with Jesus fans, they talked about the corpse.

"She been a mighty good neighbor, Lila," the woman near me rose. "One time, remember when my William cut his foot so bad on that soda bottle? well, she look after all my other little ones the whole night till we walk back home from the doctor's out Middlesex way. Then Lila say, Don't you be coming in here waking up these babies in the middle of no night, you let them sleep. She kept mine over to her house till they all awake and then she fed them a mighty fine breakfast, sent them back on home to me. Too, Lila done give my momma eighty cents, one time she couldn't pay."

"Lila," one old man with two canes called. "Had the prettiest yard on Atlantic Avenue, better'n mine and you know how nice mine is. Yeah, she got her dahlias to someway grow big as you head. Used bonemeal, some says."

They told why she never married (tending her sick mother). They said she dearly loved a moving picture show. She knew the age and facts of every movie star on-screen. Lila's say-so settled every movie bet or argument in Baby Africa.

Listening, I nodded. I soon felt I knew Lila a little, then—maybe it sounds pushy—I felt I knew her pretty well. It *was* pushy. Odd, I almost missed her. But even then I understood—I'd confused Lila with certain others: a Detroit autoworker I'd never seen alive. I mixed up this Lila person with my own ailing parents. I confused Lila with a freed slave whose burial I'd missed and maybe caused.

After the testimonies, music started again and I really threw myself into the pump and swell of hymns. I let myself go, wanting to be excellent at this. I was a silly kid hoping, his first time out, to get straight A's in Grief. But even while crooning the choruses, while practicing A-plus Amens loud, I still knew: This might be fine for today. For a change. Oh but I needed this now, oh yeah. And I would never forget it or outlast its uses; but, being white like me, I couldn't *live* here.

I might rant and sway, released toward the best of Afro-Baptist, I might be today's greatest hottest pudding of emotion—but I would always remain a tourist when it came to such display. Call me frozen, or career-oriented. Fill in the blank by saying I'm hyper-Caucasian. Some claim that just such hanging back has already turned our white race into the losing side: creatures that cannot take the heat and so keel over. Maybe we've already been outranked by those more fluid, faster moving, closer to the earth and ready to adapt, sweat, go with things.

That day I tried, though. Oh I tried to get it right.

"We hopes our white friends will feel free and speak." It was the preacher crook-ing off his varnished perch. He smiled for the first and only time that day. He bared his square white teeth in a fake, presented grin I recognized as mine. The single white lady popped up quick, then looked around and seemed to regret it. She'd stood to force herself. I knew this and felt for her as, stranded, she cleared her throat, alarmed but determined. The lady wore trim navy-blue, her foil-colored hair all in a knotty permanent. I couldn't place her name but—knowing Falls the way this ex-paperboy did—I could've told you her street address to within one block. She might've been sister to the owner of that resurrected Wedgwood.

In a girl's voice, the lady now mentioned hiring Lila-here for many years. The lady admitted how hard Lila'd worked, far above the call of duty. The lady sounded short of breath—maybe she gasped due to sadness or stage fright, both. Soon you could hardly hear her. Everybody tipped forward, trying. I did too. She went, ". . . Feel we never . . . understood or whatever what a fine person . . . we had . . . around our house till Lila got so . . . so sick last . . . June was it?" she asked the man seated beside her.

"June, yes. Lila'd fallen in our rec room. We came back on Monday. We found her. She'd knocked over liquid floorwax and was lying in it, it'd dried. And when my sons pulled her to standing, the sound was like the flooring coming up with her. She was embarrassed about having spilled. It was too awful. The first Monday she didn't turn up for work I felt our house was like . . ." the lady waited, standing, doubting her lungs. "Like . . . house . . . was . . . hollow. There was an echo, it seemed all our rugs had been taken out. My husband can tell you. Now it seems that . . . to be . . . our self—our best selves—we needed Lila there to . . . And since she . . ." This time the matron curved one palm around her throat, gulping, unable to find a voice. But she refused to sit. Her husband reached out, almost touched her back, decided against it—improved his own posture instead. You saw that the woman really wanted to sit—she knew people would forgive her. But she'd decided. She had to finish.

"Tell the troof," some old man called, rapping floorboards with two homemade walking sticks. "Jesus going to see that you get all the air you needs for speaking true. Jesus going to fan some cold truth-telling wind down into you. You watch."

The thin woman smiled back at him, nodding. Her fist now rapped her sternum, she shook her prim head sideways. Her embarrassment, I saw, was a country club white person's. Social embarrassment. She feared she looked foolish. *Being* foolish pained her less than getting caught at it by strangers, especially these decent black ones.

Still, I felt for her. Takes one to know one. "The Black-and-Blue About Being White Blues." I sat remembering Mrs. Battle in the rainstorm, drenched for me, throwing rocks under my car, scattering dogs that'd taken cover there to snap at my sogged ankles. I'd never thought of doing that. Being watched like I always was in Baby Africa—it'd never come to me that I might just kick dogs or chuck stones at them. Why'd I settled for their nipping at me? Why hadn't I properly defended myself?

"Loving Lila," the white woman tried summing up. "Might've let us love each other more, but I'm not sure that was reason enough . . . for taking up her life the way we did. And by accident almost, looking back. We gave her ten days off a year. Five of those she spent at the beachhouse with us. She cooked for us there. Which was no vacation. I see that now. Believe me, I'm living with this. We learned so much from her. Look, we loved her is all. Maybe that's the best thing anybody can teach anybody? I don't know."

She sat, face in hands then. "Amen. It'll do," somebody shouted. Heads bobbed.

The white man hopped up to remark that what his wife'd just said sure went double for him.

Then I stood. I did. I hadn't known I would. Suddenly it's like the church had sunk and left me vertical. I think the singing had made me light-headed. That song "Blessed Assurance" chanted in child voices, the white flowers' smell, white robes like makeshift wings. Those made me.

I told everybody I felt real bad about selling funeral insurance. I told why I'd

come. I admitted seeing the great beauty of this ceremony. I conceded: Negro funerals had it all over white ones—much more personal and everything. But it seemed
I'd never understand enough to help me feel quite easy with the business end of
burial. I admitted: some of my most beloved clients, they had lapsed, see? I'd let
them drift from the black into the red and then I told on them. I had. I couldn't
rescue the whole world, could I?—though, for a while, I'd given it my level best.
You try and save a drowner but if you drown too—what good is that to anybody,
you know? I said, Sure, I wanted a college education but not one built by walking
on the heads of others. I apologized for taking up their time with something not
exactly on the subject. Then I added—feeble, I knew—that Miss Lila's lilac dress
was about the finest-looking lilac dress I'd ever seen. "Amen. Ain't it, though?" two
old women, maybe twins, hollered. I sat. Breathing hard. No way would I start
sobbing like a fool, no, they were all looking. The same old man up front began
really beating floorboards with his canes, he cried back at me, "Jesus Have His Ways,
Child. Be of Comfort, Son. You going to act right. You wait. Scales going to fall off
them young eyes by-and-by. You'll see."

Then—that fast—I knew what I would do.

Again I stood. I emptied my pockets of all rolled quarters and loose change. I
yanked out every bill. I whipped the premium book from my jacket.

Mourners between the aisle and me kindly slid out. They let me step free. I walked
to the tin collection plates tucked behind massed lilies. Into one plate, I piled all my
money. About eighty-nine dollars and fifty cents, I think. Maybe more.

Then—not able not to—I dropped in the keys to my loyal Nash. I held the key
ring back up—I told everybody where my car was parked, what kind it was, what
color. "Oh Lord," somebody called. "Jesus got them Miracle-Working Ways. He
look into the whiteboy Soul. He Clean House."

I announced I wanted some kind of college scholarship set up. It'd help some
straight-A child from this church. Elders would sell my used car—that and what
cash I'd left here would at least help get things rolling. The fund would be named
to honor ... Miss Lila here. I didn't want to say Vesta Lotte Battle's name. Then
they'd know it was me that turned her in. I left.

Two ushers swung open the exits for me. One young man was smiling, face all
wet. The older gent gave me this "Who are you kidding?" stare, his mouth looked
big, postcard-sized and folded in on itself with scorn. *He* seemed right. But, soon
as sun hit me, I felt light and wonderful. Sunflowers and zinnias seemed my African
honor guard. I weighed nothing for six blocks. Though this neighborhood was
rough, no dog chased me today. I felt afraid of nobody. Nothing dared to hassle or
to nag me.

I hiked back to my folks' place. They hadn't heard me drive up, they asked what
was wrong, where'd I parked? I told them, I tried. They sat looking at each other.
Dad's latest *Life* rested open on his lap. I remember Ava Gardner was on the cover.
She's also from North Carolina, from very much the wrong side of the tracks and
with the face of a Contessa and I have always loved her. Neither of my folks could

drive. Proud, they called my wreck "Jerry's runabout." I often took them shopping in it or out to the Dairy Queen.

Now Dad laughed, removed his glasses, folded them. He had an uneducated person's respect for eyeglasses, like these were some substitute for a college degree. He set the bifocals in their little casket, snapped it shut. He kept shaking his head side to side, he told Mom, "They give our boy free encyclopedias, he throws them in the drink. Now he's gone and handed over his roadster to the colored people because they're poor. Who knows? Maybe if a boy acts like a rich man long enough, he turns into one? Sure hope so."

Then Poppa's chuckling slid, like always, right down breath's stairsteps into deep and deeper coughs till you never thought his wind would surface again. Mom jumped up and stood patting his back. It never helped but he liked it anyway. Next, Momma bent toward me, bent across Dad's leatherette easy chair. She touched the top of my hair, then one side of my neck. I felt too young then, shrunken down, just like earlier I'd felt so old and high up.

"Jerry's always had him a soft streak," Mom said, with me standing right here. "It's not soft," I snapped at her. "It's the only part I like. It's hard—and the rest of it is sloppy and extra. Don't say 'soft.' " She pitied me, knowing I was weak enough to pity others. I hated her for that.

I stumbled to my room, threw myself onto the bed, mashed my face into the chenille spread's nubbins, pretending they were Braille—I'd soon read what to do next. I just wished I hadn't left my premium book in the collection plate. I don't know. I worried what might happen to my other clients. Even with Mrs. Battle gone, I still had big responsibilities. My ledger, was it the only record for the tens of thousands that older folks had saved toward their standing on the next plane? Would they miss out on their hard-earned heaven just because I'd lost my head while feeling generous?

Two days later, the mailman brings me a package. In it, my insurance book, all the money I'd left, plus—held to a piece of cardboard by crisscrossed electrician's tape—my car keys. The cardboard said, "Parked right where it was." A note read: "We all get move sometime. Sometime we needs to think out why. If it still the same way you felt then we start up the college thing for one our young folk. If not then that OK too. Cause we all Children OF God. Either way you a man of heart. IN Christ Blood Bartered for us sinners I am Rev. T. Y. Matthews—Free-Will Afro-Baptist (Church)."

I sat down to write a check for two hundred dollars. Signing it, my hands shook—the largest check I'd ever written. I kept the ledger. And, look, I kept the car. Can you forgive me? I waited till night to go collect it. I hated being seen. My parents applauded when they heard me pull up out front again. "Pile in," I hollered and they came running like kids rasping from a touch of croup. I drove them to the Dairy Queen. They sat in back, royalty, holding hands. You'd've thought it was a Rolls, my used Nash. We said nothing the whole way out and home. They were back there, sighing, eating their cones. Driving, I breathed through my mouth, not wanting to cry. The three of us, we had been so unlucky, really. And just getting back what little was ours, it seemed some great reward to us, some justice.

NEXT DAY, I drove to Sam's office, I would turn in my book and quit. But just outside his door, I decided on collecting two more weeks. I'm not sure why. I guess I wanted to get things cleaned up for whatever poor soul Windlass Eventualities hired next. Two more Saturdays. Hounds showed no mercy. Foolish and smug of me, but I somehow thought dogs might act kinder during these last trips. I half-believed dogs would smell my sacrifice: the Miss Lila Scholarship. I hoped yard dogs would finally decide I was a friend to Baby Africa. Dogs didn't.

Again I knocked. Mrs. Battle's nosy neighbor, the hugely fat widow, peeked out. She said, "You come for your Assurance? Is you new? You look older than that last one."

"Yes ma'am, older."

From inside the darkest corner of her home, underlit by a dime-store votive candle, one Jesus grinned—dressed in powder blue and white, beard marceled just so, he had a twenty-four-carat halo that somebody really should go hock for food. He looked guilty over being so pretty on a street of such bad need. This client's payments were only two weeks overdue. She'd greeted me with a broad face so scared I didn't like to see it. Dead Lila in her box looked much more in control than this living woman. "I checks," she shook her head. "I goes and looks but I real low just now."

Watching her move, I wondered how somebody so poor could stay so mammoth.

She lumbered toward a tiny vase that showed another Jesus hammocked among clouds, arms out beside him like a diver about to leap. From here the vase sure sounded empty. She stood—eyes closed, one ear mashed against it, like listening to a seashell. Like she could hear a hundred coins trying to hatch alive in there.

"Seem like it ought to be around here." The widow moved from vase to firewood box to mantel. She shifted things. There sat an unopened jar of jam, a tartan bow topping it. A gift from Mrs. Battle? An inheritance?

"I busy checking," the woman promised.

But I stood remembering Mrs. Battle's honesty: "I ain't got no money today." "Pearl dead." "Vesta Lotte Battle tries." "I reckon you'll do what you wants." I felt I'd learned something from the old woman. I still couldn't explain quite what.

"Maybe it been stole. Yeah, stole probably," the obese woman patted around behind a sheeny Last Supper wall rug. Then she moved to a calendar that showed Christ holding out his own lit-up and dripping heart. His face looked sobered. You could see why.

"Assurance? These young boys now'll steal you blind. Ain't nobody safe. Too, I getting so I forgets. You sure it already a Saturday again? I done sunk mighty low but I still hunting. Don't you fret your pretty head none, I gone find it yet. You so pretty. Look how 'good' and yellow his hair is. Golder'n that"—and she scanned the room for her favorite picture, then pointed to the rouged Jesus who posed nearby—heartless Himself because He kept *offering* it to everybody.

Such flattery always sickened me. I really couldn't abide it. "Here," I bent, kicking over one corner of her rag rug. Since the house was dark, since her notched swollen back was toward me, it was easy to unpocket the two quarters. I picked them up, held them out to her. "These?" I said.

She turned, she made a cry, "No!" She inched forward, blinking, her jaw slack. Each huge arm now lifted from the elbow—wobbling like udders as she neared me. The sad weight hanging off her sides and breasts suddenly seemed like a burden assigned, not chosen. In the face, surprise mixed with such fear. Fear that I might take these back, fear I meant to trick her. I couldn't stand watching. *May this job end, and now, Amen. I am not fit to earn a living in this world.* "So let's see here, that's what?—fifty—five zero—cents, paid in full?" I fiddled with my black book. "Listen, there'll be a new fellow next week. Just to make sure you get full credit, you'll want to save these. Just give him these same two next week, okay? Okay."

I passed her fifty cents. All the hut's accidental sunlight, the shine from her red candle got snagged across two silver coins. Her callused hand itself, charcoal dark on its back, showed a pale pink copper color inside. It seemed that years of work for whites had rubbed the true black pigment off her palm.

Her face gleamed, the upper body rocking toward me. Moaning, she showed me my own coins—like these were two working eyes that some genius had awarded a blind woman, round things she could pop right into ruined sockets, and see again. "I still on the assurance, Assurance?"

Beside her name, I read the tally, three policies complete: Two thousand three hundred five dollars and fifty cents. "Consider yourself carried, please." I backed into daylight, glad even for the posse of sunning mongrels. They rose, stretching, grumpy at their duty. We all have our jobs.

She hid both eyes behind the heavy crook of one great arm.

I heard her weeping, then explaining to the crowd of paper Jesuses, "Your Dorothy ain't lost out after all, Savior. You done carried her over into the Promised Land of another week of Surrance and for free. I still under the coverage. Your old Dot here, she still covered, Lord."

NOW I'M GOING on sixty. It seems impossible, but years are really the bottom line, aren't they? Semi-retired, I've had the usual two heart attacks but, as with some of us who get the best cardiac specialists, I lived. Of course, as a young man, I went into business for myself. I actually did pretty well.

It came about in a strange enough way. I was working other odd jobs, saving up for law school. I'd got my BS through night courses. My parents lived to see me graduate. They were so happy about it. My father wore his reading glasses all through the ceremony. I wanted to tell my folks, "No, this is just the start . . . don't be so thrilled so early." But they were.

I sometimes wonder what they'd think if they could see where I live now. We just built a fancy guest wing onto our beach place. I designed it myself. It doubled the floor space of our original cottage. These days we don't have too much company and the addition's not that practical. I just wanted to add it on is all. The kids come down when they can get away from their jobs and such. My wife calls this wing— with its white spiral staircase, all the glass, cathedral ceilings—Gerald's Taj Mahal. My wife is from one of *the* old families around here. She stops short of calling my new annex that dreaded word of hers: "nouveau." I can't explain to her just why I had to get so flashy this time around.

Last August, she and I were on our new porch just sitting there, reading. It was late afternoon. A young white couple, strangers, wandered off the public beach. Holding hands, they crossed our property, headed toward the road. They were country kids in bathing suits, very tall, they moved well, they were as good-looking as they'd ever be. They walked right by the entrance to our new guest wing. I jumped up. "What's wrong?" Millie asked from behind me. I shook my head No. I couldn't answer for a while. In the second I'd seen one pale man and woman come up from the ocean, slowed by sand and tramping toward our fine glass house, I understood I'd built it for them. For my parents, dead these thirty-odd years, people whose idea of an annual vacation was one spendthrift afternoon at the State Fair outside Raleigh. For a second, in the late night, I thought they'd finally come home to collect.

But my career so-called, I was telling you about that. I cleaned two laundromats for a rich ill-tempered bachelor. We hardly ever saw each other. He'd leave my pay envelopes in his rural mailbox. He must've liked my work. His will left me both laundromats. I was twenty-five by then. I'd been studying law on my own. This first equity helped get me a school loan. I made Law Review at Duke. I was thirty-one when I finished.

I moved back here to Falls and bought another laundry unit. I hung up my shingle and started managing the estates of the lawyers and dentists whose widows needed help, whose Princeton sons now practiced in flashier cities. The boys'd gone off to Atlanta and New York where real fortunes could be made. Me, I stuck it out locally. In the late Fifties, I put new laundromats into the shopping centers that'd started opening nearby and all up into Virginia. Then, with our kids off in good schools, with me now spending more time managing my own holdings than other people's, I invented something.

I'd stayed polite and steady, of course—forever grateful to have a leg up in this town society-wise. To this day I follow my dead mother's advice, I still say "Please" and "Thank you very much." They still like that. And it's only now, when I no longer *have* to be polite, it's only now that people notice my manners and find them humble, touching. Odd. I got somewhat sly. I concocted (with a smart college boy's summer help) and patented (on my own) an adjustable coin plunger for commercial washers and driers. It used to be—when prices went up (as they will)—a laundromat owner had to rebuy the whole coin-activator component. With my device, the owner can just adjust his own machine's templates. He can ask whatever seems fair—and without getting soaked by the manufacturer every time he ups the load cost by a dime or a quarter. It sounds simple. It is. "Strictly a nickel and dime operation," my wife teases me. But I got there first and it has made our financial life a good bit easier.

I took over other laundry facilities. I worked all this out consciencewise: Washing helps people, right? My forty-one Carolina/Virginia locations are open to all—all who have some pocket change and the will to stay tidy. Who can argue with the beauty and value of a clean 100% cotton business shirt, pressed, brand-new, and on its hanger, ready-to-wear? How could that cause anybody pain?

Over my years in business, I've been ethical usually, and (to be fair to myself) sometimes even when it hurt. One thing I admit I'm proud of: I volunteered as an unsalaried consultant in a local class-action against the cotton mill here. Nowadays, newspapers call my parents' disease "brown lung." Then we just said, They've Got What You Get from Working Too Long in the Mill. The Wages of Wages.—Owners, clever, never let anybody *title* the sickness. That meant it wasn't real, see?—Workers won this go-round. Japanese-made filters now purify the plant, replacing its entire air supply every twenty minutes. Some new insurance benefits are in place, there's back-pay for those too broken-winded to work.

STRANGE, THOUGH TECHNICALLY I'M PRETTY WELL SET NOW, I've never really felt rich. If that's any defense! Weird that my own kids have trust funds—it's thrilling, really. Only two bothered finishing college, of course. One teaches the deaf in Savannah. Our middle daughter, Miranda, took Sarah Lawrence by storm and will enter Harvard Law this fall. Our baby girl lives in St. Louis with a black airlines mechanic who plays jazz on weekends. She says she's happy. You have to believe them. I know that her living situation shouldn't bother me. But, hey, it does bother me some, what can I say? Nobody's perfect.

Oh, and I'm not insured. Drives my estate planner absolutely crazy but, after that first experience, forget it. Insurance based on getting sick, they call Health. The kind depending on everybody's fear of death they call Life!

You can have it.

SOME SATURDAY MORNINGS here lately I wake at our beach place and I'll be half out of bed before understanding I don't have to go to work. It's almost disappointing. I'm free finally. No routes left. I still remember most every house along Sunflower Street and Atlantic Avenue, my Eventualities crew.

I HAVE A mind that holds onto such details: the one that told the same three easy riddles, the one in the metal wheelchair and wearing, for no good reason, a cowgirl hat.—A head for facts is good in a lawyer and a tinkerer like me. But you can overdo remembering. Recalling too much makes the person inefficient. As I age, early memories come clearer. I still picture many a door opening on those wizened faces. Many faces probably no older than mine now. I settle back in bed, I listen to the ocean working at reclaiming our oceanfront lot. It should soothe you, having a big white glassy house right on the beach. So I lie here looking at the patterns sunlight-on-water moves across our high white ceiling. Times, I say—low so as not to wake Millie—"That's over and done." Then I try and catch more sleep. But you know how it is, once your eyes are open, you can pretend for forty minutes but you're awake for good.

Over thirty-odd years, I've told myself to forget the insurance route. And yet, lately for no good reason, it's been coming back on me, like an overrich meal.

We all have our crimes. Right?

I REMEMBER, after Sam got hold of my list, before he rang up Cleveland with news of impounded funds, he promised me I'd done the right thing. Sam said I'd fingered fewer Overdues than any collector he could remember, especially for a *young* collector. They were really ruthless about turning in certain oldsters, these darned eager-beaver kids. Sam claimed I must be good for my clients' morale. "Thank you," I said. "Tried," I said. Since I'd personally floated many of my old folks' funeral payments for weeks, months—I *was* their morale.

"You're beginning to look better already, Jerry. Know your problem? See, you're like Charlie Chaplin or this Paul Robeson or Mrs. Roosevelt maybe—you want to be all things to all people, but you can't. Nobody can. Choose maybe four, six, tops. Think of these as job slots you've filled. You get to pick this one handful, then you really better stick your neck out—but just for them. The rest you let go. You've got to, Jerry. Of your six all-time keepers, I seriously doubt one's on this list. Don't say otherwise, Jer.—My job? I'm here to make you feel better. You haven't got the organic chemistry figured out yet. You're like me—just dripping virtue. There's no percentage in taking it to heart, son. What we're doing here is rigged, sure, but you know why, Jerry? Because it's part of the world."

Soon as he phoned in our nine worst credit risks to Cleveland—a town he called The Mistake by the Lake—Sam offered me a drink right from his bottle. This time I took it. My eyes watered. To me the stuff'd already started tasting like old couches, the smoky interiors of huts, my Baby Africa route and brown clientele distilled.—I drank and drank it so I'd sleep. My homely boss leaned back, he took his longest hardest bourbon-pull so far. Dazed, I sat in the office's half-light, drunk. Sam gulped; I kept watching his notched Adam's apple hopping and hopping like some small live thing you pity.

I quit Funerary Eventualities forty years ago. I still feel responsible for those nine who never got the warm reception they deserve. On the next plane, I mean. And, look, I don't even *believe* in the next plane, you know? Still, I understand certain basics: Everybody expects a few sure things, a bit of blessed assurance. A person wants to feel covered.

Hey, and I appreciate your listening. Really. I don't know—I've kept fretting over this, feeling it for all these years. I mean, basically I'm not all that bad of a man, am I. Am I?

I've never once credited any type of heaven. No way. But I still worry for the souls I kept from theirs.—Even now I know the names of my nine clients I squealed on. They are:

> Betty Seely
> Easton Peel
> "Junior" Turnage
> Carlisle Runyon
> Mary Irene Tatum
> Leota Saiterwaite
> P. M. Hilton
> Minna Smith
> Vesta Lotte Battle

I still try and imagine her—on hold, rocking between this world and the next. I want to either bring her back or send her on toward her proper reward. I can't.

Vesta Lotte Battle owed me $12.50.

THERE, I'VE TOLD YOU. I'll feel better. Thank you very much.

I WROTE THE STORY "Long Distance" as a result of several unrelated moments joining up in my mind. The first of these was a story told to me by a friend, about going home for Christmas and overhearing her two sisters-in-law having a quiet argument about the wrapping of Christmas presents. The sister I considered to be the more unreasonable won the argument, which spurred me into wanting to write the story. I was divorced at the time, and a second element that swam into the mix was a story told to me by a drunken date, about a conversation he had had with his former girlfriend from Japan. I found this intriguing, too, and asked his permission to use it. He gave me permission, but when I later showed him the story, he never spoke to me again. The secondhand item about the sisters-in-law returned to me again, too. After the book was published, the pastor of the church that one of the couples attended out of the blue asked the husband whether he knew me or my work, because a character in one of my stories reminded him of this man. It took about six months for that brouhaha to die down. Later I wrote a long piece for an anthology about writers and friendship called, "Can Writers Have Friends?" I do have friends, but it takes a certain amount of courage for a friend to know that he or she might turn up in a story. Good writers are ruthless, and willing to say anything.

JANE SMILEY

JANE SMILEY

Long Distance

KIRBY CHRISTIANSON IS STANDING under the shower, fiddling with the hot-water spigot and thinking four apparently simultaneous thoughts: that there is never enough hot water in this apartment, that there was always plenty of hot water in Japan, that Mieko will be here in four days, and that he is unable to control Mieko's expectations of him in any way. The thoughts of Mieko are accompanied by a feeling of anxiety as strong as the sensation of the hot water, and he would like the water to flow through him and wash it away. He turns from the shower head and bends backward, so that the stream can pour over his face.

When he shuts off the shower, the phone is ringing. A sense that it has been ringing for a long time—can a mechanical noise have a quality of desperation?—propels him naked and dripping into the living room. He picks up the phone and his caller, as he has suspected, is Mieko. Perhaps he is psychic; perhaps this is only a coincidence; or perhaps no one else has called him in the past week or so.

The connection has a crystalline clarity that tricks him into not allowing for the satellite delay. He is already annoyed after the first hello. Mieko's voice is sharp, high, very Japanese, although she speaks superb English. He says, "Hello, Mieko," and he *sounds* annoyed, as if she calls him too much, although she has only called once to give him her airline information and once to change it. Uncannily attuned to the nuances of his voice, she says, "Oh, Kirby," and falls silent.

Now there will be a flurry of tedious apologies, on both sides. He is tempted to hang up on her, call her back, and blame his telephone—faulty American technology. But he can't be certain that she is at home. So he says, "Hello, Mieko? Hello, Mieko? Hello, Mieko?" more and more loudly, as if her voice were fading. His strategy works. She shouts, "Can you hear me, Kirby? I can hear you, Kirby."

He holds the phone away from his ear. He says, "That's better. Yes, I can hear you now."

"Kirby, I cannot come. I cannot go through with my plan. My father has lung cancer, we learned this morning."

He has never met the father, has seen the mother and the sister only from a distance, at a department store.

"Can you hear me, Kirby?"

"Yes, Mieko. I don't know what to say."

"You don't have to say anything. I have said to my mother that I am happy to stay with her. She is considerably relieved."

"Can you come later, in the spring?"

"My lie was that this Melville seminar I was supposed to attend would be offered just this one time, which was why I had to go now."

"I'm sorry."

"I know that I am only giving up pleasure. I know that my father might die."

As she says this, Kirby is looking out his front window at the snowy roof of the house across the street, and he understands at once from the hopeless tone of her voice that to give up the pleasure that Mieko has promised herself is harder than to die. He understands that in his whole life he has never given up a pleasure that he cherished as much as Mieko cherished this one. He understands that in a just universe the father would rather die alone than steal such a pleasure from his daughter. All these thoughts occur simultaneously and are accompanied by a lifting of the anxiety he felt in the shower. She isn't coming. She is never coming. He is off the hook. He says, "But it's hard for you to give it up, Mieko. It is for me, too. I'm sorry."

The sympathetic tones in his voice wreck her self-control, and she begins to weep. In the five months that Kirby knew Mieko in Japan, and in the calls between them since, she has never shed a tear, hardly ever let herself be caught in a low moment, but now she weeps with absolute abandon, in long, heaving sobs, saying, "Oh, oh, oh," every so often. Once, the sounds fade, as if she has put down the phone, but he does not dare hang up, does not even dare move the phone from one ear to the other. This attentive listening is what he owes to her grief, isn't it? If she had come and he had disappointed her, as he would have, this is how she would have wept in solitude after swallowing her disappointment in front of him. But this is her father's doing, not his. He can give her a little company after all. He presses the phone so hard to his ear that it hurts. The weeping goes on for a long time and he is afraid to speak and interfere with what will certainly be her only opportunity to give way to her feelings. She gives one final wailing "Ohhh" and then begins to cough and choke. Finally she quiets, and then sighs. After a moment of silence, she says, "Kirby, you should not have listened."

"How could I hang up?"

"A Japanese man would have."

"You sound better, if you are back to comparing me with Japanese men."

"I am going to hang up now, Kirby. I am sorry not to come. Good-bye."

"Don't hang up."

"Good-bye."

"Mieko?"

"Good-bye, Kirby."

"Call me! Call me again!" He is not sure that she hears him. He looks at the phone and then puts it on the cradle.

TWO HOURS LATER he is on the highway. This is, after all, two days before Christmas, and he is on his way to spend the holidays with his two brothers and their wives and children, whom he hasn't seen in years. He has thought little about this visit, beyond buying a few presents. Mieko's coming loomed, imposing and problematic. They had planned to drive out west together—she paid an extra fare so that she could land in Minneapolis and return from San Francisco—and he had looked forward to seeing the mountains again. They had made reservations on a bus that carries tourists into Yellowstone National Park in the winter, to look at the smoky geysers and the wildlife and the snow. The trip would have seemed very American to her. Buffalo and men in cowboy boots and hats. But it seemed very Japanese to him—deep snow, dark pines, sharp mountains.

The storm rolls in suddenly, the way it sometimes does on I-35 in Iowa, startling him out of every thought except alertness. Snow swirls everywhere, blotting out the road, the other cars, sometimes even his own front end. The white of his headlights reflects back at him, so that he seems to be driving into a wall. He can hardly force himself to maintain thirty-five miles an hour, although he knows he must. To stop would be to invite a rear-end collision. And the shoulder of the road is invisible. Only the white line, just beside the left front corner of the car, reveals itself intermittently as the wind blows the snow off the pavement. He ejects the tape he is playing and turns on the radio, to the state weather station. He notices that his hand is shaking. He could be killed. The utter blankness of the snowy whirl gives him a way of imagining what it would be like to be dead. He doesn't like the feeling.

He remembers reading two winters ago about an elderly woman whose son dropped her off at her apartment. She discovered that she had forgotten her key, and with the windchill factor at eighty below zero, she froze before she got to the manager's office. The winter before that a kid who broke his legs in a snowmobile accident crawled three miles to the nearest farmhouse, no gloves, only a feed cap on his head.

Twenty below, thirty below—the papers always make a big deal of the temperature. Including wind chill, seventy, a hundred below. Kirby carries a flashlight, a down sleeping bag, a sweatshirt that reads UNIVERSITY OF NEBRASKA, gloves and mittens. His car has new tires, front-wheel drive, and plenty of antifreeze. He has a thermos of coffee. But the horror stories roll through his mind anyway. A family without boots or mittens struggles two miles to a McDonald's through high winds, blowing snow, thirty below. *Why would they travel in that weather?* Kirby always thinks when he reads the papers, but of course they do. He does. Always has.

A gust takes the car, just for a second, and Kirby grips the wheel more tightly. The same gust twists the enveloping snow aloft and reveals the Clear Lake rest stop. Kirby is tempted to stop, tempted not to. He has, after all, never died before, and he has driven through worse than this. He passes the rest stop. Lots of cars are huddled there; but then, lots of cars are still on the highway. Maybe the storm is letting up.

As soon as he is past the rest stop, he thinks of Mieko, her weeping. She might never weep like that again, even if she heard of his death. The connection in her mind between the two of them, the connection that she allowed to stretch into the future despite all his admonitions and all her resolutions, is broken now. Her weeping was the sound of its breaking. And if he died here, in the next ten minutes, how would she learn of it? His brothers wouldn't contact her, not even if she were still coming, because they didn't know she had planned to come. And if she were ever to call him back, she would get only a disconnect message and would assume that he had moved. He can think of no way that she could hear of his death, even though no one would care more than she would. These thoughts fill him with self-pity, but at least they drive out the catalogue of horror: station wagon skids into bridge abutment, two people killed, two paralyzed from the neck down, mother survives unharmed, walks to nearby farmhouse. Kirby weighs the boredom and good fellowship he will encounter sitting out the storm at a truck stop against possible tragedy. Fewer cars are on the road, more are scattered on the median strip. Inertia carries him onward. He is almost to Minnesota, after all, where they really know how to take care of the roads. He will stop at the tourist center and ask about conditions.

But he drives past the tourist center by mistake, lost in thought. He decides to stop in Faribault. But by then the snow seems to be tapering off. Considering the distance he has traveled, Minneapolis isn't far now. He checks the odometer. Only fifty miles or so. An hour and a half away, at this speed. His mind eases over the numbers with customary superhighway confidence, but at once he imagines himself reduced to walking, walking in this storm, with only a flashlight, a thermos of coffee, a University of Nebraska sweatshirt—and the distance swells to infinity. Were he reduced to his own body, his own power, it might be too far to walk just to find a telephone.

For comfort he calls up images of Japan and southern China, something he often does. These images are the one tangible gift of his travels. So many human eyes have looked upon every scene there for so many eons that every sight has an arranged quality: a flowering branch in the foreground, a precipitous mountainside in the background, a small bridge between. A path, with two women in red kimonos, that winds up a hillside. A white room with pearly rice-paper walls and a futon on the mat-covered floor, branches of cherry blossoms in a vase in the corner. They seem like postcards, but they are scenes he has actually looked upon: on a three-day trip out of Hong Kong into southern China, with some other teachers from his school on a trip to Kyoto, and at Akira's house. Akira was a fellow teacher at his school who befriended him. His house had four rooms, two Japanese style and two Western style.

He remembers, of course, other scenes of Japan—acres of buses, faces staring at his Westernness, the polite but bored rows of students in his classroom—when he is trying to decide whether to go back there. But these are not fixed, have no power; they are just memories, like memories of bars in Lincoln or the pig houses on his grandfather's farm.

AND SO, HE SURVIVES THE STORM. He pulls into the driveway of Harold's new house, one he has not seen, though it is in a neighborhood he remembers from junior high school. The storm is over. Harold has his snowblower out and is making a path from the driveway to his front door. With the noise and because his back is turned, he is unaware of Kirby's arrival. Kirby stops the car, stretches, and looks at his watch. Seven hours for a four-hour trip. Kirby lifts his shoulders and rotates his head, but does not beep his horn just yet. The fact is that he has frightened himself with the blinding snow, the miles of slick and featureless landscape, thoughts of Japan, and the thousands and thousands of miles between here and there. His car might be a marble that has rolled, only by luck, into a safe corner. He presses his fingers against his eyes and stills his breathing.

Harold turns around, grins, and shuts off the snowblower. It is a Harold identical to the Harold that Kirby has always known. Same bright snowflake ski hat, same bright ski clothing. Harold has spent his whole life skiing and ski jumping. His bushy beard grows up to the hollows of his eyes, and when he leans into the car his mustache is, as always, crusted with ice.

"Hey!" he says. He backs away, and Kirby opens the car door.

"Made it!" Kirby says. That is all he will say about the trip. The last thing he wants to do is start a discussion about near misses. Compared with some of Harold's near misses, this is nothing. In fact, near misses on the highway aren't worth mentioning unless a lot of damage has been done to the car. Kirby knows of near misses that Harold has never dared to describe to anyone besides him, because they show a pure stupidity that even Harold has the sense to be ashamed of.

At dinner, over sweet and savory Nordic fare that Kirby is used to but doesn't much like, the people around the table, his relatives, waver in the smoky candlelight, and Kirby imagines that he can feel the heat of the flames on his face. The other people at the table seem unfamiliar. Leanne, Harold's wife, he has seen only once, at their wedding. She is handsome and self-possessed-looking, but she sits at the corner of the table, like a guest in her own house. Eric sits at the head, and Mary Beth, his wife, jumps up and down to replenish the food. This assumption of primogeniture is a peculiarity of Eric's that has always annoyed Kirby, but even aside from that they have never gotten along. Eric does his best—earnest handshake and smile each time they meet, two newsy letters every year, pictures of the children (known between Harold and Kirby as "the little victims"). Eric has a Ph.D. from Columbia in American history, but he does not teach. He writes for a conservative think tank, articles that appear on the op-ed pages of newspapers and in the think tank's own publications. He specializes in "the family." Kirby and Harold have made countless jokes at Eric's expense. Kirby knows that more will be made this trip, if only in the form of conspiratorial looks, rolling eyes. Eric's hobby—Mary Beth's, too, for they share everything—is developing each nuance of his Norwegian heritage into a fully realized ostentation. Mary Beth is always busy, usually baking. That's all Kirby knows about her, and all he cares to know.

Across the table Anna, their older daughter, pale, blue-eyed, cool, seems to be staring at him, but Kirby can hardly see her. He is thinking about Mieko. Kirby looks at his watch. It is very early morning in Osaka. She is probably about to wake up. Her disappointment will have receded hardly a particle, will suck her down as soon as she thuds into consciousness. "Oh, oh, oh": he can hear her cries as clearly as if they were still vibrating in the air. He is amazed at having heard such a thing, and he looks carefully at the women around the table. Mieko would be too eager to please here, always looking after Mary Beth and Leanne, trying to divine how she might be helpful. Finally, Mary Beth would speak to her with just a hint of sharpness, and Mieko would be crushed. Her eyes would seek Kirby's for reassurance, and he would have none to give. She would be too little, smaller even than Anna, and her voice would be too high and quick. These thoughts give him such pain that he stares for relief at Kristin, Eric's youngest, age three, who is humming over her dinner. She is round-faced and paunchy, with dark hair cut straight across her forehead and straight around her collar. From time to time she and Leanne exchange merry glances.

Harold is beside him; that, at least, is familiar and good, and it touches Kirby with a pleasant sense of expectation, as if Harold, at any moment, might pass him a comic book or a stick of gum. In fact, Harold does pass him something—an icy cold beer, which cuts the sweetness of the food and seems to adjust all the figures around the table so that they stop wavering.

OF COURSE HIS EYES OPEN well before daylight, but he dares not move. He is sharing a room with Harold the younger, Eric's son, whose bed is between his and the door. He worries that if he gets up he will stumble around and crash into walls and wake Harold. The digits on the clock beside Harold's bed read 5:37, but when Kirby is quiet he can hear movement elsewhere in the house. When he closes his eyes the footsteps present themselves as a needle and thread, stitching a line through his thoughts. He has just been driving. His arms ache from gripping the wheel. The car slides diagonally across the road, toward the median. It slides and slides, through streams of cars, toward a familiar exit, the Marshalltown exit, off to the left, upward. His eyes open again. The door of the room is open, and Anna is looking in. After a moment she turns and goes away. It is 6:02. Sometime later Leanne passes with Isaac, the baby, in her arms.

Kirby cannot bear to get up and face his brothers and their families. As always, despair presents itself aesthetically. The image of Harold and Leanne's living room, matching plaid wing chairs and couch, a triple row of wooden pegs by the maple front door, seems to Kirby the image of the interior of a coffin. The idea of spending five years, ten years, a lifetime, with such furniture makes him gasp. But his own apartment, armchair facing the television, which sits on a spindly coffee table, is worse. Mary Beth and Eric's place, where he has been twice, is the worst, because it's pretentious; they have antique wooden trunks and high-backed benches painted blue with stenciled flowers in red and white. Everything, everything, they own is blue and white, or white with blue, and Nordic primitive. Now even the Japanese images he calls up are painful. The pearly white Japanese-style room in Akira's house was bitterly cold in the winter, and he spent one night there only half-sleeping, his thighs drawn to his chest, the perimeters of the bed too cold even to touch. His head throbbing, Kirby lies pinned to the bed by impossibility. He literally can't summon up a room, a stick of furniture, that he can bear to think of. Harold the younger rolls over and groans, turning his twelve-year-old face toward Kirby's. His mouth opens and he breathes noisily. It is 6:27.

At breakfast, Leanne sets a bowl of raisin bran before him, and he is struck by the elasticity of her motion. She smiles, so cool and kind that Kirby is suddenly daunted. Ten minutes later, when Anna enters the kitchen in her bathrobe, yawning, he recalls, suddenly, her appearance in the doorway to his room. Fifth grade. Only fifth grade. He can see that now, but the night before, and in the predawn darkness, she had seemed older, more threatening, the way girls get at fourteen and fifteen. "Cereal, sweetie?" Leanne says, and Anna nods, scratching. She sits down without a word and focuses on the back of the Cheerios box. Kirby decides that he was dreaming and puts the incident out of his mind; but, "sweetie"—he would like for Leanne to call him that.

Harold, of course, is at his store, managing the Christmas rush, and the house is less festive in his absence. Eric has sequestered himself in Leanne's sewing room, with his computer, and as soon as Anna stands up from breakfast, Mary Beth begins to arrange the day's kitchen schedule. Kirby rinses his cup and goes into the living room. It is nine in the morning, and the day stretches before him, empty. He walks through the plaid living room to the window, where he regards the outdoor thermometer. It reads four degrees below zero. Moments later it is five degrees below zero. Moments after that he is standing beside Harold's bar, pouring himself a glass of bourbon. He has already drunk it when Anna appears in the doorway, dressed now, and staring at him again. She makes him think of Mieko again—though the child is blond and self-contained, she is Mieko's size. Last evening, when he was thinking of Mieko, he was looking at Anna. He says, attempting jovial warmth, "Good morning, Anna. Why do you keep staring at me?"

She is startled. "I don't. I was looking at the bookshelves."

"But you stared at me last night, at dinner. And you came to the door of my room early this morning. I know because I was awake."

"No, I didn't." But then she softens, and says with eager curiosity, "Are you a socialist?"

While Kirby is trying not to laugh, he hears Mary Beth sing from the kitchen. "Anna? Your brother is going sledding. You want to go?"

Anna turns away before Kirby can answer and mounts the stairs. A "No!" floats, glassy and definite, from the second floor.

Kirby sits down in one of the plaid armchairs and gazes at an arrangement of greenery and shiny red balls and candles that sits on a table behind the couch. He gazes and gazes, contemplating the notion of Eric and Mary Beth discussing his politics and his life. He is offended. He knows that if he were to get up and do something he would stop being offended, but he gets up only to pour himself another drink. It is nearly ten. Books are around everywhere, and Kirby picks one up.

People keep opening doors and coming in, having been elsewhere. Harold comes home for lunch, Leanne and Isaac return from the grocery store and the hardware store, Harold the younger stomps in, covered with snow from sledding, eats a sandwich, and stomps out again. Eric opens the study door, takes a turn through the house, goes back into the study again. He does this three times, each time failing to speak to Kirby, who is sitting quietly. Perhaps he does not see him. He is an old man, Kirby thinks, and his ass has spread considerably in the past four years; he is thirty-six going on fifty, round-shouldered, wearing slacks rather than jeans. What a jerk.

But then Kirby's bad mood twists into him, and he lets his head drop on the back of his chair. What is a man? Kirby thinks. What is a man, what is a man? It is someone, Eric would say, who votes, owns property, has a wife, worries. It is someone, Harold would say, who can chop wood all day and fuck all night, who can lift his twenty-five-pound son above his head on the palm of his hand.

After lunch the men have all vanished again, even Isaac, who is taking a nap. In various rooms the women do things. They make no noise. Harold's house is the house of a wealthy man, Kirby realizes. It is large enough to be silent and neat most of the time, the sort of house Kirby will never own. It is Harold and Eric who are alike now. Only Kirby's being does not extend past his fingertips and toes to family, real estate, reputation.

SOMETIME IN THE AFTERNOON, when Kirby is still sitting quietly and his part of the room is shadowed by the movement of the sun to the other side of the house, Kristin comes in from the kitchen, goes straight to the sofa, pulls off one of the cushions, and begins to jump repeatedly from the cushion to the floor. When he says, "Kristin, what are you doing?" she is not startled. She says, "Jumping."

"Do you like to jump?"

She says, "It's a beautiful thing to do," in her matter-of-fact, deep, three-year-old voice. Kirby can't believe she knows what she is saying. She jumps three or four more times and then runs out again.

At dinner she is tired and tiresome. When Eric tells her to eat a bite of her meat (ham cooked with apricots), she looks him right in the face and says, "No."

"One bite," he says. "I mean it."

"No. I mean it." She looks up at him. He puts his napkin on the table and pushes back his chair. In a moment he has swept her through the doorway and up the stairs. She is screaming. A door slams and the screaming is muffled. When he comes down and seats himself, carefully laying his napkin over his slacks, Anna says, "It's her body."

The table quiets. Eric says, "What?"

"It's her body."

"What does that mean?"

"She should have control over her own body. Food. Other stuff. I don't know." She has started strong but weakens in the face of her father's glare. Eric inhales sharply, and Kirby cannot restrain himself. He says, "How can you disagree with that? It sounds self-evident to me."

"Does it? The child is three years old. How can she have control over her own body when she doesn't know anything about it? Does she go out without a coat if it's twenty below zero? Does she eat only cookies for three days? Does she wear a diaper until she's five? This is one of those phrases they are using these days. They all mean the same thing."

"What do they mean?" As Kirby speaks, Leanne and Mary Beth look up, no doubt wishing that he had a wife or a girlfriend here to restrain him. Harold looks up, too. He is grinning.

Eric shifts in his chair, uncomfortable, Kirby suddenly realizes, at being predictably stuffy once again. Eric says, "It's Christmas. Let's enjoy it."

Harold says, "Principles are principles, any day of the year."

Eric takes the bait and lets himself say, "The family is constituted for a purpose, which is the sometimes difficult socialization of children. For a certain period of their lives others control them. In early childhood others control their bodies. They are taught to control themselves. Even Freud says that the young barbarian has to be taught to relinquish his feces, sometimes by force."

"Good Lord, Eric," Leanne says.

Eric is red in the face. "Authority is a principle I believe in." He looks around the table and then at Anna, openly angry that she has gotten him into this. Across Anna's face flits a look that Kirby has seen before, has seen on Mieko's face, a combination of self-doubt and resentment molded into composure.

"Patriarchy is what you mean," Kirby says, realizing from the tone of his own voice that rage has replaced sympathy and, moreover, is about to get the better of him.

"Why not? It works."

"For some people, at a great cost. Why should daughters be sacrificed to the whims of the father?" He should stop now. He doesn't. "Just because he put his dick somewhere once or twice." The result of too many bourbons too early in the day.

"In my opinion—" Eric seems not to notice the vulgarity, but Harold, beside Kirby, snorts with pleasure.

"I don't want to talk about this," Leanne says. Kirby blushes and falls silent, knowing that he has offended her. It is one of those long holiday meals, and by the time they get up from the table, Kirby feels as if he has been sitting in a dim, candlelit corner most of his life.

There is another ritual—the Christmas Eve unwrapping of presents—and by that time Kirby realizes that he is actively intoxicated and had better watch his tone of voice and his movements. Anna hands out the gifts with a kind of rude bashfulness, and Kirby is surprised at the richness of the array: from Harold he has gotten a cotton turtleneck and a wool sweater, in bright, stylish colors; from Leanne a pair of very fancy gloves; from Isaac three pairs of Ragg wool socks; from Eric's family, as a group, a blue terry-cloth robe and sheepskin slippers. When they open his gifts, he is curious to see what the wrappings reveal: he has bought it all so long before. Almost everything is some gadget available in Japan but not yet in the States. Everyone peers and oohs and aahs. It gives Kirby a headache and a sense of his eyeballs expanding and contracting. Tomorrow night he will be on his way home again, and though he cannot bear to stay here, after all, he cannot bear to leave either.

He drifts toward the stairs, intending to go to bed, but Harold looms before him, grinning and commanding. "Your brain needs some oxygen, brother," he says. Then they are putting on their parkas, and then they are outside, in a cold so sharp that Kirby's nose, the only exposed part of him, stings. Harold strides down the driveway, slightly ahead of him, and Kirby expects him to speak, either for or against Eric, but he doesn't. He only walks. The deep snow is so solidly frozen that it squeaks beneath their boots. The only thing Harold says the whole time they are walking is, "Twenty-two below, not counting the wind chill. Feels good, doesn't it?"

"Feels dangerous," Kirby says.

"It is," Harold says.

The neighborhood is brightly decorated, and the colored lights have their effect on Kirby. For the first time in three Christmases he feels a touch of the mystery that he thinks of as the Christmas spirit. Or maybe it is love for Harold.

Back at the house, everyone has gone to bed except Leanne and Mary Beth, who are drying dishes and putting them away. They are also, Kirby realizes—after Harold strides through the kitchen and up the stairs—arguing, although with smiles and in polite tones. Kirby goes to a cabinet and lingers over getting himself a glass for milk. Mary Beth says, "Kristin will make the connection. She's old enough."

"I can't believe that."

"She saw all the presents being handed out and unwrapped. And Anna will certainly make the connection."

"Anna surely doesn't believe in Santa Claus anymore."

"Unofficially, probably not."

"It's Isaac's first Christmas," Leanne says. "He'll like all the wrappings."

"I wish you'd thought of that before you wrapped the family presents and his Santa presents in the same paper."

"That's a point, too. They're his presents. I don't think Kristin will notice them."

"If they're the only wrapped presents, she will. She notices everything."

Now Leanne turns and gazes at Mary Beth, her hands on her hips. A long silence follows. Leanne flicks a glance at Kirby, who pretends not to notice. Finally she says, "All right, Mary Beth. I'll unwrap them."

"Thank you," Mary Beth says. "I'll finish this, if you want." Kirby goes out of the kitchen and up to his bedroom. The light is already off, and Harold the younger is on his back, snoring.

WHEN HE GETS UP an hour later, too drunk to sleep, Kirby sees Leanne arranging the last of Santa's gifts under the tree. She turns the flash of her glance upon him as he passes through the living room to the kitchen. "Mmm," he says, uncomfortable, "can't sleep."

"Want some cocoa? I always make some before I go to bed."

He stops. "Yeah. Why not? Am I mistaken, or have you been up since about six A.M.?"

"About that. But I'm always wired at midnight, no matter what."

He follows her into the kitchen, remembering now that they have never conversed and wishing that he had stayed in bed. He has drunk himself stupid. Whatever words he has in him have to be summoned from very far down. He sits at the table. After a minute he puts his chin in his hand. After a long, blank, rather pleasant time, the cocoa is before him, marshmallow and all. He looks at it. When Leanne speaks, Kirby is startled, as if he had forgotten that she was there.

"Tired?" she says.

"Too much to drink."

"I noticed."

"I don't have anything more to say about it."

"I'm not asking."

He takes a sip of his cocoa. He says, "Do you all see much of Eric and family?"

"They came last Christmas. He came by himself in the summer. To a conference on the future of the family."

"And so you have to put up with him, right?"

"Harold has a three-day limit. I don't care."

"I noticed you unwrapped all Isaac's presents."

She shrugs, picks at the sole of her boot. She yawns without covering her mouth, and then says, "Oh, I'm sorry." She smiles warmly, looking right at him. "I am crazy about Kristin. Crazy enough to not chance messing up Christmas for her."

"Today she told me that jumping off a cushion was a beautiful thing to do."

Leanne smiles. "Yesterday she said that it was wonderful of me to give her a napkin. You know, I don't agree with Eric about that body stuff. I think they naturally do what is healthy for them. Somebody did an experiment with one-year-olds, gave them a range of foods to choose from, and they always chose a balanced diet. They also want to be toilet trained sooner or later. I think it's weird the way Eric thinks that every little thing is learned rather than realized."

"That's a nice phrase." He turns his cup handle so that it points away and then back in his direction. Finally he says, "Can I tell you about something?"

"Sure."

"Yesterday a friend of mine called me from Japan, a woman, to say that she couldn't come visit me. Her father has cancer. She had planned to arrive here the day after tomorrow, and we were going to take a trip out west. It isn't important, exactly. I don't know."

Leanne is silent but attentive, picking at the sole of her boot. Now that he has mentioned it, the memory of Mieko's anguish returns to him like a glaring light or a thundering noise, so enormous that he is nearly robbed of the power to speak. He pushes it out. "She can't come now, ever. She probably won't ever call or write me again. And really, this has saved her. She had all sorts of expectations that I couldn't have . . . well, wouldn't have fulfilled, and if she had come she would have been permanently compromised."

"Did you have some kind of affair when you were there?"

"For a few months. She's very pretty. I think she's the prettiest woman I've ever seen. She teaches mathematics at the school where I was teaching. After I had been with Mieko for a few weeks, I realized that no one, maybe in her whole adult life, had asked her how she was, or had put his arm around her shoulders, or had taken care of her in any way. The slightest affection was like a drug she couldn't get enough of."

"What did you feel?"

"I liked her. I really did. I was happy to see her when she came by. But she longed for me more than I have ever longed for anything."

"You were glad to leave."

"I was glad to leave."

"So what's the problem?"

"When she called yesterday, she broke down completely. I listened. I thought it was the least I could do, but now I think that she is compromised. Japanese people are very private. It scares me how much I must have embarrassed her. I look back on the spring and the summer and yesterday's call, and I see that, one by one, I broke down every single one of her strengths, everything she had equipped herself with to live in a Japanese way. I was so careful for a year and a half. I didn't date Japanese women, and I was very distant—but then I was so lonely, and she was so pretty, and I thought, well, she's twenty-seven, and she lives in this sophisticated city, Osaka. But mostly I was lonely."

Leanne gazes across the table in that way of hers, calm and considering. Finally she says, "Eric comes in for a lot of criticism around here. His style's all wrong, for one thing. And he drives Harold the younger and Anna crazy. But I've noticed something about him. He never tries to get something for nothing. I admire that."

Now Kirby looks around the room, at the plants on the windowsill, the hoarfrost on the windowpanes, the fluorescent light harsh on the stainless-steel sink, and it seems to him that all at once, now that he realizes it, his life and Mieko's have taken their final form. She is nearly too old to marry, and by the end of her father's cancer and his life she will be much too old. And himself. Himself. Leanne's cool remark has revealed his permanent smallness. He looks at his hands, first his knuckles, then his palms. He says, "It seems so dramatic to say that I will never get over this."

"Does it? To me it seems like saying that what people do is important." And though he looks at her intently, seeking some sort of pardon, she says nothing more, only picks at her boot for a moment or two, and then gets up and puts their cups in the sink. He follows her out of the kitchen, through the living room. She turns out all the lights, so that the house is utterly dark. At the bottom of the stairs, unable to see anything, he stumbles and puts his hand on her arm. She takes it, in a grasp that is dry and cool, and guides it to the banister. Then, soft and fleeting, he feels a disembodied kiss on his cheek.

I WROTE "ALMA" as I was beginning work on a novel called *Shelter*, which concerns the coming-of-age of four girls through a shared rite of passage. Two of those girls, Lenny and Alma, are sisters, and this story was my first inkling of who they were before they arrived (in the company of numerous other characters) at the isolated rural setting of the novel. As work on *Shelter* progressed, "Alma" was cut up through a particular section of the book, arranged differently, put into third person. Numerous readers have asked me to preserve it in its original, more concise, first-person form. In this version, Alma's coming-of-age has more to do with quiet realization. You might say she hears her own heart breaking, which is how many of us grow up, though we may not realize what it means until much later. The story deals head on with the burden/blessing of being the recognized and acknowledged "special child"—the confidante—in the love relationship most primary for women. All our lives, it is our mother's voice we hear in our heads, often in precise, oft-repeated phrases and stories. They say there is no love like first love, with its attendant loss and betrayal, and our love affair with her is always first, born in the self before we know we will leave her.

JAYNE ANNE PHILLIPS

JAYNE ANNE PHILLIPS

Alma

AT NIGHT THEY SHUT THE DOOR of my room. The shade of the one window was drawn, and the only light I saw was the light along the bottom of the door. It was the light of their world, a razor-thin sliver hovering in space, somewhere between yellow and white. Lying in my narrow bed, I said my name over and over, slower and faster and faster and slower. I was eleven years old: I thought my name was a code for what happened when I said the word that was me, a code for the way my breathing changed, for how the space of the room got big, bigger than the house or the town, quiet and full of crashing. Light flickered behind the closed lids of my eyes. Sudden red flashes erupted like visual sirens and disappeared, sucked deeper into the sound of flying and the lonely, vast whirl of darkness. All of inner space sang with a roar of wind. I could fling myself deeper, endlessly, and all the time my name sounded in the whisper of my voice.

I thought that's what night was for everyone, that my mother, Audrey, my father, Wes, my sister, Lenny, all tumbled into themselves, falling asleep as they fell. I imagined my parents in their double bed, lying prone and silent, their heads in the exact centers of their pillows.

And Lenny, my idol, my tormentor, was her night self in my vision, a self washed free of us. I was mesmerized if I watched her as she slept, walked into her room at night after drinking in forbidden fashion from the bathroom faucet. She was fourteen: I remember standing in the dark, looking at her, the delicious metallic taste of tap water still sharp in my mouth. Lenny looked cold, but comfortably so, as though she were meant to be cold, like marble or crystal. She slept like a nun, fearless and still, on her back, her hands at her sides, her head gently inclined to one side. Her face, expressionless, perfect and smooth, seemed a face unconcerned with possibilities, a face waiting to be alive. Her long loose hair was the color of bleached hay, hay that has weathered in fields. All day her hair was bound in a long blond swatch, a silky, blunt-cut ponytail that swung when she moved. Wes, who'd learned to barber in the Army, trimmed it once a month—Lenny in the kitchen or the yard, stalwart in her straight chair, Wes with his sharp scissors and rattail comb. My mother put newspapers under them in winter to catch the hair, but in summer the pale wisps fell into the grass and took flight on any gust of breeze. Those nights in my room, in the black fields of my vision, I imagined Lenny and our father tilting and spinning through space, Lenny seated, our father's hands in her hair. He was separate from us, a bordering country whose customs and language were mysterious, yet he was part of Lenny. Now that I'm grown, I realize they had quiet, definite rituals, unspoken, barely noticed. Aligned with him, she could not have been as lonely as I was, bearing up under Audrey's plaintive secrets, constantly told the truth.

Lenny was told nothing. She learned to understand things in a different way. Maybe Wes taught her it wasn't necessary to name, label, categorize, compile histories, argue with herself until she knew what she wanted. Our mother had to tell herself stories, recite two or three versions of an event, see where things fit. Always, she was outside what happened, alone, talking to include herself in the picture. Someone had to hear her and believe her. Audrey compiled evidence, stories to support her conclusions, and I was the jury she convinced.

I never knew your dad was an alcoholic until after I married him. The man is a secret still, but he's an alcoholic as surely as Mina Campbell is. That family has been through hell, I know all about it from hearing Nickel talk and hearing women gab. Years ago now. Your friend Delia was only three or four. Mina's still okay, but they all walk on eggs. Your dad, he just goes out and drinks and is gone, and I get a phone call from Kentucky, or that time some sheriff called, and he was in lockup at Wildwood Beach, in New Jersey. He won't ever say what happens. I think it's because he doesn't remember. It's all secrets from him as well. And I never know why he goes off. It never seems to have anything to do with me. It's all him, his whole life is him. I'm just a bystander.

IF HE WAS AWAY, Audrey carried on as though nothing were different, listening for a phone call. Always, the lines of the rooms glowed with the heat of her disappointment. My mother had wanted so desperately to do well and she had ended up with Wes, an outsider to whom nothing was relative. He compared himself to no one and he worked alone, a salesman of mining equipment. When times were bad and the mines laid off or shut down, he roamed farther and farther to sell machines, the backseat of the car stacked with thick manuals. He drove to Kentucky or the Carolinas, maybe north to Maryland, often on tips from Henry Briarley, who was his friend and cohort. He must have sold machines on the basis of similar friendships with other men, on the basis of his independence. My mother knew he was friendly with powerful men, men who passed for rich in our sphere. She envisioned being entertained in their homes, living as they lived. The fact that Lenny was friends with Cap Briarley, the daughter of the town Midas, was a further tease. Audrey could never understand why Mrs. Briarley failed to recognize her at school functions, met her attempts at conversation with a withering blankness. She couldn't think of Lenny and Cap as motherless daughters, daughters admiring of their fathers, independent, detached, open to anything, capable of disappearing. Audrey cooked Lenny's food, washed her clothes, yammered at her about chores, loved her, I suppose, but she was never in Lenny's mind. Lenny was elsewhere. She had a flat, pared-down light in her blue eyes. She wasn't eager, hungry, desirous; she couldn't be enlisted in Audrey's struggle to survive in isolation. Oh, my mother wanted so much. Even before she conspired to be loved by someone else, Wes was lost to her. She might have been happy with a salesman, a man whose nature it was to cajole and charm. Wes was the antithesis of his own profession. He wasn't ingratiating, he didn't try to please, he wasn't cheerful or optimistic. He had a solid, masculine presence and an outlaw dignity. "What does he have to feel so proud about?" my mother would muse. Men trusted him.

I wonder what Nickel Campbell knew of my father. They were acquainted; Nickel was Henry Briarley's day foreman and manager at Consol Coal, where my father dropped in two or three times a week. Nickel sat in the outer office behind a burled mahogany desk. The desk was bigger and fancier than Henry's, and I remember my father joking about it with Nickel on our back porch. My mother gave a barbecue for Wes's birthday; it may be an indication of his lack of interest that Lenny and I were allowed to invite the guests. Predictably, she invited Cap, whose parents declined to attend, and I invited Delia, whose parents did. Mina Campbell sat nursing Johnny, who was just a baby then, a year before Nickel died. It was June and the corn was in the fields, young, pale-green stalks, and the wild fields were not tangled yet with milkweed and pokeberries and their bitter, pronged stems. The sun was setting slowly and an ocher light was on the grass. Must have been Sunday, no sound of cars going by on the road past the house. There were crickets, their melodic, intermittent alarms sounding out like little cries of surprise, and farther off, the panicked warble of a cicada. I was sitting by Delia, my face in her hair, whispering; we spent years in that posture or its reverse, trained on each other like homing devices, deliciously unaware of adults except when we needed their services, or when they interrupted and demanded our attention. I remember the smell of Delia's hair, like cold vanilla, and the minuscule, starburst scars on the side of her face from chicken pox. I always thought they were pretty. I was seeing them, hearing laughter indistinguishable from my own, when I became aware of my father's voice, of the two men warily conversing at the other end of the table. It was a picnic table, unpainted and roughhewn, like the ones used in roadside parks in the Fifties. Nickel Campbell sat at the end of the bench, his hands spread on the wood beside his legs as though for balance. He wore a gold signet ring on the smallest finger of his right hand. Girls in a special club might wear such rings, in Gaither, to represent a secret. It resembled in design the plastic jewelry we collected from bubble-gum machines.

"Where did Henry get that damn desk he's got you set up in? Looks like something his wife's folks might have pressed on him."

"Oh, it's not Henry's. My desk, had it at school. My parents sent it, turned up on our porch one day in a big crate. Mina wouldn't have it in the house, so I moved it to the office. She doesn't get on with my family."

My father laughed. "You mean you had that desk as a kid? Must have been bigger than you were."

"It was, nearly," Nickel Campbell nodded.

"Schools provide desks around here. Where'd you go to school?"

"Place up in Connecticut. I lived there, pretty much. Bed, desk, clothes. I told Mina she was lucky they didn't send the bed."

"Or Henry is lucky."

"But Henry is always lucky. Luck is Henry's stock-in-trade."

He smiled wryly, felt my scrutiny, and glanced at Delia and me. He touched my hair. "Are you lucky, Alma?"

"We're lucky together," Delia answered, but her voice didn't reassure me. Her father had never really looked at me before, never seen me. He'd seemed part of the atmosphere of Delia's house, always gone to work, wedding and graduation photographs staring from the mantel in his absence. On my occasional overnight visits he sat reading by a window that looked out on railroad tracks and the overgrown athletic field of Presbyterian College. The small living room was lined with bookshelves; books were always scattered and stacked by his chair, as though he were studying for a test. He sat reading and Delia and I sat in the dining room where no one dined, where the folded dining-room table supported pots of Mina's lush, crowded spider plants. A Motorola television glittered *The Price is Right* in a corner, pots rattled in the kitchen. The baby, Johnny, not walking yet, visible through the narrow doorframe, sat on the linoleum floor and held to the porcelain leg of an old-fashioned sink. I couldn't remember that Nickel Campbell had ever spoken directly to me. Now, on my own summer porch, I felt the full force of his recognition, a questioning appraisal not deflected by the fact of my childhood. His eyes, vaguely golden, held me. And I saw that his right pupil was crossed by a dark slash.

"My dad has a cat's eye," Delia said quietly, behind me.

Then the women returned from the kitchen in a noise of bustle and conversation, a clicking of high-heeled sandals on concrete, their hands full of trays piled with cups, saucers, dessert plates, the cake lone and revered like a crown on a pillow. Lenny was carrying the baby and Cap brought the presents, peering from behind boxes wrapped in modestly celebratory papers. Her quizzical, watchful face was aglow. Nickel Campbell turned from me. The candles were on fire and we all began to sing.

I still see us, standing around the cake, and there's a shadow beside Nickel Campbell. Not a shadow of his shape, as in the child's poem we all memorized in school, but a shade, a subtle darkening, a blur in the summer air, as though he is already moving toward another evening a year later—the evening his car went off Winfield

Bridge in a gathering dusk, and the police dragged the river to find him. My mother and Nickel Campbell took plenty of chances, ignored all manner of shadows, fell into a darkness from which she emerged alone. Or not quite alone. I was with her.

THEY MET ON A SATURDAY, the week after my father's birthday, for lunch in the nearly deserted Winfield bus station. The station was just a block from Souders department store, where Audrey took us to buy school clothes. Later, during numerous fifty-minute car rides along Route 19 to Winfield, she recited details, so many images and sounds, so much story and puzzle. But that first time I didn't know how or when they'd planned it or why we were going to Souders to buy me a spring coat on sale. People from all the little towns around—Gaither, Weston, Bellington—shopped occasionally in Winfield, a real city of sixty thousand or so, a city with buildings tall enough to house elevators, a city with a real department store. We always dressed in our church clothes and good shoes to go there, and we met after shopping in the lobby of the Stonewall Jackson Hotel. Lenny and I would ride the elevators up and down, stepping out on various floors to look at the different wallpapers, the empty corridors, views of the city from the narrow corner windows of the hotel. The rooftops were black and deserted, each fitted with a windowless shack. With their waist-high walls, the roofs seemed the abandoned, tar-papered fields of another, more secretive city.

But now my mother bypassed the hotel and wide main boulevard of Winfield and pulled into the bus-station parking lot. Atop the squat brick building there stood a faded representation of a greyhound, a sign nearly as long as the buses parked behind the station. It was meant to be the classic image, sleek and anonymous, but it was hand-painted, transformed, made clumsy and real. The dog had an expression at once cartoonish and melancholy, and its form cast a shadow across our car as my mother drove slowly past, easing into a space not fully visible from the street.

"We'll have some lunch here," Audrey said.

"Here? Why don't we go to the hotel?"

She regarded me, considering. "I might want to check on a ticket."

Inside, the station was dusty and neglected, and a man slept on one of the iron benches in the waiting area. I followed my mother as she walked uncertainly toward the lunch counter, an outpost of booths toward the rear of the building. I'm sure she'd never been to the bus station. Not much came or went through Winfield, big city though it seemed to us, and the bus station was known to host rummies and bums, and the poor too poor to afford trains. Years ago, the station was closed and torn down. But I still hear my mother talking, telling a story that's finished.

I don't know how I was brave enough to be so foolish, phoning him at work that Monday. Maybe I was just desperate, not willing to go along nursing some little hope. I told him it was Audrey Swenson, please not to say anything until I was finished, that I knew he went to Winfield to do banking for Consol every Saturday, I wanted to meet him there, this week, at noon at the bus station, I wanted to talk to him . . . more than anything in the world, please if he would just not ask questions and agree. He didn't hesitate, just answered like he'd been waiting for my call, Yes, I'll see you then. He said nothing for a moment, I said nothing, but maybe I sighed, tense, relieved, some anguished sound I couldn't stifle, and he said, so calmly, It's all right. Maybe you don't know what feeling is, comfort, gratitude, until you've reached a certain point, then you'll tear out your soul for it.

He was sitting at a table by the wall, a wall maybe the height of a man's shoulder, and beyond it we could see a cafeteria counter with a steam table. She walked right up to him, holding my hand. To his credit, he feigned no surprise and gestured to indicate we should sit with him. The chairs were metal, the seats covered with the same yellow vinyl as our kitchen chairs at home. For a moment I was deeply embarrassed that we owned and used objects similar to those in a bus station, but I realized he wouldn't remember, the barbecue had been outside. I felt my mother's gloved hand at the back of my neck.

"Alma," she said to me, "you must be hungry. You go ahead and get a tray, and I'll pay for your food when I come."

I walked away from them, around the partition of the little wall. People seemed to have appeared from nowhere, maybe a bus had pulled in, and there was a line of five or six customers, one dragging a toddler. I moved along the wall behind them, and realized I could hear Nickel Campbell's voice.

They were sitting just opposite. The wall was tall enough to obscure the top of my head.

"What possessed you to bring Alma?" he said.

"I had to, really. What other excuse do I have to drive to Winfield on a Saturday or any other day?" Her voice faltered. "You mustn't worry. She'll keep it all to herself."

"What do you mean? She's like sisters with Delia."

"Yes, but—she's unusual. I can trust her, I know it. And believe me, there's no other way. I'll schedule lessons for her here, maybe, dance or something—"

"Audrey . . ." he said, in his wise, sad voice, and I moved along the wall, staring at my feet. I moved because the woman behind me was starting to edge past, and my mother was right, I was starved.

SO IT BEGAN. I don't know if my mother actually inquired about Saturday lessons in Winfield, but she invented classes in baton. I already knew how to twirl, though I was clumsy, and I had wanted a baton for some time. My mother announced that evening at the supper table that I would be taking baton on Saturday afternoons in Winfield.

Lenny looked up from her plate with interest. "You mean you want to be a majorette in high school?"

"Maybe." I shrugged. Even then, I had a feeling the lessons weren't real. Touching the lace of the tablecloth, touching the nearly black wood of the walnut table through cutouts in the lace flowers, I remembered Audrey's voice: *I'd be afraid of real lace, this is just synthetic, won't hold a stain.* And she'd shaken out a broad panel of white froth, a froth that settled and was flat and thin.

"Alma doesn't have to be a majorette," Audrey said. "I mean, unless she wants to. Baton is just good exercise, good for coordination and confidence, like dance."

"*Hmmm,*" Lenny responded. "A little coordination wouldn't hurt." She smiled a slow, close-mouthed smile, a mannerism I knew she'd learned from Cap Briarley.

"That's not your smile," I said immediately.

"What do you mean?" She waited, staring, as though trying to make sense of gibberish.

"You don't smile that way, Cap does. You're always trying to look like her, and she's always trying to look like you. But you don't look like each other, you just look like nobody real. It's horrible. I'm so sick of it."

"You are nuts," Lenny replied evenly, but she didn't look angry, only interested, considering, as though I'd hit on something the two of them might refine.

My father broke in. "How much are these lessons going to cost? And why can't she wait until junior high and take lessons for free in the school band?"

"Well," Audrey said, hesitating a beat as though she didn't want to imply I'd be no one's first choice as a twirler, "the girls have to try out to take baton in band, and most of them would already have had classes. My mother sent me a check for Alma's birthday—so she could take music lessons of some kind—but baton is cheaper than renting an instrument. I'm not saying she has to become a majorette or make it her life's work, I just thought it would be nice if she had an interest."

"Alma." Wes gave me a sardonic, amused look, a mark of affection I highly prized, though it was usually offered in collusion against my mother. "Alma, do you need an interest? And it seems to me that if your grandmother wanted to send you money, she might have sent it to you instead of to your mother."

Audrey stood up and began clearing plates. "You don't need to worry. I won't ask you to drive her. I'll take her. It'll be fun, something for the two of us." This she said for my benefit, to indicate once again that I was her special one, the one who cared for her, the one for whom she cared. She made such statements in a tone that paid homage and registered complaint, but Lenny and Wes didn't seem to hear. Her feelings were a consistent atmosphere, an expected weather that inspired no comment or reply. I was always afraid she'd leave, though I never acknowledged my fears, even to myself. Sometimes I still have the same scary dream that evolved in my mind during those years—that I'm walking through the house of my childhood, a Fifties-style ranch house with parquet floors and a long hallway, wandering from my parents' bedroom in the back, past the bathroom and Lenny's closed door, turning the corner near my own small room, desperately trying to keep my footing because the floor is moving and the walls are not stationary. I move out toward the dining room, which opens into the living room, a large space, it seemed to me then.

The blue couch and chair, the white fiberglass drapes, the braided rug on the floor, waver as though seen underwater. I make my way to the narrow kitchen, where I nearly always find my mother, but the room is empty, the counters wiped clean, the doors of the cabinets shut, the dishrag wrung out and dried stiff over the long neck of the spigot. The sink is clean, and the metal stopper is in place, washed and dried, free of the garbage she's constantly cleaning from our dirty plates. It's as though she's been released, she's gone, I've lost her.

"Mama?"

"Yes, honey."

"Am I going to get a baton?"

"Of course you are. We'll just park at the lot near the hotel and then we'll go to Craigie's."

"You mean the store that sells instruments?"

"They sell batons, too, and instruction booklets. I already phoned to be sure."

We were driving along the road to Winfield, a gentle two-lane that curved past the little towns of Peeltree and Quiet Dell ("wide spots in the road," Audrey called them) and a few farms with big, prosperous barns. Many more were scroungy and poor, the houses sagging, a dog or two chained in the yard. Later, when the interstate was built, none of them showed anymore, not the houses or the way people really lived. The new road was only for passing through, so outsiders could cross the state faster and admire the seemingly empty hills, rolling land dotted with stands of maples and oaks. That day, just less than a year before Nickel Campbell died, the trees were heavy-leaved, their foliage motionless in the heat. My mother and I kept the car windows rolled down and were assaulted by hot air redolent with the smells of hay and soil. She wore a scarf to keep her hair from blowing, and a black dress with a wide white organdy collar, the one Lenny said made her look like a Pilgrim.

That day, she wouldn't have said some of the words I remember now. She must have said them later, and surely more than once, because I know exact phrases and the inflections of her voice.

It was such a day, that first day. The air was rushing into the car but beyond that roar everything seemed hushed, hot, and still. It seems terrible that I told you so much, but is it always terrible to tell a child the truth? When I married at twenty, I believed all the fairy tales, and they didn't get me very far. I knew Lenny would hold herself apart, like Wes always did, they were born that way, like animals with protective coloring. You were so like me and I didn't ever want you to fade away and then have such trouble coming back from the dead, have to deceive and turn yourself inside out. Being with him was the worst wrong I ever did but it felt the most like belief; I still believe things he said. I don't have any shame in my mind about that time, just a still white calm like a snowfield over all the pictures and the words.

I was wearing anklets and Mary Janes and a shirtwaist dress of that color we call aqua, a minty blue with cold in it. My mother's short white gloves were folded in her lap. We always *put our best foot forward* in Winfield, as though we represented our town or our lives in a subtle contest. The day felt like a normal shopping trip, except the light coming in the windshield was whiter and too hot, like we were driving right into the sun. I squinted, staring straight ahead.

"Alma," my mother said quietly, "I'm sorry there aren't any lessons. I'll practice with you, if you want, at home."

"Are we going to have coffee at the bus station again?"

"Well, no. I thought we'd go to Craigie's and then I'll walk you over to Souders, and you can just stay there and shop by yourself. Don't go anywhere else, now. I'll meet you by the big front door, just as you go in, right at the stroke of three. All right?"

"What are you going to do?"

"I'm going to the bus station to talk to Nickel Campbell."

"What about?"

She shook her head and sighed. "I don't know, I don't know what to say to him. Listen, look in my purse and take five dollars. If you get hungry you can get a sandwich at the lunch counter. You remember where it is."

"In the basement."

She continued looking ahead into the road. "Oh, I have a notion to go with you, and order a club sandwich, and stash our shopping bags back against the wall like always."

THAT FIRST SATURDAY I drifted through the oversize revolving door of Souders and proceeded along the main aisle of the first floor, anonymous among the cosmetics counters, the mirrored displays of bottles, tubes, hair clasps. I carried the new baton in a plastic bag with a fancy handle and wished it had come in a case with a clasp; I wanted to assemble it, break it down, like a clarinet or a gun. In the hosiery department a succession of disembodied plastic legs were sheathed in different tones of smoke, cinnamon, beige. Far above their upturned ankles the ornamental tin ceilings of the old building hinted at an opulence of fifty years before, but now no one looked up; fluorescent lights hung down at a more reasonable height, and the wide marble stairs were never crowded. Everyone squeezed into the elevator in a profusion of boxes and perfumes. The cage moved, lurched to a stop, and the operator called out the floors. She was the color of oiled walnut, her voice a hoarse baritone. She was thin, small as though she held herself in from long habit, as though it was part of the job to take up as little room as possible. Half sitting, half leaning against a tall metal stood, she stood sentinel before a brass lever. Numerals lit up in neat glass buttons. With her left hand she drove the cage along its vertical route, B through 5. With her right she opened and shut the folding metal gate, latching it so the modern pneumatic doors on each floor could function with clean, short sighs. The metal gate rattled and resembled a wildly exaggerated piece of jewelry or a torture device. Through its lattice of steel triangles I watched our passage through the shaft itself and thought of tunnels, mining, a dark netherworld.

Women habitually watched the illuminated strip above the gate, but it wasn't necessary to check our position. The operator stopped at every floor unless the elevator was packed full. She was the only one who spoke. Her passengers murmured directives and thanks but never conversed. Ongoing exchanges stopped as though by mutual consent, and women snapped their purses shut with authoritative clicks. Whole families stood nearly silent, all but the youngest children quieted. The small, oblivious ones continued to jabber and sing, their voices whole and pure in the enclosure, large beyond their own expectations. Their breathy talk permeated our ascending cage. Listening, I heard their words and phrases as the lost, receding language of a home now far from me, and I understood that I was no longer a child.

1980s

BY THE TIME RONALD REAGAN was elected president, the Workshop was half a century old and the muscular prose of Bellow, Roth, and Mailer, as well as the fabulist metafictions of Barth, Pynchon, and Vonnegut had begun to give way to a wan style of American fiction described as "Minimalism." The content of this particular strain of writing was almost universally domestic. "Around the house and in the yard" fiction, Don DeLillo called it. Suddenly, it seemed, nearly everyone had a dysfunctional family and believed that the only way to write about it was in plain, direct, often overly sincere prose. By sincere I mean prose that reflects a narrative sensibility too timid to risk offending any potential reader, a narrative stance that's unwittingly sentimental and naive. In the '80s, irony, like Nixon, was in exile and politically charged fiction, like Vietnam, history.

Despite the isolation of the text called for by the New Critics, many subsequent critics such as Frederick Jameson and Edward Said argue that there is no way literature can avoid the effects of history. Therefore, is it merely coincidental that during the forgetful, evasive testimony of the Iran-Contra hearings, when truth and meaning seemed irrevocably severed from the language used in a public forum, much American fiction was politically, morally, and emotionally tentative?

Lionel Trilling's brilliant book *Sincerity and Authenticity* argued that man's speech before the Renaissance was an instrument of God. Man spoke *through* God, therefore he was always sincere, or at least perceived to be by others. As secularization overtook the West, this quality receded and man had to prove his sincerity to others. "If one spoke publicly on great matters as an individual, one's only authority was the truth of one's experience." Accompanying this sea change in society, from one that was church-based to one based on business and politics, Trilling noted the rise in autobiography, a form that pressed "toward a more searching scrutiny of the inner life."

After a few hundred years, sincerity came to be seen as a mode of expression that worked in service of the state, which is why the only ones who still go around pretending to be sincere are politicians. "Authenticity" replaced sincerity. "The work of art is itself authentic," Trilling argued, because it exists "wholly by the laws of its own being, which include the right to embody painful, ignoble, or socially inacceptable subject-matters. Similarly the artist seeks his personal authenticity in . . . his goal . . . to be as self-defining as the art object he creates." Speaking from this center of individual authenticity became the quintessential means of expression in early- and mid-twentieth-century literature. Its influence can be found in Hemingway, Kafka, Camus, and others. Authenticity was also the endgame of Romanticism. For by cutting itself off from society, which was perceived as insincere, the self imploded.

Due to the undermining of American confidence after Vietnam, the culture shifted from the '60s' "self-expression" to the '80s' "family values." The rise of the religious right also influenced the literary arena. For, just as post-Renaissance man had to prove his sincerity in public settings, the growing political conservativism of the '80s exerted a similar pressure on public utterance, urging it in from the margins toward sincere depictions of individual and domestic troubles and, with rare exceptions, away from political or cultural dissent.

Carver's influence can be felt in the stylistic and emotional inclinations of the decade's fiction. Aside from historical factors, the rise of simple sentences and first-person narrators are largely attributable, I believe, to Carver's huge presence. His style created a sense of intimacy, an intimacy, however, that was an illusion, a masterfully deployed one. In the story included in this collection, for instance, one can't have the feeling of being any closer to Myers while reading, or any more distant from him once the story is over. Carver's imitators, particularly apprentice writers for whom the artistry, invisible as it was, seemed easy to emulate, missed the distance, seeing and replicating only the directness of Carver's style. Instead of intimacy coupled with distance, the result tended toward sincerity, which is a much diminished artistic accomplishment.

Carver's imitators spawned what came to be derisively called "trailer park" fiction. In the '80s, it was difficult at the workshop level, not simply at Iowa but across the country, as well as in national literary journals, to find a story where the main character didn't drive a Toyota to the Chat N' Chew to meet Bob from K-Mart over a Slurpee. This contraction of narrative ambition confirmed Abraham Rothenberg's 1972 *Best American* assessment of American fiction's increasing penchant for domestic subject matter. As the decade's public and political language tended toward the fantastic ("Morning in America") or the duplicitous ("Read my lips, no new taxes"), much American fiction embraced the sincere style to counter the hype and hucksterism of the era.

The trouble was, sincerity limited the authorial imagination. The sincere style cannot produce an imaginary world in which an army grunt named Slothrop has erections that pinpoint locations of V-2 rocket launches. With writers too afraid of being perceived as insincere, and therefore frivolous, sincerity surrendered all the gravity and play found in great art. As Oscar Wilde said, "All bad poetry springs from genuine feeling."

"Trailer park" fiction assured us that poverty and injustice were consigned to a few marginal lives on the American landscape, and the sincere concern directed toward these lives in short stories and novels allowed us to believe that our communal compassion for the disenfranchised remained intact. But the passive style of these works was a far cry from the protest literature of the 1930s that accompanied Iowa's beginnings.

The best of Iowa's writers, as they have always done, either sidestepped or capitalized on the pitfalls of the cultural moment. Michael Cunningham did so by linking the tragedy that befalls a single family to the lost energy and idealism of the '60s; Bob Shacochis did so by revitalizing American literature's sense of international culture, venturing beyond the United States to depict a postcolonial world that earned him the American Book Award for his first collection of stories, *Easy in the Islands*. Kim Edwards and Gish Jen integrated the personal and the political with loving brilliance, making abortion, cultural dislocation, and childbearing deeply felt individual matters that also reverberate at the communal level. Ethan Canin perfectly renders the complications of his era's coming-of-age, or rite-of-passage story, in a narrative voice that leavens the best elements of sincerity with a comic sense of wisdom. Kathryn and Colin Harrison, who met at the Workshop and later married, offer dual tales of obsession, her first published story focusing on the ultimate disintegration of the Self in a woman suffering from obsessive-compulsive disorder, his living up to Tom Wolfe's call for an American Balzac, someone who takes the pulse of the culture at large, as Harrison does in his deft linkage of marital discord and a generation's fixation on entitlement and its obsession with the stock market. Finally, Pinckney Benedict makes class differences the centerpiece of his chilling story about capitalism's ability to literally buy a family's culture and history.

"WHITE ANGEL" IS AN EARLY CHAPTER from my novel *A Home at the End of the World*, published by Farrar Straus & Giroux in 1991. It was not originally written as a story, or even as a chapter that might pass for a story. Although the particular moment of violence it describes was central to the novel as a whole, I intended this chapter essentially as background, to illuminate one of the novel's four central characters.

I'd written a shorter version of what would appear as "White Angel," along with a few other chapters, and showed it all (with trepidations) to Ken Corbett, who I'd just started dating and with whom I still live, twelve years later. After reading the pages, Kenny said, "These are pretty good, why don't you send the Bobby chapter to the *New Yorker*?"

I responded with something like, "I've sent so many stories to the *New Yorker* that they've hired someone named Dan Menaker, whose job it is to return as quickly as possible anything with my name on it, with a short, regretful note enclosed so I won't feel too bad. If they didn't want those other stories of mine I can promise you they won't want one involving a nine-year-old on drugs, sex in a cemetery, and violent death."

He persevered, and I sent the chapter to Dan Menaker at the *New Yorker*, at least in part to show Kenny how quickly it would come back, in hopes that he would then understand just how difficult and frustrating my life really was and how impenetrable the forces arrayed against me. The chapter was, in fact, returned, but this time with a two-page letter from Dan not only expressing his regrets but suggesting that he call me to talk about possible changes, though he could make no promises regarding publication. He called the next day and we talked about the chapter at length, mainly about its ending, which we agreed was abrupt and unsatisfying. Over the following few weeks I came up with a conclusion of sorts—it's the story's final section, describing what happens a year after the accident—and sent it back to Dan. This time, to my astonishment, the *New Yorker* said yes.

The story's appearance, in the July 25, 1988, issue of the *New Yorker*, made more difference than I'd ever imagined. About a dozen editors called to ask if I was working on a novel, and if so, whether they could get a look at it. Roger Straus, however, called not to ask if he could see the novel but to say, essentially, that if I could write something he liked this much he'd agree to publish whatever novel I might write. It was a rare gesture of faith, and I will always adore him for it.

Here, then, is a piece of something larger that has turned out to have a surprisingly potent life of its own.

MICHAEL CUNNINGHAM

MICHAEL CUNNINGHAM

White Angel

WE LIVED THEN in Cleveland, in the middle of everything. It was the sixties—our radios sang out love all day long. This of course is history. It happened before the city of Cleveland went broke, before its river caught fire. We were four. My mother and father, Carlton, and me. Carlton turned sixteen the year I turned nine. Between us were several brothers and sisters, weak flames quenched in our mother's womb. We are not a fruitful or many-branched line. Our family name is Morrow.

Our father was a high school music teacher. Our mother taught children called "exceptional," which meant that some could name the day Christmas would fall in the year 2000 but couldn't remember to drop their pants when they peed. We lived in a tract called Woodlawn—neat one- and two-story houses painted optimistic colors. Our tract bordered a cemetery. Behind our backyard was a gully choked with brush, and beyond that, the field of smooth, polished stones. I grew up with the cemetery, and didn't mind it. It could be beautiful. A single stone angel, small-breasted and determined, rose amid the more conservative markers close to our house. Farther away, in a richer section, miniature mosques and Parthenons spoke silently to Cleveland of man's enduring accomplishments. Carlton and I played in the cemetery as children and, with a little more age, smoked joints and drank Southern Comfort there. I was, thanks to Carlton, the most criminally advanced nine-year-old in my fourth-grade class. I was going places. I made no move without his counsel.

Here is Carlton several months before his death, in an hour so alive with snow that earth and sky are identically white. He labors among the markers and I run after, stung by snow, following the light of his red knitted cap. Carlton's hair is pulled back into a ponytail, neat and economical, a perfect pinecone of hair. He is thrifty, in his way.

We have taken hits of acid with our breakfast juice. Or rather, Carlton has taken a hit and I, considering my youth, have been allowed half. This acid is called windowpane. It is for clarity of vision, as Vicks is for decongestion of the nose. Our parents are at work, earning the daily bread. We have come out into the cold so that the house, when we reenter it, will shock us with its warmth and righteousness. Carlton believes in shocks.

"I think I'm coming on to it," I call out. Carlton has on his buckskin jacket, which is worn down to the shine. On the back, across his shoulder blades, his girlfriend has stitched an electric-blue eye. As we walk I speak into the eye. "I think I feel something," I say.

"Too soon," Carlton calls back. "Stay loose, Frisco. You'll know when the time comes."

I am excited and terrified. We are into serious stuff. Carlton has done acid half a dozen times before, but I am new at it. We slipped the tabs into our mouths at breakfast, while our mother paused over the bacon. Carlton likes taking risks.

Snow collects in the engraved letters on the headstones. I lean into the wind, trying to decide whether everything around me seems strange because of the drug, or just because everything truly is strange. Three weeks earlier, a family across town had been sitting at home, watching television, when a single-engine plane fell on them. Snow swirls around us, seeming to fall up as well as down.

Carlton leads the way to our spot, the pillared entrance to a society tomb. This tomb is a palace. Stone cupids cluster on the peaked roof, with stunted, frozen wings and matrons' faces. Under the roof is a veranda, backed by cast-iron doors that lead to the house of the dead proper. In summer this veranda is cool. In winter it blocks the wind. We keep a bottle of Southern Comfort there.

Carlton finds the bottle, unscrews the cap, and takes a good, long draw. He is studded with snowflakes. He hands me the bottle and I take a more conservative drink. Even in winter, the tomb smells mossy as a well. Dead leaves and a yellow M & M's wrapper, worried by the wind, scrape on the marble floor.

"Are you scared?" Carlton asks me.

I nod. I never think of lying to him.

"Don't be, man," he says. "Fear will screw you right up. Drugs can't hurt you if you feel no fear."

I nod. We stand sheltered, passing the bottle. I lean into Carlton's certainty as if it gave off heat.

"We can do acid all the time at Woodstock," I say.

"Right on. Woodstock Nation. Yow."

"Do people *really* live there?" I ask.

"Man, you've got to stop asking that. The concert's over, but people are still there. It's the new nation. Have faith."

I nod again, satisfied. There is a different country for us to live in. I am already a new person, renamed Frisco. My old name was Robert.

"We'll do acid all the time," I say.

"You better believe we will." Carlton's face, surrounded by snow and marble, is lit. His eyes are bright as neon. Something in them tells me he can see the future, a ghost that hovers over everybody's head. In Carlton's future we all get released from our jobs and schooling. Awaiting us all, and soon, is a bright, perfect simplicity. A life among the trees by the river.

"How are you feeling, man?" he asks me.

"Great," I tell him, and it is purely the truth. Doves clatter up out of a bare tree and turn at the same instant, transforming themselves from steel to silver in the snow-blown light. I know at that moment that the drug is working. Everything before me has become suddenly, radiantly itself. How could Carlton have known this was about to happen? "Oh," I whisper. His hand settles on my shoulder.

"Stay loose, Frisco," he says. "There's not a thing in this pretty world to be afraid of. I'm here."

I am not afraid. I am astonished. I had not realized until this moment how real everything is. A twig lies on the marble at my feet, bearing a cluster of hard brown berries. The broken-off end is raw, white, fleshly. Trees are alive.

"I'm here," Carlton says again, and he is.

HOURS LATER, we are sprawled on the sofa in front of the television, ordinary as Wally and the Beav. Our mother makes dinner in the kitchen. A pot lid clangs. We are undercover agents. I am trying to conceal my amazement.

Our father is building a grandfather clock from a kit. He wants to have something to leave us, something for us to pass along. We can hear him in the basement, sawing and pounding. I know what is laid out on his sawhorses—a long raw wooden box, onto which he glues fancy moldings. A single pearl of sweat meanders down his forehead as he works. Tonight I have discovered my ability to see every room of the house at once, to know every single thing that goes on. A mouse nibbles inside the wall. Electrical wires curl behind the plaster, hidden and patient as snakes.

"Shhh," I say to Carlton, who has not said anything. He is watching television through his splayed fingers. Gunshots ping. Bullets raise chalk dust on a concrete wall. I have no idea what we are watching.

"Boys?" our mother calls from the kitchen. I can, with my new ears, hear her slap hamburger into patties. "Set the table like good citizens," she calls.

"Okay, Ma," Carlton replies, in a gorgeous imitation of normality. Our father hammers in the basement. I can feel Carlton's heart ticking. He pats my hand, to assure me that everything's perfect.

We set the table, spoon fork knife, paper napkins triangled to one side. We know the moves cold. After we are done I pause to notice the dining-room wallpaper: a golden farm, backed by mountains. Cows graze, autumn trees cast golden shade. This scene repeats itself three times, on three walls.

"Zap," Carlton whispers. "Zzzzzoom."

"Did we do it right?" I ask him.

"We did everything perfect, little son. How are you doing in there, anyway?" He raps lightly on my head.

"Perfect, I guess." I am staring at the wallpaper as if I were thinking of stepping into it.

"You guess. You guess? You and I are going to other planets, man. Come over here."

"Where?"

"Here. Come here." He leads me to the window. Outside the snow skitters, nervous and silver, under streetlamps. Ranch-style houses hoard their warmth, bleed light into the gathering snow. It is a street in Cleveland. It is our street.

"You and I are going to fly, man," Carlton whispers, close to my ear. He opens the window. Snow blows in, sparking on the carpet. "Fly," he says, and we do. For a moment we strain up and out, the black night wind blowing in our faces—we raise ourselves up off the cocoa-colored deep-pile wool-and-polyester carpet by a sliver of an inch. Sweet glory. The secret of flight is this—you have to do it immediately, before your body realizes it is defying the laws. I swear it to this day.

We both know we have taken momentary leave of the earth. It does not strike either of us as remarkable, any more than does the fact that airplanes sometimes fall from the sky, or that we have always lived in these rooms and will soon leave them. We settle back down. Carlton touches my shoulder.

"You wait, Frisco," he says. "Miracles are happening. Fucking miracles."

I nod. He pulls down the window, which reseals itself with a sucking sound. Our own faces look back at us from the cold, dark glass. Behind us, our mother drops the hamburgers sizzling into the skillet. Our father bends to his work under a hooded lightbulb, preparing the long box into which he will lay clockworks, pendulum, a face. A plane drones by overhead, invisible in the clouds. I glance nervously at Carlton. He smiles his assurance and squeezes the back of my neck.

MARCH. After the thaw. I am walking through the cemetery, thinking about my endless life. One of the beauties of living in Cleveland is that any direction feels like progress. I've memorized the map. We are by my calculations three hundred and fifty miles shy of Woodstock, New York. On this raw new day I am walking east, to the place where Carlton and I keep our bottle. I am going to have an early nip, to celebrate my bright future.

When I get to our spot I hear low moans coming from behind the tomb. I freeze, considering my choices. The sound is a long-drawn-out agony with a whip at the end, a final high C, something like "ooooooOw." A wolf's cry run backward. What decides me on investigation rather than flight is the need to make a story. In the stories my brother likes best, people always do the foolish, risky thing. I find I can reach decisions this way, by thinking of myself as a character in a story told by Carlton.

I creep around the side of the monument, cautious as a badger, pressed up close to the marble. I peer over a cherub's girlish shoulder. What I find is Carlton on the ground with his girlfriend, in an uncertain jumble of clothes and bare flesh. Carlton's jacket, the one with the embroidered eye, is draped over the stone, keeping watch.

I hunch behind the statue. I can see the girl's naked arms, and the familiar bones of Carlton's spine. The two of them moan together in the dry winter grass. Though I can't make out the girl's expression, Carlton's face is twisted and grimacing, the cords of his neck pulled tight. I had never thought the experience might be painful. I watch, trying to learn. I hold on to the cherub's cold wings.

It isn't long before Carlton catches sight of me. His eyes rove briefly, ecstatically skyward, and what do they light on but his brother's small head, sticking up next to a cherub's. We lock eyes and spend a moment in mutual decision. The girl keeps on clutching at Carlton's skinny back. He decides to smile at me. He decides to wink.

I am out of there so fast I tear up divots. I dodge among the stones, jump the gully, clear the fence into the swing-set-and-picnic-table sanctity of the back yard. Something about that wink. My heart beats fast as a sparrow's.

I go into the kitchen and find our mother washing fruit. She asks what's going on. I tell her nothing is. Nothing at all.

She sighs over an apple's imperfection. The curtains sport blue teapots. Our mother works the apple with a scrub brush. She believes they come coated with poison.

"Where's Carlton?" she asks.

"Don't know," I tell her.

"Bobby?"

"Huh?"

"What exactly is going on?"

"Nothing," I say. My heart works itself up to a hummingbird's rate, more buzz than beat.

"I think something is. Will you answer a question?"

"Okay."

"Is your brother taking drugs?"

I relax a bit. It is only drugs. I know why she's asking. Lately police cars have been browsing our house like sharks. They pause, take note, glide on. Some neighborhood crackdown. Carlton is famous in these parts.

"No," I tell her.

She faces me with the brush in one hand, an apple in the other. "You wouldn't lie to me, would you?" She knows something is up. Her nerves run through this house. She can feel dust settling on the tabletops, milk starting to turn in the refrigerator.

"No," I say.

"Something's going on," she sighs. She is a small, efficient woman who looks at things as if they give off a painful light. She grew up on a farm in Wisconsin and spent her girlhood tying up bean rows, worrying over the sun and rain. She is still trying to overcome her habit of modest expectations.

I leave the kitchen, pretending sudden interest in the cat. Our mother follows, holding her brush. She means to scrub the truth out of me. I follow the cat, his erect black tail and pink anus.

"Don't walk away when I'm talking to you," our mother says.

I keep walking, to see how far I'll get, calling, "Kittykittykitty." In the front hall, our father's homemade clock chimes the half hour. I make for the clock. I get as far as the rubber plant before she collars me.

"I told you not to walk away," she says, and cuffs me a good one with the brush. She catches me on the ear and sets it ringing. The cat is out of there quick as a quarter note.

I stand for a minute, to let her know I've received the message. Then I resume walking. She hits me again, this time on the back of the head, hard enough to make me see colors. "Will you *stop*?" she screams. Still, I keep walking. Our house runs west to east. With every step I get closer to Yasgur's farm.

CARLTON COMES HOME whistling. Our mother treats him like a guest who's overstayed. He doesn't care. He is lost in optimism. He pats her cheek and calls her "Professor." He treats her as if she were harmless, and so she is.

She never hits Carlton. She suffers him the way farm girls suffer a thieving crow, with a grudge so old and endless it borders on reverence. She gives him a scrubbed apple, and tells him what she'll do if he tracks mud on the carpet.

I am waiting in our room. He brings the smell of the cemetery with him, its old snow and wet pine needles. He rolls his eyes at me, takes a crunch of his apple. "What's happening, Frisco?" he says.

I have arranged myself loosely on my bed, trying to pull a Dylan riff out of my harmonica. I have always figured I can bluff my way into wisdom. I offer Carlton a dignified nod.

He drops onto his own bed. I can see a crushed crocus, the first of the year, stuck to the black rubber sole of his boot.

"Well, Frisco," he says. "Today you are a man."

I nod again. Is that all there is to it?

"*Yow*," Carlton says. He laughs, pleased with himself and the world. "That was so perfect."

I pick out what I can of "Blowin' in the Wind."

Carlton says, "Man, when I saw you out there spying on us I thought to myself, *yes*. Now *I'm* really here. You know what I'm saying?" He waves his apple core.

"Uh-huh," I say.

"Frisco, that was the first time her and I ever did it. I mean, we'd talked. But when we finally got down to it, there you were. My brother. Like you *knew*."

I nod, and this time for real. What happened was an adventure we had together. All right. The story is beginning to make sense.

"Aw, Frisco," Carlton says. "I'm gonna find you a girl, too. You're nine. You been a virgin too long."

"Really?" I say.

"*Man.* We'll find you a woman from the sixth grade, somebody with a little experience. We'll get stoned and all make out under the trees in the boneyard. I want to be present at your deflowering, man. You're gonna need a brother there."

I am about to ask, as casually as I can manage, about the relationship between love and bodily pain, when our mother's voice cuts into the room. "You did it," she screams: "You tracked mud all over the rug."

A family entanglement follows. Our mother brings our father, who comes and stands in the doorway with her, taking in evidence. He is a formerly handsome man. His face has been worn down by too much patience. He has lately taken up some sporty touches—a goatee, a pair of calfskin boots.

Our mother points out the trail of muddy half-moons that lead from the door to Carlton's bed. Dangling over the foot of the bed are the culprits themselves, voluptuously muddy, with Carlton's criminal feet still in them.

"You see?" she says. "You see what he thinks of me?"

Our father, a reasonable man, suggests that Carlton clean it up. Our mother finds that too small a gesture. She wants Carlton not to have done it in the first place. "I don't ask for much," she says. "I don't ask where he goes. I don't ask why the police are suddenly so interested in our house. I ask that he not track mud all over the floor. That's all." She squints in the glare of her own outrage.

"Better clean it right up," our father says to Carlton.

"And that's it?" our mother says. "He cleans up the mess, and all's forgiven?"

"Well, what do you want him to do? Lick it up?"

"I want some consideration," she says, turning helplessly to me. "That's what I want."

I shrug, at a loss. I sympathize with our mother, but am not on her team.

"All right," she says. "I just won't bother cleaning the house anymore. I'll let you men handle it. I'll sit and watch television and throw my candy wrappers on the floor."

She starts out, cutting the air like a blade. On her way she picks up a jar of pencils, looks at it and tosses the pencils on the floor. They fall like fortune-telling sticks, in pairs and crisscrosses.

Our father goes after her, calling her name. Her name is Isabel. We can hear them making their way across the house, our father calling, "Isabel, Isabel, Isabel," while our mother, pleased with the way the pencils had looked, dumps more things onto the floor.

"I hope she doesn't break the TV," I say.

"She'll do what she needs to do," Carlton tells me.

"I hate her," I say. I am not certain about that. I want to test the sound of it, to see if it's true.

"She's got more balls than any of us, Frisco," he says. "Better watch what you say about her."

I keep quiet. Soon I get up and start gathering pencils, because I prefer that to lying around trying to follow the shifting lines of allegiance. Carlton goes for a sponge and starts in on the mud.

"You get shit on the carpet, you clean it up," he says. "Simple."

The time for all my questions about love has passed, and I am not so unhip as to force a subject. I know it will come up again. I make a neat bouquet of pencils. Our mother rages through the house.

Later, after she has thrown enough and we three have picked it all up, I lie on my bed thinking things over. Carlton is on the phone to his girlfriend, talking low. Our mother, becalmed but still dangerous, cooks dinner. She sings as she cooks, some slow forties number that must have been all over the jukes when her first husband's plane went down in the Pacific. Our father plays his clarinet in the basement. That is where he goes to practice, down among his woodworking tools, the neatly hung hammers and awls that throw oversized shadows in the light of the single bulb. If I put my ear to the floor I can hear him, pulling a long low tomcat moan out of that horn. There is some strange comfort in pressing my ear to the carpet and hearing our father's music leaking up through the floorboards. Lying down, with my ear to the floor, I join in on my harmonica.

THAT SPRING our parents have a party to celebrate the sun's return. It has been a long, bitter winter and now the first wild daisies are poking up on the lawns and among the graves.

Our parents' parties are mannerly affairs. Their friends, schoolteachers all, bring wine jugs and guitars. They are Ohio hip. Though they hold jobs and meet mortgages, they think of themselves as independent spirits on a spying mission. They have agreed to impersonate teachers until they write their novels, finish their dissertations, or just save up enough money to set themselves free.

Carlton and I are the lackeys. We take coats, fetch drinks. We have done this at every party since we were small, trading on our precocity, doing a brother act. We know the moves. A big, lipsticked woman who has devoted her maidenhood to ninth-grade math calls me Mr. Right. An assistant vice principal in a Russian fur hat asks us both whether we expect to vote Democratic or Socialist. By sneaking sips I manage to get myself semi-crocked.

The reliability of the evening is derailed halfway through, however, by a half dozen of Carlton's friends. They rap on the door and I go for it, anxious as a carnival sharp to see who will step up next and swallow the illusion that I'm a kindly, sober nine-year-old child. I'm expecting callow adults and who do I find but a pack of young outlaws, big-booted and wild-haired. Carlton's girlfriend stands in front, in an outfit made up almost entirely of fringe.

"Hi, Bobby," she says confidently. She comes from New York, and is more than just locally smart.

"Hi," I say. I let them all in despite a retrograde urge to lock the door and phone the police. Three are girls, four boys. They pass me in a cloud of dope smoke and sly-eyed greeting.

What they do is invade the party. Carlton is standing on the far side of the rumpus room, picking the next album, and his girl cuts straight through the crowd to his side. She has the bones and the loose, liquid moves some people consider beautiful. She walks through that room as if she'd been sent to teach the whole party a lesson.

Carlton's face tips me off that this was planned. Our mother demands to know what's going on here. She is wearing a long dark-red dress that doesn't interfere with her shoulders. When she dresses up you can see what it is about her, or what it was. She is responsible for Carlton's beauty. I have our father's face.

Carlton does some quick talking. Though it's against our mother's better judgment, the invaders are suffered to stay. One of them, an Eddie Haskell for all his leather and hair, tells her she is looking good. She is willing to hear it.

So the outlaws, house-sanctioned, start to mingle. I work my way over to Carlton's side, the side unoccupied by his girlfriend. I would like to say something ironic and wised-up, something that will band Carlton and me against every other person in the room. I can feel the shape of the comment I have in mind but, being a tipsy nine-year-old, can't get my mouth around it. What I say is, "Shit, man."

Carlton's girl laughs at me. She considers it amusing that a little boy says "shit." I would like to tell her what I have figured out about her, but I am nine, and three-quarters gone on Tom Collinses. Even sober, I can only imagine a sharp-tongued wit.

"Hang on, Frisco," Carlton tells me. "This could turn into a real party."

I can see by the light in his eyes what is going down. He has arranged a blind date between our parents' friends and his own. It's a Woodstock move—he is plotting a future in which young and old have business together. I agree to hang on, and go to the kitchen, hoping to sneak a few knocks of gin.

There I find our father leaning up against the refrigerator. A line of butterfly-shaped magnets hovers around his head. "Are you enjoying this party?" he asks, touching his goatee. He is still getting used to being a man with a beard.

"Uh-huh."

"I am, too," he says sadly. He never meant to be a high school music teacher. The money question caught up with him.

"What do you think of this music?" he asks. Carlton has put the Stones on the turntable. Mick Jagger sings "19th Nervous Breakdown." Our father gestures in an openhanded way that takes in the room, the party, the whole house—everything the music touches.

"I like it," I say.

"So do I." He stirs his drink with his finger, and sucks on the finger.

"I *love* it," I say, too loud. Something about our father leads me to raise my voice. I want to grab handfuls of music out of the air and stuff them into my mouth.

"I'm not sure I could say I love it," he says. "I'm not sure if I could say that, no. I would say I'm friendly to its intentions. I would say that if this is the direction music is going in, I won't stand in its way."

"Uh-huh," I say. I am already anxious to get back to the party, but don't want to hurt his feelings. If he senses he's being avoided he can fall into fits of apology more terrifying than our mother's rages.

"I think I may have been too rigid with my students," our father says. "Maybe over the summer you boys could teach me a few things about the music people are listening to these days."

"Sure," I say, loudly. We spend a minute waiting for the next thing to say.

"You boys are happy, aren't you?" he asks. "Are you enjoying this party?"

"We're having a great time," I say.

"I thought you were. I am, too."

I have by this time gotten myself to within jumping distance of the door. I call out, "Well, good-bye," and dive back into the party.

Something has happened in my small absence. The party has started to roll. Call it an accident of history and the weather. Carlton's friends are on decent behavior, and our parents' friends have decided to give up some of their wine-and-folk-song propriety to see what they can learn. Carlton is dancing with a vice principal's wife. Carlton's friend Frank, with his ancient-child face and IQ in the low sixties, dances with our mother. I see that our father has followed me out of the kitchen. He positions himself at the party's edge; I jump into its center. I invite the fuchsia-lipped math teacher to dance. She is only too happy. She is big and graceful as a parade float, and I steer her effortlessly out into the middle of everything. My mother, who is known around school for Sicilian discipline, dances freely, which is news to everybody. There is no getting around her beauty.

The night rises higher and higher. A wildness sets in. Carlton throws new music on the turntable—Janis Joplin, the Doors, the Dead. The future shines for everyone, rich with the possibility of more nights exactly like this. Even our father is pressed into dancing, which he does like a flightless bird, all flapping arms and potbelly. Still, he dances. Our mother has a kiss for him.

Finally I nod out on the sofa, blissful under the drinks. I am dreaming of flight when our mother comes and touches my shoulder. I smile up into her flushed, smiling face.

"It's hours past your bedtime," she says, all velvet motherliness. I nod. I can't dispute the fact.

She keeps on nudging my shoulder. I am a moment or two apprehending the fact that she actually wants me to leave the party and go to bed. "No," I tell her.

"Yes," she smiles.

"No," I say cordially, experimentally. This new mother can dance, and flirt. Who knows what else she might allow?

"Yes." The velvet motherliness leaves her voice. She means business, business of the usual kind. I get myself out of there and no excuses this time. I am exactly nine and running from my bedtime as I'd run from death.

I run to Carlton for protection. He is laughing with his girl, a sweaty question mark of hair plastered to his forehead. I plow into him so hard he nearly goes over.

"Whoa, Frisco," he says. He takes me up under the arms and swings me a half-turn. Our mother plucks me out of his hands and sets me down, with a good farm-style hold on the back of my neck.

"Say good night, Bobby," she says. She adds, for the benefit of Carlton's girl, "He should have been in bed before this party started."

"*No*," I holler. I try to twist loose, but our mother has a grip that could crack walnuts.

Carlton's girl tosses her hair and says, "Good night, baby." She smiles a victor's smile. She smooths the stray hair off Carlton's forehead.

"*No*," I scream again. Something about the way she touches his hair. Our mother calls our father, who comes and scoops me up and starts out of the room with me, holding me like the live bomb I am. Before I go I lock eyes with Carlton. He shrugs and says, "Night, man." Our father hustles me out. I do not take it bravely. I leave flailing, too furious to cry, dribbling a slimy thread of horrible-child's spittle.

Later I lie alone on my narrow bed, feeling the music hum in the coiled springs. Life is cracking open right there in our house. People are changing. By tomorrow, no one will be quite the same. How can they let me miss it? I dream up revenge against our parents, and worse for Carlton. He is the one who could have saved me. He could have banded with me against them. What I can't forgive is his shrug, his mild-eyed "Night, man." He has joined the adults. He has made himself bigger, and taken size from me. As the Doors thump "Strange Days," I hope something awful happens to him. I say so to myself.

Around midnight, dim-witted Frank announces he has seen a flying saucer hovering over the backyard. I can hear his deep, excited voice all the way in my room. He says it's like a blinking, luminous cloud. I hear half the party struggling out through the sliding glass door in a disorganized, whooping knot. By that time everyone is so delirious a flying saucer would be just what was expected. That much celebration would logically attract an answering happiness from across the stars.

I get out of bed and sneak down the hall. I will not miss alien visitors for anyone, not even at the cost of our mother's wrath or our father's disappointment. I stop at the end of the hallway, though, embarrassed to be in pajamas. If there really are aliens, they will think I'm the lowest member of the house. While I hesitate over whether to go back to my room to change, people start coming back inside, talking about a trick of the mist and an airplane. People resume their dancing.

Carlton must have jumped the back fence. He must have wanted to be there alone, singular, in case they decided to take somebody with them. A few nights later

I will go out and stand where he would have been standing. On the far side of the gully, now a river swollen with melted snow, the cemetery will gleam like a lost city. The moon will be full. I will hang around just as Carlton must have, hypnotized by the silver light on the stones, the white angel raising her arms up across the river.

According to our parents the mystery is why he ran back to the house full tilt. Something in the graveyard may have scared him, he may have needed to break its spell, but I think it's more likely that when he came back to himself he just couldn't wait to get back to the music and the people, the noisy disorder of continuing life.

Somebody has shut the sliding glass door. Carlton's girlfriend looks lazily out, touching base with her own reflection. I look, too. Carlton is running toward the house. I hesitate. Then I figure he can bump his nose. It will be a good joke on him. I let him keep coming. His girlfriend sees him through her own reflection, starts to scream a warning just as Carlton hits the glass.

It is an explosion. Triangles of glass fly brightly through the room. I think for him it must be more surprising than painful, like hitting water from a great height. He stands blinking for a moment. The whole party stops, stares, getting its bearings. Bob Dylan sings "Just Like a Woman." Carlton reaches up curiously to take out the shard of glass that is stuck in his neck, and that is when the blood starts. It shoots out of him. Our mother screams. Carlton steps forward into his girlfriend's arms and the two of them fall together. Our mother throws herself down on top of him and the girl. People shout their accident wisdom. Don't lift him. Call an ambulance. I watch from the hallway. Carlton's blood spurts, soaking into the carpet, spattering people's clothes. Our mother and father both try to plug the wound with their hands, but the blood just shoots between their fingers. Carlton looks more puzzled than anything, as if he can't quite follow this turn of events. "It's all right," our father tells him, trying to stop the blood. "It's all right, just don't move, it's all right." Carlton nods, and holds our father's hand. His eyes take on an astonished light. Our mother screams, "Is anybody *doing* anything?" What comes out of Carlton grows darker, almost black. I watch. Our father tries to get a hold on Carlton's neck while Carlton keeps trying to take his hand. Our mother's hair is matted with blood. It runs down her face. Carlton's girl holds him to her breasts, touches his hair, whispers in his ear.

He is gone by the time the ambulance gets there. You can see the life drain out of him. When his face goes slack our mother wails. A part of her flies wailing through the house, where it will wail and rage forever. I feel our mother pass through me on her way out. She covers Carlton's body with her own.

HE IS BURIED in the cemetery out back. Years have passed—we are living in the future, and it's turned out differently from what we'd planned. Our mother has established her life of separateness behind the guest-room door. Our father mutters his greetings to the door as he passes.

One April night, almost a year to the day after Carlton's accident, I hear cautious footsteps shuffling across the living-room floor after midnight. I run out eagerly, thinking of ghosts, but find only our father in moth-colored pajamas. He looks unsteadily at the dark air in front of him.

"Hi, Dad," I say from the doorway.

He looks in my direction. "Yes?"

"It's me. Bobby."

"Oh, Bobby," he says. "What are you doing up, young man?"

"Nothing," I tell him. "Dad?"

"Yes, son."

"Maybe you better come back to bed. Okay?"

"Maybe I had," he says. "I just came out here for a drink of water, but I seem to have gotten turned around in the darkness. Yes, maybe I better had."

I take his hand and lead him down the hall to his room. The grandfather clock chimes the quarter hour.

"Sorry," our father says.

I get him into bed. "There," I say. "Okay?"

"Perfect. Could not be better."

"Okay. Good night."

"Good night. Bobby?"

"Uh-huh?"

"Why don't you stay a minute?" he says. "We could have ourselves a talk, you and me. How would that be?"

"Okay," I say. I sit on the edge of his mattress. His bedside clock ticks off the minutes.

I can hear the low rasp of his breathing. Around our house, the Ohio night chirps and buzzes. The small gray finger of Carlton's stone pokes up among the others, within sight of the angel's blank white eyes. Above us, airplanes and satellites sparkle. People are flying even now toward New York or California, to take up lives of risk and invention.

I stay until our father has worked his way into a muttering sleep.

Carlton's girlfriend moved to Denver with her family a month before. I never learned what it was she'd whispered to him. Though she'd kept her head admirably during the accident, she lost her head afterward. She cried so hard at the funeral that she had to be taken away by her mother—an older, redder-haired version of her. She started seeing a psychiatrist three times a week. Everyone, including my parents, talked about how hard it was for her, to have held a dying boy in her arms at that age. I'm grateful to her for holding my brother while he died, but I never once heard her mention the fact that though she had been through something terrible, at least she was still alive and going places. At least she had protected herself by trying to warn him. I can appreciate the intricacies of her pain. But as long as she was in Cleveland, I could never look her straight in the face. I couldn't talk about the wounds she suffered: I can't even write her name.

AFTER GRADUATING from the University of Missouri journalism school in 1973, I lived in the Caribbean for a year, working on the island of Providencia with two spear fishermen, Raimundo Lung and his partner Gabriel, before sailing home, enlisting in the Peace Corps, and returning to the West Indies as an agricultural journalist.

Robertson Davies once wrote that a man in his youth has several fathers, and his biological one isn't necessarily his most significant. I had three: the one who fathered my flesh; a professor in Missouri—William Peden is his name—who fathered my passion to be a writer; and Mundo, the third and most adroit, a penniless black fisherman, the father of my spiritual point of view, who taught me how to persevere in the face of hardship and never be afraid of life.

One thing about Mundo: he was, and is, clairvoyant. Years later, as a student at the Iowa Writers' Workshop, I was compelled to write about this power of his, fictionalizing the truth of events I was unable to comprehend, and although I had crafted an alter ego for myself, I was unable to give Mundo any other name—or reality—but his own. In life, Mundo had always been larger than life. The same goes for duppy-haunted Providencia, rubbing itself so intimately against nature. The islands have always played "Twilight Zone" tricks on me, suggesting, among other things, that there were moments of mysticism inherent in the human act of expression, including the act of writing, moments of prophecy, moments of hyperlucidity, moments that would reach out to tear a souvenir off the coattails of the future. Where does an imagination come from? I found myself asking on Providencia, but the island always answered back with a riddle—*Where does reality come from?*—and a biblical reproach: In the beginning was the Word. It's the language, dummy. The narrative might be domestic or political, but there was no other link between real events and the imagination but language and nature.

By the way, "Mundo's Sign" was the only story I ever wrote at the Workshop that was dismissed outright by my instructor. Your style reminds me, he sneered, of that drunk who wrote that volcano thing in Mexico. My style is nothing like Malcolm Lowry's, but I appreciated the backhanded compliment.

BOB SHACOCHIS

IN THE FADING DARKNESS, the small boats, twelve in all, were dragged into the water from the camp on Southwest Cay. Masts were stepped quickly and the sails unfurled in the placid security of the coral lagoon. Wind-filled and ghost-white, they rounded the leeward edge of the cay and scattered in all directions across the fishing banks.

Bowen was in the bow of Mundo's catboat, huddled against the cool dawn breeze. He and Gabriel faced each other, their knees bumping together, but Gabriel lay back relaxing, his arms spread out along the gunnels as if he sat in a bathtub. Mundo was in the stern, his brown flesh sallow without true light, eyes and cheeks puffy, evidence that he had not slept well. Bowen hugged himself, his head down, shivering as the veiled pastel sun lifted from the sea behind him. A bird landed on his shoulder.

"Doan move, mahn," said Gabriel. "Daht is good luck."

The white man turned his head slowly to look at the bird. It was a green finch, little enough to fit in his hand. Through his T-shirt, Bowen felt the light pricking pressure of the bird's claws as it balanced to the rock of the boat.

"A bird never landed on me before," he said.

"Daht is good luck," Gabriel insisted. "Good fah de boat."

The bird fluttered from Bowen's shoulder to the gunnel and then hopped down between his feet, pecking at flecks of dried fish. It ran rodentlike under Gabriel's seat, in and out of sight in the shadows.

"Keep you head down low, Mistah Bone," Mundo said. The word *Mistah* was a joke, a taunt that Bowen had finally to accept. A friendship with Mundo had not been easily established. Bowen had come to Providence because he had heard that sea turtles were still numerous in the waters of the archipelago. They were something he wanted to know about, creatures whose habits informed his own pursuits, the omnibus sciences that made his life what it was, a quest for worlds lost or hidden, for knowledge unavailable to ordinary lives. His interviews with the fishermen led him to Raimundo Bell, the man most respected on Providence Island for his abilities in the water. Mundo had no interest in him at first beyond a natural suspicion, but Bowen offered to trade a share of the everyday work for a seat in Mundo's boat. If it was a question of proving oneself, Bowen did so, he hoped, through his sweat and dirtiness and exhaustion. The difference in the lives of the two men gradually diminished until they took each other for granted. Still, Bowen could not talk Mundo out of calling him *Mistah*, or pronouncing it in a tone that underscored the conspicuous nature of their relationship.

Mundo balanced upright in the back of the boat, the two rudder lines gathered from behind him, held in his big hands like the reins of a horse. "Gabriel?" he warned. Mundo was rarely more than laconic and yet Gabriel always responded precisely. Mundo stooped down, dark and solid, steering for extra wind.

"Yes," Gabriel answered, rising up. "Goin speedify directly, mahn." He began to coil in the mainsheet. The boat heeled and pressed into the tinted water, going faster, bracing the men against the windward hull. Mundo jibed the boat. Once the sail had luffed Gabriel allowed the boom to swing over, combing the back of Bowen's hair. The canvas inhaled again and held the breath. Bowen sat up straight and repositioned his weight in the boat. He could see the sunrise now, chalked with lavender towers of clouds lining up away from it. The light was like a warm hand on his face.

Behind them they heard the slapping of another sail as it dumped wind. "Look dere," said Gabriel. "Ezekiel turnin ahcross, too,"

"Daht bitch," Mundo grumbled, and twisting his neck he shouted back, "Ezekiel, you old piece ah fuck, you tink you cahn race me, mahn?"

Ezekiel would not answer, nor would he look toward them. Within minutes he had let his boat fall far in their wake. Months ago, Bowen had approached Ezekiel because he heard the doddering fisherman had once caught a malatta hawksbill, a crossbreed between a hawksbill and a green turtle that the experts Bowen had read insisted was only mythical, a tall tale. He wanted to know if they were wrong. Mundo said he himself had shot a malatta, two years ago on the fishing banks in Serrana, and that he had seen the one Ezekiel had netted before it was butchered and sold to the Japanese. When Bowen went to Ezekiel for verification, the old man was incoherent, a pathetic figure who could not focus his memory. Bowen pitied him out loud to Mundo. Mundo said *Daht mahn steal from de mouth of he children. He beat de wife fah rum money. Mahn, when de devil need feelin sorry fah?*

"Mundo, where you goin, mahn?" Gabriel finally asked. Bowen had watched him fidgeting, building up to the question until he was certain of their course. Gabriel was a handsome man and knew it well, shaving his sideburns into broad flairs and wearing a gold cross on a thin strand of wire around his neck. He had once told Bowen he was too good-looking to be a fisherman, that he would like to work in a shop or as a waiter. But on Providence there was no other work but fishing for a man who did not own land. Mundo didn't seem to care though. Mundo loved the sea and never questioned what it brought him or what it took away.

"Mundo, you sleepin?"

"Jewfish Hole," Mundo said, spitting into the water and watching it twirl out of sight. "Headed up daht way."

"True? Not Five Shillin Cay?"

"No."

Gabriel licked his teeth and asked why not. Last night after supper they had discussed where they might fish today. Mundo had argued that if the wind stayed the direction it was, they must sail for Five Shilling Cay or Aguadilla Reef instead of closer waters. That was fine with Bowen because he wanted to go ashore on the cay and see what there was in a place where man never came. *Light bulb, whiskey bottle, piece ah plahstic baby, dead fumey stuff ahnd birds*, Mundo told him. Maybe a malatta hawksbill, too, Bowen added, and Mundo had said *De malatta can be anywheres, mahn. Daht's only luck.*

"Mundo, wake up now. Dis a bahd wind fah Jewfish Hole."

Mundo peered at them both through hooded eyes. "I get a sign," he said. Bowen wondered what he was talking about. Mundo stared past him, out of the boat, measuring the waters of Serrana as if these eighty square miles of unmarked banks were city streets he had grown up on. He veered several degrees off the wind; Gabriel automatically trimmed the sail.

"So you get a sign, Mundo?" Gabriel probed.

"Yeah."

"What's that supposed to be?" Bowen wanted to know. Perhaps the two men were humoring each other to pass the slothful time of the sail. Mundo was too serious and impassive this morning. He should have been singing. He liked to sing when they were sailing: Jim Reeves, Bing-Bing, salsa, anything.

"I get a dream lahst night daht was a sign."

Bowen sniffed at this revelation, fretting. Back on Providence, Mundo didn't play the lottery so he never talked about his dreams like those who did. The town would stir in the morning and somebody would be claiming they had a dream, a good one, and then the dreambook would be consulted, a finger-worn copy published in Harlem in 1928, and the dreams figured out. *No, I tellin you, a white horse is six, de white cow is two six, ahnd a white lady is six one one. In dis dream you see a white lady milkin a white cow? Oh ho! De lady come first, so daht six one one two six. No, I tellin you, is de lady come first, mahn, not de cow. If blahck on de cow, daht six two.* A boy would be sent running to Alvaro's shop to buy the number. But Mundo always said the lottery was foolish.

Bowen dipped his hand over the side to feel the water. He liked the unworried, surging speed of the catboat, the white and rose and amber colors of the bottom refracted and blurry, just colors streaming by through the window of the surface. "Is that so?" Bowen asked. "You had a dream?" Mundo said yeah.

"I didn't know you dreamed, Mundo," Bowen said. "Did you dream you saw a white lady wearing a white dress riding a white jackass?"

"Mistah Bone think you makin joke, Mundo," said Gabriel. "He believe you jokifyin."

Mundo's eyes sparked, showing Bowen the hubris he saw in many black men. "Dis a sign fah dis place only," he replied harshly. He was moodier than Bowen had ever seen him. This place, Bowen thought. This place wasn't a place at all. It was wide open. It was openness, sunlight shattered blue and unstopped in all directions. There was another world beneath, a mint-cool wilderness, treacherous and lush, but here on the surface the boat pushed into an empty seascape.

"No kidding?" Bowen asked.

"No."

"What's the sign?"

"Fuck a mahn."

"Oh yeah?" Bowen said incredulously.

"Fuck a mahn."

"Daht a funny sign, Mundo," said Gabriel.

"What's he talking about?" Bowen asked Gabriel almost incidentally, squinting beyond him to study Mundo. His skin was slicker now in the sun and the light stuck across Mundo's narrow face in sharp pieces, leaving him cheekbones but no cheeks and emphasizing his stolid mouth, lips parted but no teeth visible. Bowen expected Mundo to grin at him but he didn't. His distance seemed acted out, like part of a magician's masquerade. He's playing with me, Bowen thought. No, he decided, looking at him again, he's serious.

"So Mundo, you fuck a mahn, eh?" Gabriel said.

"Yeah, boy," Mundo answered. He began to uncurl his arms and legs from the tight ball he sat in and warmed up to his story. "I dream I fuck a mahn. I stayin in Costa Rica, in Puerto Limon, when I play basebahll in de leagues, ahnd I stayin in dis residencia. Dis girlie mahn come to visit wit a bottle of aguardiente. We drink de bottle, den I fuck him."

"Oh ho," said Gabriel, as if he were saying, Yes, I see.

Mundo navigated the boat through a porcelain blue channel that furrowed between two ridges of coral. Outside the reef, the water deepened abruptly, a darkening translucence. The waves rose to one-third the height of the mast. They were on the open sea now, outside the coral walls. The faraway sail of Ezekiel's boat had disappeared. Mundo followed the reef northward. Already the sun was strong and Bowen was acutely aware of its power to stupefy. Before the words dried up in his mouth and his mind muddled, he wanted to know what it was about the dream that meant something to Mundo.

"You dreamed you fucked a man," he said cautiously. "What does that mean? What kind of a sign is that?"

"A good one," replied Mundo.

The bird reappeared on Mundo's knee. He made a quick grab for it, but the finch was in the air, scooting low over the waves.

"Come again next day," Gabriel called after it. The bird hooked east toward whatever land might lie that way.

The mystery had become too much for Bowen. He mimicked Alvaro the bookie and his high rapid voice, like a little dog's: "Costa Rica, dat's two oh one; mon's arsehole, dat's nought; drinkin aguardiente, dat's oh oh oh. Boy, you get a nice numbah dere, Mundo. Put a fiver on it, mon."

Mundo's weak smile made Bowen feel patronized. The black man blinked ostentatiously, widening his hidden eyes as if only now he had reason to come awake, to come away from the dream.

"No, let me tell you, Mistah Bone. Dis sign mean I must shoot a big he hawksbill," Mundo said emphatically. He raised his thick right forearm. His fist clenched, the dark muscles flexed from elbow to wrist. "Big!" he said.

"Mistah Bone doan believe," said Gabriel in a sad, false voice. He nodded at Bowen. "He is a sci-ahnce mahn. He only see sci-*ahnce*." Then Gabriel laughed, pushing Bowen's knee good-naturedly.

Hearing Mundo and Gabriel talk about the sign made Bowen feel for a moment that he had lost all contact with them. He leaned forward earnestly, resting his forearms along his bare thighs. He could not resist speaking and yet he hesitated, sure that he was being drawn into trouble.

"Tell me, you can shoot a hawksbill turtle because you dreamed you assholed somebody?" An image of the dream flicked through his mind: Mundo bent over slim, tar-black buttocks, mounting like a beast, the *girlie mahn* in a stupor, slurring a languid, corrupt Castilian. "How is that?"

"How you mean, mahn?" Mundo looked keenly at Bowen, a challenging eyebrow cocked, teasing him with a crooked smile, ready to invite Bowen into his house and then beat him at dominoes all night long. "You evah fuck a mahn, Mistah Bone?"

"No," Bowen said immediately. He was surprised that the question had embarrassed him so easily, as if it exposed a level of manhood he had not achieved.

"Mistah Bone want to investigate everyting, but he doan fuck a mahn yet?" Gabriel said, his voice scaling to a parody of a question.

"Some men just be like womahn. Gabriel—right?"

"Daht's true. It's de same, mahn."

"Oh, Christ," Bowen said, shaking his head ruefully. He tried to play along. "Let's let it all out."

"So Mistah Bone," Mundo continued, "you evah take a womahn like daht?"

"My God."

"You doan like it?"

Bowen folded his arms across his chest and refused to answer. There were pieces of himself he did not wish to share, even in a game. To be forced to this realization, to admit that something in him would instinctively retreat into rock like a sea anemone, made him angry.

"Mistah Bone," Mundo said, "when we reach bahck to Providence we find you a mahn to fuck." Gabriel winked at Bowen.

"No thanks," Bowen answered coolly. "You two black queers."

Separating himself from the conversation, Mundo came up off his seat to look around. Bowen wondered how he could know where they were when there was absolutely nothing out there to sight on. Mundo sat back down, rocking rhythmically from side to side, letting the waves loosen his shoulders and neck, danced by the sea.

"Fuck fucka fucka mahn," he chanted.

"Sail the boat."

"Sailin like a real bitch right now."

"Black man bullshit. Jungle stuff."

"Uh-oh, Mundo. Mistah Bone vexed now wit dis dream bodderation."

"All right. All right. Enough," Bowen declared. "Do that trick, shoot the turtle, then I'll start fucking men. Maybe you first, Gabriel."

"Oh me God, Mundo." Gabriel laughed. "Look what you talk Mistah Bone into."

"He gettin de picture now, boy," Mundo said. "You doan worry, Gabriel. Mistah Bone lookin hahd to fuck dis bunch ah guys bahck in de States who say malatta hawksbill a make-believe. You not hear him say so?"

"I got the picture now, so let's drop all this somethingness out of nothingness."

"Pretty talk," said Gabriel.

Bowen resented his ambition described through such a coarse metaphor, but now that the point had been made, he felt comfortable again with the two black men. Mundo said nothing more but sat quietly like a schoolboy with an expression of overbearing innocence.

They sailed for another twenty minutes, cutting progressively nearer to the reef until they were only yards away from the foam left behind by the waves that broke across the shallow coral. Then the reef bowled inward, pinched by a channel which they rode through into calmer water. After a short distance, Mundo tacked back toward the inside of the main reef, and when they were a couple of miles down-current from the channel, he steered into the wind.

"Come, you workin today, mahn?" Mundo called. Bowen looked at him stupidly. He had let himself fall into a daze, the light, like thick crystals growing on the water, overcoming him. His deeply tanned skin felt scratchy and sore and gluey.

"Get de sail, mahn. Quick."

Bowen jerked himself out of his lethargy and stood up, holding the gunnels for balance. He concentrated on his equilibrium, judging how the water moved the boat until he was sure of himself, straightened up, and then leapt from the bottom of the boat to his seat. He grabbed the mast with one hand and extended the other one out toward Gabriel. Gabriel stood behind him, rolling the sailcloth onto the boom as far as he could, passing it to Bowen until the flour-sack sail was furled around the wood and the boom was parallel with the mast.

"Gabriel, watch out," Bowen said.

"You okay, Mistah Bone. You become ahn expert."

But Bowen wanted to know that Gabriel was ready if he should lose his footing in the pitch of the boat. He lashed the boom and mast tight together with the sheet line, grunting as it took all his strength to lift the long heavy mast from its step. He rested the butt on the seat, spread his arms on the poles like a weight lifter and lowered the mast slowly to Gabriel and then Mundo, who had their arms up ready to receive it.

When the mast was down, they passed it back to Mundo far enough so he could get it under the seats to stow. Bowen pulled the two handmade oars from the gear in the bottom of the boat. Slipping them through the rope oarlocks midway on each gunnel, he jammed them back into the boat and left them ready while the boat drifted. It was still early in the morning.

"Sun hot," Gabriel said. He always said this before he set to work.

"Daht's right."

"Watah too cool," he said, cupping his hand into the sea and splashing his face. Bowen stood up to negotiate a piss with the churning of the boat but remained there for some minutes prick in hand, unable to relax.

"Mahn, jump in de sea if you want a piss."

He removed his shirt and sat down with his legs over the gunnel. Mundo and Gabriel leaned to the opposite hull to counterbalance the canoelike boat and then quickly leaned back after Bowen hefted himself over the side. He let himself sink a few feet below the keel, felt the temperature subtly change, cooler and cooler until it was all the same, the blue pressure bearing against him completely. He opened his eyes briefly, welcoming the rough bite of the salt that took away his drowsiness. He kicked back to the surface, spinning in slow circles for the pleasure of it, relieved himself and struggled back into the boat. Without a diving mask to clearly see what else was there with him, he did not like to stay in the water long. No matter how casual Mundo and Gabriel could be around sharks, Bowen couldn't muster the same aloofness. They chided him about this, but still, Mundo wore a cummerbund of old sheet around his waist for bandaging in case of trouble. And Gabriel's left arm was arced with purple scars across his bicep. *Ahn eel do daht. Shark doan molest mahn. It's true.*

Bowen dried his face and hands on his shirt and put it back on as protection against the sun. Underneath the bow seat he kept an oatmeal tin. He stretched and found it, unscrewing the lid. Inside, wrapped in a plastic bag to keep out moisture, were a pack of Pielrojas, a box of matches, the precious spear points, and a sack of hard candy labeled simply *Dulces* which he had bought at Alvaro's right before the fishermen had set sail on the *Orion* from Providence eight days ago. The candy had turned gummy in the sea air. He took a red piece and bit into its waxy surface, chewing vigorously and swallowing the whole lump without determining its flavor. The sweetness took the salty, sour heat out of his mouth. Mundo asked for a Pielroja and Bowen lit one for him, smoking it down a bit before he passed it along with the point for Mundo's spear. Bowen switched places with Gabriel and began to row, bringing the boat around into the current, pulling against the tide just enough to stay where they were.

The black men silently outfitted themselves and to Bowen they already had the grim look of hunters on them. The cigarette jutted straight out like a weapon in Mundo's tight lips. He propped his long metal gun between his legs and unclasped its spear, screwing on the point, securing the catch line, and then set the gun aside while he pulled black flippers snug on his white-soled feet. Bowen watched him; each piece of equipment he added on seemed to alter his humanness, and now, more so than with the dream business, Mundo was becoming inaccessible, the friendship between them a triviality. From under his seat the fisherman took his diving mask and spit on the inside of the glass, spreading the tobacco-flecked phlegm with his fingers to prevent the glass from fogging. He washed the mask out in the sea and adjusted it to rest on his forehead, pressing into the short curls of his hair, not kinky hair like Gabriel's but more Latin, straighter and oily. He sucked the ash of the cigarette down next to his lips, knocking the butt off into the water with his tongue before it burned him. He exhaled deeply, and then inhaled, and then exhaled normally. Turtles made that same noise when they sounded for air, thought Bowen, that sudden, single gasp of inhalation bobbing out of the sea from nowhere. Mundo's eyes were featureless, without pupils, the irises dark, without color. Go fuck your big turtle, Bowen said to himself. He began to see that the prophecy was an easy one—like a handsome man boasting he would seduce an available woman—because there were plenty of turtles in the water. This was their mating season, the end of the hurricanes. They had come from all over the ocean to return here to breed.

"Ahll right," Mundo said softly, and pulled his mask down over his eyes and nose. He was out of the boat promptly, disappearing below the surface.

Gabriel procrastinated, sharpening the point of his spear on the block of limestone they carried in the boat. Bowen heard Mundo purge his snorkel. Looking over his shoulder to check the diver's position, he began to row.

"Wait a minute, Mistah Bone," Gabriel said. He slung his legs over the side and crossed himself vaguely, lifting the crucifix from his chest to kiss. He fitted the mouthpiece of the snorkel behind his lips and they bulged apishly. Splashing into the water, face down, the gun ready, he turned a spiral to examine what was there below him.

Bowen pulled ahead six times and then paused, unable to locate Mundo. Gabriel was to Bowen's left, kicking mechanically into the two-knot current, his gun cradled from elbow to elbow. Mundo surfaced ten yards ahead, going down again like a porpoise. Bowen went after him, quickly over the glossy boil that marked Mundo's dive.

He leaned out of the boat and looked down. Below him in about eight fathoms of water he could see Mundo in pieces, distorted fragments of motion rising and coalescing into human shape, the curve of his dark back floating up to him, the red faded trunks looking like raw skin under the water.

His back broke the surface first, a long brown bubble, smooth and headless. The snorkel poked up, gargled and wheezed. There was a moment's calm before the water in front of the diver was flying apart, twisting and scattering and white. Blood swelled olive-green from the center of it all. Mundo fought for control over something Bowen had not yet fully seen. Again there was quiet. And then this: Mundo's torso suddenly out of the water, pendulous beside the boat, his arm dipping the spear down inside and letting a slab of great, furious life slide off it at Bowen's feet. The fish was as long as the arm that had released it, violently thrashing, the fan of its dorsal spines sharp enough to cut through leather. Bowen fell back off his seat, drawing his legs out of the way.

"Jesus."

He found the ironwood mallet and bent over, striking at the fish, unable to hit it effectively. Blood and bits of rubbery tissue sprayed on his chest. Finally its movements slowed and he was able to direct a clean blow to the broad, bull-like slope of its head.

"Goddammit."

The shot had not been clean. The spear had struck behind the head but too low to hit the spinal cord. It had entered through the huge gills—thus the excess of blood now in the boat—and come out on the other side below the pectoral fin. The blood all over Bowen made him feel filthy. He was stone-eyed now, full of his job. Mundo's head popped over the gunnel. He was amused.

"You like daht one, mahn?"

"Shoot better," Bowen said.

Mundo laughed wickedly and sank out of sight. Bowen could hear the click of the spear sliding into the latch of the trigger as Mundo reloaded the spring-action gun against the hull of the boat. Gabriel was calling. He held his spear in the air, a lobster skewered on the end of it. Bowen was there in a minute, screwing off the flanged spear point to take the catch into the boat.

He set the oars and stood up to rearrange the gear under his seat. Mundo's fish was a grouper, by Bowen's estimate twenty-five to thirty pounds. To shield it from the sun he tugged it into the cleared space below the seat. The lobster was thrown into the stern behind a coil of rope. He used to put the lobsters with the fish, but if they weren't dead they kept crawling out from beneath him and he would stab his feet on the thorns of their shells. Before he could sit down again Gabriel was beside the boat with another lobster.

"Four more in de hole, boy. I tellin you, de bird was good luck."

Bowen hovered over Gabriel until the diver had brought up the remaining lot. It took some time and only then did Bowen search for Mundo. He spotted him far off, impatiently waving the boat forward. The muscles in Bowen's arms cramped from the fast rowing. By the time he reached him, Mundo had his face back down in the water, staying afloat with his fins. Bowen had to shout to get his attention. Mundo raised his head, a glare in his eyes exaggerated by the mask. He lifted a fish up and hurled it into the boat.

"What's the matter?" Bowen asked defensively. "Sharks?"

"Keep up, mahn. Keep up."

"Yeah, yeah." Bowen shrugged off Mundo's admonishment. It was impossible to stay with both divers unless both divers stayed together. He took his own mask and held it on top of the water, providing a small round view of the scene below. There were no dark, darting shadows, nothing ominous at all.

Mundo swam crosscurrent into deeper water, his flippers continuously paddling the surface. In pursuit of something beneath him he doubled back and sped past the boat headed in the opposite direction. He vanished as Bowen put all his effort into turning the boat around, determined to keep on top of the action. He heard the rasp then, a sound like a vacuum filling with air. Off the starboard he saw the green, pale-throated head of the turtle bouncing in the swell and he understood Mundo's urgency, because two or three turtles would double the value of a day's work. He couldn't see Mundo, but he knew the man was carefully ascending beneath the creature, taking slow aim. The turtle lurched forward and tried to submerge as the spear shot through one of its hind flippers. Mundo surfaced, hauling the spear line in until the turtle was beside him, hopelessly struggling to shake the iron rod from its leg. Bowen was right there.

"Nice work," Bowen said. "You did it."

Mundo handed the gun to Bowen. While Bowen held the turtle by the rim of its shell, Mundo wrestled to extract the spear. Once he had succeeded in unscrewing the point, it slid out easily from the thin flesh of the flipper.

"He's a big one."

"Not so big."

"He's a male and pretty big. That was your sign."

"Nah," Mundo grunted.

"Close enough."

"Dis no hawksbill. Lift him up now."

The green turtle weighed close to a hundred pounds. Bowen almost fell out of the boat pulling him in. The turtle banged down the curve of the hull, its flippers clawing for water that wasn't there, a dull calloused scrape across the wood, its mouth gasping, the lower mandible unlocked like an old man's jaw. I'll be damned, thought Bowen, this was the biggest turtle their boat had brought in here on the banks. Only two loggerheads netted by the boat with the old men were bigger.

He turned the heavy green on its back. The yellow plates of its belly glowed like pinewood. He set his feet on them, feeling the turtle's cold-bloodedness. Its sea-smell was clean, without mucus or secretion. From inside a wooden toolbox Bowen took the small bundle of palm fronds that every Providence fishing boat carried. He pulled two short strands from it. Grabbing one of the turtle's anterior flippers, he placed it against the hull and with the tip of his diving knife punched a small hole through the glazed flesh that formed the shape of a man's hand with the fingers fused together. He did the same to the flipper behind it and then threaded the cuts with a frond, tying the ends off in a square knot. With its fore and hind legs thus bound, the turtle was immobile.

Prayin from both ends, the fishermen called this.

"Why don't you use fishing line?" Bowen had asked when he first saw Gabriel bind a turtle.

"Palm leaf nice," Gabriel told him. "Turtle ahpreciate daht."

Bowen rowed on, occasionally pausing to fill the calabash bailer with seawater and cool the turtle that now suffered the sun. The first time he did this the turtle curled its head and appeared to look at him. Bowen turned away. It made him feel foolish but he did not like to see a sea turtle's eyes. The eyes were too mammalian and expressive, a more vivid brown than the eyes of a human being, lugubrious. They teared out of water, salty silk tears beading down the reptilian scales, and he did not like to see it. In the ocean there was no movement with more grace, no ballet more perfect, than the turtle's.

The men worked for several more hours before switching. Mundo shot another turtle, an average-size hawksbill which Bowen tied and was able to fit under the seat. There was a long period with no luck. Then, like a magic returning, the divers found fish again. The boat began to fill up.

Bowen tended to the divers, the citric tang of sweat in his nostrils, his eyes closed now and then to soothe them from the glare. His blue trunks and white T-shirt were smeared with blood and the gray slime that came off the fish. Trailing the swimmers, his back to them as he rowed forward, he counted the strokes of the oars, an empty meditation broken by the need to cool the turtles or take another fish into the boat. Alone again he would look up, his thoughts not yet refocused on his labor, and be startled by the uncut geography of the sea, the desolate beauty, the isolation.

The sun was straight up and fierce. Patches of wind blew off the glassy veneer of the surface. The waves lumped high enough to conceal the divers if they weren't close to the boat. Mundo and Gabriel trod water together, talking in bursts, their snorkels jutting out from under their chins. Bowen came over to them. Hours in the sea had made Mundo look younger, Gabriel older. They clung to the side of the boat.

"Mistah Bone, dis Jewfish Hole a pretty spot. Come give Gabriel a rest."

Bowen stowed the oars and went to the bow for his diving gear, anxious to leave the confinement of the boat, the blind sense of being denied something others took for granted. They would not always let him fish. They had spent their lives on the water; for all his effort, Bowen could not begin to match their skill. On a good day, though, he would take over for Gabriel. Mundo had an appetite for the reef and knew that Bowen, more than Gabriel ever would, felt the same way. There were times when he would come and hurry Bowen out of the boat if there was something extraordinary he wanted the white man to see. They swam together like two farm boys at a carnival, exploring everywhere, the joy of it all and the mystery running between them like an electric ribbon.

Bowen lowered himself into the water after Gabriel was settled in the boat. His ears filled with the steady fizzing static of the ocean moving against its cup of earth.

The reef seemed scooped out here, forming a wide horseshoe-shaped arena, ten fathoms deep in the middle where they were, the bottom tiering up in shaggy clusters of coral until the perimeter shallowed in a dense thicket of staghorn branches. A school of fry, a long cloud of flashing arrows, passed with the current toward them herded by watchful barracuda. It parted and reclosed around the divers, obscuring them from each other's sight for several moments.

The sandy paths of the surge channels wove through the swaying flora on the bottom, continuing up like white banners from the open end of the pool where the water gathered more dimension and the channels disappeared into a fog of infinite blue. Here the current pushed in from outside the reef.

They started to swim. Bowen followed Mundo's lead. Gabriel stopped them with a shout.

"Mundo, me see a boat."

Mundo swam like a dog with his head up and coughed out his snorkel: "Who?"

"Cahn't see. He way up, mahn."

Mundo stuck his head back in the water, uninterested in this news. He led them closer to the coral walls, turning again into the current when the water reached about forty feet, the depth at which Bowen managed best. They swam toward the wide mouth of the canyon which kept expanding as they kicked onward. Beyond, the visibility closed and faded, a chiaroscuro lanced by drifting shafts of sunlight. The blank distance shadowed and materialized into shapes, accumulating more and more detail as they moved ahead.

Bowen swam with his gun out in front of him like a soldier on patrol. Surveying an isolated button of brain coral, Mundo pointed to the antennae of a spiny lobster. Bowen jackknifed and dove, missed the first shot. On the second shot he took aim more carefully. There was a screeching sound of old armor when he yanked the lobster from its den. He ascended quickly, fighting for the sterling surface as he ran out of air. Gabriel came alongside.

"I see two guys," he reported, taking the spear from Bowen and removing the point. "Maybe daht's Ezekiel." Bowen didn't respond. It wasn't so unusual to see another of the boats off in the distance during the course of the day. The fact that the boat was close enough for Gabriel to see the men in it didn't mean anything to Bowen. He reloaded his gun and swam away to catch up with Mundo.

Together they continued ahead, frequently descending to inspect a cave or niche in the polychromatic reef. Fish were everywhere but they sought only those that appealed to the restaurants of the mainland. Cutting in and out of a gray forest of gorgonian coral, a mako shark rose toward them curiously but then stopped halfway and returned to its prowling. The shark was too small and too preoccupied to worry Bowen; still, he had tensed upon first seeing it, and adrenaline drove into his heart. Mundo plummeted down, found the shark interested in a red snapper nosing in the silt for food, and shot the fish. The shark skirted away when Mundo jabbed at it with his empty gun. The boat was there when he surfaced.

"It's Ezekiel," Gabriel told the two of them. He slipped a hand into the gills of the fish and took it from Mundo. "Ahnd Henry Billings. Dey driftin on de current from down de outside."

"Turtlin," Mundo said. He handed his spear to Bowen while he defogged his mask.

Ezekiel and Henry were too old to dive anymore—*divin squeeze up a mahn's insides*—but they came along on expeditions to the banks to line fish, net turtles, and collect conchs from the shallows. They did not mingle much with the other fishermen who were mostly young and scorned the insipidness of fishing with a hand line and hook. Gaunt and unhealthy, Ezekiel looked like a wrinkled black puppet, simian with lackluster eyes. He suffered the bitter condescension of the islanders because he was too much a drunkard. Most people treated Henry Billings, round and smooth-faced, as though he were a moron. Bowen had never heard him speak a word, and neither had anybody else for more than twenty years.

"Dey lookin excited, boy," Gabriel said, standing up to get a better view. Bowen and Mundo could not see the other boat from the water. "Ezekiel buryin he head in de glahss, ahnd Henry rowin hahd hahd like he racin home fah pussy."

Mundo pushed away from the boat, followed by Bowen, who had trouble catching his breath. They were now approaching the same windward channel in the barrier reef that they had sailed through earlier in the morning. The water doubled in depth, the bottom became more sand than coral. Bowen kicked harder to keep up with Mundo as the current increased. It tugged against him relentlessly and he began to tire. He halted and pressed himself out of the water as far as possible but could not see Mundo over the swell of the waves. He tried to move ahead again, grew discouraged and let the tide sweep him back to the boat.

Gabriel helped him aboard. Bowen saw that they were going out through the channel while Ezekiel's boat was steering in a hundred and fifty feet or so in front of them off the port. Mundo was almost halfway between the two boats, still headed straight upcurrent.

"Dey on de trail," Gabriel said. They watched Ezekiel take one hand off the waterglass and reach behind himself to grasp an iron-hooped net used to catch turtles. Ezekiel called back to Henry, urging him forward. He held the net over the bow, waiting for position. Mundo spun in the water. He looked quickly around and then back at his own boat. Bowen saw him, imagined he saw the calculating look in his enlarged eyes. He stood on the aft seat and waved his arms at the diver. Mundo put his head back down and charged across the channel, angling toward Ezekiel's boat.

"Mundo!"

Bowen was not certain if Mundo realized Ezekiel's boat was so close. He yelled again.

"Mundo!"

Ezekiel positioned the net and dropped it. Mundo was past the center of the channel and nearing the other boat. In an instant he was out of sight under the water. Perched in front of the boat, his face hidden by the wooden sides of the waterglass, Ezekiel became more and more animated until he had come to his feet, his head still stuck ostrichlike in the box. He took one hand off the glass to shake his fist.

"Mundo," he shouted in a garbled voice, difficult to understand. "Mundo. Wha de fuck!"

"Oh, shit," Gabriel said. "Look Ezekiel dere bein so voicetrous. Mahn, he cryin a lot of nonsense, you know."

Mundo had been down for about two minutes and his limit was four. Bowen pulled on his mask and rolled over the side of the boat, biting down on the mouthpiece of his snorkel just as he hit the water. Son of a bitch, he said to himself, seeing what was happening below.

Suspended in deep water six or seven fathoms down, Mundo labored to free the turtle from Ezekiel's net. One hind flipper was loose, pierced by the spear and sea-anchored by the gun which Mundo had let drop. The diver held the turtle by the stub of its penis-tail and used his free hand to untangle the netting from the other back flipper. Bent around the turtle so his feet were in front of him, he kicked himself backward to resist Ezekiel's effort to raise the net. The turtle's flipper finally pulled clear and flailed wildly about.

With one set of flippers extended, the turtle was easily Mundo's length, the caramel and yellow carapace twice the man's width. Its great size magnified by the thick lens of water, the turtle seemed unreal, like a comic-book monster, to Bowen. Mundo moved spiritedly, hovering now on the back of the turtle. He reached for a front flipper but the turtle fought him. Each time he worked the limb out of the net the turtle jerked and recaught itself. The diver sprung off the turtle as if he were a rider being dismounted into the sky. He exhaled as he ascended, silver spheres of air boiling from his mouth, forming a column which he appeared to climb hand over hand to the surface. Bowen heard the agonized suck of his inhalation— "Mundo!" this from Ezekiel—and then he was down again.

By the time Mundo was back to the turtle, Ezekiel had hauled the net up nearer to the surface. Bowen dived to help his partner but he had entered the water without his fins and could not make the depth. At the bottom of his descent, he saw Mundo bend the turtle's left flipper back through the net and wrench it over the shell. As Bowen turned upward, he heard the crack of the turtle's elbow joint dislocating.

Gabriel threw Bowen his fins. By the time he had them on, the turtle was out of the net, its two foreflippers dangling awkwardly, the third flipper weighted by the spear, the fourth performing its sad ballet. Mundo dipped below the turtle, retrieving the gun that hung from the spear by its line. He swam sluggishly toward the air with the turtle in tow by its impaled flipper. Bowen watched them rise. The sight of the black man and the turtle was like a dream-borne image floating in cool ether. The bright surface gleamed like the edge of sleep, the head of the leviathan turned from it toward the indigo mouth of the channel that sloped down and down and away.

They came up between the two boats. Ezekiel began his protest.

"Daht my hawksbill, Mundo. Wha hahppen, mahn? Wha hahppen?"

"Here now, Ezekiel," Gabriel shouted back. "You makin a mess ah noise, boy. Stop dis ugliness."

Mundo kept his back to Ezekiel's boat and would not answer the charge. He dragged the spear line in, bringing the turtle between him and Bowen. Both men caught hold of opposite sides of the shell and waited for Gabriel to position himself. The turtle wagged its huge head back and forth out of the water.

"Wha hahppen, mahn?"

"Ezekiel," Gabriel said across the negligible distance between the boats. "You shut up."

"Wha hahppen, mahn?"

"Shut up now or come here ahnd take some licks."

Mundo and Bowen faced each other over the mound of the carapace. Blood clotted on the side of Mundo's face.

"Doan move up too high, Mistah Bone," Mundo warned. "Keep in de middle or he snahp you."

"You're bleeding some."

Mundo grinned. To Bowen his grin seemed to celebrate only mischievousness.

"Did you shoot him," Bowen asked quietly, "before they netted him?"

"You have to guess, mahn?" The tone of Mundo's voice didn't answer Bowen but simply posed the question. Bowen suspected that the net had reached the turtle before Mundo had but there was no way to prove it. Only Mundo and Ezekiel knew for sure.

"This is a fucking big turtle," he said.

It took them awhile to get the hawksbill into the boat. Ezekiel and Henry raised their mast and set sail for the camp on Southwest Cay. Gabriel restepped their own mast to give them more room in the bottom of the boat, but even so they had to remove the middle seat to fit the turtle in. Bowen straddled the shell. He subdued the flippers and tied them off with palm fronds. He was shivering unconsciously, a condition Gabriel called *dog-leg*. When Mundo joined them the boat sank low in the water. He took his seat in the stern and stared thoughtfully at the turtle as if he were preparing to interrogate it.

"Dis beast must weigh tree hundred pounds, Mundo," Gabriel proclaimed.

"Daht's good luck."

All at once Bowen was throbbing, tired, hungry and thirsty. The oatmeal can and water bottle were buried in the chaos of fish and rope; he had no energy to look for them.

Gabriel unfurled the sail and changed places with Bowen on the turtle to work the sheet line. They began the long sail back. Because there were only a few inches of freeboard left to the boat Mundo would not let Gabriel trim the sail too tightly. The boat plugged languidly through the head seas. When they were on a direct course, Gabriel put the sheet line between his horny toes and stepped on it to keep it in place. He and Bowen scaled the fish and cleaned them, dropping the guts overboard into the water that was still clear but now colorless again, the blue gone out of it with the beginning of twilight. *Come, shark, come,* Gabriel said each time. *Here's a nice piece ah food. I treat you good, you know.* Mundo sang country-and-western songs, throwing all the melodrama he could into them. The air became steely and dense with haze.

They entered the lagoon shortly after dark. For some time they had been seeing a flickering bright light coming from the camp; even from a mile off at sea it cast a wobbly, liquid thread of illumination that ran out from the cay to their boat. It was obvious now that someone had built a large bonfire on the shore, and as Mundo steered into the shallows and they prepared to beach, a man moved out of the darkness into the firelight, the flames curling above his head. To Bowen the silhouette was crippled—the shadow of a beggar.

"Mundo," Gabriel said. "Ezekiel want to make a cry, mahn."

Mundo thieved the hawksbill from him, Ezekiel shouted crazily. The other fishermen gathered around him now. *Mundo teef de hawksbill. Wha hahppen, Mundo? Henry, come tell dem, mahn.* But Henry would not come out of the darkness and speak. As they dragged the boat ashore, the fishermen moved down next to the water to help them and to have a look at the big turtle. Amid the crowd, the talking all at once, the three of them were solemn and efficient, anxious for an end to the work. Ezekiel pushed forward, keeping the boat between himself and Mundo.

"Wha hahppen, Mundo?" he said witlessly. "Wha hahppen, mahn? You fuck me."

Mundo would not acknowledge him but spoke instead to the other men assembled around the boat. He looked predatory in the changing light of the fire, dangerous.

"I shoot de hawksbill," Mundo said. "You see it dere in my boat. De hell wit daht bitch Ezekiel." He wouldn't say anything more. Together he and Bowen lifted the two big turtles out of the boat and placed them gently in the sand. The old man yelled a lot but Bowen could not understand what he was saying. Colbert, a fisherman from the same village as Ezekiel, called out boldly from the group.

"Gabriel, speak up, mahn."

Gabriel talked softly as though to counterbalance Mundo's bitter disdain for Ezekiel. Although he would not speculate about what happened in the water, he explained how on their way out in the morning Mundo had revealed his dream, and how the bird had flown into the boat. Immediately the excitement returned. The dream and the bird inflated the drama and the importance of the dispute, and this pleased the onlookers. Someone called for Bowen to tell what he knew. Most of the men stopped arguing to hear him. Bowen was reluctant to speak, aware of his difference and how it would distort what he said to them, how it would become a story that began, *Ahnd den de white mahn say . . .*

"It was like Gabriel said. Mundo told us he had a dream about fucking a man. He said this was a sign that meant he was to shoot a big male hawksbill. There's the turtle right there."

"Sci-*ahnce* mahn doan carry faith in dreams," someone yelled at him. "Dreams is fah peoples like we."

"That's so, but this one came true, didn't it," Bowen said calmly.

Ezekiel shoved forward toward him. "No," he shouted. "Dis dream a lie. Mundo teef de hawksbill. Wha hahppen, Mundo?"

"The dream is no lie," Bowen said, unable to avoid his irritation. He hated the way the focus had been transformed entirely onto him. It seemed that everyone except Mundo was ready to grant him the full authority of his judgment because he was white and educated.

"Yes," a voice agreed. "But you see Mundo shoot de hawksbill before de net reach?"

Gabriel spoke before anyone else could. "Mahn, what de fuck it mattah? De dream come true. Daht's daht. Quit dis fuss."

Bowen bent over into the boat to collect the spear guns, wary that Ezekiel would see only him, blame only him, and that if there was uncertainty on his face he must hide it from them, because he knew now what he had to say. On the sail back Mundo and the turtle wouldn't leave his mind. There was the dream, as undeniable as it was incomprehensible, a coincidence announcing itself, a magic somehow conspired between man and beast.

Out of the corner of his eye he saw Mundo watching him. Bowen wished he could know what the black man was thinking, but he had no intuition for what was at stake between them. His only clear impulse was to protect the mystery of the dream.

"Mundo shot the turtle. The net wasn't there yet."

"You see it, mahn?"

"That's how it happened."

"You see it hahppen daht way?"

"I'm telling you what I know."

Bowen's proclamation put an end to it. Everyone agreed then that the hawksbill was Mundo's. Ezekiel wouldn't be quiet, but he walked away from them anyway, still shouting passionately, and others shouted back at him to shut up. The men went back to their cooking fires to have their suppers. The three of them were alone again. As they finished unloading the boat, Mundo whispered to Gabriel, "Mistah Bone find a mahn to fuck."

"Oh ho," said Gabriel, turning around to see if Bowen had heard. "Maybe next he get a sign, too. Mistah Bone—right?"

No guilt burned into him, or sympathy for Ezekiel. The dream was more important than what he had or had not seen. Mundo had come to the turtle first, through the dream, and that could not be changed, not by Bowen, not by Ezekiel's net. It frightened him that something so intangible could become so absolute in his mind. He confronted Mundo.

"Was I wrong?"

"You must decide, mahn. But you doan has to lie fah me."

"I did it because of the dream."

"Maybe daht's so," Mundo said, watching Bowen carefully. "Maybe you find out someting."

"I should have stayed out of it," he said.

"No, mahn, you was right, so you must fuck Ezekiel so. De hawksbill was mine no mattah what you say to dem."

They picked up their gear and hauled it to camp. While Gabriel prepared to cook their supper, Bowen found his tape measure, notebook and pencil and went with Mundo back to the boat. Together they carried the turtles down the beach and set them under the narrow thatched ramada built by the fishermen to shelter them from the sun. Bowen tallied the ones brought in today by all the boats, measured the length and width of their shells, counted the dorsal plates, recording the sex and species. As always, he checked for the milk-white markings of a malatta hawksbill. Mundo scratched his initials into the chests of his turtles with a diving knife.

"Damn," Bowen said, finished with his notes. "No malatta."

"Daht's only luck, mahn. Have faith."

The firelight rubbed weakly on the carapaces and spun small gold drops orbiting in the eyes of the turtles. Their flippers crooked front to back underneath the rows of shells, the palm fronds pinning them firmly together in a frozen clap, an endless prayer.

"I goin bahck."

"All right. I'll be there in a while."

Bowen did not know why he wanted to stay with the turtles but he lay down in the broken coral, too tired to help with supper, and listened to the sea creatures take their air, the gasping litany that committed them to the surface and to men. He saw them in the sea again, male and female clasped together, hawksbill and green turtle, the plates of their shells flush. They would join each other in this embrace and mate, drifting in the shallows, pushing up together to breathe, the female en-circled by the flippers of the male for a day and a night until the mythical pas de deux ended and a new form conceived from different bloods. Then they would unlock to spend a year alone in the sea. The images stopped there and he felt himself falling asleep. He did not want to sleep here in the ramada with the turtles so he rose and walked back to camp, to the men and to the pleasure of food. The sea pulled back off the reef, its tidal sucking audible, the air brought down through coral bones and exhaled again and again.

"THE STORY OF MY LIFE" began on a visit to Iowa, sparked by a newspaper article. It's a very American story, but I wouldn't have written it if I hadn't spent so many years living outside the United States during the early 1990s, a time when attacks on abortion clinics and doctors were growing increasingly brazen and violent. On each visit to the United States, I was confronted by something strange, shocking—in the case of this article, small children being made to block a clinic driveway. I wondered about those children, how it would feel to grow up in this atmosphere, complicit in events before they could fully comprehend them.

I made some notes, jotted down a few rough ideas. It was a busy time, and I soon put these aside, somewhat glad to be distracted. I knew this story would be risky, and difficult to write. But it persisted, as the necessary stories always do. Two summers later I was in Buffalo, New York, preparing to leave for a year in Cambodia, and each morning I drove past a clinic clustered with protesters. One day, suddenly, mysteriously, I had the voice of this young girl. *You'd know me if you saw me.* But just who was she? What was her story? I went straight to the University of Buffalo library and wrote the first several pages in a breathless rush, possessed by this character and the need to find out what had happened.

I'm grateful to Lois Rosenthal of *Story* for her ardent support of this piece, and to Holly Hunter for her powerful and evocative reading at Symphony Space.

KIM EDWARDS

YOU'D KNOW ME if you saw me. Maybe not right away. But you'd stop, lots of people do. I bet you'd look back twice at me, and wonder. I'd be an image lingering in your thoughts for days to come, nagging, like a forgotten name on the edge of your mind, like an unwelcome memory twisting up through dreams. Then you'd catch a glimpse of me on television, or gazing at you from a poster as you hurried down the sidewalk, and you'd remember. I'd come into your mind like a vision then, a bright and terrifying light.

Some people see it in an instant. They call out to me and stop me on the street. I have felt their hands, their vivid glances, the demanding pressure of their embraces. They have kissed my fingertips, have fallen to their knees and wept, have clustered around me, drawing the attention of a crowd. Once a girl even grabbed my arm in the parking lot at school. I still remember the darkness in her eyes, the panic clinging to her skin like mist, the way she begged me to give her a blessing, to relieve her of her great sin, as if I had a direct line right to God.

"Hey no," I told her, shrugging her away. "You've got that wrong. You're thinking of my mother."

YOU'VE SEEN my mother too, guaranteed. See her now, the star of the evening news, standing with several hundred other people in a parking lot in Buffalo. It is hot for May, the first fierce blast of summer, and heat waves rise around these people, making them shimmer on the screen. But that, of course, is pure illusion. The truth is, these people never waver, they never miss a step. Theirs is a holy path, a righteous vision, and if they must stand for twelve hours a day in the blinding heat, thirty days in a row, then they will do it like a penance, they will not think twice. This

Buffalo clinic is at the edge of the university, and the protesters with their graphic signs draw increasing crowds. For days we have watched the news clips: ceaseless praying, bottles of red paint splattering brick walls, scared young women being escorted through the hostile crowd by clinic workers in bright vests. Mounting tension, yes, the sharp edges of impending violence, but still it has been a minor protest, something witnessed by motorists on their way to work, then forgotten until the evening news.

It is nothing compared to what will happen now that my mother has arrived.

See her. She is young still, long-boned and slender, with blond hair that swings at the level of her chin. She favors pastels, crisp cottons, skirts that brush against the calf, shirtwaist dresses and sweater sets. On the evening news the cameras pick her out, her pale yellow dress only a few shades darker than her hair, the white collar setting off her tan face, her sapphire eyes. Unlike the others with their signs, their chanting anger, my mother is serene. It is clear right away that while she is with this crowd, she is not of it. Her five assistants, surrounding her tightly like petals on a stamen, guide her slowly to the steps. The banners rustle in the hot wind, fluttering above the famous posters.

See me, then, my sweet smile, my innocence. It is a black-and-white shot, a close-up, taken three years ago when I was just fourteen. My mother strides before these posters, passing in front of one of me after another, and when she pauses alone at the center of the steps, when she turns her face to the cheering crowd and smiles, you can see it. The resemblance was striking even then, and now it is uncanny. In the past three years my cheekbones have become more pronounced, my eyes seem wider. We could, and sometimes do, pass for sisters. My mother waves her hand and starts to speak.

"Fellow sinners," she says, and the crowd roars.

"TURN IT OFF, why don't you?" Sam says. We are sitting together on the sofa, drinking Coca-Cola and eating animal crackers. We've lined the elephants up, trunk to tail, across the coffee table. Sam's eyes are the same deep blue as my mother's, and the dark curls on his head are repeated, again and again, down his wide chest. When I don't answer he turns and presses his hand against my cheek, then kisses me, hard, until I have to pull away from him.

We look at each other for a long moment. When Sam finally speaks, his voice is deliberately grave and pompous, twisting the scriptures to his own advantage.

"Nichola," he says, drawing a finger slowly down my arm. "Your body is such a mystery to me." There is longing in his voice, yes, but his eyes are teasing, testing. He knows I know these verses, the ones my mother always uses to begin. *My body is no mystery to Thee, for Thou didst knit me together in my mother's womb.* He must also know that it seems near sacrilege to me, what he says, the way he says it. And truly I am flushed with his audacity, the breathless danger of his words. I am thrilled with it. Sam watches my face, smiles, runs his hand down my bare arm.

"You know what comes later," I remind him, hearing my mother's voice rising in the background. *"Deliver me from evil men.* Remember?"

He laughs and leans forward to kiss me again, his hand groping for the remote control. I get to it first and sit up straight, keeping a distance between us. I am saving myself, I am trying to, though Sam Rush insists there is no need because one day we will marry.

"Not now," I tell him, inching up the volume. "She's just about to tell the story of my life. It's the best part."

Sam catches my wrist and pulls the remote control from my fingers. The TV snaps off and my mother disappears to where she really is, 257 miles away.

"You're wrong," he says, sliding his hands across my shoulders, pressing his lips against my collarbone.

"What do you mean?"

"That's not the story of your life," he whispers. I feel his breath on my skin, insistent, pressing the words. "This is."

MY MOTHER WORRIES, or ought to. After all, I have her looks, her blond beauty, her narrow hips. I have her inclinations. But my mother has a high and shining faith. This is what she tells me every time she leaves the house. She holds my face in her two hands and says *You'll be good, Nichola, I know that. I have the strongest faith in you, I know you are not a wild girl like I was.*

Well, it is true in a way, I am not a wild girl like she was. Sam Rush is the only boyfriend I have ever had. And for a long time I was even good like she means. Those were the days when she used to take me with her, traveling around the country from one demonstration to another, standing in the rain or snow or blazing heat. There are snapshots of my mother and me from those days. In many of them I am just a toddler perched on her hip, while she squints into the camera, gripping half a banner in her free hand. She wore pantsuits, all creaseless polyester, with wide cuffs at the wrists and ankles. She had maxi-skirts and shiny boots and her hair was long then, falling down her back like the thin silk of corn. For years she was just a part-time protester, like anybody else. But then she got religion, and got famous, all in a single afternoon.

I was five years old that day. I remember it, the heat and the crowd, my mother's pale blue dress, and the way she held me tightly when the preacher started speaking. "Amen," my mother said. "Amen, oh yes, AMEN." I remember the expression on her face, the way her eyes closed shut and her lips parted. I remember how we moved so suddenly toward the steps where the preacher stood with his microphone, leading everyone in prayer. Another moment and we were up there with him. My mother put me down and turned to the crowd. When she took the microphone from the startled preacher and began to speak, something happened. She called my name and touched my hair, and then she said *I am a sinner, I have come here today to tell you about my sin.* People sighed, then, they drew in closer. Their faces filled with rapture.

I know my memory on these points is pure, not a story that was told to me, or one that I saw much later on a film. We have a copy of the newsreel now, down in the archives, and it is still a shock each time I watch it and see how many things I missed. I felt so safe, standing up there with my mother, but I was too young to really understand. I didn't see the anger on the preacher's face as my mother wooed his congregation. I don't remember how the crowd changed beneath her voice and followed her, forming a circle before the clinic doors and lying down. I did not even notice when the police arrived and began hauling them away. But on the film, it happens. My mother and the preacher pray while the circle around them is steadily eroded. I see myself, as the circle shrinks, lifted up and handed blindly into the crowd, to a woman with a patchwork skirt who smelled very clean, like lemons. And then, I see on film the most important thing I missed that day. I see the way my mother rose to power. She stands right by the preacher, praying hard, until just he and she are left. That handsome preacher glances at my mother, this interloper, this surprise. It's clear he's thinking that she will be taken first. He expects her to be humble, to concede the stage to him. My mother sees his look and her voice lifts. She closes her eyes and takes a step back. Just a small step, but it's enough. The police reach the preacher first. He stops praying, startled, when they touch his arm, and suddenly it is just my mother speaking, her eyes open now, sustaining the crowd with the power of her voice alone.

People rise up sometimes, start their lives anew. That day it happened to my mother. She burned pure and rose high above the others, like ash borne lightly on a flame. When they came for her she did not cease her prayers. When they touched her she went limp and heavy in their arms. Her dress swept the ground and her sweet voice lifted, and on the news that night she seemed almost angelic. They carried her away still praying, and the crowd parted like a sea to let her pass.

People rise up, but they fall down too. That preacher, for instance, fell so far that he disappeared completely. Others are famous one month, gone the next. They hesitate when boldness is required, they grow vain and self-important and go too far. Sometimes, they sin. In those days before she rose herself, my mother watched them, and she learned. She is smart, careful, and courageous, and her story gives her power when she steps before a crowd. Still, she says, it is a brutal business we are in. There are always those who would like to see her slip. She trusts no one, except for me.

Which is why, when I hear raised voices in her office one afternoon, I pause in the hallway to listen as they talk.

"No, it's too much," Gary Peterson, her chief assistant says. He is a young man with a thin mustache and a great ambition, a man who is a constant worry to my mother. "If we go that far we'll alienate half the country."

I glimpse my mother, standing behind the desk with her arms folded, frowning. "You saw what happened in Florida," she insists. "A clinic closed, and not a soul arrested."

A cleared throat then, a low and unfamiliar voice I can't quite hear. I know what they are talking about, however. I watched it with my mother on TV. In Florida they piped butyric acid through holes in the clinic walls. Soon everyone spilled out, doctors and nurses, secretaries and patients, vomiting and choking, the building ruined with that smell of sewer gas and rancid meat. My mother watched this happen, amazed and also envious. "That's bold," she said, turning off the TV and pacing across the office. "That's *innovative*. We're losing ground, I'm afraid, with the same old approach. We have to do something stunning before we fade away entirely."

And so I wonder, standing there, what idea she has asked them to consider now.

"It's too risky," another voice insists.

"Is it?" she asks. "When we consider the children who would be rescued?"

"Or lost," Gary Peterson interjects. "If we fail."

They go on. I lean against the wall, listening to their voices, and press my hand against my lips. It smells of Sam, a clean salty smell of skin, the old vinyl of his car. In another week or so my mother goes to Kansas City, and Sam has put it to me clearly: He wants to come and stay with me while she's away. He's going crazy, that's what he says, he can't wait any longer. He says it's now or never. I told him I would think about it, let him know.

"Anyway," I hear Gary Peterson say. "Your plan involves Nichola, who isn't exactly reliable these days."

The men laugh and I go still, feeling myself flush bright with anger. They are talking about a year ago in Albany, about the day Gary Peterson made children block the clinic driveway. "Go on," he said to me, though I was sixteen, older than the others. He put his arm around me. Gary Peterson, tall and strong and slender, with his green eyes and steady smile. I felt his hand on my shoulder. "Go on, Nichola, please, these little boys and girls need someone like you to be a leader." The pavement was hot and dusty, scattered with trash, and the cars barely slowed when they swept in from the street. I was scared. But Gary Peterson was so handsome, so good, and he leaned over and whispered in my ear. "Go on, Nichola," he said. "Be a leader." And he kissed me on the cheek.

I was drawn in then. I remember thinking that my mother was a leader, and I would be one too. Plus I could feel his lips on my skin long after he had stepped away. I looked to where my mother was speaking on the steps. The protest was going very badly, just a few stragglers with signs, and I knew she needed help. And so I did it. I spread myself out on the asphalt in a line with all the others. The sun beat down. Some of the little ones started crying, so I led them in a song. We sang "Onward Christian Soldiers." It was the only song I could remember all the words to. Everyone got excited, and someone called in the TV crews. I could see them arriving from the corner of my eyes, circling us with their black cameras. That film is in the archives now, thirty of us lying there, singing. All those sweet small voices.

The camera crew was well established by the time the first doctor got back from lunch. She cruised into the driveway, determined to speed past the growing group of protesters, and almost ran over the smallest child, who was lying at the end of the row. Her car squealed to a stop near that girl's left arm. She got out of her car, livid and trembling, and went right up to my mother, grabbed her arm. I stopped singing so I could listen. That doctor was so angry.

"What in the name of heaven," she said, "do you think you are doing? If you believe in life, as you claim, then you do not put innocent lives at risk. You do not!"

My mother was calm, in a white dress, angelic. "Close your doors," she said. "Repent. The Lord will forgive even you, a murderess."

"And if I had hit that child?" the doctor demanded. She was a small woman, delicate, with smooth gray hair to her shoulders, and yet she shook my mother's arm with a power born of fury. "If my brakes had failed? Who would have been a murderess then?"

Lying there on the hot asphalt, I saw her point. The others were too little to understand, but I was sixteen, and suddenly I saw the danger very clearly. Other cars were pulling up, and there we were, a pavement of soft flesh. Their tires could flatten us in a second. Gary Peterson was hovering near the cameras, talking to the reporters. More crews had come, and the crowd was growing, and I could see that he was very pleased. If one of us were hit, I thought, we would make the national, maybe the international news. I was suddenly very frightened. I waited for my mother to recognize this, to understand the danger, but she was intent on making her point in front of the doctor and a dozen TV cameras.

"Repent," my mother yelled. "Repent and save the children!"

As she spoke another car drove up, too fast and unsuspecting, and bumped the back of the first. The doctor's car jerked forward a foot, so that the last little girl was lying with her arm against the doctor's tire, the bumper hanging over her face. She was crying hard, but without making a sound, she was so scared. That was when I stood up. "Hey, Nichola." Gary Peterson was shouting, and then he was standing next to me, grabbing my arm. "Get back down," he hissed at me, still smiling. "No one's going to get hurt." But already I could feel him fixing bruises on my arm. "No," I said, "I won't." And when he tried to force me, I screamed. That's all it took—the cameras were on us. He let me go, he had to, and stood there while I helped those children up, one by one, brushed them off, and led them out of danger. We made the national news that night after all. My mother was upset for days, but Gary Peterson, who made the front page of several papers, was quite pleased.

It's because I am so angry that I step into the doorway.

"Nichola!" my mother says. She must see from my face that I have overheard the conversation. She nods at me seriously and asks me to come in. "There you are, honey. Come say hello to Mr. Amherst and Mr. Strand and of course to Gary. They are here to discuss the upcoming work in Kansas City." She glances at them then, and smiles, suddenly calm, almost flirtatious, all the tension gone from her face. "We're having a little disagreement," she adds.

They smile at this small joke, and look soberly at me. We get all kinds of people here, from the real religious freaks to the bored rich ladies from the suburbs, and I can tell which is which by the way they react whenever I show up. The religious people, they get all emotional. They say, *so that's your little girl, your baby that was saved, oh she is sweet.* Some of the ladies even weep to see me, the living embodiment of all their strivings and beliefs. These men, though, are not moved. In fact, they seem uncomfortable, as if I remind them of something they'd rather not know. My mother calls me her secret weapon when dealing with such people. Against these men, with their college degrees, their congregations, their ways of doing things, I am my mother's strength. Because there is no one who can argue when they see me, the walking, talking evidence of my mother's great sacrifice for life.

"Nichola," my mother says softly, glancing at the men. "I wonder if you could help us out."

"Sure," I say. "What do you need?"

"These gentlemen would like to know—just as a sort of general inquiry—exactly what you are prepared to do, Nichola? What I mean to say is that there's some concern, after the incident in Albany, about your level of commitment."

Our eyes meet. I know that I can help her. And even though I feel a little sick, as if a whiff of butyric acid were puffing through the air vents as we speak, I do.

"I'd do whatever I could to help," I say. This is not exactly a lie, I decide.

"Anything?" Gary Peterson repeats. He looks at me hard. "Think about it, Nichola. It's important. You'd do anything we asked?"

I open my mouth to speak, but the next words won't come. I keep remembering the hot asphalt against my back, the little voices singing. My mother's expression is serious now, a frown streaks her forehead. This is a test, and it will hurt her if I fail. I close my eyes, trying to think what to do.

Nichola. I remember Sam's touch, the way his words sometimes have double meanings. *Your body is a mystery to me.*

And then I open my eyes again and look straight at them, because suddenly I know a way to tell the truth, yet still convince them.

"Look," I say. "You know I am His instrument on earth."

Gary's eyes narrow, but my mother smiles and puts her arm around me, a swift triumphant hug, before anyone can speak.

"You see," she says. She is beaming. "I told you we could count on Nichola."

Something shifts in the room, then. Something changes. My mother has won some victory, I don't know what exactly.

"Perhaps you're right," Mr. Amherst says as I am leaving. I hurry, relieved to get away. Whatever they are planning doesn't matter, because I already told my mother I won't go to Kansas City. "Perhaps it would be best to escalate the action, to make an unforgettable impact, as you suggest."

I smile, heading up the stairs. I smile because my mother is winning her argument, thanks to me. And more, I smile because today Sam Rush kissed the inside of my elbows and said that he could not live without me, that the blood is always pounding, pounding in his brain these days. Thanks to me.

"YOU ARE ASKING for trouble with that outfit," my mother says the next day, when Sam drops me off after school.

I flush, wondering if my lips are red, like they feel. Parked in his car, we argued for an hour, and Sam was so angry that I started to get scared. He kissed me at the end of it, so hard I couldn't breathe, and told me to decide tonight, no later. *You love me,* he insisted, gripping my arm like Gary did. *You know you do.*

"Nichola," my mother insists, "that sweater is too tight, and your skirt is too short. It's provocative."

"Everyone dresses this way," I tell her, which is not entirely true.

My mother shakes her head and sighs. "Sit down, Nichola," she says. We are in the kitchen, and she gets up to make some coffee. She looks so ordinary, so much like any other mother might look. It is hard to connect her with the woman on TV who can hold a crowd of thousands enthralled. It is hard to picture her standing on a platform, offering up the story of my life, and hers, to the tired crusaders. For that is when she tells it, when people are growing weary, when the energy begins to lag, when "Amazing Grace" goes terribly off-key and the day is as hot or as cold as it will get. She stands up on the stage then with her hand on my shoulder and says, "This is my daughter Nichola. I want to tell you the story of her life, of how the Lord spoke through her, and thus saved me."

She tells them how it started, how she was young and beautiful and wild, so arrogant that she believed herself immune to the consequences of her sins. From the stage she gives them details to gasp about, how beautiful she was, how drop-dead gorgeous. How many men pursued her and how far she let them go, how high she climbed on the ladder of her ignorance, until the world below seemed nothing but a mirage which never would concern her. They envy her a little, despite themselves, and after a while they begin to hate her just a little too—for her beauty, for the power that it gave her. My mother makes them feel this way on purpose, so that when she tells them of her fall they can shake their heads with secret pleasure, they can murmur to each other that she got what she deserved.

My mother knows her audience. In her weakness lies her strength. She tells them how she wound up a few months later, pregnant of course, abandoned by her family and her friends. They sigh then, they feel her pain, her panic. They understand the loneliness she felt. When my mother flees on a Greyhound bus the crowd is with her. They wander by her side through the darkest corners of an unfamiliar city. She grows fearful, yes, and desperate. They, too, grow numb and lose hope, and finally they climb with her to the top of the tallest building she can find. They stand at the edge, feeling the wind in their hair and the rock-bottom desperation in their hearts, and they swallow as she looks at the city below and prepares herself to jump.

It is such a long way down. She is so afraid. And she, poor sinner, is so beyond herself that she does on impulse what she would never plan: she prays. She whispers words into that wind. She takes another step, still praying. And that is when the miracle occurs.

An ordinary sort of miracle, my mother says, for she heard no voices, saw no visions, experienced no physical transformation. No, on that day the Lord simply spoke to her through me. She tells how she grew dizzy suddenly. From hunger, she thought then, or maybe from the height, but she has realized since that it was nothing less than the hand of grace, a divine and timely intervention. She stumbled and fell against the guard rail, sliding on the wire mesh, scraping her arm. Brightness swirled before her. She put one hand on the cold concrete and the other on her stomach and she closed her eyes against that sudden, rising light. For a moment the world was still, and that was when it happened. A small thing, really. An ordinary thing. Just this: for the first time, she felt me move. A single kick, a small hand flailing. Once, and then again. It was that simple. She opened her eyes and put both hands against her flesh, waiting. Still, as if listening. Yes, again.

At this point she pauses for a moment on the speaker's platform, her head still bowed. Her voice has gone soft and shaky with this story, but now she lifts her slender arms up to the sky and shouts *Hallelujah, on that day the Lord was with me, and intervened, everything was saved.*

"Nichola," my mother says now, sitting down across from me and pouring cream into her coffee. I watch it swirl, brown gold, in her cup. "Nichola, it's not that I don't trust you, baby. But I know about temptation. I know it is great, at your age. Next week I am going to do that mission work in Kansas City, and I want you to come with me. It will be like the old days, Nichola, you and me. We could stop in Chicago on the way home, and go shopping."

She offers this last one because she can read my face, like a mirror face to hers, but with opposite emotions.

"Oh Nichola," she says wistfully. "Why not? We used to have such fun."

She is right, I guess. I used to think it was fun. I sat on the stage with my mother and watched her speak. I felt the pressure of all those eyes, moving from the posters and back to me, as my mother told our story. That was when I was still a kid, though, and it was before the protests got so strong, so ugly.

"Look, I already told you. I'm too busy to go to Kansas City."

"Nichola," she says, an edge of impatience in her voice. "I promised people that you would."

"Well, unpromise them," I say. "They won't care. It's you they come to see."

"Oh, Nichola," she protests. "People always ask for you. Specifically for you."

"I can't," I say. I'm thinking of the heat, the hours of standing in the group of prayer supporters, of the way there is no telling, anymore, what anyone will do. "I'm so busy. I've got a term paper due. The junior prom is in three weeks. I just don't think I can leave all that right now."

"Leave school, or leave Sam?" my mother asks.

I'm starting to blush, I can feel it moving up my cheeks, and my mother is looking at me with her gentle eyes that seem to know everything, everything about me. I fold my arms, my left hand covering the place where Sam held on to me so hard, and then I say the one thing that I know for sure will change the subject.

"You know, I've been wondering about my father again," I tell her.

My mother's face hardens. I watch it happen, imagining my own features growing still and thick like that.

"Nichola," she says. "As far as your father is concerned, you don't exist."

"But he knows about me, right? And don't you think I have a right to meet him?"

"Oh, he knows," she says. "He knows."

She pauses, looking at me with narrowed eyes, the same expression she wore in the office, negotiating about Kansas City with Gary and the others. Her face clears then, and she leans forward with a sigh.

"All right," she says. "What if I told you that you'd get to meet your father, if you come with me to Kansas City?"

"What are you saying?" I ask. Despite myself my heart is beating faster. This is the first time she has ever admitted that he is alive. "Is that where he lives?"

She shrugs. She knows she has my interest now. "Maybe," she says. "He may live there. Or maybe he lives right here, or in another city altogether." She sits back and looks at me. "I don't think that you should meet him, Nichola. I think once you do, you'll wish you hadn't. I'm keeping it from you for your own good, you know. I just don't want you to get hurt."

She waits for me to say what I have said every other time: that she is right, that I don't want to meet him after all.

"All right," she says at last, when I don't speak. "All right then. Here's the deal. Come with me to Kansas City, Nichola. Do exactly what I ask there. And then, I promise, I'll tell you all about him."

I sit still for a moment, tempted, but thinking also of the dense crowds, the stink of sweat in air already thick with hate, with tension. I try to imagine a face for the father I've never known. I think of Sam, of the answer he's expecting, and how afraid I am right now to tell him anything but yes. My mother waits, tapping her fingers against her empty cup. I wonder why she wants so much for me to go. I remember what I promised in her office.

"I don't want to do anything . . . anything terrible," I tell her. I say this so stupidly, but my mother understands. Her face softens.

"Oh Nichola," she says. "Is that what this is about? I know how much you hated that business with Gary. It won't be anything like that, I promise you." She leans forward and puts her hand on my arm, speaking in a confidential voice. I can smell the coffee on her breath, her flowery perfume. "It's true I need you to do something, Nichola. Something special. But it's not a terrible thing, and anyway it's more that I just need your support, hon. It's going to be big, this protest. The very biggest yet. It would mean such a lot to me if you were there."

It is because she asks like this that I can't say no. I hesitate. That is my mistake.

She gives me the smile she uses for the cameras, and pushes back the chair, stands up.

"Thank you," she says. "I prayed for this. You won't regret it, honey."

It's true that for a few minutes I feel good. It's only when she's gone that I realize how much I have given, how little I have gained. It's only then that the first slow burn of my anger begins.

MY MOTHER'S BEDROOM is done in rose and cream. A few years ago, when she started getting paid a lot to do Christian TV talk shows, she hired a decorator to redesign the whole house with a professional look. The decorator was one of those angular women with severe tastes, and you can see her mark everywhere else— black-and-white motifs, tubular furniture, everything modern and businesslike. It's only my mother's room that is different, soft, with layers of pillows and white carpet so thick it feels as though you are walking on a cloud. Sometimes I close my eyes and imagine I could fall right through. I wonder if this is how my mother thinks of heaven, a room like white chocolate with a strawberry nougat center.

I know where she keeps things. I have sat on her bed, amid a dozen quilted and ruffled pillows, and watched her paste newspaper photos into her private scrapbook. She trusts me, the one person in her life she says she can trust, and I would not have imagined that I'd dig into her secrets.

Still, when my mother leaves the next day, when she phones me from downtown and I know for sure she is safely away, I go into her bedroom. I know just where to look. The box is in the closet, wedged into the corner, and I pull it out from beneath my mother's dresses. It smells of her perfume. I untie the string and lift the things out carefully, the scrapbooks and the yearbooks, the photos and the letters. I note their order. I arrange them precisely on the carpet.

At first I am so excited that I can barely concentrate. I pick up each letter feeling lucky, as if the secrets inside are giving off a kind of heat. In fact, however, I find absolutely nothing, and soon enough my excitement begins to fade. Still, I keep on looking, pausing only once when the phone rings and Sam's voice floats into the room on the answering machine. "Nichola," he says. "I'm sorry. You know you are everything to me." I listen, holding still, feeling shaky. I told him not to call today. I listen, but I don't pick up the phone. Once he hangs up I go back to the papers on the floor.

I read. I sort. I skim. Much of it is boring. I sift through a pile of checkbooks, old receipts, a stack of unsorted pictures of people I have never met. I shuffle through the letters from her fans. It's just by chance that I see the one that matters. The handwriting is so like mine, so like my mother's, that I stop. I turn it over twice, feeling the cool linen paper in my hands, the neat slit across the top. I slide the letter out, and money, two hundred dollars in twenty-dollar bills, falls into my lap. I unfold the paper slowly, and then I begin to tremble as I read.

I don't know if you got my other letters. I can only hope that they have reached you. I don't understand why you would do this, run off without a word. Yes, we were upset at your news but we are your family. We will stand by you. I am sending money and I am begging you, Valarie, to come home. I cannot bear to think about you out there in the world with our little grandbaby, in need of anything.

I put the letter down and finger the bills, old, still crisp. My mother told me that they kicked her out, that they severed ties with her forever. At least, that is what she always says, speaking to the crowd, how she begged them to forgive her and they would not. How she was cast out into the world for her sins, alone to wander. I came up here looking for my father, but I sit instead for a long time with that letter in my lap, wondering about my grandparents, who they are and where, and whether or not they have ever seen me on TV. Sam phones again. I hear the longing in his voice, the little flares of anger too, and I do not answer. Instead, I read that letter again, and yet again. The return address is smeared, difficult to decipher, but the postmark helps: it was sent from Seattle, and dated six months after I was born. Seattle, a place that I have never been. I put the letter aside and go through everything again. I look hard, but there is nothing else from them.

I am still sitting there a long time later, studying that letter, when the fax comes through. There's a business line downstairs, but my mother keeps this one for sensitive communications that she does not want her secretary—or Gary Peterson—to see. It has never occurred to me that she might not want me to see them either, so when it falls from the machine I'm hardly even curious. I'm still thinking about the grandparents I always thought disowned us. I'm trying to figure out how I can find them. I scan the fax, which is from Kansas City. It starts out with the usual stuff, hotel reservations and demonstration times, and I'm about to toss it down when I see this line:

So glad that Nichola has seen the light at last.

What light?

I read. The words seem to shift and change shape beneath my eyes. As with the letter, I have to read it several times before I can get the meaning straight and clear in my mind. I'm sure that in all my life I have never read so slowly, or been so scared. For in my hands I have their plans for Kansas City. The usual plans at first, and then references to their bold plan too, the one that will keep them in the news. I can see at last why my mother needs so much for me to join them. Like pieces of white ice, her lies melt clear in my hands, and suddenly I see her true intentions. What did she promise me? *It's a small thing, not terrible, not at all.* But it is terrible. Oh yes. It's the worst thing yet.

Suddenly the room seems so sweet to me, stifling, that I have to get out. I feel I am inhaling sugar, and it hurts. I leave the fax on the carpet with the other papers, and outside I lean against the narrow black banister, breathing deeply. I am so grateful for the clean lines, the clarity, the sudden black and white. Because it is obvious to me now that what I have taken to be the story of my life is not that at all. It is not my life, but my mother's life, her long anger and relentless ambition, that has brought us to this moment, to where we are.

KANSAS CITY SWELTERS in the heat, and every day my mother speaks of sin, her voice a flaming arrow. The crowd listens and ignites. The National Guard spills out of trucks and the nation waits, to see how this protest, the longest and ugliest in the history of the movement, will end. I wait too, watching from the fringes as she steps from her cluster of bodyguards, smiling shyly at the crowd, which cheers, enraptured, ready to believe. *I am just a sinner,* she begins, softly, and I look right at her as the crowd responds; I whisper *that's right, you are a sinner and a manipulating liar too.* She goes on speaking to the nation. I watch her, as if for the first time; I see and even admire her skill at this, her poise. For the very first time I see her clearly. I watch her, and I wait to see if she will make me do this evil thing.

It is on the third day that she leaves the stage and comes to me. It is late afternoon and her face is tanned dark. There is sweat on her forehead and above her upper lip. When she puts her arm around me her skin feels slick. She seems tired, but exhilarated too, for the protest is going very well. *Don't ask,* I think. Maybe she just wants to go for dinner. *Please, don't ask.*

"Come on, Nichola," she says. "It's time for you to do that favor."

We take two cars, the one with me and Gary and my mother, the second with tinted windows and three men I've never met. We drive for a long time, it seems, maybe half an hour, and as we reach the suburbs they tell me what they want me to do. It is, as my mother said, a simple task, and if I did not know better I would do it without flinching, I would not think twice.

"Okay, Nichola," Gary says, stopping on a suburban block where lawn sprinklers are hissing against the sidewalks and the trees are large and quiet. The other car parks in front of us. "It's about a block down, number 3489. She comes out every night at 8:30 to walk the dog. You know what to say?"

"Yes," I tell them, swallowing hard. "I know."

"Good luck," my mother says. "We'll be praying."

"Yes," I say, getting out of the car. "I know."

I walk slowly through the dying sunlight, feeling their eyes on me. Number 3489 is big but ordinary, with fake white pillars and a wide lawn, flower beds. There is no sign of a teenage girl. I keep walking, but slowly, because I am scared and because I do not know yet what I'm going to do. Behind me in the car my mother trusts that I will keep my word, and before me in the house the doctor and his family finish dinner, do the dishes, glad that today, at least, no protesters have gathered on the lawn. You can see where the flowers are all crushed from other times. There are bars on the lower windows, too. In a few minutes the daughter will come out of the house with her Scottish terrier on a leash and take him for a walk. My job is simple. I must walk with her, make her pause, and talk to her. About the dog, about videos, about anything that will distract her so she doesn't see them coming. That is all. Such a small thing they have asked of me, a five-minute conversation. They have not told me the rest, but I know.

At the end of the block I pause, turn around, start back. It is 8:35 and I can see the sun glinting off the chrome edges of the two parked cars. This time when I near the house two people are outside, on the lawn. I hesitate by the hedge. A man is squatting by his car, soaping up the sides. A bucket and a hose lie next to him on the ground. The car is old and kind of beat up, too, more like Sam's car than my mother's. On the thick grass a small white dog is running here and there, sniffing at bushes and spots in the lawn, while the young girl whistles and calls to him. The dog's name is Benjy. I do not know the girl's name, though her father is Dr. Sinclair. At the demonstration they emphasize his name. *Sin*clair, *Sin*clair. His daughter has short hair and is wearing a T-shirt, shorts, and sneakers. She is holding a leash in her hand.

Suddenly, her father, who has been washing the car with his hose, stands up and sprays a little water at her back. She shouts out in surprise, then turns around, laughing, letting the water rain down around her. The little dog runs over, jumping up, trying to get in on the fun, and suddenly I wonder what it would be like to be that girl, to have grown up in this ordinary house. I know I should walk away, but I can't. I can't get enough of looking at them. In fact, I stare so long and so hard that the father finally sees me. Our eyes meet and he turns his head, suddenly alert. I start walking across the lawn then, trying not to think.

"Hi," I say, when I get close enough.

"Hi," the girl says, looking at me curiously. Her father smiles, thinking I'm a friend of hers. I had this idea that they would know me right away, like I know them. I thought that they would look at me and see my mother, but they don't. They just stare. I'm so surprised by this that for a moment I can't think of what to say. So I just stand there, looking at this doctor. I have only seen him from afar, as he darted from his car into the clinic. Now I notice how small his ears are, how many wrinkles there are around his eyes. His smile fades as the silence grows between us. He takes a small but perceptible step closer to his daughter.

"Can we help you?" he asks. Despite his wariness, he is kind.

"Look," I say. I glance back at the road and then reach up and release my hair, shake it out to my shoulders. They ought to know me now, it should strike their faces like ice water. They should turn and flee without another word from me. But they do not. The doctor gives me an odd look, true, and glances past me then, to the quiet street, the row of bushes that hides his house. There is nothing there. Not yet. They are waiting. He looks back at me, and after a long moment more, he speaks.

"What is it?" he asks. His voice is very gentle.

His daughter picks up the little dog and smiles at me, to help me speak. She is younger than I am. I think about how they want to shove her into the back of the second car and drive away. A few hours in a dark place, and then they'll let her go. They don't want to hurt her, though I'm sure they are prepared for anything to happen. Scare her yes, they want to do that. They intend to show her the wrath of the heavens, and to this end the men in the car are waiting with their ski masks and their Bibles. Perhaps she will be saved, but that's not the point. What they really want is to terrify her father, to make him repent for the lives that he has taken. They want the world to know that there are no limits in this battle.

I look straight at the doctor then. I don't smile. "Dr. Sinclair," I say. "You should know better than to trust a stranger. It's very dangerous. Especially tonight. I wouldn't walk that dog."

I'm ready to say more, but he understands at last. He reaches for his daughter, and they hurry to the house, leaving the bucket of water, the hose still running. I see the front door close and hear it lock behind them, and I wonder if they watch from their barred windows as I walk through their backyard to the alley, then out of sight. I walk for miles like this, between the quiet yards of strangers, and when it's finally dark I get on the first city bus that I see.

It's hard to do this. I know I'm leaving everything behind. My mother and Sam, my whole life until this day. But it was not really my life, I know that now, it was always just the reflections of the lives of other people. I finger the letter my grandmother wrote, the money folded neatly. Seventeen years is a long time. They may not be there anymore. They may not want to see me if they are. But it is the only place I can imagine to begin.

Already, though, I miss my mother. I will always miss her, the force of her persuasion, her strong will. I wonder how long she will wait before she realizes that I've failed her, that I've gone. Outside the window Kansas City rushes past. The air is black and hot, and sprinklers hiss against the sidewalks. The bus travels fast, a lean gray shadow between the streetlights, and elsewhere in the dark Sam gives up on me and turns away. I imagine that my mother waits much longer. It seems to me I know the exact moment when she finally sees the truth. She sighs, and presses her hands against her face. Gary Peterson starts the car without another word. They drive off, and at that moment I suddenly feel the pressure ease. The other people on the bus don't notice, but all this time I have been growing lighter and emptier, until at last I feel myself emerge.

See me then, for the first time.

You do not know me.

I am just a young woman, passing through your life like the wind.

A STUDENT OF MINE at Iowa once explained that her paper was going to be late because she was working on a special project for homecoming: a ten-foot-high Hawkeye head, this was, made out of corn kernels. I can't remember whether I gave her an extension, and I don't think I ever saw the completed product, her pièce de résistance. But whenever I am at work on a novel, I think of that student and picture her patiently gluing on corn kernels. How many kernels did it take to do that Hawkeye? Thousands? Tens of thousands? Millions? As I write along, I am always struck at how little I knew about the novel-writing enterprise, back at Iowa—so little that I did not recognize that student, with her fanatical patience, as kin.

Partly this is because I was strictly a story writer at the time and knew only the galloping joy and quick arrival of the short story. Now I know both pleasures—the brave haul of long work and the hop-around-the-block of short—and find that each is made sweeter by the other. I wrote "Birthmates" on a break from my second novel, *Mona in the Promised Land*—and what a break it was. Even now I can remember how beautifully that story seemed to lay itself out, and how sorry I was to finish it; I returned to *Mona* with no small reluctance. The novel was less daunting an enterprise for having been neglected a while, though, and I found that although I had many corn kernels to go, I could suddenly at least see—eureka!—where they all went.

GISH JEN

GISH JEN

Birthmates

THIS WAS WHAT responsibility meant in a dinosaur industry, toward the end of yet another quarter of bad-to-worse news: You called the travel agent back, and even though there was indeed an economy room in the hotel where the conference was being held, a room overlooking the cooling towers, you asked if there wasn't something still cheaper. And when Marie the new girl came back with something amazingly cheap, you took it—only to discover, as Art Woo was discovering now, that the doors were locked after nine o'clock. The neighborhood had looked not great but not bad, and the building itself, regular enough. Brick, four stories, a rolled-up awning. A bright-lit hotel logo, with a raised-plastic, smiling sun. But there was a kind of crossbar rigged across the inside of the glass door, and that was not at all regular. A two-by-four, it appeared, wrapped in rust-colored carpet. Above this, inside the glass, hung a small gray sign. If the taxi had not left, Art might not have rung the buzzer, as per the instructions.

But the taxi had indeed left, and the longer Art huddled on the stoop in the clumpy December snow, the emptier and more poorly lit the street appeared. His buzz was answered by an enormous black man wearing a neck brace. The shoulder seams of the man's blue waffle-weave jacket were visibly straining; around the brace was tied a necktie, which reached only a third of the way down his chest. All the same, it was neatly fastened together with a hotel-logo tie tack about two inches from the bottom. The tie tack was smiling; the man was not. He held his smooth, round face perfectly expressionless, and he lowered his gaze at every opportunity—not so that it was rude, but so that it was clear he wasn't selling anything to anybody. Regulation tie, thought Art, regulation jacket. He wondered if the man would turn surly soon enough.

For Art had come to few conclusions about life in his thirty-eight years, but this was one of them—that men turned surly when their clothes didn't fit them. This man, though, belied the rule. He was courteous, almost formal in demeanor; and if the lobby seemed not only too small for him, like his jacket, but also too much like a bus station, what with its smoked mirror wall, and its linoleum, and its fake wood, and its vending machines, what did that matter to Art? The sitting area looked as though it was in the process of being cleaned—the sixties Scandinavian chairs and couch and coffee table were pulled every which way, as if by someone hellbent on the dust balls. Still, Art proceeded with his check-in. He was going with his gut here. Here, as in any business situation, he was looking foremost at the personnel; and the man with the neck brace had put him at some ease. It wasn't until after Art had taken his credit card back that he noticed, above the check-out desk, a wooden plaque from a neighborhood association. He squinted at its brass face plate: FEWEST CUSTOMER INJURIES, 1972–73.

What about the years since '73? Had the hotel gotten more dangerous since then, or had other hotels gotten safer? Maybe neither. For all he knew, the neighborhood association had dissolved and was no longer distributing plaques. Art reminded himself that in life, some signs were no signs. It's what he used to tell his ex-wife, Lisa—Lisa who loved to read everything into everything; Lisa who was attuned. She left him on a day when she saw a tree get split by lightning. Of course, that was an extraordinary thing to see. An event of a lifetime. Lisa said the tree had sizzled. He wished he had seen it, too. But what did it mean, except that the tree had been the tallest in the neighborhood, and was no longer? It meant nothing; ditto with the plaque. Art made his decision, which perhaps was not the right decision. Perhaps he should have looked for another hotel.

But it was late—on the way out, his plane had sat on the runway, just sat and sat, as if it were never going to take off—and God only knew what he would have ended up paying if he had relied on a cabbie to simply bring him somewhere else. Forget twice—it could have been three, four times what he would have paid for that room with the view of the cooling towers, easy. At this hour, after all, and that was a conference rate.

So he double-locked his door instead. He checked behind the hollow-core doors of the closet, and under the steel-frame bed, and also in the swirly green shower-stall unit. He checked behind the seascapes, to be sure there weren't any peepholes. That *Psycho*—how he wished he'd never seen that movie. Why hadn't anyone ever told him that movies could come back to haunt you? No one had warned him. The window opened onto a fire escape; not much he could do about that except check the window locks, big help that those were—a sure deterrent for the subset of all burglars that was burglars too skittish to break glass. Which was what percent of intruders, probably? Ten percent? Fifteen? He closed the drapes, then decided he would be more comfortable with the drapes open. He wanted to be able to see what approached, if anything did. He unplugged the handset of his phone from the rest, a calculated risk. On the one hand, he wouldn't be able to call the police if there was an intruder. On the other, he would be armed. He had read somewhere a story about a woman who threw the handset of her phone at an attacker, and killed him. Needless to say, there had been some luck involved in that eventuality. Still, Art thought (a) surely he could throw as hard as that woman, and (b) even without the luck, his throw would most likely be hard enough to at least slow up an intruder. Especially since this was an old handset, the hefty kind that made you feel the seriousness of human communication. In a newer hotel, he probably would have had a new phone, with lots of buttons he would never use but which would make him feel he had many resources at his disposal. In the hotel where the conference was, there were probably buttons for the health club, and for the concierge, and for the three restaurants, and for room service. He tried not to think about this as he went to sleep, clutching the handset.

He did not sleep well.

In the morning he debated whether to take the handset with him into the elevator. Again he wished he hadn't seen so many movies. It was movies that made him think, that made him imagine things like, *What if in the elevator?* Of course, a handset was an awkward thing to hide. It wasn't like a knife, say, that could be whipped out of nowhere. Even a pistol at least fit in a guy's pocket. Whereas a telephone handset did not. All the same, he brought it with him. He tried to carry it casually, as if he were going out for a run and using it for a hand weight, or as if he were in the telephone business.

He strode down the hall. Victims shuffled; that's what everybody said. A lot of mugging had to do with nonverbal cues, which is why Lisa used to walk tall after dark, sending vibes. For this he used to tease her. If she was so worried, she should lift weights and run, the way he did; that, he maintained, was the substantive way of helping oneself. She had agreed. For a while they had met after work at the gym. That was before she dropped a weight on her toe and decided she preferred to sip piña coladas and watch. Naturally, he grunted on. But to what avail? Who could appreciate his pectorals through his suit and overcoat? Pectorals had no deterrent value, that was what he was thinking now. And he was, though not short, not tall. He continued striding. Sending vibes. He was definitely going to eat in the dining room of the hotel where the conference was being held, he decided. What's more, he was going to have a full American breakfast, with bacon and eggs, none of this Continental breakfast bullshit.

In truth, he had always considered the sight of men eating croissants slightly ridiculous, especially at the beginning, when for the first bite they had to maneuver the point of the crescent into their mouths. No matter what a person did, he ended up with an asymmetrical mouthful of pastry, which he then had to relocate with his tongue to a more central location, and this made him look less purposive than he might. Also, croissants were more apt than other breakfast foods to spray little flakes all over one's clean dark suit. Art himself had accordingly never ordered a croissant in any working situation, and he believed that attention to this sort of detail was how it was that he had not lost his job like so many of his colleagues.

This was, in other words, how it was that he was still working in his fitfully dying industry, and was now carrying a telephone handset with him into the elevator. Art braced himself as the elevator doors opened slowly, jerkily, in the low-gear manner of elevator doors in the Third World. He strode in, and was surrounded by, of all things, children. Down in the lobby, too, there were children, and here and there, women he knew to be mothers by their looks of dogged exasperation. A welfare hotel! He laughed out loud. Almost everyone was black, the white children stood out like little missed opportunities of the type that made Art's boss throw his tennis racket across the room. Of course, the racket was always in its padded protective cover and not in much danger of getting injured, though the person in whose vicinity it was aimed sometimes was. Art once suffered what he rather hoped would turn out to be a broken nose, but was only a bone bruise with so little skin discoloration that people had a hard time believing the incident had actually taken place. Yet it had. *Don't talk to me about fault, bottom line it's you Japs who are responsible for this whole fucking mess,* his boss had said—this though what was the matter with min-icomputers, really, was personal computers. A wholly American phenomenon. And of course, Art could have sued over this incident if he could have proved that it had happened. Some people, most notably Lisa, thought he certainly ought to have at least quit.

But he didn't sue and he didn't quit. He took his tennis racket on the nose, so to speak, and when the next day his boss apologized for losing control, Art said he understood. And when his boss said that Art shouldn't take what he said personally, in fact he knew Art was not a Jap, but a Chink, plus he had called someone else a lazy wop just that morning, it was just his style, Art said again that he understood. And then Art said that he hoped his boss would remember Art's great understanding come promotion time. Which his boss did, to Art's satisfaction. In Art's view, this was a victory. In Art's view, he had perceived leverage where others would only perceive affront. He had maintained a certain perspective.

But this certain perspective was, in addition to the tree, why Lisa left him. He thought of that now, the children underfoot, his handset in hand. So many children. It was as if he were seeing before him all the children he would never have. He stood a moment, paralyzed; his heart lost its muscle. A child in a red running suit ran by, almost grabbed the handset out of Art's grasp; then another, in a brown jacket with a hood. He looked up to see a group of grade-school boys arrayed about the seating area, watching. Already he had become the object of a dare, apparently—there was so little else in the way of diversion in the lobby—and realizing this, he felt renewed enough to want to laugh again. When a particularly small child swung by in his turn—a child of maybe five or six, small enough to be wearing snowpants—Art almost tossed the handset to him, but thought better of the idea. Who wanted to be charged for a missing phone?

As it was, Art wondered if he shouldn't put the handset back in his room rather than carry it around all day. For what was he going to do at the hotel where the conference was, check it? He imagined himself running into Billy Shore—that was his counterpart at Info-Edge, his competitor in the insurance market. A man with no management ability, and no technical background either. But he could offer customers a personal computer option, which Art could not; and what's more, Billy had been a quarterback in college. This meant he strutted around as though it still mattered that he had connected with his tight end in the final minutes of what Art could not help but think of as the Wilde-Beastie game. And it meant that Billy was sure to ask him, *What are you doing with a phone in your hand? Talking to yourself again?* Making everyone around them laugh.

Billy was that kind of guy. He had come up through sales, and was always cracking a certain type of joke—about drinking, or sex, or how much the wife shopped. Of course, he never used those words. He never called things by their plain names. He always talked in terms of knocking back some brewskis, or running the triple option, or doing some damage. He made assumptions as though it were a basic bodily function: of course his knowledge was the common knowledge. Of course people understood what it was that he was referring to so delicately. *Listen, champ,* he said, putting his arm around you. If he was smug, it was in an affable kind of way. *So what do you think the poor people are doing tonight?* Billy not only spoke what Art called Mainstreamese, he spoke such a pure dialect of it that Art once asked him if he realized that he was a pollster's delight. He spoke the thoughts of thousands, Art told him, he breathed their very words. Naturally, Billy did not respond, except to say, *What's that?* and turn away. He rubbed his torso as he turned, as if ruffling his chest hairs through the long-staple cotton. Primate behavior, Lisa used to call this. It was her belief that neckties evolved in order to check this very motion, uncivilized as it was. She also believed that this was the sort of thing you never saw Asian men do—at least not if they were brought up properly.

Was that true? Art wasn't so sure. Lisa had grown up on the West Coast, she was full of Asian consciousness; whereas all he knew was that no one had so much as smiled politely at his pollster remark. On the other hand, the first time Art was introduced to Billy, and Billy said, *Art Woo, how's that for a nice Pole-ack name,* everyone broke right up in great rolling guffaws. Of course, they laughed the way people laughed at conferences, which was not because something was really funny, but because it was part of being a good guy, and because they didn't want to appear to have missed their cue.

The phone, the phone. If only Art could fit it in his briefcase! But his briefcase was overstuffed; it was always overstuffed; really, it was too bad he had the slim silhouette type, and hard-side besides. Italian. That was Lisa's doing, she thought the fatter kind made him look like a salesman. Not that there was really anything the matter with that, in his view. Billy Shore notwithstanding, sales were important. But she was the liberal arts type, Lisa was, the type who did not like to think about money, but only about her feelings. Money was not money to her, but support, and then a means of support much inferior to hand-holding or other forms of finger play. She did not believe in a modern-day economy, in which everyone played a part in a large and complex whole that introduced efficiencies that at least theoretically raised everyone's standard of living. She believed in expressing herself. Also in taking classes, and in knitting. There was nothing, she believed, like taking a walk in the autumn woods wearing a hand-knit sweater. Of course, she did look beautiful in them, especially the violet ones. That was her color—Asians are winters, she always said—and sometimes she liked to wear the smallest smidgeon of matching violet eyeliner, even though it was, as she put it, less than organic to wear eyeliner on a hike.

Little Snowpants ran at Art again, going for the knees—*a tackle,* thought Art, as he went down; Red Running Suit snatched away the handset and went sprinting off, triumphant. Teamwork! The children chortled together; how could Art not smile a little, even if they had gotten his overcoat dirty? He brushed himself off, ambled over.

"Hey, guys," he said. "That was some move back there."

"Ching chang polly wolly wing wong," said Little Snowpants.

"Now, now, that's no way to talk," said Art.

"Go to hell!" Brown Jacket pulled at the corners of his eyes to make them slanty.

"Listen up," said Art. "I'll make you a deal." Really he only meant to get the handset back, so as to avoid getting charged for it.

But the next thing he knew, something had hit his head with a crack, and he was out.

LISA HAD LEFT in a more or less amicable way. She had not called a lawyer, or a mover; she had simply pressed his hands with both of hers and, in her most California voice, said, *Let's be nice.* And then she had asked him if he wouldn't help her move her boxes, at least the heavy ones that really were too much for her. He had helped. He had carried the heavy boxes, and also the less heavy ones. Being a weight lifter, after all. He had sorted books and rolled glasses into pieces of newspaper, feeling all the while like a statistic. A member of the modern age, a story for their friends to rake over, and all because he had not gone with Lisa to her grieving group. Or at least that was the official beginning of the trouble; probably the real beginning had been when Lisa—no, *they*—had trouble getting pregnant. When they decided to, as the saying went, do infertility. Or had he done the deciding, as Lisa later maintained? He had thought it was a joint decision, though it was true that he had done the analysis that led to the joint decision. He had been the one to figure the odds, to do the projections. He had drawn the decision tree, according to whose branches they had nothing to lose by going ahead.

Neither one of them had realized then how much would be involved—the tests, the procedures, the drugs, the ultrasounds. Lisa's arms were black and blue from having her blood drawn every day, and before long he was giving practice shots to an orange, that he might prick her some more. He was telling her to take a breath so that on the exhale he could poke her in the buttocks. This was no longer practice, and neither was it like poking an orange. The first time, he broke out in such a sweat that his vision blurred and he had to blink, with the result that he pulled the needle out slowly and crookedly, occasioning a most unorangelike cry. The second time, he wore a sweatband. Later he jabbed her like nothing; her ovaries swelled to the point where he could feel them through her jeans.

He still had the used syringes—snapped in half and stored, as per their doctor's recommendation, in plastic soda bottles. She had left him those. Bottles of medical waste, to be disposed of responsibly, meaning that he was probably stuck with them, ha-ha, for the rest of his life. A little souvenir of this stage of their marriage, his equivalent of the pile of knit goods she had to show for the ordeal; for through it all, she had knit, as if to gently demonstrate an alternative use of needles. Sweaters, sweaters, but also baby blankets, mostly to give away, only one or two to keep. She couldn't help herself. There was anesthesia, and egg harvesting, and anesthesia and implanting, until she finally did get pregnant, twice, and then a third time she went to four and a half months before they found a problem. On the amnio, it showed up, brittle bone disease—a genetic abnormality such as could happen to anyone.

He steeled himself for another attempt; she grieved. And this was the difference between them, that he saw hope still, some feeble, skeletal hope, where she saw loss. She called the fetus her baby, though it was not a baby, just a baby-to-be, as he tried to say; as even the grieving-group facilitator tried to say. She said he didn't understand, couldn't possibly understand, it was something you understood with your body, and it was not his body but hers that knew the baby, loved the baby, lost the baby. In the grieving class the women agreed. They commiserated. They bonded, subtly affirming their common biology by doing 85 percent of the talking. The room was painted mauve—a feminine color that seemed to support them in their process. At times it seemed that the potted palms were female, too, nodding, nodding, though really their sympathy was just rising air from the heating vents. Other husbands started missing sessions—they never talked, anyway, you hardly noticed their absence—and finally he missed some also. One, maybe two, for real reasons, nothing cooked up. But the truth was, as Lisa sensed, that he thought she had lost perspective. They could try again, after all. What did it help to despair? Look, they knew they could get pregnant and, what's more, sustain the pregnancy. That was progress. But she was like an island in her grief, a retreating island, if there was such a thing, receding to the horizon of their marriage, and then to its vanishing point.

OF COURSE, he had missed her terribly at first; now he missed her still, but more sporadically. At odd moments, for example now, waking up in a strange room with ice on his head. He was lying on an unmade bed just like the bed in his room, except that everywhere around it were heaps of what looked to be blankets and clothes. The only clothes on a hanger were his jacket and overcoat; these hung neatly, side by side, in the otherwise empty closet. There was also an extra table in this room, with a two-burner hot plate, a pan on top of that, and a pile of dishes. A brown cube refrigerator. The drapes were closed; a chair had been pulled up close to him; the bedside light was on. A woman was leaning into its circle, mopping his brow. *Don't you move, now.* She was the shade of black Lisa used to call mochaccino, and she was wearing a blue flowered apron. Kind eyes, and a long face—the kind of face where you could see the muscles of the jaw working alongside the cheekbone. An upper lip like an archery bow, and a graying Afro, shortish. She smelled of smoke. Nothing unusual except that she was so very thin, about the thinnest person he had ever seen, and yet she was cooking something—burning something, it smelled like, though maybe it was just a hair fallen onto the heating element. She stood up to tend the pan. The acrid smell faded. He saw powder on the table. It was white, a plastic bagful. His eyes widened. He sank back, trying to figure out what to do. His head pulsed. Tylenol, he needed, two. Lisa always took one because she was convinced the dosages recommended were based on large male specimens; and though she had never said that she thought he ought to keep it to one also, not being so tall, he was adamant about taking two. Two, two, two. He wanted his drugs, he wanted them now. And his own drugs, that was, not somebody else's.

"Those kids kind of rough," said the woman. "They getting to that age. I told them one of these days somebody gonna get hurt, and sure enough, they knocked you right out. You might as well been hit with a bowling ball. I never saw anything like it. We called the man, but they got other things on their mind besides to come see about trouble here. Nobody shot, so they went on down to the Dunkin' Donuts. They know they can count on a ruckus there." She winked. "How you feeling? That egg hurt?"

He felt his head. A lump sat right on top of it, incongruous as something left by a glacier. What were those called, those stray boulders you saw perched in hair-raising positions? On cliffs?

"I feel like I died and came back to life head-first," he said.

"I'm going make you something nice. Make you feel a whole lot better."

"Uh," said Art. "If you don't mind, I'd rather just have a Tylenol. You got any Tylenol? I had some in my briefcase. If I still have my briefcase."

"Your what?"

"My briefcase," said Art again, with a panicky feeling. "Do you know what happened to my briefcase?"

"Oh, it's right by the door. I'll get it, don't move."

And then there it was, his briefcase, its familiar hard-sided, Italian slenderness resting right on his stomach. He clutched it. "Thank you," he whispered.

"You need help with that thing?"

"No," said Art, but when he opened the case, it slid, and everything spilled out—his notes, his files, his papers. All that figuring—how strange his concerns looked here, on this brown shag carpet.

"Here," said the woman, and again—"I'll get it, don't move"—as gently, beautifully, she gathered up all the folders and put them in the case. There was an odd, almost practiced finesse to her movements; the files could have been cards in a card dealer's hands. "I used to be a nurse," she explained, as if reading his mind. "I picked up a few folders in my time. Here's the Tylenol."

"I'll have two."

"Course you will," she said. "Two Tylenol and some hot milk with honey. Hope you don't mind the powdered, we just got moved here, we don't have no supplies. I used to be a nurse, but I don't got no milk and I don't got no Tylenol, my guests got to bring their own. How you like that."

Art laughed as much as he could. "You got honey, though, how's that?"

"I don't know, it got left here by somebody," said the nurse. "Hope there's nothing growing in it."

Art laughed again, then let her help him sit up to take his pills. The nurse—her name was Cindy—plumped his pillows. She administered his milk. Then she sat— very close to him, it seemed—and chatted amiably about this and that. How she wasn't going to be staying at the hotel for too long, how her kids had had to switch schools, how she wasn't afraid to take in a strange, injured man. After all, she grew up in the projects, she could take care of herself. She showed him her switchblade, which had somebody's initials carved on it, she didn't know whose. She had never used it, she said, somebody gave it to her. And that somebody didn't know whose initials those were, either, she said, at least so far as she knew. Then she lit a cigarette and smoked while he told her first about his conference and then about how he had ended up at the hotel by mistake. He told her the latter with some hesitation, hoping he wasn't offending her. But she wasn't offended. She laughed with a cough, emitting a series of smoke puffs.

"Sure must've been a shock," she said. "Land up in a place like this. This no place for a nice boy like you."

That stung a little. *Boy!* But more than the stinging, he felt something else. "What about you? It's no place for you, either, you and your kids."

"Maybe so," she said. "But that's how the Almighty planned it, right? You folk rise up while we set and watch." She said this with so little rancor, with something so like intimacy, that it almost seemed an invitation of sorts.

BUT MAYBE HE WAS KIDDING HIMSELF. Maybe he was assuming things, just like Billy Shore, just like men throughout the ages. Projecting desire where there was none, assigning and imagining, and in juicy detail. Being Asian didn't exempt him from that. *You folk.* Art was late, but it didn't much matter. This conference was being held in conjunction with a much larger conference, the real draw; the idea being that maybe between workshops and on breaks, the conferees would drift down and see what minicomputers could do for them. That mostly meant lunch.

In the meantime, things were totally dead, allowing Art to appreciate just how much the trade show floor had shrunk—down to a fraction of what it had been in previous years, and the booths were not what they had been, either. It used to be that the floor was crammed with the fanciest booths on the market; Art's used to be twenty by twenty. It took days to put together. Now you saw blank spots on the floor where exhibitors didn't even bother to show up, and those weren't even as demoralizing as some of the makeshift jobbies—exhibit booths that looked like high school science fair projects. They might as well have been made out of cardboard and Magic Marker. Art himself had a booth you could buy from an airplane catalog, the kind that rolled up into cordura bags. And people were stingy with brochures now, too. Gone were the twelve-page, four-color affairs; now the pamphlets were four-page, two-color, with extra-bold graphics for attempted pizzazz, and not everybody got one, only people who were serious.

Art set up. Then, even though he should have been manning his spot, he drifted from booth to booth, saying hello to people he should have seen at breakfast. They were happy to see him, to talk shop, to pop some grapes off the old grapevine. Really, if he weren't staying in a welfare hotel, he would have felt downright respected. *You folk.* What folk did Cindy mean? Maybe she was just being matter-of-fact, keeping her perspective. Although how could anyone be so matter-of-fact about something so bitter? He wondered this even as he took his imaginative liberties with her. These began with a knock on her door and coursed through some hot times but ended (what a good boy he was) with him rescuing her and her children (he wondered how many there were) from their dead-end life. What was the matter with him, that he could not imagine mating without legal sanction? His libido was not what it should be, clearly, or at least it was not what Billy Shore's was. Art tried to think *game plan,* but in truth he could not even identify what a triple option would be in this case. All he knew was that, assuming, to begin with, that she was willing, he couldn't sleep with a woman like Cindy and then leave her flat. She could *you folk* him, he could never *us folk* her.

He played with some software at a neighboring booth; it appeared interesting enough but kept crashing so he couldn't tell too much. Then he dutifully returned to his own booth, where he was visited by a number of people he knew, people with whom he was friendly enough. The sort of people to whom he might have shown pictures of his children. He considered telling one or two of them about the events of the morning. Not about the invitation that might not have been an invitation, but about finding himself in a welfare hotel and being beaned with his own telephone. Phrases drifted through his head. *Not so bad as you'd think. You'd be surprised how friendly the people are. Unpretentious. Though, of course, no health club.* But in the end the subject simply did not come up and did not come up until he realized that he was keeping it to himself, and that he was committing more resources to this task than he had readily available. He felt invaded—as if he had been infected by a self-replicating bug. Something that was iterating and iterating, growing and growing, crowding out everything else in the CPU. The secret was intolerable; it was bound to spill out of him sooner or later. He just hoped it wouldn't be sooner.

He just hoped it wouldn't be to Billy Shore, for whom he began to search, so as to be certain to avoid him.

Art had asked about Billy at the various booths, but no one had seen him; his absence was weird. It spooked Art. When finally some real live conferees stopped by to see his wares, he had trouble concentrating; everywhere in the conversation he was missing opportunities, he knew it. And all because his CPU was full of iterating nonsense. Not too long ago, in looking over some database software in which was loaded certain fun facts about people in the industry, Art had looked up Billy, and discovered that he had been born the same day Art was, only four years later. It just figured that Billy would be younger. That was irritating. But Art was happy for the information, too. He had made a note of it, so that when he ran into Billy at this conference, he would remember to kid him about their birthdays. Now, he rehearsed. *Have I got a surprise for you. I always knew you were a Leo. I believe this makes us birthmates.* Anything not to mention the welfare hotel and all that had happened to him there.

IN THE END, he did not run into Billy at all. In the end, he wondered about Billy all day, only to finally learn that Billy had moved on to a new job in the Valley, with a start-up. In personal computers, naturally. A good move, no matter what kind of beating he took on his house.

"Life is about the long term," said Ernie Ford, the informant. "And let's face it, there is no long term here."

Art agreed as warmly as he could. In one way, he was delighted that his competitor had left—if nothing else, that would mean a certain amount of disarray at Info-Edge. The insurance market was, unfortunately, some 40 percent of his business, and he could use any advantage he could get. Another bonus was that Art was never going to have to see Billy again. Billy his birthmate, with his jokes and his Main-streamese. Still, Art felt depressed.

"We should all have gotten out before this," he said.

"Truer words were never spoke," said Ernie. Ernie had never been a particular friend of Art's, but somehow, talking about Billy was making him chummier. It was as if Billy were a force even in his absence. "I tell you, I'd have packed my bags by now if it weren't for the wife, the kids—they don't want to leave their friends, you know? Plus the oldest is a junior in high school, we can't afford for him to move now, he's got to stay put and make those nice grades so he can make a nice college. Meaning I've got to stay, if it means pushing McMuffins for Ronald McDonald. But now you . . ."

"Maybe I should go," said Art.

"Definitely, you should go," said Ernie. "What's keeping you?"

"Nothing," said Art. "I'm divorced now. And that's that, right? Sometimes people get undivorced, but you can't exactly count on it."

"Go," said Ernie. "Take my advice. If I hear of anything, I'll send it your way."

"Thanks," said Art.

But of course, he did not expect that Ernie would really turn anything up. It had been a long time since anyone had called him or anybody else he knew of; too many people had gotten stranded, and they were too desperate. Everybody knew it. Also, the survivors were looked upon with suspicion. Anybody who was any good had jumped ship early, that was the conventional wisdom. There was Art, struggling to hold on to his job, only to discover that there were times you didn't want to hold on to your job, times to maneuver for the golden parachute and jump. That was another thing no one had told him, that sometimes it spoke well of you to be fired. Who would have figured that? Sometimes it seemed to Art that he knew nothing at all, that he had dug his own grave and didn't even know to lie down in it, he was still trying to stand up.

A few more warm-blooded conferees at the end of the day—at least they were polite. Then, as he was packing up to go back to the hotel, a mega-surprise. A headhunter approached him, a friend of Ernest's, he said.

"Ernest?" said Art. "Oh, Ernie! Ford! Of course!"

The headhunter was a round, ruddy man with a ring of hair like St. Francis of Assisi, and sure enough, a handful of bread crumbs: A great opportunity, he said. Right now he had to run, but he knew just the guy Art had to meet, a guy who was coming in that evening. For something else, it happened, but he also needed someone like Art. Needed him yesterday, really. Should've been a priority, the guy realized that now, had said so the other day. It might just be a match. Maybe a quick breakfast in the A.M.? Could he call in an hour or so? Art said, *Of course.* And when St. Francis asked his room number, Art hesitated, but then gave the name of the welfare hotel. How would St. Francis know what kind of hotel it was? Art gave the name out confidently, making his manner count. He almost didn't make it to the conference at all, he said. Being so busy. It was only at the last minute that he realized he could do it—things moved around, he found an opening and figured what the hell. But it was too late to book the conference hotel, he explained. That was why he was staying elsewhere.

Success. All day Art's mind had been churning; suddenly it seemed to empty. He might as well have been Billy, born on the same day as Art was, but in another year, under different stars. How much simpler things seemed. He did not labor on two, three, six tasks at once, multiprocessing. He knew one thing at a time, and that thing just now was that the day was a victory. And all because he had kept his mouth shut. He had said nothing; he had kept his cool. He walked briskly back to the hotel. He crossed the lobby in a no-nonsense manner. An impervious man. He did not knock on Cindy's door. He was moving on, moving west. There would be a good job there, and a new life. Perhaps he would take up tennis. Perhaps he would own a Jacuzzi. Perhaps he would learn to like all those peculiar foods they ate out there, like jicama, and seaweed. Perhaps he would go macrobiotic.

It wasn't until he got to his room that he remembered that his telephone had no handset.

He sat on his bed. There was a noise at his window, followed, sure enough, by someone's shadow. He wasn't even surprised. Anyway, the fellow wasn't stopping at his room, at least not on this trip. That was luck. *You folk,* Cindy had said, taking back the ice bag. Art could see her perspective; she was right. He was luckier than she, by far. But just now, as the shadow crossed his window again, he thought mostly about how unarmed he was. If he had a telephone, he would probably call Lisa—that was how big a pool seemed to be forming around him, all of a sudden; an ocean, it seemed. Also, he would call the police. But first he would call Lisa, and see how she felt about his possibly moving west. *Quite possibly,* he would say, not wanting to make it sound as though he was calling her for nothing, not wanting to make it sound as though he was awash, at sea, perhaps drowning. He would not want to sound like a haunted man; he would not want to sound as though he was calling from a welfare hotel, years too late, to say, *Yes, that was a baby, it would have been a baby.* For he could not help now but recall the doctor explaining about that child, a boy, who had appeared so mysteriously perfect in the ultrasound. Transparent, he had looked, and gelatinous, all soft head and quick heart; but he would have, in being born, broken every bone in his body.

I LEFT IOWA at the end of the M.F.A. program having written almost nothing. Just two short stories, both of them in the same month of my final year. I'd heard over and over that it was typical not to write until one had been out of the program for quite a while, but I assumed this was nothing more than a kind dismissal. I left Iowa convinced that I had failed as a writer.

What I did then was go to medical school. There, confronted with the necessity of memorizing the origin of all twenty-seven carbons in the cholesterol molecule, I began again to write fiction. I registered for an undergraduate creative writing course—not telling anyone that I already possessed an M.F.A.—and during that semester I wrote five new short stories. "The Year of Getting to Know Us" was one of them. It was originally called "Twelve Angles of the Heart," in reference to the twelve leads of the electrocardiogram, which I had just then been studying. My teacher urged me to change the title, which I did—though now, in retrospect, I wish I had kept the original.

ETHAN CANIN

ETHAN CANIN

The Year of Getting to Know Us

I TOLD MY FATHER not to worry, that love is what matters, and that in the end,
when he is loosed from his body, he can look back and say without blinking that
he did all right by me, his son, and that I loved him.

And he said, "Don't talk about things you know nothing about."

We were in San Francisco, in a hospital room. IV tubes were plugged into my
father's arms; little round Band-Aids were on his chest. Next to his bed was a table
with a vase of yellow roses and a card that my wife, Anne, had brought him. On the
front of the card was a photograph of a golf green. On the wall above my father's
head an electric monitor traced his heartbeat. He was watching the news on a TV
that stood in the corner next to his girlfriend, Lorraine. Lorraine was reading a
magazine.

I was watching his heartbeat. It seemed all right to me: the blips made steady
peaks and drops, moved across the screen, went out at one end, and then came back
at the other. It seemed that this was all a heart could do. I'm an English teacher,
though, and I don't know much about it.

"It looks strong," I'd said to my mother that afternoon over the phone. She was
in Pasadena. "It's going right across, pretty steady. Big bumps. Solid."

"Is he eating all right?"

"I think so."

"Is *she* there?"

"Is Lorraine here, you mean?"

She paused. "Yes, Lorraine."

"No," I said. "She's not."

"Your poor father," she whispered.

I'M AN ONLY CHILD, and I grew up in a big wood-frame house on Huron Avenue in Pasadena, California. The house had three empty bedrooms and in the backyard a section of grass that had been stripped and leveled, then seeded and mowed like a putting green. Twice a week a Mexican gardener came to trim it, wearing special moccasins my father had bought him. They had soft hide soles that left no imprints.

My father was in love with golf. He played seven times every week and talked about the game as if it were a science that he was about to figure out. "Cut through the outer rim for a high iron," he used to say at dinner, looking out the window into the yard while my mother passed him the carved-wood salad bowl, or "In hot weather hit a high-compression ball." When conversations paused, he made little putting motions with his hands. He was a top amateur and in another situation might have been a pro. When I was sixteen, the year I was arrested, he let me caddie for the first time. Before that all I knew about golf was his clubs—the Spalding made-to-measure woods and irons, Dynamiter sand wedge, St. Andrews putter—which he kept in an Abercrombie & Fitch bag in the trunk of his Lincoln, and the white leather shoes with long tongues and screw-in spikes, which he stored upside down in the hall closet. When he wasn't playing, he covered the club heads with socks that had little yellow dingo balls on the ends.

He never taught me to play. I was a decent athlete—could run, catch, throw a perfect spiral—but he never took me to the golf course. In the summer he played every day. Sometimes my mother asked if he would take me along with him. "Why should I?" he answered. "Neither of us would like it."

Every afternoon after work he played nine holes; he played eighteen on Saturday, and nine again on Sunday morning. On Sunday afternoon, at four o'clock, he went for a drive by himself in his white Lincoln Continental. Nobody was allowed to come with him on the drives. He was usually gone for a couple of hours. "Today I drove in the country," he would say at dinner, as he put out his cigarette, or "This afternoon I looked at the ocean," and we were to take from this that he had driven north on the coastal highway. He almost never said more, and across our blue-and-white tablecloth, when I looked at him, my silent father, I imagined in his eyes a pure gaze with which he read the waves and currents of the sea. He had made a fortune in business and owed it to being able to see the truth in any situation. For this reason, he said, he liked to drive with all the windows down. When he returned from his trips his face was red from the wind and his thinning hair lay fitfully on his head. My mother baked on Sunday afternoons while he was gone, walnut pies or macaroons that she prepared on the kitchen counter, which looked out over his putting green.

I TEACH ENGLISH in a high school now, and my wife, Anne, is a journalist. I've played golf a half-dozen times in ten years and don't like it any more than most beginners, though the two or three times I've hit a drive that sails, that takes flight with its own power, I've felt something that I think must be unique to the game. These were the drives my father used to hit. Explosions off the tee, bird flights. But golf isn't my game, and it never has been, and I wouldn't think about it at all if not for my father.

Anne and I were visiting in California, first my mother, in Los Angeles, and then my father and Lorraine, north in Sausalito, and Anne suggested that I ask him to play nine holes one morning. She'd been wanting me to talk to him. It's part of the project we've started, part of her theory of what's wrong—although I don't think that much is. She had told me that twenty-five years changes things, and since we had the time, why not go out to California.

She said, "It's not too late to talk to him."

MY BEST FRIEND in high school was named Nickie Apple. Nickie had a thick chest and a voice that had been damaged somehow, made a little hoarse, and sometimes people thought he was twenty years old. He lived in a four-story house that had a separate floor for the kids. It was the top story, and his father, who was divorced and a lawyer, had agreed never to come up there. That was where we sat around after school. Because of the agreement, no parents were there, only kids. Nine or ten of us, usually. Some of them had slept the night on the big pillows that were scattered against the walls: friends of his older brothers', in Stetson hats and flannel shirts; girls I had never seen before.

Nickie and I went to Shrier Academy, where all the students carried around blue-and-gray notebooks embossed with the school's heraldic seal. SUMUS PRIMI the seal said. Our gray wool sweaters said it; our green exam books said it; the rear window decal my mother brought home said it. My father wouldn't put the sticker on the Lincoln, so she pressed it onto the window above her kitchen sink instead. ІМІЯЧ ꙄUMUꙄ I read whenever I washed my hands. At Shrier we learned Latin in the eighth grade and art history in the ninth, and in the tenth I started getting into some trouble. Little things: cigarettes, graffiti. Mr. Goldman, the student counselor, called my mother in for a premonition visit. "I have a premonition about Leonard," he told her in the counseling office one afternoon in the warm October when I was sixteen. The office was full of plants and had five floor-to-ceiling windows that let in sun like a greenhouse. They looked over grassy, bushless knolls. "I just have a feeling about him."

That October he started talking to me about it. He called me in and asked me why I was friends with Nickie Apple, a boy going nowhere. I was looking out the big windows, opening and closing my fists beneath the desk top. He said, "Lenny, you're a bright kid—what are you trying to tell us?" And I said, "Nothing. I'm not trying to tell you anything."

Then we started stealing, Nickie and I. He did it first, and took things I didn't expect: steaks, expensive cuts that we cooked on a grill by the window in the top story of his house; garden machinery; luggage. We didn't sell it and we didn't use it, but every afternoon we went someplace new. In November he distracted a store clerk and I took a necklace that we thought was diamonds. In December we went for a ride in someone else's car, and over Christmas vacation, when only gardeners were on the school grounds, we threw ten rocks, one by one, as if we'd paid for them at a carnival stand, through the five windows in Mr. Goldman's office.

"YOU LOOK LIKE A TRAIN STATION," I said to my father as he lay in the hospital bed. "All those lines coming and going everywhere."

He looked at me. I put some things down, tried to make a little bustle. I could see Anne standing in the hall just beyond the door.

"Are you comfortable, Dad?"

"What do you mean, 'comfortable'? My heart's full of holes, leaking all over the place. Am I comfortable? No, I'm dying."

"You're not dying," I said, and I sat down next to him. "You'll be swinging the five iron in two weeks."

I touched one of the tubes in his arm. Where it entered the vein, the needle disappeared under a piece of tape. I hated the sight of this. I moved the bedsheets a little bit, tucked them in. Anne had wanted me to be alone with him. She was in the hall, waiting to head off Lorraine.

"What's the matter with her?" he asked, pointing at Anne.

"She thought we might want to talk."

"What's so urgent?"

Anne and I had discussed it the night before. "Tell him what you feel," she said. "Tell him you love him." We were eating dinner in a fish restaurant. "Or if you don't love him, tell him you don't."

"Look, Pop," I said now.

"What?"

I was forty-two years old. We were in a hospital and he had tubes in his arms. All kinds of everything: needles, air, tape. I said it again.

"Look, Pop."

ANNE AND I have seen a counselor, who told me that I had to learn to accept kindness from people. He saw Anne and me together, then Anne alone, then me. Children's toys were scattered on the floor of his office. "You sound as if you don't want to let people near you," he said. "Right?"

"I'm a reasonably happy man," I answered.

I hadn't wanted to see the counselor. Anne and I have been married seven years, and sometimes I think the history of marriage can be written like this: People Want Too Much. Anne and I have suffered no plague; we sleep late two mornings a week; we laugh at most of the same things; we have a decent house in a suburb of Boston, where, after the commuter traffic has eased, a quiet descends and the world is at peace. She writes for a newspaper, and I teach the children of lawyers and insurance men. At times I'm alone, and need to be alone; at times she does too. But I can always count on a moment, sometimes once in a day, sometimes more, when I see her patting down the sheets on the bed, or watering the front window violets, and I am struck by the good fortune of my life.

Still, Anne says I don't feel things.

It comes up at dinner, outside in the yard, in airports as we wait for planes. You don't let yourself feel, she tells me; and I tell her that I think it's a crazy thing, all this talk about feeling. What do the African Bushmen say? They say, Will we eat tomorrow? Will there be rain?

WHEN I WAS SIXTEEN, sitting in the back seat of a squad car, the policeman stopped in front of our house on Huron Avenue, turned around against the headrest, and asked me if I was sure this was where I lived.

"Yes, sir," I said.

He spoke through a metal grate. "Your daddy owns this house?"

"Yes, sir."

"But for some reason you don't like windows."

He got out and opened my door, and we walked up the porch steps. The swirling lights on the squad car were making crazy patterns in the French panes of the living room bays. He knocked. "What's your daddy do?"

I heard lights snapping on, my mother moving through the house. "He's in business," I said. "But he won't be home now." The policeman wrote something on his notepad. I saw my mother's eye through the glass in the door, and then the locks were being unlatched, one by one, from the top.

WHEN ANNE AND I CAME to California to visit, we stayed at my mother's for three days. On her refrigerator door was a calendar with men's names marked on it—dinner dates, theater—and I knew this was done for our benefit. My mother has been alone for fifteen years. She's still thin, and her eyes still water, and I noticed that books were lying open all through the house. Thick paperbacks—*Doctor Zhivago*, *The Thorn Birds*—in the bathroom and the studio and the bedroom. We never mentioned my father, but at the end of our stay, when we had packed the car for our drive north along the coast, after she'd hugged us both and we'd backed out of the driveway, she came down off the lawn into the street, her arms crossed over her chest, leaned into the window, and said, "You might say hello to your father for me."

We made the drive north on Highway 1. We passed mission towns, fields of butter lettuce, long stretches of pumpkin farms south of San Francisco. It was the first time we were going to see my father with Lorraine. She was a hairdresser. He'd met her a few years after coming north, and one of the first things they'd done together was take a trip around the world. We got postcards from the Nile delta and Bangkok. When I was young, my father had never taken us out of California.

His house in Sausalito was on a cliff above a finger of San Francisco Bay. A new Lincoln stood in the carport. In his bedroom was a teak-framed king-size waterbed, and on the walls were bits of African artwork—opium pipes, metal figurines. Lorraine looked the same age as Anne. One wall of the living room was glass, and after the first night's dinner, while we sat on the leather sofa watching tankers and yachts move under the Golden Gate Bridge, my father put down his Scotch and water, touched his jaw, and said, "Lenny, call Dr. Farmer."

It was his second one. The first had been two years earlier, on the golf course in Monterey, where he'd had to kneel, then sit, then lie down on the fairway.

AT DINNER the night after I was arrested, my mother introduced her idea. "We're going to try something," she said. She had brought out a chicken casserole, and it was steaming in front of her. "That's what we're going to do. Max, are you listening? This next year, starting tonight, is going to be the year of getting to know us better." She stopped speaking and dished my father some chicken.

"What do you mean?" I asked.

"I mean it will be to a small extent a theme year. Nothing that's going to change every day of our lives, but in this next year I thought we'd all make an attempt to get to know each other better. Especially you, Leonard. Dad and I are going to make a better effort to know you."

"I'm not sure what you mean," said my father.

"All kinds of things, Max. We'll go to movies together, and Lenny can throw a party here at the house. And I personally would like to take a trip, all of us together, to the American Southwest."

"Sounds all right to me," I said.

"And Max," she said, "you can take Lenny with you to play golf. For example." She looked at my father.

"Neither of us would like it," he said.

"Lenny never sees you."

I looked out the window. The trees were turning, dropping their leaves onto the putting green. I didn't care what he said, one way or the other. My mother spooned a chicken thigh onto my plate and covered it with sauce. "All right," my father said. "He can caddie."

"And as preparation for our trip," my mother said, "can you take him on your Sunday rides?"

My father took off his glasses. "The Southwest," he said, wiping the lenses with a napkin, "is exactly like any other part of the country."

ANNE HAD AN AFFAIR once with a man she met on an assignment. He was young, much younger than either of us—in his late twenties, I would say from the one time I saw him. I saw them because one day on the road home I passed Anne's car in the lot of a Denny's restaurant. I parked around the block and went in to surprise her. I took a table at the back, but from my seat in the corner I didn't realize for several minutes that the youngish-looking woman leaning forward and whispering to the man with a beard was my wife.

I didn't get up and pull the man out with me into the parking lot, or even join them at the table, as I have since thought might have been a good idea. Instead I sat and watched them. I could see that under the table they were holding hands. His back was to me, and I noticed that it was broad, as mine is not. I remember thinking that she probably liked this broadness. Other than that, though, I didn't feel very much. I ordered another cup of coffee just to hear myself talk, but my voice wasn't quavering or fearful. When the waitress left, I took out a napkin and wrote on it, "You are a forty-year-old man with no children and your wife is having an affair." Then I put some money on the table and left the restaurant.

"I think we should see somebody," Anne said to me a few weeks later. It was a Sunday morning, and we were eating breakfast on the porch.

"About what?" I asked.

ON A SUNDAY afternoon when I was sixteen I went out to the garage with a plan my mother had given me. That morning my father had washed the Lincoln. He had detergent-scrubbed the finish and then sun-dried it on Huron Avenue, so that in the workshop light of the garage its highlights shone. The windshield molding, the grille, the chrome side markers, had been cloth-dried to erase water spots. The keys hung from their magnetic sling near the door to the kitchen. I took them out and opened the trunk. Then I hung them up again and sat on the rear quarter panel to consider what to do. It was almost four o'clock. The trunk of my father's car was large enough for a half-dozen suitcases and had been upholstered in a gray medium-pile carpet that was cut to hug the wheel wells and the spare-tire berth. In one corner, fastened down by straps, was his toolbox, and along the back lay the golf bag. In the shadows the yellow dingos of the club socks looked like baby chicks. He was going to come out in a few minutes. I reached in, took off four of the club socks, and made a pillow for my head. Then I stepped into the trunk. The shocks bounced once and stopped. I lay down with my head propped on the quarter panel and my feet resting in the taillight berth, and then I reached up, slammed down the trunk, and was in the dark.

This didn't frighten me. When I was very young, I liked to sleep with the shades drawn and the door closed so that no light entered my room. I used to hold my hand in front of my eyes and see if I could imagine its presence. It was too dark to see anything. I was blind then, lying in my bed, listening for every sound. I used to move my hand back and forth, close to my eyes, until I had the sensation that it was there but had in some way been amputated. I had heard of soldiers who had lost limbs but still felt them attached. Now I held my open hand before my eyes. It was dense black inside the trunk, colorless, without light.

When my father started the car, all the sounds were huge, magnified as if they were inside my own skull. The metal scratched, creaked, slammed when he got in; the bolt of the starter shook all the way through to the trunk; the idle rose and leveled; then the gears changed and the car lurched. I heard the garage door glide up. Then it curled into its housing, bumped once, began descending again. The seams of the trunk lid lightened in the sun. We were in the street now, heading downhill. I lay back and felt the road, listened to the gravel pocking in the wheel wells.

I followed our route in my mind. Left off Huron onto Telscher, where the car bottomed in the rain gulley as we turned, then up the hill to Santa Ana. As we waited for the light, the idle made its change, shifting down, so that below my head I heard the individual piston blasts in the exhaust pipe. Left on Santa Ana, counting the flat stretches where I felt my father tap the brakes, numbering the intersections as we headed west toward the ocean. I heard cars pull up next to us, accelerate, slow down, make turns. Bits of gravel echoed inside the quarter panels. I pulled off more club socks and enlarged my pillow. We slowed down, stopped, and then we accelerated, the soft piston explosions becoming a hiss as we turned onto the Pasadena freeway.

"Dad's rides," my mother had said to me the night before, as I lay in bed, "would be a good way for him to get to know you." It was the first week of the year of getting to know us better. She was sitting at my desk.

"But he won't let me go," I said.

"You're right." She moved some things around on a shelf. The room wasn't quite dark, and I could see the outline of her white blouse. "I talked to Mr. Goldman," she said.

"Mr. Goldman doesn't know me."

"He says you're angry." My mother stood up, and I watched her white blouse move to the window. She pulled back the shade until a triangle of light from the streetlamp fell on my sheets. "Are you angry?"

"I don't know," I said. "I don't think so."

"I don't think so either." She replaced the shade, came over and kissed me on the forehead, and then went out into the hall. In the dark I looked for my hand.

A few minutes later the door opened again. She put her head in. "If he won't let you come," she said, "sneak along."

On the freeway the thermal seams whizzed and popped in my ears. The ride had smoothed out now, as the shocks settled into the high speed, hardly dipping on curves, muffling everything as if we were under water. As far as I could tell, we were still driving west, toward the ocean. I sat halfway up and rested my back against the golf bag. I could see shapes now inside the trunk. When we slowed down and the blinker went on, I attempted bearings, but the sun was the same in all directions and the trunk lid was without shadow. We braked hard. I felt the car leave the freeway. We made turns. We went straight. Then more turns, and as we slowed down and I was stretching out, uncurling my body along the diagonal, we made a sharp right onto gravel and pulled over and stopped.

My father opened the door. The car dipped and rocked, shuddered. The engine clicked. Then the passenger door opened. I waited.

If I heard her voice today, twenty-six years later, I would recognize it.

"Angel," she said.

I heard the weight of their bodies sliding across the back seat, first hers, then his. They weren't three feet away. I curled up, crouched into the low space between the golf bag and the back of the passenger compartment. There were two firm points in the cushion where it was displaced. As I lay there, I went over the voice again in my head: it was nobody I knew. I heard a laugh from her, and then something low from him. I felt the shift of the trunk's false rear, and then, as I lay behind them, I heard the contact: the crinkle of clothing, arms wrapping, and the half-delicate, muscular sounds. It was like hearing a television in the next room. His voice once more, and then the rising of their breath, slow; a minute of this, maybe another; then shifting again, the friction of cloth on the leather seat and the car's soft rocking. "Dad," I whispered. Then rocking again; my father's sudden panting, harder and harder, his half-words. The car shook violently. "Dad," I whispered. I shouted, "Dad!"

The door opened.

His steps kicked up gravel. I heard jingling metal, the sound of the key in the trunk lock. He was standing over me in an explosion of light.

He said, "Put back the club socks."

I did and got out of the car to stand next to him. He rubbed his hands down the front of his shirt.

"What the hell," he said.

"I was in the trunk."

"I know," he said. "What the goddamn."

THE YEAR I GRADUATED from college, I found a job teaching junior high school in Boston. The school was a cement building with small windows well up from the street, and dark classrooms in which I spent a lot of time maintaining discipline. In the middle of an afternoon that first winter a boy knocked on my door to tell me I had a phone call. I knew who it was going to be.

"Dad's gone," my mother said.

He'd taken his things in the Lincoln, she told me, and driven away that morning before dawn. On the kitchen table he'd left a note and some cash. "A lot of cash," my mother added, lowering her voice. "Twenty thousand dollars."

I imagined the sheaf of bills on our breakfast table, held down by the ceramic butter dish, the bank notes ruffling in the breeze from the louvered windows that opened onto his green. In the note he said he had gone north and would call her when he'd settled. It was December. I told my mother that I would visit in a week, when school was out for Christmas. I told her to go to her sister's and stay there, and then I said that I was working and had to get back to my class. She didn't say anything on the other end of the line, and in the silence I imagined my father crisscrossing the state of California, driving north, stopping in Palm Springs and Carmel, the Lincoln riding low with the weight.

"Leonard," my mother said, "did you know anything like this was happening?"

DURING THE SPRING of the year of getting to know us better I caddied for him a few times. On Saturdays he played early in the morning, when the course was mostly empty and the grass was still wet from the night. I learned to fetch the higher irons as the sun rose over the back nine and the ball, on drying ground, rolled farther. He hit skybound approach shots with backspin, chips that bit into the green and stopped. He played in a foursome with three other men, and in the locker room, as they changed their shoes, they told jokes and poked one another in the belly. The lockers were shiny green metal, the floor clean white tiles that clicked under the shoe spikes. Beneath the mirrors were jars of combs in green disinfectant. When I combed my hair with them it stayed in place and smelled like limes.

We were on the course at dawn. At the first fairway the other men dug in their spikes, shifted their weight from leg to leg, dummy-swung at an empty tee while my father lit a cigarette and looked out over the hole. "The big gun," he said to me, or, if it was a par three, "The lady." He stepped on his cigarette. I wiped the head with the club sock before I handed it to him. When he took the club, he felt its balance point, rested it on one finger, and then, in slow motion, he gripped the shaft. Left hand first, then right, the fingers wrapping pinkie to index. Then he leaned down over the ball. On a perfect drive the tee flew straight up in the air and landed in front of his feet.

OVER THE WEEKEND his heart lost its rhythm for a few seconds. It happened Saturday night, when Anne and I were at the house in Sausalito, and we didn't hear about it until Sunday. "Ventricular fibrillation," the intern said. "Circus movements." The condition was always a danger after a heart attack. He had been given a shock and his heartbeat had returned to normal.

"But I'll be honest with you," the intern said. We were in the hall. He looked down, touched his stethoscope. "It isn't a good sign."

The heart gets bigger as it dies, he told me. Soon it spreads across the x-ray. He brought me with him to a room and showed me strips of paper with the electric tracings: certain formations. The muscle was dying in patches, he said. He said things might get better, they might not.

My mother called that afternoon. "Should I come up?"

"He was a bastard to you," I said.

When Lorraine and Anne were eating dinner, I found the intern again. "I want to know," I said. "Tell me the truth." The intern was tall and thin, sick-looking himself. So were the other doctors I had seen around the place. Everything in that hospital was pale—the walls, the coats, the skin.

He said, "What truth?"

I told him that I'd been reading about heart disease. I'd read about EKGs, knew about the medicines—lidocaine, propranolol. I knew that the lungs filled up with water, that heart failure was death by drowning. I said, "The truth about my father."

THE AFTERNOON I had hidden in the trunk, we came home while my mother was cooking dinner. I walked up the path from the garage behind my father, watching the pearls of sweat on his neck. He was whistling a tune. At the door he kissed my mother's cheek. He touched the small of her back. She was cooking vegetables, and the steam had fogged up the kitchen windows and dampened her hair. My father sat down in the chair by the window and opened the newspaper. I thought of the way the trunk rear had shifted when he and the woman had moved into the back of the Lincoln. My mother was smiling.

"Well?" she said.

"What's for dinner?" I asked.

"Well?" she said again.

"It's chicken," I said. "Isn't it?"

"Max, aren't you going to tell me if anything unusual happened today?"

My father didn't look up from the newspaper. "Did anything unusual happen today?" he said. He turned the page, folded it back smartly. "Why don't you ask Lenny?"

She smiled at me.

"I surprised him," I said. Then I turned and looked out the window.

"I HAVE SOMETHING to tell you," Anne said to me one Sunday morning in the fifth year of our marriage. We were lying in bed. I knew what was coming.

"I already know," I said.

"What do you already know?"

"I know about your lover."

She didn't say anything.

"It's all right," I said.

It was winter. The sky was gray, and although the sun had risen only a few hours earlier, it seemed like late afternoon. I waited for Anne to say something more. We were silent for several minutes. Then she said, "I wanted to hurt you." She got out of bed and began straightening out the bureau. She pulled my sweaters from the drawer and refolded them. She returned all our shoes to the closet. Then she came back to the bed, sat down, and began to cry. Her back was toward me. It shook with her gasps, and I put my hand out and touched her. "It's all right," I said.

"We only saw each other a few times," she answered. "I'd take it back if I could. I'd make it never happen."

"I know you would."

"For some reason I thought I couldn't really hurt you."

She had stopped crying. I looked out the window at the tree branches hung low with snow. It didn't seem I had to say anything.

"I don't know why I thought I couldn't hurt you," she said. "Of course I can hurt you."

"I forgive you."

Her back was still toward me. Outside, a few snowflakes drifted up in the air.

"*Did* I hurt you?"

"Yes, you did. I saw you two in a restaurant."

"Where?"

"At Denny's."

"No," she said. "I mean, where did I hurt you?"

THE NIGHT HE DIED, Anne stayed awake with me in bed. "Tell me about him," she said.

"What about?"

"Stories. Tell me what it was like growing up, things you did together."

"We didn't do that much," I said. "I caddied for him. He taught me things about golf."

That night I never went to sleep. Lorraine was at a friend's apartment and we were alone in my father's empty house, but we pulled out the sheets anyway, and the two wool blankets, and we lay on the fold-out sofa in the den. I told stories about my father until I couldn't think of any more, and then I talked about my mother until Anne fell asleep.

In the middle of the night I got up and went into the living room. Through the glass I could see lights across the water, the bridges, Belvedere and San Francisco, ships. It was clear outside, and when I walked out to the cement carport the sky was lit with stars. The breeze moved inside my nightclothes. Next to the garage the Lincoln stood half-lit in the porch floodlight. I opened the door and got in. The seats were red leather and smelled of limes and cigarettes. I rolled down the window and took the key from the glove compartment. I thought of writing a note for Anne, but didn't. Instead I coasted down the driveway in neutral and didn't close the door or turn on the lights until the bottom of the hill, or start the engine until I had swung around the corner, so that the house was out of sight and the brine smell of the marina was coming through the open windows of the car. The pistons were almost silent.

I felt urgent, though I had no route in mind. I ran one stop sign, then one red light, and when I reached the ramp onto Highway 101, I squeezed the accelerator and felt the surge of the fuel-injected, computer-sparked V-8. The dash lights glowed. I drove south and crossed over the Golden Gate Bridge at seventy miles an hour, its suspension cables swaying in the wind and the span rocking slowly, ocean to bay. The lanes were narrow. Reflectors zinged when the wheels strayed. If Anne woke, she might come out to the living room and then check for me outside. A light rain began to fall. Drops wet my knees, splattered my cheek. I kept the window open and turned on the radio; the car filled up with wind and music. Brass sounds. Trumpets. Sounds that filled my heart.

The Lincoln drove like a dream. South of San Francisco the road opened up, and in the gulley of a shallow hill I took it up over a hundred. The arrow nosed rightward in the dash. Shapes flattened out. "Dad," I said. The wind sounds changed pitch. I said, "The year of getting to know us." Signposts and power poles were flying by. Only a few cars were on the road, and most moved over before I arrived. In the mirror I could see the faces as I passed. I went through San Mateo, Pacifica, Redwood City, until, underneath a concrete overpass, the radio began pulling in static and I realized that I might die at this speed. I slowed down. At seventy drizzle wandered in the windows again. At fifty-five the scenery stopped moving. In Menlo Park I got off the freeway.

It was dark still, and off the interstate I found myself on a road without street-lights. It entered the center of town and then left again, curving up into shallow hills. The houses were large on either side. They were spaced far apart, three and four stories tall, with white shutters or ornament work that shone in the perimeter of the Lincoln's headlamps. The yards were large, dotted with eucalyptus and laurel. Here and there a light was on. Sometimes I saw faces: someone on an upstairs balcony; a man inside the breakfast room, awake at this hour, peering through the glass to see what car could be passing. I drove slowly, and when I came to a high school with its low buildings and long athletic field I pulled over and stopped.

The drizzle had become mist. I left the headlights on and got out and stood on the grass. I thought, This is the night your father has passed. I looked up at the lightening sky. I said it, "This is the night your father has passed," but I didn't feel what I thought I would. Just the wind on my throat, the chill of the morning. A pickup drove by and flashed its lights at me on the lawn. Then I went to the trunk of the Lincoln, because this was what my father would have done, and I got out the golf bag. It was heavier than I remembered, and the leather was stiff in the cool air. On the damp sod I set up: dimpled white ball, yellow tee. My father would have swung, would have hit drives the length of the football field, high irons that disappeared into the gray sky, but as I stood there I didn't even take the clubs out of the bag. Instead I imagined his stance. I pictured the even weight, the deliberate grip, and after I had stood there for a few moments, I picked up the ball and tee, replaced them in the bag, and drove home to my wife.

THE YEAR I WAS SIXTEEN we never made it to the American Southwest. My mother bought maps anyway, and planned our trip, talking to me about it at night in the dark, taking us in her mind across the Colorado River at the California border, where the water was opal green, into Arizona and along the stretch of desert highway to New Mexico. There, she said, the canyons were a mile deep. The road was lined with sagebrush and a type of cactus, jumping cholla, that launched its spines. Above the desert, where a man could die of dehydration in an afternoon and a morning, the peaks of the Rocky Mountains turned blue with sun and ice.

We didn't ever go. Every weekend my father played golf, and at last, in August, my parents agreed to a compromise. One Sunday morning, before I started the eleventh grade, we drove north in the Lincoln to a state park along the ocean. Above the shore the cliffs were planted with ice plant to resist erosion. Pelicans soared in the thermal currents. My mother had made chicken sandwiches, which we ate on the beach, and after lunch, while I looked at the crabs and swaying fronds in the tide pools, my parents walked to the base of the cliffs. I watched their progress on the shallow dunes. Once when I looked, my father was holding her in his arms and they were kissing.

She bent backward in his hands. I looked into the tide pool where, on the surface, the blue sky, the clouds, the reddish cliffs, were shining. Below them rock crabs scurried between submerged stones. The afternoon my father found me in the trunk, he introduced me to the woman in the back seat. Her name was Christine. She smelled of perfume. The gravel drive where we had parked was behind a warehouse, and after we shook hands through the open window of the car, she got out and went inside. It was low and long, and the metal door slammed behind her. On the drive home, wind blowing all around us in the car, my father and I didn't say much. I watched his hands on the steering wheel. They were big and red-knuckled, the hands of a butcher or a carpenter, and I tried to imagine them on the bend of Christine's back.

Later that afternoon on the beach, while my mother walked along the shore, my father and I climbed a steep trail up the cliffs. From above, where we stood in the carpet of ice plant, we could see the hue of the Pacific change to a more translucent blue—the drop-off and the outline of the shoal where the breakers rose. I tried to see what my father was seeing as he gazed out over the water. He picked up a rock and tossed it over the cliff. "You know," he said without looking at me, "you could be all right on the course." We approached the edge of the palisade, where the ice plant thinned into eroded cuts of sand. "Listen," he said. "We're here on this trip so we can get to know each other a little bit." A hundred yards below us waves broke on the rocks. He lowered his voice. "But I'm not sure about that. Anyway, you don't *have* to get to know me. You know why?"

"Why?" I asked.

"You don't have to get to know me," he said, "because one day you're going to grow up and then you're going to *be* me." He looked at me and then out over the water. "So what I'm going to do is teach you how to hit." He picked up a long stick and put it in my hand. Then he showed me the backswing. "You've got to know one thing to drive a golf ball," he told me, "and that's that the club is part of you." He stood behind me and showed me how to keep the left arm still. "The club is your hand," he said. "It's your bone. It's your whole arm and your skeleton and your heart." Below us on the beach I could see my mother walking the waterline. We took cut after cut, and he taught me to visualize the impact, to sense it. He told me to whittle down the point of energy so that the ball would fly. When I swung he held my head in position. "Don't just watch," he said. "*See.*" I looked. The ice plant was watery-looking and fat, and at the edge of my vision I could see the tips of my father's shoes. I was sixteen years old and waiting for the next thing he would tell me.

THIS IS THE ONLY INSTANCE I can remember when I knew the ending of a story before I started writing it. I was lying in bed one night when, for some reason, the final scene came to me. I usually have no idea where I'm going with a short story—I just arrive at an opening sentence and let it grow, bit by bit, from there, so that I don't know the ending until I actually find myself writing it. And then I usually rewrite or tinker with the final paragraphs for quite some time before it seems to click. It was an unusual experience for me to write toward an ending I had in mind. I honestly don't recall anymore where the idea of writing about a woman who'd had a mastectomy came from. This story is the story of mine I feel most attached to because I felt the ending was risky—I liked it, but I was nervous about it because I could feel that I was on thin ice, attempting not to crash from the sublime to the ridiculous. I wasn't at all sure what the reaction to the story, and particularly to the ending, would be; I was afraid it was a little "over the top." But I stuck by it. I read a quote by David Jauss once about the best fiction "playing chicken with melo-drama." It was a line I took to heart and also took heart from. I did have more trouble than usual getting the story published, but I won a Wisconsin Creative Writing Institute Fellowship on the basis of this story—which managed to keep me from starving for another year, so I'm grateful to the story (and to the University of Wisconsin) for that. I also got a call from a women's magazine editor asking me if I'd be interesting in writing an article on women who had been through mastec-tomies because she felt that I had an unusual feeling for the experience, even though I had not experienced breast cancer myself. I thanked her but said I wasn't really interested in writing a nonfiction piece. The aspect of the story I enjoyed most was getting to wax rhapsodic about breasts. And exploring the notion that when you experience a loss, you gravitate toward the person who most fully appreciates the thing that's lost. A connoisseur, of sorts. There's a sort of empathetic intimacy there. Rather than turning toward someone who tries to tell you that it's really not that important in the cosmic scheme of things.

MARLY SWICK

MARLY SWICK

The Zealous Mourner

"YOU'RE ALIVE," David said, "that's the main thing. That's all that really matters."

"Your wife is disfigured, your only wife has only one breast. Doesn't that matter to you?"

"Of course it *matters* . . ." David paused, confused. "But it's not the *main* thing. There are degrees of tragedy. I can live with this."

"Well, that makes one of us," Louise said, snapping off the light.

"Christ," he sighed into the darkness. "You'd think you were Jayne Mansfield, some airhead bimbo, not an intelligent, successful professional woman. I married you because I—"

"Jayne Mansfield was decapitated," she interrupted. "That must be the worst." Louise's hand flew to the empty place on her chest. It felt to her fingers like a crater, although she knew it was just flat. Since the operation, she had spent considerable mental time weighing the relative gravity of various possible disfigurements and impairments: the loss of an eye versus the loss of a leg, arm, voice, hearing. One day she had even dug up an old insurance policy and studied the cash awards—fifty thousand for an eye, ten thousand for an arm, no mention of breasts.

"You'd think you'd been decapitated. You should be glad you've got brains, interests. You're a *tenured professor,* for chrissakes. When's the last time—"

"Just *shut up,*" she shouted. "Please."

"All right." He rolled over, his back to her, and yanked the blanket over to his side. "But I really think you should call Alice," he said for the hundredth time. "Good-night."

"Good-night." She kissed the back of his neck, a guilt kiss. "Maybe I'll call Alice in the morning," she lied.

Alice was her therapist. She had helped Louise through some rocky times, but

Louise had no desire to talk about this particular affliction with Alice or any other therapist. The mind, the spirit, who cared? It was her *body,* her perfect body with all its flaws, she wanted back. She was tired of the mind, hers and everyone else's. She thought maybe if she had it all to do over again she'd become a tennis star, or at the very least an aerobics instructor. And maybe she'd stay married to Teddy Flynn. Which was another good reason to steer clear of Alice. Alice would make her talk about Teddy, try to analyze the dreams. Since the operation, she had started dreaming about her ex-husband for the first time in years. They were only married for two years, twenty years ago, and she'd only married him because her mother had died of cancer that spring and she was all alone. No father (he had died years earlier). No sister, no brother. Alone. Although at the time, of course, that's not how she saw it. At the time it was all hot summer evenings and clandestine skinny-dipping and sad songs on the car radio and aftershave that smelled manly—like someone strong and capable of taking care of you forever—and the scratch of stubble against her cheek, the taste of rum and Coca-Cola, his lips nuzzling her breasts like candy.

The Teddy dreams were erotic and at the same time a little sad, as if mournful, romantic music were playing in the background, and Louise did not want them analyzed, reduced to archetype, by Alice or anyone else. She just wanted to keep dreaming them.

In his sleep David hunkered against her backside and draped a heavy arm over her waist. His hand sleepwalked up her belly toward her chest until she intercepted it and slid it back down—like a teenage virgin, only in reverse. In those days the trick was to keep their hands *above* the waist. The boys were like babies you had to distract from danger with bright, shiny objects. Whenever one seemed too intent upon tugging off her underpants, she would pop a breast out of her bra and wave it around beguilingly until his attention shifted safely upward. With Teddy Flynn it was different. She never had to resort to such maneuvers. From a family of flat-chested women, fresh from Vietnam and a series of R & R flings with small-boned Asian bar girls, he'd seemed stunned, dazed, by the sight of her generous American breasts. Night after night, parked on some dark lovers' lane even though she lived alone in an empty house full of empty beds, he paid such court to her mammary glands that she began to feel like a mermaid. Eventually her neglected lower half began to thrash and demand its share of attention until they finally did IT, and she decided THIS MUST BE LOVE.

Two years later she'd decided THIS COULDN'T BE LOVE. How odd, she'd thought: it had taken her two days to work up the courage to marry him and two years to work up the courage to divorce him. She couldn't believe how much harder it was to say "I don't" than "I do." The day she finally left him, he stood at the front door watching her get in her car, the same car he'd sold her two years earlier. He reminded her of a dog—a big, sad, obedient dog that someone parks on the curb and orders, "Stay!" For a long time after that she didn't much like herself. When she told her life story to new friends and lovers, she edited out the part about having been married. She took the snapshots of her and Teddy out of her photo albums and hid them. She hadn't even told David about her brief first marriage until after she'd moved in with him and he'd stumbled across the snapshots of Teddy while searching through the closet for the heating pad.

"Who are they?" he'd said, staring at a picture of Teddy and her cutting the wedding cake, as if he expected her to tell him she had an identical twin sister she'd neglected to mention.

"A *used-car salesman*," he'd laughed when she told him. "Come on. I know you're kidding."

Suddenly she had a need to see those pictures again. The digital dial blinked 3:15, but she didn't care. She didn't have to wake up early anymore. She had extended her semester's leave of absence indefinitely even though everyone, *everyone*, had told her that was exactly what she should *not* do if she wanted to get back on track, back to her old self. Her old self minus a breast, that is. No one mentioned that. Except the trickle of volunteers, women with one or both breasts missing, women who had been in her shoes and who came to talk to her like a special maimed branch of the Welcome Wagon. One woman sat on the edge of Louise's hospital bed, holding her hand and talking earnestly about the miracle of survival. Every thirty seconds or so she would squeeze Louise's hand hard, as if pumping something into her. Another woman, who visited her at home one afternoon, yanked the bedclothes off and asked Louise just who she thought she was to lie around feeling so sorry for herself when she had a nice home and husband and fancy job?—giving Louise the distinct impression that this woman, a double mastectomee, had none of the above. Yet another woman, younger and more glamorous, came with tiny twin daughters dressed in identical pink bathing suits, like animated Valentines. They were on their way to the beach, she'd explained, a strategy calculated to show Louise that the good life goes on. As she was leaving, she'd pulled down the strap of her black tank suit and exhibited her breast to Louise. "Reconstructed," she'd said. "Not bad, do you think?" She'd asked Louise if she wanted to feel it and Louise had said no, although she did. "A lot of the Hollywood stars go to him. He has a special back entrance his nurse showed me." One of the pink twins wet her pants and the woman departed hastily, slipping the plastic surgeon's card in the mailbox on her way out. That night Louise made fun of the woman to David. They were eating take-out Chinese food and he was laughing, nervously pleased that she seemed to be regaining her sense of humor, when she'd stopped suddenly and shivered. "I used to be a nice person," she said. "Didn't I?"

"Of course, of course you were. Are." Tears sprang to his eyes and he had reached for her, and she had held him at bay with a chopstick. It left a fiery dot of sweet and sour sauce on the snowy breast of his white shirt. He'd stormed out to the kitchen, muttering to himself. A second later he'd loomed in the doorway, sponge in hand, and said, "If you don't call Alice right now, I'm going to call her for you. And drive you to the appointment myself."

She continued eating her rice.

"Well, what do you have to say to that?" he'd demanded, anxiously biting his cuticle—a habit she had broken him of back in graduate school.

"You can lead a horse to water but you can't make her drink."

"God!" he'd pounded his fist against the door frame. "God, you piss me off!"

"I'm sorry." She had finished her rice and moved on to what was left of his.

"And I have news for you." He waited for her to look up at him. "You were *never* all that nice."

"I was too."

"Oh yeah? What about Tommy Flynn? Why don't you ask that poor schmuck just how nice you were?" He marched over and grabbed the telephone receiver and brandished it until he felt foolish and set it down again in its cradle.

"Maybe I just will, as a matter of fact," she said. "I've been having these dreams about him lately. Pleasant dreams. *Very* pleasant dreams. And his name is *Teddy,* as in bear."

DAVID WAS A SOUND SLEEPER. He had two modes—on and off. She always felt the instant he woke up. It was like a furnace kicking on in the basement. She could hear his mind rumbling beside hers on the pillow. Conversely, when he was asleep, there was nothing—she doubted that even a brain scan would pick up any activity. She slid out from under his arm, quietly closed the bedroom door, and turned on the hall light. The two photo albums were buried under a heap of racquets—tennis, badminton, squash, racquetball. She carried an album into the bathroom, locked the door, sat down on the toilet lid, and flipped through the slightly sticky pages, passing by snapshots of college, of a summer trip to England, Scotland, and Wales (with her mother), and of her small candy-colored wedding—everyone managing to look simultaneously stiff and wilted in their best clothes in the ninety-five-degree heat—hurriedly flipping the pages until she was at Lake Tahoe with Teddy on their honeymoon.

They had arrived in the late afternoon, unpacked—she had insisted on unpacking his suitcase in a fit of wifely domesticity—and made love before dinner. She remembered his being miffed by all her giggling every time his empty stomach grumbled. In between giggling fits she murmured apologetic reassurances. Passion spent, they showered and dressed and debated restaurants—Italian, Chinese, steak, and seafood. She was straining, arms akimbo behind her back, to hook her black bra when he reached over and said, "Let me." She let her arms hang loosely at her sides, enjoying this classic bit of married life, when he suddenly slid the bra off and tossed it onto the bathroom floor where it skidded into a puddle.

"You don't need that," he said. "It's 1966. California. The natural look."

"But—"

"Do it for me. Your loving husband. Please."

She had looked at their image in the mirror, like some multiarmed Indian deity. He was standing behind her, his hands caressing her unbound breasts with such a sweet, contented expression on his face.

"Okay, I guess," she'd giggled.

He kissed the back of her neck.

They went to an Italian place on the highway and she remembered holding the large red menu over her breasts while they gave the waiter their order. She also remembered driving back to the hotel with her legs squeezed tight, her bladder painfully full, because she had been too self-conscious to saunter all the way back to the ladies' room with her breasts bobbing like buoys beneath her thin summer dress. But by the end of the week she was playing volleyball on the shore and parading around in skimpy T-shirts, bestowing breezy, oblivious smiles on the oglers as Teddy puffed with pride of ownership.

There was one snapshot she particularly liked. They were standing in front of the yellow Mustang, the car he'd sold her. The car door was open and you could almost hear the radio playing. A sliver of blue lake floated in the background and Teddy's arms cinched her waist, swinging her round and round. His tanned, muscled arms were pushing her breasts up, and they threatened to spill over the top of her strapless sundress like foam over the rim of a glass.

She slid the snapshot out from behind the cloudy plastic page. As her fingertips traced the pneumatic curve of her glossy breasts, she could hear her mother's patient voice telling her not to touch the image, to hold the picture by the edges—like so— and suddenly, more than anything, she wished her mother were asleep in the next room, wished she could see her mother for one minute, wished she could feel her soft hands, hear her cluck of sympathy. But her mother was dead, of cancer, and Louise was alive. Lucky to be alive. That's what everyone kept telling her, and she didn't get it because she never for one second thought she was going to die. Louise had watched her mother on her sickbed and had come to the conclusion that no one ever really believes they're going to die until they're already dead, and then it's too late to worry. What it's not too late to worry about is everything just short of death.

"WHAT'RE YOU DOING?" David cleared his throat, scratched his groin, and squinted into the bright bathroom. "At this hour."

"Nothing. I couldn't sleep." She hastily jammed the picture back into the album and feigned a yawn. He reached for the album and shook it until the loose picture fluttered out. She stomped on it with her bare foot, but it slid easily out from under her toes.

He glanced at it and sighed. "I have to pee." He handed the picture back to her. "If you'd be so kind."

She stood up and he raised the toilet seat, careful not to brush against her. She remembered the orange-robed monk she had accidentally bumped into on the crowded ferry in Bangkok, the horrified look in his eyes as she smiled apologetically and reached out her arm to steady him. Later she read in a guidebook that the monks were forbidden to touch females and that the Thai women scrupulously gave them wide berth. She was in her strident feminist phase back then and had gone wild when she read that.

"From now on every monk I see I'm going to pat his ass."

"No, you're not," David said calmly. "It's a cultural difference and we respect cultural differences."

She'd stuck her tongue out at him and he'd patted her ass, and she'd socked him in the gut and they'd ended up rolling around on the bed, an hour of athletic sex that left them lying sweaty and exhausted, contentedly immobile, on top of a pile of crinkled maps and train schedules.

They had not made love now in over four months, since right before the operation. Her fault. He could not have behaved more heroically, showering her with flowers, champagne, lacy negligees, compliments, protestations of love. Yet she'd thought he protested too much. Such romantic fuss was not like him. They had been colleagues before lovers. Their marriage had flourished in the glow of reading lamps, not candlelight, and although they had always enjoyed each other in bed, the fact that they were of the opposite sex had always seemed like more of a boon than a necessity. So it made no sense to her now that the loss of a single breast could cause this rift between them. But it had.

On her way out of the bathroom she hit the light switch, then paused in the semidark to admire him naked for a moment, one of those alabaster gods peeing in a Roman birdbath.

"You should have an affair," she said.

"Don't tell me what to do. You're not my mother."

She laughed. He could still make her laugh. That was something at least.

He flushed the toilet. "What makes you so sure that I haven't, that I'm not?" He followed her down the hall to the bedroom.

"Because I know you."

"And what is it you know?" He waited until she was settled back in bed and then climbed in delicately on the other side.

"I know you couldn't stand thinking of yourself as the sort of unenlightened schmuck who cheats on his wife after her mastectomy."

"You don't give me much credit." He rolled over, his back to her.

For the first time it occurred to her that maybe there actually was someone else, another woman who listened sympathetically while he confided to her the details of his dismal home life. The thought of this other woman judging her filled Louise with white-hot indignation. Who was *she* to judge *her* until she had walked in Louise's shoes? Then it suddenly occurred to her that it would be just like David to find someone who *had* walked in her shoes, just to make her look bad, to leave her no room for argument. She imagined David lying in bed with the glamorous blond with the reconstructed breast, the two matching little Valentine girls sound asleep, innocently sucking their identical thumbs, in the next room.

"Don't blame yourself, Dave," she'd stroke his mussed hair and whisper into his ear. "You've done everything anyone could do. It's her. It's just her. She's a sick woman, Dave."

"But I'm her husband," he'd protest. "I'm an intelligent, sensitive man, not some macho jerk. I should be able to help."

"Some women just don't want to heal, Dave. They're like emotional hemophiliacs. They'll bleed all over you if you give them half a chance." She'd slide her hand under the covers until she found what she was looking for, and he'd bestir himself to show his gratitude.

Gratitude. She remembered this odd habit of Teddy's. He used to thank her after they made love. Every time without fail, he would kiss one breast and say "thank" and the other breast and say "you." It got on her nerves after a while, and finally she blew up and screamed, "For chrissakes don't thank me! It's not like I'm doing you some big favor." He got that wounded-deer look in his eyes and said, "Okay. I'm sorry." After that he stopped thanking her aloud, but she could tell he was still thinking it, and the silence was louder than the spoken words.

"What did you *see* in him?" David asked her once. "I don't get it." He was staring at one of those Polaroid Christmas cards that Teddy had sent her. The color picture on the card showed a paunchier Teddy with his new wife, Lorraine, and their ten-month-old baby, Brian Jeffrey. The card had arrived out of the blue six years after their divorce and represented the sum total of their communication over the years.

While she was busy chopping an onion, David affixed the card to the refrigerator with a sushi magnet and printed at the bottom, "Would you buy a used car from this man?"

"You're a disgusting snob," she'd said when she'd turned around and noticed it finally. "And if you want to know the truth, I'd trust him over you any day." She'd snatched the picture off the refrigerator and slid it into her pocket, then resumed mincing the onion with a new threat of violence. "He was the sweetest, gentlest, most selfless person I've ever known. Absolutely no ego. No personal ambition. Not like our kind. A kind of latter-day saint, really." Her eyes were tearing, her nose sniffling. "Needless to say I didn't appreciate him at the time. I didn't think he was smart enough for me. One afternoon we went down to the Motor Vehicle Department to take our written driving tests together. I got 100 percent and he flunked. When I saw that big red *F*, I felt humiliated. I felt contempt. And that's when I knew for sure I was going to leave him. Over a stupid grade on a stupid driving test. And the irony was, he was the best driver in the world, the very best." She wiped her eyes, then blew her nose in a paper towel. She knew she sounded like some maudlin drunk. David stared at her amazed, not quite daring to laugh.

AT DAWN she was still awake, watching the darkness fade to gray, listening to the birds' clatter. She feigned sleep while David showered and dressed and foraged in the kitchen. As soon as the front door shut behind him, she fell asleep. When she woke up, she was alone and smiling. The smile faded along with whatever she was dreaming, leaving only a vague afterimage of Teddy and a vast parking lot full of toy cars, like a parking lot glimpsed from an airplane. It was late. The bed was ablaze with sunlight, and she was sweating in her flannel nightgown. As she peeled the nightgown off over her head, her naked body exuded the odor of old coffee grounds. She threw on the sweatpants and sweatshirt that she had worn the day before and probably the day before that. Then she walked out to the kitchen, poured herself some coffee, and sat. She had no plans for the day. There was nothing she had to or wanted to do. She looked lazily at the hand-painted calendar hanging on the wall opposite her, a gift from a former student, and saw that in some former lifetime she had drawn a line through the first three days of this week and scrawled in the title of a conference at UCLA she had planned to attend. For an instant she could remember, relive, sitting here in the kitchen, skimming the brochure, and hastily penciling in the dates on her calendar. For an instant she was possessed by the spirit, the spirit of her former busy, confident self. It was as if some dervish had lifted her up, whirled her around, and then dropped her back to earth, stunned and winded.

Louise suddenly felt an ache in her left breast, the one that wasn't there. She frequently felt some sensation there. She knew it was a common phenomenon—the phantom limb. Everyone had heard about amputees who could still feel their missing arms and legs. She had read about one man, a Vietnam vet with his leg amputated at the thigh, who kept waking up at night to scratch the sole of his missing foot. The itch eventually drove him insane. This reminded her of an off-the-wall joke she'd heard on Johnny Carson: my girlfriend has poison ivy of the brain—the only way she can scratch is to think of sandpaper.

The summer she married Teddy she had picked some wildflowers and come down with the ugliest case of poison ivy ever. Her fingers blistered and swelled like sausages. Three times a day Teddy would patiently swab her hands with Calomine lotion and then tenderly position a cottonball between each of her fingers to keep them from chafing against each other. She sat there in the rocker on the front porch like some splay-fingered queen of Sheba, restless and whiny, while he cooked the dinner and washed the dishes, whistling away just as cheerful as could be. It was after dark by the time he joined her out on the porch. She was complaining about the itching when suddenly he leaned over and unbuttoned her blouse and parted it like a curtain so he could look at her bare breasts. "Are you *crazy*? Button it," she hissed at him. She clawed clumsily at the front of her blouse, her fingers too swollen to maneuver the tiny mother-of-pearl buttons. Neighbors were passing by on their evening constitutionals, and although her chair was angled facing the house, she was sure they could see. "Lovely evening!" he called out. "Just enjoying the view." He smiled and winked at her. She frowned and muttered at first, but pretty soon she was aroused, so aroused she wouldn't have murmured a peep of protest if he'd stripped her naked right there on the front porch in full view of passersby. They let it build like that for just as long as they could withstand the heat, then tore inside and went at it like a house afire.

Afterward he lay quietly with his head on her breasts humming that song "Louise." Then they took a long hot shower together. Every now and then he'd hold one of her breasts to his lips like a microphone and warble some silly song until she slapped his hand away. She used to sigh and wonder if all men carried on like such fools. She found it hard to imagine Jean-Paul Sartre, for instance, clowning around with Simone de Beauvoir's tits. She fantasized having silent, sophisticated, highbrow sex with pale, bespectacled men. Years later, one of the things that most attracted her to David was his dignity in bed. That and the fact that he seemed virtually indifferent to her large breasts.

So how—the thought cracked like a whip in her brain—could she now expect him to grasp the enormity of the loss? She had chosen him for his very lack of fanaticism, and now suddenly she wanted him to mourn like a true zealot. It wasn't his fault. He was simply miscast. The right man for the wrong job. It was perfectly obvious.

She leapt up from the table, suddenly energized, and hurried into the bathroom. Moving quickly and mechanically, she showered and dressed and packed a small suitcase. On the way through the kitchen to the garage, she scribbled a hasty note to her husband—

Back in a couple days. Don't worry.
It's not your fault. Love you.

—and stuck it on the refrigerator with the sushi magnet.

IT WAS AFTER MIDNIGHT, raining lightly, when she took the Petaluma Boulevard South exit off of 101. Her shoulders and lower back ached from the nine straight hours of freeway driving, but other than that the trip was a blur, as if she'd been suspended in a trance. A trance that had not yet worn off. It was too late to call him this evening, she knew, yet she continued down Petaluma Boulevard, away from the strip of highway motels, and turned left onto D Street. Even though she had not heard from him in over a decade, she knew in her bones he would still be living in the same house, and in fact, as she pulled up to the curb and looked across the street at the one lighted window on the second floor—their old bedroom, her mother's old bedroom—she saw him stand up, look out at the street for a moment almost as if he sensed something, and then shut the window. As simple as that. She was so tired she could barely keep her eyes open as she headed back out to the highway, back to the lonely little strip of motels.

The next morning she was jostled out of a deep, dreamless sleep by voices in the next room. For an instant she thought she was back in the hospital, but then she heard a car door slam right outside her window and she remembered. She got up and dressed, dressing more carefully than she had in some time. She arranged her dark hair so as to hide the gray streaks and put on lipstick, then wiped it off. She wanted to look as much like she had back then as possible, and back then she had not worn makeup. She left her things in the motel room and drove to some bright, anonymous place on the highway for coffee. Although she'd had nine straight hours alone in the car to think, she didn't have much of a plan really. She felt as if she were obeying some more powerful will than her own. She sat there calmly, drinking her coffee, waiting for some voice from the wilderness to tell her what to do next. Go ye forth and . . . The waitress brought her the bill.

It was a cool, sunny day, crisp as new money. Perfect car-selling weather. Teddy had always said you had to work twice as hard to sell a car in the rain. She headed out toward McBride Buick and Olds on the west end of town. Although it seemed almost inconceivable that anyone could work in the same place for twenty years— she thought of her address book, crossed out and written over as her friends moved on to better jobs, bigger houses—it seemed entirely possible that Teddy had stayed put, had remained loyal to Walter McBride. When she arrived at the corner where the car lot used to be, her heart sank. There was a minimall with a donut shop, auto parts, 60 Minute Photo, and a deli—all catty-corner to a huge new Toyota dealership. She parked and went into the auto parts store, looked around for the oldest clerk, and asked him whether McBride Motors still existed.

"Oh sure," he said. "They're out on the highway now. Practically in Novato." He drew her a little map.

He was such a nice man and her relief was so great to hear the place still existed that she grabbed the first recognizable item she saw—a pair of sunglasses—and said, "I'll take these." She didn't realize they were mirrored until she glanced in the donut shop window on the way back to her car and was startled to see herself.

The map was precise and detailed, and she found the new location without any trouble. McBride Motors was twice its former size but still only half the size of the new Toyota place. She drove over toward the service area and parked inconspicuously, as if waiting for someone. She kept her new sunglasses on. A couple of young salesmen were out on the lot talking animatedly with prospective customers. She felt conspicuous and unpatriotic in her silver Saab. Except for the anachronistic cars, she could have been in some time warp. She was beginning to feel like Peggy Sue in that Francis Ford Coppola movie, filmed right here in Petaluma, in fact, about an unhappily married woman who gets conked on the head at her high school reunion and winds up back at Petaluma High. The trance was beginning to wear thin around the edges. She was thinking about getting the hell out of there when the voice in the wilderness said, "Wait!" She paused with her hand on the ignition key, and then she saw him. He was wearing a suit and talking with two younger salesmen. It was evident from the younger men's demeanor that he was their boss.

This surprised her. Somehow she had never thought of Teddy climbing the success ladder along with everyone else. He looked, actually, thinner and more fit than in the Christmas picture he had sent her years ago.

A mechanic walked over, wiping his hands on a greasy rag, and asked her if she needed help. "No," she smiled ingratiatingly, "I'm just waiting for a friend." When she looked back over at the sales office, Teddy and one of the younger salesmen were climbing into a shiny red car. Lunchtime, she supposed. She noticed the mechanic glancing back over his shoulder at her suspiciously. She supposed she couldn't very well hope to sit here all day without attracting attention. It was now or never. She could telephone, wait until he came back from lunch and then call, but she thought some physical proof of her presence, her nearness, was necessary. She took one of her cards from her wallet and was about to scribble a note on the back when she thought no. The card said "Dr. Louise Jensen" and would only serve to remind him of all the time that had passed and all the differences between them. She tossed the card on the floor and tore off a large white scrap from a McDonald's bag.

> Dear Teddy,
>   I'm here in Petaluma. I drove up here just to see you. Please meet me at the Buckhorn when you get off, around 5? 6? I'll wait. I won't leave til you get there, so please come.
>
>   Louise

She thought about giving him the name of her motel, where he could leave a message, but she did not want to make it easy for him not to come. Better he should think of her sitting alone at the Buckhorn waiting. She walked over to the young salesman who was left, handed him the folded note, and asked him if he would please give the note to Mr. Flynn. "It's very important," she said as she turned to go. "Business. You won't forget?"

"Right. I'll see to it personally." He made a big show of tucking the note carefully in his wallet.

She could tell by the way he watched her get back into her car just what sort of business he thought it was. Well that was stupid, she thought as she drove away. Small town like this. He was probably the wife's kid brother.

AT A QUARTER TO FIVE she was sitting in a booth at the Buckhorn nursing a draft beer. She disliked beer, but she figured that Teddy would order one and she didn't like the image of herself sipping white wine while he chugged on a beer. The afternoon was a blur. It would take a shot of sodium pentothal to make her remember how she'd managed to while away the past four and a half hours since leaving the car lot. Her brain revved and idled as she waited. Her hands and feet felt like ice, but she was sweating underneath her chamois shirt and bulky tweed jacket, which she kept buttoned as if he could walk right in, take one look at her, and tell what had happened, what was missing. The Man with X-ray Eyes. One of the two loud, beefy men at the bar was giving her the bold eye. She frowned down at her beer and got some morbid, vengeful pleasure out of imagining letting him coax her into bed and the look of horrified shock on his beer-bloated face as his hand groped under her sweater.

At 5:30 she ordered a second beer. It did not occur to her to wonder what she would do if he didn't show, because she knew he would. It was just a matter of when, when he could get away. Then an awful thought occurred to her: what if he didn't come alone? What if he brought along one of the young salesmen or, worse yet, his wife? Teddy was the above-board, open-book type. He didn't know the meaning of the word intrigue. She got up and went to the ladies' room—the beer seemed to pass straight through her—and when she walked back out to the main room, there he was, standing uncertainly at the front of the bar, alone. He stiffened when he saw her, and she suddenly wondered what she was doing there. Four hundred miles from home. An image of the pay phone hanging next to the ladies' room flashed in her brain, and she fought a quick urge to run back there and dial David or Alice and have them talk her back home, the way air controllers sometimes talk lost pilots safely back to earth.

Teddy followed her back to her booth.

"Thanks for coming," she said.

"I was surprised, you know, out of the blue like that. How long's it been?" He took a sip of his wine. "Almost twenty years. I recognized the handwriting, though, right away." He paused for a long minute, nervously fingering his tie, waiting for her to explain herself.

"Give me a minute," she said. She downed the rest of her beer and signaled the waitress for another. She wasn't half drunk enough.

"So," he frowned. "You look good, real good."

"Come on. I look like hell." She started in on the new beer. Her hands were shaking and she sloshed some on the table.

"No, not at all. A little tired maybe," he conceded, blotting the spilled beer with his napkin. "You were always hard on yourself."

"And on you."

He shrugged. "I'm married now. Again."

"You mean since Lorraine?"

"No. I mean Lorraine. Fourteen years. How did you know her name?" He looked a little paranoid, as if he suddenly suspected her of something.

"Christmas card one year."

"Oh." He smiled, relieved. "We have two kids. Brian and Amy."

God, she groaned to herself, waiting for him to pull out the wallet and the pictures. For this she drove four hundred miles. She reached across the table and grasped his hand to prevent him from reaching for the wallet. Embarrassed, he glanced over at the bar for a moment, then slipped his hand out from under hers. She started to cry quietly.

He sat there looking at her, seemingly paralyzed by cross impulses. She could imagine the battle going on in his soul: the impulse to be loyal to his wife on the one hand, the impulse to give comfort on the other.

"Come back to my motel room with me," she whispered, staring down at her hands now folded primly in her lap. "Please. Just this once." She pressed her leg against his under the table. "I need you to."

Automatically he moved his leg away, then let it drift slowly toward hers again, just barely touching. "I don't know what to say," he said. "I'm happily married. I thought you were married." Suddenly a light seemed to dawn. "That's it, isn't it? You're getting a divorce."

She shook her head. "David's fine."

"Oh. Good." He seemed deflated, overtaxed, at a loss. He finished off his wine and glanced at his watch. "Lorraine will be worried. I'm sorry." He started to reach in his pocket for his wallet, this time to pay. He put enough bills on the table to cover her, too.

"Thanks," she mumbled.

"I'm sorry," he said again. "I am."

He stood up and self-consciously struggled into his raincoat. "Look. Would you like to come over for dinner? I could call Lorraine and say, well, she . . ."

"No. No thank you. That's very sweet, though."

He shrugged and looked relieved but still hesitant to walk off and leave her like this—alone, in a bar, crying into her beer.

"Could you give me a lift to my motel?" she asked suddenly. "If you're not too late already."

"Sure. No problem." He seemed overjoyed to be given a concrete way to help. "How'd you get here?"

"Cab," she lied, as she followed him out to the parking lot past her Saab and got into the shiny red car she'd seen earlier in the day.

He turned on the radio and they didn't say much during the short ride to her motel. He attempted some chitchat about how Petaluma was changing—skyrocketing property values, gourmet restaurants, etc.—but when she didn't respond, he fell silent. She was sunk inside herself, straining to hear the voice in the wilderness, summoning her courage.

"Here." She pointed at a neon sign up ahead.

He swerved into the poorly lit, deserted parking lot, gravel flying.

"There." She pointed to a room on the end.

He coasted to a halt in front of her door. "Not exactly the Ritz," he joked. "I figured you'd be a millionaire by now. Or at least married to one."

"Do it now," the voice said. "Now."

"Come inside," she coaxed. "Just for a minute."

"No," he shook his head. "I can't. I'm sorry." He sighed and reached across her and opened the door.

"Please. I have to explain the way I'm acting. I have to show you." She started unbuttoning her jacket.

"Jesus," he groaned and rested his forehead against the steering wheel.

She finished the jacket and started in on her shirt buttons.

"Jesus *Christ*, what're you doing?" He scrambled out of the car and walked around to her side of the car. "You're crazy. I'm going to call your husband myself and tell him to come and get you 'cause you're just not yourself."

He held her jacket shut and half-dragged, half-carried her into the motel room, dropped her on the nearest twin bed, and then turned his back to her, fumbling in the dark to find the lamp switch.

"Shit, where is that fucking thing?" he cursed and muttered as he frisked the pole lamp.

It was comical, and she surprised herself by bursting into laughter. The light blinked on and he turned to glare at her, face flushed scarlet from exertion and exasperation. She stopped laughing and watched his expression change as he got a good look at her sitting there, stock-still, with her blouse gaping open. The color bleached out of his face, and he sank down on the edge of the twin bed opposite her.

"I've been dreaming about you," she said. "Ever since it happened. You were always so crazy about them. Treated them like pets."

"I used to drive you crazy. You used to threaten to handcuff me."

"Yeah. How the mighty have fallen." She caught a glimpse of herself in the large wall mirror and winced. "God." She buttoned a couple of buttons of her blouse and smoothed her wild hair. "I apologize. I have no right. I don't know what I'm doing really. I really don't know. I really don't. Last night I parked in front of your house. There was a light on upstairs in the bedroom, my mother's old bedroom. And all of a sudden I had this idea that I was your little girl asleep in my old room and you and my mother were about to go to sleep in her room, your room—our old room, yours and mine—and for a second I felt so safe. So comforted. For a second it all made sense, you know, like dream logic, and then it all fell apart. I don't know. I just don't know anything anymore. And now I can't seem to stop talking. I really can't." She paused for breath, hoping he'd say something. He didn't. She sighed. "You can go. You don't have to stay. I know she's waiting for—"

"Shhh. Be still." He sounded like a stern father.

"Sorry." She bowed her head meekly.

He leaned over and kissed her firmly on the lips as if to seal them shut, then rocked back and waited to see if she had anything else to say. She kept quiet. He smiled and knelt on the floor in front of her and unbuttoned her blouse.

"Beautiful," he whispered, "unique. The world's most perfect breast." He stroked her breast and gently pressed his lips to it.

"*No.*" She shoved him away, wrenched her shirt free, and scrambled to button it. A button fell loose in her hand. She looked at it sadly for an instant, as if it were a tooth, then hurled it across the room. It nicked the mirror and bounced onto the carpet. "Shit!" Holding her blouse bunched together in the front, she crouched down on all fours and raked her fingers frantically through the red shag.

"Forget it. It doesn't matter." He grabbed her hands and wrestled her slowly down onto her back and pinned her there until her resistance snapped like a wishbone. Then, clumsily, he lowered himself down beside her and held her to him like a child, rocking her back and forth as if she were crying. But she wasn't. It was him. He was crying noisily, just as she had imagined he would be. A wonderful, terrible racket, more comforting than any lullaby. She closed her eyes and listened.

IF NEW YORK CITY can be seen as a vast, unkillable organism ever-changing yet always recognizable as the same neon-eyed, stone-skinned monster—and if the American money-madness of the 1980s and 1990s can be understood as a cultural virus, then this story might be a needle biopsy of a time and a place. Or, at least I so hoped. "The Commuter" was written in late 1993 in two parts for *Worth*, a glossy monthly magazine devoted to a higher contemplation of money and its manners, and if there is a slightly feverish quality to the prose, it is due to the fact that when the first half of the story went to press, I did not know how the second half would resolve itself. Although the story was quite consciously written about the kind of people who might find themselves reading a magazine such as *Worth*, I hoped to subvert their valuing of what things were worth what, perhaps even demonstrating that when large sums suddenly arrive, they are often on the end of a pointed stick.

COLIN HARRISON

COLIN HARRISON

The Commuter

BUFFALO GRASS, Nicholas Wren told himself as he gazed out of the commuter train at the gray doomscape of the Bronx. He'd definitely go with the buffalo grass. It wasn't an easy choice—there was much to be said for the Kentucky bluegrass variety called Baron, or Citation II, a perennial ryegrass resistant to aphids and webworms. Around him the other riders rattled their newspapers and flipped through printouts and memos as the train flashed past block after block of abandoned buildings. No, he decided, it had to be buffalo grass—soft, apple-green buffalo grass that formed a tight sod, needed little water, and grew to a maximum of six inches and then stopped! The stuff had been developed by some obscure genius at Texas A&M. He'd mow only three times a summer! He pictured, what—two, three acres? Lisa and the kids, Frisbees, maybe a dog. He'd get out there on a John Deere and remember the bold wager that had catapulted them out of the city. It was a bet, in fact, that he was going to place today.

Outside in the February cold, graffiti ribboned along the walls next to the tracks, continuing even into the tunnels. The train car was dirty and overheated, with a mood of futility—a hundred-odd souls hurtling toward the very same moment 24 hours hence. Did they suffer the same pressing anxiety he and Lisa felt? For the last few years, the two of them had entertained the idea of fleeing their cramped condo 30 minutes north of New York City and moving back to Lisa's hometown outside of Cincinnati—a place where someone could buy a five-bedroom Victorian for around $160,000 and actually know the mailman by name. But now there was a certain urgency; there had been an incident two weeks ago—a nasty incident—and Lisa was desperate to leave.

He and his wife had realized, of course, that the entire metropolitan area was slipping into barbarity. Only a month ago, three youths in ski masks had blundered onto the very train Nicholas was riding, the 7:48 from Croton-Harmon, a mere two cars forward of him, shot one round of a 9-mm pistol into the roof, and nervously relieved a dozen riders of their money and watches before fleeing. And one of the secretaries at Belton Associates, the engineering consulting firm where Nicholas worked, had been brutally raped in her apartment and was now on indefinite leave.

But none of this had prepared them for what had happened to Lisa outside the Grand Union. How could it? The van had bumped the back of her Camry, and when Lisa looked up in her rearview mirror, she hadn't liked what she saw. No, not a bit. The men were already out of the van, she'd later told Nicholas tearfully, and they looked strangely angry, considering *they'd* hit *her,* and anyway, what were two men in a rust-eaten van doing in a suburban shopping center? She'd shifted into first gear and hit the gas, but even so, one of them got the passenger door open, a hand and gun coming in first, with the words "Give it up, bitch, give it—" But he was a second too late, and the Camry kicked him back against the rear door. By then Lisa was going 40 miles an hour across the parking lot.

Later as they'd examined the damage to the rear bumper, Nicholas had seen the fear in Lisa's face. The van incident was just the latest proof that they were living in a landscape of bad possibility, that the hour was late. It was time to go.

There was one problem: money. Perhaps $8,000 for a mover, plus six months' living expenses while he and Lisa found work, a minimum of $30,000. If, as he hoped, he started his own consulting business, he'd need another $20,000, at least. And because banks would be less eager to lend to people without jobs, they'd need a sizable down payment on a house—say $50,000. This came to $108,000, which they could scrape up. Barely. But there were other costs: Lisa would insist on busing the kids into the private school she'd attended in Cincinnati. Two kids, two tuitions—another $18,000 a year, and Nicholas needed that money now, in case it took a while to get a business rolling.

But this wasn't all: Lisa's mother—lucid, stoic, and 68 years old—suffered from diabetes. She had lost one foot already, and was sliding as the months went by. This was another reason Lisa wanted to move back to Ohio soon. Her mother, whose assets amounted to $11,000 and a small farmhouse with a rotting roof, would soon need skilled nursing care on a daily basis, which Medicare wouldn't pay for. If they could unload the farmhouse (for maybe $35,000, if anyone was foolish enough to buy it), her mother might eventually qualify for Medicaid. Yet there were more problems: The local nursing home, a private facility ten miles away run by a large Texas-based corporation, had a six-year waiting list for Medicaid patients. But Nicholas had heard that if one was willing to fork over $28,000 a year—cheap by New York standards—then this outfit would smile and miraculously find a bed. The other option was a private-duty nurse—three hours a day at $22 an hour was $66 a day, or about $24,000 a year. Which didn't include the time and expense of trips to a dialysis center every other day and which meant that Lisa could probably not work full time.

When it was all said and done, Nicholas figured he needed at least $200,000 in hand if they were going to move to Ohio. Their net worth was more than that, but if they couldn't unload their condo (built in the mid-'80s with such greedy haste that the wallboard was actually falling off its framing), then the move was just about impossible. Their condo village, Nicholas had found out, had nine units more or less identical to theirs for sale. Three had been on the market for more than 18 months. People hated condos now, knew they were a bum deal. To make matters worse, Nicholas and Lisa's place needed perhaps $4,000 or $5,000 in work to make it ready for the market. If he couldn't sell the condo quickly, there was no other source of $200,000 cash. Certainly not his and Lisa's salaries. Her part-time work in a small local law firm brought in $26,000, and he was due to make $88,000 this year. While $114,000 had once sounded ample, it now provided just enough for a mortgage payment, a vacation each summer, and perhaps new bikes for the kids every year or two.

And what about making money in the stock market? The averages had gone up through most of '93, but Nicholas felt the market was dicey in even the best of times. Last June, one of the personal-finance magazines had recommended Nike stock at $69 a share. The projected 18-month return? Forty-seven percent. "A terrific buy," the text had trumpeted and so Nicholas bought 100 shares. But when he'd finally dumped the stock in the first week of October, it was down to 45½. He'd lost only $2,300, but the experience just confirmed his belief that the market was in a strange time. Each new high brought the voices of doom from the financial press, and while he wasn't sure he agreed with them, the market felt choppy and capricious, and he knew that any play he could make had better be specific—not an attempt to time the market or bet on interest rates (though he *had* predicted November's carnage in the bond market). As for commodities, it was a devil's game he'd never played. He'd once read that the price of corn was affected by no fewer than 14 unrelated factors, including the price of fertilizer and who was in power in Moscow.

What he needed was to make money in some way that departed from the honest but meager buy-and-hold strategy. And he needed it soon. The family budget didn't have much breathing room—nothing left over for, say, Broadway tickets or anything that might make Lisa feel that her life was the one she wanted. She was great with the kids, dutiful toward him, but he could see that inwardly she felt that her existence had become *forgettable*. And as he'd discovered bitterly only a week before, her one avenue of solace did not include him.

AFTER ARRIVING IN GRAND CENTRAL, Nicholas walked from the train toward his office on 47th Street—just another man in a winter coat and scarf. In the lobby he ran into Hal Gruber, the senior vice president.

"You remember we've got the monthly meeting," Gruber said.

"Ten o'clock."

"I got the first readings on that Culver City location," Gruber said, raising his eyebrows.

"What was it, 1,000, 1,200?"

"Eighteen-fifty."

"Will they shield?" Nicholas asked.

"They don't know. The owner's daughter works 16 feet from the highest reading."

Belton Associates had pioneered the growing specialty of electromagnetic-field consulting, one of four firms with national reputations. Every few weeks another office building around the country was discovered to harbor a cancer cluster among its employees, and scientific evidence increasingly suggested that electromagnetic fields created by power cables within the buildings might be the cause. There was, for example, the Ford House Office Building in Washington, D.C., which had 12 cases of cancer, five of them brain tumors, among its 500 employees. Or the cluster of brain-tumor deaths at the *St. Louis Post-Dispatch* in Missouri. And now, female emergency medical technicians in New York City were complaining that their Motorola 800 MHz radios were affecting their menstrual cycles.

All this bad news was good news for Belton Associates, which consulted with companies that were designing new buildings, telling them how offices should be laid out in respect to phone lines, transformers, cables, and electrical-service equipment. The firm also conferred with companies that suspected the potential for EMF health problems among their employees. Sometimes electrical equipment could be shielded, at other times offices could be reconfigured, and occasionally, if EMFs reached high enough levels, companies were forced to abandon buildings to avoid litigation by their employees.

It was Nicholas's responsibility to coordinate and oversee Belton's nine technical teams as they moved through various consulting projects nationally. He knew where they were and the severity of the EMF problems in each location—worst in raised-floor buildings with huge power requirements to run air conditioning, computers, phones, lights. In his five years at Belton, he'd gradually discerned an intriguing pattern. So intriguing he hadn't mentioned it to anyone else at the firm.

The companies most disrupted by EMF tended to be in office buildings built between 1978 (after it became clear that new buildings would have as many computers as people, thereby requiring higher power levels) and 1989 (when design-phase EMF shielding became more typical). Most commercial buildings erected in this time were service companies dealing with information—banks, insurance offices, 800-number phone operations—and, Nicholas had observed, when operations crucial to the company's cash flow were affected by EMF problems, something happened: Profits dropped. The effect was most pronounced in smaller companies that were forced to heavily modify or move out of their chief offices.

Because the companies did not want to alarm their employees, they would generally proceed quietly with the office closings, often attributing them to other causes—say, restructuring or consolidation—with the result being that the analysts who followed the stock sometimes didn't know of the disruption until weeks or months after it had occurred. On several occasions, Nicholas had watched in amazement as stock pickers touted certain small-cap companies that were about to take huge hits to their cash flows. Locked into their spreadsheets, pressured to issue buy and sell recommendations on stocks every day, the last thing they'd know about would be what was actually happening at the company.

But if *he* knew a company was in trouble, then he could short the stock. He'd merely borrow a certain number of shares of the company, immediately sell those shares, and then wait for the stock to drop to a certain price, at which point he'd buy back the same number of shares and return them to the lender, pocketing the difference between the proceeds from the sale of borrowed stock and the cost to replace it.

The difficulty, of course, was that he couldn't trade on information he knew about Belton's client companies—that was insider trading. (And when he thought about *that,* invariably the theme song to *Cops* would pipe into his head: "Bad boy! Bad boy! What you gonna do, what you gonna do when they come for you?") So he dutifully read the industry publication that came to his office every month, a newsletter with dense columns of minuscule type that updated the latest research, hoping to spot a small, publicly traded company with EMF troubles. Several prospects had appeared, but he'd discarded them as shorting possibilities—the affected operations weren't critical enough, other positive profit news would counteract the EMF effect, or other negative news would surpass the EMF effect. Sooner or later an opportunity would come along—it had to.

Meanwhile, the "Ohio scenario," as Nicholas referred to it, had become increasingly desirable over the last few months, and he'd realized that if a shorting opportunity came along, he'd better have some money ready. In fact, considering what he wanted to do he'd need every dime. He and Lisa's regular savings were minimal, under $15,000. But his wife's grandmother had died five years back, leaving Lisa about $19,000, and Lisa had asked him to invest it, which he had, choosing one of the less speculative health-care funds, buying on the fallbacks in price that occurred whenever the media carried a surge of stories on health-care reform. Then the media would become interested in something else and the health-care stocks would climb back. In three years, he'd turned that original $19,000 into $37,000. When the Japanese stock market had dropped off the cliff in '92, he'd waited with fiendish patience, watching the Nikkei average fall into the grave (to 14,309 to be exact), then finally taken all of the $37,000 and bought into a Pacific index fund that same August, just before the Japanese government announced it was going to "fix" its own stock market with various tricks. Fourteen months later he was up 47 percent and gleefully sold out with just over $54,000.

But he needed a bigger stake, much bigger. So in October he'd tapped out his credit cards for another $12,000 in cash. The carrying cost on that debt was negligible—less than $200 a month. He also borrowed $65,000 from his mother. That gave him a grand total of $146,000 to play with. Yet this still wasn't enough for the white-knuckle wager he had in mind. So as a final measure, he'd refinanced the condo, hitting the interest-rate cycle close to the bottom at 6.75 percent for a 30-year mortgage. The condo was worth $310,000, and he and Lisa had owed $110,000 on the old mortgage, leaving $200,000 in equity. The bank had allowed him to pull $150,000 out of that, giving him a new mortgage for $260,000, which sounded like a hell of a lot to carry, but at 6.75 percent it was about $2,000 a month—not so bad. "Going to put that money to work?" the bank's lawyer had inquired at the closing.

Yes, sir. With the $150,000 from the refi, he now had $296,000. Through the end of the year, he'd funneled each piece of money into his brokerage account as it had been received, and so now all of it, with accumulated interest, was sleeping peacefully at a tooth-rattling 3 percent—a little more than $298,000. It would seem that he could just use this sum to move to Ohio, but that meant carrying the $260,000 condo mortgage while buying a house in Ohio—too much. Nor could he carry the mortgage by renting out the condo, because that was strictly prohibited by the homeowners association. No, the $296,000 could only be understood as a short-term fund with which to leverage more money. All he needed was an opportunity. The fall had trudged along, and the stock and bond markets kept hitting new highs, making him second-guess himself. Had he made a huge mistake? Even the *idiots* were making money!

But then something extraordinarily lucky happened.

Just four days before, he'd gone to the annual EMF conference in Miami. By now it was something of a chore yet a good excuse to get away, and Belton Associates picked up the tab. He wasn't scientist but he was management, and Ralph Belton liked to think that his management people were up on their engineering research. Besides, all of Belton's main competitors would have people there—Cross Tek, Crane Associates, Kimmel Engineering.

So he'd gone, pinning his name tag to his shirt each morning, attending the presentations of papers, jawboning with the other conferees afterward. On the last day, in the morning session, old Lawrence Davis, Crane's chief engineer, had given his presentation. Davis, whose head radiated wiry red hair, liked to show off the difficult cases he was tackling on behalf of Crane Associates. Nicholas had considered skipping Davis's presentation (instead lying in bed and watching CNN or one of the soft-porn films on the hotel TV), but ever the dutiful soldier, he'd dragged himself down to the hotel's conference center along with about 25 others—most of them engineers.

Standing next to the podium and using computer graphics projected on a large screen, Davis sawed on about the usual things: new frequency-measuring equipment, shielding configurations. Nicholas slumped in his chair, letting his mind resonate with the hotel's drumming ventilation system. After dozing off at one point, his head lolling backward, he forced himself to sit up, if only to be polite and appear professional.

And *that* was when he heard old Davis describe the latest instance of his own glory. Crane Associates, Davis boasted, had received a call from a Seattle-area data-processing company, RemoteCount, Inc. The company's processing facility had a grid-pattern EMF with peak measurements of 3,029 mG—a genuinely shocking figure. Davis moved briskly toward the relevant scientific question, but Nicholas got the gist of what had happened: After signing a consulting agreement and performing an initial examination of the premises, Crane Associates had argued to the RemoteCount executives that the company was running a huge litigation risk by continuing to allow its 1,400 employees to work in the building. Shielding of the electrical equipment wouldn't work, according to Davis, for the power grid ran throughout the entire structure, even directly beneath one of the ladies' restrooms. Crane had presented data about brain-cancer latency rates and EMF exposure, Davis went on, the conclusion being that after nine years of operation, the RemoteCount facility was just about to enter a 20-year window of higher probability for a brain-cancer cluster. Davis didn't need to say any more. Nicholas could guess that the RemoteCount executives had consulted their legal counsel about potential liability costs and then, upon getting the estimate, freaked out.

At this point, he sat upright in his chair in the auditorium. Assuming that RemoteCount was publicly traded, here was a company that fit his paradigm (key operations affected, information-based) and—*and*!—presented no insider-trading problem! He was learning about RemoteCount in an open forum! Just 25 sleepy engineers, but open to the public! Advertised in the industry journals! Pay your $1,395 for the three-day conference! They let *anyone* in! Davis was scratching his scraggly red hair and describing how he planned to tear apart the entire power system of the RemoteCount operation! The company had big, big problems!

But wait. When had all this been discovered? From the ninth row of the small auditorium, Nicholas raised his hand.

"Yes?" Davis frowned at the interruption. "A question?"

"This may be getting a bit ahead, but I'm curious to know whether the situation in Tucson you described earlier would be helpful in evaluating—"

"*Yes,*" old Davis blurted, happy that someone was paying such close attention, "yes, we *were* able to modify the model and apply it directly."

"So this Seattle situation wasn't recent?" Nicholas asked slyly from his seat. An open forum! Anyone can attend!

Davis frowned. From a scientific point of view, the question was irrelevant. "Oh, no, quite recent," he said, turning back to the screen. "Last week, actually."

The information was new! Davis rambled to his conclusion, and then while the rest of the audience shuffled obediently toward the hotel's restaurant for a lunch of overcooked vegetables and soggy fish, Nicholas fled to his room and called Jane Chung, his broker. She confirmed that RemoteCount was public, traded over-the-counter on the Nasdaq. Shortly thereafter she called back, with a certain excitement in her voice: RemoteCount was a thriving data-processing company, deriving all of its income from two sources—sorting out medical-insurance claims and, recently, organizing creditors' claims against large companies that had fallen into Chapter 11. Handling the bankruptcy claims against a major airline, for example, RemoteCount had recently processed no fewer than 357,000 pieces of paper. All of this activity transpired in RemoteCount's huge data-operations center east of Seattle, where, as Davis had said, 1,400 people peered into screens all day long. There was no other facility. It didn't take a genius to figure out that shutting down the building meant RemoteCount could not process claims, which meant that the company *could not make any money.* RemoteCount's cash flow was about to hit a wall! Of course, the company would be forced to establish some kind of temporary processing center, but it would take weeks—months!—to find such a facility, and more time before a computer network was installed, people transferred, retrained, and so on.

But when would the brokers learn of the problem? They certainly hadn't yet, Jane had said, for the stock had floated merrily along at around $47 a share for months, held largely by big West Coast pension funds—Calpers, Oregon Public Employees, Washington State.

"The fourth-quarter numbers are out soon," Jane added. "They could start dumping then."

"But it could happen sooner, right?"

"Conceivably, someone else in that room figured out the same thing you did," Jane said. "You want that, remember. But it means you have to move quickly to borrow the RemoteCount at 47."

"There were guys in the room from a lot of small West Coast start-ups—specialized engineering companies, system-service companies, companies like that."

"That supports my point. They could *easily* be on the pension committee of their company, and they would know if their company held RemoteCount stock."

"Maybe they're sitting on some decent profits," Nicholas mused.

"Well, the stock *has* done nicely. It was at 38 a year ago. *Somebody's* been buying. . . ." Jane was reading. "There's a good future growth feeling about the stock . . . but you could say it's overpriced. . . . The p/e is 41, so you *could* make an argument about it being overpriced."

She interrupted herself. "Nicholas, someone at that conference could call the benefits manager at his company tomorrow, telling them RemoteCount has big problems, dump it immediately."

"What would happen?"

"You'd have the regional pension funds seeing that, getting on the phone, and calling around to ask why, and then maybe the big pensions in New York would catch on, TIAA-CREF, and then the technology funds might—"

"How far could it go down?"

"That's impossible to answer," she told him. "But I've seen stocks lose half their value in one day. If a few major institutional investors want out, suddenly there's no market to prop up the price."

Yes, yes, yes, Nicholas had muttered to himself yesterday on the plane from Miami back to New York, *and suddenly there's no market to prop up the price.*

NOW, IN THE FEW MINUTES before the ten o'clock meeting at Belton started, he closed his office door and called Jane Chung again. "I want to do it," he told her. "I thought about it all night."

"How much?"

"The whole account, 298 and whatever."

"I checked this morning with our stock loan department. We don't have any RemoteCount to loan out. So they'll have to call around, see if they can find some to borrow."

"Jane, I'm worried the stock'll drop and I won't—"

"Just be patient," she said. "Give me a few hours." There was a pause. "And, hey, you *do* realize that if we do this and you're wrong, if the stock goes up instead—"

"Then I'm screwed. I'm burning thousand-dollar bills."

"Yes."

"Just find the stock for me, Jane. I'll call you after lunch."

At his computer, he did the math one last time. Because of various margin rules, he figured he'd be able to actually borrow about $270,000 worth of RemoteCount stock—at $47 a share, some 5,700 shares—from whatever unsuspecting source was located by Jane's stock loan department. She'd sell the stock for him as soon as it was borrowed, and if all went right, he'd watch RemoteCount's stock begin to drop. The farther the better. Would it start soon? At the bottom, if he could hit it, he'd buy back the 5,700 shares. Every dollar the stock price dropped would generate $5,700 of profit, more or less, after Jane's commissions. If the stock dropped 10 points, $57,000 in profit; 15 points, $85,500, and so on. How far could it go? If RemoteCount lost three months' worth of income, it still had to pay its executives, service its bank debt of $105 million and bond payments, and pay consultants like Crane Associates. Even laying off people cost money. Moreover, the firm might permanently lose business as its clients shifted their accounts to other providers—some of them the newer, low-cost data-processing outfits in the Caribbean, Ireland, places where labor was much cheaper. RemoteCount might not only post a sizable annual loss but be seriously weakened. Any analyst would realize that RemoteCount stock might not pay a dividend in 1994, and that would be another reason to dump it. Who would buy a stock in a company like that? Bottom-fishers, vulture funds. But they would let the stock fall to sickening levels. Could it fall to $10 or even $5 a share? Nicholas pulled out his calculator; if the stock fell to 5, and he sold then, he'd be looking at almost $240,000. Stranger things had happened in life. Those who never wager never win, he reassured himself. Life is a sequence of bets.

IT WAS AFTER 11:30 when he finally turned his attention to the *other* matter at hand. His wife was having an affair—sneaking into the city when the kids were in school. He'd discovered it only a week ago, shortly after the van incident in the supermarket lot. She'd forgotten—or chosen not—to erase a phone-machine message before he came home one evening: "Monday at noon," the voice crooned, "I'll be the man with the unlit cigarette and the maroon scarf." Ha. Such wit. Such style. Such an asshole—the self-appreciating voice belonged to Richard Chambers, a former neighbor who'd recently moved back into the city. Chambers was an officer at the Ford Foundation. He drank exotic Kashmiri tea and liked to talk about his collection of African masks. Lisa had always found him charming, and now, no doubt, met him at his apartment, perhaps a hotel. Maybe a different hotel each week, just for thrills. (The excitement in the elevator, the fresh bed.) There'd been signs, of course—yes, he'd been a fool not to see them: the aloof expression on Lisa's face, a renewed interest in wearing high heels. The extra hundred miles or so on the car's odometer each month. Or, most sickeningly, the night they were in bed a month or two back and she'd pinched his nipples while he was on top of her—seemed excited by it. *Someone has taught her this*, he'd thought.

He decided not to confront her just yet; in market-theory terms, he had inside information but was choosing not to act upon it. He didn't blame Lisa, not exactly. Maybe she'd been worrying that despite all their talk about moving to Ohio, they'd never do it, in which case she had stepped outside the marriage for a little excitement. Maybe she figured that they *would* move to Ohio and she'd better have some fun now. Maybe—aah, maybe he'd let himself go to pot. He was, after all, 30 pounds heavier than when they married, and sometimes when he caught a glimpse of himself in a store window, he was mystified by what he saw: a 37-year-old man in an overcoat, hair receding, face softened by too many lunches at Grand Central's Oyster Bar, too many hours pushing paper.

But what to do? Over the weekend, before his trip to Miami, Nicholas had shuffled around the house pondering the question while Lisa was out with the kids. He'd combed through the junk in the basement, staring at his wife's black winter coat in the closet, even sticking his hand in the pocket, finding nothing. He'd seen this situation a couple times with his friends—the wife and husband went through a long agony of confrontation and confession, sometimes breaking up. Such protracted suffering didn't appeal to him, seemed destructive, even. And the hell with therapists. Therapists were *consultants*, for God's sake, and he knew how useful consultants were.

It had occurred to him, wandering the house, peering into the refrigerator, that if he could destroy his wife's relationship with Chambers *remotely*, then he could avoid a conflagration at home. At the same time, his stock play, a quarter-million dollars out of nowhere if it worked, might get Lisa excited about replanting the family and the marriage in Ohio. Then, staring at a drawer of outgrown baby clothes, an idea came to him. It was clear, it was quick, it was full of emotional violence, and it hinted that Nicholas Wren was a strange and desperate man who might stop at nothing. And, most important, it was perfect for such a fastidious soul as Richard Chambers.

He called up Chambers from Miami and asked him to lunch after his return. "I thought we'd better have a little talk," Nicholas said calmly, knowing Chambers would understand why. "Yes, of course," Chambers replied, attempting to sound at ease. "I have a three o'clock meeting. Perhaps I should reschedule. . . ." Nicholas let these words hang there and die. "No," he answered, "I think we'll be done quickly."

IT WOULD BE a bit of ugly business, but that made Nicholas happy. Life is a series of bets. Sell Chambers, buy buffalo grass. They'd agreed to meet at Giverney, a quiet out-of-the-way place in the Village. Very elegant. Once inside, past the freshly cut flowers, the girl checking the reservation book was genuinely French and arrogant about her beauty; her scrutiny was frank, for she was deciding whether patrons were to be dumped close to the windows near the street, the restaurant's crass zone of easily pleased tourists, or to be graciously ushered back past stacks of French bread and bottles of sweet after-dinner wines to the quiet enclosed garden court in the back, where bankers quietly delivered the bad news to their clients or Wall Street men enjoyed a discreet lunch with their mistresses.

When Nicholas arrived at the restaurant, he told the hostess he preferred the garden. And they looked away. In New York, if you look away, that's the indication you expect no difficulty, that your preference has been expressed and your mind is now on to more important matters. Nicholas was in his good gray suit and a black tie with flecks of red, and the hostess showed him back to the garden.

Chambers came in a minute later, a dapper walking stick of a man. Nicholas hated to admit it, but he understood why Lisa found him attractive. Chambers was a studied presence. He had fine features and soft hands. He was a man who'd spent years building his surfaces; he planned his conversations days in advance; he spent a long time choosing shoes; he had a lengthy opinion about American foreign policy toward Haiti. Of course Lisa found Chambers interesting and mysterious; her own husband didn't shave over the weekends, farted to amuse the kids, arrived at the dinner table with house paint on his hands, and had long since lost his manners in bed.

He stood and extended his hand as Chambers approached. Sitting down now. Very polite. Suppressed mannerisms, smoothing the tie repetitively, etc. The waiter arrived.

"They have a very good steak here," Nicholas said.

"We'll both have it then," Chambers agreed heartily. "Despite the impact on the heart."

"Despite that, yes."

"You've been well?" Chambers offered, with no hint of irony. "The consulting . . . the electromagnetic thing prospering?"

"Terrific, very good. And the foundation? Giving away millions every day?"

"We do have some innovative projects underway, in fact," Chambers answered, a man who dictated too many letters. "We're less prescriptive than in the past, and perhaps we work better with the local officials and citizenry."

"Do you get down to Latin America much anymore?" Nicholas asked.

"Maybe twice a year now. The larger projects mostly."

From there it went to NAFTA, with Chambers dilating on the effects at the village level: acceleration of change—more jobs, less traditional culture. Then, after his soup, Nicholas put down his spoon. "Of course you know that I asked you to lunch here because you're screwing my wife."

Silence. Their eyes met. Two men in fine suits.

"Yes," Chambers said. "Yes. Well, I—"

"No, please, don't say anything more," Nicholas interrupted. "No explanation is necessary. I see your attraction to her—I am her husband, after all."

Chambers seemed relieved, yet puzzled. Is this all there would be? his eyes seemed to say.

The steak was served, and for a few minutes they busied themselves with that. The knife and fork, the butter on the potato. Then Nicholas slipped his hand into his breast pocket. Chambers appeared alarmed. A gun? No, of course not. They were civilized men. Nicholas pulled out a small white envelope.

"If you are going to continue to do what you are *doing,* I think you should look at these," he said.

Chambers waited warily.

"You see, I want to hasten your perceptions, Richard." Nicholas slid the envelope across the table.

Chambers opened it. Inside was a small stack of photographs.

"The first," Nicholas said, "is when Lisa had Tommy."

The delivery room at Lexington Hospital. A clinical shot, between the knees, as the baby crowned. In the photo, Lisa was huge; 40 pounds heavier than she was now, her ankles thick, her face bloated (yet Nicholas had thought she was beautiful, truly). Overhead lights reflecting off her kneecaps. The doctor's green gloved fingers could be seen spreading Lisa's labia to reveal something that looked like a wet, whitish tennis ball.

"Huh," said Chambers.

The next picture was a close-up of Lisa straining as she pushed the baby. Her face was a mask of veins, sickening, magnificent, one eye shut, the other a slit of suffering consciousness.

"I took all of these," Nicholas said evenly. "I was there."

Chambers turned to the next photo, which, Nicholas knew (for he had carefully arranged the sequence), was taken at a slightly different angle than the first; it showed Lisa straining again, a full body shot, the nurse urging her, the fetus a monstrous rise of a belly. Her chin was up in the air and her arms thrust back above her head, gripping the top of the delivery table. Pushing. Pushing for all she was ever going to be worth.

"Of course, the first baby is usually more painful," Nicholas said. "Plus this was back labor, the baby pounding the spinal nerve. It was very bad here, actually. Lisa wouldn't take the epidural."

Here Chambers paused. He'd been chewing his steak. He swallowed what was in his mouth with uncomfortable awareness and looked up at Nicholas.

"She screamed so much she was about to vomit. I told the anesthesiologist to just put in the goddamned needle."

The next photo showed the head of the baby outside of the labia, supported by the doctor's hand. The wincing face of the baby was elongated from labor and covered with white gunk from inside the womb. The struggle in the baby's face suggested that the outcome was in doubt; in fact, Tommy had been vigorous from his first breath.

Now Chambers twisted his watch around his wrist as if handcuffed by it.

"Have a look at the rest," Nicholas said.

"Well, I—"

"Just look at them, Richard."

There were six or seven more photos, and Chambers grimaced with each one: healthy baby being suctioned; umbilical cord; Tommy resting on Lisa's breasts, his face a wrinkled monkey mask that she was kissing; and the last, a shot of Lisa and Nicholas holding the baby together.

Chambers slipped the photos back into the white envelope and sucked at his teeth contemplatively. A waiter appeared, offering coffee. No thanks. Some dessert, gentlemen? They declined. Chambers handed back the envelope.

"I also have a set for my daughter." Nicholas said, patting his breast pocket. "Tommy was easy, but Sally came out blue."

Chambers touched his napkin to his mouth.

"Did Lisa ever mention that Sally came out blue?"

Chambers shook his head silently.

"The umbilical cord was around her neck. They couldn't slip it off. Lisa was frantic, terrified. The doctor had to—"

"Okay," Chambers interrupted, a wince flashing across his face. He got the point. There were other possibilities, he seemed to be thinking, there were other women. He appeared to understand that the whole affair could only get messy from now on. He'd not quite imagined the graphic quality—the *horror* of it. If they had been his children, that might be another matter. The photos had seemed so . . . so *veterinary*. . . . This was Lisa, this was where—

The two men sat in silence. Around them was the tinkle of silverware on plates, the bustle of waiters, the musical hum of conversation. Nicholas knew that he'd won, but he did not feel triumphant. It sickened him that he'd had to do this. The moments when his son and daughter had been born had been the happiest of his life. And now he would always think of this lunch.

"So—" Nicholas began, but the waiter arrived with the check. Chambers pulled it toward himself.

"I'll take it." He gave a brisk nod that suggested this was the most efficient way to conclude.

And that was that. The men left the restaurant separately, Nicholas second. He paused outside at the steps and watched Chambers march away down the narrow street with the brisk step of someone who knows he has just eluded disaster, just sold out at the top of the market.

UPTOWN, IN HIS OFFICE, Jane Chung's number was busy. He left messages. Had she found the RemoteCount stock? What was happening to the price? He waited, agonized. Finally she called, shortly after four.

"Don't worry," she said, "the price didn't move yet. And I actually found the shares. A wirehouse out west, Monroe Securities."

"Never heard of them."

"It's a house with a small investment bank that specializes in local and regional IPOs. They handled RemoteCount's IPO four years ago."

"I don't get it."

"They're still sitting on stock they couldn't sell."

"Are they suspicious?" he asked.

"They might be, but to them it's easy money."

"What are the terms?"

"The stock is callable at any time. The running fee is 3 percent of average daily market price, calculated and paid monthly."

"Three percent a month?"

"Yes. Now our house rule is that we must have 10 percent overage in case we have to mark to market."

"You mean if the stock goes up and I'm toast."

"Right. But I'll put in a buy-stop at 50. That would be about a 6 percent loss."

"A mere 17 or 18 thousand dollars."

"Well, the math works out a bit differently," Jane said. "You have a little more than $298,000 in your account. I'm setting aside $27,090 for our overage rule, which leaves 271, and I'm setting aside another 3 percent of that—about 8,000—to take care of the Monroe fee."

"What am I left with?"

"Two sixty-three."

He was tired of waiting for the rest of his life to begin. "All right. Do it."

"You're *sure?*"

"Yes. Just get that sell order in quick."

"You'll send me a letter that directs—"

"Already typed," he said. "I'll fax it in about a minute."

After Nicholas hung up the phone, he walked down the hallway to the office fax machine, past the usual afternoon chatter: Ewing looked good last night, the new De Niro movie, Clinton making promises. He slipped his letter of instruction into the tray and watched it feed through. For a moment he considered yanking the sheet out of the machine. But he calmed himself. The fax finished. He retrieved the letter and returned to his office.

He glanced at his watch and realized he'd better get moving if he wanted to catch the 5:14 home. Right now Lisa would be watching the local news in the kitchen—the murders and fires and scandal. He wondered if she knew him anymore. Perhaps he didn't know himself anymore, except that he was a man pulling on his winter coat in a lighted office in the dark sky high above the street. His dreams had become transsubstantiated into digital pulses that even now were across the city somewhere, moved onward from Jane into another bright current of dreams that itself flowed through another computer, another trader. In time those pulses would come back to him, revealed for what they had become. As nothing—mere expirations of hope. Or as an odd, terrifying, exultant form of energy: Money.

II

NICHOLAS WREN was sitting in the backseat of a late-model Chrysler Fifth Avenue, speeding north through a gray winter morning on I-270, a spotless ten-lane artery spoking out from Washington, D.C., and *again* he was agonizing over the price of RemoteCount stock. Again!—when he should be worrying about this morning's presentation, which, potentially, promised a huge contract, a bigger annual bonus, possible promotion. All he could think about was RemoteCount.

HADN'T HIS ANALYSIS BEEN CORRECT? Hadn't he weighed all the factors? Oh, but if he'd known how nerve-racking this business was going to be, well, then he'd never have—*No!* That was *not* the way to be thinking. He *had* to have faith! *Faith!* Without it he'd be lost. It had been three trading days since Jane Chung, his broker, had executed the order, and since then nothing! Well, yesterday the stock had crept up, just half a point, just enough to terrorize him, and before getting the 5:14 home, he'd needed to stop off at a bar outside New York's Grand Central and knock back a couple just to relax.

And now the market had been open for nearly an hour, and he didn't know what was happening! "Don't turn into a quote junkie on me, Nicholas," Jane had warned. "If there's anything important, I'll let you know." In other words, don't bug me. Jane was right; he needed to maintain his composure. He looked out the window hoping for distraction. The highway flowed through the newest paradigm of American civilization—gleaming exurban office parks, townhouses rolling over what used to be cornfields, the landscape tidy as a microchip. He hated it. What he wanted was an Ohio farmhouse tucked away on a bumpy lane, a couple of old maples in front.

Now wasn't the time to be thinking of this. In a few minutes the car would pull into the parking lot of Girardi Corp. According to the research prepared by Nicholas's office, Girardi had grown from an $18 million house contractor to a $277 million office-complex developer. The Washington metropolitan area had kept growing through the Bush recession. Why? Its traditional suburbs, like Chevy Chase, were insanely expensive; the federal government's payroll kept growing; D.C. itself was more or less segregated; and the city was staggeringly violent, even by New York standards. And the newer suburbs were far enough north that one could actually commute to Baltimore—for a developer, what could be better? Too bad Girardi was privately held.

The company had seven projects in the pipeline, each worth more than $40 million, and some of its younger executives had begun to worry about electromagnetic-field radiation—which is where Belton came in.

Nicholas was here to propose to Girardi Sr. a consulting arrangement—a three-year training and project-oversight deal. Belton Associates would train Girardi engineers and architects to avoid high-level EMFs in their new building. It could mean a lot of money for the firm. Just yesterday, Bart Belton himself had come by Nicholas's office to ramble on about how the deal might help them get more business in the Washington market, develop a relationship with a deep-pockets company, even create the possibility for joint—

But the RemoteCount stock! What *was* it doing? He leaned toward the driver. "How long before we get there?"

"We got about nine, ten minutes."

Time enough to call Jane. He hoped that RemoteCount had already started to drift downward. He picked up the car's cellular phone. Jane was there on the first ring.

"Jane, hi, I'm in D.C. this morning."

"I'm surprised you didn't call me from the shuttle."

"We were landing. The phones didn't work. How's it look?"

"Well, the market's started to rise on the lower oil prices . . . wait a sec. . . ." He could hear her tap her keys. "All right, here—well, no, RemoteCount's up a quarter point."

"On top of yesterday's half point."

"Well, the Labor Department released some numbers saying more people have jobs. That means more insurance claims for RemoteCount to process. Good for the stock."

He straightened his tie. "Not good for me, Jane."

"I'd say not."

Up three quarters of a point, multiplied by the 5,700 shares; he was down about $4,300. He wasn't about to panic, right? *Scared money always loses.* Some investment guru had said that. *To contemplate panic is to panic.* Sounded like a Chinese philosopher. "Jane, you mind if I give you a call at the end of the day?"

"Nicholas, if there's any kind of significant action, I'll call."

"You can leave it on my voice mail in New York."

Next he phoned Lisa at the small law office where she worked part time in their suburb outside New York City. It was a general-purpose law firm, but Lisa had developed an odd specialty—examining the medical depositions of people who had been in car accidents.

"Hi," he said. "You just get in?"

"Few minutes ago," she answered.

"How'd you sleep?"

"Well enough." Her every word a bomb thrown in his direction.

"What do you have going today? More human misery?"

"Yes, Nicholas, more misery."

Fake charm was only going to get him trouble. "I think I can make it home just after dinner. I'll try to make the 4 P.M. shuttle."

"Okay."

"Okay?" he pressed.

"Yeah, okay."

"Is that an 'Okay, that's great, it'll be nice to see you?' Or 'Okay, try to choose a plane that has no working engines?' "

"Nicholas, we've both got long days ahead of us."

"Oh, come on. I got my sad ass up at five o'clock this morning in the cold, and I'm just looking for a little cheap affection from my wife."

He heard her sigh, followed by a long pause as she considered what level of conflict she wished to pursue.

"I've got to get off," she said. "I'm expecting a call from London."

"Kids fine?"

"They're fine. Tommy said he had a nightmare."

"What did he—"

"I've got to get off here, Nicholas. I've got to get off."

"Okay. We should see a movie sometime."

"Yeah, we should. Bye."

He hung up. Things would get better with Lisa after the RemoteCount deal. That was one of his operating principles. If the deal worked, then he might appear to her as more than the irritating man who got off the train each night and ate dinner in her dining room. *To contemplate panic is to panic.* Perhaps that applied to a marriage, too.

THE CAR ROLLED into the Girardi Corp. office cluster, and a minute later he was gulping coffee in a huge conference room, wondering again if RemoteCount had started to fall, and then all the Girardi executives came in and he forced himself to concentrate on the business at hand—which he did, performing quite a nice sell job on old Girardi Sr., a big-bellied man with hands that had once grasped hammers and power saws. Girardi Sr. seemed skeptical of anything he could not touch himself, but he had clearly seen the worry in the faces of his young vice presidents who were helping him make so much money.

So Girardi Sr. was receptive, and Nicholas—thinking ahead to the home he'd soon be buying in Ohio—even slipped in a question about what kind of seed Girardi

Corp. used in the lawns around its office parks. Girardi brightened. "Kentucky bluegrass," he boomed. "Stick it in on any kinda soil."

With the obvious success of the meeting, Nicholas was hoping he could shrug off RemoteCount's three-quarters-of-a-point rise. *Worry and you're lost; believe and you've won,* he'd heard a failed television star profess on a late-night infomercial, and so, no, he was *not* going to worry. He believed in his heart that once RemoteCount's EMF troubles became more widely known, the stock would drop. Jane had said that most of the RemoteCount stock was held by the pension funds and they'd probably dump it all at once, causing the stock to nosedive. So he'd sit tight. RemoteCount would drift along at 47, okay, maybe 48, and suddenly drop. Maybe he'd graph the stock's falling price on his Mac using the Microsoft Excel 4.0 that he'd bootlegged from the office. No problem. He wouldn't even bother Jane at the end of the day.

HE CALLED HER from the shuttle at 4 P.M.

"Forty-eight and an eighth," she said.

"What? Why?"

"The broad market is really up today. People are buying everything. The Dow was up 53 points after lunch and settled back up 39."

"But why RemoteCount? Wal-Mart or McDonald's or something I could understand, but—"

"Hey, Nicholas, I just trade them, right?" Jane said irritably. "But you know, one of the pension funds could have taken a profit somewhere in a big position in another stock and decided to pick up some interesting smaller stocks, and they just bought a rising RemoteCount price until they filled their position. That could be it."

He hung up and did the math; he was down $6,400. His stop order was at 50, and suddenly that seemed rather close.

HE TRAMPED INSIDE the front door just after 7 P.M., as the kids were getting in the bath, and hollered upstairs to say he was home, then tossed his briefcase on the floor and floated into the living room. In the kitchen he ate the rest of the kids' vegetables and rice out of the pot and idly pressed the play button of the phone machine to see who might have called: nothing. You never knew what could turn up—this was how he'd learned about Lisa's recent (and presumably terminated) affair with Richard Chambers. Ever since Nicholas's brutal little lunch with Chambers a week ago, he could only assume that Chambers had immediately cut short the relationship. And as much as he wanted to confront Lisa about the whole thing, perhaps it was better to wait until they moved. New York would seem like a million miles away. Maybe he'd stoically never even bring it up. Or maybe he liked keeping the secret—it let him stay angry at his wife.

Upstairs, he stuck his head into the bathroom, and there they were, Lisa bent over the tub reading a book, Sally and Tommy in the warm suds, their little chests and shoulders above the bubbles.

"Hi," he said. "How's my kids?"

"We're almost ready here," Lisa said, flipping the page.

"Okay."

She pushed her dark hair out of her face and looked at him, waiting. Even in her exhaustion, she was still lovely, still someone he admired and wanted to please. But a marriage, he now understood, was not just a static condition; it was a series of marriages between the same two people, and these days theirs was weakened by his inattention to her, burdened by children and work, and poisoned by her affair. They needed a new start, they needed hope, they needed RemoteCount to drop by 20 points. But maybe he could say something pleasant, signal his willingness not to fight. "There's a lot of building going on outside Washington."

She nodded, faking interest in this comment. "I'm glad you're back."

Did he believe her? He wasn't sure.

"Me, too," he mumbled.

In the bedroom, he flipped through the mail. The usual bills, the usual junk mail—solicitations for investment newsletters and credit cards, catalogs for women's dresses and Japanese power tools. Then Tommy, his five-year-old, ran into the bedroom, hair wet, trailing his towel.

"Dad, do dead people all die lying down?" he asked.

"I don't know, Tommy. That's kind of a strange question."

"Billy Meyer says all dead people when they die, they have their tongues sticking out."

"I don't think so." He toweled off his boy's back. "Let's get your pajamas."

"Billy Meyer told me in school."

"Has Billy Meyer seen a lot of dead people?"

"He was with his mom, and they saw a dead man lying on the sidewalk."

"He saw that?" Nicholas said, aghast.

"Billy says they all die with their eyes shut and if—and if they forget to shut them, then the bugs eat the eyeballs."

He looked at his boy and at the smoothness of his cheeks and the odd wet cowlick and his bright eyes and breathless patter.

"Don't worry about it, pal, okay?"

From the bathroom came the happy sounds of Sally and Lisa finishing up. He and Lisa had made various parenting mistakes—too long in the crib for Tommy, too early with the play group with Sally—but they'd gotten bedtime down, never varying the ritual. The kids actually seemed to like going to sleep. Lisa came into the bedroom, followed by Sally, who marched around the room in chubby excitement, her skin pink and warm. His wife flipped a diaper on the bed, and he swooped Sally up, held her gently on her back, dabbed a pinch of Balmex on her rear and put on the diaper. He'd once calculated that they'd spent nearly $5,000 on Pampers—good reason to buy Proctor and Gamble; he'd ask Jane about the stock. Now the kids ran around in their pajamas for a few minutes, and then Nicholas got down on his hands and knees like he always did and Tommy flew onto his back for an "executive ride," which meant that Tommy rode on Nicholas over to the bed, where he leapt dramatically into the covers.

Sally was in her little bed, and then Lisa turned the light out, and Sally, like she always did, asked, "Night-light?" And Nicholas answered, "Yes, sweetie, it's on, let's go to sleep," and the kids settled down while he sang "Take Me Out to the Ball Game," one of the few songs he knew by heart. While he warbled, "Buy me some peanuts and Crackerjack, I don't care if we ever go back . . ." he wondered what he would do if RemoteCount went any higher. A few punk 25-year-old fund managers who knew more about Air Jordans than they did stocks could have a look at RemoteCount tomorrow and start buying for the hell of it; Jane's stop-loss order would kick in at $50 a share and he'd be finished—out of the game with a $17,000 loss, his foolishness confirmed.

LATER, HE FOUND LISA IN BED READING.

"Well?" he said. "How about a romantic interlude?"

"Can I finish my chapter?"

"Sure."

He took off his clothes and got into bed naked, laying his hands on his stomach. He'd lose weight once they moved to Ohio. Start running again, biking at least. Then he felt the weight of his wife as she got beneath the covers, and they lay quietly there for a few minutes as they both made the long transit from their respective thoughts toward each other. When he finally rolled toward her, he hoped that she wouldn't be thinking of Richard Chambers, his beguiling smile, his toned buttocks, and so on.

Twenty minutes later, after Lisa had returned from the bathroom and he'd pulled on a T-shirt and underwear, he drifted in a fugue state, a half dream, in which he saw a new car skidding sideways across a wet road in slow motion. The wet skin of the car, the brilliant spray, the poetry of advertising. The dark figure behind the windshield was him. He liked the Ford Taurus. He was driving and turned off up a long driveway that led to a classic white farmhouse. The buffalo grass made a thick green carpet around the house. The stuff didn't need much water. He'd plant a nice row of flowering trees—Sargent crab apples, perhaps, or flowering white dogwoods (*Comus florida*). Or the rare magnolia hybrid Pink Goblet, a vigorous grower, according to the catalog, plantable in USDA zones 6–9. Pruning them was something of an art—

"Nicholas," came Lisa's voice in the dark, "I was trying to buy Tommy some shoes today and they wouldn't take the Visa."

"You usually use the MasterCard," he said sleepily, tasting his pillow.

"Yes, that's true, but not because there isn't one dime of credit on the Visa. I haven't been using it, so that means you—"

"There's a $5,000 cash advance on the Visa."

"Why, may I ask?"

Yes, why? he wondered. "I borrowed it to make an investment."

"What kind of investment?"

He sighed. Tasted his own breath, already sour.

"I've put together a—it's an idea to make some money. I think I can actually make some money at it. I've thought it out, Lisa."

She sat up next to him. "What'd you do with the money from the refinancing?"

He rolled onto his back. "It's sitting in the brokerage account."

"All of it?"

"Every dime, Lisa."

She seemed to be thinking, ordering her questions. She had a disciplined mind, his wife, and he had always known that she was smarter than he was. "What about that money I inherited and you put into health-care stocks?"

"That's in cash, in the brokerage account."

"Is the credit card advance in the brokerage account, too?"

"Yes."

"Is there more?"

"More in the account?"

She sighed in fury. "*Yes,* more in the account, more you haven't told me?"

"I borrowed some money from the other credit cards, and my mom sent me a check, actually."

"Your mother?"

"She lent me—us—65,000."

"How much is in the account?"

He didn't want to tell her; he wanted to keep the thing close to himself. "Just under 300,000."

"What?" Lisa's voice rose.

"Just under—"

"Three hundred thousand dollars?"

He nodded.

"What are you doing?" she cried. "That's our money!"

"I know."

"But why's there all this borrowed money and all our other assets in one account, in one place?"

"I'm making a play, Lisa. I'm shorting a stock."

"You're what—?"

"It's called RemoteCount. It's a small data-processing company that trades on Nasdaq. It's totally overvalued—I think it's a great opportunity." He paused for a breath. "I've borrowed 5,700 shares of RemoteCount and concurrently executed a sell order for the same number of shares, and now I'm waiting."

"But you never discussed this with me! That's outrageous."

He could feel her shifting in the bed, gathering herself up, her breathing accelerating.

"Yes," he announced into the dark. "It's outrageous, the whole goddamn thing is goddamn outrageous."

"You never told me!" she screamed. "You could lose it all!"

"I'm not going to lose it."

"How do you know?" she cried anxiously.

"At most I'll lose only a part of it. I have a stop-loss order in."

"You think—"

"Don't worry," he said. "I've spent a long time putting this thing together. You're just going to have to trust me."

"Trust you?" she screamed.

"Yes." He leaned close to her face in a way that was not affectionate, and she drew back. With one hand he reached up to the light above the bed and switched it on; both of them winced in the sudden brightness. "Yes, Lisa," he said slowly. "The same way that I've trusted you."

FOR THREE MORE DAYS, nothing happened. RemoteCount flicked up and down, feigning a run-up here, dropping three-eighths there. He began to hate the stock as if it were a human being who was being purposefully cruel. Meanwhile, despite the argument over RemoteCount, Lisa was warmer toward him, and they had even hired a sitter one night and slipped out to see *The Piano,* which had a couple of hot scenes between Holly Hunter and Harvey Keitel—a couple of hot *adulterous* scenes, Nicholas noted. In the darkness of the movie theater he slipped a glance at Lisa. Her face was a mask of rapture as the two naked bodies embraced on the huge screen. He looked away.

But when they got home, she said she wanted to apologize for her outburst a few nights back. "You should have discussed the idea with me, but I guess I could have reacted better," she said, getting him a beer from the refrigerator. "I mean, I didn't catch all the details, but it sounds like a pretty smart deal."

What accounted for Lisa's sudden pleasantness? Having just seen that movie, he thought bitterly, she believed in true love tonight. Then again, he had been something of a jerk not to tell her of the RemoteCount play. He'd try to be agreeable. "I'm just waiting for it to drop," he said.

"Will you explain the whole thing to me again? I got so worked up the other night that I was hardly listening."

She listened intently as he laid out the whole play. She was a good listener and quickly caught on.

"How much do you think we could make?" Lisa asked. "Maybe twenty or thirty thousand?"

"Hard to say." It would be better not to get her hopes up too high. "If it went well, *really* well, and the stock dropped to $30 a share, say, that would be about $97,000."

His wife stared at him. "Really?"

"Really."

THE NEXT AFTERNOON, he got an urgent call from Jane.

"Nicholas, it's at 49¾, and my guess is that it'll hit 50 any time."

"What's going on? Why didn't you call me when it hit 49?"

"Because it happened fast. One of the technology analysts gave it a buy this morning."

"He's an asshole. Now, look, you should have called me immediately—"

"Nicholas, you have a stop order at 50. I don't *have* to call you—you have *already* decided what you're doing. I called as a matter of courtesy—"

"Cancel the stop-loss," he ordered suddenly.

"What?"

"Cancel it," he insisted. "Don't sell at 50."

"Wait a minute, you worked out how much you were willing to lose."

"I'm changing my mind."

"This is *not* the way to make decisions. You're not a professional trader."

"Cancel the stop-loss. Please do it now."

"And what," said Jane, exasperated, "should I replace it with?"

Yes, of course, she had to put in *some* kind of stop-loss order.

"What's my margin here? I had some kind of 10 percent overage in my account, right?"

"It was 10 percent of 47, which is 4.7, which, rounded down, is four and five-eighths. If you add that to 47—"

"Put in the stop-loss at 51½."

"That leaves you exactly *one-eighth* of a point. We can't do this again."

"Yes."

"You don't have *any* more money, Nicholas. If it hits 51½, I'm not going to listen to any noise about sticking more money into your account."

He heard the anger in her voice. "Yes, Jane."

"Now you better fax me instructions to cancel the stop-loss at 50 and to put in a new one at 51½."

Which he did. At the end of the day he called Jane to get the quote. Sure, he was being an asshole, but it was his money on the line; he'd bought the right to be an asshole. But there was no answer. Jane was gone for the day.

THAT NIGHT he forced himself not to call the brokerage for the price and instead watched the CNN business report, and of course, there was no mention of why RemoteCount had gone up and how far. Who cared? Nobody. It was a nothing stock. Perhaps ten people in America *really* cared—got sweaty balls—thinking about RemoteCount, and six of them were probably RemoteCount executives. *They* knew the stock was going to tank. He'd seen this pattern. It had to happen. The company made all of its money with 1,400 people sitting in front of screens in one large facility in Seattle that had EMF readings above 3,000 mG. RemoteCount would be forced to shut down and tear the hell out of the building in order to correct the problem. The RemoteCount executives were all cheats and liars afraid to tell their stockholders what was happening to the company. They were sitting at home and telling their wives they'd better not buy the Lexus right now. They couldn't sell their own RemoteCount holdings, of course, because that might be insider trading and also could trigger the landslide. Nicholas hated them. They were killing him.

THE NEXT MORNING he walked outside in the cold in his bathrobe, ripped the *Times* out of its plastic bag, snatched the business section, folded the rest of the paper under his arm, and flipped to the stock tables. RemoteCount had closed at 51¼. Death! Somebody was buying the stock! Today the price would probably vibrate up to 51½, and there would be nothing he could do about it! Jane's computers would sell his position, and the effect of the whole insane fantasy would have been that he had *given away* $18,000—what was that? A Ford Taurus? No. The Taurus ran higher. But certainly a Ford Aerostar minivan. Driver's-side airbag, antilock braking system. I'll take it in Cayman green with mocha interior trim.

When he got to the office, Hal Gruber, his immediate boss, came in. "Girardi called Belton last night."

Nicholas looked up. He'd forgotten about Girardi Corp.

"What'd he say?"

"What did he say?" Gruber exclaimed. "He said he wanted to do a three-year deal, and he asked if we were thinking of expanding in Washington, D.C., and needed investors!"

"Really?"

Gruber slapped him on the shoulder and shook his hand. "I don't know what you said to him down there but jeez, Nicholas, great job. Really great job. Jeez, I mean, Belton was really pleased."

Nicholas arranged his features into something resembling a hearty grin. What did it mean, really? Two bosses pleased, a few more pieces of candy in the Christmas bonus. He was still inconsolable. After Gruber left, he pushed the paper around on his desk absentmindedly. He had no interest in calling Jane. Why hasten the bad news? How would he face Lisa? She'd been so excited, *so happy*, when he'd told her the workings of the RemoteCount play. She'd talked about Ohio, how nice it would be to live near her mother again. Take care of her. And the kids would love being in the country. He'd let all of them down.

So, right before lunch, when he received the phone message that Jane had just called, he wondered how he would ever get Lisa and the kids out of the city. He couldn't work for Belton Associates the rest of his life. He wanted *out*, he wanted grass. There had been another incident in their neighborhood recently, a hit-and-run with some Bronx kids whacked out on drugs. A four-year-old was on a respirator, severe brain swelling. When the cops arrived, it got even worse. The kids in the car inexplicably started shooting at them, and the police had been forced to shoot two of the kids. And Billy Meyer had seen a dead man on the sidewalk. And that lunatic had killed a bunch of people on the Long Island Railroad a few months back. This was 1994. What would it be like in 1999? Perhaps he was never going to get his kids and wife out of the sinkhole of New York City. His loss on RemoteCount made the goal even more . . . remote. Ha, no pun intended! *Hell,* he thought, *get it over with.* Life is a series of bets, and sometimes you lose! Yes! He knew that all along! Ha! He shut his office door and punched Jane's speed-dial button on his console.

"Jane?"

"Nicholas, finally! RemoteCount is down to around 38!"

"What?"

"I tried you when it hit 46," she said in excitement. "They're dumping on the West Coast. Calpers sold its entire position."

"Anybody else selling yet?"

"I can't find out. I got a couple of calls in. . . . Wait, here it is—the volume is *huge,* it's at 36¾. The Seattle paper has a long story on closing the facility this morning," Jane said excitedly. "That's what kicked it off. Let me read you the article; I had the whole thing faxed to me. It just came out. Here, it's their business writer. 'Employees leaving the building yesterday afternoon, some carrying personal items, expressed complete shock at the announcement and worried about making a living in the coming months. "They said they don't know when they're going to let us in again," said Shanelle Johnson, a data entry clerk.' "

"Does it say anything about the stock?" Nicholas asked.

"It quotes a local analyst who says that he expects that the company will lose market share."

"Yeah, I guess so. They'll have *no* market for at least six months."

"Wait, also, he says that he expects the company's debt will be downgraded."

"Call me when you get another price, okay?"

He almost called Lisa; no, he thought, better to wait until the deal is finished; he'd go home that evening and give her the exact figure, down to the penny. Instead he went out and treated himself to a big lunch at the Oyster Bar, and then felt too happy to go back to the office. So he wandered into a hardware store two avenues to the east and charged up a new shovel, rake, trowel, and leather work gloves. Sure, it was silly! But wasn't life!

And just as he returned at 3 P.M., Jane called again.

"The stock's at 13. Someone bought 3,000 shares at 13."

"Thirteen?" It seemed impossible.

"You're making serious money here, Nicholas. All the pensions are dumping. They're being quite ruthless, positioning themselves for a bounce."

"We have to sell on an uptick, right?"

"Yes."

"Should I sell now?"

A pause.

"No," she said. "Our guy who specializes in technology stocks says he thinks the 3,000 shares is someone trying to stabilize the stock, somebody who owns a lot more still. See, it's only been bought a couple of times on the way down. You got something like a million shares in sell orders, and he says that only about 80,000 have been *bought*."

"I don't get it—"

"There are no buy orders. Our own guy is calling some of his clients who might want to make a play on the stock on the way up."

"Trying to hit the bottom, knowing that when the company pulls itself back together the stock could do well?"

"That's the idea," she said. "Now, for you—I want instructions to buy on an uptick at anything less than 10."

"But it's at 13."

"Oh, I think it could go lower."

"But—" He stopped himself from asking why she thought that. Jane might have guessed at the rough price that the other broker at her firm would suggest to his own trading clients. They'd know the fundamentals of the company and decide to buy at a certain price, which would make a market for the stock again. The sudden buying volume might attract more buying. But now he was scared and wanted to get out. "How about 11½?"

"Okay," Jane said. "I'll call when I've got the uptick. Under 11 is going to be no problem is my guess."

HER GUESS WAS good. She called 40 minutes later.

"You're famous around here."

"Jane?"

"Nine and an eighth."

"Jesus."

"It's one of the best shorts I've ever seen," she told him. "And one of the most *obscure*, too."

He wasn't interested in her praise, just his money. "You bought at 9⅛?"

"Five thousand at 9 and the rest at 9⅛. It was heading back up pretty fast."

"When will my account be settled?"

"Three days."

"This happened? I'm done, I don't have to worry anymore?"

"Go out and buy a bottle of champagne."

Well, yes. They'd soon be buying all kinds of things! But first he'd call Lisa! Get a sitter, babe, we're going out for dinner. Better yet, come into the city and we'll see a show, maybe *Angels in America,* which from its title sounded optimistic, good fun. But there was no answer. Tommy was old enough to pick up the phone. Strange. He left a message saying he'd be home soon with big news. Maybe they went out, but Lisa usually ran her errands after picking the kids up from school. He always called at the end of the day. He felt both irritated and fearful. Perhaps someone had broken into the house, perhaps—he pushed back the possibilities. He glanced at his watch; 4:56 P.M. If the kids had been picked up at the end of their day, at 2:50 P.M., then that meant that all was normal up to that point. Then again, if they hadn't been picked up, the school would have called him, since his office number was on the emergency form. He got the number of the school, dialed it, and reached the lower-school principal's office.

He quickly explained to the principal, Mrs. Kroeber, that he was checking to see that his wife had picked up their kids. Was there any way she could check?

"If your children were still here, I would know about it," she said firmly.

"Right. Of course."

"Are you worried about them?"

"Well, no, I have no reason. . . . I called home, and there's no answer."

Mrs. Kroeber didn't respond. There was an appraising silence on the other end of the line. He knew she saw all kinds of family situations.

"Let me check something," she finally said.

While he waited he worked out Jane Chung's commission. It was figured on the number of shares bought and sold and came out to just over $3,200, which seemed pretty slim pickings when you considered that she had helped to put $216,000 into his pocket. But then again, he and not Jane had taken all the risk, so—

"Mr. Wren, your children never came to school today."

"What?"

"I said your children didn't come to school today. All absences are reported by 10 A.M. by the teachers. I checked our daily sheet, and they never came to school. Mrs. Costello downstairs called around 11, she says, but there was no answer at your home. So I suggest that you—"

But he was already hanging up and pulling on his coat.

THE CAMRY was not in the driveway as he huffed along the sidewalk from the train station. The house was dark. He fumbled for his keys in the cold, pushed through the front door. "Lisa?" he called, flicking on lights. But nothing. Inside, on the dining-room table, set at his place, were some papers. He snatched them up. First: Letterhead from the law firm where Lisa worked, addressed to him, his eyes flitting to the crucial sentence: "has retained my services to assist in the preparation of divorce filings before the New York State Supreme Court, County of Westchester. . . ." Two pages later, the formal filing: WHEREAS, Lisa Wren, legal wife of Nicholas Wren, residing at . . . seeks a no-fault judgment in the matter of . . ."

He sat down.

She was gone, the kids in the back of the Camry, headed where? Ohio, he assumed. He knew he could walk upstairs and find that the suitcases were not in the closet and that the kids' dressers would be missing a lot of clothes, that Lisa had probably taken some of her jewelry, a few photo albums. But where had she gone? He could only assume that she was halfway to Ohio, maybe spending the night somewhere in Pennsylvania, maybe at a Motel 6—whose stock had really done well two years ago. They'd arrive at her mother's house the next afternoon.

But when had they left? The kids had not been in school all day, which suggested she'd left that morning, just after him. He looked at the date on the law-firm letter. Today. Of course, the papers had been prepared ahead of time. Just a word-processing file at the law firm—change the names and addresses and blow up a family. He examined the second page of the letter, which helpfully summarized the key tenets of New York State divorce law. Joint divisible assets, etc. Then: "Although the brokerage account at . . . represented by Ms. Jane Chung is listed in your name only, it quite clearly falls within the joint property of the marriage and no further trading, liquidating of positions, reinvestment, etc. may be done in this account without the advance written agreement of Lisa Wren. Kindly have your attorney forward to me a complete accounting of 1) all sums invested, 2) dividends or interest received, and 3) capital gains . . ."

He flipped the papers to the table, then picked them up and reread them. It was all very clear. Why had she given up on him? Things had been bad, but they hadn't even discussed . . . *this*. He wandered into the kitchen, frowning. Was there something in this he had missed? He was blasted by shock; yes, he would no doubt be drinking later that night; yes, he was falling into a crevasse of grief, but, before that happened, before he gave himself over to all of it, there was . . . *something* . . . a logical question, an irritating matter of sequence. The papers were dated that day, signed by the attorney. Attorneys didn't falsify dates. The papers had been signed today, picked up at the law office. That meant that Lisa had *not* left for Ohio immediately after he'd departed for work. She'd driven to the law office with the kids in the car and picked up the papers about the time the office opened, 9:30 or 10. Then, he figured, she'd driven back to the house, dropped off the papers, loaded the car, then gotten started on the day's long drive. He drifted over to the sink, looked at the plastic children's cups in the drainer, cartoon figures dancing across them. All Disney licensing. The stock had been murdered recently, the parent company taking huge losses on the EuroDisney park that had flopped in France. Chairman Eisner hadn't even been awarded a bonus.

Nicholas Wren looked, for no reason, into his kitchen sink. Resting on the stainless steel edge of the drain, poised to fall in, was a lima bean. Wrinkled and pale green. Lisa had cooked it for Sally, he knew, and as if to commune with his children even as they sped through the dark night away from him, he picked up the lima bean and placed it between his teeth.

And bit. The bean was warm. Or rather, it was *not cold*. Dinner! They had eaten dinner at home! Lisa had fed Tommy and Sally dinner and then left for Ohio. Maybe an hour ago! But why leave so late? Why delay? It was sort of hard on the kids, and Lisa would have them foremost in her mind. Clearly she had *planned* to leave earlier in the day, but then been delayed. Second thoughts? Her mother telling her not to come? Richard Chambers making a swan song? He went over to the phone. It blinked with a message ready. He hit the play button. Maybe this was it. Maybe she and Chambers—"Hi, it's me," came his own voice, made hopeful by the certainty of money, "and I have some big news—" How pathetic and foolish he sounded. Then he had another idea. Perhaps Lisa had called her mother to say she would be leaving later than expected. He hit the phone's redial number. A sequence of tones followed—enough, he could tell, that the number wasn't local. If her mother picked up, he's somberly tell her he knew that Lisa and the kids were on their way and would she please ask Lisa to at least call him when they arrived safely. Then he would not have to worry that—

"Quotronex," a woman's voice answered, "is pleased to serve your investment-information needs. For today's closing stock prices on the New York Stock Exchange, press one, *now*. For the American Stock Exchange, press two, *now*. For Nasdaq, press three, *now*. For Chicago Mercantile and other commodity exchanges, press four, *now*. For—"

He pressed three.

"You are calling from 914-555-6734. If you would like a price and volume update on your last inquiry, press one, *now*. If you want the price and volume of a different stock, press two, *now*. If you would like—"

He pressed one.

"You previous inquiry was . . . *today* . . . at . . . *four-thirty-two* . . . P.M. . . . for the stock symbol R . . . E . . . M . . . C . . . —" RemoteCount. ". . . Which closed at . . . *eleven* . . . and . . . *three-eighths* . . . on volume of . . . *six* . . . hundred thousand—"

He hung up. Lisa had been following the price! No doubt she'd been tracking the RemoteCount price ever since he explained the play to her. And surely she'd called for a quote that morning and seen that the price was dropping. And called back. Been a quote junkie all day. Just like him. As the price dropped, it would have been more difficult to leave for Ohio. Oh, yes, it must have been an exciting day for her. He shook his head at the beauty of it all. He'd asked her to trust him, and she had. And then she'd locked in her gain, serving the papers on him just after his short play had succeeded. Yes, he'd always known she was smarter! Ha, ha! What a smart wife he had! He took a pencil and paper from next to the phone and did a few calculations. Their gross worth minus their debts, today's profits, after commissions, multiplied by their federal tax rate, which was the one applied to short-term capital gains. A certain symmetricality to the figures emerged, give or take ten thousand. . . . Why, yes, he figured, how unusual, how strange, that when he and Lisa came to divide up their assets, today's winnings would constitute half their holdings, which meant—and this was what finally broke Nicholas Wren on that February night after his train ride home from the city—that the magnificent profits of his brilliant short play would become exactly what he had never imagined: his divorce settlement, proof of a family destroyed.

THIS STORY, FIRST PUBLISHED in 1988, was never revised. I wrote it in 1986, while at the Workshop, and have since avoided it, not only because it's the one piece I haven't pushed and polished into a shape far different from its inception. I was afraid that much of what I've costumed, propped, and obfuscated in novels many times rewritten would be naked and immediately available in this odd, early attempt, a story produced in one ill-considered burst. The fear that being human means to be alone, at once horribly conscious of that loneliness and denying it; the dangers of a religious sensibility turned inward, day by day dismantling and emptying the world; the desire for purity—the flight from sin and stain—that ends in sterility and death: I could go on, but as I feared, my obsessions are all here on the page, unmasked, obvious. . . .

KATHRYN HARRISON

KATHRYN HARRISON

Planting

FIRST THE ROOM in which I sleep and eat and prepare my meals, in which I work. I have this room and I have the other, the bathroom. Nothing I own produces dust or lint and that is an advantage in this. I have eliminated curtains and rugs and tablecloths. I have no sheets or blankets. I sleep in my uniform. Outer garments I wash every two days, lately more often. My underwear is disposable and I incinerate it.

It will be difficult, what I am trying to do, to have everything clean and ready at once. I start with the ceiling. It is not generally supposed that ceilings get dirty. That is because no one bothers to clean them. But they are greasy and little hairs stick in the grease, and dust as well. When I finish, it is very white and like a wide plateau of fresh snow, just fallen. Upside down I see it with my head tipped far back, like winter sleeping clean and white. All the trees are stripped bare in the winter: there are no more leaves to drop and rot. The black earth is covered clean and white and empty like hospital sheets.

In the middle of the ceiling there is one fluorescent light, square, and I lift the four panels of milky glass out of their aluminum frame and take them to the bathtub. No matter how often one cleans a light, there are always dead insects in it under the glass. Before washing them, I take the panels outside and tilt them over the sidewalk, and the gray wings and legs and bodies, now dry like husks and all dismembered, slip off and fall around my shoes.

With the light off, I take out the long tubular bulbs and dust them and then soap them carefully and then rinse and dry them. The square hole in the ceiling I clean with a solution of Pine-Sol and water and I make sure to dry it thoroughly. When the fixture is reassembled and I turn it on, the light comes through strong and clear and almost blue. It is the color of moonlight but lacking its softness, its apology. It is a hundred times brighter. With that light I can see everything clearly and I can clean.

Now the walls, which are painted a high-gloss white and are unmarked. Nothing hangs on them, only one window, two doors break them. I wash the walls starting at the top. They look clean before I begin, but the water runs down in a thin gray tide, pushing before it fly dirt and grime, little hairs.

The smell of pine cleanser fills my chest and throat and head. It burns the inside of my nose, my eyes water. Already my fingers are white and shriveled at the tips, withered. I wring out my cloth in the bucket and go over each surface again and again, I do not know how many times. It takes all day.

Then the doors and especially the doorknobs. When I lost my job, I had to take a test and three times there was the question: are you afraid of germs on doorknobs? I had not been afraid of them, but truthfully, the question did awaken in me the understanding that this was a reasonable fear. I know from my work that doorknobs can be very dirty. So I said yes, I was afraid. I said yes three times.

That is the trick with those tests. Over and over the same question is repeated to see if one's answers are consistent. On the test is the question, Do you believe in hell and damnation? There are only two possible answers: yes or no. I wanted to say yes, I did believe, but it was not that simple. I wanted to say more, but there was no room. The last time I took that test it was administered at a computer terminal in a windowless office, the questions rolling up on the screen. The case-worker explained that I might choose only one of two keys in response to each question: X for yes, O for no. There was no space for any comment.

Now the furniture. I have thrown almost everything away, dispensed with knick-knacks, burnt the papers, given away the books. The magazines are stacked neatly on the steps outside apartment number four. Perhaps its occupant will want them. Each shelf is straight and still and bare. The bookcase is empty. There is a smell in that corner that is stale like the breath of someone who has not eaten. When I do not eat, I cup my hands over my face and exhale through my mouth, then I breathe in again through my nose to smell the emptiness inside me. It smells like that, the bookcase, empty and slightly rank.

I dump the pail of dirty water down the toilet and draw another bucketful clean from the spout in the tub. More Pine-Sol and a fresh cloth. It says one should not use pine cleanser on wood, but I do. I like the smell and I use it on everything. I used it on the window and it never streaked the glass, although the label warned that it might.

Besides the shelves and the bookcase I have a chest of drawers for my clothes, and I clean that, too. It has three drawers, but I use only one. The others are empty and attract dust even though I run my vacuum cleaner through them each week, using the little round brush attachment that is intended for furnishings. This time, after I vacuum, I have decided to wash inside the drawers with the pine solution and then stand them out to dry.

I store my underwear in the top drawer. Stacked neatly to the left are a few sets for the next day or so, and I take them in their plastic packages and place them on one of the clean bookshelves. When it is empty, I take out the top drawer and wash it first, then the second and the third; and then the chest itself I scrub without the drawers inside. When it is all cleaned and dry, I reassemble the dresser and replace the packages of underwear. Before shutting the top drawer, I lay my face down in it so close that the plastic wrap on the underwear makes my cheek perspire. I inhale deeply and smell nothing but Pine-Sol. That is good, that is what I want.

On top of the dresser, in the center, I set the box in which I keep a few important things. I have dusted and polished the box. It is square and made of wood with a lining of green felt and has my initials cut into the front. The contents themselves I do not need to clean. They stay untouched inside under the tightly fitting lid. My mother's ring and one long curl of her hair tied together with string. If I am not gentle when touching it, the hair, shining and smooth, slips out of the string. Two syringes that I took from the hospital. I have never used them and have no purpose for a syringe, but I like them because they are sealed in plastic so tight and clean and sure that not even a microbe is inside that wrapper, just the plastic chamber and the bright winking needle. And there are some other things I have saved: an old driver's license with an image of me as I looked before but which I no longer resemble, a gold-plated pendant with an imitation sapphire, one earring with a real pearl. And finally, one tiny envelope of ten apple seeds ready for planting. These are the only things I keep and they are safe in the box on top of my dresser.

Now I can wash the table and chair where I work and eat. They are metal and collapsible, both of them, and tend to pinch fingers in the folding and unfolding of them. I take them one at a time to the bathroom and into the tub where they stand, the table mostly folded, the chair open. I go over and over them with Brillo pads—it takes a whole box—and then Pine-Sol, and then I can use the detachable shower-head, the sprayer on the end of a hose, and rinse them until the water runs clear. I leave them in the bathroom to dry while I wash the floor.

I have wanted one of those floors like they have in public showers, all tiled with a drain in a depression in the middle. That is the ideal floor to wash. I could scrub and wash and rinse until the water fell down the drain clear and sweet. I once worked as a janitor at a public school—that was before I worked at Redimaid and was given this uniform—and the bathroom was always the best to clean. I knew it was good when I was finished, not like the halls. The halls I could never get clean.

My floor is linoleum, white in squares with black lines printed into the vinyl. It looks like tiles until you are down on your hands and knees and then it is just another kind of plastic. I like plastic, though, and vinyl and Naugahyde, because they are washable. Anything I cannot wash I throw away, like my white leather work shoes. I rubbed and rubbed and bits and pieces kept coming off onto the rag, the surface of the leather deteriorating into grainy smudges on the cloth. I threw them out and bought plastic shoes. I wear no socks because, like underwear, the only time hosiery is ever really clean, I think, is before it has ever been worn.

I wash the floor three times: once to cut the grease, again to remove the dirt, and once more to be safe. Each time takes a lot of water and a lot of Pine-Sol and then even more water. It is very difficult in the drying, and there are quantities of towels to be washed in the process. The washer and dryer in the building are not large-capacity machines and so I must do several loads. So the floor, then, takes another day.

After it is done, I have come to the third day of the cleaning and I damp-mop the ceiling and the walls and go over the shelves again. So far everything is still clean. I put the table and chair back where they belong. No bugs have gotten into the light.

The refrigerator hums in the clean still white square of the room where I work and eat and sleep. I unplug it now. I defrosted and cleaned it first, before anything, before the ceiling even, because fasting is part of the cleaning and part of the getting ready and I have stopped eating. Since I did not need food anymore, I left some on the landing by the mailboxes and threw the perishables away. All those onions in the drawer by the sink, sprouting pale green fingers and gently touching one another, they lay in a pile of dry brown skins. I had forgotten them waiting there in the dark. Later, after I put them in the trashcan, I thought again of each onion growing, its fingers reaching in the dark to learn what was there.

I washed all inside the refrigerator, the walls and the door. Each hollow cup where each egg had been, I polished with a cloth. I took the little doors off the butter and cheese compartments and soaked them in the bathtub with the vegetable drawers, the meat bin, the shelves, and the ice trays. Then I reassembled all the pieces and plugged it back in. It ran for three days empty, humming in self-purification, but now I am unplugging it and leaving the door ajar.

I have my bed yet to do, but that is simple. I do not use a mattress made from cloth and springs and padding because they spawn dust and are not easy to clean. Before I disposed of the last one, I saw on its surface and in the indentations around each button a film of dust that was not dust. It was gray and soft and could only have been the accretion of skin cells sloughing off my body as it slept heavy and unknowing there. The mattress was old and there was a long hollow where I had lain so many nights. That dip in the frayed brocade was darker and greasier than the edges. Just to look at it made my armpits go cold and the saliva start at the back of my mouth, the way you feel just before you get sick.

Now I have a plastic pneumatic pad. It is like a raft and I am comfortable sleeping on it. It is readily deflatable and washable, and once a week I take it into the shower with me. That way it stays clean. I stood it in the bathroom while I was washing the floor, but now, having just disinfected it with rubbing alcohol, I put it back in its place under the window.

All that is left in this room are the cupboards and the hotplate and the small counter beside the refrigerator where I fixed my meals. The cupboard is empty and I begin by prying up the tacks that hold down the paper shelf liners. It looks like plain white butcher paper, but it is rubberized on one side and the other is treated with a chemical that discourages weevils and roaches. I have never had any of those insects in my home, but it is good to be safe. My apartment is in the basement; the one window is high and squat and wide and does not open. I am afraid that any hole dug out of the earth could become infested in the summer, no matter how fastidious its occupant. I have had ants, but only a few, and rarely. I spray for insects; I use an aerosol product that delivers poisonous foam to corners and crevices by means of a thin plastic tube.

The tacks come up with difficulty, pulling my fingernails away from the flesh. When all the paper is up I suck my tender fingers and taste cleanser. It reminds me to brush my teeth and I do. I brush often and use dental floss twice a day and still, even when one does not eat, there is a yellow film that builds up. When I hold the used floss up to the light I can see where it has turned yellow, and if I hold it up to my nose it smells like bad breath.

The shelf paper is gone and there are crumbs and stains underneath. I am so careful and keep everything wrapped so tightly—I use hundreds of Ziploc bags— and I wash each bottle and jar before putting it away, but incredibly there are yet stains and crumbs. I scrub each shelf and the doors and the walls of the cupboards.

The hotplate has a brown crust in the drip pan under the burner. I try and I try but I cannot get it off, not even with steel wool. The burners themselves look dirty and gray with spots in places. It is astounding how dirt can withstand the heat, but it does. I turn the hotplate on high just to burn off the dirt, but that does not work, so I throw the whole thing away. Last week I disposed of the toaster oven. I had broken the coil trying to clean it, and a sliver of glass from the tube around the element cut my finger. The blood came out onto my wet knuckles. Threading through the creases in the skin, hot and red and alive, a web of color spread over my hand and frightened me. Bleeding has always made me afraid.

The toaster oven and the hotplate do not matter because I have stopped eating and I do not need those things anymore. For that matter, I have no use for the refrigerator either, but it does not belong to me, I cannot throw it away.

There is a knock at the door, tentative, feeble almost, and from its familiar three taps and then two, I know that it is my landlady. I recognize the outline of her head on the glass panel set into the door.

"Miss Vernon," she says, "Miss Vernon?"

I crouch down near the stove and am very quiet, hardly breathing.

"Miss Vernon?"

My head is between my knees, my arms around my legs. Even the steady noise of my pulse quiets and slows.

"Miss Vernon," she is shouting now, "I'm leaving your rent receipt in your mailbox."

We go through this for each month's check. I am not sure that she knows I am at home, for I never answer, but if not, why does she persist in speaking to me?

One floor up, there is the noise of the metal lid to the mailbox falling shut; it bounces, the sound echoing against the concrete stairs, and then silence. I look up, and through my window I can see outside to the sky so quiet and pale pale blue. The clouds are floating stillborn. They move slowly to the edge of the window and disappear.

I wait a few minutes to be sure she is really gone, that she has not come back to my door. There is no sound of her feet. She wears rubber-soled houseshoes—plush and pink on top with little flowers machine-stitched into the velour—they make just a faint whisper of sound on the stairs, and so I must wait to be certain. When I know she is not there, outside, when I am sure that she too does not crouch silently and listen, I can stand and go back to my cleaning.

The counter has not been used since last I washed it, but I scrub it over again anyway. I use last week's toothbrush on the grout, brushing and brushing until all the bristles bend back and then there is no point in going on. The tile on this counter was new last year, and the man who laid it said, yes, one could keep it from getting dirty and gray. There is a silicon solution with which to paint it. I bought the solution and painted it twice, but it did not work absolutely. I am so very careful, but the grout is stained in places, stained but not soiled. I smell it to be sure.

Now this room in which I live is clean. I take down my glass from the shelf—I keep only one because more just gather dust—and pour myself sixteen ounces of distilled water. The glass I use is like a beaker and has measurements in ounces marked on one side, in milliliters on the other. The water I drink is distilled by ionization, a process of evaporating impure water and then collecting its vapor. Afterwards there is nothing in it, it is clean and tastes like the bottle it comes in. This is all I drink, and I like to think of it bringing nothing to my body, nothing that might contaminate me. When I give myself enemas, which I do each night—I learned about them in the hospital—I use tap water as many times as I can stand it, and then finally I use the distilled.

I know there are a lot of impurities in water from the city's reservoir—I have seen them. I am not sure what they are, but when I hold a glass of tap water up to the light it is frightening how many little things are suspended in it, moving slowly and unconsciously there in the glass, swimming to the edges and then gradually sinking to the bottom. And those are only the things one can see. There are other worse things, worse because they are invisible, but I know they are there. Distilled water is clean and it is all I drink. I drink it and drink it, as much as I can stand, so that I always urinate clear. To test myself, I empty my bladder into my glass and hold my urine up to the light. I cannot eliminate the odor entirely, but if it smells too strongly of ammonia, I know I must try to drink more. I use over two gallons of distilled water each day, I brush my teeth in it.

Only the bathroom is left now, and that will not be difficult. I clean it each day anyway. It is small and has no window. Even better, it is tiled from floor to ceiling. The only trouble is that the grout is old and stained. I have tried and tried but I cannot make it white. Today, this time, when I want it to be perfect, I use straight Clorox. I empty the metal medicine cabinet and pull out the glass shelves. I put all its contents in the tub. The same with the things from the cupboard under the sink:

the toilet paper, the cans of Ajax, the towels and the enema bag and hose; they all go into the bathtub.

Then the surfaces: the walls, the floor, the sink, the cabinet, the cupboard, the counter, the towel rack, the door, the doorknob, the hook on the back of the door. I go over everything with a pad soaked in Clorox. The fumes are overwhelming, they make me faint. I am weak anyway, I have eaten nothing for days, and the things I do to cleanse my intestines each night before I go to bed are exhausting. I wake up tired. Still, I have the strength to do my work, to prepare myself and my home.

When everything is covered with Clorox, I let it stand for a few minutes and then I rinse it well and dry it. On my hands and knees I clean the toilet, all around in the bowl and under the seat and up under the edge. It is white and it does not smell, but I clean it just the same. When I finish the toilet, I do the sink with Ajax and then the cupboard under the sink with Pine-Sol. After that I can put all the things that are sitting in the tub away in their places, and then I can do the bathtub itself.

I always clean the tub and the shower when I bathe myself. I take off my clothing and my paper underwear. They are all of them dirty and this time I am going to burn the outer ones as well. I bundle them together and wrap them all in the white uniform and, wearing only a paper robe, the kind with a blue plastic sash like that nurse gives me in the doctor's office, I take them to the other basement room. Standing together just outside my door are my plastic shoes and I put them on to leave my apartment, and then take them off again as I enter. In this way my feet stay clean and do not touch the cement floor. I am sure no one eats there by the furnace, but to a bare foot it always feels as if there are crumbs on the floor, crumbs and dust and strange little hairs as if animals had been there in the heat and had begun to shed their heavy coats.

In the furthest corner is the black furnace with its small door, and into its flames I push all my clothes, the only clothes I own. They make no sound as they burn, but there is an unpleasant, faintly acid smell as the polyester melts and smokes. I stand there in the heat for a few moments, the heat of my uniform burning, and then I check, opening the hot metal door, to be sure that everything has been destroyed.

I can hear the footsteps of the other tenants. Each time someone crosses the floor, the ceiling over the basement creaks. But no one ever comes down here, not unless there is some problem with the heat or a pipe bursts or someone is moving in or out and needs access to the storage area. I am not afraid to be in this room.

One last time I look inside the furnace door: there is a bright badge of orange, nothing left of my clothing, not even ashes.

Back in the bathroom I gather all that I need for the shower: cleansers and cloths and a brush for the grout and the tile, Ajax and sponges for the tub, soap and a razor and the enema apparatus for myself.

First is the tub. I do it standing on the sponges and moving my feet around in slow circles through the gritty paste of the cleanser, a generous amount of Ajax and about two cups of water from the faucet. My legs with my weight on top of them are much stronger than my arms which are thin and tired as well. A few seasons ago, I had a plant in this basement apartment but it did not get enough sun and its leaves dropped. Its stems which reached for the window, begging light, were long and thin and so pale they were almost colorless. When I look at my arms I think of that plant that died.

Soon the tub is clean, and I scrub the walls and the faucet and I rinse everything over and over with the detachable shower head. I run my fingers over each surface to make sure none of the grains from the cleanser remain.

Now I am ready to wash myself. I soap my body once all over with deodorant soap and I leave the lather on until it begins to burn a little in the more sensitive areas. Then I wash again, one part at a time. Since hair is so hard to keep really clean, I shave it all off. I read in a biology textbook once about follicle mites, tiny parasites invisible to the naked eye. They live in human hair follicles. It does not matter how much one washes, they are still there. I cannot be sure that shaving helps, but it might. When I began I had a hard time shaving certain parts of my body, especially my head, the back of it, that tender place right above the neck where the skull curves in, and at the very top inside my thighs. But I am so used to shaving each day now that I never need a mirror and I can do it very quickly. I start with my legs, the left one first. I use a new disposable razor each time and it is fast and smooth. Shaving takes no time at all. Except for my genitals, those I nick every once in a while, and I have to proceed very slowly, pulling the skin taut with my left hand and shaving with the right. Inside the little folds of skin which are impossible to shave completely, I use a tweezer to pluck any hair that I miss. When I am clean-shaven I wash once more and then sit on the floor of the tub and let the water run over and over every part of me until I am ready for the enema.

It used to be that I did not think so much about being clean on the inside. I concentrated on my home and my skin. Now I fast and drink only distilled water and I use the enema every night. Now I can imagine the whole long trail of my intestines, wet and empty, pink and clean. With one of those scopes, a tiny camera on the end of a wire, like a snail's eye, goggling, with one of those a doctor could see inside me that I was clean and empty and pure, as pure as the day I was born. There is nothing in me now. The water pours over my hairless skull and into my ears. It makes the sound of a storm and finds each secret place of me. I let the bathtub fill, and up inside me creeps the water. It trickles out again, disappointed, when I stand to reach for the enema apparatus.

I fill the rubber bag and turn on my side.

Last night and tonight, after days of eating nothing, the enemas are just part of a routine of bathing. The water goes in and comes out clean and clear, over and over. I start with soapy water which burns, especially lately when I have been so empty, but I wash all the soap away. It is not so bad and the cramps stop after a while. Just when I think I cannot stand it any longer, they stop. Tonight I do it just for the pleasure of routine, of ritual, and of knowing that I am empty and clean. I am content imagining that pure slippery pink track coiling and unfurling empty within me.

I am tired when I finish. This bathing is exhausting, but when I finish I can know that I am clean. And now I am almost ready. The towel is white and big and wound around me like a sheet. It covers me from head to toe. My skin, tender and stripped of its oil from the soap that I use, I blot instead of rubbing. When I am dry, I hang up the towel and go to the other room to put on my underwear. I have one last set and I tear off the plastic wrappers from the two pieces, the underpants and the shirt. My fingers are tired; they shake and make it difficult to remove each delicate garment from its package. If I pull at the plastic roughly or carelessly, the underwear might tear as well and be wasted. That is not good. I put my legs through the pants slowly and deliberately; in this way they do not rip. When they are on the fit is not good, but by no means uncomfortable. Since they have no elastic there is a thin white string threaded through the top which I pull tight and tie closed.

I am clean and my home is clean. Everything is ready. I check all the surfaces and in the drawers and cupboards, under the toilet seat, around the faucets. Just once more I look at each thing. There are no bugs in the light. With the refrigerator unplugged, the room is very quiet. It is like a becalmed vessel, sails slack, unmoving, waiting for the wind.

And I have never heard such silence before. I stand still in my own home and listen. All there is is the noise inside my own head, the heavy drum of blood in my ears.

Now I am ready, with everything clean and my home in perfect order, with my body washed and my teeth brushed and all through me clean from my mouth to the end of me. When I urinate, it is clear like water. It even tastes like water. I am ready.

From the box on top of the chest of drawers I take my envelope of seeds. There are ten of them and I shake them out onto my clean palm where they lie, a small and silent promise. I count them several times, and turn them over and over. I close them in my hand and rattle them like seeds inside a dry pod. They click together.

One last time I check each one to be sure of the uninterrupted seam closing its hull, the slight bulge of each side, brown and glossy and smooth. They are perfect. In the silence they speak to me of the spring and of new life. When I hold them to my nose they smell like the thaw, like the snow melting and dripping and running in the April mud.

My heart clenches with my fists and then beats wildly, a sound like feet drumming down the fire escape.

I turn out the light and go to my bed on the floor with my seeds in my hand. It is darker than I have ever known it to be. I am afloat now in the black still night of an endless calm, my pulse rocking me. In that immense dark I hold my seeds close to my chest, to where I can feel them tight inside my hand, that one hand a fist inside the other. For a moment I pray, and then I swallow them.

Without water they travel slowly down my throat and I am aware of each one and its blind trip inside me to where it lodges in the clean ripe bed of my intestines. There, inside me, is the blood meal and the bone meal which I have watched the gardener pour over the soil, turning it under with his shovel. I will make these seeds live. Like those onions in the drawer, they will grow without my seeing them, green fingers reaching toward my heart and searching for light.

Outside I hear the noise of a breeze. Soft at first, the sound of a child blowing over the lip of an empty glass bottle, a gentle sound, almost of calling. Then the air moves with more force. Dry leaves stir in the flower bed and rustle against my window.

I lie back on my bed in the empty shadow of my room, my hands crossed over my chest. At my window there is a faint stirring of light, as if a gray wing were spread above me. All else is dark: the complete eternal night that exists under the soil and at the roots. Already my seed inside me is coming to life. In the red, deep earth of my belly, my blood and my life are coming to new life.

The breeze yet rises, becomes a wind. Oppressive before, the silence is now broken, air lowing around the walls of my home, and I can rest. I sleep with my head back and my mouth open, breathing.

In the spring, a bud will come forth over my tongue.

THE WRITER WHO PREFACES his own work runs the risk of proving himself beyond a shadow of a doubt to be a worthless horse's ass. You're here with this book in your hands, presumably, to read stories. If you wanted to have some yahoo yap at you about his personal life, you'd have picked up some other book, or you'd be doing something else altogether. Watching television, perhaps.

Still, here I am, a writer with a preface. A potential horse's ass.

And yet, it seems to me, there's something worth my considering, and perhaps writing about, in this republication of a story written when I was still a teenager. I'm not a teenager anymore, far from it. I'm a college professor now, something I never imagined myself being—it was the farthest thing from my mind, teaching!—when I wrote "The Sutton Pie Safe."

"The Sutton Pie Safe" was compulsively, obsessively written, as I recall, drafted in a single energetic sleepless twenty-four-hour period, when nothing but the story at hand mattered. Most of my early stories were written that way. I was a kid from West Virginia who wanted people to know about the place I'd grown up in. I was terribly, terribly homesick, going to college in New Jersey, and nothing else seemed quite as important to me as that strange, mountainous place, that ruin full of idiosyncratic, ferociously proud, ignorant people.

My stories come to me more slowly now, with reluctance, and there are many other things that I have come to care about. I have a family, and professional ambitions, concerns that pull me away from my work as nothing did in those first fierce early days—the days of "The Sutton Pie Safe"—when I discovered the labor of reinventing the mountain country from which I came.

I miss it. I miss the clarity of purpose that drove me as I wrote "The Sutton Pie

Safe." The conviction that I was preserving a time and a place that would soon be gone, beyond redemption. (And they are gone.)

I miss being a boy.

Of course I do. Of course I miss it. What man doesn't? As I said earlier: a horse's ass.

PINCKNEY BENEDICT

A BLACKSNAKE LAY stretched out on the cracked slab of concrete near the diesel tank. It kept still in a spot of sun. It had drawn clear membranes across its eyes, had puffed its glistening scales a little, soaking up the heat of the day. It must have been three feet long.

"There's one, dad," I said, pointing at it. My father was staring at the old pole barn, listening to the birds in the loft as they chattered and swooped from one sagging rafter to another. The pole barn was leaning hard to one side, the west wall buckling under. The next big summer storm would probably knock it down. The winter had been hard, the snows heavy, and the weight had snapped the ridepole. I wondered where we would put that summer's hay.

"Where is he?" my dad asked. He held the cut-down .410 in one hand, the short barrel cradled in the crook of his elbow, stock tight against his bare ribs. We were looking for copperheads to kill, but I thought maybe I could coax my dad into shooting the sleeping blacksnake. I loved the crack of the gun, the smell of sulphur from the opened breech. Again I pointed to the snake.

"Whew," he said, "that's a big one there. What do you figure, two, two and a half feet?" "Three," I said. "Three at least." He grunted.

"You gonna kill it?" I asked.

"Boys want to kill everything, don't they?" he said to me, grinning. Then, more seriously, "Not too good an idea to kill a blacksnake. They keep the mice down, the rats. Better than a cat, really, a good-sized blacksnake."

He stood, considering the unmoving snake, his lips pursed. He tapped the stock of the gun against his forearm. Behind us, past the line of willow trees near the house, I heard the crunch of gravel in the driveway. Somebody was driving up. We both turned to watch as the car stopped next to the smokehouse. It was a big car,

Buick Riviera, and I could see that the metallic flake finish had taken a beating on the way up our lane.

My father started forward, then stopped. A woman got out of the car, a tall woman in a blue sun dress. She looked over the car at us, half waved. She had honey-colored hair that hung to her shoulders, and beautiful, well-muscled arms. Her wave was uncertain. When I looked at my dad, he seemed embarrassed to have been caught without a shirt. He raised the gun in a salute, decided that wasn't right, lowered the gun and waved his other hand instead.

It was too far to talk without shouting, so we didn't say anything, and neither did the woman. We all stood there a minute longer. Then I started over toward her.

"Boy," my dad said. I stopped. "Don't you want to get that snake?" he said.

"Thought it wasn't good to kill blacksnakes," I said. I gestured toward the house. "Who is she?" I asked.

"Friend of your mother's," he said. His eyes were on her. She had turned from us, was at the screen porch. I could see her talking through the mesh to my mother, nodding her head. She had a purse in her hand, waved it to emphasize something she was saying. "Your mom'll take care of her," my dad said. The woman opened the porch door, entered. The blue sun dress was pretty much backless, and I watched her go. Once she was on the porch, she was no more than a silhouette.

"Sure is pretty," I said to my father. "Yeah," he said. He snapped the .410's safety off, stepped over to the diesel pump. The snake sensed his coming, turned hooded eyes on him. The sensitive tongue flicked from the curved mouth, testing the air, the warm concrete. For just a second, I saw the pink inner lining of the mouth, saw the rows of tiny, backward-curving fangs. "When I was ten, just about your age," my dad said, leveling the gun at the snake, "my daddy killed a big old blacksnake out in our backyard."

The snake, with reluctance, started to crawl from the spot of sun. My dad steadied the gun on it with both hands. It was a short weapon, the barrel and stock both cut down. It couldn't have measured more than twenty inches overall. Easy to carry, quick to use: perfect for snake. "He killed that blacksnake, pegged the skin out, and give it to me for a belt," my dad said. He closed one eye, squeezed the trigger.

The shot tore the head off the snake. At the sound, a couple of barn swallows flew from the haymow, streaked around the barn, swept back into the dark loft. I watched the body of the snake vibrate and twitch, watched it crawl rapidly away from the place where it had died. It moved more quickly than I'd seen it move that afternoon. The blood was dark, darker than beets or raspberry juice. My dad snapped the bolt of the gun open, and the spent cartridge bounced on the concrete. When the snake's body twisted toward me, I stepped away from it.

My dad picked the snake up from the mess of its head. The dead snake, long and heavy, threw a couple of coils over his wrist. He shook them off, shook the body of the snake out straight, let it hang down from his hand. It was longer than one of his legs. "Wore that belt for a lot of years," he said, and I noticed that my ears were ringing. It took me a second to understand what he was talking about. "Wore it 'til it fell apart." He offered the snake to me, but I didn't want to touch it. He laughed.

"Let's go show your mother," he said, walking past me toward the house. I thought of the woman in the sun dress, wondered what she would think of the blacksnake. I followed my dad, watching the snake. Its movements were slowing now, lapsing into a rhythmic twitching along the whole length of its body.

As we passed the smokehouse and the parked Riviera, I asked him, "What's her name?" He looked at the car, back at me. I could hear my mother's voice, and the voice of the other woman, couldn't hear what they were saying.

"Hanson," he said. "Mrs. Hanson. Judge Hanson's wife." Judge Hanson was a circuit court judge in the county seat; he'd talked at my school once, a big man wearing a three-piece suit, even though the day had been hot. It seemed to me that his wife must be a good deal younger than he was.

The snake in my father's hand was motionless now, hung straight down toward the earth. His fingers were smeared with gore, and a line of blood streaked his chest.

"Why'd you kill the blacksnake?" I asked him. "After what you said, about rats and all?" I was still surprised he'd done it. He looked at me, and for a moment I didn't think he was going to answer me.

He reached for the doorknob with his free hand, twisted it. "Thought you'd know," he said. "My daddy made a belt for me. I'm gonna make one for you."

THE WOMAN in the sun dress, Mrs. Hanson, was talking to my mother when we entered the porch. "I was talking to Karen Spangler the other day," she said. My mother, sitting at the other end of the screen porch, nodded. Mrs. Spangler was one of our regular egg customers, came out about once every two weeks, just for a minute. Mrs. Hanson continued. "She says that you all have just the best eggs, and the Judge and I wondered if you might possibly . . ." She let the sentence trail off, turned to my father.

"Why, hello, Mr. Albright," she said. She saw the snake, but she had poise: she didn't react. My father nodded at her. "Mrs. Hanson," he said. He held the snake up for my mother to see. "Look here, Sara," he said. "Found this one sunning himself out near the diesel pump."

My mother stood. "You don't want to bring that thing on the porch, Jack," she said. She was a small woman, my mother, with quick movements, deft reactions. There was anger in her eyes.

"Thought I'd make a belt out of it for the boy," my dad said, ignoring her. He waved the snake, and a drop of blood fell from his hand to the floor. "You remember that old snakeskin belt I had?"

Mrs. Hanson came over to me, and I could smell her perfume. Her skin was tan, lightly freckled. "I don't think we've met," she said to me, like I was a man, and not just a boy. I tried to look her straight in the eye, found I couldn't. "No'm," I said. "Don't think we have."

"His name's Cates," my mother said. "He's ten." I didn't like it that she answered for me. Mrs. Hanson nodded, held out her hand. "Pleased to meet you, Cates," she said. I took her hand, shook it, realized I probably wasn't supposed to shake a lady's hand. I pulled back, noticed the grime under my fingernails, the dust on the backs of my hands. "Pleased," I said, and Mrs. Hanson gave out a laugh that was like nothing I'd ever heard from a woman before, loud and happy.

"You've a fine boy there," she said to my dad. I bent my head. To my father, my mother said, "Why don't you take that snake out of here, Jack. And get a shirt on. We've got company."

He darted a look at her. Then he waved the snake in the air, to point out to everybody what a fine, big blacksnake it was. He opened the screen door, leaned out, and dropped the snake in a coiled heap next to the steps. It looked almost alive lying there, the sheen of the sun still on the dark scales. "Mrs. Hanson," he said, and went on into the house. He let the door slam behind him, and I could hear him as he climbed the stairs inside.

Once he was gone, Mrs. Hanson seemed to settle back, to become more businesslike. "The Judge and I certainly would appreciate the opportunity to buy some of your eggs." She sat down in one of the cane-bottom chairs we kept on the porch in summer, set her purse down beside her. "But Sara—may I call you Sara?" she asked, and my mother nodded. "Something else has brought me here as well." My mother sat forward in her chair, interested to hear. I leaned forward too, and Mrs. Hanson shot a glance my way. I could tell she wasn't sure she wanted me there.

"Sara," she said, "you have a Sutton pie safe." She pointed across the porch, and at first I thought she meant the upright freezer that stood there. Then I saw she was pointing at the old breadbox.

My mother looked at it. "Well, it's a pie safe," she said. "Sutton, I don't know—"

"Oh, yes, it's a Sutton," Mrs. Hanson said. "Mrs. Spangler told me so, and I can tell she was right." Mrs. Spangler, so far as I knew, had never said anything to us about a pie safe. Mrs. Hanson rose, knelt in front of the thing, touched first one part of it and then another.

"Here, you see," she said, pointing to the lower right corner of one of the pie safe's doors. We'd always called it a breadbox, kept all kinds of things in it: canned goods, my dad's ammunition and his reloading kit, things that needed to be kept cool in winter. The pie safe was made of cherry wood—you could tell even through the paint—with a pair of doors on the front. The doors had tin panels, and there were designs punched in the tin, swirls and circles and I don't know what all. I looked at the place where she was pointing. "SS" I saw, stamped into the wood. The letters were mostly filled with paint; I'd never noticed them before.

Mrs. Hanson patted the thing, picked a chip of paint off it. My mother and I watched her. "Of course," Mrs. Hanson said, "this paint will have to come off. Oh, a complete refinishing job, I imagine. How lovely!" She sounded thrilled. She ran her hands down the tin, feeling the holes where the metal-punch had gone through.

"Damn," she said, and I was surprised to hear her curse. "What's the matter?" my mother asked. Mrs. Hanson looked closely at the tin on the front of the pie safe. "It's been reversed," she said. "The tin panels on the front, you see how the holes were punched in? It wasn't put together that way, you know. When they punched this design in the tin, they poked it through from the back to the front, so the points were outside the pie safe."

"Oh," my mother said, sounding deflated. It sounded ridiculous to me. I couldn't figure why anyone would care which way the tin was put on the thing.

"Sometimes country people do that, reverse the tin panels," Mrs. Hanson said in a low voice, as if she weren't talking to country people. My mother didn't disagree. "Still, though," Mrs. Hanson said, "it is a Sutton, and I must have it. What will you take for it?"

I guess I should have known that she was angling to buy the thing all along, but still it surprised me. It surprised my mother too. "Take for it?" she said.

"Yes," Mrs. Hanson said, "it's our anniversary next week—mine and the Judge's—and I just know he would be thrilled with a Sutton piece. Especially one of the pie safes. Of course, I don't think it'll be possible to have it refinished by then, but he'll see the possibilities."

"I don't know," my mother said, and I couldn't believe she was considering the idea. "Is it worth a lot?" It was an odd way to arrive at a price, and I laughed. Both women looked at me as if they had forgotten that I was on the porch with them. I wondered what my father would say when he came down from putting on a shirt.

Mrs. Hanson turned back to my mother. "Oh, yes," she said. "Samuel Sutton was quite a workman, very famous throughout the Valley. People are vying to buy his pieces. And here I've found one all for myself. And the Judge." Then, as if understanding that she wasn't being wise, she said, "Of course, the damage to it, the tin and all; that does lower the value a great deal. And the paint." My father had painted the breadbox, the pie safe, when it had been in the kitchen years ago, to match the walls. We'd since moved it out to the porch, when my mother picked up a free-standing cupboard she liked better.

"I don't know," my mother said. "After all, we don't use it much anymore, just let it sit out here. And if you really want it . . ." She sounded worried. She knew my father wasn't going to be pleased with the idea. "We should wait, ask my husband." Mrs. Hanson reached into her handbag, looking for her checkbook. I knew it wasn't going to be that easy.

"Didn't that belong to Granddad?" I asked my mother. She looked at me, didn't answer. "Dad's dad?" I said, pressing.

"It was in my husband's family," my mother said to Mrs. Hanson. "He might not like it."

"Could we say, then, three hundred dollars? Would that be possible?" Mrs. Hanson asked. She wasn't going to give up. Just then, my father opened the door and stepped out of the house onto the porch. He had washed his hands, put on a blue chambray shirt, one I'd given him for Christmas.

"Three hundred dollars?" my father said. "Three hundred dollars for what?" I saw my mother's face set into hard lines; she was determined to oppose him.

"She wants to buy the pie safe," my mother said. Her voice was soft, but not afraid.

My father walked over to the breadbox, struck the tin with two fingers. "This?" he said. "You're going to pay three hundred for this?" Both my mother and Mrs. Hanson nodded. "I think that's a fair enough price, Mr. Albright," Mrs. Hanson said. I noticed she didn't call him Jack.

"You could use it to get someone over to help you work on the barn," my mother said. My father didn't even look at her. I moved to his side.

"Didn't know the breadbox was for sale," he said. "Didn't know that it would be worth that much if it was for sale."

"My father owned that," he said. "Bought it for my mother, for this house, when they were first married." He turned to my mother. "You know that," he said.

"But what do we use it for, Jack?" she asked. "We use the barn. We need the barn. More than some pie safe."

My father put his hand on my shoulder. "You're not going to leave me anything, are you?" he said to my mother. She flushed, gestured at Mrs. Hanson. Mrs. Hanson managed to look unflustered.

My dad looked at Mrs. Hanson. Her calm seemed to infuriate him. "We aren't merchants," he said. "And this isn't a furniture shop." He turned to me. "Is it, boy?" I nodded, then shook my head no, not sure which was the correct response. "Mrs. Hanson," my mother began. You could tell she didn't like my father talking like that to Mrs. Hanson, who was a guest in her home.

"Don't apologize for me, Sara," my dad said. "Go ahead and sell the damn breadbox if you want, but just don't apologize for me." My mother opened her mouth, shut it again.

"Boy," he said to me, "you want a snakeskin belt like I was talking about? Like my daddy made?" He gestured out the porch door, to where the headless snake lay. A big fly, colored like blue glass, was crawling on the body.

"Yes, sir," I said, glad not to have to look at the high color rising in Mrs. Hanson's cheeks.

"You come out back with me, then, and I'll show you how to skin it, how to stretch the hide. How'd that be?" Neither my mother nor Mrs. Hanson said a word. My dad pushed me ahead of him, and I headed out the door.

As he came after me, he turned and spoke through the screen. "I'll tell you something, Mrs. Hanson," he said. "You ought not to try to buy what hasn't been put up for sale."

OUTSIDE, MY FATHER groped in his pocket for a second, came up with his old Barlow knife, flicked the blade out. "You hold the snake for me," he said. "We'll take that skin right off him." He held out the body to me. I hesitated, reached out and took it.

It was heavy and rope-like, cool and limp in my hands. The scales were dry as sand. "Set it down there," my dad said, "and hold it stretched out tight." I set the snake down.

"Belly up," my dad said. "We don't want to mess up the scales on his back. That's what makes a snakeskin belt so nice, so shiny, them back scales." I rolled the snake. The scales on the sausage-like belly were light-colored, looked soft, and I prodded them with a forefinger. The skin rasped against my fingernail.

"Here we go," my father said, and pressed the blade of the knife against the belly of the snake. He always kept the knife razor-sharp, had a whetstone at the house he kept specially for it. I looked away. The knife made a sound as it went in; I thought I could hear him slicing through muscle, thought I could hear the small, cartilaginous ribs giving way under the blade.

Mrs. Hanson left the porch, and I could tell from the way she was walking that she must have gotten what she wanted. She moved with a bounce in her step. She looked over at us where we were kneeling, shook her hair back out of her face, smiled. My father paused in his cutting for a second when he heard the car door open. Mrs. Hanson backed the Buick around, headed back down the lane, toward the highway. A couple of low-hanging branches lashed the windshield as she went.

My mother stood on the porch, an outline behind the mesh of the screen, watching her go. When the car was out of sight, she turned and went back into the house.

My father gave a low laugh. When I looked at him, he was holding something gray between two fingers, dangled it back and forth in front of my face. "I'll be damned," he said. I looked down at the snake, the open stomach cavity, realized that he was holding a dead mouse by its tail. "No wonder that snake was so sleepy," my dad said. "He just ate." I stood, turned away from him.

"What's the matter?" he asked. I didn't answer. "You aren't gonna let that bother you," he said, and there was disdain in his voice. I put my arms over the top rail of the board fence around our yard, leaned my weight on it. I closed my eyes, saying nothing.

My father lowered his voice. "Thought you wanted that belt," he said. I wanted to turn to him, tell him that I did want the belt, just to give me a minute. I wasn't sure I could trust my voice not to break. "Guess not," he said.

Once again, I heard the sound of the knife, two quick cuts. I turned to look, saw that he had deftly sliced the body of the snake, had carved it into three nearly equal sections. It looked like pieces of bicycle tire lying there, bloody bicycle tire. My father rose, wiped his hands on his jeans.

"You think about that, boy," he said. "You think about that, next time you decide you want something." He walked past me, not toward the house, but toward the ruined barn.

IN 1987, AFTER stewarding the Workshop admirably for seventeen years, John Leggett stepped aside, and National Book Award finalist Frank Conroy, honored for his classic memoir *Stop-Time,* assumed direction of the program. Applications in fiction alone approached 500 annually by the beginning of the '90s, despite the fact that over 300 creative writing programs based on Iowa's model now existed nation-wide. Like Wall Street in the '80s and '90s, M.F.A. programs experienced the longest bull market in the field's history. Applications swelled to 800 under Conroy's pursuit of the best young writers in the country. With less than 3 percent of all fiction applicants accepted, gaining admission to the Iowa Workshop became statistically more difficult than getting into Harvard Medical School.

The "growth business" nature of creative writing programs, coupled with Amer-ican fiction's drift toward sincere realism as its dominant narrative voice and dys-functional families as its prevailing subject, brought a new round of denunciations against the Workshop method. Tom Wolfe lamented the dearth of the sprawling, ambitious social novel, which he dubbed the "billion-footed beast" in a 1989 *Harper's* essay. Another critic sniped that he doubted *Gravity's Rainbow* could be written as homework. It's true that, at times, it seemed as if creative writing programs existed only to churn out new teachers of creative writing who would start new programs to produce new students until everyone was issued a social security number and an M.F.A. degree at birth.

But there is, I believe, a more generous interpretation of this situation. By the '90s, writers, even literature itself—that complicated, living thing despised by those frustrated morticians, the literary theorists—increasingly had nowhere else to turn. If writers are readers moved to emulation, then neither the conventional academy, with its Derrida-crazed turn toward the quickly passé deconstruction movement, nor the culture at large offered serious readers a community, a locus for a dialogue about literature, only continual announcements about the death and ephemerality of literature, and rack after rack of Stephen King novels.

Political correctness also had a chilling effect on American literature, encouraging the rise of sincerity. How could one risk portraying a racist character, or attempt to write empathetically through the point of view of a character of another race or culture or gender, without also taking the risk of offending someone? Given this, how far off was the death of imagination so gleefully salivated over by deconstructionists? If imagination is the source of human freedom, then banning empathy as a means of imaginatively understanding one another poses a threat to liberty.

But, as conspiracy mavens everywhere have long understood, political correctness was a conservative creation designed to paralyze liberals with endless infighting over male patriarchy and victimization while the real fights—the separation of rich and poor, and the consolidation of corporate power—slithered along unnoticed. Or is this just a fiction of mine, something I imagined? Something similar to a novelistic curiosity about the federal government's approval of Prozac and other SSRI antidepressants—which help millions but also promote passivity, stifle the metaphoric thinking necessary to writing literature, and occasionally cause short-term memory loss—approval that a novelist would notice was granted virtually the same year Contragate and the '87 stock market "crash" threatened the republic's serenity. Oscar Wilde said, "Man is least himself when he talks in his own person. Give him a mask and he will tell you the truth. The truth of metaphysics is the truth of masks." Existential and historical speculation is what makes literature necessary. Not *right*, necessary. And the vitality inherent in that "billion-footed beast" of a novel Wolfe advocated sometimes requires a digression, which this has been.

The end of empathy and the rise of sincerity encouraged the "memoir explosion" of the '90s, a phenomenon that has been widely but not very astutely noted. In the age of political correctness, empathy turned even further inward. All it found was the dregs of the Self, a "remaindered" item from the Romantic movement. Sincerity seemed to promise a way of reestablishing a sense of community by sharing one's victim status with others, in a style guaranteed not to offend anyone. The sixteenth and seventeenth centuries, Trilling wrote in *Sincerity and Authenticity*, "may be taken as virtually definitive of the psychological changes to which historians point . . . men became individuals." Before this period man "did not have an awareness of . . . internal space." The blooming of man as an individual produced autobiographies such as Rousseau's *Confessions*.

Memoirs share an interesting historical link with autobiographies. History impacts literature, and history itself is often determined by advances in technology. The "French psychoanalyst Jacques Lacan," Trilling noted, "believes that the development of the '*Je*' was advanced by the manufacture of mirrors." This sudden sense of I-ness spurred the autobiographical impulse. "The subject of autobiography," Trilling said, "is just such a self, bent on revealing himself in all his truth, bent, that is to say, on demonstrating his sincerity. His conception of his private and uniquely interesting individuality, together with his impulse to reveal his self, are . . . his response to the newly available sense of an audience," one created by the decline of the church.

In the electronic hall of mirrors that the '90s became, memoirs were a reaction to the exact opposite phenomenon that produced autobiographies. Rather than coming into a sense of individuality and Self, the memoirist felt these twin qualities of modern civilization fading. The various extensions of the media—radio, newspapers, magazines, TV, the Web—have diminished, if not completely dismantled, the concept of the private, individual Self who valued, according to Trilling, sincerity as a quality of "supreme importance in the moral life . . . of Western culture for some four hundred years." Many memoirists have tried to reassert sincerity as a viable, regenerative strategy for literature. But, "Every profound spirit needs a mask," Nietzsche wrote. Yes, he was ultimately insane. But memoirists who resist the mask never achieve "one of the beneficences of art," namely a "detachment achieved through irony."

"Man only plays," Schiller said, "when he is in the fullest sense of the word a human being, and he is only fully a human being when he plays." Irony requires a sense of play, rather than a commitment to sincerity. Play is the exact quality that distinguishes Frank Conroy's inimitable memoir *Stop-Time*. In it, he plays music, plays with his yo-yo, plays around with the literary structure of a *Bildungsroman*. The result is a work of art, made distinctive by Trilling's notion of "detachment achieved through irony," which is the narrative stance that frames the book from the opening scene's car crash to the bile and laughter coming up through the narrator's throat at the story's close.

Given the gossip-fevered, money-centered era that memoirs thrived in, it's easy to see that, as a form, the memoir surrendered literature's sense of ironic play and replaced it with self-exposure as a form of currency. For with the imaginary, fictive Self discredited not only by literary theorists but by a culture in which the Self seemed not to fully exist unless the media was covering it, memoirs exchanged epiphanies that yielded meaning for revealed secrets. Instead of Joyce's "radiant shining forth," the more egregious memoirs offered revelations of tawdry indiscretions and tales of 12-step redemption, a phenomenon that culminated in the conservative movement's Ur text, *The Starr Report*, our end-of-the-millennium *Scarlet Letter*.

Of course, I'm joking. Or am I? Fiction keeps alive what one of the great champions of literature Milan Kundera calls philosophical speculation on the nature of human existence. Literature cannot promise 20 percent annualized returns on investments. It cannot promise peace or bring about the end of injustice. It can't even promise to stay in print. Literature is a frail, mortal, imperfect thing, which forever makes it the perfect mirror for the human condition.

My 1990s classmates, all of whom I know too well to comment on, have done a brave and magnificent job of continuing to polish and hold up the "postmodern" hall of mirrors to American culture. This decade represents the vibrancy and variety of work by writers who, like others before them, have given over their lives to sustained faith in the necessity and nobility of literature. A faith that continues to burn brightly in Iowa City as the century ends, and one that will, like Faulkner's great spirit Dilsey, endure.

I CAME TO THE WORKSHOP in August of 1988. The state of Iowa was no mystery to me: my mother is a native; my parents met there; I had family living still in Des Moines. Nearly everything else was. I had never lived on my own, never exactly thought about becoming "A Writer" (as opposed to a person who sometimes wrote). Allan Gurganus was my first Workshop teacher at Iowa, and if he'd suggested car selling instead of fiction writing, today I'd probably have a Chevy dealership somewhere: I believed everything he said, since I was particularly credulous and he so inspirational, and so eloquent. He told us we were lucky to be writers, and though in some dark moments I have a hard time remembering this, I have never been able to completely forget it.

Plus every month I went to Des Moines to see my grandmother. That in itself made me a better writer.

Lucky, too, to meet the kinds of people I met in Iowa and have kept as friends ever since. Many of my dearest friends and best readers are Workshop classmates. The Workshop has a reputation for being competitive, even cutthroat. Some of my friends there even felt that it was, but I can't say that I ever noticed: my buddies there were kind to me and to each other, full of good advice and love.

ELIZABETH MCCRACKEN

ELIZABETH McCRACKEN

Here's Your Hat What's Your Hurry

AUNT HELEN BECK was square-shouldered and prone to headaches. She stretched out on sofas too short for her, and let her feet climb walls or rest on end tables or knock over plants. The children in the houses she visited told Aunt Helen Beck Stories, first to their friends, then to their own children, who sometimes got to meet the old lady in real life and collect their own tales, the same ones: the healing power of molasses; the letters she dictated to dead relatives. Her fondness for reciting James Whitcomb Reilly or any morbid poet with three names: Edgar Allan Poe, Edward Arlington Robinson. She said she knew James Whitcomb Reilly when she was a girl in Indianapolis and had once presented him with a bouquet of flowers at a school pageant. He was drunk.

After a while, everyone Aunt Helen Beck knew was dead, and so she wrote a lot of letters, dictated to the children, who, despite being terrified of the enormous old lady on the sofa, loved scribbling down: "Dear Arthur. You have been dead fifty years and I still don't forgive you." Aunt Helen Beck would hold a small change purse in her hand and shake it as she spoke; it was leather gone green with age. Aunt Helen Beck said there were two pennies in it, though she would never show them to anybody.

"I have had these pennies for sixty-five years," she'd say. "I intend to be buried with them."

Aunt Helen Beck had many intentions about her death. She was about being dead the way some people are about being British—she wasn't, and it seemed she never would be, but it was clearly something she aspired to, since all the people she respected were.

I AM YOUR AUNT HELEN BECK.

That was how she began every call, no matter who answered the phone. It was important to say it as if they should remember her, though of course, having never met her, they rarely did.

Aunt Helen Beck, they'd say. How are you?

Tell the truth, she'd answer, not so good. I'm in Springfield (or Delta Bay, or Cedar Rapids, or Yrma), and I need a place to stay.

Sometimes she'd explain that she was about to visit a friend who had now suddenly fallen ill. If she had stayed with one of their siblings, she'd mention that. They'd come in a pick-up truck or a sedan or a ramshackle station wagon, and when they spotted the one old woman likewise looking for a stranger, she could see their alarm. It was as if they were scanning a dictionary page for a word they'd just heard for the first time: Good Lord. You mean *that's* how it's spelled?

Aunt Helen Beck always liked that moment. She was bigger than anyone ever assumed she'd be; she looked as if she might still be growing, her hands and knees outsize, like a teenager's. People thought women were like dogs: the big ones were expected to die, until all that was left were the small, fussy sorts, the ones with nervous stomachs and improbable hair.

Then she got in the car with them and they drove home.

This time, it was a boat she stepped off, the ferry to Orcas Island, in Puget Sound. Already she could spot Ford and his wife, Chris: they kept still, looking through the crowd only with their eyes. Ford held his wife's hand. Aunt Helen Beck had stayed with Abbie, Ford's sister, a few years before. That's when she'd gotten Ford's address, and back then an island had sounded too far away to visit. Now she was beginning to run out of places.

Aunt Helen Beck walked straight up to them, one arm extended, without any doubt. In the other hand she carried a suitcase as if it weighed nothing at all.

"Ford," said Aunt Helen Beck. They both jumped. "And Chris." She bent down a bit to allow Chris a kiss on the cheek, but made it clear she did not want another kiss anytime in the near future. Ford took her suitcase instead.

She saw them take her in, her navy blue suit, clean shirt, none of the usual old lady fripperies: no perfume, makeup, or glasses. Her gray hair was short and close to her head. She looked like a nun who had decided, after much thought, that as a matter of fact she'd always preferred cleanliness over godliness.

"You have a beard," Aunt Helen Beck said to Ford.

"Glory be," he said, touching his chin. "Actually, yes. I do."

"Your cousin Edward was fond of his beard, too. I always thought that bearded men were hiding something, but I have been assured that that's not true."

"I hope not," said Chris. She was a copper-headed, freckled woman dressed just like her husband, in blue jeans and a dark long-sleeved T-shirt.

"Just parked over here," Ford said.

Chris climbed in the bed of the truck. Ford tried to help Aunt Helen Beck up into the cab, but she wouldn't allow it. He walked around and got in.

"So." Ford tapped the steering wheel, then turned the key in the ignition. "How long do you think you'll be with us?"

Aunt Helen Beck looked at him. "Here's your hat what's your hurry, is that how it is?"

"No," he said. "No. I was just wondering—"

"Well, I don't know whether or not I like you. It would be premature for me to make a prediction. I might want to turn around soon as we get to your house."

"I hope," said Ford, a little sincerity forced into his voice, "that you'll give us more of a chance than that."

"Done," said Aunt Helen Beck.

She looked at his profile, at the sun coming through his beard. In fact, he was hiding things. There were acne scars on the parts of his cheeks that were out in the open; and it was clear that if you poked your finger straight into his beard, it would be a while before you hit any semblance of a chin.

"Here." Aunt Helen Beck reached into her pocket and pulled out a small framed photograph of a mustached man standing in front of a painted arbor. "For you," she said. "Your great-grandfather. My uncle Patrick Corrigan. Not my blood uncle, of course, but I was very fond of him always." She held it up. "You do look like him."

Ford looked at it out of the corner of his eye. "Nice-looking man," he said. "Thank you. Sure you want to give that up?"

"I always bring a present to my hosts," said Aunt Helen Beck.

They pulled up a rocky drive that jostled Aunt Helen Beck's bones, still sore from traveling. An old trailer flashed by, the round sort that had always looked to her like a thermos bottle, as if the people inside needed protection against rot. Then a house showed itself around a bend, halfway up the big hill. It looked like a good house, solid and small. Aunt Helen Beck had stayed in better, perhaps, but she had certainly stayed in much worse.

"This must be the place," said Ford, pulling on the brake.

She heard a child say to Chris, "You're ridin' in back like a *dog*."

Chris barked a response, then came around to the door to help Aunt Helen Beck out. The child, who had white-blond hair halfway down its back, ran around with her.

"Who's that?" the child asked, pointing.

"Who are you?" Aunt Helen Beck replied, and then, because she couldn't tell, "Are you a little boy or a little girl?" They dressed them alike, these days.

"I'm a *boy*," he said.

"Your hair's too long," she told him.

"I like my hair. My mother cuts it for me."

"Your mother is falling down on the job," said Aunt Helen Beck. "Come to me and I'll do better." She grabbed her suitcase, which Ford took from her. "I'm your Aunt Helen Beck," she told the boy.

"He's not ours," said Ford, swinging the suitcase over his shoulder. "He lives in that trailer we just passed."

"Good," she said.

They went around back and walked into a bright kitchen, full of the sorts of long skinny plants Aunt Helen Beck had always distrusted: they looked like they wanted to ruffle your hair or sample your cooking. The boy followed them into the house. He flopped down on the couch; Aunt Helen Beck couldn't blame him. A child who lived in a trailer surely thought that furniture was a luxury.

"So," she said. "What's your name?"

"Mercury," he said.

"I beg your pardon?"

Ford shrugged. "His mother likes planets."

"I like vegetables," said Aunt Helen Beck, "but I wouldn't name my child Rutabaga. But—" she squinted at Ford, "—I suppose that someone named after a car isn't shocked."

"The theater, actually," said Ford.

"Huh," said Aunt Helen Beck. She turned to her niece. "Christopher Columbus, I presume?"

Chris just blushed.

"In my day," said Aunt Helen Beck, "we settled on a dead uncle and were done with it."

Mercury took off one of his shoes. "When you have children," he recited, "you can name them anything you want."

THE HOUSE was a small prefab; Aunt Helen Beck had never heard of such a thing. The guest room down the hall was decorated with a number of faded bedspreads: on the narrow cot, as drapes, suspended from the ceiling like something in a harem. The furniture was otherwise sparse and functional; Ford explained that he had made some of it himself and was thinking of taking up caning. There was a picture window in the living room with a view of both Puget Sound and the silver trailer. According to Ford, Mercury's mother, Gaia, had casual attitudes toward marriage and having children. So far she'd had Mercury, Jupiter, Venus, and Saturn, and seemed bent on assembling her own galaxy, though God help the child named Pluto or Uranus. The kids were all as blond and airy as Gaia, and constantly orbited Chris and Ford's flower patch, dirty and nosy as trowels.

"Ford's cooking dinner tonight," Chris said. "What do you like to eat?"

"Nothing, really," said Aunt Helen Beck. "But I'll eat anything anyhow."

In the kitchen, Ford was pulling pots and boxes out of cupboards. "I'd thought I'd make some quinoa," he said. "The grain of the ancient Aztecs."

"Of who?" Aunt Helen Beck asked. She and Chris sat down at the kitchen table.

"Aztecs," said Ford. "Or. Incas? Ancient somebodies. The guy at the store told me. I think you'll like it."

"Because I'm ancient, no doubt."

"No, no," said Ford. But Chris laughed and touched Aunt Helen Beck's forearm lightly.

"No, really," Ford said. "Somebody ancient really did eat this stuff."

"But did they like it?" asked Chris, giggling.

"Not you, too," said Ford. "Okay. Rice? It's tricky, Aunt Helen Beck: we're vegetarians."

"As am I," said Aunt Helen Beck. "I knew you seemed sensible."

"Beans and rice it is," said Ford. He set out his things carefully: first garlic, then spices; he poured the rice into a glass measuring cup and then into a strainer. "No time to soak beans," he said under his breath, "so we'll just used canned," and Aunt Helen Beck could tell that he was a convert to careful diet: once upon a time he went through this sort of ritual with substances that were not so good for him. She had seen that sort of thing in plenty of houses.

"So where were you taking the bus from?" Chris asked her.

"From Vallejo." Aunt Helen Beck got up and opened a drawer, looking for silverware. When she found it, she started setting the table.

"Leave that," Ford said. "We'll do it."

Aunt Helen Beck ignored him. She said to Chris, "Usually I travel by car, but my car broke down about a month ago and I had to leave it behind."

"That's terrible," said Chris. "Are you going to get another one?"

"I can't tell. This car was a gift, so I suppose if someone wants to give me another I'll take it."

Chris tried to take a fork from Aunt Helen Beck's hand, but failed. "You're making me feel guilty," she said.

"Your guilt I can do nothing about," said Aunt Helen Beck. "The table I can."

"You're from Vallejo?" asked Ford.

"Heavens, no," said Aunt Helen Beck. "My niece Marlene lives there. I was just visiting her. And before that I was with Abbie, and before that I was with my dear cousin Audrey, who passed away."

"Oh dear," said Chris. "While you were visiting?"

"Yes, I'm sorry to say." Aunt Helen Beck straightened one of the placemats that was already on the table. "She gave me the car—she left it to me; she left everything to me. I think perhaps Audrey was my closest friend, though I didn't meet her until we were both grown women. In fact, I read her husband's obituary and realized this was a cousin and called her to offer my condolences, that's how we met. I visited Audrey often."

"How long had you been there when she died?" Chris asked.

"Five years. When you're seventy-four, the people you know are dying or dead. One gets used to it."

Ford rummaged in a kitchen drawer for a spoon. "Where do you call home now?"

Aunt Helen Beck picked up a fork and set it back down decisively. "All set here," she said. "Ready when you are."

AFTER AUNT HELEN BECK had cleared the table, washed the dishes, and wiped down the table, the three of them sat around the kitchen table. Aunt Helen Beck rattled her little purse.

"There must be a story behind that," Chris said.

"My brother made it for me." Aunt Helen Beck stopped shaking it but didn't open her palm to let them see.

"Another relative!" said Ford. "Where's he now?"

"He died very young. My brother," said Aunt Helen Beck, "was a child preacher. He toured the South with my father. Beautiful child, Georgie. Famous, too. Before he died, he made me this purse for my birthday and put two pennies in it. I've kept it with me ever since."

"Nice to know there's spirituality in the family," said Ford.

Aunt Helen Beck waved her hand. "My father made him preach, and Georgie was smart and pretty. Children are not spiritual, in my opinion."

But the voice she used when she wanted to shut people up had no effect on him. "Why, Aunt Helen Beck," he said. "Children are spiritual creatures. It's why they're unpredictable."

"No," she said. "There's a difference between being spiritual and just being willful. Some people never learn that." She looked at him deliberately.

Chris laughed. "Don't get him started, Aunt Helen Beck. He's full of theories."

"So's Aunt Helen Beck, I have a feeling," said Ford.

She smiled back. "I'm sure we have a lot to talk about." She could tell he was flattered by that: he was the type of man who wanted to be invited to join every club there was. Even hers.

AUNT HELEN BECK worked hard at all the things that convinced people to let her stay. She got up early to bake bread, examined the books that were on the shelves and referred to them in conversation. She did dishes immediately; cooked for herself; went to bed early and pretended to sleep soundly.

She charmed Mercury, at least. He adored her, and started playing in the yard less and in the house more. She instructed Mercury to behave, she threatened him with poems about goblins that stole nasty children, and he seemed eager to be taken, and asked her if she were the head goblin.

"He's a good kid," Chris told her. "Just restless."

"Perhaps," said Aunt Helen Beck, but she smiled. She was fond of Mercury, though the brother and sister old enough to walk struck her as colorless and dull.

Children did not interest her until they were six: Aunt Helen Beck liked conversation.

She got that in abundance from Ford. He was a glib young man, too free and easy. Aunt Helen Beck had expected him to be reserved, since when she'd stayed with his sister he left a message on the answering machine: "Oh hell, Ab," he said. "You got a machine? Well. Hate these things. Guess I'll just write." Aunt Helen Beck had assumed that meant he wouldn't brook any nonsense, when really he just preferred his own special stock. He admired Indians—both sorts—and wrote poetry that he tacked to the doorjambs of the house, frequently addressed to "The Earth," or, "The Goddess." It took Aunt Helen Beck some time to discover that this second wasn't a pet name for his wife.

She was the reason Aunt Helen Beck wanted to stay. Chris stayed home all day to make her necklaces, which she sold through some of the shops and galleries in town. Sometimes, Ford helped with the beading, but Aunt Helen Beck noticed his impatience: he threw all the good beads together, and ended up with chunky clashed messes. His wife knew how to spell the dazzle with tiny beads and knots. Aunt Helen Beck noted with approval that Chris was quiet and perennially embarrassed: an attractive quality in a woman, and something, she knew, that had always been lacking in herself.

AFTER A WEEK, she let Chris catch her making a phone call in the kitchen.

"I thought I might come to visit," said Aunt Helen Beck into the phone. "Oh. Well, no, of course you're busy. Might I help? No, you're welcome, I just thought I might be useful. Some other time, perhaps. In a month or so." She hung up the phone.

"Aunt Helen Beck," said Chris. "You don't have anywhere to stay, do you?"

"I'm sure I'll find some place—"

"Stay here. We like having you, there's plenty of room—"

"Can't stay forever," said Aunt Helen Beck.

"Well," said Chris. She thought it over. "For a while, at least. For as long as you like. Why not?"

"Dear me," said Aunt Helen Beck. "You're sure to think of a reason eventually."

AFTER DINNER each night, Chris and Ford went in the living room and watched the sun set over the Sound and tried to get her to join them. They sat with arms around each other, and though Aunt Helen Beck did not strictly approve of that sort of public display, she did not object. She liked people in love: they were slow-witted and cheerful. They never asked her again how long she planned to stay.

Sometimes, she stood in the door of the living room, and the three of them looked at the trailer standing between them and the Sound. Ford liked to pretend he knew what was going on in there, and made up stories.

"About now," he said, "Gaia has fed them and bathed them—"

"Bathed them?" asked Aunt Helen Beck. "There's a tub in that tiny thing?"

"A little shower," he said. "Or she's taken them to the lake to swim. And one of them—probably Venus, since she's stubborn and a flirt—is refusing to get dressed and is bouncing off the walls, stark naked."

"And so Gaia is singing a getting-dressed song," said Chris.

"And Jupiter's crying," said Ford. "Because it's not a very good song."

Aunt Helen Beck shook her head. "All those people in one little house. I'm not sure I approve."

"What's to approve?" asked Ford. "She leads her life and she's happy. And they're good kids, so she must be doing something right."

"How does she make her way in the world?"

"Oh, the way anybody does around here. Part-time work, barter. She works a couple of days a week at the Healing Arts Center."

"Healing?" asked Aunt Helen Beck. "Physical healing?"

"Reiki. Rolfing. That sort of thing. Laying on of hands, really. Perhaps not so different from what your brother did, Aunt Helen Beck."

"My brother," she said, "was a child of God."

"Well, everybody's got their own idea of God," said Ford. "Anyhow, Gaia's good at what she does. She fixes things. Maybe—" he looked at her with teasing eyes, "—you should go to her sometime."

Aunt Helen Beck said, "I was not under the impression I needed fixing."

"EAT THIS."

Mercury closed his mouth around the spoon of molasses.

"Mmmmm." He licked the spoon all over, including the handle.

"You think that's good?" she asked.

"Yes," he said. Chris and Ford were in town, shopping, and Mercury had elected to follow Aunt Helen Beck through the house as she cleaned and straightened. His brother and sister had been outside, throwing dirt at the window, until she had dispatched him to tell them to stop.

"If you think that tastes good," she said, "I'm afraid something's wrong with you. You must be part dog, to think everything's good to eat."

"Maybe I am a dog," he said; he lay down on the living room floor, his hair fanning out behind him.

"How old are you, Mercury?"

"Seven."

"Do you know how to write?"

"Yes," he said peevishly.

"Well then." She looked around for a piece of paper. "Would you like to write a letter for me?"

"Who to?"

"Kneel down here," she said, pointing to the coffee table, "and I'll tell you what to say." She found a pencil and some lined paper in a drawer and gave them to him, then tried to stretch out on the sofa, a tiny loveseat. She bent her knees over the arm and let her feet dangle. "All right. Put down just what I tell you. Here we go. 'Dear Mac. Of course, we haven't spoken for a while. That is understandable.' Do you have that?"

"Yes." His head was bent over the paper and he was holding the pencil like a needle, very delicately. His hair, that ridiculous hair, hid his face. She imagined he was concentrating.

" 'But I need to tell you this: I'm still mad about what you said to me when last we met. Furious. You know what I'm talking about.' "

"What's in your hand?" Mercury asked, still writing. She figured he was stalling for time while he caught up to her words.

"It's a purse. A little boy made it for me a long time ago."

Mercury turned to look. "Any money in it?"

All little boys know what purses are for, thought Aunt Helen Beck: in each and every one a Fort Knox.

"Two pennies," she said. "Let's get back to work."

"Where does this guy live?" Mercury started writing again.

"He's dead," said Aunt Helen Beck.

"You can't write to dead people." He put down his pencil and turned around again.

"Why not?"

"They're *dead.*"

"That only means they can't read," she told him. "It has nothing to do with what I can or cannot do. Let's see how you're doing." She sat up; the arm of the loveseat was cutting off the circulation to her feet.

He leaned away so she could see, and what she saw was this, in pale letters because he did not bear down: MERCURY MERCURY MERCURY KABOOM I LOVE YOU.

"Well," she said, because he had tried his best. "I might have put that last part down anyway."

IN THE MORNING, when she slipped her hand into the pocket for Georgie's purse, it was gone. She took her hand out of her pocket, put it back in, took it out, back in again. It was not in her pocket.

Not in her pocket, where it always was; not on top of the dresser or tucked in her suitcase. Not anywhere in the kitchen, not even on the floor near the edges along the baseboards, which is where she was looking when Chris walked in.

"Aunt Helen Beck," Chris said, alarmed. "What's the matter?"

"Somebody's taken Georgie's purse. I can't find it anywhere."

"I'm sure it's around." Chris dropped to her knees beside Aunt Helen Beck.

"I can't find it." She hadn't ever been without the purse; it was one of her organs, it was vital. "I have to find it," she said.

"We will, we will." Chris had caught her worry. "I'll look in the living room." She crawled toward the other room just as Mercury came in the door. He laughed to see the grown-ups on all fours. Chris, looking over one shoulder, asked, "Have you seen Aunt Helen Beck's purse?"

"No," he said, too quickly.

"You're sure," said Aunt Helen Beck. She did not want to frighten him, but suddenly understood that he was the one who must have taken it. Who is as sneaky as a little boy? Who is more interested in other people's belongings?

"It's in your pocket," he said.

"No it isn't," she said, still on her hands and knees, still looking at him squarely. "If you have it, Mercury, I would very much like it back." She wished that just once, in all those houses she'd been in, she had picked up the child psychology book that was always sandwiched between Shakespeare and Tolstoy. Just use common sense, she'd always advised, but common sense, she now realized, had little to do with real life.

"It's not in my pockets," she said again.

"I don't have it," said Mercury, inching toward the door.

"Merc—" Chris began.

"I don't!" he yelled, and he ran out.

They sat back on their heels. Aunt Helen Beck rubbed the tops of her thighs slowly, in an effort not to cry. It didn't work, which surprised her.

"Oh, Aunt Helen Beck." Chris shuffle-crawled over to her, and laid one hand on her shoulder.

"What will become of me without it?"

"If he has it, I'm sure he'll bring it back. He's an honest kid, and he sees how much it means to you."

But Aunt Helen Beck could not see that happening. Little boys lose things. They trade them or bury them or give them to their sisters to chew on. The walls of the purse were the only walls she'd ever owned, and she'd allowed them to be taken away. She would have told another person in the same situation, You're allowed to be careless once in eight decades. She could not believe so herself.

"AUNT HELEN BECK, your talisman," Ford said when he found out. "I'm so sorry. Maybe Merc's got it and he'll bring it back." He sat down on the loveseat beside her. "Listen. Maybe we can make a stand-in."

Aunt Helen Beck leaned away from him and looked out the window at the silver trailer, and envied the woman's life there. Gaia was surely surrounded by things she owned: big jars of rice, children. To keep your family in such a small place now struck her as intelligent; it was like making your whole life a locket.

"I don't mean replace," said Ford. "But it was a symbol. Now you need another symbol, something to stand for Georgie and how much you love him."

"Georgie Beck died when he was seven. There is nothing in this world that he touched except that purse."

"Earth's the same," he said. "Same then as now. We'll make a little pillow of earth."

Aunt Helen Beck turned to look at him, and was startled at how close he sat. She could easily have hit him. Some common damp dirt for Georgie? But then she saw Ford was sad and desperate over the whole thing and somehow wanted to help.

"No thank you," she said.

Thereafter, Mercury kept his distance. One little boy was dead and gone; the other had done something she was not sure she could ever forgive. Her anger at him did not make the loss of his company any easier to bear: you always miss the person who breaks your heart. A few nights later, she caught a glimpse of him outside of the trailer, staring up at the house, as if he were a miniature general considering the best means of attack.

FORD WENT DOWN to the trailer to talk to Gaia, who said that she hadn't seen it, would keep her eye out. "She'll do her best," Ford said.

Even as he said it, Aunt Helen Beck felt herself change. She had been, up until that moment, in the same mood her entire life. The panic that engulfed her now was unfamiliar and frightening. She felt there must be a pill, something she could eat, that would clear it up. Or a pair of hands that put upon her would restore her to the way she used to be. But a pill worked its way through you, hands departed your skin. They were no replacement for the one thing she'd always owned.

Now she sat still to watch the sun set every night with Chris and Ford, and admired the family pictures that had always lined the walls. Those nights, she talked a streak, about nothing in particular. There was an affectionate recklessness to what she said: she spoke of people from her past, and family.

"I once knew a woman with twenty-one children," she said to Chris.

"Good Lord," said Chris. "That doesn't seem possible."

"It's true," said Aunt Helen Beck. "She was a collector. They weren't all hers; she just fancied them and took them in and when she tired of one, threw him out and got another."

"She sounds like a sad case," said Chris.

"Perhaps. Despite it all, I loved my mother."

"Your mother?"

"Yes," said Aunt Helen Beck. "We are discussing my mother."

And later, when Ford asked her what she did for Christmas as a child, she said, "Nothing. I always wanted to celebrate it, but my people are Jewish."

"What?" asked Ford. "What part of the family?"

"All sides. My grandfather was a rabbi." He looked confused, so she added, "Orthodox."

"I never knew we had any Judaism in the family," he said.

"You might not," she began, and then she caught herself. "You might not have been told," she said. "People used to like to cover that up, you know."

"But I thought your brother was a preacher—"

"Half-brother," she said quickly, her lightness gone. "And I don't want to talk about it. Have a care, Ford." Frequently she'd turn like that, from nostalgia straight into anger. Ford and Chris grew wary of her, and started going to bed earlier and earlier. She could hear them talk about her—her name again and again, because Aunt Helen Beck could not be reduced to a handful of pronouns. She didn't care to listen closely.

"We're glad to have you here," Chris would tell Aunt Helen Beck in the morning, coming in for a careful half hug. Aunt Helen Beck could feel heat coming off the younger woman's body. With her copper curls, her freckles exactly the same color, white skin underneath, Chris reminded Aunt Helen Beck of some pale cake left too long in the oven. She even smelled that way, delicate and warm, as if a sudden loud noise could make her collapse.

Did people always radiate such heat, or any heat? Did their temperatures vary? Aunt Helen Beck had never noticed before. She wanted to steal up behind Chris, or Ford, let a long breath loose across their skin to cool them before touching, cautiously, a quick furtive tap with her fingertips before allowing her whole palm to rest.

Sometimes, she would feel suddenly fearless and loving, put a hand on Ford's shoulder, give Chris a pat on the cheek, leave them notes in the bathroom signed with a heart. The one day they all went into town, she drifted off from them and returned with licorice, ginseng tea, a little trial-size packet of vitamins.

"Happy un-birthday," she said. "Have an un-birthday present."

Ford laughed, and said, "Aunt Helen Beck, you're all right."

"Just all right?" she asked. All he did was laugh again in his horsey way, but she really did want to know. She had tried all her life to be a good person, but how could she judge her success unless other people let her know? She knew she was not a good listener, supposed she got impatient at times. That's what having standards will get you, she thought: restless. It was one of the reasons she went visiting. Every person saw her a different way, and once she divined their opinion—bossy old lady or lovable crank or sometimes, she hoped, even nice plain honest woman—she wondered what someone else might think. She wondered if two people who knew her at separate times would agree.

Still, she felt now, for the first time, all it would take would be one person saying, Aunt Helen Beck, here's where you belong, and she'd stay in a minute.

SHE DIDN'T HEAR the boy walk into the room until he said, "I want you to cut my hair."

"Hello, Mercury," she said. He hadn't been in the house in the two weeks since the purse had gone missing. She looked at him and hoped that he had it tucked in his pocket, though she still felt so wretched about its loss she was no longer sure even the thing itself would help.

"I want you to cut my hair, please."

"Why?" asked Aunt Helen Beck, but even as she asked, she eyed the blond fall of hair, thought about how it would feel, giving way to the pressure of a pair of scissors.

"Too long," he said.

"Get your mother to do it."

"She won't."

"Well then, perhaps you shouldn't."

"It's too long," he said. "Please? It makes me look like a girl. You said so."

"It makes you look like Mercury."

He took a deep breath. "Aunt Helen Beck, please cut my hair."

"What will you do with it?" she asked.

He pleated his nose at her.

"That's a lot of loose hair you'll have. Will you throw it in the ocean? Wear it as a bracelet?"

"I don't want it," he said.

"Well," said Aunt Helen Beck. "We'll see."

His hair was dry and light, like some rare delicate vegetable that couldn't possibly be nourishing but is rumored to cure cancer. She had to sit down to reach. He didn't make a noise, though she felt him wince every time he heard the scissors shut. She could only find the kitchen shears, and they were a little rusted at the heart.

"It's coming fine," she said.

She did not understand why she was doing such a thing, but it improved her; she felt herself return to normal every time the blades slid into a kiss.

"What will your mother say?" she asked.

"I don't care."

Finally, she finished.

"You're handsomer than I thought you were. Would you like a mirror?"

Mercury ran one hand up the back of his head, smiling at the bristle of it. Aunt Helen Beck knew a few things about hair cutting, and she realized it was not modesty when she thought: Well, I certainly botched this job.

"Feels weird," he said, which is when Chris and Ford came through the door.

"Shit," said Chris. She put her hands to her face, as if to steady her head.

"I like it," Mercury said.

"How do you know?" asked Aunt Helen Beck. "Run look in a mirror and then decide."

"Shit," said Ford.

"It's cool," Merc said, returning.

Aunt Helen Beck picked up Merc's hair, which she had braided and secured with rubber bands before she took the first cut. "I'm going to keep this," she said quietly. She started to look for a broom to sweep up the thin scraps on the floor.

Ford put his hand on Mercury's head; the boy leaned into the touch and rubbed his head against Ford's palm.

"I know you're upset," Chris said. She sat down at the kitchen table. "But why on earth?"

"He asked me," she answered. "You know I have never been able to refuse a child."

THAT EVENING, they approached her. "Aunt Helen Beck," Ford said. "I think we need to talk."

They took the loveseat; she sat in a chair across from them, feeling the curl of hair in her pocket.

"Tell me again," said Ford. "How are we related, precisely?"

"Your great-grandfather," she began, but then she realized it was gone. Usually, she knew everything, every uncle, but now she couldn't remember anything about Ford's family, and hers therefore, except that she imagined they were Irish. "He came from Ireland," she said. "He was a doctor."

"And?" said Ford.

"He was a magician," she said, changing her mind.

Ford sighed. "A witch doctor, maybe?"

"A flim-flam artist," she said. "A snake-oil salesman. Perhaps not really a doctor."

"No," said Ford. "Flim-flam runs in the family, huh?" He smiled; Chris poked him in the side.

"I called Abbie," said Ford, "and we discussed the possibility, and then I called the rest of my family and, Aunt Helen Beck—you're not related to us."

"Why, Ford."

Ford rubbed his beard. She could not tell whether he was enjoying this or whether he was truly sympathetic. "Maybe a family friend," he said. "I mean, maybe you grew up calling one of my relatives uncle. Family friend's enough, if you're a close one."

She knew that it wasn't. If it were, she could call up anybody and say, I once knew your mother. All that would get her was a cup of coffee, and besides, she'd have to know about college or DAR days or wasn't the wedding beautiful. She was silent.

"I thought so," Ford said.

"I can't believe this." Chris stared at the floor, then looked up. "You're a liar," she said.

Ford touched his wife's arm. "Now, listen—"

"You're one, too. You told me you remembered her. When she first called, you said, Oh yes, my dear Aunt Helen. And how long have you known this without telling me?"

"I'm not a liar," said Aunt Helen Beck.

Chris just shook her head.

"I took that picture you gave me out of its frame," said Ford, softly. "And it says on the back, Holland, school play. Even the guy's mustache is fake."

Aunt Helen Beck sat up straight in the chair, arranged her legs, smoothed her skirt.

"How did you choose us?" Ford asked.

"Well," she said. "I was at the public library, and Abbie had donated some magazines. They were good magazines."

Ford laughed out loud, but Chris looked bitterly disappointed. Which struck Aunt Helen Beck as unfair; she'd never claimed to have been related to Chris.

"I can't believe you made it all up," said Chris. "I can't believe you took advantage of us like this."

"I didn't make it all up," she said.

"You came in and told us sad stories that weren't even true. You made up this tragic dead brother—"

"Georgie Beck was real," said Aunt Helen Beck. "And everything I said I felt about him I did."

"Will you please, please tell us the truth, just for a minute?"

"It would be nice," said Ford.

Aunt Helen Beck looked at her and then at Ford and then out the window.

"It was my first visit. I'd heard he was sick—he was a famous child, and I heard this in my hometown, my real hometown. He'd preached there before and caused a sensation and people said what a shame it was. And so I went and knocked on the door and called myself cousin. I was a child myself, sixteen. Back then," she said, looking at them, "it was even easier. I really did nurse him, but he died anyway, and I took the purse—" Here she returned to the window, certain of herself in a way she had not been since the purse had been lost. "He'd made it for his brother, I think, and I took it and his name besides, and I left."

"You're a fraud," said Chris.

Aunt Helen Beck sat still. Flashes jumped off the water with such regularity that the sparkle looked somehow mechanical, as if it were worked by a crank. "He told me he loved me," she said. " 'God loves you, too,' but I told him to say the first part again.

"This is all the truth." She looked at them. "I suppose I'll leave in the morning."

"You don't—" said Ford.

Chris said, "It would be for the best."

They left her in her chair, said they imagined she'd rather pack alone. Though what she wanted to pack, of course, was nowhere in the house. She had never been caught before—never accused, anyway—and some part of her had stopped worrying about it. She couldn't bear the thought of leaving, of any more travel, certainly not without Georgie's purse. For a moment, she supposed the most useful thing for her to do was to die.

But she had no interest in dying. At least, she did not want to start soon. She felt her life was a course of study with the obvious terminal degree; to hurry it meant being somehow unprepared. She had asked them not to turn her in to the police, and Chris, who had softened a bit, said of course not.

"You're obviously harmless," she said before she went to bed. Then she said, "Be careful. You live pretty dangerously."

Aunt Helen Beck said, "I have been living dangerously for some time."

THAT NIGHT, she took a brass candlestick from the whatnot shelf in the living room; she always had to take something to give to her next host—a little gift, an heirloom. It made her feel like the families really were somehow related.

Leaving would not be easy. Usually, she left clean, as if each little life were a railroad car and she was simply walking through to the back. This time, she had left things behind: Georgie Beck, and information. She felt a wind across her legs; something new was starting. Aunt Helen Beck did not believe in fate, but she did think that you made mistakes according to what you wanted in your heart, and she could not understand what it was she wanted this time, what she was trying to tell herself.

She stayed up all night, wanting to see the light playing off the silver trailer one more time; she forgot that the sun rose on the other side of the island. Intent on catching the sun itself she barely noticed the growing light, as if she were a detective intent on nabbing a single criminal when in truth conspiracy was all around her. Suddenly it was morning. Time to go, she thought; she certainly didn't intend to face Chris and Ford again. Aunt Helen Beck picked up her suitcase, felt the candlestick roll in the bottom. Already she could tell she hadn't taken enough.

Outside the air was cold and wet. She began to walk down the hill, stepping sideways so she wouldn't slip in the mud.

"Hey," she heard somebody say.

It was Mercury. He stepped out from behind a tree, dressed in the clothes he'd been wearing the night before; a few hair clippings glistened on his shirt. Really, she thought, you could see why his mother kept his hair long: jug ears. Big as planets orbiting his head. Not a good-looking boy after all.

He scratched the back of his neck. "Hello."

"Good morning." Aunt Helen Beck set her suitcase down. "You're up early."

He blinked at her. She couldn't tell whether or not he was angry over the haircut. "You're still asleep, looks like," she said. "You're grumpy."

He picked up a stone and turned it over in his hand. "Nope." Then he looked at her. "My mother says I can't come in till I grow some hair back."

"She left you out all night?"

Mercury shrugged and nodded at the same time, stepping closer. Aunt Helen Beck leaned down in the mud and put a hand on one side of the boy's head. He was damp to the touch, like something blown off a tree in bad weather. She saw in his eyes an old, familiar expression: I could go now, it wouldn't make any difference, my family album might as well be the phone book, so long.

She lightly took hold of one of those extraordinary ears—it was like a hand itself, like a purse, like something that could hold a great deal.

"Tell me, Mercury," said Aunt Helen Beck. "Tell me—are you fond of travel?"

AS A STUDENT in Iowa City, I spent time in the Foxhead, a small, one-room tavern that was known as a writers' bar. The place was a meeting ground of alcohol, intelligence, neuroses, and sensitivity. Anything was liable to happen—and did. People shot pool, played poker, danced on the bar, went out back to smoke pot, smooched in cars, engaged in huge arguments, and had the occasional fistfight. Of course, I participated in none of that.

My purpose was to hear stories, and one night I heard a dandy from a nurse who'd gotten off work at the hospital down the street, the hospital where my children were born, and the hospital that Denis Johnson wrote about in his story "Emergency." The nurse had as a patient an old soy farmer who was dying. He had told her that fifty years before, he'd made his first trip out of Iowa to fetch a dead relative in the back of his pickup truck. I made a few notes on a bar napkin and thought it would make a terrific plot for a short story one day.

A year later a friend took me to Chicago for the first time. We went to the Checkerboard, a blues club in the South Side, where we were the only white people in the place. Nobody seemed to mind. The band was Magic Slim and the Teardrops.

I was thirty-four years old and it was the first time I'd ever heard live blues. It knocked me for a bugwinder. One of the songs concerned a man who'd given a woman a wig as a gift and wanted it back after they had a fight. I made a few notes on a bar napkin and thought it would make a terrific plot for a short story one day.

The next day we drove back to Iowa, and I wrote "Out of the Woods." I owe thanks to a white nurse, a black musician, a dying farmer, and Craig Collins, who introduced me to the blues.

CHRIS OFFUTT

GERALD OPENED HIS FRONT DOOR at dawn, wearing only a quickly drawn-on pair of jeans. His wife's four brothers stood in the ground fog that filtered along the ridge. The oldest brother had become family spokesman after the father's death, and Gerald waited for him to speak. The mother was still boss, but everything had to filter through a man.

"It's Ory," the oldest one said. "He got shot and is in the hospital. Somebody's got to fetch him."

The brothers looked at Gerald from below their eyebrows. Going after Ory wasn't a chore anyone wanted, and Gerald was new to the family, married to Kay, the only sister. He still needed to prove his worth. If he brought Ory home, maybe they'd cut the barrier that kept him on the edge of things, like he was nothing but a third or fourth cousin.

"Where's he at?" Gerald said.

"Wahoo, Nebraska. Ory said it would take two days but was easy to find."

"My rig won't make it."

"You can take the old Ford. She'll run till doomsday."

"Who shot him?"

The oldest brother flashed him a mean look. The rest were back to looking down, as if they were carpenters gauging the amount of linoleum needed for a job.

"Some woman," the oldest brother said.

Kay began to cry. The brothers left and Gerald sat on the couch beside Kay. She hugged her knees and bit a thumbnail, gasping in a throaty way that reminded him of the sounds she made in bed. He reached for her. She shrugged from his hand, then allowed his touch.

"Him leaving never made sense," Kay said. "He hadn't done nothing and nobody was after him. He didn't tell nary a soul why. Just up and went. Be ten years come fall."

"I'll go get him," Gerald whispered.

"You don't care to?"

"No."

"For my family?"

"For you."

She snuggled against him, her damp face pressed to his neck. She was tiny inside the robe. He opened the front and she pushed against his leg.

The next day he left in the black pickup. Gerald was thirty years old and had never been out of the county. He wore a suit that was snug in the shoulders and short in the legs. It had belonged to his father, but he didn't figure anyone would notice. He wished he owned a tie. The dogwoods and redbuds had already lost their spring color. The air was hot. In four hours he was in Indiana, where the land was flat as a playing card. There was nowhere to hide, no safety at all. Even the sun was too bright. He didn't understand how Ory could stand such open ground.

Illinois was equally flat but with less green to it. Gerald realized that he was driving through a season, watching spring in reverse. The Illinois dirt was black as manure and he pulled over to examine it. The earth was moist and rich. It smelled of life. He let it trickle between his fingers, thinking of the hard clay dirt at home. He decided to stop and get some of this good dirt on the way back.

He drove all day and crossed the Mississippi River at night. At a rest area, he unrolled a blanket and lay down. He was cold. Above him the stars were strewn across the sky. They seemed to be moving down, threatening to press him against the ground. Something bright cut across the night, and he thought someone had shot at him until he realized it was a shooting star. The hills at home blocked so much sky that he'd never seen one. He watched the vast prairie night until fading into sleep.

The eerie light of a flatland dawn woke him early. The sun wasn't visible and the world seemed to glow from within. There were no birds to hear. He could see his breath. He drove west and left the interstate at Wahoo and found the hospital easily. A nurse took him to a small room. Everything was white and the walls seemed to emit a low hum. He couldn't place the smell. A man came into the room wearing a white coat. He spoke with an accent.

"I am Dr. Gupte. You are with the family of Mr. Gowan?"

"You're the doctor?"

"Yes." He sighed and opened a manila folder. "I'm afraid Mr. Gowan has left us."

"Done out, huh. Where to?"

"I'm afraid that is not the circumstance."

"It's not."

"No, he had a pulmonary thromboembolism."

"Is that American?"

"I'm afraid you will excuse me."

Dr. Gupte left the room and Gerald wondered who the funny little man really was. He pulled open a drawer. Inside was a small mallet with a triangular head made of soft rubber, perfect for nothing. A cop came in the room, and Gerald slowly closed the drawer.

"I'm Sheriff Johnson. You the next of kin?"

"Gerald Bolin."

They watched each other in the tiny room under the artificial light. Gerald didn't like cops. They got to carry a gun, drive fast, and fight. Anybody else got thrown in the pokey for doing the same thing.

"Dr. Gupte asked me to come in," the sheriff said.

"He really is a doctor?"

"He's from Pakistan."

"Run out of your own, huh."

"Look, Mr. Bolin. Your brother-in-law got a blood clot that went to his lung. He died from it."

Gerald cleared his throat, scanned the floor for somewhere to spit, then swallowed it. He rubbed his eyes.

"Say he's dead."

The sheriff nodded.

"That damn doctor ain't worth his hide, is he."

"There's some things to clear up."

The sheriff drove Gerald to his office, a small space with a desk and two chairs. A calendar hung from the wall. The room reminded Gerald of the hospital without the smell.

"Ory was on a tear," the sheriff said. "He was drinking and wrecked his car at his girlfriend's house. She wouldn't let him in and he broke the door open. They started arguing and she shot him."

"And he got the blood clot."

The sheriff nodded.

"Did he not have a job?" Gerald said.

"No. And there's some money problems. He went through a fence and hit a light post. He owed back rent at a rooming house. Plus the hospital."

"Car bad hurt?"

"It runs."

"Did he own anything?"

"Clothes, a knife, suitcase, a little twenty-two pistol, a pair of boots, and a radio."

"What all does he owe?"

"Twelve hundred dollars."

Gerald walked to the window. He thought of his wife and all her family waiting for him. They'd given him a little money, but he'd need it for gas on the ride back.

"Can I see her?" he said.

"Who?"

"The woman that shot him."

The sheriff led him across the street to a tan building made of stone. Near the eaves were narrow slits to let light in. They went through heavy doors into a common room with a TV set and a pay phone. Four cells formed one wall. A woman sat on a bunk in one of the cells, reading a magazine. She wore an orange jumpsuit that was too big for her.

"Melanie," the sheriff said. "You have a visitor. Ory's brother-in-law."

The sheriff left and Gerald stared through the bars. Her hair was dark purple. One side was long, the other shaved. Each ear had several small gold hoops in a row that reminded Gerald of a guide for a harness. A gold ring pierced her left nostril. She had a black eye. He wanted to watch her for a long time, but looked at his boots instead.

"Hidy," he said.

She rolled the magazine into a tube and held it to her good eye, looking at Gerald.

"I come for Ory," Gerald said, "but he died on me. Just thought I'd talk to you a minute."

"I didn't kill him."

"I know it."

"I only shot him."

"A blood clot killed him."

"Do you want to screw me?"

Gerald shook his head, his face turning red. She seemed too young to talk that way, too young for jail, too young for Ory.

"Let me have a cigarette," she said.

He passed one through the bars and she took it without touching his hand. A chain was tattooed around her wrist. She inhaled twin lines of smoke from her mouth into her nose. The ash was long and red. She sucked at the filter, lifting her lips to prevent them from getting burned. She blew a smoke ring. Gerald had never seen anyone get so much out of a single cigarette.

"Wish it was menthol," she said. "Ory smoked menthol."

"Well."

"What do you want," she said.

"I don't know. Nothing I don't guess."

"Me neither, except out of here."

"Don't reckon I can help you there."

"You talk just like Ory did."

"How come you to shoot him?"

"We had a fight, and he like, came over drunk. He wanted something he gave me and I wouldn't give it back. It was mine. He busted the lock and started tearing everything up, you know, looking for it. I had a little pistol in my vanity and I like, got it out."

Melanie finished the cigarette and he gave her another one, careful not to look at the ring in her nose. Behind her was a stainless steel toilet with a sink on top where the tank should be. When you washed your hands, it flushed the toilet. He thought of the jail at home with its putrid hole in the floor and no sink at all.

"What was it he was wanting so bad?"

"A wig," she said. "It was blond and he liked me to wear it. Sometimes I wore it in bed."

"You shot him over a wig."

"I was scared. He kept screaming, 'Give me back my wig.' So I, you know, shot him. Just once. If I knew he'd get that blood clot, I wouldn't have done it."

Gerald wondered how old she was but didn't want to insult her by asking. He felt sorry for her.

"He give you that eye?"

"The cops did. They think me and Ory sell dope but we don't, not really. Nothing heavy. Just to, like, friends."

"Why do you do that?" he said.

"Deal?"

"No. Cut your hair and stick that thing in your nose."

"Shut up," she said. She began yelling. "I don't need you. Get away from me. Get out of here!"

The sheriff came into the common room and took Gerald outside. The sky was dark with the smell of rain. He wanted to stand there until the storm swept over him, rinsing him of the jail. He underwent a sudden sense of vertigo, and for a moment he didn't know where he was, only that he was two days from anything familiar. He didn't even know where his truck was.

"She's a hard one," the sheriff said.

"I don't want no charges pressed against her."

"That's not up to you."

"She didn't kill him."

"I don't know about Kentucky," the sherrif said, "but in Nebraska, shooting people's a crime. Look, there's been a big wreck on Ninety-two and five people are coming to the hospital. They need the space. We got to get your brother-in-law to a funeral home."

"Can't afford it."

"The hospital's worse. It charges by the day."

"What in case I take his stuff and leave."

"The county'll bury him."

"That'll run you how much?"

"About a thousand."

"That's a lot of money."

The sheriff nodded.

"Tell you what," Gerald said. "I'll sell you his car for one dollar. You can use it to pay off what all he owes. There's that radio and I'll throw in a hundred cash."

"You can't buy a body."

"It ain't yours to sell or mine to buy. I just want to get him home. Family wants him."

"I don't know if it's legal."

"He ain't the first person to die somewhere else. My cousin's aunt came in on a train after getting killed in a wreck. They set her off at the Rocksalt station. She was in a box."

The sheriff puffed his cheeks and blew air. He went to his office and dialed the courthouse and asked for a notary public. Half an hour later the car belonged to the city of Wahoo. It was a Chevelle and for a moment Gerald wondered if he'd made a mistake. They were pretty good cars.

The sheriff drove them to the hospital. Gerald pulled the money out and started counting.

"Keep it," the sheriff said.

"Give it to Melanie. She wants menthol cigarettes."

"You and Ory aren't a whole lot alike, are you."

"I never knew him that good."

"The only man I saw give money away was my daddy."

"Was he rich?"

"No," said the sheriff, "Daddy was a farmer."

"You all worked this flat land?"

"It worked him right back into it."

Gerald followed the sheriff into the hospital and signed several forms. An orderly wheeled in a gurney with the body on it, covered with a white cloth. He pushed it to an exit beside the emergency room. Three ambulances came into the lot and paramedics began moving the injured people into the hospital. The orderlies left the gurney and went to help. A state police car stopped behind the ambulances.

"I have to talk to them," the sheriff said. "Then I'll get an ambulance to drop the body down at the train station."

Gerald nodded, as the sheriff left the car and walked to the state trooper. Nobody was looking at Gerald. He pushed the gurney into the lot and along the side of the building. A breeze rippled the cloth that covered Ory. Gerald held it down with one hand but the gurney went crooked. He let go of the cloth and righted the gurney and the wind blew the cloth away. Ory was stretched out naked with a hole in his side. He didn't look dead, but Gerald didn't think he looked too good either. He looked like a man with a bad hangover that he might shake by dinner.

Gerald dropped the tailgate of his pickup and dragged Ory into the truck. He threw his blanket over him and weighted the corners with tire tools, the spare, and a coal shovel. Outside of town, he tied the blanket down with wire and haystring, and drove the rest of the day. In Illinois, he stopped and lay down beside the truck. Without the blanket he was cold, but he didn't feel right about taking it back from Ory. Gerald thought about the blond wig, how Ory had asked Melanie to wear it. He wondered if it made a difference when they were in bed.

He woke with frost on him. A buzzard circled high above the truck. He drove into the rising sun, thinking that he'd done everything backward. No matter when he drove, he was always aimed at the sun. Mist lifted above the land as the frost gave way. At the next exit, Gerald left the interstate for a farm road and parked beneath a cottonwood that stood beside a plowed field.

He carried the shovel over a wire fence. The dirt was loose and easy to take. It would make a fine garden at home. His body took over, grateful for the labor after three days of driving. A pair of redwing blackbirds sat on a power line, courting each other. Gerald wondered how birds knew to go with their own kind. Maybe Ory knew he was in the wrong tree and that's why he wanted Melanie to wear a wig. Gerald tried to imagine her with blond hair. He suddenly understood that he wanted her, had wanted her at the jailhouse. He couldn't figure why. It bothered him that he had so much desire for a woman he didn't consider attractive.

He climbed in the back and mounded the dirt to balance the load. As he traveled south, he reentered spring. The buds of softwood trees turned pale green. Flocks of starlings moved over him in a dark cloud, heading north. By nightfall, he crossed the Ohio River into Kentucky. In four hours he'd be home. He was getting sleepy, but coffee had stopped doing him any good. He slid into a zone of the road, letting the rhythm of motion enter his body. A loud noise made him jerk upright. He thought he'd had a flat until he saw that he'd drifted across the breakdown lane and onto the edge of the median. He parked and lay down in the bench seat. He was lucky not to have been killed. The law would have a hard time with that—two dead men, one naked and already stiff, and a load of dirt.

When he woke, it was light and he felt tired already. At a gas station he stared at the rest room mirror, thinking that he looked like the third day of a three-day drunk. The suit was ruined. He combed his hair with water and stepped into the sun. A dog was in the back of his pickup, digging. Gerald yelled, looking for something to grab. The dog saw him and jumped off the truck and loped away. Gerald shoved dirt over Ory's exposed hand. A man came behind him.

"Shoo-eee," the man said. "You waited long enough didn't you."

Gerald grunted. He was smoothing the dirt, replacing the weights along the blanket's edge. The man spoke again.

"Had to take one to the renderers myself last week. Got some kind of bug that killed it in three days. Vet said it was a new one on him."

"A new one."

"I put mine in a garbage bag. Keeps the smell in better than dirt."

"It does."

"Did yours up and not eat, then lay down and start breathing hard?"

"More or less."

"It's the same thing. A malady, the vet called it."

"A malady."

Gerald got in the truck and decided not to stop until he was home. The stench was bad and getting worse. He wondered if breathing a bad smell made your lungs stink. The land started to roll, the crests rising higher as he traveled east. The sun was very hot. It seemed to him as if summer had arrived while he was gone. He'd been to winter and back.

Deep in the hills, he left the interstate for a blacktop road that turned to dirt, following the twists of a creek. He stopped at the foot of his wife's home hill. Kay would be up there, at her mom's house with all her family. They would feed him, give him bourbon, wait for him to tell what happened. He brushed off his suit and thought about the events, collecting them in sequence. He told the story in his head. He thought some more, then practiced it again. Ory had quit drinking and had a good job as manager of a department store. He'd gotten engaged to a woman he'd met at church, but had held off telling the family until he could bring her home. She was nice as pie, blond-headed. He was teaching her to shoot a pistol and it went off by accident. She was tore all to pieces about it. He'd never seen anyone in such bad shape. All she did was cry. It was a malady.

Gerald drove slowly up the hill. Later, he could tell the truth to the oldest brother, who'd tell the rest. They'd appreciate his public lie and he'd be in with the family. He parked in the yard beside his mother-in-law's house. Dogs ran toward the truck, then kids. Adults stepped onto the porch and Gerald could see them looking for Ory in the cab. Kay came out of the house. She smiled at him, the same small smile that she always used, and he wondered how she'd look in a wig.

He got out of the truck and waited. Everything was the same—the house, the trees, the people. He recognized the leaves and the outline of the branches against the sky. He knew how the light would fall, where the shadows would go. The smell of the woods was familiar. It would be this way forever. Abruptly, as if doused by water, he knew why Ory had left.

TO ME THIS STORY was about ending my work with short stories. It came at the end of the book because I was fed up with short work and its restrictions and decided perversely to write something with a kind of sweep I knew, in advance, didn't belong in a story. To me, it was a kind of bad manners. Midway through—a figure of speech, since this story, in the writing, offered nothing but a vast feverish insomniac middle—I realized that I was looking forward, into the next project, getting ready to follow these same people into a novel. This hope allayed the anxiety I was fighting as I finished both the story and the collection as a whole and also answered an anxiety about my life generally, namely, what next? So I chose the fairly corny title "Open House" to mark and claim a new ambition for myself.

CHARLES D'AMBROSIO

CHARLES D'AMBROSIO

Open House

THE LAST TIME I'd seen him he'd behaved like one of those wolf-boys, those kids suckled and reared in the wild by animals, and I was never sure, during the ten confusing minutes I stood on the lawn, whether or not he recognized me. He asked me when I was going to relinquish my disease, which made me think either he was speaking rhetorically or confusing me with my brother Miles, who is schizophrenic and lives in a halfway. Then he seemed to have a moment of lucidity, and called me a loser for dropping out of college. He had trouble breathing and rasped and swore like someone twitched by demons on a downtown corner. All the flowers, in the hanging baskets, in the clay pots, in the whiskey barrel, were dead and hissing dryly in the wind, so it was true, apparently, that he had watered the garden with gasoline. The security chain on the door remained slotted. Inside, through the crack, he gasped, he yelled, he mixed the Latinate with potty talk, calling my sisters complicitous cunts and my mother a vituperative bitch. His shouting had always had the effect of diminishing me, the sheer volume of it taking away the ground I stood on, for it would sound as if he were screaming across the country or into the past, to someone, at any rate, who was not present, and the longer I remained there, listening, the more deranged I felt. He had a certain emotional vigor that turned his head purple, and all during that most recent visit, his head was purple. When I was a kid he'd put that purple head in my face and grab my jaw and tell me, "If you were me you'd be dead because my father would have killed you." Driving away, I had that feeling, of echoes within echoes.

Certain he was finally and forever crazy, and in need of professional help, I called his shrink, Dr. Headberry, but that poor, harassed pill dispenser had been fired, or dismissed, and then, about a week later, my father tried to take his suffering public. He came to church dressed in his version of sackcloth and ashes—tin pants, snake boots, a wool coat with suede ovals at the elbows, and a plaid cap with foam earflaps. These things had long ago been banished to hooks in the garage, and smelled, I knew, of motor oil and grass clippings and the dusty, forgotten odor of fabrics that have gone damp and dried, then gone damp again and dried again, endlessly over the years. He'd locked away his guns after my brother Jackie (as my father liked to say) sucked a barrel—shoved a twelve-gauge Mossberg back in his tonsil area and opened his skull against the bedroom wall.

While both my older brothers were evidently fucked up, I, as the baby of the family, was luckily buffered by my four sisters. If it wasn't for them, I knew I'd be way more of a mental clodhopper than I was, or dead or crazy. Karen, Lucy, Meg, and especially Roxy, they all had this special way, this oddball interest in good places to paddle canoes, and herb remedies, and parks where you could take safe walks in the dark, and sardonyx and black fire opals, and weird healing practices, and crow feathers and chips of eggshells, and numerology, and playing records backward, and food that didn't come out of a can or box. My father thought they were witches. Roxy carried a bull thistle in a tea infuser chained around her neck. The Salish Indians believed thistles would ward off bad luck, and the Scots believed they would keep away the enemy. Roxy gave me a thistle of my own and once she gave me a pomegranate. I'd never seen one before, and I was surprised that someone could think of me, sitting downstairs in Jackie's room, on Jackie's old bed, and bring me a gift out of nowhere, and for no reason. A pomegranate. *Out of nowhere, and for no reason!* Isn't it perfect, she asked, and it was.

I watched my father from across the aisle. He knelt in a pew with his head bowed and his hands hung limply over the backrest as though he'd been clamped into a pillory. Lawyers for both sides had called me, asking if I'd testify if the divorce went to trial, but I had no idea what I'd say if I were being deposed. He looked drunk and sleepy and wired, and also penitent in this odd, remembered way, as if he were still trying to fool some buzzard-backed nun from his childhood. He wiped sweat from his brow with a wrinkled hankie, mopped the back of his neck, held the thing like a flag of truce as he folded his hands for prayer. During the Offertory he began crying or weeping—weeping, I guess, because there was something stagey about it. He beat the butt of his palm against his head, lifted his eyes to the Cross, and said, "Oh God, oh God, my God."

"I wish I could be crucified," my father had told me over the phone, the day after he was served papers. "That's really the only way to settle these things."

Despite the lunacy of pitting his agony against the agony of Jesus Christ, I now decided he wasn't crazy. This was calculated. He'd come to menace and harass my mother. For years church had been her only bastion and retreat and he'd come as a trespasser to violate it, to pollute its purity and calm, to take it away from her, and make it ugly like everything else in our life, and that's what I'd tell the lawyers. I was no disciple or defender of the church and no big fan of the snobs who weekly attended Mass. With its pale green walls and polished pine benches and high windows of distorted glass it seemed a place for lame rummage sales, a place where fussy old men sold boxes of yesterday's best-sellers, soup ladles, and wide neckties. The young seemed old, and the old seemed ancient—widowers in pleated pants who had retired into a sallow golden age, bereft men with nothing to do but sip their pensions like weak tea in a waiting room whose only door opened on death. And the women—some so fanatically dedicated to a pre–Vatican II universe they still wore hats within the nave, and if they'd forgotten a scarf or hat, they'd unclasp their purses and find a Kleenex and bobby-pin that to their hair. Arranged in the pews, these solemn women with toilet paper pinned to their heads looked like planted rows of petunias. Yet that Saturday, as my father crudely interrupted the service, I considered the possibility that the heart and soul of any faith is absurdity, and that these ridiculous, otherworldly women, with their silly gestures, might just be saints.

The Mass stopped and everyone turned from the altar and stared at him. Everyone—the Greys, the Hams, the Wooleys, Mrs. Kayhew and the Grands and the Stones, etc. Also the priest, the altar boys. It was a caesura that filled with whisperings of disbelief and doubt, and only my mother, who was the Eucharistic minister and sat in the sanctuary, remained quiet and calm. She laced her hands together and buried them like a dead bird in her lap. Sitting in her chair, icily withdrawn, she looked as she did when I was a child and dinner was not going well, evenings when my father occupied the head of the table like a cigar store Indian and silence settled in our bones and we could hear little else but the tink-tink of fork tines and the sound of chewing and it was painful to swallow. Those nights I wouldn't eat the hard things, the raw carrots or bread sticks, for fear of making a noise, and my mother wouldn't eat at all. My mother liked to say that silence had made her a very slender woman, and it was true, she was slim and at sixty still looked girlish in blue jeans.

The priest drank wine from the chalice and, wiping the rim, held the cup to my mother's lips. He leaned toward her, whispered something in her ear, and she shook her head deliberately. Together they stepped down to the Communion rail. My father waited until the line dwindled down, then lifted himself awkwardly, stumbling up the aisle alone. I saw Mrs. Grand lay a hand on her husband, restraining him. My father stood, swaying a little, before my mother. Later, after my mother returned from her trip to Texas, she would tell me it was not her place to judge, and certainly not her role as the morning's Eucharistic minister. Her faith gave her the ability not to judge anything, even movies. To me, as an outsider, and someone without any faith at all, the scene at the Communion rail seemed a show of profound strength, but my father, later, would say he only went up there to prove what a chickenshit she was. The church was dead quiet. My mother lifted the Eucharist as you would a bright, promised coin, holding it slightly above eye level, and my father looked up. "Body and Blood of Christ," she said, and he responded, "Amen," and then she very carefully set the host on his waiting tongue.

After the blessing my mother left the sanctuary and knelt in the front pew. The door in the vestibule had been jammed open with a rubber wedge and a cool wet wind circulated through church, stirring the lace edge of the altar cloth and the sprigs of white gladiolas in their fluted gold standards. Her friends filed out, and cars left the lot. She remained kneeling on the padded hassock and prayed with her eyes shut and with her eyes shut she heard, from the vestibule, the ruffle of the priest's soutane as the black skirt swept the floor, and then the hurried, plodding steps of my father. She remained still and continued to pray.

"She denied me and she denied me," my father said to the priest. "She denied me even the simplest things a husband requires."

The priest gestured helplessly toward the confessionals—the penalty boxes, my father called them, those two upright coffins in the corner of the church. Probably it crossed the priest's mind that the formality of this arrangement might help contain my father's apparent madness. A closed door, at the very least, might muffle his complaint. My father didn't often go out in public because he thought people didn't like him, and when he did socialize, out of nervousness and excessive drinking, he was a terrible gasbag, and most people did try to avoid him, and so the fact that he'd come to church, and made such an awful ruckus, now swayed me back in the direction of the idea that he must be crazy. I was about to step in, but the priest waved me away.

"Even bedtime pleasures."

The priest said, "I'm sure there's more to the story."

"Don't tell me about stories," my father responded. "Calumny is one of the seven deadly sins."

"No it isn't," the priest said, firmly.

My father ignored him, shouting at my mother.

"How dare you judge me! You call yourself Christians!"

The altar boy returned to snuff the candles and collect the cruets of wine and water. My mother could smell the curls of black smoke rising from the burnt wicks. With her eyes closed, she felt as though she could lift herself up, she could rise away and soar, as she said her prayers, on the whispered fluttering wing beat of words, away, away, away . . . while my father stared after her from what then seemed a lifetime of hatred. She did not move. Her skin was pale to the point of appearing blue. Her fingers, interlaced, were delicate and weak. She was as still in her pew as the pale crucified Christ floating high above the sanctuary, but she was gone.

"Goddamn you to hell," my father screamed on his way out the door.

I HADN'T DROPPED out of school. In early March the bursar asked me to withdraw until the outstanding balance on my tuition bill was paid. I stuffed a rucksack with clothes and left campus that night. I was relieved. My lisp made me quiet and shy, embarrassed at the sound of myself, and also something of a hostile shit. People gathered in their dorms, smoked bong hits under batik bedspreads that breathed, and endlessly analyzed their families. I couldn't do it. The soft sibilance of my voice didn't square with what I had to say, and I felt paralyzed by a pressure, a sense that if I started talking there was a good chance I'd never stop. To cure this, or get around it, I had signed up for a writing course, but dropped it when I couldn't figure out the economy of a story, the lifeboat ethics of it—who got pitched in with the sharks, who got rescued. By the end of January I had stopped attending classes, and only turned in the written assignments, and sometime in February I pulled the curtains and lay in bed for a week.

I left school without telling anyone, in part because as a rule, a policy, I never say good-bye. The night I walked off campus was quiet, I remember, that country quiet where every sound seems to have a distinct place in the world, as arranged as notes in a Bach sonata, and by the next morning I'd hitched to Altoona, Wisconsin. From there I hopped a freight train home to Seattle. Twice as the train crossed trestles over the Yellowstone and then later over the Clark Fork I considered jumping off to do some fishing, but the divorce was already in progress and I was convinced my father was going to destroy the contents of our house. (He did: he burned the christening dress we'd been baptized in, he tossed our photo albums, etc.) Back in Seattle I rented a shoe-box room and got a job busing tables at a restaurant owned by two lesbians I knew from day one would eventually fire me. (They did.) I spent most nights hunched over my vice, drinking beer and tying flies, filling one box with hare's ears and pheasant tails, and another with size 16 Blue-winged Olives and Pale Morning Duns. My only plan in the world right then was to hop a train to Livingston, hitch into the park, and fish the Firehole near the west end of Fountain Flats, a place that was a favorite of both Miles and Jackie. After that, after Memorial Day, I planned to take my tent and stove and live in the park all season. (Which I did, until I woke one morning with my tent sagging like a collapsed parachute and was driven out by snow in mid-October.)

The only things I wanted out of our house were Miles's old fly rod and the original fifteen and a half pages of Jackie's suicide note.

REALTOR'S SIGNS had been staked into the front and side yards, and a sandwich board stood spraddled on the sidewalk. "Open House," it said, "Sunday," and the lead agent's name was Cynthia. My father's beat spy car was parked in the drive, the passenger door lashed shut with loops of clothesline, the landau top half-scalped, peeling back to raw metal. For weeks he'd been tailing my mother around town in this battered, rust-bitten Plymouth. Was this corny or dangerous? In the last days, as the end drew near, he'd thrown her down the stairs, grated her arm with a grapefruit knife—but the end had been drawing near regularly for twenty years, my entire life, and the tragic end of it all was the very rhythm of our hearts, and if two of my sisters, Roxy and Karen, hadn't finally abducted my mother, hadn't dragged her out of the house, she would have stayed, I bet, and would still be getting chased around the house with knives and screamed at.

I was the youngest of seven children, and my family's history had always been my future, a past I was growing into and inheriting, a finished world, a place where the choices had been made, irrevocably. As a result I was never very interested in the riddle of heredity or the way dysteleology can become design. I arrived too late to believe any other world existed. I was fourteen when Miles started living either on Western Avenue behind the Skyway coat factory or at the VA or in a series of ratty halfway houses, and by now I just assumed the voices Miles heard would speak to me also. I was sixteen when Jackie killed himself. At twenty, I assumed madness would visit me, and so would suicide. I assumed they would approach quietly and hold out their hands and claim me and take me where they had taken my brothers. Miles had tried to kill himself too, driven by his voices to jump off the Aurora Bridge, but he'd survived. Frequently, obsessively, I fantasized sitting on the bridge railing and shooting myself in the head. That way in one moment I'd bring my brothers together in me. I was convinced I'd know them in that way. And my father? Would I know him? Could I even describe him? Often my father couldn't take a shit unless my mother held his hand. But I couldn't really imagine that.

I looked up, and there he was, framed in the open window of Miles's old bedroom.

"You can't come in," he shouted. "My lawyer guy said nobody can come in the house. Not you, not anybody. I'm sorry, I know it sounds stupid, but too many negative things redound in my direction."

"I came to get my stuff," I said.

"I have to insulate me totally."

He disappeared from the window and reappeared at the back door. He opened it a crack, steel chain still slotted.

"We did this last week," I said.

"You can't come in. I'm sorry, too many negative things. You're all complicitous with your mother. I didn't want this. It wasn't my idea. I wanted to work it out. There's family solutions to family problems, but this, this is appalling and obscene, it's immoral."

"I have a key," I said.

"Not anymore you don't. I changed the locks."

The back porch was lined with clay pots full of dead marigolds, woolly brown swabs on black stalks.

"What's wrong?" I asked.

"Wrong? Nothing's wrong except your mother's got me by the fucking balls. She's got her hooks in me but I'm fine."

I picked up one of the clay pots and put my nose to the soil and it had the cold smell of gasoline.

"Did you pour gas on the flowers?"

"That's just more of your mother's calumny."

"I think we should call Dr. Headberry," I said.

"Headberry? I just talked with him. Headberry says I have no real problems. He's got your mother analyzed perfectly, though. It's ugly. She's got control of my life."

He was lying about Headberry, of course, and unless something happened we were going to continue having the kind of conversation that you have when there's only one seat left on the bus.

"Let me in."

"I don't understand the ugliness—the enormity of the entire process. So many hooks there—they've got control of my life."

I dropped the pot, letting it shatter on the porch, and started walking back out to my truck.

"This is against my better instinct," my father said. He closed the door and slipped the chain off. "It's against everything I know and against my lawyer's advice too."

"Thanks," I said. I nodded out toward the Realtor's sign. "There's an open house tomorrow."

"Yeah, yeah," he said. "Well, I guess you're here and you're coming in and we'll talk and maybe have a drink and then you'll leave. So let's start. Come on in."

Except for boxers drooping off his ass, he was naked. His hunting outfit was piled on a shelf in the kitchen.

He shook his head, and scratched the thick, knotted hair on his chest, then rubbed his arms, his stubbled face.

"Feel like my veins are turning into worms," he said.

"Why'd you come to church?"

"Hey, don't forget I let you in," he said. He grabbed his coat off the shelf and pulled a piece of paper out of the pocket. "I got the restraining order right here. I take it with me everywhere I go. I felt the need to talk to a priest." He scratched the pale insides of his arm, and examined the legal document. "I don't think the law applies to a church," he said. "Once you get inside you have asylum."

He returned the paper to his coat pocket and then picked up the kitchen garbage can, reached his hand in, and pushed aside newspapers, a tuna can, a melon rind.

"See?" he said.

He meant to show me a prescription bottle at the bottom of the can. I lifted it out, gave it a rattle, and held it to the light.

"There's one left," I said.

"I quit," he said. "Thirty-five years and now I've kicked 'em cold turkey."

My father never talked about his own father, and the oldest story he ever told me about himself was of the way snow whipped off Lake Erie in August of 1953, great blinding gusts and rolling drifts, the summer landscape sculpted into a sea of white. Fantastic! A miracle! Naturally, of course, it hadn't been August. He'd been hospitalized, locked up in a Cleveland sanatorium and then shocked out of his mind for six months, and the snow was falling in January, the day of his release. Why, in telling me this, had he left the story in its state of confusion? Now I thought of the snow in August. At the time electroconvulsive therapy was an experimental procedure and current thinking called for barbiturates in long-term intractable cases. That, then, was science and the bold sci-fi future. My father, the day of his release, filled his prescription at a corner druggist and renewed it regularly, like his subscription to the *Wall Street Journal,* for the next thirty-five years.

"When d'you quit?"

"It's a booger, man," he said, clawing at his arms and again at the matted hair on his chest. "I tried watching TV. Then I tried taking a shower and banging my head against the wall."

"You just now tossed these," I said.

"Why the fuck do you think I'm traipsing around the house naked?" he shouted. "My clothes were driving me crazy, that's why."

"I'd like to call Headberry."

He scratched himself some more. "Worms, man. I feel like I could explode. You want a drink?"

The gin and limes and a tray of melting ice were already out on the sink counter. He fixed us two drinks and we sat at the dining table. Across the street the Grand and Wooley families walked out onto their adjoining lawns. A badminton net was strung across the property line on metal stakes. The kids, some of them my age, stood on one side, and the parents stood on the other. Everybody carried rackets and Mr. Wooley, in chinos and a pink shirt, opened a canister of birdies. Bill Grand said something and Bill Wooley leaned back and aimed a silent laugh at the sky.

"I hate those redundant bastards," my father commented.

"You don't even know them."

"Sure I do, you know one, you know 'em all." He sipped his drink with fine relish. "Where's your mother going?"

It surprised me that he knew she was going anywhere, and I was caught off guard.

"I'm not saying," I said, and now there was a secret between us.

"She's having an affair."

"Mom? Mom's not having an affair."

"What makes you so sure?"

"Who with, then?"

My father looked away, out the window. "Jesus Christ, probably." He sucked an ice cube out of his drink and bit it, spitting glassy splinters. "She's got me by the nuts."

"Hardly," I said. "You're free."

"Free? Free my ass. You know, I've never been to the rain forest—isn't that a phenomena? She's mortgaged my work effort."

For the longest time I thought this was an old bromide all fathers told their kids. Don't mortgage my work effort. No one in this house is going to mortgage my work effort. Roxy took me to the dictionary and explained. *Mort,* she said, means dead. And *gage,* she said, means security.

"That doesn't make any sense," I told him now.

"No? Okay, fine. What's up with you?"

I guessed we were going to ignore the scene at church. Somehow we had agreed to forget it.

"I had a dream about you last night."

"Other people's dreams are boring."

"I was over here, in the kitchen. You were trying to give me some medicine, like when I was a kid, with a squeeze dropper. Like liquid aspirin. But I wasn't a kid anymore. You were holding the back of my head and telling me to open my mouth. 'Open up,' you said, and when I did, you put a gun in my mouth and kept saying, 'Thataboy, take your medicine. Take your medicine, you'll feel better.' "

"Goddamnit," he said.

"It's just a dream."

"Let's talk about something else. You hear the latest about Mr. Kayhew?"

"No, what?"

"You knew a blood vessel popped in his head? Up in an airplane, up there behind the curtain, first class, knowing the Kayhews. He wasn't dead, just in a coma. I heard they rented him his own apartment and he lived there in a coma."

"I didn't know."

"I'm practically there myself."

I must have made a face.

"What? I'm serious. When I die I'll be exploded to shit. People'll look in the box and say, 'Good God, what the hell killed him?' "

My dad sipped his drink again, keeping an eye on me over the lip of his glass.

"Just everything," he said, answering himself. "Anyway, Kayhew's out."

"Out?"

"He was in a coma."

"You told me that," I said. "So he's out of it now?"

"I guess. I guess you could say that. He's dead."

"That's not what people usually mean when they say someone comes out of a coma."

"Well, it's a little-discussed medical fact, but dying is the other way out."

After a moment, he said, "We were friends, you know, me and Kayhew. Not great friends, but I liked him all right and he liked me. I think he liked me. He never actually said he liked me, but anyway, the point is, I read his obit—he was much beloved, survived by, all that phoney baloney—and he was only sixty-five years old. Sixty-five. That's six years older than me. You know how many days that is?"

"Do you?" I said.

"Two thousand one hundred and ninety," my father said. "Given my habits, I figure I've got two thousand days left." He raised his eyebrows. "This is one of them." He shrugged. "How's your drink? You want another? I'm having another."

"I'll hold off," I said.

But he made me a drink anyway. When he returned to the table, a cigarette dangled from his lips.

"Smoking?"

"Two thousand days, man. Who gives a crap?"

I left the split seeds and floating pulp of my old drink and started the new one.

I held the glass to the light and the fresh gin at that moment seemed to be the clearest thing I'd ever seen in my life.

"Miles used to say certain streams were gin clear," I said. "That's how he'd describe them."

"I hate fishing."

"I was only remembering. It was just something to say."

"I've worked in insurance all my life," he said. "The actuarial tables are incredibly accurate. They'll nail you to the wall just about every time. You can read those things and then call a mortician and make an appointment. Like Jackie."

Jackie's last day, his last hour, was an obsessive concern of mine. I'd reconstructed it. I knew where he went, who he talked to, the last tape he played in his stereo ("Johnny Was," by Stiff Little Fingers). The night Jackie shot himself my mother had come into his bedroom. He was at his desk, writing. It was shortly after eight-thirty. He wore a green and gray flannel shirt, blue jeans with blown-out knees, black army boots. Jackie wouldn't turn around and face her. She went back upstairs to tell my father something was strange, that Jackie had a shotgun in his room. "I'm watching a TV show," he said, "don't interrupt me. And close the door when you leave." But that doesn't really explain. What he told my mother that night he told her every night. Without the punctuation of Jackie's death the night of November twenty-sixth, and all the information I'd gathered about it, would mean nothing. But at four-thirty in the morning when the police lights pulsed in the graying air and a couple cops stood on the lawn discussing the case I ran out there in my pj's. "It wasn't suicide," I screamed at them. "It was murder!"

"You want a smoke?" My dad waved his pack of Pall Malls at me. He went to the kitchen and fished in the garbage can and set the tuna can between us. "No ashtrays. I quit these buggers to save money. I calculated it out that I was spending two hundred bucks a year on cigs. That was when I only made two hundred a month. A whole month's salary. So I quit."

"Where's the rug?" I asked.

I had just felt with my feet below the dining table that the oriental rug wasn't there.

"What? The rug, I don't know."

"That's weird," I said. "All my life it was under the table and now it's gone."

"Crazy, huh?"

I finished my drink, stood, and said, "I'm gonna split. First I want to get some stuff."

"Stay here," my dad said. "I can't have you running around the house."

"It's my house too."

"On what piece of paper does it say this is your house?"

"There's only two things I want."

"Look, sit down. Okay? Sit down. Let's have another drink."

"I want Miles's fly rod. You don't fish and I want it."

"It's yours, you can have it. Okay? Jesus. I hate fishing. Fishing makes me feel fucking hopeless."

"And the christening dress, I want that too."

"I'm not sure where that is," my dad said.

"Crazy, huh?"

"Yeah, it's fucking nuts."

Out the window the Grands and Wooleys were playing badminton in the lowering light. I could faintly hear their shouts and cries as they chased the birdie. The gray air seemed to be filling the house like rising water.

My dad said, "It's wild."

I waited for him to say what was wild, but he only looked out the window.

"What?"

"I can't make the data stand still."

My father sipped his drink meditatively and watched.

"So what's your mother doing in Texas?" he asked.

"How do you know she's going to Texas?"

"She went to the travel agent. She used our credit card to charge the ticket. That's how."

"You put on quite a show at church this morning."

"A show?"

I was starting to feel hazy, blurred. "Yeah, a show. You almost looked like somebody in need of pity."

I shook a Pall Mall from the pack, lit it. My dad watched the badminton game wind down. The Wooleys and the Grands seemed to be running around their lawn swatting flies. Cheers went up, moans, cries, but I could no longer see what they were chasing. It was too dark. A clock ticked in the living room and the refrigerator buzzed and a wind must have risen because behind me a branch scratched the window. A car turned the corner.

"I'll get that stuff," I said.

"You know what the agent told me? Cynthia—that's her name, Cynthia—she told me the place had bad vibes."

"I don't get it."

"We'll have to sell below the appraised value," my dad said. "We won't get near the asking price. They all know Jackie killed himself in the basement, they know Miles is crazy, they know all that shit."

"They? Who's they?"

"People." He looked at me. He smiled grimly. "Do what you have to do. I'm having another drink. This gin is something, huh?"

Our basement was a museum housing a collection of all the usual artifacts. In bins and racks, we had baseball bats, broken skis, tennis rackets with warped guts, wingless gliders, golf clubs, aquariums, hula hoops, a bowling ball, and several orange life jackets my dad had purchased at a lawn sale, along with an old O'Brien water ski and a gas can, all with the idea, a very sudden, impulsive idea, that he'd buy a boat, too. For weeks after we saw boats gleaming in showrooms or parked on trailers in someone's driveway or heading out to sea or docked at a slip in the Union Bay Marina. I don't know what happened to that idea, but here were four faded life jackets, hooked on tenpenny nails. Along a rickety wooden shelf were cases of canned peas and corn and thirty-weight oil, a box of powdered milk, several bottles of novitiate wine—bulk items of a big family. In boxes were tools, tools to fix everything, from loose chair legs to leaky faucets. C-clamps, crimpers, a circular saw. With a tool in his hand, my dad was no better than a caveman. He couldn't fix anything. He usually ended up clubbing whatever wouldn't work, breaking it worse. But he loved tools, he strolled through hardware stores handling trouble lights and blue hacksaw blades with the enthusiasm other people might reserve for the Louvre.

I found what I was looking for: a polished cherry wood case, narrow and about two and half feet long. I brought it upstairs and turned on a light. I popped the hasp, and opened the box. The inside was lined with crushed velvet, and hand-carved bridges at either end held the rod in place. I lifted the butt end out, cradled the sanded cork in my hand. The cane was pale blond, unmarred by knots or coarse grain, and the lacquer, gin clear, seemed only to draw out the bamboo's simplicity; the reel seat was rosewood, the fittings nickel-plated; the guides gleamed; the ferrules were wrapped in blue and green thread, winding in a spiral pattern. I heard the ice in my dad's glass clink, and then he was there, looking at the rod over my shoulder. I turned the rod in my hand. Miles had called the whole family down to his workbench in the basement the day he signed it. He used a Chinese brush from which he'd clipped all but a single horsehair. I remember watching him do it, the way he held one hand steady with the other while, miraculously, his name looped across the cane in a single stroke.

"That's art. That's a piece of work," I said.

"Not bad for a crazy fuck," my dad said.

"He wasn't crazy then." I angled the rod in the light. "It's just the opposite of how he is now. It's simple."

"Have another drink?"

"No," I said.

From the kitchen, Dad said, "You planning a trip?"

"Wyoming," I said. "I'm gonna live in the park all season."

"That's stupid," Dad said. "Here's your gin."

"I said no. What's stupid about it? I go there every year."

"What about school?"

"What about it?"

"Don't look at me that way," my father said. "I'm broke."

"Anyway, it's where I tossed Jackie's ashes," I said. After he'd been cremated, we were each given an envelope of ashes, just a pinch—you'd throw more oregano in a pot of spaghetti sauce.

"Where?"

"Well, you've never been there, so it's hard to describe."

"Hey, guy, it's good to see you."

"You're drunk."

"I don't think I've talked to anyone for ten days, two weeks."

"You're talking pretty good tonight."

"I guess I am. Imagine if you were God and had to listen to all this."

AND THEN I MUST HAVE SAID YES. I should have gone back to the shoe box, and there were four or five opportunities to say no, no, I've had enough, I got what I wanted, see you. But the evening kept opening up, wider and wider, accepting every vague word and half-assed idea. Everything was finding a place; there was a room at every inn. The night became like a fairy tale in which every juncture is answered with a yes and the children hold hands and merrily march down the dark trail into a furnace. The gin ran clear, the tuna can was full of stubbed Pall Malls, I was drunk and awake and my dad was drunk and awake, and the space was there, yawning, and something had to happen.

"Tell me where your mother is?" Dad was saying.

"No way," I insisted.

"Tell me."

"Okay," I said. I squinted a teasing look across the table. "I'll trade you."

"You already got the fly rod."

"I want the original of Jackie's letter."

"Can't do it. I don't know where it is."

"Oh well—"

"All right."

"Get it," I said.

"You don't trust me?"

"Oh, I don't think so."

When he brought the letter back I checked to make sure all fifteen and a half pages were there, licking my fingers and counting them like bills.

Then I said, "She's gone to see an angel."

"An angel, huh?"

"In the bark of a tree, a cottonwood. In the middle of a junkyard somewhere in Texas. There's been reports, so she's going to see for herself."

"It's been in the papers. I've read about that angel." He lit a cigarette, waved the smoke from his face. "Hey, we got coffee stains in the carpet look like angels. We got angels in this house."

A bus passed out front. An old habit, I looked through the window to see if any of my brothers and sisters were coming home.

"Your mother was never anything but a whore. She got me fired off my job. All slander."

"The reason you were fired is because no one likes you. You're an asshole—that's actually a quote."

"Who said that? Markula?"

"I'm not telling."

"I got something else to give you," my father said.

He disappeared again and when he returned to the table he set the shotgun and a box of shells in front of me.

I said, "That's the gun."

"Cops took this as evidence," my father said. "Suicide's a crime. Evidence? Heigh-ho—but I got it back."

IN THE GARAGE we gathered up gunnysacks, some twine, and a flashlight, and loaded everything into the Plymouth.

"Me and Miles used to do this," my dad said, as we drove away.

"I'm not too big on guns," I said.

"Neither was Jackie. You took after him on that."

"I hope not."

"A gun doesn't mean anything."

"Huh?"

"Take a caveman," my father said. "You put a short arm of some sort, a .38 or what have you, you put it on the ground with some other stuff, like a rock and a sewing machine and a banana. Ordinary things. What's the caveman going to do? Huh? He's not going to look at the banana and think, oh, this'd be good on corn-flakes. He's not going to take the sewing machine and stitch up a tutu. And he's not going to look at the gun and think, maybe I'll blow my head off. You see what I'm saying."

I thought I did, and then I was sure I didn't.

"I'm nearly broke," my dad said.

"No you're not."

"I thought I'd be living with more dignity by this time, but it's not turning out that way."

"You're lying," I said. It wasn't an accusation, more like a statement. We were stopped at a four-way intersection. My father steadied his hands by curling them tightly around the wheel.

"Maybe I should do the Jackie thing," he said.

"Fuck you," I said. The words just popped out of my mouth, like a champagne cork. Now my hands were trembling and I put them in my coat pocket. "Don't ever say that again."

"Why are you so pissed all of a sudden?"

"Let's just go. Let's get those birds."

I've read and reread Jackie's letter to us, I've searched the final paragraph for a summation. Now I had the original. The letter is long. In it he lists the things he likes: wolves and trains, the Skagit River, coasting a bike down Market Street to Ballard. He talks about my mom, dad, my four sisters, and Miles, but at no time does he mention me. Toward the last few pages I sense a creepy mortmain, as if my father's hand is folded over his, guiding the pen across the page, line by line. Is he trying to say something about himself, or about my father? The letter goes on for fifteen and a half long, tightly scrawled pages, but I'm drawn to the end, even though I know the outcome. I look at the last word and think of the moment when he put down the pen and picked up the gun and pulled the trigger. How much time passed? Had he been thinking it over? To pull the trigger he would have used the same finger he used to press the pen against the paper. What went on in that space? Between the pen and the gun?

UNDER THE FREEWAY we found a cement ledge. A sleepy cooing came from the recess, the occasional flutter of beating wings. It sounded like a nursery at naptime.

"You stay down here," Dad said. "I'll hand the birds to you."

He chinned himself onto the ledge, grunting loudly. He wiped shit off his hands and I passed him the flashlight. He aimed the beam at the birds, a row of them squatting along the ledge. The first bird was mottled gray and brown with beady eyes like drops of melted chocolate. Its eyes remained wide open, stunned and tranced, staring into the beam, unable to move or turn away from the white light. Dad stroked the bird's throat gently. "Come to Papa," he said, and when he'd soothed it somewhat he grabbed it by the neck and passed it down to me. I could feel its heart beating in my hand. I slipped the bird into the gunnysack. The pigeon flopped around, trying to orient itself. Dad jacklit another and another. Some were white as doves, others black as crows. After we'd bagged five birds I tied off the first sack with twine and started a new one. Dad handed me five more paralyzed pigeons and then jumped down.

"That ought to do it," he said. He brushed molted gray feathers from his face, from his arms. "Look at that," he said.

The sacks were alive with confused pigeons, two blobs rolling down the hill. You could see the birds struggling to take off, stupidly beating against the burlap. We ran after them, two drunks at a pigeon rodeo, each grabbing a sack.

We put the birds in the backseat of the car. I picked a downy feather from my father's ear.

"You still pissed?" he said.

"Don't make hollow threats."

"You think it was hollow?"

"I've heard it before."

"Feel like it was just yesterday I was driving around the woods with the Beauty Queen, trying to get my hand up her skirt."

My father laughed. The Beauty Queen was my mother. She'd been Miss Spanaway in 1954.

"Well," he said, gesturing broadly with a sweep of the bottle, "I did. Seven kids. One dead, one crazy. Four girls who don't want a damn thing to do with me. Then you. What the fuck's wrong with you, I wonder?"

"We going?"

The pigeons were insane, jumping around inside the sacks. A crazy burlap aviary. My father got out of the car, took the sacks, and spun the birds in circles. When he put them back in the seat, they were quiet.

"You're the only one left. You'll bury me," my father said. "You'll have to write my obituary."

GENERALLY MY FATHER was what people call a paper killer. He drove to a firing range and clamped on ear protection and stood in a port lined with blue baffle shield and shot two-bit targets. Bull's-eyes, black silhouettes, now and then the joke target of a dictator's face in profile. At the end of an afternoon of shooting, he'd roll up and rubberband his targets, tacking the best to a wall in his den, like trophies. "You shoot against your old self," he'd told me. Of the boys, it was my crazy brother Miles who enjoyed guns. Jackie hated them. The first and only time he'd ever fired a gun the barrel was in his mouth. Obviously, you don't need to be a sharpshooter to kill yourself. Even before Jackie, I'd never liked guns. My father sensed this hesitance, and took me out to the woods, trying to teach me to see things and then trying to get me to shoot them out of the trees. Squirrels, robins. The only time I'd actually fired a gun with him was at a gravel pit. He stood behind me and watched as I leveled his bolt-action .22 at a row of pop cans. He calmly gave me directions, but I quickly aimed high and pinched off a round, missing, then chambering another round and missing again, spent shells skittering at my feet in brassy flashes, until I dry-fired and knew the gun was empty. I was ten years old and it was the first time I'd ever felt like I was not in control of myself. I'd been feeling the urge to turn around and shoot my father.

It was near dawn when we parked at the gravel pit. I hadn't been there in ten years and it was now abandoned, a maze of packed dirt roads, each ending in a cul-de-sac of bitten earth. I carried the pigeons and the gin and Dad carried the gun. The sky was just beginning to pale with a metallic dawn light outlining a dark fringe of trees. We sat down.

"Can't drink like I used to," Dad said.

I raised an eyebrow. "How'd you use to?"

"I didn't mean I don't drink like I used to," he said. "Just I can't." He coughed up a laugh, breathing in short, swift rasps. He lit a cigarette. "My lawyer call you?"

"He did."

"You gonna testify?"

I thought about it, briefly, as shapes in the gravel pit took on solidity. People were using it as a dump. Washing machines, the odd chair, boxes and lawn bags, bent and twisted gutters, a suitcase.

"I wouldn't let it go to trial," I said.

"You mean I don't have a chance?"

I imagined my father's life caught up in the snare of the law, the courts, in the web of family history, in all those things whose severest weapon is consistency, and I knew he would not fare well.

"I'd settle."

My father nodded. He pointed the shotgun at the gunnysack of pigeons.

"Better than skeet," he said.

"I'll release them."

"You don't want to shoot? You want, you can go first."

I looked at the gun, resting across my father's lap. I knew no magic inhered in the piece itself, that it was just a shotgun, but even though I could convince myself that the thing housed no resident boogie, I wouldn't touch it.

"I'll just do the birds," I said.

I carried both sacks about fifty yards away, intensely aware that my back was turned to my father. A spot at the base of my neck grew hot. My heart beat in a way that made me conscious of it. I untied the knot on the first sack and gently cradled a pigeon in my palm. I covered its eyes and looked at my father. He nodded. I spun the bird in circles, round and round, and then I set it down. It fell over. The next few moments were kind of vaudevillian. The pigeon flapped its wings, raising a cloud of dust, scooting sideways over the ground, pratfalling, and then it took flight, rising drunkenly in the air, executing a few goofy loops and turns. By instinct the pigeon appeared to know it was supposed to fly, but couldn't figure out the up and down of it. It smashed to the ground, leaden, then rose again. Before it could gain equilibrium and fly level, I heard the deep percussive blast of the shotgun, and the pigeon jerked back, propelled by the impact, and fell like a limp dishrag from the sky. Immediately I grabbed another bird. Its heart raced in my palm. Dad gave the nod. I spun it around and released it, watching as it rose just so far and then exploded in a flak burst of gray feathers. Each time, for the moment I held the bird, I could feel its life, the heart and the breastbones and the soft cooing in its throat, but there really was no moment of decision on my part, no hesitation, as I released the bird. I tossed another into the air, watching it struggle wildly against falling, then rise erratically, lifting above the trees, and get blown out of the sky.

"Take a shot," my dad said.

"No thanks," I said.

He came to me, and we sat down again. He drank from the gin and passed the bottle.

"This used to be open country out here," he said. "But I think we're inside the city limits now. I think we're in the suburbs."

I took a drink, and said, "You know the christening dress? All of us were baptized in that. Mom was, and Grandpa too."

"Yeah, so?"

"Where is it?"

"She'll get an annulment. Everything to nothing in the eyes—"
I interrupted. "But we'll never see it again, right?"
When he didn't answer, I said, "Let's head out."
"There's one more pigeon left."
I folded open the sack and let the bird go. It walked around, head bobbing, among the dead ones.

MY FATHER, on Thorazine, always became childlike. He walked in slanted, head-long, stumbling bursts that ended when he smacked into walls or collapsed in a heap on the carpet. He hid in closets, he broke his head open falling down stairs. We cleaned up after him, we mopped piss off the bathroom floor, we helped my mother wipe his muddied ass. At dinner, we wrapped a bedsheet around his neck and spoon-fed him pureed carrots and canned spaghetti and pale green peas we mushed with a fork. We fought over the chance to feed him, played airplane games with the zooming spoon. He babbled and sputtered and sometimes through the Thorazine fog the rudiments of language bubbled up. Once while the nine of us sat at the table, silently eating our dinner, he began to mumble, and we all leaned forward to listen. "Fuck you," he said. "Fuck you. Fuck you. Fuck you." My mother pushed another spoonful of mashed potato in his mouth and it burbled back out in a fuck-you.

As the youngest I was never left alone with my father, never left to care for him by myself—except once, and briefly. Everyone was out and I remember the strange-ness of being in the house alone with him. I asked him, did he want to watch TV? When he was crazy, the television ran constantly. I flipped the dial from sports to cartoons to network coverage of the last lunar mission, Apollo 17. Then he spoke—it was a miracle, like hearing a child's first words. He wanted me to go through the house and gather up all the sunglasses I could find. Despite his ongoing bouts of insanity, he was still my father, no crazier than the dads in the Old Testament, and I obeyed him. I thought it was a game. I tore through the house. "Thataboy," he shouted whenever I found a new pair of glasses. I gathered up Jackie's wire rims, a pair of aviators and blocky tortoiseshells, the girls' red and yellow and green plastic Disney glasses. Ski goggles, protective eyewear. My father arranged them on the floor, shuffled them one way, then another way, and then he asked, "Who do you think we can call about these glasses?" I said I didn't think there was anyone. And he said, "Well, I guess we're sitting ducks, then. I guess there's no hope. Isn't there anybody we can call?"

This memory came back to me at the open house. My father had put on his good suit and Sunday shoes but perversely decided not to wear his glasses. Immediately he looked lost. He stumbled around the house, filling shallow dishes with salted nuts, setting out a card table with potato chips and pretzels and pop. There were so many things missing from the house, things like family photos and favorite sympathy cards, things that had earned their places on the wall, on the fireplace mantel, simply by virtue of having always been there, that my father seemed spatially confused, and kept rearranging his dishes of nuts, putting them down on the coffee table, then the end table, then setting them back in their original spots.

"Sit down," I said.

"I'm not supposed to be here," my father said. "Cynthia asked me to vacate for a while."

Cynthia, the agent, was openly miffed when she saw my father. She introduced prospective buyers to me and then quickly moved on. I tagged along. She had a proprietary air as she showed the first few strangers through the house. She took a young, childless couple upstairs and showed them the master bedroom. She stood by the window and pointed to the view, the long sloping hill, the mountains in the west, offering this vista as a possibility for the future. We toured the kitchen, the living room. Then we all went downstairs, to the basement. Half of it was unfinished and the other half was paneled in knotty pine. While the Realtor talked about turning the basement into a rumpus room, I lifted the lid of an old Te-Amo cigar box and found some pennies and pen caps, a few buttons, a harmonica, and several hypodermics. When he was fifteen and sixteen, Jackie had been a junkie, and he'd shoot up in the basement. I'd find him downstairs, nodded off, a needle dangling from his arm. It seemed like ages ago now, my childhood. I closed the box.

The most earnest and eager buyers showed up early, followed by a few dreamers who obviously couldn't make a reasonable offer. By afternoon, though, the tone of things changed. I was standing at the picture window when I saw Mrs. Wooley stroll up the walkway. She was wearing a short skirt and heels. She rang the doorbell and I let her in.

"Bobby," she said. "I'm surprised to see you."

She was an intimate of my mother's and had to have known, of course, that I'd left school. She had a daughter my age finishing up at Yale.

"Nice to see you, Mrs. Wooley," I said.

"Call me Lois," she said. "I think you can do that now."

I offered her a drink. She looked at her watch and said, "No, thank you."

She bit her lip, and a little pink came off on her teeth.

"Last time I saw you," she said, "was at the funeral."

"You thinking of buying the house?"

"I was just in the neighborhood."

"Aren't you always? You live across the street."

"Lois, Lois," I heard my father say. He clasped her hand and smiled warmly. "It's been forever. How are you?" He looked down at his feet, and said, "Things have been crazy."

"Yes," Mrs. Wooley said.

Mrs. Kayhew tottered across the street and walked up the stone steps to our porch as if avoiding cracks. And shortly after, Mrs. Greyham followed, along with several other women from the neighborhood. My father greeted each of them with the same warm, somewhat chastened smile and then, like a docent, he led the entire group on a tour of our house. He was especially kind to Mrs. Kayhew, our next-door neighbor. He took her arm in his and guided her up the stairs. Mrs. Kayhew turned her yellow face toward my father, holding it up at a precise angle, as if her blue eyes were pools of water she didn't want to spill.

The little group stood on the upstairs landing. All the bedroom doors were closed, and the thickly coated brown paint gave them a certain feel, as if they'd been sealed shut a long time ago.

My father nudged a crucifix with his foot. He'd knocked it off the wall the day he came home to find my mother gone. The brass Jesus had come unnailed, and was wedged between two spikes in the banister. Mrs. Greyham looked at the cross and then at my father. I waited to hear the lie he would tell.

"I knocked it off the wall," Dad said.

My dad hitched his trousers and bent down on one knee. He picked up the cross and the Jesus and held them, one in each hand, and then tried to fit them together.

He opened his bedroom door, and all the women stepped in. He showed them the deck and the half bath and the big closet still filled with my mother's clothes. The big king bed still held the outline of my father in the wrinkled sheets, an intaglio of a head and legs and an arm stretching out toward the other pillow. He looked down at the impression, as if he might slip right back into bed, occupying the mold of himself.

My father offered to make a pot of tea.

"Tea?" I blurted out.

"That's okay," my dad said.

But none of these women had come to see the house, which was unexceptional; they'd come to see him. They were ready to leave.

I asked my father if he'd like to have a drink. The last light faded from the day and the street lamps were flickering to life. My father seemed dispirited.

"I think I'll just sit," he said. He pointed to his chair in the living room and then followed his index finger. He sat down and removed his wing tips, his navy socks, and began massaging his feet.

"Boy, they're sore," he said, squeezing his toes.

He sat in the dark, very quietly, as if he'd discovered a still point.

"Any buyers?"

"Huh? Oh, maybe."

I went to the kitchen and fished my dad's last barbiturate from the garbage can. I rattled the amber bottle and popped the top and dry-swallowed the pill. I used to steal them out of his medicine cabinet all the time. The thing about barbiturates is they make you feel caressed or gently held, your skin humming all over with the touch of a thousand fingers. I sat at the dining table and took apart Miles's old reel, dabbing drops of Remington gun oil on the pawls, and then went outside and rigged up the fly rod, drawing the line through the guides. I stripped out twenty-five feet of line and began false casting. At first I was out of practice, throwing wide loops that dipped low on the backcast and piled up on the forecast, but with each stroke

I made a minor adjustment and soon I could feel the rhythm, marking time. To Mrs. Wooley across the street I might have looked like a man sending semaphore to a distant ship. I worked the line until I was casting forty, fifty feet, and the back-and-forth motion felt substantial, bending the rod down to the butt. I took up a couple of extra coils in my left hand and shot those forward. The line sailed smoothly through the guides and unfurled across the street.

Holding Miles's rod in my hand, I thought of him, my surviving, wrecked brother. A few weeks after he jumped from the Aurora Bridge, I decided, one night, to walk out there. I'm terrified of heights, and I walked slowly out onto the bridge, step by step, my hand rubbing the dirty railing, until I'd made it midway onto the span. My legs weakened, my hands shook and burned with sweat. I had not yet looked down but I didn't need to; the fear rose toward me. I closed my eyes and felt the gritty wind suctioned by oncoming traffic. I heard the clack of tires over the concrete, the screech of a seagull. When I looked down, some three hundred feet, where the black water of Union Bay glinted with city lights, I couldn't move, I froze. My legs wouldn't work. I felt the fall in my stomach, an opening up and a hollowing out. I couldn't move forward up the bridge, or back where I'd come from. I couldn't let go of the rail. I might have been there for an hour, easy, when a woman, out walking her dog, came by. My fear of heights overcame my normal fear of speaking to strangers, and I told her I couldn't move. "I'm afraid," I said, pointing over the edge. She switched the leash to her other hand. "I thought I could cross," I explained. The woman took my hand. She talked us across, I know, because I remember the sound of her voice, but I have no idea what she said, and on the other side of the bridge I thanked her ridiculously, over and over, and the next day I rode the bus back to the bridge to pick up my truck.

My father came out. He was barefoot, but otherwise he still wore the suit. He scratched the back of his hand, and looked over his shoulders at our house. I lifted the line off the street and started casting again.

"I'll never settle," he said.

"Your choice, I guess."

I kept casting, working the rod back and forth, the line flowing gently in watery curls, whispering over our heads.

"It's beautiful," my father said. "Like haiku."

"Let me give it a try," he said.

I let the line fall and stood behind him, closing his hand around the cork, then closing my hand over his.

"LILACS" WAS INSPIRED by a patient with AIDS whom I took care of in Johnson City, Tennessee. He had monstrous lesions of Kaposi's sarcoma on his face and a manner so obnoxious and so deliberately antagonistic that it made it tricky to see beyond this and recognize his particular form of bravery. Other elements of the story borrow from my experience with HIV clinics—particularly the waiting rooms—in Boston and Iowa. I began with the character and his anger and went along for the ride. Bobby's endurance and determination were all that he had left that was of any value to him; he had no medical options, and no amount of money could buy him more time. His diatribe with Clovis surprised me as much as it must have Clovis; it was, however, despite being cruel, also an act of love, a legacy to another young man from the rural South who had escaped to the big city to find anonymity and freedom only to encounter this unforgiving virus. Bobby's actions in the story exceeded all permissible boundaries. But what are permissible boundaries when you are dying of AIDS? The story came out in one quick rush and then underwent several revisions, the most significant of which was I changed to the present tense the better to convey a sense of urgency. Mary Evans, who is my agent, and Daniel Menaker at the *New Yorker* helped me considerably through numerous revisions. I think we all were cautious about tinkering with Bobby, fearful that in his testy, irascible state, Bobby would tell us to butt out.

ABRAHAM VERGHESE

ABRAHAM VERGHESE

Lilacs

BOBBY SITS UP on the side of the bed. He feels weak, spinny-headed, and hollow. In a little while he tugs at the bedspread and wraps it around himself. Using the chest of drawers and the television for handholds, he stumbles to the air-conditioning unit below the window. He leans over the gray box, turning his head away from the cold blast, fumbling till he finds the concealed door to the control panel, and then blindly punches buttons till it turns off.

He draws the curtain back cautiously. He stares out at the motel parking lot for several minutes, focusing on any movement that might suggest he is being watched. Over the high wall behind the parking lot he sees the blue-green span of Tobin Bridge and, beyond that, the Boston skyline. The parking lot has filled up overnight. He sees Massachusetts plates, New Hampshire plates—an Indiana plate on a jeep reads HOOSIER HOSPITALITY.

FIRST IN THE WAITING ROOM. That would be on his license plate. If he had a car. When he walked into the motel lobby the previous night, it had smelled of coriander. The manager, an Indian, had stared at him with alarm. "No vehicle?" he said. Behind the counter, a door stood open, revealing a woman's fat leg on a recliner; a silver toe ring looked welded onto her second toe. There were the murmurs of a TV and the shrill voices of children speaking in another language. Bobby peeled three hundred-dollar bills from his roll, and the man's manner softened considerably. "What it is happened to your face?" the man asked, coming close to Bobby. The woman in the recliner stuck her head around to look.

"Oh, I was born this way," Bobby had answered. He had smiled at the fat woman, who quickly retracted her head.

THE BATHROOM IS COLD. He brushes his teeth with the bedspread still wrapped around him. He tries not to look into the mirror. Why look? Better to remember himself as he used to be. As he is in the photograph in the briefcase—a photograph Primo took. It is from Myrtle Beach, the summer of 1973, when he was twenty-one years old. In the photograph his hair comes down to his shoulders. He is bare-chested, sitting sideways on Primo's '64 Harley, one hand on the tank and the other resting lightly on his thigh—his own thigh. He is smiling—a strong smile, a smile of certainty. Primo had said something to make him smile, something flattering, and his Fu Manchu mustache looks innocent, young. In the background is Primo's airplane, and beyond that, faintly, the sea, though in the photograph it blurs with the blue of the sky. Carolina blue.

In those days, Bobby worked as a manager in the Myrtle Mystery Mall, selling tokens for the peephole dioramas, supervising the soda and trinket concessions, keeping the lines flowing through the Dinosaur Cyclorama, shooing out the couples who lingered in the dark recesses of the Polynesian Fire-Walk of Love. He was ten years old the first summer his parents brought him to Myrtle Beach. They drove down from Spartanburg and rented a "cottage" (in reality, a double-wide trailer) for two weeks in late July, in what became an annual family ritual. Bobby, an only child, distracted, suffering again that summer with bad eczema, spent most of his time and all of his allowance in the Myrtle Mystery Mall. He thrilled to its dark, paneled interiors, the dim, red glow of the Chinese lanterns, the labyrinth of doors and corridors leading to exhibits, but most of all he thrilled to being part of the clique of boys who hung around in their flowery sports shirts and shades and seemed unofficially to preside over the whole phantasmagoria. They encour-aged him to disobey the HANDS OFF sign on the Iron Maiden in the Gallery of Torture; they laughed when he tested the blade edge of the guillotine with his tongue; and later, sitting in a prop room, they let him sip from the silver hip flask that they were passing around—a mark of his acceptance. He much pre-ferred their company to baking on the beach with his parents or sitting mute in the backseat while his father, talking nonstop, inched the Buick into the family cavalcade that went up and down the strip in search of a different fast-food joint for the evening.

The year his father died, Bobby dropped out of the English honors program at Appalachian State and moved to Myrtle Beach, landing a job in his old hangout. Every day, Bobby caught triptychs of himself in the Distortion Gallery; Bobbys were catapulted out of one mirror and reeled back into another: thin Bobbys, fat Bobbys. In the evenings, Bobby went to the Connection, and there he saw himself reflected in the eyes of guys from Johnson City, Fayetteville, Raleigh, wherever. They would cluster around him, buy him drinks, while he looked over the tops of their heads. One night he saw Primo come in, look around, and leave before Bobby could get near him—it was the only time Bobby had seen a better-looking man than himself in the place. Primo had returned in an hour, dressed in leather. This time Bobby walked over, scattering the people around them.

"If I had known," Bobby said, fingering the straps on Primo's shoulders, "I would have worn my skins."

"It's not too late," Primo said. They didn't make it out of the parking lot.

HE RINSES OFF the toothbrush. He has no razor, and, in any case, his beard barely grows anymore. He runs a washcloth over his face and works the corners of his eyes. His eyelashes have grown long and translucent and have curled up at the ends—a side effect of AZT, according to Dr. Chatupadia. Of the six doctors in the clinic at Boston Metropolitan, four are from India, one is from Pakistan, and one is a Palestinian. Chatupadia, who has been Bobby's physician ever since Bobby moved to Boston nine years ago, took a photograph of Bobby's closed eyelids with the eyelashes dangling and sent it to *The New England Journal of Medicine*. Chatupadia was disappointed when they sent the photograph back, saying that what it showed was now a well-described side effect of AZT. He showed the letter to Bobby. " 'Well-described,' they are calling it, Bobby!" he said, pronouncing it *Boobee*. "These people," Chatupadia said, and he wagged his head from side to side, letting the silence stand for all the injustice in his life and Bobby's life. Bobby agreed. *These people* . . .

These people had no place for Bobby. These people were waiting for him to die. Even Chatupadia seemed to regard his longevity, his hanging on despite plummeting weight and daily fevers, as an aberration. He was a bird without wings, suspended in midair, defying the ground below. His Social Security supplement, even with Medicaid, could not support him. It didn't cover the medications for the infections—the opportunists—that threatened to kill him before the AIDS virus did. Five days earlier, after waiting for three months, Bobby was turned down from the only multicenter interferon trial in Boston. Because his white-blood-cell count was too low, Chatupadia said.

"But my count is low *because* of the AIDS!"

"So sorry, Boobee. They won't allow it."

The other interferon trial in the United States was in Durham. He didn't have the money to go to Durham, but he called anyway, not telling them his white count. "Sorry, we are fully enrolled," a tired male voice had said. "And the study protocol only allows our own patients—our own AZT failures—to be enrolled."

"What if I came down there and waited on your doorstep?" Bobby asked.

They had a waiting list of three hundred. The doorstep was full.

"Just give me *some* of the drug! You don't understand—I have no more rope to hang on to."

But they couldn't. Protocol.

These people . . . But Bobby cannot give up. He cannot. He will not give them that satisfaction. He will go to the clinic today, as he has done every Wednesday these nine years. He will be first in the waiting room, as always. He will sit there and show everyone that he lacks neither determination nor, as of last night, money. And he will remind them of their impotence.

"We are an army of Boobees, an army with overgrown eyelashes," Bobby says to the shrouded figure in the mirror. His voice echoes in the bathroom, and he speaks even louder: "Across this great country, our army is converging on city hospitals. We will assemble in the waiting rooms. We will wait for the clinics to open. We will be treated—we Americans—by our Indian, our Pakistani, our Filipino, our Palestinian doctors: the drones. Upstairs, the queen bees will be working on the cure, appearing on television, writing for the journals."

Someone bangs on the wall next door. "Fuck you!" Bobby shouts, but he has lost enthusiasm for his speech.

He pulls his T-shirt on, trying not to snag it on his Hickman catheter. The catheter enters above his right nipple and then tunnels under the skin to pierce the large vein beneath his collarbone and extend through it till it reaches the vein just above his heart. For two years the Hickman has been his lifeline. It has spared him countless needles; blood for testing has been drawn out of it, and all his intravenous medicine, at home and in the hospital, administered through it. He has not used the catheter in two days; the solution he injects to keep it open is in the refrigerator in the South End apartment he abandoned in such haste the previous day. The catheter has probably clotted off, he thinks.

He turns on the TV as he dresses. He flips past the local news stations, half expecting to see his mug flash on the screen, and stops at CNN. He presses the mute button as Miss Cheekbones talks. He speaks for her: "An overgrowth of eyelashes is being described among persons infected with the AIDS virus who are on the anti-AIDS drug AZT." Here she flashes her dimples, and Bobby continues. "Concern is being expressed by advocates that this will result in people being identified in their workplace as infected with the AIDS virus. . . ." He remembers his father watching boxing on television with the volume turned off, providing ringside commentary in his loud voice: "Muñoz, once again pounding the body, coming straight ahead, hooking to the ribs—Styles make fights, wouldn't you say, Mary? you couldn't find two more different fighters. Concinni hasn't stopped moving, dodging, backpedaling, weaving—Oh! Concinni is tagged with a left! He's in trouble! He's down! Good night, sweet prince!"

He picks up the briefcase. It is burgundy and made of soft leather; it belonged to Michael. Michael moved into the apartment soon after Primo moved out. Michael did research on mice at the Genecor Research Center—mice with heart disease. He got sick and moved back to Iowa, leaving everything: his medicine, his furniture, his briefcase.

The bag has handles that slide out. In the outer, zippered pocket is Bobby's birth certificate, his living will, his prescriptions, a yellow pad, and a pen. Inside the bag is the gun. And thick wads of hundred-dollar bills. He takes the gun out—Primo's gun. In his hand it looks animate and repulsive. He regrets having it; he regrets having needed it. He walks around the room, looking for a place to hide it. He has a vision of a child discovering the gun, examining it, playing with it. Reluctantly, he puts it back in the briefcase.

HE LEAVES the motel after a last look around. He takes a bus and gets off near MIT, near the hospital. A mist is rising off the river. He walks onto the bridge on Massachusetts Avenue. Halfway across, the muscles of his calves begin to hurt. These are not my muscles, he thinks as he reaches down to touch them. This is not my pain. He leans over the railing and looks down at the water. A purple reflection of his face flashes at him, and he pulls away from the railing.

He starts walking again, watching his feet: one boot with silver chain, the other plain; left, right, left, right. This is the only way to do it, he thinks—something Primo never understood. He is angry when he thinks of Primo, and Michael. Primo gave up almost at once. Primo had made the move to Boston with Bobby, in search of better AIDS care, but had bolted from the clinic after the first visit, terrified by the sight of a cachectic young man in the waiting room. Primo's only fight—before he was hospitalized—was to take wild risks in his plane. He tried Dead Man's Stalls and Cuban Eights in the Cessna until they took away his license. Later, Bobby heard from others—because they had separated by then; the path Bobby had chosen to deal with the disease made Primo and his fatalism impossible to be around—that Primo began to cruise, spreading it, poisoning as many others as he could, as if it would ease his own pain. This had enraged Bobby so much that he did not attend Primo's funeral. Primo's mother called him afterward, screamed at him, accused him of killing her son. Michael gave up in a different way: he left one morning, saying that the magic of being in Waterloo, Iowa, eating his mama's cooking, going to the high-school ballgames, doing whatever one did in Waterloo, Iowa, would somehow save him. It didn't.

Meanwhile, Bobby had tried it all: AZT, then DDI, now DDC. And ganciclovir. And the underground Compound Q. And intravenous protein feeds. And aerosol pentamidine. He had meditated—he still did. He had gone macrobiotic until he could no longer swallow. "Oh, I may die," he shouts at a car that passes by, "but not without a goddamn fight!"

Near the Christian Science Building, Bobby jams one toe between the stones of the retaining wall and climbs up to reach some lilacs that hang from a bush. It is more effort than he thought it would be. He gets the flowers, but his shoulder hurts. He hears the woman's voice before he sees her. "Those are pretty flowers. But you should leave them on the tree."

She wears a track suit and tennis shoes; her gray hair peeks out from under a scarf. A handkerchief is tightly wadded in her hand, and she is breathless. Bobby holds the flowers out to her; it freezes whatever else she was going to say, and she breaks into a shy smile. He drops slowly to one knee. He imagines he catches the scent of her perspiration, sees the steam rising off her body. "The official flower of our state, ma'am."

"You shouldn't have done that," she says, her hands reaching for one cluster, "but they are beautiful."

"Aren't you going to ask me what state?"

"Are you all right?"

He gets up and rubs his shoulder. It is on his tongue to say "the State of Immunodeficiency." Instead, he says, "No, I'm not all right."

Her smile melts into an expression of concern. She moves her feet, conscious that she has tarried too long already, but feels obliged to ask: "Can I do anything?"

"Are you a magician?" Bobby asks. "Never mind. No, you can't do anything. Thank you for stopping, though. Thank you."

She waves and walks away briskly, her elbows pumping high, her lockstep gait quickening; she turns when she nears the bridge, and smiles.

Bobby watches her till she is out of sight; he feels the anger return again. It comes in waves and crashes over him. Yesterday, rage at the mindless bills, the dunning letters, and—finally—the cutting off of his telephone and electricity had carried him downtown. He had seen his reflection as he tore into the Bank of Boylston—a whirling dervish in a black coat, with gun drawn. He almost shot at the reflection. Could a face really be that purple? He braced himself, expecting to be challenged at any moment. Instead, they pushed money bundles at him, even gave him a bag to stuff them in. When the bag was full, he shouted, "What now? What now?" but none of the prone figures would move. "What now?" he cried to the camera on the ceiling.

Too late he remembers that he could have given the woman some of the money.

HE RESTS OUTSIDE the hospital by the dry fountain that is full of butts and matchsticks. Then he starts walking again, against the flow of traffic as the eleven-to-seven nurses head for the parking lot. He bypasses the main entrance and goes into the tunnel and walks down it to the Kass Memorial Building and then takes the elevator to the fifth floor. He walks past patients' rooms smelling of Lysol and bacon. In the nurses' lounge the coffee is fresh, and he pours himself a cup, then snaps open drawer after drawer until he finds some sugar. He empties six packets into his cup.

Two people in white come in. One male, one female. One black, one white.

"Who are you?" one asks.

"Who are you?" he replies.

"We work here."

"*We work here,*" Bobby says. Such complacency, such arrogance, he thinks. "And I am a walking skeleton. I'm a voodoo doll. I own this hospital." They look confused. He explains: "I'm your three square meals a day."

His hands are full now, what with the lilacs and the coffee and the briefcase. He moves toward the nurses and they step quickly aside.

Bobby goes down the stairs to the second floor and then through a long hallway, past dark labs and locked offices, until he reaches the clinic waiting room. Before the first sip of coffee is past his throat, before he can even sit down, he feels his intestines start to writhe, and he hurries for the men's room.

Back in the waiting room, he takes one lilac stalk and leans over the counter, over the patient-register book, and wedges the stalk between the printer stand and the printer. Laurelei will keep it there all day. She says that whenever she thinks of lilacs or smells them she thinks of him.

He tries breathing and meditation. He wants to feel the prana ebb and flow. *Ommmmm.* His mind strays and he brings it back. *Ommmmm.* But there is only anger. *Ommmmm.* He thinks of his job as a short-order cook in Hoboken, ten years ago, while Primo was enrolled in a six-month course for his commercial license. It was fluid motion for Bobby—a moving line walked past him and they called the tune while he danced. He was the ballerina of Niko's in Hoboken, cracking eggs, flipping hotcakes, buttering toast, sliding the dishes down the counter. Oronfrio, the manager, said he didn't know why Bobby bothered with the men when he could have had any of the women. "Because I can have any of the men," Bobby would say, flipping a morsel of scrambled egg into the air and catching it on his tongue, all the while looking into Oronfrio's eyes. *Ommmmm.* He thinks of his mother in Spartanburg and how she must shudder when she thinks of him with Primo. *That's right, Mama. I was his blushing bride. He did to me more or less what Dad did to you.* She will be surprised when she gets the money he sent her. She will draw the shades and walk around the living room talking to herself, tormented by the knowledge of where the money came from and what she ought to do, and by her greed for the money and her wish to burrow in her house and deny his existence. He laughs aloud, and gives up the idea of meditation.

THREE GUYS COME in; two of them are a couple he knows from the waiting room. They run a bar in the South End. Bobby remembers buying some dope from one of them a year ago. The third one—the new one—is not quite with them. He signs in and sits two seats away from Bobby while the couple sign in. Bobby smells after-shave on the new guy, but beneath it is a sour, unwashed smell. It is the smell of fear, Bobby thinks; it irritates him. Laurelei arrives behind the desk and turns pale when she sees Bobby. "Thanks," she stammers when the dope dealer comments on the flowers. "Bobby brings them in," she adds, and looks at Bobby fearfully. Bobby waves back and points at the rest of the flowers, which he has arranged in a soda can on the windowsill, but Laurelei runs into the inner office.

"The official AIDS flower," Bobby says to the new guy, pointing to the lilacs. The new guy looks at the lilacs and then at the purple growths on Bobby's face. "Get it?" Bobby asks, touching the biggest growth, over his right eyelid. "Lilacs out of the dead land. Get it?"

The new guy just blinks. The disease is not choosy, Bobby thinks; this kid is dumb as a coal bucket.

The new guy tries to ignore Bobby. He shakes out a cigarette with trembling fingers. There is a ring with a turquoise stone on his pinky, and his nails are long. They would be elegant in a different setting from the Metropolitan Hospital clinic.

His brown hair is slicked back in a "wet look"—a style that Primo favored years before it became commonplace. Bobby moves over to sit next to him.

"You didn't really have a bath, did you?" Bobby asks. "Your hair looks like you had a bath, but you didn't. And you hurried with your breakfast—doughnuts on the way? How did I know? The powdered sugar on your mustache. I'm Bobby, by the way." The new guy has the cigarette in one hand and a lighter in the other. "You can't smoke here. You can shake my hand, though. You can't get it by shaking my hand. Besides, you already got it."

The new guy puts the lighter away and Bobby shakes his hand. The hand feels crumbly, fragile, but it is its sweatiness that primes Bobby, forces him to take more interest in this boy.

"You must be Clovis," Bobby says. "I saw the register. 'Clovis: Forty-five.' Forty-five minutes is for new patients. Must be you. Let me guess. You tested positive—what, two years ago? And you were positive before that but didn't want the test. And now you wake up in the night and you feel cold and you put on socks and wrap your head up, and then in an hour you drench the sheets. And then you feel cold again. That's why you didn't shower, right? You were cold when it was time to have the shower. Am I right? You're shit scared, am I right?"

Clovis tries to get up. "Sit down," Bobby says to him. "You can't afford not to listen to me. You need to listen to me. I'm a survivor—nine years. If you don't want to live, just keep walking. That's better. Let's begin." Bobby puts both his hands round Clovis's forearm and twists the skin in opposite directions; Clovis yelps. "That's called a barber's twist, Clovis. Keep your eyes on the skin." A shower of fine red dots makes a bracelet on Clovis's forearm. "Oh, oh! You know what that means, don't you? Your platelets are low. You're farther along than you thought, Clovis. Good thing you came today." Clovis's face shrivels.

Clovis's acquaintances are getting out. Clovis tries to rise again. His eyes plead with the couple, who are standing at the door, but Bobby takes the gun out of the briefcase and sets it on the chair. "Clovis is with me," Bobby tells them. "And don't roll your eyes at me, honey. You guys don't look so hot yourselves. You got a way to make him live? I can make him live. What have you got?" The couple hurry out.

Bobby looks at Clovis; he wonders why he is bothering with this kid. Has Clovis become his hostage? In return for what? Bobby gets up and bolts the door. He paces around and then sits down. He has no doubt the police will be here soon. He takes one of Clovis's cigarettes and lights it and hands it to Clovis. "You can smoke now, Clovis. Everything has changed." He sits down and thinks awhile and then picks his words carefully.

"You don't know how special I am, Clovis. I am a nine-year survivor. I've beaten the odds; I am way over the median survival. Look it up, if you want. I'm the only nine-year guy in this clinic. And it wasn't luck either, Clovis. I fought for every fucking bit of it; I *scrapped* for it; I *took* all the responsibility."

Clovis is listening; the fear and gloom that were on his face are momentarily erased.

"Level with me, Clovis. What is the scariest thing about this whole business? That you can die from it? Death? Bang, bang? You probably will die from it, right?" Clovis's eyes get big. "And that fear is what kept you from being tested? And that fear is still there—right?" Clovis's eyes get even wider. Bobby takes out his yellow pad and pencil. He pats Clovis's hand. "The only way to beat this is to lose your fear, Clovis," he says kindly. "The fear doesn't do you any good. In fact the fear can kill you before the disease does. It's like most anything else in life: lose your fear and it can't touch you."

Bobby massages Clovis's hand, trying to imagine what it is like to be a Clovis. What does a Clovis really feel? He sees a LOSER, LOSER, LOSER sign flash across Clovis's face. Clovis is giving up, retreating again. Clovis is ugly, Bobby thinks. The dimples are really pimples, he has dandruff on his eyelashes, his face is oily. Clovis tries to withdraw his hand. Bobby considers stopping but feels obliged to continue; let the kid have the message, for what it's worth.

"It's not illegal to hold hands—is it, Clovis? Okay, I'm going to let go of your hand. I want you to answer a series of questions for me. I'll write down your answers on paper, and then you put that paper in your pocket and carry it with you. Then—trust me—you will have conquered death. It worked for me. Okay? First of all, where do you want to die?"

Clovis's chin is quivering. Bobby makes lines and draws columns on the paper. He is aware of the absolute silence in the building. "I'm asking you where you want to die. In the hospital? At home? On the street? You live with those guys, right? You all came in the same car, right? You work in the bar for them, right? A little dope, a little head—Hey, I know. So, you ready to die with them, in their apartment? In the South End? Or you want to die at your own house, in your mama's arms? Or do you want to die with me?" Clovis begins to open his mouth, but no answer seems forthcoming. "With Mama," Bobby whispers for him. He uses a southern accent. Childlike and *very* southern. "With Mama? Let me guess—Alabama? Tennessee? Okay, you want to die with Mama? You need to write that down, Clovis. Get that down on paper. Otherwise they'll dump you in Roxbury Cemetery. Okay, so you want to die at home. Now, what do you want them to do with your body?"

Clovis is weeping now, his face in his hands, and Bobby strokes the ducktail, his fingers coming away greasy. "It boils down to do you want to be cremated or buried?" Bobby busies himself writing on the yellow sheet. He is aware of the sirens approaching the parking lot outside, but he concentrates on the paper:

BODY	Home	x	Away	
DISPOSAL	Bury		Cremate	x
SERVICE	Yes	x	No	
MUSIC				
TOMBSTONE				

"I personally can't stand the thought of waking up one day to find I'm locked in a pine box with rats nibbling at my eye sockets. If I was you I would go for cremation. It's cheaper, easier for your family."

Clovis is sniffling and carrying on. Bobby lets the *X* remain where it is. Cremation for Clovis.

"Music? I assume you want a service—so, music. See, that's something you can control. Music: what do you want them to play? Come on, Clovis—music?

" 'Rocky Top,' Clovis? 'Rocky Top you'll always be, Home sweet home to me, Good old Rocky Top, Rocky Top, Tennessee.' " Singing the song makes Bobby laugh. He gets up and tries to clog but can't move his feet quickly enough. "Good choice, Clovis! 'Rocky Top' it shall be." He writes in "Rocky Top." He lets go of the pad to hold Clovis's hand again, because Clovis is trying to get away. Clovis sits down on the floor, his hand in Bobby's grasp.

"The eulogy, Clovis! Don't forget the eulogy. What do you want them to say? Okay, okay, you can think about that. But the tombstone, the grave marker. That *has* to be your choice. 'Clovis. Our beloved son—' "

Clovis breaks loose. He unbolts the door, pulls it open, and runs around the corner.

"Wait, Clovis! Put this paper in your pocket."

BOBBY PICKS UP the gun but then tosses it out the window. He sits on the floor and carefully folds the paper into an airplane. His body is rocking back and forth with concentration. When he is done, he stands up and looks out the window. He is astonished by the crowd below. He sees Chatupadia and waves. He slowly pushes the window wide open and stands on a chair. With a flick of the wrist he sails the plane out. It is a wonderful plane—the best he has ever made. It catches an updraft and rises in a tight spiral. Bobby is drawn to the window: the yellow plane is still climbing. Bobby steps out on the sill and cranes his neck to follow it. Finally, when it can climb no more, it banks into a lazy left turn. He is aware of voices yelling at him, but they are drowned out by the roar of the plane's engine. He imagines himself as the pilot. The plane finds another updraft. Bobby increases the power to full throttle and points the nose straight up. Gravity works against him, and he watches the airspeed indicator drop rapidly. Just before the plane shudders to a stop, he applies full rudder. He has timed it exactly, and his plane makes a perfect Hammerhead turn, rotating on the tip of one wing. Now he points the nose at the crowd below. He sees his airspeed rise again. The wings shudder and the wind whips at his face. He puts his finger on the fire button. "Coming at you!" he shouts.

GIVEN THE STRICT realism that permeates much contemporary American fiction, Susan Power's "A Hole in the Sheets" offers a perfect example of how to establish authority, or credibility, in what would seem an otherwise somewhat fantastic situation. Between the main character, who has various powers, and the reader, she places an "outsider," one not familiar with the Native American world she is entering for the first time. The effect created is that the reader's initial doubt is the "outsider's" initial doubt. And as it is surrendered for the character over the course of the story, so too is it relinquished by the reader.

TOM GRIMES

SUSAN POWER

A Hole in the Sheets

JEANNETTE MCVAY'S PERFUME set the dogs barking. It was Chanel No. 5, and I should know, because I once had enough of it to fill my porcelain tub. I had a sudden whim to submerge my flesh in its sweetness and sent my boyfriend of the time, Roger Bonnin—his pockets bulging with lease money—into Bismarck to fetch me some of that nectar. I went in slow, made it a misery, and when the liquid closed over me, with just my head poking out like the olive in a cocktail, I knew I was something spun of gold or mined from a vein of precious rock. I knew I was special. Which Jeannette McVay was not, though intoxicated by her own spirit of misadventure.

"Hello-o-o, there's no be-ell," she sang in a bright voice too bleakly cheery to hide her fear. I let the dogs—two fierce brothers named Gall and Crazy Horse—lunge and scratch at the kitchen door; I could hear claws raking the screen. Their growls were crushed gravel in their throats.

"Okay, pipe down," I said when I was finally bored.

I didn't let that girl in right away. I'd seen her step out of Herod Small War's blood-colored Pontiac, which was bottom-heavy as a matron, and that old criminal was not someone I called friend. *What's he landed on my door?* I wondered, not eager to find out.

Jeannette's Chanel fragrance entered my house before she did. She was wary of the dogs and hampered by the tallest suitcase I'd ever seen, the sleek texture and color of a shark.

"This isn't a rooming house, despite what you may have been told," I said.

"Oh, I know," she puffed. "I take this wherever I go, because home is with me at this moment."

"You've just told me more than I wanted to hear," I said. I thought it would make her pause on the back porch, but she moved ahead and dragged that monster suitcase into my kitchen. "If I weren't Sioux, I'd walk you through the house and usher you right out the front door," I told the girl. "But as it is, I'm Dakota, and that means I'm going to feed you something first."

She laughed at that, and I stopped to watch her because her mouth was like a balloon releasing air. "I didn't know you had such a sense of humor," she said. I had the idea she didn't mean me personally but was making some vague reference to my people. I opened a can of commodity peaches, letting my little finger trail in the syrup so I could taste it. I placed a bowl of the sweet fruit before her, and a glass of cool water. "This is the best," she sighed. We sat in silence for the next few minutes while she finished that bowl, and a second, and a third.

Jeannette McVay, as she turned out to be, was tall and bony, like a set of wooden rulers tacked together to make a stick-figure girl. She had one brown hair for every blond one, and all of it was pulled back into a limp ponytail, thin as a pencil. She had eyes the color of tarnished nickels and skin that looked stained and yellow like a smoker's fingers, but the balls of her cheeks popped out in bright happy circles, wearing a faint wash of pink as if she'd pinched them.

"What a generous lady you are," she said when the can of peaches was gone.

"You speak too soon," I warned.

"You must be wondering what this is all about, this intrusion." She laughed again, and I could smell the peaches. "Well, let me lay it all out to get you even." Before she began her explanation, Jeannette put on eyeglasses with heavy black frames that swept up at the corners into wings. The glasses didn't fit properly, so she was constantly adjusting them, her cuticle-bitten finger pushing them onto the bridge of her nose.

"What's this?" I said. "You need to see the words as they come out of your mouth?"

"No," she said, all serious. "I want to see *you*." So I was quiet, and she chattered like a ground squirrel, her head tipped to one side and then to the other, her thin yellow hands pressed between her knees.

"I come from Pennsylvania," she told me. "A little town you wouldn't know, although it has its share of moguls who flatter themselves they're running the world. Well, maybe they are." She paused here and looked at me as if to inquire: *What do you think about that?*

I didn't even blink.

"So this is the boring part," she continued. "My father is a work-obsessed dad who hasn't said more than five words to me since giving me life, and my mother is a country club mental with a waist smaller than Scarlett O'Hara's and a brain pickled in Long Island iced tea. She's said plenty to me, none of it pertinent. The good news is that I spent the last four years of my life at a girls' college, East Coast but *not* Pennsylvania, a place where everything is relevant, an issue. I studied archaeology, and that led to anthropology and mythology. I'm going to go to graduate school, but first I thought I'd do some work in the field, get firsthand experience and go out there to meet humanity rather than just slip it under a microscope or flash slides of it across some institutional-green wall." Jeannette sipped her water and sloshed it in the glass. One tiny swell washed over the lip and spattered her skirt.

"My parents think I'm part of a team of graduates—you know, complete with funding and dorm rooms and ancient chaperones. They think I flew, but I took the bus all the way to Bismarck and then hitched to the reservation, and let me say, that was a thesis in and of itself." Jeannette laughed as she sipped.

"I thought this was going to be a thing about death: dead culture, dead language, dead God. I came out here to record the funeral, so to speak. Collect data on how a people integrate this kind of loss into their souls. And you know what? I found all this activity and vitality and living mythology. I feel like I've stumbled upon a secret."

My daughter Crystal suddenly charged into the kitchen, having just returned from school. She was a freshman in high school, and her canvas bookbag was heavy with texts. I noticed for the first time that her school uniform—a green plaid jumper—was almost obscenely tight; it was a girl's size, while she was nearly a woman. She rinsed her hands in the sink and splashed water on her face. She'd brought the smell of springtime into the warm kitchen, and it made my ankles itch.

"Come meet our company," I said. "A visitor from the East." Crystal looked as uninterested as I felt. She shook Jeannette's hand but quickly backed out of the kitchen and went upstairs. I heard the phonograph hum as it warmed up and then strains of that number I called the oily song because the lyrics were all about slipping and sliding.

"I have to get this down," Jeannette mumbled. "A Sioux girl listening to Little Richard."

I am not considered a patient woman. "You have yet to place yourself in my kitchen," I said.

Jeannette put down her spiral notebook, its metal spine crooked and tortured-looking. "That's right. We're not there yet," she said. She nudged her glasses higher.

"When I first got here and asked about your religion and your medicine people, I was sent straightaway to Herod Small War. He was nice enough, but prejudiced against women. I was barred from his sweat lodge and couldn't take part in his Yuwipi ceremony because I was on my period. When I argued with him and told him about a few little developments, such as a woman's right to vote, he told me I could not vote my way into his ceremony or his sweat lodge. What's the use of studying with someone like that, who excludes me, doesn't recognize me as a full-functioning peer? So I asked about the women, and they told me: you." Jeannette removed her glasses and pulled out the tail of her cotton shirt to clean them. When she repositioned them on her nose, crescents of fog smudged the lenses. Jeannette was a sphere of heat; I could feel the mercury rising.

"I was told such stories—they were legends really, but alive and moving upon this earth. I absorbed the tales, marveled that you were nothing less than Aphrodite,

Goddess of Desire, with her magic girdle that helped her spell the other deities and mortal men. But think how wonderful this is, because you're not in some book or reclining on Mount Olympus. You're right here in the kitchen, serving me peaches!"

Jeannette reached for my hand, but I anticipated her move and clasped my hands to form a single fist. The girl pinched the scarred wooden table instead. Steam enveloped her lenses, so I couldn't see her eyes when she whispered urgently: "Anna Thunder, I want to get to know you, understand you, see you in action. You are modern magic and miracles I was raised to think were passé—no, worse than that: were gone forever. In short, I am here because I revere you."

I was no Aphrodite, Goddess of Desire, and I never wore a girdle in my whole life, though I have spread until my sitting end is broad as Texas. I was fifty-one years old, and my face was pleated by early disaster—what people so innocently call "hard times." I was not one to gaze long in the mirror beyond parting my hair in a straight line, and I knew the tips of my fingers were squashed-looking from so many years of beadwork, but my breath was sweet with the taste of wild plums and my eyes were black as those cut into gambling dice, and if I looked into a man I could lower a line so skillfully it would hook his heart. Then I would jerk it right out of his throat. I collected so many I kept thinking I would get my fill of them, but I never did.

Medicine pulsed within me, shot through my veins, and I don't mean the kind a doctor pumps into the body. I didn't practice good medicine or bad medicine, or a weak magic summoned by poems; I simply had potent blood inherited from my grandmother's sister, Red Dress. And there were times when it pained me like a fire, or froze me like a rock, and any weaker person would have crawled toward death.

Jeannette McVay, that little white girl with pennies in her penny loafers and a plaid kilt fastened with what looked like a diaper pin, could see this power in me, and it raised her temperature. Her nickel eyes rubbed against mine, flint striking flint, and sparks shot around the kitchen. *Everybody duck,* I thought to myself, and had to pull a smile through all those wrinkles.

I will be the first to say it: Jeannette McVay appealed to my vanity. And who *wouldn't* enjoy being admired, quoted, chronicled? One cannot be a pariah without feeling the effects, and the very qualities my neighbors feared were those Jeannette valued. I allowed her to stay in my house for an unspecified period of time, and when I learned that she'd picked up a colony of head lice in her travels, I spent several evenings combing them out with kerosene.

"That feels so wonderful, it's worth the experience of lice," Jeannette murmured as I worked through her hair in sections.

I thought to myself, *This is what it's like to have a daughter,* because my own daughter was increasingly withdrawn, always putting a door between us.

"Crystal, your dinner is ready," I had to call every evening, only to watch her take it upstairs to eat in her bedroom like an invalid. I would have welcomed rebellion, but this was a complicated surrender. If I insisted she have dinner in my company at the kitchen table, she ate furtively, in pecks and nibbles, her brown eyes growing larger by the minute until they looked capable of sliding across her face like runny eggs skidding off a plate.

Two weeks after Jeannette made her appearance, I scolded Crystal, telling her: "You should stick around and listen like this little *wašičun* girl. This is your story I'm telling, not just mine."

"I have a test tomorrow," she whispered, and although she was taller than her mother, she had backed so far into her shadow she seemed small enough for me to settle on my palm. My daughter was the color of a chestnut mare, and her eyes rolled white like a shy pony's to avoid my gaze. It was too easy to dip into those eyes; I looked away. Jeannette was furiously chewing gum—it sounded like a string of firecrackers set off in her mouth—while she studied samples of my beadwork: a few pairs of moccasins and a child's vest.

"Be careful what you throw away," I told my daughter. "Be cautious with your spirit, because it can fill up with the wrong things. I will tell you a secret," I murmured. Crystal flinched, and it was all I could do not to slap her. The scent of plums left my mouth. "Too many people don't believe in their souls, don't recognize them when they feel the spirit twist against their heart or snap across their brain. And some that do believe hand their spirits over to the care of others, just give them blithely away, though they may be tightfisted when it comes to their coins. I own my spirit. Can you say that? How many can say that? How many have fingered that cobweb veil? I've fingered yours. I know its texture. It tastes like bitter apricots."

Crystal stumbled toward the stairs, collapsing into her shadow. "I have a test," she sobbed.

"You will have many," I tried to assure her. But she had already glided up the steps and melted into the walls of her room.

That night I couldn't sleep, though I had plumped the pillows and folded down the quilt, which was too heavy for the mild air. My daughter's thoughts were noisy on the other side of my bedroom wall. Her mind was full of children's voices: a whining, a litany of complaints, a chain of foolish songs. I wanted hinges and a latch worked beneath her hair so I could smother all that noise.

It wasn't until morning that I slipped into a light, anguished doze; every muscle was tense and cramping, my fists strangling the sheets and teeth chewing the pillow. I dreamt it was my daughter's ear caught between my teeth and I was beading her thoughts, picking into her brain with my needle. And oh, the sparkling cells were easy to string!

I am beading you a medallion, I told her. *A new brave heart for you to wear around your neck.* But when I awakened there were no beads, no busy needle, and my daughter's thoughts were scattered throughout the house, uncollected, an explosion of them like shattered glass.

SPRING HAD NEARLY ENDED. It was a balmy morning, and I was already seated on my back porch, welcoming the crimson light. I was busy braiding the tassels of wild turnips to chain their bulbs together. I sang an old Dakota song to encourage the sun in its rising:

> She came in a red dress,
> that sacred woman.
> She was a warrior in a red dress.

I had a deep drum voice I could throw for some distance. On this morning I cast it to the ground so it sounded as if my notes came from a hole in the earth. When I saw a storm of dust washing toward me, I thought my song had stirred the creatures from their burrows. But moments later I noticed the mud-speckled blue vehicle ripping through the center of that cloud. It was Calvin Wind Soldier of the tribal police. I continued my work and pushed my voice to drum harder, until I made those spinning tires vibrate. The car barreled down the gravel road, spitting rocks, and looked as though it would crunch its way right through my house. I stood my ground. Finally it rolled to a stop just outside my unpainted fence, nudging it lightly like a horse against its hitching post. Some former boyfriend of mine, whose name has gone down the well, had decided to build that fence, but he couldn't have lasted long, because the pickets extended for about five feet and then ended in space, attached to nothing, leaning this way and that like broken teeth.

Two figures emerged from the car: Calvin Wind Soldier, fresh as rain, his black hair lightly oiled and holster creaking, and Jeannette McVay, naked but for a towel.

"I threw my clothes out the window," she said. "But not my shoes." They dangled from her fingers. "I've got narrow feet, hard to find a good size, so I won't make a statement with these. But the rest went flying!"

Calvin moved past her as if she weren't there. He walked to the porch and rested one foot on the bottom step. "Did you put her up to this?" he asked me.

"I don't know what she's done, but you can tell me over a cup of coffee," I said.

"Can't." Calvin shook his head. "There's a carnival setting up in town, and the crazies will be trailing onto the reservation. She can tell you what happened. I'm not sure I understand. Keep an eye on her. If she's staying here, then she's your responsibility."

I stood up and walked over to Calvin Wind Soldier. I set the string of wild turnips across his shoulder and held out my hand. He shook it lightly, barely touching, which is the proper way. "You take those home," I told him.

Calvin thanked me and patted the turnips. "Soup tonight," he said. He looked into my eyes.

It felt as though the morning went cold, the air became blades sharpening their edges against my skin. I almost trembled. I almost told him: *I forgot what it's like to see eyes clean of fear*. I soaked in that look, and after Calvin drove away, I watched the dust trail him like smoke. I watched it hover, fall, and settle.

Jeannette stalked through the kitchen, her bare feet slapping the dull yellow linoleum. "We heard you, Anna, from way back," she said. "Your voice was coming from everywhere, and even though I was mad, hopping mad, I registered that this was another one of those unaccountable things you do. I wished I had a recording device. I liked the way it surrounded me and filled me up and said, *Jeannette, I am bigger than you and come from someplace you know nothing about*." The girl stopped pacing to pluck a splinter from the pad of her heel.

"So tell me why you're doing a striptease on the highway," I prompted.

"No, I was already stripped," she said, as if that explained everything. "I was determined to take part in a sweat, to rid myself of the last vestiges of East Coast snobbery and foolishness, of my petty issues, which I well know are nothing compared to the struggles I see around here. But let me point out before I continue that I think it's an accomplishment for me to even realize this. My folks would never get it that a balloon payment on the mortgage, or busted Waterford crystal, isn't the be-all and end-all."

Jeannette dropped suddenly on her haunches to kiss my dogs, which she had won over with baby talk and beef jerky. "I walked all the way over to Herod Small War's place. I know his schedule. I know he likes to start the day off with a sweat. He and Archie Iron Necklace and Bill Good Voice Elk. They got it going pretty good, and their assistant was busy heating more rocks, when I stepped inside there."

"Wearing what?" I asked.

"Wearing me, just me. I took my clothes off at the entrance. But there was so much smoke it wasn't a show or anything."

"They must have liked that," I said.

"You would think that they would finally see my pure sincerity, the depth of my respect and willingness to learn. But they are blind as my parents. Herod flapped his hand and told me, 'Shoo.' Like I was some fly. 'Shoo. Shoo. Men and women don't share a sweat.'

"I said, 'So if I was some white guy who probably didn't even believe in any of this, you'd welcome me with open arms?' At least he was honest. He said, 'No. If you were a white guy I'd give you a bloody nose.' Then the assistant called Calvin to bring me back here, and I was protesting. I wouldn't budge. They put me in the car and gave me my clothes. They're out there somewhere." She waved at the distant road.

I wagged my head at the girl. "Jeannette McVay, why do you need these men?"

"I could ask you the same thing," she said.

Later that day she questioned me: "Why is it that people take their spiritual matters to Herod Small War even though he doesn't have one shred of your control, while your name they speak in whispers? It's a thing against women, right?"

"That's easy," I told Jeannette. "Herod waits for them to come to him, waits for their tears and their sad little stories, their confusion and illnesses, their fear of death. I enter before they invite me in."

CALVIN'S SQUARE FACE was before me as I worked in my garden. I crumbled soil in my hand and imagined its soft rushing motion was like his shiny hair slipping through my fingers. Straight flat eyebrows stretched across his face like the even line of the horizon, and his eyes rose beneath them like two black suns. I caressed his skin as I collected the tomatoes and said his name in Dakota: "Tate Akičita." I dug with my trowel and planted that name alongside the parsley.

"Anna, I made lemonade," I heard Jeannette call from the kitchen. I left Calvin, and the name buried in my garden. "You've been preoccupied," Jeannette said. "Is it the stunt bothering you? I won't try it again."

I held lemonade on my tongue, cool and sweet and bitter. I shook my head. "I'm just recalling stories."

"Tell me, tell me," she murmured. She pulled her chair closer to me and nearly spilled her lemonade.

"This is an old story, from a hundred years ago," I began. I told her about my grandmother's sister, Red Dress, who had been a woman warrior. "She killed a number of U.S. Army soldiers," I said. Jeannette tittered like a lark sparrow. She hugged her knees to her chest and wiggled her bare toes.

I talked about the love between this woman and a Dakota warrior named Ghost Horse. "That policeman who brought you back this morning, Calvin Wind Soldier, is descended from him. Ghost Horse's brother was Calvin's great-grandfather. Ghost Horse was *heyo'ka*, one of our old-time clowns. Today people refer to them as contraries, because they had to work in opposites." I told Jeannette she better not dream about the thunderbirds who rule the sky, or she too would have to appease them with perverse behavior that antagonized people.

"I think I already do that," she said.

"My stories never have a happy ending," I warned the girl. I proceeded to tell her that the lovers never came together, that some believed they were still searching for one another in the open country.

"It's like Cathy and Heathcliff," she interrupted.

I nodded. "Yes, it is a little like *Wuthering Heights*."

"You know that book?"

"I knew it once."

Jeannette pressed her thumbnail into her knee. She was curious; I could see the fog creep across her lenses. But I would not say more on the subject. That is a road I left behind me and will not travel again, for anyone.

JEANNETTE DRAGGED AROUND the house all day, morose. I told her to take a hot shower, that would surely draw Pennsylvania out of her pores, but she didn't even smile.

"We're going to the carnival," I announced, promising: "We're going to cheer you up." I knocked on Crystal's door. I could see her so plainly through the wood grain it was like X-ray vision. I knew she was huddled on her bed, surrounded by books and magazines that did nothing to transport her. "Come with us to the carnival," I said through the door. "We're going to make some mischief."

"No," she answered. "My finals are coming up next week."

Your finals are useless knowledge, I wanted to tell her, but I was suddenly tired. *My blood is somewhere inside you, percolating,* I thought to myself. *It will show in time.* So I let her close up like a box.

The carnival was in full swing by the time we arrived. The rides were lit, streaking neon colors against the night sky. Shells of sunflower seeds crackled beneath our feet, and lean dogs prowled behind the concession stands. Jeannette pointed out two of them fighting over a hamburger bun.

"I've never seen such a people for dogs, they're everywhere roaming loose," she said. "But I thought your tribe liked to eat them too. Have you ever tasted dog meat?"

"I only eat poodles," I said. Jeannette laughed a beat too late.

She pitched tennis balls at tin cans, and I chewed corn dogs, my eyes scanning the crowd. Finally I saw him, one arm wrapped around his young wife, the other draped over his sister-in-law's shoulder. The women were twin sisters but very different. Calvin's wife, Lydia, was nearly six feet tall, and graceful in her body. She wore her long braids pinned around her ears like a little Swiss girl, and she never wore lipstick or any paint on her face but it was bright with color. Her dark eyes reflected light the way people say only white can. Calvin seemed drawn to their shine; he searched them again and again. Evelyn looked much older than her sister. She was half a head shorter than Lydia, and her body sagged with fatigue. The lashes rimming her eyes were short spikes, and her hair was a dense thicket. I didn't often see her with Calvin and Lydia. She was usually in the company of a rodeo cowboy named Philbert, but their romance was such an up-and-down drama it was difficult to keep current. I was surprised to hear Evelyn laugh. It cut me. I became angry with the three of them: their careless pace, the tangle of their arms, their breezy voices.

I watched as Lydia tucked her slim hand in Calvin's back pocket. *It's empty,* I told that foolish, untroubled girl. *Nothing is there.*

As I walked across the carnival grounds, I was like Moses parting the Red Sea; my neighbors swept to either side, watchful, humming like wasps. The only one to stagger in my path was Chester Brush Horns. He stood with his head down and hands thrust deep in his pockets.

"What is it, Chester?" I asked him.

"No money," he said, his eyes still on the ground. "I could sure use some smokes too."

"I can do that," I said.

I was so weary and blue I took the trouble to collect Chester Brush Horns. It was no triumph, for he was pliant, his mind a crushed bird. I don't remember what the damage was—a car accident, a beating, or a drunken fall from a window. It didn't really matter. He was handsome in pieces, but the placement was all wrong. His features were crowded around the center of his face, orbiting his nose the way darts cluster around the target. But he was strong, and smiling now at the promise of tobacco. And it was so easy to dole out the cigarettes one at a time, stealing a pinch of the shredded leaves and dropping the flakes in my dress pocket.

"I want to ride the Ferris wheel," I told him. I bought two tickets, and Chester's hand was already seeking mine before we lifted into the night air. When our car reached the top and I looked out from our point of light at the dark land, I felt a sudden pull. Gravity sucked at the soles of my shoes, and I was heavy, a lodestone drawn toward the earth. It was a delicious moment. I think the attraction messed up the works, for the Ferris wheel became stuck, with our car riding at the top. Men hollered up at us: "We'll get it going again in no time." But I was unconcerned.

"Entertain me," I said to my companion.

Chester Brush Horns stood up in our car and bowed to me. He placed one hand on the seat and the other on the metal back, and carefully lifted his legs into a handstand. He puffed happily on the cigarette clenched between his teeth, and except for the tension in his arms, he looked peaceful. I heard gasps, but no one shouted.

"Pull him in," someone muttered from another car.

I smiled to myself and tried to spot my house in the distant shadows. I flicked the ash from Chester's cigarette when it burned down. "You could have been an acrobat," I told him.

And then, just to make things interesting, I gently set the car to rocking.

THE NEXT MORNING I woke in a bed of ashes, and my bedroom was gray with a pall of smoke. Chester Brush Horns, whose sense of balance was now legend, coughed himself awake.

"I hear Jeannette making breakfast," I told him. "If you want something to eat, you better get it now." He looked so disoriented I pointed to the door. His hair fell forward, covering his face, and he dressed silently.

"You're a serious smoker," I said. "It's going to get you in trouble one of these days." Chester Brush Horns didn't perch on my bed to pull on his boots, but gathered them, together with his socks, and hugged the bundle against his chest. He crept toward the door lightly, on his toes, as if I were still sleeping. So I said, "I'm awake now, Chester. You can go ahead."

He sprang for the doorknob and nearly dropped his boots as he struggled with the lock. The door flew open, slammed shut, and there I was, obscured by the haze, filling my lungs with acrid air. I knew Jeannette was alone at breakfast, just as I was certain that Chester Brush Horns was running down the gravel-sharp road, barefoot, shirttails flying, still clutching his socks and his boots.

JEANNETTE OPENED THE BEDROOM WINDOW and beat the air with her skinny hands. "How can you breathe?" she complained. She was wearing crisp cotton pajamas and her winged eyeglasses. I waved her over to the bed.

"That guy took off from here like a bat out of hell," she said.

"I bet he did." I chuckled.

"You made him do that last night, didn't you?" she asked me. "I looked up and saw him rising out of that car. People were grumbling, you should have heard them. I thought they were going to string you up. To defend you, I said, 'He's a grown man.' But by that time it was all over."

"No one's going to string me up," I said with conviction. "You pay attention now," I told Jeannette, my voice low and steady. She scooted closer. "I am going to right a wrong of history." It felt strange to speak my thoughts; I had never announced my intentions before. The room filled with quiet, became heavy; I thought my bones would collapse and settle beneath the rest of me. My heart stopped in that moment, I know it did, until my hand massaged the spot and my voice exploded the silence: "You just watch."

CALVIN WIND SOLDIER, whose name was planted in my garden and whose ancestor had so dearly loved mine, would find his way into my arms. We would close the unhappy circle, change the ending of that story I had been told so many times it seemed like my own life read back to me. Calvin was half my age, but I would live forever. I would never leave him. Already I could hear him calling me, "*Unči*"— grandmother—and we would laugh at how ridiculous that was, because my hands and knees could clamp like vises. I was so caught up in this dream, I felt it was already accomplished. *Not yet, old girl,* an inner voice warned. *Not yet.*

This would take a special skill, a profound concentration. Calvin Wind Soldier would not be trapped by powder in his soup or loose tobacco. He would not slump forward if I clapped my hands, or spend his last penny to purchase some desire I whispered in his ear. I closed myself in the bedroom and walked the floor. Jeannette brought me lunch on a tray, but I didn't touch it. I listened so closely to myself I heard my heart talking. *Simple is best,* it told me. *Plain is powerful.*

At sunset I stood in the yard, breathless, spade in hand. *Look at this wash of colors,* I told Calvin. *Look at how the sky is painting itself.*

How sad, I thought, *that even now Calvin Wind Soldier is oblivious to his coming happiness.* I dug into the ground with my spade, used my foot to plunge it into the mother's dark flesh. When the hole was a foot deep I knelt beside it and placed two objects in its mouth: an old rattlesnake rattle, once used as a baby's toy, and a wild plum that was not yet ripe. Then I covered them with a heavy rock so the dogs wouldn't be able to disturb them, and replaced the dirt.

Tonight I will find him, I said. And an instant later the sun ducked its head.

I sat right on the ground in my housedress, rocked myself to the beat of my heart. At some point I fell over onto my back, and the night sky pressed me down. Was I falling? The stars were spinning and the moon whirled, flat as a dime, and the grass below me grew into the weave of my dress. I heard the rattle hissing in the ground. I smelled the plum. As I clutched dirt in my fists and pointed my feet at the back door, just a few steps away, I journeyed to Calvin Wind Soldier's house. He was sitting out front on a truck tire.

"Lydia is going to paint this," he told me. "She's going to grow flowers in it like a planter."

"Lydia is yesterday," I said. "Anna is tomorrow." My dress had patch pockets, and I raided them now, removed the rattlesnake rattle and the green plum. "My auntie Red Dress was a friend to snakes," I told the young man. "She wore their rattles in her hair to hear their voices. Your uncle loved her and planted a plum tree in her honor, but the fruit has gone untasted."

Calvin grinned at me, and I did not like to see his white teeth bared that way. I shouted, "Calvin Wind Soldier, I am claiming you!"

He held a finger to his lips. "Lydia isn't feeling well, and she is sleeping," he said. "I don't want your noise to wake her."

The ground trembled then, and the sky was black muslin—I wanted to tear it down the middle. "Where is your respect?" I bellowed. But that was too desperate. I made my voice a song. I crooned: "Wind Soldier, I am here to claim you. Wind Soldier, Anna is here."

"Of course you are," a third voice cackled. "We had a feeling you would come." An old man stepped from the house's shadow. It was Herod Small War, Jeannette's nemesis.

"Old man, you are nosy," I told him.

"Old woman, you are greedy. You go on home now and stop this mischief." Herod smiled, and I could see his back teeth were missing. His white hair glimmered in the moonlight. "I can make a few things," he was telling me. "You're not the only one. See this belt Calvin's wearing? I gave it to him a long time ago and told him to wear it."

I looked at the piece of leather threaded through the loops of Calvin's blue jeans. It was snakeskin, not some common cowhide. The scales glistened with oil; I thought I saw them flex.

"You will not make your way past this belt," Herod continued. "Your fingers will slip and fumble and shake, and you will just embarrass yourself. I think you should go on home and leave this man to his wife. Remember who you came from. Your people didn't approve of this kind of fooling around."

"Enough," I said. "I am too old for you to be lecturing." My daughter would have been surprised at my control. I knew she thought I was a cyclone spinning disaster, losing itself in its own fury. But I was deep calm, the cold dark water you find at the bottom of the sea.

I put away the rattle and the plum, held out my hands to show their emptiness. "You are too clever for me," I said. "Old man, you have more tricks than I thought possible." Herod grinned and shifted his weight. His body ached, the joints giving him pain; I could hear the flesh moan. I nearly felt pity for the aged man and his foolish manipulations, for the young man still seated on the tire, thinking all the time about his sleeping wife and how he would slip into bed beside her.

"I am gone," I said. I had turned my back, but I could hear them smile at one another. I knew the two men would sleep well that night, give themselves up to their dreams. Their hearts were peaceful because they didn't know the thing that powered me.

LATER THAT NIGHT, when I came back to myself, I was cradled in my daughter's arms.

"Mama, why are you doing this?" she cried. Her tears fell onto my eyelids and slid across my cheeks. "I thought you were dead when I saw you stretched out on the ground."

I opened my eyes then and saw an oblong patch of light—the gaping back door of my house. Jeannette was standing in the doorway, flanked by the dogs. Her eyes looked strange to me, enormous and unblinking, until I realized I was staring at her glasses. I was in no hurry to move from my daughter's embrace. I reclined there, my empty hands in empty pockets, my eyes loose, rolling this way and that way, my tongue trapped.

"Little spider, let me go," I finally said, and Crystal released me so quickly I doubted I had ever been held. But that was good; I had to be firm with myself. "Fate will never ride me again," I told Crystal. "I broke that horse a long time ago and kicked it with my heels. I had to take my own spirit in hand, or it would have shriveled like gauze held to a flame, been consumed, and my mind would be in too many pieces for me to scrape together. So I am here, working my fate, driving it before it has the chance to drive me."

Jeannette stepped forward, out of the light. She hurried down the back steps. "What was that?" she called to me. "What was it you said?"

I held out my hand to Crystal and, with her help, rose to my feet. I was not a tall woman, but that night I grew. I was flying without leaving the earth. I shot into the darkness, higher and higher, until the clouds circled my breasts, the stars lightly burned my skin like embers falling to flesh, and the planet I stood on was a turquoise stone too small for a ring. I answered Jeannette, though she had disappeared far below me.

"I am Providence," I said.

MY PEOPLE DON'T always turn out for celebrations—weddings and graduations— but they will travel hundreds of miles for a funeral. A good wake becomes a family reunion, maybe even a political caucus; feasts are spread, matches made, sometimes children conceived, when we come together to honor the dead. So when I heard that old Albert Elk Nation had departed this life, I became alert as the dogs. I could predict where my neighbors would be that night: congregating in the cavernous paneled meeting hall on the second floor of the tribal agency building. They would converge to shed their tears, eat their food, sing honor songs.

A month had passed since the night Herod Small War turned me away, and in that time I had mapped futures in my head, decided how a number of lives would turn. Jeannette asked me questions: "What will you do? How will it work?" And I answered plainly, letting her document my activities as if this were all a scientific experiment performed in a lab. She was so excited she was losing weight, just the opposite of Crystal, who increasingly craved soft starchy foods that rounded her figure, blurred her edges, made her less visible to my eyes.

But the things I did I managed alone, striding from empty house to empty house, using nothing more than a needle, thread, and a small pair of scissors. When my neighbors had left for the wake, I went first to Calvin Wind Soldier's house, entering boldly through the front door, which in those days was never locked. I found the bedroom in mere seconds and decided that the left side of the bed was his, because when my people dance as couples around the drum, the men are on the left and the women on the right. This was the side I revealed, though carefully, disturbing as little of the coverlet as possible; I would have to smooth the bedding when my work was done.

I imagined what Calvin would look like in that bed, how his body would relax against the mattress. I traced with my finger a small area on the sheet, a space I thought of as the Region of Lust. I crimped the material at its center and, with sharp scissors, snipped a piece of the fabric, such a small swatch my little finger couldn't push through the resulting hole.

Half a mile away, in the bedroom of a clean but flimsy shack, I repeated the process, only this time I worked on the right side of the bed, the woman's side, and repaired the tiny hole I'd just made, with the fabric from Calvin's sheet. It was so easy I was almost disappointed. Both sets of sheets were white, and the damage invisible unless you knew where to look. I had to return to Calvin Wind Soldier's place to mend his sheet with the material I'd taken from the other bed. I cut the thread. I restored order.

Perhaps my hands could not get past the belt he was wearing, perhaps they would remain lonely and never work happiness on Calvin Wind Soldier, but he would soon learn that there were other prying fingers and warm palms ready to touch him.

I WAS NOT a witness to the affair I had manipulated. I could only imagine the details. I don't know how many times Calvin Wind Soldier was late coming home to his wife or quick to leave her in the morning so that he could meet her twin sister, Evelyn, in some private spot. Maybe they used the back of his police car, feeling all the while like furtive criminals, or desecrated the top of Angry Butte, where young men went to cry for a vision. The only thing I knew for sure was that I had filled these young people with hurtful desires, changed the course of their destinies, because, after all, I could do it.

As I lay in bed at night, I thought to myself, *Perhaps right now Evelyn's bramble hair is scratching Calvin's face, as he flicks the blunt edges of her eyelashes with his tongue, tastes the tears leaking from her eyes.* I was sure their bodies would be heavy and their mouths would burn, and their limbs would ache and ache because there was no release in all this; the want would start up again as soon as they were apart. Sometimes I spoke to Lydia in the dark: *Isn't it funny how things end up? You're so young and beautiful and, everyone says, sweet, and now your arms are empty as mine. We are widows together.*

Slowly, gradually, like draining batteries, the cheating couple must have lost desire. The wonder of it is, my triumph was only beginning, for there would be a child. And he would have Calvin Wind Soldier's square face and even brow, but his hair would grow in tangled brown waves like his mother's.

JEANNETTE MCVAY had given up her perfume and become so skinny her shoulder blades protruded like budding wings. Summer was almost over, but its heat was still oppressive, and Crystal had taken to wearing a towel around her neck. Only Jeannette, whose body temperature must have lowered with her dwindling flesh, looked supremely cool. She was the one who brought the news from town, finding me in the kitchen at my beadwork.

"Evelyn is pregnant," she announced.

"Well, she's been shacking up with that goofy cowboy," I said. I was convinced of my success and didn't have to look for credit.

"You know that baby isn't his," Jeannette said. "She kicked him out months ago, and he's been down in South Dakota ever since." I thought she would crow, but she looked sober, a little troubled even.

"Yes," I admitted, "that child is my creature."

Jeannette shuddered, and it was so hot that day the movement appeared strange. "You really do what they say you do," she finally whispered.

Dakota people have an acute awareness of cycles, the patterns in time. I opened a can of commodity peaches and poured the fruit and the rich syrup into a bowl. I handed it to the girl. She was slow to eat, the first taste no more than her tongue grazing the spoon. But midway through the bowl she gained her appetite and soon asked for another serving, and another. The peaches were gone; the juice glistened on her chin, and she sucked it from her fingers. I realized that on this day, months after Jeannette McVay first entered my house, we had traveled only one step. The girl who came to me eager to discover a modern mythology had not really believed in it any more than she trusted that Aphrodite would show up at our next powwow wearing nothing but a dance shawl and her magic girdle. I don't know what finally convinced her. Everything that happened in my life could be explained in those bland terms that comfort the faithless. But there was no mistaking the pure fear I saw in her eyes.

"I am not a bedtime story," I told her now. "I am not a dream."

I was suddenly angry. I reached out and pinched what little flesh remained on her arm. "Feel that? Feel me? Remember Pennsylvania and your college in the East, and the buses, all the buses you took to get out here?" She nodded. "That is all a legend from the past, and here you are where things happen. It is so real now it is a nightmare, am I right?"

Jeannette was still and silent. The warm air was like broth; it didn't move. We were caught in a spell of dense lethargy, and it was Crystal, emerging from her upstairs bedroom, who finally ended the painful moment.

"Tell her," I said to Crystal. "Tell her that what happens in this house is not imagined."

Crystal's lips trembled. "Oh, Jeannette," she stammered. "You aren't asleep, and this isn't a story." She stopped there. She squeezed Jeannette's shoulder with her hand.

I looked at the girls, my girls, and nodded. "It's about time," I scolded. "Now we're all starting from the same place."

THE NEXT MORNING Jeannette dragged her shark-colored suitcase down the stairs and left it at the back door. "Herod Small War's coming to pick me up," she said. "I guess he's forgiven me, or maybe he just thinks I'm a lost cause and will be glad to see me go. Anyway, he said he'll drive me into town and then he has some relative there who will get me to the bus."

I knew all this, I had heard her make the call, so I just smiled placidly. "I could have driven you," I said.

"Oh, no. You've done so much for me already. It's a terrible cliché to say so, but honestly I don't know how I'll repay you for taking me into your family the way you did. My parents would never do something like that for a stranger."

She jabbered on this way, nervous, glancing out the window for plumes of dust signaling Herod's arrival. I was so calm and certain of the future; I remember humming to myself. I called to the dogs: "Get out here and say good-bye. Your little friend is taking off." They came to lick her hands and roll their eyes with great sadness. "So dramatic," I teased. "I don't know which they'll miss more. You or the beef jerky."

Crystal failed to appear, but it didn't surprise me. "Don't mind her," I told Jeannette. "She's at that moony age when everything is a little purple. She won't get her mind back for a couple of years."

Herod Small War didn't come up to the house, and I didn't step outside. There was danger between us, and though it didn't frighten me, I thought it best to leave that package unexplored.

"Good-bye," said Jeannette. "Good-bye, good-bye." She was chirping with relief, and new strength gathered in her arms—she lifted the heavy suitcase as if it were packed with feathers. We shook hands in the doorway, my expression solemn while she descended the steps, walked to Herod's car, then disappeared into the Pontiac.

I felt the smile break after Herod drove away. Laughter gripped me, exploded from my diaphragm, shook and shook until my body convulsed. I fell to the floor. I cried weak tears, lost control of my bladder, burned myself with all the salty fluid from my body, and still I laughed.

That girl left so lightly, so certain of her escape, she didn't feel my thumb on the crown of her head. "It isn't good to be a sound sleeper in this house," I told her now, wheezing. I thought of her narrow feet, their difficult size, and the prized penny loafers she tucked so neatly beneath her bed. I remembered how the night before, anticipating this betrayal, I had crept into her room and borrowed those shoes. I pried up the insoles with a screwdriver and sprinkled loose reservation soil inside the loafers. I glued the insoles back in place and returned the shoes.

Jeannette McVay might make it to town, but there would be no bus. She would find herself incapable of leaving the reservation. She would struggle with herself, would probably cry. She would pack and unpack and live out of a suitcase. She would take a lover and every night tell him, "I am leaving." But she would never get very far. I laughed in my kitchen, already hearing the question that would rise to her lips again and again: "Why can't I leave when I long to leave?"

I was ready with the answer she would never hear. "Because I have willed it. And I am not a fairy tale."

I WROTE THE first draft of "Brownsville" during my first visit to New Orleans. It seems like a long time ago now. At the time I was tired of things as they were in my life and was looking for something else. When the voice in "Brownsville" started up I knew I had found what I was looking for. Gordon Lish bought it for *The Quarterly*; it was my first published story.

For me, being at Iowa was the right thing at the right time. I'd been living in New York City for fifteen years, and it was always a struggle to get the time to work on fiction. I did it, but it was like building a tunnel underwater. Your surroundings were always flooding in on you. In Iowa, fiction was what was on the menu, and I gorged myself. It was great to be out in the country, too, after all those years of hard right angles and bus exhaust. When I went out I expected no more than time to write and and read, which I had, but I also learned so much from the writers who taught there—Frank Conroy, Jim McPherson, Margot Livesey, Debbie Eisenberg, and Rob Cohen, in particular. Plus I don't think any other graduate program presented such a stream of writers coming through town, for readings and workshops— Saul Bellow, Robert Stone, John Wideman, Ted Solotaroff—too many to mention, really. I miss it all, even though I'm enjoying myself and working well (I hope) in New Orleans. I miss picking up the week's stories on Friday and reading them over the weekend. I miss being able to go down to the Foxhead, or George's, and know that everybody else, or almost everybody, had spent some part of the day at the desk, too.

TOM PIAZZA

TOM PIAZZA

Brownsville

I'VE BEEN TRYING to get to Brownsville, Texas, for weeks. Right now it's a hundred degrees in New Orleans and the gays are running down Chartres Street with no shirts on, trying to stay young. I'm not running anymore. When I get to Brownsville I'm going to sit down in the middle of the street, and that will be the end of the line.

Ten in the morning and they're playing a Schubert piano trio on the tape and the breeze is blowing in from the street and I'm sobbing into a napkin. "L. G.," she used to say, "you think I'm a mess? You're a mess, too, L. G." That was a consolation to her.

The walls in this café have been stained by patches of seeping water that will never dry, and the plaster has fallen away in swatches that look like silhouettes of countries nobody's ever heard of. Pictures of Napoleon are all over the place: Napoleon blowing it at Waterloo, Napoleon holding his dick on St. Helena, Napoleon sitting in some subtropical café thinking about the past, getting drunk, plotting revenge.

I picture Brownsville as a place under a merciless sun, where one-eyed dogs stand in the middle of dusty, empty streets staring at you and a hot breeze blows inside your shirt and there's nowhere to go. It's always noon, and there are no explanations required. I'm going to Brownsville exactly because I've got no reason to go there. Anybody asks me why Brownsville—there's no fucking answer. That's why I'm going there.

Last night I slept with a woman who had hair down to her ankles and a shotgun in her bathtub and all the mirrors in her room rattled when she laughed. She was good to me; I'll never say a bad word about her. There's always a history, though;

her daughter was sleeping on a blanket in the dining room. It would have been perfect except for that.

The past keeps rising up here; the water table is too high. All around the Quarter groups of tourists float like clumps of sewage. The black carriage drivers pull their fringed carts full of white people from nowhere up to the corner outside and tell them how Jean Lafitte and Andrew Jackson plotted things out, as if the driver knew them personally. The conventioneers sit under the carriage awning, looking around with the crazed, vacant stare of babies, shaded by history, then move on.

The sun is getting higher, the shadows are shortening, the moisture is steaming off the sidewalks. The Schubert, or Debussy, or whatever it is, has turned into an oboe rhapsody, with French horns and bassoons quacking and palmetto bugs crawling across the tile floor, making clicking sounds that I can't hear because the music is too loud. If she didn't love me, why didn't she just tell me so? I asked her why she lied to me and she said she was afraid to tell me the truth. In other words it was my fault. She doesn't even have a friend named Debbie.

I keep trying to look at what's right in front of me. I want to stop trying to mess with the past. The last thing she said to me was, "I have to get this other call." But I'm not going to think about her.

One cloth napkin.

One butter knife.

One fork.

One frosted glass containing partly melted ice and a slice of cucumber. Another frosted glass with similar contents. Where's the waiter? A small menu, marked with coffee along one edge. Breeze from a ceiling fan. Three Germans at the next table. The pictures of Napoleon must make them nervous. A waiter on a stool, leaning back against the wall by the ice chest, hair already pasted to his forehead with sweat.

A white Cadillac just backed into a car parked right outside, making a loud noise and partly caving in the wooden column supporting the balcony above the sidewalk. People are getting up and walking to the door, looking. The driver is black and is wearing a full Indian costume, plumes mushrooming as he gets out to look. He is about seventy years old; a five-year-old boy waits in the front seat. The driver gets back into the Cadillac and drives off.

One coffee mug at the next table. One crumpled pack of Winstons.

Hopeless.

I saw a sign once, on a building outside Albuquerque, that read ALL AMERICAN SELF-STORAGE. If you could just pay a fee somewhere and put yourself in a warehouse, just for a night.

Brownsville.

I picture a little booth at the edge of town, with a bored-looking woman sitting in it. You pay fifty cents and leave everything you can remember in a box with her. You walk down Main Street at high noon, wearing a leather vest, on the balls of your feet. The one-eyed dogs bark and shy away, walking sideways, eyeing you. You walk into the saloon, which is cool and dark, and order a bourbon. You look in the mirror behind the bar and talk to yourself in the second person. Maybe it would be better to stay outside in the sun.

Here is what morning is like in New Orleans. Just before the sky starts getting light, the last freight train inches its way through Ville Platte and the stars have drifted off to sleep. Slowly, the sky exhales its darkness and the trees look black against the deep blue over Gentilly. The houses along Felicity Street, and farther out toward Audubon Park, are cool to the touch, and dew covers the flower beds. A taxi pulls up to a traffic light, looks, goes through. The smell of buttered toast disappears around the corner and televisions are going in the kitchens of the black section. The St. Charles trolley, as unbelievable as it was yesterday, shuttles its first serious load toward the business district. Later, the men will have taken their jackets off and folded them in their laps, staring out the streetcar windows, caught in that dream. Already the first shoeshine boys are out hustling on Bourbon Street, and the first dixieland band is playing for the after-breakfast tourists, and the first conventioneers are climbing into carriages at Jackson Square, and the Vietnamese waitresses at the Cafe du Monde are getting off their all-night shifts, and luggage is lined up on the sidewalk outside the Hyatt.

If there was just some way to stay in it, to be there and see it without starting in. If there was just some way to wipe the slate clean. As soon as I can, I'm going to pay my tab and step outside. I'm closing my accounts and going to Brownsville. I'll leave everything at the edge of town. I'm going to walk in and take it from there.

I BEGAN WRITING "Pipa's Story" during my second year in the workshop, while house-sitting over winter break for faculty poet Marvin Bell. I don't know if I was encouraged by the excitement of living in a real poet's house or by the marvelous darkness of the Iowan December, but something compelled me into a magical narrative that spun along even while I did the historical research necessary for its completion.

"Pipa's Story" seemed to almost write itself, following the lines of the ancient fairy tales that I grew up reading during similar snowy winters in Wisconsin, where I was born and raised. Writing this story raised a question that I am continuing to explore as I read the work of Junichiro Tanizaki, Kazuo Ishiguro, and Chang Ailing: Are there quintessentially "Eastern" and "Western" narratives, and if so, how can they be combined into a narrative that speaks to people of both sides of the world?

LAN SAMANTHA CHANG

MY MOTHER WORKED in charms. She could brew a drink to brighten eyes or warm the womb. She knew of a douche that would likely bring a male child, and a potion to chase away unborn children. Except in emergencies, she gathered her own herbs and animal parts. I was not allowed to help.

The villagers said she had learned her craft from a Miao tribeswoman. A group of Miao—strangers from the west—had stayed in our village for a few months, shortly after my father's death. My mother had mixed potions to forget, wandering in the woods to learn where mushrooms grew. My earliest memories are of watching the smoke from her kettle: white smoke, blue, gray, and black smoke.

When I was a child she seemed all-powerful, and although time passed and I grew tall, she continued to loom over me until I thought I would disappear if I could not get away from her shadow. When I was nineteen, I decided to leave the village. For days I watched my mother stir a mixture over the stove-kettle. Finally I gathered the courage to speak.

"I will go to Shanghai and work for a family there," I said to her back. "I'll send you an envelope filled with money at New Year."

My mother added a bowl of ice that hissed and crackled against whatever was in the pot. Then she turned to look into me. I forced myself to look back into her black eyes.

"Sit down," she told me, gesturing to the wooden chair by the window.

I sat and watched her strain the cooling potion into a wooden bowl. Then she unbraided my hair and combed it, dipping the comb into the potion. It was a warm evening in early spring. The room glowed white in the light of the half-moon.

"What is the potion?" I asked.

"It is a mixture to make you ready for departure."

I lost a breath. My mother tugged and pulled at me, braiding my hair into one thick plait.

"There are herbs here to protect you against bodily harm from illness, loss of energy, and unclear thinking. There are also herbs that will fix your memory, your past. You will never forget me here, no matter how far away you go."

She wrapped the end of my braid around and around with red thread. "You want to leave," she said. "You have my permission if you make one promise to me."

"I promise," I said. Anything if she would let me go.

She looked out the window to make sure that no one was standing by. "Come here," she said. I followed her to a corner of the room, where it was dark.

Three steps from the corner my mother knelt down and began digging into the dirt with a spoon. She unearthed a small box, muddy but with dull tin showing in patches. We walked to the window, where we could see. My mother opened the box, took something out, and handed it to me. It was a lump, smaller than the palm of my hand, wrapped in rough cotton.

"Open it," she said.

I unfolded the cloth. Inside glowed a pinkish stone, a craggy piece of our mountain.

"Lao Fu will take you to Shanghai," my mother said. "Find work with a family named Wen. They have a large household and probably many servants. You're still rough, straight from the country, and they may not want to hire you, but I'm sure you can persuade them. Don't tell them that you're from this village, and don't tell them my name."

"Why not?"

"That doesn't concern you. If you don't like working for the Wens, you may leave and go wherever you like, but before you leave, you must do this one thing for me."

"What is it?"

"Find the heart of the house," she said. "It's a huge, modern place. I am sure. Wen will have become involved with Western business, and he will have a large Western-style house. You'll have to spend some time searching. Let the house seep around you; listen for its rhythm. Before three months are up, find the center and hide this stone there."

"What are you talking about?" I asked rudely. "I never learned anything about houses. You never told me. How would I know?"

My mother didn't scold me but squatted on the floor and looked into the beam of pale moonlight.

"Tell me," she said, "where the heart of our own house is."

I thought for a minute. Then I pointed to the middle of the floor.

"No," she said. "The physical center is not what I mean."

I sighed. Our house—a hut, really—was quite small, and as far as I could tell had no other center. We had a table, our beds, two old chairs. The corner shelf held storybooks: *Dream of the Red Chamber* and *Outlaws of the Marsh,* that my mother had been teaching me to read for years. Our house had no male presence, because my father had died before I was born. My mother earned our living. I thought about my mother, her long gray braid hanging down her back, hunched before the stove-kettle full of glowing coals.

"The fire," I said. "The stove is the heart of our house."

My mother nodded. "Good," she said.

At her praise I felt cold and heavy. "What is this about?"

She shook her head. "It's better if you don't know," she said. "It was before you were born. Your deed will be the end of it." She stood up and walked to the window again. "It's something that happened long ago."

I LEFT with the stone sewn into my pocket. I rode in a cart with Lao Fu, my mother's old friend, who was bringing medicine roots to sell around the city. These roots were much like ginseng, and grew wild on our mountain. I watched Lao Fu's thick, arthritic hands on the reins, carelessly guiding his spotted horse. Now and then he flicked a tattered whip. In those days it took weeks to reach Shanghai. Lao Fu didn't usually make such long trips. He was taking me as a favor to my mother, who often rubbed an ointment into his knuckles. We didn't speak for hours, by which time the most familiar mountains had grown pale blue in the distance and we were surrounded by shapes I had seen before only from far away. Then Lao Fu turned an eye to me.

"You're a *nenggan* girl, Pipa," he said in his rusty voice. "A capable, dutiful girl. Traveling hundreds of miles in order to help your mother."

He smiled, exposing four brown teeth. I glared at the stains on his gray beard and I wished that someone else were driving me, someone I had never met. Even in this remote region the lines of the surrounding hills seemed to shape my mother's face. The stone in my pocket, my secret, weighed so heavily I could hardly sit upright. I wanted to rip it out of my smock and fling it into the next river. She would never know.

But when we reached Shanghai I felt so terrified by my first view of the great port that I held onto the stone like a talisman. I sat close to Lao Fu, dreading our approach to the Wen house, where he would leave me. The city seemed to whirl past. The wide streets were cluttered with travelers—in carts like ours, but also in rickshaws and automobiles. I had never seen either before, nor had I seen the kind of people, foreigners, who rode in them.

In those days foreigners were everywhere: stiff soldiers in uniforms from England and America, businessmen from Russia, hurrying in and out of large, square Western buildings. I sat paralyzed, blocking my ears against the roaring, honking automobiles. I turned away from the rickshawmen, their faces drawn, their feet slap-slapping against the pavement. We stopped at an intersection. I saw a man with yellow eyes lurch toward our cart. Lao Fu twitched his whip in that direction. "Opium," he said. "Don't look."

On another corner I spotted a powerfully built Chinese man dressed in Western clothes, his short, glossy hair oiled back from his forehead. He was talking to three foreigners, standing as straight as any of them. For a moment he seemed to stare at our cart, at Lao Fu adjusting a strap on the harness. Then he looked away.

As we went on the shops and businesses gave way to houses: tall brick boxes set back from the road, with no round doorways or Chinese courtyards. Shining black automobiles veered around us. One of them nearly struck the horse. I turned to Lao Fu in alarm, but he merely shook his head and guided our cart closer to the side of the road.

"Lao Fu, where are we?"

"Close."

After one more street he turned right. The horse clip-clopped around a long bend, and suddenly we were twenty yards from an entrance to an immense house built of brick and wood. I saw a woman watching us from a window. Lao Fu stopped the cart.

"Here you are, Pipa. That door is the servants' entrance." I stared at my lap. "*Xialai.* Get down. I'll take your bundle."

I climbed from the cart, my legs stiff, clutching the stone in my pocket. Lao Fu came around the back of the cart holding my blue cotton bundle.

"Go in," he said. I wrinkled my mouth to hold back tears. "You will be all right," he said. "I'll be in the surrounding towns for a few months. I'll come visit you."

We faced each other and bobbed our heads. Lao Fu climbed back onto his cart and picked up the reins. He nodded again before turning away.

I stood watching his cart go back around the bend. I realized that I had said good-bye to the last of the village, and to my mother. After years of avoiding her sight, I had gone to a place where she could not see me. Suddenly I was filled with an emotion so terrible that I turned and vomited at the side of the road.

A VERY PRETTY GIRL stood at the servants' door, waiting. She wore black pants and a clean white blouse. From the way her hair was done, I guessed that she had been the one looking out the window.

"Are you all right?" she asked in a low, pleasant voice. Close up, I stood a head taller than she.

"Yes," I said. I clutched my bundle. "I want to work here."

Her glance darted over my rough cotton clothes. "Come in," she said. "Clean up inside. You should bathe, and change. Then I'll introduce you to the house-keeper."

I walked into the great house and smelled the warm, rich odor of food and spices. We stood in a square room lined with wood. A door to my right opened into a hallway. I could see at the end a room where a number of people were chopping vegetables.

"Come here quickly," whispered the girl, darting toward another doorway. She led me to a very white, shining room with a long white basin on four feet. I had never seen a bathtub before, and I stopped to stare. The girl, who said her name was Meilan, turned two silver fixtures at one end of the tub, and steaming water poured out of a pipe. She held a huge towel in front of me so that I wouldn't be embarrassed while she stayed in the room.

I took off my dirty traveling clothes and stepped into the tub. The warm water rushed around my body, erasing the village dirt. I unbraided my hair, and my mother's spells were washed away in a swirl of steam. I felt myself changing, like a tadpole, and I looked at my hands and limbs as if they were new.

Behind her towel Meilan chattered away.

"Of course they'll hire you; the family just moved into this new residence, and they need servants. They hired me only three months ago. I'll have you fixed up so that no one will think twice."

"Why did you come to work here?" I asked.

"I'm from Beijing. My mother died giving birth to me, and my father was in the Kuomindang Army. He died last year in the fighting. I am an orphan. I had to find work. This is a good place. The master is rich and good-looking. Supervision is not very strict."

After a minute I asked, "Fighting? What fighting?"

"You really are from far away! There's been terrible fighting, not in Shanghai, but maybe soon!" Her voice dropped, and I had to lean close to the towel in order to hear.

"I don't know anything about these events," I said. "Our village is so remote, even the Japanese ignored it."

When I was finished, she found a pair of black trousers and a white shirt that were both a little too small for me. "We'll get some others after you've started," she said. "I'll steal them from the closet."

"Thank you for helping me," I said.

Meilan smiled. "This is nothing," she answered. "There is plenty here; why not share it? And besides, you look like a nice person." She picked up my old blue cotton smock. "Do you want this saved?"

I thought of the stone sewn into the pocket. "No," I said.

WEN LIVED ON one of the most stylish new streets in Shanghai. For weeks I marveled at his house; I had never even dreamed of anything like it. The rooms were broad and tall, with glossy, patterned wooden floors built by English carpenters and covered with flowered Persian carpets. English curtains draped down by long windows, deep red velvet curtains with gold-colored tasseled cords. Everything in that house was new, from the mysterious electric lights to the great wooden tubs in the kitchen, filled with live clams in salt water in case one of the family should have a craving for them.

The housekeeper, Lu Taitai, was an immense older woman whose face lay as still as a mud bog. When she was very angry, she would slowly lift one fat finger into the air. I lived in terror of her. I was the newest of thirty servants, so unskilled that at first I worked in the servants' quarters, which, as Meilan pointed out, had to be kept clean along with the rest of the house. Meilan's swift hands and pretty face had earned her a job on the third floor, where the family lived. I imagined that the upstairs must be a magical place.

"Can you show me the upper floors?" I asked her once, as we ate dinner at one end of the long servants' table.

She looked right and left before answering. "We have to watch out for Lu Taitai," she said. "And it's harder to get away with things upstairs. The women have sharp eyes. If I have a chance, I'll take you."

"What women?" I asked. "The servant women?"

Meilan put down her chopsticks. "Pipa," she said, "the master has four wives." She smiled. "Stop blushing, and keep eating."

I looked at the table. We ate what Wen and his family left. The night before, they had feasted on duck done ten ways, and there was a pile of crackling duck skins, which I had discovered I particularly liked. There were also jelled duck eggs, pigeon eggs in sauce, shrimps with chicken and peas, chicken and scallops with ginger, scallops in sauce, salted prawns, spicy prawns, late oysters, early asparagus, several other vegetable dishes, and a great fish that lay on its side, barely touched. I thought that if a man was wealthy enough to serve four dishes for each member of the family, then perhaps four wives was to be expected.

A FEW WEEKS later Lu Taitai was suddenly called away to her home province.

"Good," Meilan said. By flirting with the second housekeeper, she arranged for me to bring tea to the master upstairs in his library, during a meeting with some of his Western associates.

"If it weren't for you, I would be lost," I said when I thanked her. "I've been here for a month and I've never seen him."

"Well," she said, "he's very good-looking. I can see why the women fall for him: rich, handsome, and powerful! But even so, I don't think I'd want to be the object of his attention. I have a feeling he's not very kind—that he simply doesn't take kindness, or certain human feelings, into account. Of course, he seldom looks at people like you and me. We can only watch. But if that's what you want, my dear friend Pipa, you shall have it." And she made me practice several times with the bamboo tea tray.

On the day of the meeting, we waited to hear the men's heavy shoes start up the staircase. "Go up now," Meilan said. She fixed some of the coarse hair that had escaped from my pinned-up braid. The cook's assistant stared with grim disapproval while I balanced the tray.

For the first time I climbed the polished staircase.

The second floor was quiet. The carpet melted under my feet. Meilan had instructed me: "Turn left at the top, go down two doors, and you've reached the library." The heavy, unfamiliar tray hindered my progress; delicate teacups slid on their bits of lace. I reached the library door, braced the tray as securely as possible against my hip, and knocked.

"Come in," said a resonant male voice.

I looked at the big china knob. How could I possibly turn it? I moved to brace my feet and felt the smooth wood tray slide against my blouse.

Suddenly the door opened and a man stood over me, holding a book in one hand. For a moment I forgot my manners and stared. I had seen him before: the arrogant man whom I had noticed while riding with Lao Fu on my first day in Shanghai. Now he stood and looked at my face, my blouse, my hands holding the tray. I felt as if a piece of burning ash had been put down my back. I gasped; the tray tilted in my hands. The house with its soft rugs fought against me, making me lose my balance. Hot tea spilled on the master's arm and over the book he carried.

"*Duibuqi*," I gasped, hastily putting down the ruined tray. I grabbed an embroidered linen napkin and reached to dry his arm.

"I'm fine," he said. "Dry this." He handed me the book, and even in my horror it occurred to me that this man must have strength not to so much as flinch at the boiling water. I waited for him to scold me, or even strike me, but he did not move.

"*Duibuqi*," I repeated, and indeed at that moment I did not think I could ever look him in the face again. I wiped the pages. "*Xianggang Falu*," I read aloud. Why was he studying Hong Kong laws?

"You can read," he said.

"My mother taught me," I blurted out.

"Then you'll still be of some use to us," he said. "It's obvious you're not a good maid. Come in."

I tiptoed into the room. Opposite me stood three crowded bookshelves. The foreigners sat at the end, before the fireplace.

"You're tall," said Wen. "You can read. Find the books I want and bring them over. Find me the volume about transportation on the Yangtze and the Grand Canal."

I turned to the shelves, my hands sweating. Wen went back to the fireplace.

"If you want factual proof, I'll give it to you," I heard him say to the foreigners. "But I guarantee, they'll wait. They've won too many battles too quickly. They need to regroup. It will be months before they reach Shanghai, maybe a year. You needn't worry."

Someone coughed. "Oh, certainly, certainly." This man spoke Chinese with difficulty. "It's just that we have received some—reports from further north. Of course," he continued, searching for the words, "we're not worried about them. The Kuomindang troops have regrouped themselves to defend our side of the Yangtze. . . . We are just—making sure that we understand the situation."

"Those who flee are fools," Wen said. "I tell you, it's not time to leave yet. They would never touch a foreigner. Remember, the longer you stay, the more you'll make."

"And you as well," said one of the men.

"You can believe me." Wen's voice grew hard. "I know what Mao will do. I'm one of them. I was born a peasant, you know."

In the bottom right corner of the shelf I spotted a blue volume on waterways, which I pulled and brought to Wen. I watched as he studied the book, the firelight flickering on his face, and I could sense his force, his intelligence and cunning.

"Ha!" he said, pointing to a line of characters. "You see, I was correct." He showed the book to one of the Western gentlemen, who squinted, nervously stroking his blond beard.

"What does it say, Stanton?" one of them asked.

"Ah, yes! Mr. Wen is correct," Stanton said. I wondered if he could read characters well enough to know what he was talking about.

"Now," Wen said, "about those collections. I'll have the first half to you by Monday next week." He turned to me. "You can go now," he said. "I'll call you the next time there is a meeting."

As I left the library, I saw the tea tray sitting in the hallway. I bent down to pick it up.

"What are you doing?" asked a musical, imperious voice.

I straightened. I had not heard her walk across the carpet. She was tiny, beautiful, with large eyes and a curved lower lip like an orange slice. She wore a qipao of shimmering sea-green silk.

"I came with the tea," I tried to explain. "I was helping in the library."

"Helping," she said. Her eyes flickered up and down my body.

"Getting books."

Her lower lip swelled with dissatisfaction. She walked past me to the library door. "Are they still inside?"

I nodded.

She lifted her chin. "Hmph!" she said. "Get back downstairs."

I picked up the tray and hurried away, cold tea splashing on the carpet.

Downstairs, Meilan waited for me.

"I was worried!" she cried. But when I explained what had happened, she smiled and patted my arm. "Now you've earned your job in the house. No more rag-pushing for you!" Her eyes sparkled.

"YOUR MOTHER WILL want to know how you are doing," Lao Fu said.

I didn't answer. Lao Fu guided his horse past two arguing street peddlers. He had returned to the city and come by to take me on a ride. I felt ashamed that the others would see me with him, with his patched clothes and shabby cart. But it was a beautiful day in May. The fresh warm air reminded me how seldom I had a chance to go outside, now that I was working at the Wen house.

"Before we left, she asked me to check on you," Lao Fu said, "and to ask you if you kept your promise."

"Why is everything so crowded?" I asked, changing the subject. Even on the quieter streets we could not drive in a straight line.

"In the past few months more and more people north of us have fled the Red Army, seeking safety."

"Where is the Army now?"

"Since the end of the year it has been waiting north of the Yangtze River."

I remembered the conversation in the library. "What will happen when it moves south again?"

Lao Fu looked at me, and I saw his cloudy cataracts. "Things will change."

"How will they change?"

"Ah," he said. "Who knows? These days I demand only coppers in payment. The Kuomindang is crumbling. Why won't you answer your mother's question?"

"I don't have time to think about her anymore," I said.

Lao Fu ignored me. "Look over there," he said. "A decent noodle house, and not too busy. Let's have lunch."

After we had taken care of the cart and horse, we stood for a minute outside the noodle shop, watching the people on the street. A thin man carrying a large wicker basket shuffled close to us. "*Zhuan qian, zhuan qian,*" he repeated under his breath. Lao Fu nodded and handed him a few coppers. The man opened his basket and counted out sixteen bundles of paper money. They nodded at each other, and we entered the dark, noisy noodle shop.

"You see?" Lao Fu said as we sat down at a corner table. "By the time we leave, those coppers will be worth sixteen and a half bundles of paper money."

I felt as if he were saying these things to make a point against me. Stubbornly I folded my hands in my lap.

"What will happen when the Communist Army reaches this city?" Lao Fu lit his long pipe. "They'll go after people like your master, rich people who flourished under the Kuomindang by working with foreign capitalists. There's a word for your master, Pipa. He's an *ermaozi,* a comprador."

"He's a peasant," I said. "He's a former peasant who used his wits to make a fortune for himself, to move away from his village."

"Ha," Lao Fu said. He fitted his pipe between his four stubby teeth. "You're a young girl, Pipa. You're young, and the world is a strange place."

I scowled and took a sip of the tea that a greasy-haired, smudge-faced woman had flung on the table.

"What difference do his origins make to you?" I asked. "You're here with a message from my mother. You don't know Master Wen or anything about him."

"But I do know him," Lao Fu said. "I used to know him well."

I stared at my wavering saucer of tea.

"When he was a young man in the village, we used to call him Xiao Niu, Little Bull. He was once a friend of your father's."

There was a terrible pounding in my ears. Lao Fu's rusty voice sounded like a shout. I waited for him to stop, but he continued. "Some people forget their histories, but they don't realize that others remember," he said. "Not everyone forgets the wrongs they've suffered."

He raised the saucer to his mouth. His loud slurp brought me back to my senses.

"What do you mean?" I forced out the words.

"Ah. Well, this is an old story. Something that happened before you were born. It is, shall I say, a village secret."

"There aren't any secrets in the village."

"Well, it's possible. There were only four of us who knew. One died, one has forgotten, and two of us have chosen not to tell. That is, until now."

At that moment the woman brought us two broad, steaming bowls of noodle soup. Lao Fu nodded. "Good. Eat."

I took a spoonful of soup, waiting. The food and even the serving utensils were so much coarser than what I had grown used to.

Lao Fu began. "Your father and mother were the two village orphans. No one arranged their marriage. When they wed, it was a love match."

He took a mouthful of noodles and went on. My father, he said, was gentle and kind. He had spent years learning to read in his spare time; he sat and daydreamed over his meals. My mother was clever, forceful. She never rested. And she had an astounding talent that everyone in the village knew about. If an object was lost, my mother could almost always find it. On the mountains she understood the natural order and discovered more medicine roots than anyone else. It was she who suggested that she and my father supplement their income by collecting medicine roots. Xiao Niu and Lao Fu agreed to help them.

"There was one problem," Lao Fu said. "Perhaps because she was so sure of herself, your mother underestimated Xiao Niu. He was a ruthless, ambitious boy who wanted to be the best at everything. And the more he saw of your mother, the more he wanted her as well. He desired her. He wanted to stop her constant thinking and doing; he wanted her to think and do only for him.

"Your mother was not beautiful, but she had so much vitality that she was impossible to ignore. She knew that Xiao Niu wanted her, but she thought she could control him. This goaded Xiao Niu until he couldn't bear it."

One cloudy fall day the four of them had gone to dig for medicine roots. For part of the day they worked together. All morning Xiao Niu watched my mother out of the corner of his eye. After lunch my mother suggested that they split up and search on different parts of the mountain. And Xiao Niu suggested he and my father go off together.

That afternoon the fog grew so thick that my mother and Lao Fu, working close together, could hardly see each other. It was very quiet. The path became almost impossible to find; trees and stones looked like people and animals. If it hadn't been for my mother, Lao Fu said, they might not have found the pathway down the mountain, back to the village.

When they reached the village, my mother waited for Xiao Niu and my father to return. She built a fire, cooked the evening meal. But the other two did not come back. She began to worry. Finally, after the gray fog had turned dark, Xiao Niu stopped by our hut.

"Where's Dangbei?" he asked.

"What do you mean?" my mother said. "I thought he was with you."

"He left early," Xiao Niu told her. "He decided to go back to the village."

All that night my mother waited, but my father did not come home.

The next day my mother went out on the mountain, in the fog, searching for him. She looked and looked, but she could not find him. Finally some men from the village had to force her to stay inside—she was pregnant, after all. Then winter set in.

"All winter, your mother mourned," Lao Fu said. "She would only speak to me and Xiao Niu. Xiao Niu asked her to marry him, but she refused to discuss anything until your father's body was discovered. That spring, right before you were born, the villagers found him at the bottom of a ravine, lying on a bed of pinkish stones. After the birth your mother insisted on going up on the mountain to look upon the spot where they had found his body.

"Now here is the secret," Lao Fu said. "Your mother told only me. After seeing the site where your father's body was discovered, she felt certain that he had not gotten there on his own. If the two of them had gone to dig in the place Xiao Niu had described, your father would not have died where his body was found."

"How did she know?" I asked. "On foggy days in our mountains, a person could wander anywhere."

"I asked her. 'I know Dangbei,' she said. 'He would never have gotten lost there,' she said. And I believed her. She knew the mountains. I felt foolish and angry. So much had been going on right under my nose, and I had not understood."

He looked at me. I ignored him, studying my soup. "I was younger those days, and I hated being wrong about things," he said.

"That summer Xiao Niu again asked her to marry him. She accused him of killing Dangbei, and Xiao Niu left the village. He disappeared for years, and when we heard about him next, he had taken the name of Wen."

After this my mother had begun to brood before the stove, to speak to Miao travelers and learn their arts. She was unable to forget what had been lost.

"Now," Lao Fu said when the story was finished and our bowls were empty, "when I return to the village, your mother will ask me if you have kept your promise to her."

I looked at him. He leaned toward me; a noodle hung from his beard. I felt my eyes grow hot with confusion and anger. Despite my own intentions, my loyalties had changed. He had cast her shadow over me again, and I could not forgive him.

"Leave me alone!" I said. "You tell my mother that I will not keep my promise to her. None of this has anything to do with me. I'm far away, and she can't reach me. She can't make me do what I don't want to do. Besides, it's impossible now."

Lao Fu's wrinkled lids lowered. He nodded. "You do what you must do. I'll be in the city another week—"

"Don't visit me anymore," I said.

BACK AT WEN'S house the servants were getting ready for an important business dinner. I looked for Meilan. I wanted to talk to her, but the second housekeeper gave me a pile of rags and some scented oil, and put me to work on the yards of rich wood paneling in the sitting room and dining room.

As I wiped and polished, certain thoughts traced themselves over and over in my mind. The scented oil filled my nostrils, reminding me of my mother's potions. I remembered her sorting out bundles of herbs on our wooden table, her frown deepening in the firelight. She had loved my father, whom I had never met. For years I had secretly believed that the purpose of her herbs, her potions, and her utterances, was not to help the others but to keep me near her. But now it seemed that even my flight from her fit into some incomprehensible design. I began to see that Lao Fu was right. I was young; the world was a mystery.

I finished the woodwork and walked into the hall. And for the first time I noticed something odd about Wen's house. I saw the great house, with its women and servants, as a testimony to the unquenchable desire of its master, desire that destroyed all obstacles and then discarded them. The house seemed raw and unexplained, as if it were hiding its origin. The rooms were big and empty: too clean, too new, too cold. I looked down the hall at the dozen servants cleaning and sweeping as if there were more than dirt to get rid of.

As I entered the dining room, one of the rags dropped out of my hands and fell to the wooden floor with a small thud. I knelt down to pick it up, but then I stopped, crouching, and stared at the rough blue cotton fabric.

Snatching the rag, I sprang up and ran toward the staircase. I had to find Meilan, my friend, and tell her what had happened. I needed to hear what she would say. I had to see her. I pounded up the stairs, past the second floor, and up to the family quarters.

The upstairs was lit by the fading light from a few windows. I had never been up so high before, but I remembered the stories from the servants' table: the four wives each in a suite of rooms, and at one end the master's room, near a separate staircase to the outside door, so he could get away. The doors were closed. Sweet scents of soap and perfume filled the air. They must all be getting ready for dinner. I would never find Meilan.

I heard a doorknob turn, then another door open and shut. I saw two doors at the north end, and one was ajar. I hurried toward it and ran straight into Meilan coming out. When I saw her face, I forgot to think for a moment.

"What's wrong?" I cried.

Meilan buried her face in her hands. "Oh!" she sobbed. "It's terrible—I have to get away from here! I can't work here anymore."

"What happened?" I asked. She clutched herself around the waist and ran down the hall. I followed her down the two flights of stairs, rushing past a few surprised-looking servants. "Meilan," I begged, "let me help you!"

She ran into the room we shared with some other servants.

"Please let me help you," I said. "You're always so kind to me."

"Do you have a clean shirt?" she whimpered, her arms still crossed. "Mine are in the wash."

"It'll be too big," I said. But I handed her one. She reached for it, and I saw the rip in the one that she had on. She took off her torn shirt. I saw four blue bruises, in the shape of fingerprints, on her arm. More bruises were on her chest.

Then I knew what I had to do. I found a pair of scissors and cut the stone from the rag I still held in my hand. I went back up the stairs, past the second floor and the library, up to the third floor. The door to the master's room was still ajar. The shades were closed, but I made out a huge square shape in the semi-darkness. I walked to the great canopied bed, and I hid the stone inside it.

When I came back downstairs, Meilan and her things were gone.

LATE THAT NIGHT I was asked to work in the library. My eyes smarting with weariness, I searched the tall bookcases in the flickering light from the fireplace.

"You're making a mistake," I heard him say. "They won't harm you or your business. You'd be better off staying in China and keeping what you have. There's no telling what will happen if you run off and leave everything."

The men by the fire said nothing.

"They would never touch you," he said.

After a minute, one of the foreigners spoke. "What will happen to you, Wen? Where are you burying your money? How much of it have you sent abroad?"

"I told you," Wen said. "How could they betray one of their own kind? They won't get me."

Finally I found the book he wanted, and he dismissed me for the evening. The room was utterly silent as I left.

I went downstairs, put on my nightclothes, and lay in bed.

When I shut my eyes, I found that I had grown as light as a straw. I floated high on the wind over Wen's great house and back to where I had come from. I soared over the rich green Yangtze Delta, with its fishermen and rice paddies, following the broad river as it narrowed into rushing rapids, and then continuing westward toward the mountains of my village. Evening fell; the stars wheeled over my head. When I landed, the air smelled of thawed earth and sweet plum blossoms. I walked quietly down the dark road, past the well, and to the corner where my mother's hut stood, slightly sagging.

I looked through the window. Her face was deeply grooved, bloodless with concentration. She had unbraided her long gray hair. She sat cross-legged in the firelight in front of a group of small paper figures. Her voice rattled into the air, making an incantation. She swayed, muttering low deep sounds under her breath, an endless curse word. I looked at the firepot; coals glowed through the slits in its iron sides. I watched through the window until my vision faded into smoke.

Sometime after midnight I was awakened by the sound of gunfire. It was May 12, and the Communist Army had reached the outskirts of Shanghai.

CONSIDERING THE EVENTS that have since taken place in China and the world, my own story is small and not very interesting. But it is mine. Like ginseng roots, our buried pasts have different shapes. I never saw my mother again. After Lao Fu rescued me from Wen's house, I fled to Taiwan. A year later I met up with a man from our village who told me what had happened there: the Communists had reached the village a few months after the fall of Shanghai, and they had executed my mother as a witch.

In Taiwan, I worked at a library. Now I shelve books in the Chinese collection at an American university. I have a husband and two children who both attended college. We own our own small house. I don't keep the house too clean, and I tried not to frighten my daughters the way my mother frightened me. But there are things I can't forget, and things my family knows they should never do. They do not light fires in the fireplace, not even if I won't be home for hours. For the smell of smoke, the faintest trace, reminds me of my mother.

I see her brooding over her past and I remember that it's not wise to look back too long and deep at what has gone. It is not wise to think of Shanghai, the broad houses now shabby and sectioned off for twenty families. Or to dwell too long on my friend Meilan and her generosity. Or to remember the fire that the Communists started when they reached our section of the city.

The flames leaped through the house, feeding themselves along the expensive wood paneling, ruffling the curtains, exploding the leaded-glass windows. I stood outside with the other servants and watched the sparks and ashes fly up into the night. We looked on as four soldiers led our master out onto the lawn. The soldiers wore red stars on their caps. They struck the back of his knees to make him kneel to them. He knelt with his head high and with anger burning in his face. One of them raised a long machete, twirling the knife so the blunt side came down on the back of his neck to make him fall forward. There was a moment when we were silent; only flames moved. Then the soldier raised his arm again, and the sharp blade sliced all our lives in two.

I WAS JUST A YOUNGSTER in the Workshop when I wrote this story, and while I can't remember anything particularly interesting about how or why I wrote it, maybe I can say something about how it was received by those who first read it. It was the second story I submitted for my first Workshop class, which was captained by the esteemed director Frank Conroy. Frank had dismissed my first offering as the worst kind of amateurish yearnings, so I wasn't hopeful about the reception "Buckeye" would get.

For the first fifteen minutes of class, Frank allowed my fellow writers to do what comes natural in a Workshop class—they tore the story to bits. Frank fidgeted, shook his head sadly, and finally, when he could take no more, held up his hands to halt the proceedings and announced that "Buckeye the Elder" was a perfect story, there was not a flaw or blemish in it, not even a comma out of place, and no amount of second-guessing and nit-picking would change that. Send this story off right away, he urged me, and it will certainly be published.

I will never forget the looks of utter hatred my fellow writers gave me that day. While I can't agree with Frank that "Buckeye" is in any way a perfect story, it *was* published by the first magazine I sent it to. *Playboy* thought it was good enough to win first place in their college fiction competition. My wildest dreams had come true: my story would be published not only in a big, fancy magazine, but in a big, fancy magazine full of beautiful women in various stages of undress. What could be more perfect?

BRADY UDALL

THINGS I LEARNED ABOUT Buckeye a few minutes before he broke my collarbone: he is twenty-five years old, in love with my older sister, a native of Wisconsin and therefore a Badger. "Not really a Buckeye at all," he explained, sitting in my father's recliner and paging through a book about UFOs and other unsolved mysteries. "But I keep the name for respect of the man who gave it to me, my father and the most loyal alumnus Ohio State ever produced."

Buckeye had stopped by earlier this afternoon to visit my sister, Simone, whom he had been seeing over the past week or so. Though Simone had yammered all about him over the dinner table, it was the first time I'd actually met him. When he arrived, Simone wasn't back from her class at the beauty college and I was the only one in the house. Buckeye came inside for a few minutes and talked to me like I was someone he'd known since childhood. He showed me old black-and-white photos of his parents, a gold tooth he found on the floor of a bar in Detroit, a ticket stub autographed by Marty Robbins. Among other things, we talked about his passion for rugby and he invited me out to the front yard for a few lessons on rules and technique. Everything went fine until tackling came up. He positioned himself in front of me and instructed me to try to get around him and he would demonstrate the proper way to wrap up the ball player and drag him down. I did what I was told and ended up with two hundred-plus pounds worth of Buckeye driving my shoulder into the hard dirt. We both heard the snap, clear as you please.

"Was that you?" Buckeye said, already picking me up and setting me on my feet. My left shoulder sagged and I couldn't move my arm but there wasn't an alarming amount of pain. Buckeye helped me to the porch and brought out the phone so I could call my mother, who is on her way over right now to pick me up and take me to the hospital.

I'm sitting in one of the porch rocking chairs and Buckeye is standing next to me, nervously shifting his feet. He is the picture of guilt and worry; he puts his face in his hands, paces up and down the steps, comes back over to inspect my shoulder for the dozenth time. There is a considerable lump where the fractured bone is pushing up against the skin.

A grim-faced Buckeye says, "Snapped in two, not a doubt in this world."

He puts his face right into mine as if he's trying to see something behind my eyes. "You aren't in shock are you?" he says. "You don't want an ambulance?"

"I'm okay," I say. Other than being a little light-headed, I feel pretty good. There is something gratifying about having a serious injury and no serious pain to go with it. More than anything, I'm worried about Buckeye, who is acting like he's just committed murder. He's asked me twice now if I wouldn't just let him swing me over his shoulders and run me over to the hospital himself.

"Where is my self-control?" he questions the rain gutter. "Why can't I get a hold of my situations?" He turns to me and says, "There's no excuses, none, but I'm used to tackling guys three times your size, God forgive me. I didn't think you'd go down that easy."

Buckeye has a point. I am almost as tall as he is but am at least sixty pounds lighter. All I really feel right now is embarrassment for going down so easy. I tell him that it was nobody's fault, that my parents are generally reasonable people, and that my sister will probably like him all that much more.

Buckeye doesn't look at all comforted. He keeps up his pacing. He thinks aloud with his chin in his chest, mumbling into the collar of his shirt as if there is someone down there listening. He rubs his head with his big knobby hands and gives himself a good tongue-lashing. There is an ungainly energy to the way he moves. He is thick in some places, thin in others and has joints like those on a backhoe. He's barrel-chested, has elongated piano player's fingers and is missing a good portion of his left ear which was ground off by the cleat of a stampeding Polynesian at the Midwest Rugby Invitationals. I can't explain this, but I'm feeling quite pleased that Buckeye has broken my shoulder.

When my mother pulls up in her new Lincoln, Buckeye picks up me and the chair I'm in. With long, smooth strides he delivers me to the car, all the time saying some sort of prayer, asking the Lord to bless me, heal me, and help me forgive.

ONE OF THE MORE IMPORTANT THINGS that Buckeye didn't tell me about himself that first day was that he is a newly baptized Mormon. I've found out this is the only reason my parents ever let him within rock-throwing distance of my sister. As far as my parents are concerned, solid Baptists that they are, either you're with Jesus or you're against him. I guess they figured that Buckeye, as close as he might be to the dividing line, is on the right side.

In the week that has passed since the accident, Buckeye has turned our house into a carnival. The night we came home from the hospital, me straight-backed and awkward in my brace and Buckeye still asking forgiveness every once in awhile, we had a celebration—in honor of who or what I still can't be sure. We ordered pizza and my folks, who almost never drink, made banana daiquiris while Simone held hands with Buckeye and sipped ginger ale. Later, my daiquiri-inspired father, once a 163-pound district champion in high school, coaxed Buckeye into a wrestling match in the front room. While my sister squealed and my mother screeched about hospital bills and further injury, Buckeye wore a big easy grin and let my father pin him solidly on our mint-green carpet.

I suppose there were two things going on: we were officially sanctioning Buckeye's relationship with Simone and at the same time commemorating my fractured clavicle, the first manly injury I've ever suffered. Despite and possibly because of the aspirations of my sports-mad father, I am the type of son who gets straight A's and likes to sit in his room and make models of spaceships. My father dreamed I would play for the Celtics one day. Right now, having just finished my sophomore year in high school, my only aspiration is to write a best-selling fantasy novel.

My sister goes to beauty school, which is a huge disappointment to my pediatrician mother. Simone can't bear to tell people that my father distills sewer water for a living. Even though I love them, I sincerely believe my parents to be narrowminded religious fanatics and as for Simone, I think beauty school might be an intellectual stretch. As far as I can tell, our family is nothing more than a bunch of people living in the same house who are disappointed in each other.

But we all love Buckeye. He's the only thing we agree on. The fact that Simone and my parents would go for someone like him is surprising when you consider the coarse look he has about him, the kind of look you see on people in bus stations and in the backs of fruit trucks. Maybe it's his fine set of teeth that salvages him from looking like an out-and-out redneck.

Tonight Buckeye is taking me on a drive. Since we first met, Buckeye has spent more time with me than he has with Simone. My parents think this is a good idea; I don't have many friends and they think he will have a positive effect on their agnostic, asocial son. We are in his rust-cratered vehicle that might have been an Oldsmobile at one time. Buckeye has just finished a day's work as a pantyhose salesman and smells like the perfume of the women he talks to on porches and doorsteps. He sells revolutionary no-run stockings that carry a lifetime guarantee. He's got stacks of them in the backseat. At eighteen dollars a pair, he assures these women, they are certainly a bargain. He is happy and loose and driving all over the road. He has just brought me up to date on his teenage years, his father's death, the thirteen states he's lived in and the twenty-two jobs he's held since then.

"Got it all up here," he says, tapping his forehead. "Don't let a day slide by without detailed documentation." Over the past few days I've noticed Buckeye has a way of speaking that makes people pause. One minute he sounds like a West Texas oil grunt, the next like a semi-educated Midwesterner. Buckeye is a constant surprise.

"Why move around so much?" I wonder. "And why come to Texas?"

He says, "I just move, no reason that I can think of. For one thing, I'm here looking for my older brother Bud. He loves the Cowboys and fine women. He could very well be in the vicinity."

"How'd your father die?" I say.

"His heart attacked him. Then his liver committed suicide and the rest of his organs just gave up after that. Too much drinking. That's when I left Wisconsin for good."

We are passing smelters and gas stations and trailers that sit back off the road. This is a part of Tyler I've never seen before. He pulls the old car into the parking lot of a huge wooden structure with a sign that says "The Ranch" in big matchstick letters. The sun is just going down but the place is lit up like Las Vegas. There is a fleet of dirty pickups overrunning the parking lot.

We find a space in the back and Buckeye leads me through a loading dock and into the kitchen where a trio of Hispanic ladies is doing dishes. He stops and chatters at them in a mixture of bad Spanish and hand gestures. "Come on," he says to me. "I'm going to show you the man I once was."

We go out into the main part which is as big as a ballroom. There are two round bars out in the middle of it and a few raised platforms where some half-dressed women are dancing. Chairs and tables are scattered all along the edges. The music is so loud I can feel it bouncing off my chest. Buckeye nods and wags his finger and smiles at everybody we pass and they respond like old friends. Buckeye, who's been in Tyler less than a month, does this everywhere we go and if you didn't know any better you'd think he was acquainted with every citizen in town.

We find an empty table against the wall right next to one of the dancers. She has on lacy black panties and a cutoff T-shirt that is barely sufficient to hold in all of her equipment. Buckeye politely says hello, but she doesn't even look our way.

This is the first bar I've ever been in and I like the feel of it. Buckeye orders Cokes and buffalo wings for us both and surveys the place, once in awhile raising a hand to acknowledge someone he sees. Even though I've lived in Texas since I was born, I've never seen so many oversized belt buckles in one place.

"This is the first time I've been back here since my baptism," he says. "I used to spend most of my nonworking hours in this barn."

While he has told me about a lot of things, he's never said anything about his conversion. The only reason I even know about it is that I overheard my parents discussing Buckeye's worthiness to date my sister.

"Why did you get baptized?" I say.

Buckeye squints through the smoke and his voice takes on an unusual amount of gravity. "This used to be me, sitting right here and drinking till my teeth fell out. I was one of these people—not good, not bad, sincerely trying to make things as easy as possible. A place like this draws you in, pulls at you."

I watch the girl in the panties gyrating above us and I think I can see what he's getting at.

He continues: "But this ain't all there is. Simply is not. There's more to it than this. You've got to figure out what's right and what's wrong and then you've got to make a stand. Most people don't want to put out the effort. I'm telling you, I know it's not easy. Goodness has a call that's hard to hear."

I nod, not to indicate that I understand what he's saying, but as a signal for him to keep going. Even though I've had my fair share of experience with them, I've never understood religious people.

"Do you know what life's about? The *why* of the whole thing?" Buckeye says.

"No more than anybody else," I say.

"Do you think you'll ever know?"

"Maybe someday."

Buckeye holds up a half-eaten chicken wing for emphasis. "Exactly," he says through a full mouth. "I could scratch my balls forever if I had the time." He finishes off the rest of his chicken and shrugs. "To know, you have to do. You have to get out there and take action, put your beliefs to the test. Sitting around on your duff will get you nothing better than a case of the hemorrhoids."

"If you're such a believer, why don't you go around like my parents do, spouting scripture and all that?" I reason that if I just keep asking questions I will eventually get Buckeye figured out.

"For one thing," Buckeye says flatly, "and you don't need to go telling this to anybody else, but I'm not much of a reader."

I raise my eyebrows.

"Look here," he says, taking the menu from between the ketchup and sugar bottles. He points at something on it and says, "This is 'a', this is a 't' and here's a 'g.' This says 'hamburger'—I know that one. Oh, and this is 'beer.' I learned that early on." He looks up at me. "Nope, I can't read, not really. I never stayed put long enough to get an education. But I'm smart enough to fool anybody."

If this were a movie and not real life I would feel terrible for Buckeye—maybe I would vow to teach him to read, give him self-worth, help him become a complete human being. For the climax he would win the national spelling bee or something. But this is reality and as I look across the table at Buckeye, I can see that his illiteracy doesn't bother him a bit. In fact, he looks rather pleased with himself.

"Like I've been telling you, it's not the reading, it's not the saying. It's only the doing I'm interested in. Do it, do it, do it," Buckeye says, hammering each "do it" into the table with his Coke bottle. He leans into his chair, a wide grin overtaking his face. "But sometimes it certainly is nice to kick back and listen to the music."

We sit there quiet for awhile, me doing my best not to stare at the dancer and Buckeye with his head back and eyes closed, sniffing the air with the deep concentration of a wine judge. A pretty woman in jeans and a flannel shirt comes up behind Buckeye and asks him to dance. There are only a few couples out on the floor. Most everybody else is sitting at their tables, drinking and yelling at each other over the music.

"Thanks but no thanks," Buckeye says.

The woman looks over at me. "What about you?" she says.

I panic. My face gets hot and I begin to fidget. "No, no," I say. "No, thank you."

The woman seems amused by us and our Cokes. She takes a long look at both of us with her hands on the back of an empty chair.

"Go ahead," Buckeye says. "I'll hold down the fort."

I shake my head and look down into my lap. "That's quite all right," I say. I don't know how to dance and the brace I'm wearing makes me walk like I've got arthritis.

Buckeye sighs, smiles, gets up and leads the woman out onto the floor. She puts her head on his chest and I watch them drift away, swaying to the beat of a song about good love gone bad.

When the song is over Buckeye comes back with a flushed face and a look of exasperation. He says, "You see what I mean? That girl wanted things and for me to do them to her. She wanted these things done as soon as possible. She asked me if I didn't want to load her bases." He plops down in his chair and drains his Coke with one huge swallow. It doesn't even make him blink.

On our way home he pulls into the deserted front lot of a drive-in movie theater and floors the accelerator, yanking the steering wheel all the way over to the left and holding it there. He yells, "Carnival ride!" and the car goes round and round, pinning me to the passenger door, spitting up geysers of dust and creaking and groaning as if it might fly into pieces at any second. When he finally throws on the brakes, we sit there, the great cloud of dust we made settling down on the car, making ticking noises on the roof. The world continues to hurtle around me and I can feel my stomach throbbing like a heart.

Buckeye looks over at me, his head swaying back and forth a little and says, "Now doesn't that make you feel like you've had too much to drink?"

SIMONE AND I are on the roof. It's somewhere around midnight and there are bats zooming around our heads. We can hear the *swish* as they pass. I have only a pair of shorts on and Simone is wearing an oversized T-shirt. The warm grainy tar paper holds us against the steep incline of the roof like Velcro. Old pipes have forced us out here. Right now these pipes, the ones that run through the north walls of our turn-of-the-century house, are engaged in their semiannual vibrational moaning. According to the plumber, this condition has to do with drastic changes in temperature; either we could pay thousands of dollars to have the pipes replaced or we could put up with a little annoying moaning once in awhile.

With my sister's windows closed it sounds like someone crying in the hallway at the top of the stairs. My parents, with extra years of practice under their belts, have learned to sleep through it.

Simone and I are actually engaged in something that resembles conversation. Naturally, we are talking about Buckeye. If Buckeye has done nothing else, he has given us something to talk about.

For the first time in her life Simone seems to be seriously in love. She's had boyfriends before, but Simone is the type of girl who will break up with a guy because she doesn't like the way his clothes match. She's known Buckeye for all of three weeks and is already talking about names for their children. All of this without anything close to sexual contact. "Do you really think he likes me?"

This is a question I've been asked before. "Difficult to say," I tell her. In my young life I've learned the advantages of ambivalence.

Actually, I've asked Buckeye directly how he felt for my sister and this is the response I got: "I have feelings for her, feelings that could make an Eskimo sweat, but as far as feelings go, these simply aren't the right kind. There's a control problem I'm worried about."

"He truly loves the Lord," Simone says into the night. My sister, who wouldn't know a Bible from the menu at Denny's, thinks this is beautiful.

Over the past couple of weeks I've begun to see the struggle that is going on with Buckeye, in which the Lord is surely involved. Buckeye never says anything about it, never lets on, but it's there. It's a battle that pits Buckeye the Badger against Buckeye the Mormon. Buckeye told me that in his old life as the Badger he never stole anything, never lied without first making sure he didn't have a choice, got drunk once in awhile, fought some, cussed quite a bit and had only the women that wanted him. Now, as a Mormon, there is a whole list of things he has to avoid including coffee, tea, sex, tobacco, swearing, and as Buckeye puts it, "anything else unbecoming that smacks of the natural man."

To increase his strength and defenses, Buckeye has taken to denying himself, testing his willpower in various ways. I've seen him go without food for two full days. While he watches TV he holds his breath for as long as he can, doesn't use the bathroom until he's within seconds of making a mess. As part of his rugby training, he bought an old tractor tire, filled it with rocks, made a rope harness for it and every morning drags it through the streets from his neighborhood to ours, which is at least three miles. When he comes inside he is covered with sweat but will not accept liquid of any kind. Before taking a shower he goes out onto the driveway and does a hundred pushups on his knuckles.

Since they've met, Buckeye has not so much as touched my sister except for some innocent hand-holding. Considering that he practically lives at our house and already seems like a brother-in-law, I find this a little weird. Buckeye and his non-contact love is making Simone deranged and I must say I'm enjoying it. The funny thing is, I think it's having the same effect on him. There are times when Buckeye, once perpetually casual as blue jeans, cannot stay in one spot for more than a few seconds. He moves around like someone worried about being picked off by a sniper. He will become suddenly emotional, worse than certain menstruating women I'm related to: pissed off one minute, joyful the next. All of this is not lost on Buckeye. In his calmer and more rational moments he has come to theorize that a bum gland somewhere in his brain is responsible.

I sit back and listen to the pipes moaning like mating animals behind the walls. Hummingbird Lane, the street I've lived on my entire life, stretches off both ways into darkness. The clouds are low and the lights of the city reflect off them, giving everything a green, murky glow. Next to me my sister is chatting with herself, talking about the intrigues of beauty school, some of the inane deeds of my parents, her feeling and plans for Buckeye.

"Do you think I should get baptized?" she says. "Do you think he'd want me to?"

I snort.

"What?" she says. "Just because you're an atheist or something."

"I'm not an atheist," I tell her. "I'm just not looking for any more burdens than I already have."

THE NEXT MORNING, on Sunday, Buckeye comes to our house a newly ordained elder. I come upstairs just in time to hear him explain to Simone and my parents that he has been endowed with the power to baptize, to preach the gospel, to lay on the administering of hands, to heal. It's the first time I've seen him in his Sunday clothes: striped shirt, blaring polyester tie and shoes that glitter so brightly you'd think they'd been shined by a Marine. He's wearing some kind of potent cologne that makes my eyes tear up if I get too close. Damn me if the phrase doesn't apply: Buckeye looks born again. As if he'd just been pulled from the womb and scrubbed a glowing pink.

"Gosh dang," Buckeye says, "do I feel nice."

I can handle Buckeye the Badger and Buckeye the Mormon, but Buckeye the Elder? When I think of elders I imagine bent, bearded men who are old enough to have the right to speak mysterious nonsense.

I have to admit, however, that he looks almost holy. He's on a high, he's ready to raise the dead. He puts up his dukes and performs some intricate Mohammed Ali footwork—something he does when he's feeling particularly successful. We all watch him in wonder. My parents, just back from prayer meeting themselves, look particularly awed.

After lunch, once Buckeye has left, we settle down for our "Sabbath family conversation." Usually it's not so much a conversation as it is an excuse for us to yell at each other in a constructive format. As always, my father calls the meeting to order and then my mother, who is a diabetic, begins by sighing and apologizing for the mess the house has been in for the past few weeks; her insulin intake has been adjusted and she hasn't been feeling well. This is just her way of blaming us for not helping out more. Simone breaks in and tries to defend herself by reminding everyone she's done the dishes twice this week, my father snaps at her for not letting my mother finish and things take their natural course from there. Simone whines, my mother rubs her temples, my father asks the Lord why we can't be a happy Christian family and I smirk and finish off my pistachio ice cream. Whenever Buckeye is not around, it seems, we go right back to normal.

Not only does Buckeye keep our household happy and lighthearted with his presence, but he has also avoided any religious confrontation with my folks. Buckeye is not naturally religious like my parents, and he doesn't say much at all, just goes about his business, quietly believing what the folks at the Mormon church teach him. This doesn't keep Mom and Dad from loving him more than anybody. I hope it doesn't sound too bitter of me to say he's the son they never had. Buckeye goes fishing with my father (I'm squeamish about putting live things on hooks) and is currently educating my mother on how to grow a successful vegetable garden. They believe a boy as well-mannered and decent as Buckeye could not be fooled by "those Mormons" for long. They are just biding their time until Buckeye comes to his spiritual senses. Then they will dazzle him with the special brand of truth found only in the Holton Hills Reformed Baptist Church, the church where they were not only saved, but where they met and eventually got married. They've tried to get Pastor Wild and Buckeye in the house at the same time but so far it hasn't worked out. Up until now, though, I would have to say that Buckeye has done most of the dazzling.

ONE OF MY BIGGEST WORRIES is that I will be sterile. I don't know why I think about this; I am young and have never come close to having a girl. About a year ago I was perusing the public library and found a book all about sterility and the affliction it causes in people's lives. The book said that for some people, it is a tragedy that transcends all others. In what seems to be some sort of fateful coincidence I went home and turned on the TV and there was Phil Donahue discussing this very topic with four very downtrodden-looking men and their unfulfilled wives. I didn't sleep that night and I worried about it for weeks. I even thought about secretly going to the doctor and having myself checked. I guess I believe my life has been just a little too tragedy-free for my own comfort.

This is what I'm thinking about with a rifle in my hands and Buckeye at my side. We are in a swamp looking for something to shoot. One of the big attractions of the Mormon church for Buckeye was that they don't have any outright prohibitions against shooting things. Buckeye has two rifles and a handgun he keeps under the front seat of his Oldsmobile. I've got a .22 (something larger might aggravate my shoulder) and Buckeye is toting some kind of high-caliber hunting rifle that he says could take the head off a rhino. My parents took Simone to a fashion show in Dallas, so today it's just me and Buckeye, out for a little manly fun.

I'm not sure, but it doesn't seem as if we're actually hunting anything special. The afternoon is sticky full of bugs and the chirping of birds tumbles down out of old moss-laden trees. A few squirrels whiz by and a thick black snake crosses our path, but Buckeye doesn't even notice. I guess if something worthwhile comes along, we'll shoot it.

I tell Buckeye about my sterility worries. He and I share secrets. I suppose this is something women do all the time, but I've never tried it with any of the few friends

I have. This sterility thing is my last big one and probably the one that embarrasses me the most. When I get through the entire explanation Buckeye looks at me twice and laughs.

"You've never popped your cork with a girl?" he says. The expression on his face would lead me to believe that he finds this idea pretty incredible. I am really embarrassed now. I walk faster, tripping through the underbrush so Buckeye can't see all the blood rushing into my face. Buckeye picks up his pace and stays right with me. He says, "Being sterile would have been a blessing for me at your age. I used to lay pipe all over the place, and while nobody can be sure, there's a good chance I'm somebody's papa."

I stop and look at him. With Buckeye, it's more and more secrets all the time. A few days ago he told me that on a few nights of the year he can see the ghost of his mother.

"What do you mean, 'nobody can be sure?' " I say.

"With the kind of girls I used to do things with, nothing was certain. The only way you could get even a vague idea was to wait and see what color the kid came out to be."

There's a good chance Buckeye's the father of children he doesn't even know and I've got baseless worries about being sterile. Buckeye points his gun at a crow passing overhead. He follows it across the sky and says, "Don't get upset about that anyway. This is the modern world. You could have the most worthless sperm on record and there'd be a way to get around it. They've got drugs and lasers that can do just about anything. Like I say, a guy your age should only have worries about getting his cork popped. Your problem is you read too much."

I must have a confused look on my face because Buckeye stops so he can explain himself. With a blunt finger he diagrams the path of his argument on my chest. "Now there's having fun when you're young and aren't supposed to know better, and then there's the time when you've got to come to terms with things, line your ducks up in a row. You've got to have sin before there's repentance. I should know about that. Get it all out of you now. You're holding back for no good reason I can see. Some people hold it in until they're middle-aged and then explode. And frankly, I believe there's nothing quite as ugly as that."

We clamber through the brush for awhile, me trying to reason through what I've just heard and Buckeye whistling bluegrass tunes and aiming at trees. I haven't seen him this relaxed in a long time. We come into a clearing where an old car sits on its axles in a patch of undergrowth. Remarkably, all its windows are still intact and we simply can't resist the temptation to fill the thing full of holes. We're blazing away at that sorry car, filled with the macho euphoria that comes with making loud noises and destroying things, when a Ford pickup barrels into the clearing on a dirt road just to the south of us. A skinny old geezer with a grease-caked hat pulled down over his eyes jumps out.

To get where we are, we had to crawl through a number of barbed wire fences and there is not a lot of doubt we're on somebody's land. The way the old man is walking toward us, holding his rifle out in front of him, would suggest that he is that somebody, and he's not happy that we're on his property. "You sons of bitches," he growls once he's within earshot.

"How do you do," Buckeye says back.

The man stops about twenty feet away from us, puts the gun up to his shoulder and points it first at Buckeye, then at me. I have never been on the business end of a firearm before and the experience is definitely edifying. You get weak in the knees and take account of all the deeds of your life.

"This is it," the man says. He's so mad he's shaking. My attention never wavers from the end of that gun.

"Is there some problem we don't know about?" Buckeye says, still holding his gun in the crook of his arm. I have already dropped my weapon and am debating on whether or not to put my hands up.

"You damn shits!" the man nearly screeches. It's obvious he doesn't like the tone of Buckeye's voice. I wish Buckeye would notice this also.

"You come in here and wreck my property and shoot up my things and then give me this polite talk. I'm either going to take you to jail right now or shoot you where you stand and throw you in the river. I'm trying to decide."

This guy appears absolutely serious. He is weathered and bent and has a face full of scars; he looks capable of a list of things worse than murder. I begin to compose what I know will be a short and futile speech, something about the merits of mercy, but before I can deliver it Buckeye sighs and points his rifle at the old man.

"This is a perfect example of what my Uncle Lester Lewis, retired lieutenant colonel, likes to call 'mutually assured destruction.' He loves the idea. We can both stay or we can both go. As for myself, this is as good a time as any. I'm in the process of putting things right with my Maker. What about you?"

I watch the fire go out of the old man's eyes and his face get slack and pasty. He keeps his gun up but doesn't answer.

"Shall we put down our guns or stand here all day?" Buckeye says happily.

The man slowly backs up, keeping his gun trained on Buckeye. By the time he makes it back to his pickup, Buckeye has already lowered his gun. "I'm calling the police right now!" the man yells, his voice cracking into a whole range of different octaves. "They're going to put you shits away for good!"

Buckeye swings his gun up and shoots once over the man's head. As the pickup scrambles away over gravel and clumps of weeds, Buckeye shoots three or four times into the dirt behind it, sending up small *poofs* of dust. We watch the truck disappear into the trees and I work on getting my lungs functional again. Buckeye retrieves my gun and hands it to me. "We better get," he says.

We thrash through the trees and underbrush until we find the car. Buckeye drives the thing like he's playing a video game, flipping the gearshift and spinning the steering wheel. He works the gas and brake pedals with both feet and shouts at the narrow dirt road when it doesn't curve the way he expects. We skid off the road once in awhile, ending the life of a young tree, maybe, or putting a wheel into a ditch, but Buckeye never lets up. By the time we make it back to the highway we hear sirens.

"I guess that old cooter wasn't pulling our short and curlies," Buckeye says. He is clearly enjoying all this—his eyes are bright and a little frenzied. I have my head out the window in case I vomit.

Once we get back to civilization Buckeye slows down and we meander along like we're out to buy a carton of milk at the grocery store. The sirens have faded away and I don't even have a theory as to where we might be until Buckeye takes a shortcut between two warehouses and we end up in the parking lot of The Ranch. The place is deserted except for a rusty VW Bug.

"Never been here this early in the day, but it's got to be open," Buckeye says, still panting. I shrug, not yet feeling capable of forming words. It's three in the afternoon.

"When's the last time you had a nice cold beer?" Buckeye says a little wistfully.

"Never, really," I admit after a few seconds. What I don't admit to is that I've never even tasted any form of liquor in all my life. My parents have banned Simone and me from drinking alcohol until we reach the legal drinking age. Then, they say, we can decide for ourselves. Unlike Simone, I've never felt the need to defy my parents on this account. When I get together with my few friends we usually eat pizza and play Dungeons and Dragons. No one has ever suggested something like beer. Since I've known Buckeye, I've discovered what a sorry excuse for a teenager I am.

Buckeye shakes his head and whistles in disbelief. I guess we surprise each other. "Then let's go get you a beer," he says. "You're thirsty, aren't you? I'll settle for a Coke."

The front doors, big wooden affairs that swing both ways, are locked with a padlock and chain. Buckeye smiles at me and knocks on one of the doors. "There's got to be somebody in there. I know some of the people that work here. They'll get us set up."

Buckeye knocks for awhile longer but doesn't get any results. He peers through a window, goes back to the doors and pounds on them with both fists, producing a hollow booming noise that sounds like cannons from a distance. He kicks at the door and punches it a few times, leaving bright red circle-shaped scrapes on the tops of his knuckles.

"What is this?" he yells. "What is this? Hey!"

He throws his shoulder into the place where the doors meet. The doors buckle inward, making a metallic crunching noise, but the chain doesn't give. I try to tell Buckeye that I'm really not that thirsty, but he doesn't hear me. He hurls his body into the doors again, then stalks around and picks up a three-foot-high wooden cowboy next to the cement path that leads to the entrance. This squat, goofy-looking guy was carved out of a single block of wood and holds up a sign that says, "Come on in!" Buckeye emits a tearing groan and pitches it underhand against the door and succeeds only in breaking the cowboy's handlebar mustache. Buckeye has a kind of possessed look on his face, his eyes vacant, the cords in his neck taut like ropes. He picks the cowboy up again, readies himself for another throw, then drops it at his feet. He stares at me for a few seconds, his features falling into a vaguely pained expression, and sits down on the top step. He sets the cowboy upright and his hands tremble as he fiddles with the mustache, trying to make the broken part stay. He is red all over and sweating.

"I guess I'll have to owe you that beer," he says.

SIMONE, MY FATHER and I are sitting around the dinner table and staring at the food on our plates. We're all distraught; we poke at our enchiladas and don't look at each other. The past forty-eight hours have been rough on us: first, my mother's diabetic episode and now Buckeye has disappeared.

My mother is upstairs, resting. The doctors told her not to get out of bed for a week. Since yesterday morning old ladies from the church have been bringing over food, flowers and get-well cards in waves. In the kitchen we have casseroles stacked into pyramids.

As for Buckeye, nobody has seen him in two days. He hasn't called or answered his phone. My father has just returned from the boardinghouse where Buckeye rents a room and the owner told him that she hadn't seen Buckeye either, but it was against her policy to let strangers look in the rooms.

"One more day and we'll have to call the police," my father says. He's made this exact statement at least three times now.

Simone, distressed as she is, cannot get any food in her mouth. She looks down at the food on her plate as if it's something she can't fully comprehend. She gets a good forkful of enchiladas halfway to her mouth before she loses incentive and drops the fork back onto her plate. I think it's the first time in her twenty-one years that she's had to deal with real-life problems more serious than the loss of a contact lens.

It all started three days ago, one day after the incident with the guns. I spent that entire morning nursing an irrational fear that somehow the police were going to track us down and there would be a patrol car pulling up outside the house any minute. I was the only one home except for my mother, who had taken the day off sick from work and was sleeping upstairs.

I holed myself up in my basement bedroom to watch TV and read my books. At about four o'clock I heard a knock at the front door and nearly passed out from fright. I had read in magazines what happens in prisons to young clean people like me. I was sure that trespassing and destruction of property, not to mention shooting in the general direction of the owner, would get Buckeye and me some serious time in the pen.

The knocking came again and then someone opened the front door. I pictured a police officer coming in our house with his pistol drawn. I turned off the light in my room, hid myself in the closet, and listened to the footsteps upstairs. It took me only a few seconds to recognize the heavy shuffling gait of Buckeye.

Feeling relieved and a little ridiculous, I ran upstairs to find Buckeye going down the hall toward my parents' room.

"Hey, bubba," he said when he saw me. "Nobody answered the door so I let myself in. Simone told me your mother's sick. I've got something for her." He held up a mason jar filled with a dark green substance.

"She's just tired," I said. "What is that?"

"It's got vitamins and minerals," he said. "Best thing in the world for sick and tired people. My grandpop taught me how to make it. All natural, no artificial flavors or colors although it could probably use some. It smells like what you might find in a baby's diaper and doesn't taste much better."

"Mom's sleeping," I said. "She told me not to wake her up unless there was an emergency."

"How long's she been asleep?" Buckeye said.

"Pretty much the whole day," I told him.

Buckeye looked at his watch. "That's not good. She needs to have something to eat. Nutrients and things."

I shrugged and Buckeye shrugged back. He looked worried and a little run-down himself. His hair flopped aimlessly around on his head. He rubbed the jar in his hands like it was a magic lamp.

"You could leave it and I'll give it to her. Or you can wait until she wakes up. Simone will be home pretty soon."

Buckeye looked at me and weighed his options. Then he turned on his heels, walked right up to my parents' bedroom door and rapped on it firmly. I deserted the hallway for the kitchen, not wanting to be implicated in this in any way. I was there only a few seconds when Buckeye appeared, short of breath and a peaked look on his face.

"Something's wrong," he said. "Your mother."

My mother was lying still on the bed, her eyes open, unblinking, staring at nothing. Her skin was pale and glossy and her swollen tongue was hanging out of her mouth and covered with white splotches. I stood in the doorway while Buckeye telephoned an ambulance. "Mama?" I called from where I was standing. For some reason I couldn't make myself go any closer.

I walked out into the front yard and nearly fell on my face. Everything went black for a moment. I thought I'd gone blind. When my sight came back the world looked so sharp and real it hurt. I picked up a rock from the flower planter and chucked it at the Conley's big bay window across the street. I guess I figured that if my mother was dead, no one could blame me for doing something like that. I had always felt a special distaste for Mr. Conley and his fat sweating wife. I missed the window and the rock made a hollow thump on the fiberglass siding of the house. I cursed my uncoordinated body. If I had played Little League like my father had wanted all those years ago, that window would have been history.

I reeled around in the front yard until my father and the ambulance showed up. My mind didn't want to approach the idea that my mother might be lying deceased in her bed, so I didn't go near the house to find out. I hung out in the corner of the yard and swung dangerously back and forth in the lilac bushes. I watched the ambulance pull up and the paramedics run into my house followed a few minutes later by my father, who didn't even look my way. Neighbors were beginning to appear. I noticed their bald and liver-spotted heads poking out of windows and screen doors.

After a little while my father came out and found me sitting in the gardenias. He told me that my mother was not dead, but that she had had a severe diabetic reaction. "Too much insulin, not enough food," he said, wiping his eyes. "Why doesn't she take care of herself?"

I'd seen my mother have minor reactions, when she would get numb all over and forget what her name was and we'd have to make her eat candy or drink soda until she became better, but nothing like this. My father put his hand on my back and guided me inside where the paramedics were strapping her onto a stretcher. She didn't look any better than before.

"She's not dead," I said. I was honestly having trouble believing my father. I thought he might be trying to pull a fast one on me, saving me from immediate grief and shock. To me, my mother looked as dead as anything I'd ever seen, as dead as my aunt Sally in her coffin a few years ago, dense and filmy, like a figure carved from wax.

My father looked at me, his eyes moist and drawn, and shook his head. "She's serious, Lord help her, but she'll make it," he said. "I'm going to the hospital with her. I'll call you when I get there. Go and pray for her. That's what she needs from you."

I watched them load her into the ambulance and then went upstairs to pray. I had never really prayed in all my life, though I'd mouthed the words in Sunday school. But my father said that was what my mother needed, and helpless and lost as I felt, I couldn't come up with anything better to do.

I found Buckeye in my sister's room kneeling at the side of the bed. My first irrational thought was that he might be doing something questionable in there, looking through her underwear, etc., but then he started speaking and there was no doubt that I was listening to a prayer. He had his face pushed into his hands but his voice came at me as if he were talking to me through a pipe. I can't remember a word he said, only that he pleaded for my mother's life and health in a way that made it impossible for me to move away from the door and leave him to his privacy. I forgot myself completely and stood dumbly above the stairs, my hand resting on the doorknob.

Buckeye rocked on his knees and talked to the Lord. If it is possible to be humble and demanding at the same time, Buckeye was pulling it off: he dug the heels of his hands into his forehead and called on the Almighty in a near shout. He asked questions and seemed to get answers. He pleaded for mercy. He chattered on for minutes, lost in something that seemed to range from elation to despair. I have never heard anything like that, never felt that way before. Light was going up and down my spine and hitting the backs of my eyes. I don't think it's stretching it to say that for a few moments, I was genuinely certain that God, who or whatever He may be, was in that room. Despite myself, I had to peek around the door to make sure there was really nobody in there except Buckeye.

After Buckeye finished, I stumbled into my parents' room and sat on their bed. I put my hand on the place my mother's body had made an indentation in the sheets and picked the hairs off her pillow. Buckeye's prayer had been enough; I didn't think I could add much more. I sat there and mumbled aloud to no one in particular that I backed up everything Buckeye had said, one hundred percent.

We went to the hospital and after an eternity of reading women's magazines and listening to Simone's sobbing, a doctor came out and told us that it looked like my mother would be fine, that we were lucky we found her when we did because if we had let her sleep another half hour she certainly wouldn't have made it. Simone began to sob even louder and I looked at Buckeye, but he didn't react to what the doctor said. He slumped in his chair and looked terribly tired. Relief sucked everything out of me and left me so weak that I couldn't help but let loose a few stray tears myself.

While my father filled out insurance forms, Buckeye mumbled something about needing to get some sleep. He gave Simone a kiss on the forehead and patted my father and me on the back and wandered away into the dark halls of the hospital. That was the last any of us saw of him.

My mother's nearly buying the farm and the disappearance of Buckeye, the family hero, has thrown us all into a state. I poke at a mound of Jell-O with my fork and say, "I bet he's just had a good run of luck selling pantyhose. By now he's probably selling them to squaws in Oklahoma." I don't really know why I say things like this. I guess it's because I'm the baby of the family, a teenager, and making flippant, smart-ass remarks is part of my job.

My father shakes his head in resigned paternal disappointment and Simone bares her teeth and throws me a look of such hate that I'm unable to make another comment. My father asks me why I don't go to my room and do something worthwhile. I decide to take his advice. Simone looks like she's meditating violence. I thump down the stairs, turn up my stereo as loud as it will go, lie down on my bed and stare at the ceiling. Before I go to sleep I imagine sending words to heaven, having the clouds open up before me, revealing a light so brilliant I can't make out what's inside.

I'M AWAKENED by a sound like a manhole cover being slid from its place. It's dark in my room, the music is off and someone has put a blanket over me. Most likely my father, who occasionally acts quite motherly when my mother is not able to. There is a scrape and a thud and I twist around to see Buckeye stuffed into the small window well on the other side of the room, looking at me through the glass.

He has pushed away the wrought-iron grate that covers the well and is squatting in the dead leaves and spider webs that cover the bottom of it. Buckeye is just a big jumble of shadow and moonlight, but I can still make out his unmistakable smile. I get up and slide open the window.

"Good evening," Buckeye whispers, polite as ever. He presses his palms against the screen. "I didn't want to wake you up, but I brought you something. Do you want to come out here?"

I run upstairs, go out the front door and find Buckeye trying to lift himself out of the window well onto the grass. I help him up and say, "Where have you been?"

When Buckeye straightens up and faces me, I get a strong whiff of alcohol and old sweat. He acts like he didn't hear my question. He holds up a finger, indicating for me to wait a moment, and goes to his car, leaning to the right just a little. He comes back with a case of Stroh's and bestows it on me as if it's a red pillow with the crown jewels on top. "This is that beer I owe you," he says, his voice gritty and raw with drink. "I wanted to get you a keg of the good-tasting stuff, but I couldn't find any this late."

We stand in the wet grass and look at each other. His lower lip is split and swollen, his half-ear is a mottled purple and he's got what looks like lipstick smudged on his chin. His boots are muddy and he's wearing the same clothes he had on three days ago.

"Your mother okay?" he says.

"She's fine. They want her to stay in bed a week or so."

"Simone?"

"She's been crying a lot."

For a long time he just stands there, his face gone slack, and looks past me to the dark house. "Everybody asleep in there?"

I look at my watch. It's almost three-thirty in the morning. "I guess so," I say.

Buckeye says, "Hey, let's take a load off. Looks like you're about to drop that beer." We walk over to the porch and sit down on the front steps. I keep the case in my lap, not really knowing what to do with it. Buckeye pulls off two cans, pops them open, hands one to me.

I have the first beer of my life sitting on our front porch with Buckeye. It's warm and sour but not too bad. I feel strange, like I haven't completely come out of sleep. I have so many questions looping through my brain that I can't concentrate on one long enough to ask it. Buckeye takes a big breath and looks down into his hands. "What can I say?" he whispers. "I thought I was getting along fine and the next thing I know I'm face down in the dirt, right back where I started from. I can't remember much, but I just let loose. I lost my strength for just a minute and that's all it takes. For awhile there I didn't even want to behave." He gets up, walks out to the willow tree and touches its leaves with his fingers, comes back to sit down. "I think I got ahead of myself. This time I've got to take things slower."

"Are you going somewhere?" I ask. It seems to be the only question that means anything right now.

"I don't know. I'll keep looking for Bud. He's the only brother I've got that I'm aware of. I've just got to get away, start things over again."

Not having anything to say, I nod. We have a couple more beers together and stare into the distance. I want to tell Buckeye about hearing him pray for my mother, thinking it might change something, but I can't coax out the words. Finally, Buckeye stands up and whacks some imaginary dust from his pants. "I'd leave a note for Simone and your folks . . . ," he says.

"I'll tell them," I say.

"Lord," Buckeye says. "Damn."

He sticks his big hand out for a shake, a habit he picked up from the Mormons, and gives me a knuckle-popping squeeze. As he walks away on the cement path toward his car, the inside of my chest feels as big as a room and I have an over-powering desire to tackle him, take his legs out, pay him back for my collarbone, hold him down and tell him what a goddamned bastard I think he is. This feeling stays with me for all of five seconds, then bottoms out and leaves me as I was before, the owner of one long list of emotions: sorry that it had to turn out this way for everybody; relieved that Buckeye is back to his natural self; pleased that he came to see me before he left; afraid of what life will be like without having him around.

Buckeye starts up his battle wagon and instead of just driving slowly away into the distance, which would probably be the appropriate thing to do under these circumstances, he gets the car going in a tight circle, four, five times around in the middle of the quiet street, muffler rattling, tires squealing and bumping the curb, horn blowing, a hubcap flying into somebody's yard—all for my benefit.

I go into the house before the last rumbles of Buckeye's car die away. I take my case of beer and hide it under my bed, already planning the hell-raising beer party I'll have with some of my friends. I figure it's about time we did something like that. On the way down the stairs, I wobble a little and bump into things, feeling like the whole house is pitching beneath my feet. All at once it hits me that I'm officially roasted. Gratified, I go back upstairs and into my father's den where he keeps the typewriter I've never seen him use.

I feed some paper into the dusty old machine and begin typing. I've decided not to tell anyone about Buckeye's last visit; it will be the final secret between us. Instead, I go to work composing the letter Buckeye would certainly have left had he learned to write. I address it to Simone and just let things flow. I don't really try to imitate Buckeye's voice, but somehow I can feel it coming out in a crusty kind of eloquence. Even though I've always been someone who's highly aware of grammar and punc-tuation, I let sentence after sentence go by without employing so much as a comma. I tell Simone everything Buckeye could have felt and then some. I tell her how much she means to me and always will. I tell her what a peach she is. I'm shameless, really. I include my parents and thank them for everything, inform them that as far as I'm concerned, no two more Christian people ever walked the earth. I philosophize about goodness and badness and the sweet sorrow of parting. As I type, I imagine my family reading this at the breakfast table and the heartache compressing their faces, emotion rising in them so full that they are choked into speechlessness. This image spurs me on and I clack away on the keys like a single-minded idiot. When I'm finished, I've got two and a half pages and nothing left to say. A little stunned, I sit in my father's chair and strain in the dim light to see what I've just written. Until now, I've never been aware of what being drunk can do for one's writing ability.

I take the letter out on the front porch and tack it to our front door, feeling ridiculously like Martin Luther, charged with conviction and fear. I go back inside and try to go to sleep but I'm restless—the blood inside me is hammering against my ribs and the ends of my fingers, the house is too dark and cramped. Instead of going up the stairs, I push out my window screen and climb out the well and begin to run around the house, the sun a little higher in the sky every time I come around into the front yard. I feel light-headed and weightless and I run until my lungs are raw, trying to get the alcohol out of my veins before my parents wake up.

I'D WANTED TO WRITE about religious experience for a long time before writing "Speaking in Tongues." What I found most intriguing about people who have grown up in very religious environments is their tendency to have a split self; a self that cannot help remaining faithful to religion even while rebelling against it, rebelling against it even while ostensibly remaining faithful.

ZZ PACKER

AT FOURTEEN AND SEVENTEEN respectively, Tia and Marcelle were too old to sit with the children, but neither had yet spoken in tongues, so they could not sit with the adults of the Hope and Grace Apostolic Church of the Fire Baptized. Tia had only known Marcelle since the summer, but already Marcelle had developed the contemptuous languor of a zoo animal whose cage had been banged by too many people. Tia held onto her straight face, the face that always wondered what would come next, but Marcelle smirked as she watched the stoic congregation, simmering in a broth of perspiration and overzealously applied *eau de toilette*.

"Brother Lamont!" the pastor said to the man standing, "How has the Lord been good to you this week?"

Brother Lamont rubbed his beard. "Brothers and Sisters, y'all know me and my wife, Sister Benita, been trying to have a baby."

"Yes, Lord," a woman quietly encouraged.

"Well, I was out in the yard, mowing the grass, and up come this grasshopper."

"Tell it!" another woman shouted, flapping her fan.

"And Laaaawd!" Brother Lamont wiped his face and shook his head as if he could not bear to continue, "Laaaawd. That grasshopper *spoke* to me. I could hear the *angel of the Lord* in his little bitty chirpings! That grasshopper say to me, he say, 'Lamont Taylor. Benita gone have a little baby boy!'"

He waved his hand in the air and bent his head back as though he were about to call out for help. "Church! I'm here to tell you that *God* is a *Good* God!"

"Yes He is!" the church replied.

Brother Lamont turned around and like someone who's awakened to find himself in a place other than his bed, stamped his feet with each word. "Y'all-did-not-hear-me! I say *God is a good God*!"

"Yes He is!" the church dutifully rejoined; the organist pounced on the chords of "On Christ the Solid Rock I Stand" as if to say to his rows of slippery plastic keys, "Take *this!* And *this! And this!*" When the music had quickened to a galloping triple time, whole pews were up on their feet. Some were in the aisle, where they danced gospel versions of Irish jigs. Others were speaking in tongues, their unintelligible sounds like records played in reverse, jumbled as quickly as auctioneers rattling off prices.

After Brother Lamont, Sister Nancy Cannon stood up and testified how the Lord had filled her pantry with Spam when her paycheck ran out; an eight-year-old girl explained how her chicken pox had gone away when she'd said the Lord's Prayer in pig Latin.

As Tia's grandmother stood up to be recognized by the pastor, Marcelle rolled her eyes with boredom. Tia's grandmother's own glaucomic eye, looking like Earth as seen from space, trained itself on the pulpit while the good eye strayed over the flora and fauna–inspired towers of women's hats.

Tia sat and watched. Though other girls Tia's age had begun speaking in tongues, Tia had not and could not. As Pastor Bender reminded his church every Sunday, speaking in tongues could not be faked. "Brothers and sisters, the Lord don't like no half-shouting! You must speak in those fiery tongues! You gotta *shout,* to get it *out! Applaud* your *God!* You have to *sing* to your *King!*"

You could only speak in tongues when all worldly matters were off your mind, or else there was no room for God. To do that, you had to be thinking about him, praising him, or singing to him. She tried at church and she tried at home, but nothing worked. In her room, she would genuflect, pushing her head against her bed ruffle, reciting scriptures, praying, singing, concluding it all with a deep, waiting silence. But nothing would come out. Her only solace was that Marcelle was three years older and had never spoken in tongues either.

Tia watched the masses writhe and dance and shout. There was a clamor like a barnyard of animals being squeezed into a closet. There were "Hallelujahs" and the "Glory be to Gods" and singing and the *a-chinga chinga chinga chinga* of the tambourines. Meanwhile, twenty or so people were speaking in tongues. Some flailed their arms like children having temper tantrums, others spun about as though they were cyclones, and still others ran the length of the church, back and forth, eyes closed, tears streaming down their faces—all the while jabbering in a language that sounded like none other on earth.

Marcelle went to the bathroom, leaving Tia alone on their pew with Rebecca, the half-witted girl who flashed a nonstop grin. On the opposite pews, Tia's grandmother yelled, "Glory be to God!" She stood up and jerked back as though whiplashed, and the artificial gardenias wreathing her hat quivered.

THAT FALL, Tia and Marcelle went to school together. School was just beginning, but already the students had sectioned off: black girls traded pocket mirrors, lip-sticking themselves like four-year-olds who mercilessly crayon one spot to a waxy patch. White girls posed against their lockers as though waiting to audition for parts in a play.

In Alabama, fall meant summer heat in a school without an air conditioner. Tia and Marcelle swished through the halls in their long-sleeved blouses and ankle-length skirts, the eyes of fellow students caught and followed them. Everyone else was wearing shorts, and most girls, if they could get away with it, wore tank tops, pulling them as far as they would stretch over their navels before entering class. The girls watched Tia and Marcelle, covered neck to toe in heavy fabric, as if they were observing two Inuit hunters, attired in anoraks and kamisks, having wandered from some arctic region and into the halls of Rutherford B. Hayes Senior High.

Women and girls who were members of Hope and Grace Apostolic Church of the Fire Baptized had to cover themselves completely. They did not wear pants, ever. Jewelry—save functional timepieces—was considered unnecessary adornment; wearing makeup was a proclamation of harlotry. Once, Tia bought a tube of cherry lipgloss and forgot it in the pocket of her skirt. Her grandmother found it while doing the laundry and marched into the kitchen where Tia was mixing cornmeal and egg whites for corn bread. Soap slid in sudsy pendants down her grandmother's arms as she held up the tube with disgusted fingers, as though it were a hair she'd found in a restaurant meal.

"There is," her grandmother said, dropping the lipgloss in the trash, "no Revlon in heaven."

MARCELLE BRUSHED PAST someone on the school hall and a boy called out, "Holy Roller!"

Marcelle smiled presidentially and tipped an imaginary hat. Tia sighed, feeling the eyes on her. It was impossible to blend in with the crowd of students, so she walked briskly, tugging on Marcelle's arm. Tia knew Marcelle was taking in the whole scene: the concrete block walls freshly coated in the hue of bad weather; the boys convening outside the men's bathroom; the teachers standing by their doorways like sunglassless Secret Service agents; the artlessly student-drawn propaganda posters, one of which was featured repeatedly on the drab walls every few feet, declaring, "Rutherford B. Hayes—You Have to Love It!"

The stares of students grew more intense, and all reacquaintance greetings and pubescent catcalls diminished to a murmured hush as Tia and Marcelle passed by. Tia grabbed Marcelle's arm to urge her more quickly through the throng, but Marcelle refused to be hurried.

"Look!" she yelled a bit too loudly to a girl. The girl jumped back as Marcelle pointed to the sign on the wall and exclaimed, "Rutherford B. Hayes—You Have to Love It!" The girl's eyes widened in confusion as others around her pressed their books against their chests.

Marcelle pointed to the signs on the wall, and with each yell she transformed it into the imperative: "Rutherford B. Hayes—You *Have* to Love It!" The personal: "Rutherford B. Hayes—You Have to Love It!" The passionate: "Rutherford B. Hayes—You Have to *Love It!*" The students retreated when Marcelle's index finger landed on them, cringing as if she were a witch casting a spell, but gradually they began to see the propaganda posters in the light Marcelle had seen them: an opportunity for sarcasm and derision.

There were nearly ten signs along one hallway, and students began to rip the signs from the walls. Girls stood atop each other's shoulders in sloppy cheerleader pyramids, the topmost ones ripping the signs from where they were snugly attached, tearing the posters into confetti. Boys leapt up to the signs as if going for a slam dunk, snatched them from the walls, then shredded them. Everyone whooped and yelled, and amidst it all, Marcelle strode down the poster-strewn path, stretching out her arms as though she were about to burst into a tune from *The Sound of Music*.

Whoever called Marcelle a Holy Roller was swept into the mad joy of chaos; the comment itself was forgotten. Tia was equally forgotten. In the ecstasy of it all, Marcelle had not noticed when Tia slinked into the girl's restroom, to wait for the bell to ring.

IN JUNIOR HIGH SCHOOL, Tia had survived by speaking as little as possible. Tia lived outside the district of the schools other Hope and Grace Church children attended, and had decided that at her own school, the best tactic, by far, was to remain friendless. One girl, attempting to draw Tia out of her shell, invited her to a birthday party. All the invited girls would go to a movie then return to the birthday girl's house for ice cream and cake. Tia had to refuse, and was too embarrassed to explain to the girl that her church forbade going to the movies. People at Hope and Grace believed that movies were celluloid lies. The girl—and all the girl's friends—never spoke to Tia again.

And as if this were not enough, she had to take gym. Since she could only wear skirts that came down to her ankles and blouses that covered her wrists, Tia could not run track, she could not play badminton, she could not climb the gym ropes. Her grandmother met with the gym teacher and the principal, and the compromise was that Tia would be exempt from the gym dress code of T-shirts and shorts as long as she wore the proper shoes. But she would still have to "participate." This, Tia decided, was worse than death. Once, Tia had jumped aside to avoid being hit in dodgeball and got caught in the folds of her skirt, sprawling onto the polished gym floor.

BAND WAS THE ONLY CLASS Tia and Marcelle shared. Tia had found a clarinet, left behind from when her mother had gone to Atlanta. Her mother had become a heroin addict and Tia had not seen her in over eight years. When Tia was retrieving one of her grandmother's hats from the closet, there it was, a clarinet case with her mother's name etched on the hard leather exterior in awkward, cavemanlike scratches. It was the perfect opportunity to get out of the gym requirement after her inglorious fall. She played in the junior high band for a year and a half, and although she never made first clarinet, she had mastered the basics.

Marcelle never wanted to be in Hayes Senior High's band, but there she was, in the clarinet row, a few people down from Tia, tooting along with the rest of them. Marcelle had been allowed to skip an entire grade, and band was the only elective that fit into her schedule. On the last day of the first week of school, it was obvious that the band conductor had grown tired of hearing the same notes of "The Marriage of Figaro" slaughtered mercilessly by the tubas, squeaked out by the clarinets and breathily spittled from the flutes. After only ten minutes of rehearsal, Mr. Sherman gave the class a written assignment.

"Take out a sheet of paper and write an analysis of each instrument's role in the band." Mr. Sherman produced a newspaper from his briefcase and began to read.

Everyone grumbled, but once their notebooks were out, they began to write quietly. Marcelle took out her paper, looking up to the ceiling for inspiration as though she were about to draft a ballad, and wrote, speaking all the while:

"The trumpets bleat vociferously, but unfortunately, their skill does not match their volume."

Mr. Sherman peered above the newspaper and searched for the voice, but Marcelle's head was already studiously trained on the paper again. "This," he droned to the class in general, "is a *silent* assignment."

But Marcelle did not seem to hear Mr. Sherman.

"The tubas, though easily the most resounding instrument, fart out a series of whole notes, lasting for bars and bars of sheet music, adding an interminable weight to the piece, offering no relief."

The class laughed as Mr. Sherman folded his paper, slapping it down on his conductor's stand, marching up to Marcelle and taking her by the arm.

"You will stop right now or be thrown out of here forever!"

"Oh. I'm sorry, I didn't know I was talking." Marcelle made a face of harsh self-reproval. Mr. Sherman stood guard over her. Marcelle continued to write. When she'd finished a few lines silently, she said, "The percussion section is also one big flaw—the bass's insipid boom, the snares' insistent, insectlike tapping, the quads faltering cadences—"

Mr. Sherman had her by the arm, escorting her from the room, but Marcelle continued her diatribe while being led to the door.

"—THE OCCASIONAL CYMBAL CRASH, ALWAYS A BIT TOO LATE—"

"You will not have the privilege of—"

"—ALL SEEM IN CONCERT TO DO THEIR BEST TO OVERPOWER THE PRISSY, PRIMA-DONNA FLUTES—"

She was at the door, Mr. Sherman's arm around hers tightly, hotly whispering something to her.

"THE CLARINETS ARE ALWAYS UNDERAPPRECIATED—"

Tia sat in her second-clarinet chair, wondering if it would be the first time she'd see a man cry.

"AND THIS MUSICAL IMPOVERISHMENT MANIFESTS ITSELF IN A DISTINCTLY WOODWIND *BITCHINESS*."

Mr. Sherman slammed the door, with Marcelle on the other side. Though she was suspended from school for three days, Mr. Sherman would not, could not, repeat Marcelle's exact words over the phone, so her mother never found out about the cursing. Marcelle got her wish. She was out of band forever.

OF THE THREE columns of pews, the Ladies of the Lord Sunday School class always sat in the column next to the stained-glass windows. As the sunlight grew noontime fierce, Jesus' robe would whitely illumine; in the heat of the day, shadows of insects buzzed in front of Paul as if to mock the man, trapped forever in translucent mosaic, with no hope of ever reaching Damascus.

Sister Gwendolyn sat behind a table a few yards away from the windows. Sister Gwendolyn took her job as Sunday School teacher and directrix of adolescent girls seriously, as evidenced by the number of pencils she laid out on her table. She displayed ten or twelve pencils each Sunday, and since they had never been used, all of them retained their sharp, groomed points. She presided over them like an octopus, her balloonlike head, her absence of neck.

Marcelle was sitting next to Tia, reading a passage from the lesson: "God's Special Message for Teens." Tia sat still and quiet, but she was not looking at the Sunday School book in her lap. She gazed at the stained-glass Paul. Behind his frozen image of sudden blindness and supplication, cars swooshed on Jackson Street. The drone of the cars outside allowed her mind to slip further and further away from Sister Gwendolyn and the other girls in the class.

The leaves outside the stained-glass windows rustled, screening out the sunlight, turning the picture of Paul dark and opaque. After the other girls in Sunday School had read their passages, Marcelle kicked Tia's shin, then pointed to the passage Tia was to supposed to read.

"God's Special Message for Teens," Tia read. Sister Gwendolyn looked at her own book, puzzled.

"No," Marcelle whispered, "I already read that." Marcelle tapped her pencil on a passage four paragraphs down the page. Next to the passage, there was a picture of a young Jesus sitting on a grassy hill with a dreamy Nazarene look in his eyes. Marcelle leaned over Tia's book as though the words in Tia's book were somehow different and more engrossing than her own. Marcelle began to draw a cartoon bubble above Jesus' head. Tia read the passage.

As a teen, you may believe that no one understands your problems. You may say to yourself, "I'm all alone." But this is NOT TRUE! God understands your problems. Remember, Jesus was a teen, just like you! Modern teens face many challenges, but just think: when Jesus was a teen, he already knew he would have to save the world from SIN. And as though that weren't enough, he had homework, too—just like you!

All the Sunday School books Tia had read were written this way, but this was the first time they seemed outright ludicrous to her. Tia stopped and looked up from the page, glancing at Sister Gwendolyn. Sister Gwendolyn held her book out in front as if she were about to begin singing carols from it. "Continue," she said.

Marcelle now had the book in her lap and Tia had to lean over to see the words. Marcelle made an arrow from the word "homework" to the cartoon bubble she'd drawn. In the bubble next to Jesus' head she'd written out the formula for a quadratic equation.

Tia tried to swallow her smile, furtively glancing from the quadratic equation–dreaming Jesus to Sister Gwendolyn, who let out a piqued sigh and put her book down.

"Tia, Marcelle is busy taking notes and you can't even concentrate on a simple passage. *Read.* Please."

Tia continued, trying to read with a revitalized sense of duty.

You, being a teenager, may be asked to drink alcohol, smoke drugs and other things, or "have a little fun." DON'T DO IT! Doing these things may seem "far out" and "groovy," but they are not only dangerous to your health, they are also dangerous to your life as a Christian. When someone asks you to go to a party, you should ask yourself, "Would Jesus go to this party?" If he wouldn't, then that's God's way of telling you that the party is not for you.

When Tia finished, Marcelle was putting the final touches on her crude drawing of three drunks, asking the sketch of Jesus to attend their party.

Though Tia did not laugh very loud, nor for a long time, the other nine girls, including Marcelle, looked at her, their eyes blinking the slow and steady concerned flashes of car hazard lights. Sister Gwendolyn rolled her arms: "Sister Townsend, it's evident *you* haven't spoken in tongues with the Lord. May I remind you that the fool hath said in his heart, *there is no God.*"

DURING THE INTERIM between Sunday School and Morning Worship, some church members stood about in clusters greeting one another as though they had not just seen each other minutes ago in Sunday School. Usually, Tia went outside where she talked with Marcelle, but that Sunday she knew she was in trouble. She'd steered her grandmother away from Sister Gwendolyn for four nights of Weekday Worship, and that morning, Sister Gwendolyn had pointedly skipped over Tia when passages were read in Sunday School. Tia searched the sanctuary, trying to get to her grandmother before Sister Gwendolyn did.

Sister Gwendolyn was already talking, and at each angry quake of Sister Gwendolyn's curls, Tia's grandmother furrowed her eyebrows more deeply, shook her head more heartily, and gripped her Bible more tightly to her chest as though the goodness of all its printed pages could ward off a heart attack.

As her grandmother searched the sanctuary for her, Tia wondered whether it was so awful to have laughed in Sunday School. Was it so bad that Marcelle had used the word "bitchiness"? What if someone led a good life, but didn't speak in tongues? Would that person go to hell? Were all women who wore pants and makeup going to hell? The fool hath said in his heart, 'there is no God,' but Tia had not even questioned the existence of God. She knew He was, He *is,* but somehow Sister Gwendolyn—and now her grandmother for sure—thought she was an atheist. The dove-colored hats of the two women drifted away from each other, but Tia could see their trains of thought in unison, advancing to their shared conclusion with the efficiency of tiny black ants in a line, wending toward the same mammoth crumb of bread: Tia did not Believe, thus Tia Laughed in her Heart, thus Tia was not able to Speak in Tongues.

THAT SUNDAY was perfect walking weather. As Tia and her grandmother walked home from church, the seamless sky was hung in a blue that Tia associated with pictures of Greece, where it was especially important for the sky to make a contrast with the whitewashed walls of a small Grecian town. Once they had gotten off the main road, Tia and her grandmother approached that part of Montgomery where the sun always seemed to live. Stout pastel houses lined the streets like presents waiting to be opened, then gave way to a stretch of wood only as wide as a highway. Oaks spread their huge, trophy-shaped crowns, and bayberry branches unfolded like fans. Beyond this was bottlebrush weed, and beyond the weed, the endless green nap of the cemetery.

Tia's grandmother did not mention her conversation with Sister Gwendolyn. Instead she hummed a tune so old, only a handful in their church would have remembered it.

"I want," Tia said, "to live with my mother."

Her grandmother did not stop humming, nor did she signal in any way she'd heard Tia.

It seemed as though her grandmother never really heard her. Tia remembered when she was eleven and had dreamt that her grandmother died. In her dream, she was at the funeral, and though the church members wore black and cried quiet tears, Tia could not cry at all. Tia woke up and crept into her grandmother's room, then laid beside her grandmother like she did when she was younger; like she did before her grandmother finally allowed her to sleep in her mother's old bedroom. She could not tell her grandmother what she had dreamt, so she simply said, "I am afraid."

Her grandmother took her Bible from her nightstand and made Tia read the Twenty-third Psalm, beginning with, "The Lord is my Shepherd, I shall not want." When Tia read the section, *Yea, though I walk through the valley of the shadow of death, I will fear no evil,* she remembered her dream, and began crying. Her grandmother made Tia recite the psalm while Tia sat in a hard chair beside the bed.

"Your mother turned bad, too," her grandmother said, and her expression was that of one who has swallowed a teaspoon of bitter medicine. "Couldn't get through a verse of scripture. The devil claims children. This I know."

THEY CONTINUED DOWN the road they would come up again for Sunday Evening Worship. They went home and ate a silent dinner, then went back to church.

Dusk had fallen when they reached the church, but Tia would not enter the doorway until she knew that her grandmother had fully understood what she'd said earlier that day.

"I'm going to live with my mother."

"I heard you when you said it before." Her grandmother did not look at her at all, and Tia did not know whether this refusal to acknowledge her meant deliberation or flat-out disapproval.

They entered the church, and when Sister Gwendolyn greeted them, sucking in her rolling belly, Tia's grandmother took her hat off, wiped the sweat from her brow, then adjusted the hat back onto her head. She nodded to Sister Gwendolyn.

"Do what you have to do."

SISTER GWENDOLYN had Tia in a headlock. Her hold was like a wrench on a tricky bolt, and for several moments Tia sat in the only chair in the dark hymnbook closet, refusing to say anything. Sister Gwendolyn breathed in and out through those same flared, bullish nostrils that sent the pencils on her table gently rolling in Sunday School.

"Do you believe that you will ever receive the Holy Ghost?"

She could hear Sister Gwendolyn's nostrils suck in the musty air, and as Sister Gwendolyn exhaled, Tia heard the congregation filing into the sanctuary for evening service. Soon a tambourine would begin ringing, and the choir would sing. Robin-breasted women would swell their bosoms, inhaling God. The voices of the old men would boom. Sister Gwendolyn still held Tia's head, and all two hundred pounds of the older woman compressed itself upon the girl.

"Sister Townsend!" Sister Gwendolyn shouted, her hands still on Tia's forehead, still on the back of her skull, and with no room to move, Tia's throat grew stiff and sick with the fear that she would never breathe normally again.

"Christ died on the Cross for you at Calvary. Did you know that?" Sister Gwendolyn pushed something hard into Tia's chest. The smell of the hymnbooks, musty with years of palm sweat, the anointing oil, Sister Gwendolyn's perfume of crushed flowers and cough syrup—were buoyed by the heat of the closet, and marched across Tia's brain with the brazenness of the trumpet section blaring *Firebird*.

"Jesus died for you. He died for you. And you laugh in Sunday School. At Jesus."

Sister Gwendolyn pushed Tia's head against the wall. Tia tried to squirm away, but could not.

"I want you to say the Lord's Prayer for me, Tia," Sister Gwendolyn whispered. Then, careful to say the words in the same tone as she had before, as if any modulation in tempo would have invested the words with a different meaning, she repeated, "I want you to say the Lord's Prayer. I want you to say it until you cry tears for Jesus."

AFTER HAVING BEEN let out of the hymnbook closet, Tia sat down at her regular pew. Marcelle stared straight ahead. Rebecca, the half-witted girl on the other end, was standing, rattling her tambourine to no particular beat, her smiling head nodding like an eager puppy.

The song ended, and everyone took to their seats, fanning themselves while Pastor Bender thumbed the pages to the evening Bible selection. Rebecca still stood, happily banging her tambourine for a full minute after the rest of the church had stopped singing. Tia slid next to Rebecca and pried the tambourine from the girl's sweaty hands. Rebecca smiled widely as Tia guided her to her seat.

TIA DID NOT board the bus until morning. She had stuffed all that would fit into her backpack without looking suspicious: five skirts, five blouses, stockings, all the underwear she owned, deodorant, a toothbrush, a washcloth, soap. She opened her clarinet case and laid her sheet music atop the clarinet pieces. She stashed her books under her bed and thought about how it might be her last time smelling the lemony Murphy's oil soap that rose from the cool hardwood floor. She had thirty-four dollars. A ticket to Atlanta cost thirty-two.

Tia walked all the way to the Montgomery Greyhound bus station. The workers were on strike, but the scabs crossed the picket lines, pretending that they weren't about to do what they were about to do.

On the way to Atlanta, an old man on the bus smelling of fruity muscatel and wet wool sat across the aisle from Tia, brushing a network of knotty hair with the backside of his hand.

"Gotta comb?" he asked.

Tia did have a comb. When she stopped to tell Marcelle she was leaving, Marcelle had given her twenty dollars along with her school lunch, a sewing kit, some Kaopectate, and one of those ten-cent combs so small that it was always getting lost. "Here's a comb," she said to the man, unzipping a pouch on her backpack. It would never get through the man's knots of hair, but the man had faith and began the painful process of pulling out hair between grunts.

Before reaching Atlanta, the bus driver took an exit and switched to low gear. The machinery of the bus fought against moving so slowly, moaning until the bus let out a *psssst* when it came to a complete stop in a Burger King parking lot.

"Ten minutes, folks," the driver said. Before he could even open the door, people pushed impatiently down the aisle.

The driver stepped outside and lit a cigarette while passengers hustled into the Burger King. Tia did not want to spend her money quickly, so she stayed in her seat and watched the bus driver walk to the parking lot's edge where weeds rose up in a growth of densely packed stalks. It seemed as though the driver was sizing up the weeds to see if the brush would make a path for him. Tia could only see the back of his head, but she thought she knew what he was thinking. His back was turned on the bus and he seemed to be thinking, *I will leave you all behind, and then where will you be? I will enter this here growth of weed and disappear forever.*

"Go," Tia whispered, looking out the window. "Go." She was rooting for him, knowing she would be the only person who understood what he was doing and why, until she saw the driver unzip his pants and loose his urine in a series of arcs so elaborate, he seemed to be spelling out his name.

Tia turned her head, though she had not seen that thing on him that she was not supposed to see. The old man who had sat next to her returned, drunkenly thanking someone who'd apparently been begged into buying him a cheeseburger. Before he sat down, he pointed a finger at Tia as if recognizing a friend he hadn't seen in a long time and said, "Hey!" Tia turned her head away from the man and looked out the window where she saw the driver toss his cigarette onto the ground.

Everyone came back with Whoppers and Cokes. The driver yawned, making motions for dawdlers to hurry back onto the bus. He boarded the bus, sat in his seat, and looked at his watch.

"We'll be pulling into Atlanta, Georgia, about fifteen minutes after our scheduled arrival." He closed the door and swung into a slow reverse when somebody in the back of the bus reminded him that a guy was still in the Burger King.

"Ten minutes," said the bus driver. "I'm no joke, folks. I say ten minutes, that means ten minutes." He turned out of the parking lot.

"That ain't right!" said a small woman with greasy curls.

"Sho ain't," said another.

"Lordy, lordy. Buses sure have changed," said the white woman sitting next to Tia. Tia was about to agree, although she hadn't ridden on a bus since she'd last seen her mother, but then she realized that the white woman was talking to herself. "*No* kind of manners."

The bus had just made the turn out onto the main road toward the highway when the abandoned passenger came flying out of the Burger King with his bag of food.

"He's just back there, man. Wait for him!" someone said. The bus driver continued at a slow crawl toward the interstate sign. The abandoned man crossed the road, and a car he'd dodged honked madly, just missing him. Once he'd gotten on the right side of the road, catching up to the bus just a few yards from the door, the bus driver stopped in the middle of the street.

The man, exhausted, stopped running and lowered his head to catch his breath. He finally raised it and walked slowly toward the bus. Just as he'd made it inches from the door, the driver kicked into drive again.

"No he didn't!" a woman squealed incredulously to her seatmate.

"Girrrrl. We should report this one! Report his ass to the Greyhound people!"

The abandoned man began running once more, and the whole busload of passengers were either pressed against the windows or standing in the aisle, holding onto the backs of seats.

"Run! Run! Run!" they chanted to the man who was already running. The bus driver stopped for the man once more—another tease—and drove off again. This time the passengers began yelling at the bus driver, cursing him while he checked his rearview mirror to make sure no one was about to hit him.

Tia could not believe that all the passengers—none of whom, she assumed, knew the man—had so quickly and loudly championed him. The church members of Hope and Grace had always referred to nonchurch members as The World, as in, "The World is full of sin," or "The World is evil." She had seen instances when this was not the case. A cafeteria worker had waved her pass when she'd forgotten her lunch money, a boy once walked her home and smiled during her silences. Tia thought of these kindnesses as passing showers; refreshing, yet brief. But this kindness, everyone shouting, as though their words alone could encourage the man, came with the force of a storm.

The third time the driver stopped, he opened the door. A man in his late forties wearing a thin jacket boarded the bus to wild cheering. He was having no success at trying to keep saliva in his mouth, and whatever food he'd had in the bag had fallen out. He heaved, trying to stare at the driver murderously, mouth twisted. Tears streamed down his face while people applauded as he passed them in the aisle. He took his seat and the man next to him clamped a manly, consoling arm around him.

"Let *me* off!" said an indignant white woman up front, "I cannot *believe* you would treat someone this way! *Sinner!*" The woman stood in the aisle, and sunlight cast a matte sheen throughout her proud lilac beehive. Cars waiting to get onto the turn for the interstate honked their horns.

"You want to get off, lady?" the driver dared. He scratched his nose and opened the door again. The woman stood there, trapped and fuming.

"If you're going to get off, get off. If not, kindly sit down so we can arrive at our destination on time." The driver closed the door and turned onto the road, which curved before it merged into the highway. The woman stood with the unsteady frailty of a propped-up paper doll, and the motion of the bus thrust her down the aisle. People braced her, their hands extending to help her up like an old-time baptism.

"All I can say," hollered one woman, "is that you is WRONG, Mr. Bus Driver. I don't know who you or Mr. Greyhound is, but you is both *wrong*."

THE NEARLY ABANDONED man's celebrity faded as people stumbled out of the bus and into hot, gleaming Atlanta. Tia stood in the Atlanta bus station as streams of people with destinations whizzed past her, bumped into her, crowded around her. She found a carousel of phones and set down her clarinet case and backpack. She hefted the white pages onto her knee, trying to find her mother's last name: Dunlovey. Then she realized that Atlanta had two separate phone books, each over a thousand pages. The one she'd first picked up covered only the last half of the alphabet. She lifted up the correct phone book and saw about fifteen Dunloveys, no Rosalyns, but two "R"s.

The first R Dunlovey she called, a white woman's voice answered the phone. Tia didn't even bother asking for her mother's name and immediately apologized for having called the wrong number. The second R Dunlovey she called, a black man's voice answered the phone. Her immediate thought was that her mother would not be living with a man, and that if she was, his name would be the one listed. Then she realized that her mother probably lived by rules that did not resemble rules at all.

"Yeah," the voice said, "Who is it?"

"I'm looking for Rosalyn Dunlovey."

"I'm asking who you *is*, not who you *want*." In the background she heard screaming children. Something smashed, and the phone on the other end tumbled and fell. The man shouted for the children to shut up, and more things smashed in the distance. She held the phone toward its upright cradle, about to hang up.

"This is Tia," she said, waiting, hoping that kindness would enter the man's voice.

"Well, Tia, there's a Rosa here, but no Rosalyn. How you know Rosa?"

Tia had never heard her grandmother call her mother Rosa. If her mother had a shortened name, it would have been Roz, not Rosa. But then, she'd never heard her grandmother mention her mother at all. And her mother wouldn't have kids. But kids were not impossible to have, and these kids sounded like they were four or five. Tia didn't want to think about it. She preferred the image of her mother on an anonymous street corner, shooting up heroin, to that of her mother having a real life and not having visited her in Montgomery, especially to be with this man who had no telephone etiquette.

Then she understood: this could not be her mother. For the first time it occurred to her that her mother might be dead.

"I'm sorry. I have the wrong number."

"Wait a minute," the man said, suddenly buttering his words, "you sound good. Rosa ain't gone be off work till ten. Why don't you come—"

Tia hung up. She closed her eyes. She did not know why she'd expected there to be less people, less noise, less ugliness when she opened them again, but she had. She picked up her clarinet and put on her backpack, then took in the scene so that she would not forget what she'd just learned: expectation is what you assume will happen, based on what you see. Hope is also an assumption, made with your eyes closed.

SHE DECIDED that she'd leave the bus station and call hotels from pay phones elsewhere.

"What's your price range?" one hotel desk clerk asked.

Tia had never deliberately lied to anyone. She could say ten dollars, and it wouldn't be a lie.

"Ten dollars?" the desk clerk said. She whistled, high and arch. This desk clerk had been the only one out of nearly ten who'd even stayed on the phone with Tia after she'd announced how much money she had.

"What you're looking for is a motel. You're looking for, like, a roach motel." The clerk laughed, and when Tia did not laugh also, the clerk softly said, "Heh, I was just kidding."

Tia pictured her grandmother in the kitchen, singing along with the gospel station on the radio. Right about now, she would notice that Tia was late coming home from school.

"OK. Are you trying to find a job here or something?"

Yes. That was it. She was looking for a job. She obviously would have to start looking for a job.

"Yes, I am. Do you have one?"

"Honey, I got two jobs, but they're mine. I would gladly give 'em to you if I didn't have these goddamn bill collectors to feed. How old are you?"

Tia told the woman that she was fourteen.

"You a runaway."

She called the places the clerk told her to call. The YWCA said they didn't have rooms, just a swimming pool. She had booked a room with the Atlanta Dream Youth Hostel for fifteen dollars until their desk clerk told her to be sure to bring two forms of I.D.

"I don't have an I.D."

"Well, we can't give you a room. You need two forms of I.D."

Tia wanted to know why, and the clerk told her, "to prove that you are who you say you are."

"But I told you. I'm Tia Townsend."

"But we need pictures. Like a driver's license. Or a passport. We need picture identification."

"Why do you need a picture?" Tia asked. "You'll see me when I get there."

BY NIGHTTIME, she had walked around most of downtown Atlanta and ridden five MARTA buses. She plopped down in a hard McDonald's chair before she even thought about ordering food. She laid her head on the table, then propped her chin up, watching the people as they pretended they had not just stared at her.

It had rained during the day, and newspapers were not enough to cover her. She'd slipped in mud taking the shortcut over the small hill on her way into the McDonald's, and she was too tired to go to the restroom to change. She knew her hair was a mess, and remembered she'd given Marcelle's comb away to the man on the Greyhound.

Only the day before, her grandmother forced her to pray for two hours straight after they'd come home from church, and most of her half hour of silent prayer included thinking of a way to get to Atlanta. Now that she was in Atlanta, she prayed, her head bowed over the table's yellow formica.

When Tia lifted her head, she saw that one man did not even pretend to look away from her. He wore one of those nylon running suits that swished with every movement, and his gaze was unflagging. She was too tired not to stare back. His plastic straw daintily gurgled up the last bit of whatever was in the cup, and he grinned as though he were proud of this accomplishment.

"Rough day?"

Tia nodded and smiled.

"Well, keep your pretty self smiling." He got up and tossed his cup in the trash. He spoke a few words to the bored cashier, then swished out the door.

When Tia finally summoned the energy to order her food, taking out her remaining fourteen dollars from where she kept it—inside a sock, safety-pinned in a skirt pocket—the girl waved her hand.

"It's free," the girl said.

"Thank you," Tia said. "Thank you so much." She wanted to tell the McDonald's girl that God—or someone or something, whatever it was that drizzled good down upon the world—would bless her. "Thank you."

"I ain't do nothing. He paid for it." The girl pushed the tray of food toward Tia as though the meal had offended her in some way.

At first Tia thought "He" meant God. For people at church, "He" always meant God. "He touched me," they said, "He spoke to me," they yelled, "He visited me last night," they whispered. But people In the World, Tia knew, never used "He" to refer to God.

" 'He' who?"

The girl waved a lazy hand toward the door. "That man that just left. Dezi. It's on him."

The man who'd spoken to her, who'd said she was pretty. The last time anyone had called her pretty was when she was five years old and her mother lay next to her on a stained, sheetless mattress and said, "You so pretty." Tia remembered smiling. Her mother was probably gone on heroin. Her eyes were glazed, their whites not white at all, but a stained yellow, her hand patting Tia's face a bit more roughly than she must have intended. "You so pretty, you so pretty. Pretty, pretty, pretty," she repeated, like she was trying to jog her memory of a song. Before her mother fell asleep, she drew Tia closer to her, her breath reeking of vomit.

TAVERNS AND BARS lined Virginia Avenue, their interiors leaking a dim tungsten glow. Tia passed restaurants where waiters and waitresses navigated the round li- nened tables like dragonflies zipping atop mazes of lily pads. An Oriental grocery advertised itself in both English and Chinese, the pictograms of the latter a complex darning of saber-shaped strokes, windswept in every direction but down. The large window displayed an oversized bird of some sort, hanging by its feet, its corpse glossed molasses-black down to its headless neck.

Though the stores and bars tried their best to be inviting, she knew none of them were inviting her. Tia walked down the sidewalk, against the northward flow of pedestrian traffic. She found a pay phone and looked up R Dunlovey again. When she called, a young boy answered the phone.

"Hello!" the voice shouted, loud and confident, as if this were one of the few words he was proud to be able to pronounce.

"Hello," Tia said, "may I speak to your mother?"

The phone on the other end clattered, and as the child searched for his mother, Tia tried to figure out a way to find out whether the woman was her mother without telling the woman that she might be her daughter. After almost a full minute, she heard a sibling argument over a popsicle ensue in the distance, and hung up the phone.

She turned onto another street, then another, and another, until she entered a residential section where it looked like bills were paid on time. Then she saw the quiet streets as Marcelle might have seen them, and suddenly she knew what she would do. She walked past cars in the neighborhood, checking to see which ones were locked. After the first car alarm, she panicked, her clarinet banging against her side for the four whole blocks she ran.

She began to look for cars with clubs on their steering wheels. These, she dis- covered, were not locked nearly as often as the ones without, and when she brushed past them, no alarms sounded.

She picked the one with the plushest-looking seats, but it turned out the seats did not matter. If she didn't want anyone noticing her, she'd have to lie on the floor and cover herself. The floor was matted with what seemed like a week's worth of old newspapers, and she arranged these on herself in a thin tissuey blanket.

From a rip in the paper, she could see out the window. The sky remained a muddy purple brown, refusing to turn black and starry the way it did in Alabama. The lights from downtown winked at her, and the crescent moon looked like some- one's castaway cuticle, thrown up to God.

TIA WAS CERTAIN the morning sun would wake her before the owner got into the car to go to work. Instead the car door slammed, the engine started up, and over her face, the sun lit both the front and back of the newspaper.

The car began moving. Tia wished whoever was driving would hum or turn on the radio so she could stretch herself without the crinkling noise of paper being heard. She felt paralyzed, a vague tingle in her leg. If she could not get her circulation going soon, she feared it would stay limp and immobile forever. Then the person—a white woman—began singing to herself.

> Is this love, is this love
> is this love, is this love
> that I'm feeling . . .

Tia stretched and scratched. She could hear the newspaper crinkle and tear, but she didn't think the woman would be able to hear it over her singing.

Tia stopped scratching, a moment after the woman stopped singing. The silence in the car seemed to double. The car swerved and came to a halt.

The front door opened, but did not slam shut. The back door opened, and Tia could feel a draft of air rush up her skirt. She sat up. The woman screamed and ran down the sidewalk. The rest was all confusion in Tia's mind: at some point Tia got out of the car, running in the opposite direction, tugging her backpack behind her like it was a child who couldn't keep up. The woman had fallen onto the concrete and amid her screams, Tia realized she'd left her clarinet in the car. By the time she recovered it, the woman's hyperventilating and repeated pointing had sent two men running after her.

Only when the men had given up running after her and she had given up running from them, did she slump next to a dumpster amid pizza crusts, half-eaten sausages, and scampering cockroaches.

Her blouse sleeve was dotted with blood the whole length of her forearm. After she'd cleaned up in the public restroom, raking her hair as well as she could with her fingers, she walked by a man playing a saxophone. His case was open, and as people passed by, they dropped money inside. Tia headed toward an unshaded spot in a park where the clouds formed islands and peninsulas in a sky the color of suburban swimming pools. Tia opened her clarinet case and began to play. For the first hour, no one put money in her case, so instead of trying to play through the whole *Marriage of Figaro,* most of which consisted of uneventful passages for clarinets, she waited until she saw people approaching before she began to play, concentrating on the dramatic swells and crests. Then the change began to fall.

TO CELEBRATE, she went back to the same McDonald's. She was on her second Big Mac when the man named Dezi tapped on the window. He came inside, ordered a Coke, and sat across from her.

"You're looking more upbeat than before." He looked like he might have been thirty, or maybe a year or so younger, his head shaved to a bulletlike smoothness.

"Yeah," she said, "well, thanks for yesterday."

He looked as though he were trying to remember what he'd done that was so remarkable.

"Oh. *That*. Sweetheart, don't even worry about it. I take care of people I like, and I knew I liked you when I first saw you." Dezi sucked on his straw, but he looked at Tia as though he were making sure she wouldn't suddenly leave.

"You a church girl," he said. He nodded his head knowingly, and his lips slowly parted to reveal beautiful white teeth, one capped with gold.

When she had played her clarinet in the park, she was under the impression that she'd finally figured everything out. That she'd finally learned how to blend in with the normal world.

"No. I'm not," she answered, lying before she'd even realized it. It was the first lie she'd ever told, and it slipped from her mouth easily, as though it had been waiting to get out all along.

"Well, you just look real—I don't know. Special. You look real special."

HE FINGERED HIS THIN GOLD CHAIN and plucked out the cross attached to it from under his shirt.

"See. I'm real tight with God, *you know?*" He held up two joined fingers to signify their close relationship.

"Uh huh." She was getting tired of the conversation and nausea swelled inside her. She had wanted to get away, but he was making it more and more obvious to her how very different she was. She tried looking out the window, picking up her burger with an expression of renewed interest, but he kept staring, and the more he stared at her, the more troubled his face became.

"Your arm," he said, "What happened?"

In the park, she'd rolled her blouse sleeves to her elbows to air the wide scrape on her arm, and now she saw that it looked worse than before. Her brown skin had been stripped away to reveal the raw pink flesh under it.

"I don't know," she said absently, not wanting to go into the details of the day: the screaming woman, the men chasing her.

"That could get infected. You got to get that cleaned up. Where you live? I'll take you home."

She ate the rest of her burger. "That's alright. I live a long ways away."

Dezi wiggled his finger in his ear. "What's your name?"

She hesitated, then told him.

"Alright, Tia. Let me put it this way. I know you don't have a place to stay. Let's just say I try to watch over people." He studied her face to make sure she was following him. "I'll make sure that it gets disinfected. But if you want to sleep on the street—fine." Dezi held his hands up like a man who had nothing to hide being searched by the police. "You can sleep on the street, but I'd rather you didn't."

She glanced at Dezi's chain, thinking that a guy who wore a cross and paid for her meal couldn't be all that bad.

DEZI DROVE HER to his apartment on Martin Luther King Drive. He drove a tan Celica, and the whole ride he talked on a cellular phone using the deep low voice of a midnight deejay. The presumptuous, hyphenated store names of the Virginia Highlands gave way to grillwork-caged liquor stores with names like "Max's" and "The Place" and more to the point, "Liquor Here." Some businesses gave no indication as to what they might be selling, their signposts were signless, their neon neonless, and anything that looked as though it might give outsiders a peek at the scenery within was painted black. Other windows held a mirrory tint so that passing cars turned into blurry heat-wave mirages.

The only spots of color were the billboards and the prostitutes. The billboards all advertised Kools or Newports, and against the green backdrops, beautiful black people wore toy-colored clothes. They were depicted sledding, or skiing, or doing some other activity involving snow, all of them somehow managing to hold onto their cigarettes.

The prostitutes—Tia assumed they were prostitutes—wiped sweat from their faces, bouncing up and down in patchwork rabbit-fur jackets. Some slinked about in candy-colored outfits, desperately trying to appear as though they weren't scouting for tricks so much as eagerly willing to give men who cruised up to their curbs tourist information.

The children seemed unaware that anything was wrong. A chubby girl with hundreds of corkscrew curls springing about her shoulders wielded a snaky water-spouting hose, sending a throng of shirtless kids flying into alleys and abandoned lots. On a sidewalk, a Puerto Rican–looking kid bounced a ball to a black kid, and the black kid caught the ball with one hand, taking a drag off a cigarette with the other.

"Here it is," Dezi announced, parking the car. "The famous Stanford Gardens."

She shut the car door, not knowing if he was joking or not. The closest thing to a garden she saw were the geraniums a few people tried to grow from windowsill mayonnaise jars. Dezi laughed and took her hand. "C'mon Miss Tia, laugh sometime."

She could not laugh when he'd taken her hand as though he'd known her her whole life. She took her hand from his and pretended to attend to her scrape.

"I wonder if it'll heal?" she said, knowing that it would, but needing something to say to account for her hand's removal.

"I'll take care a that." He put his hand around her shoulder as though she were his prom date, and before she could think of a way to remove it, a group of kids appeared, wreathing about them.

A little boy about seven years old with smooth brown skin and hair as straight as an Indian was apparently the leader of the group. "Dez-zeeeee!" he singsonged, blocking their path. Dezi playfully tried to fake the boy out, but Dezi would not let go of Tia, dragging her along like a Siamese twin. "Go away, Gerard. Can't you see I got a young lady here who ain't used to little hoodlums stinking up the way?"

All the children except the one named Gerard made twinkling voodoo motions with their fingers.

"Oooooo! Dezi's got a new wo-maaaaan!"

The boy named Gerard flicked his palm open while his entourage clung to Dezi. They hugged his legs, pulled on his arms, all the time squealing his name.

Gerard's face turned serious while the others laughed and shouted.

"Gimme some money," the boy said, his palm still out, "the kind that folds."

"Nuh uh. Not today."

The other kids all began to plead with outstretched palms, explaining why they needed money.

"My tooth be hurting me and I need some candy to make the pain go away."

"See that spot? See that spot on my arm? Doctor say that spot gone kill me. He say money make it go away, though."

"I-I need to b-b-buy me some p-p-pop. M-m-my m-m-mama said she ain't gone buy me n-n-no more pop 'cause I wet the b-b-b-bed."

While everyone else made fun of the kid who was stuttering to explain that he did not *really* wet the bed, Gerard kept his face wise and smileless, his hand out-stretched.

"I'll tell," he said to Dezi, his eyes steady. "I *will* tell."

Dezi turned to Tia. He grinned the same overzealous smile black Montgomerians shined whenever faced with speaking to whites. Her grandmother disparagingly called it a "get-along" grin, as in, "put up, shut up, and get along with the white folks." She'd never seen her grandmother grin that way, and Tia developed a crumb of respect for her.

"These kids," Dezi said, shaking his head with mock weariness. He pulled out a folded, rubber-banded wad of money from his pocket. He tugged some bills from inside the wad's folded center. The kids stopped making fun of the boy who peed in the bed and crowded around Dezi and Tia so closely that she could smell their sticky kid fragrance; the silence was so profound that only the canned laughter from a faraway TV could be heard. Dezi handed them each a five.

"And don't be bothering me no more!" he yelled.

DEZI PILOTED HER through a maze of walkways and into his apartment. Tia could not shake the sight of that bundle of money. It was at least twice over what she'd seen on the collection plate at church, and after Dezi had sat her down and gone into the bathroom to get alcohol for her wound, she stood up. He walked out carrying an alcohol-soaked cotton ball.

"Listen," she said, "I really should go. Really."

He looked at her as if this were impossible.

"No. I don't think you should go."

She had half-expected for his voice to be velvety, the way it was on the car phone, or for him to ask her *why* she had to go in a tone that begged for her to stay, but he had said the words in distinct unequivocating chops. He took her arm and she struggled from him. His grip was firm, and he swabbed the alcohol onto the scrape. "Atlanta's a dangerous city."

She sniffed tears up her nose, and her face was hot. He sat her down on the couch, and for a moment, she did not know if the touch she felt was the velour of the couch or his hand. He wiped her tears away.

"It'll only sting for a little while," he said, his voice soft and instructional.

She began to think of ways she would die. He pulled her close to him, and the strength of his cologne seemed as threatening as the heat of his arm next to her.

"You don't trust me, do you?"

He laughed and hugged her like she were his daughter. She added up the years, and at the age her mother had had her, Dezi could have easily been her father's age, had she ever known her father. All she had of her father was his last name. Dezi kissed the top of her head.

"You beautiful. You know that? You don't, do you? I can tell you don't. But you are."

He rocked her for several minutes, and when her heartbeat had calmed, she realized she was no longer afraid. She still thought he would kill her, but she'd grown tired of fearing that, and simply waited for it to happen.

Dezi got up and stretched, then sat on the floor, facing her.

"I'm making you nervous, so I'll sit right here." He sat for a few minutes in their silence, then smiled shyly like it was his first date and he didn't know what to do next.

"You're a drug dealer." She said it with an unflinching matter-of-factness. She said it the way one would declare someone a Catholic or a human being. She folded her legs Indian-style, tucking her skirt under her knees. Her eyes closed, imagining him pulling out a gun and shooting her. She opened them to find him in the same position. She waited.

He looked about the apartment with the disinterest of one bored with the decor. "Yeah," he said.

She asked what it was like to deal drugs.

"It's fucked up. What more do you want me to say?"

Dezi got up and cooked a slab of steak, while she sat being perfectly still on the couch. It was the first time in a long while that she'd stopped moving.

He offered her some steak. It was tough, chewy and oversalted; his recipe was to add generous shakes of every spice he had available.

"How'd you get here?" he asked.

She told him about church, about Marcelle and Sister Gwendolyn. She told him about the bus ride and not being able to find a place to stay, about sleeping in the woman's car and being chased. She told him about her mother. Tia's words came out by the gallon and her hands had a habit of boiling up at the most exciting moments and then finally asked, "Do you know a woman named Rosalyn Dunlovey?"

He looked up to the ceiling and then a wave of recognition crossed his face.

"Yeah. Is she like, sort a medium height? Long hair like yours? Pretty brown eyes?"

"Yes!" Tia said. She jumped off the couch. "Where is she? She's alive?"

Dezi laughed and waved his hand. "Naw. I don't know her."

Tia's smile capsized. She began to hit him with slapping blows wherever she could. He took both her hands.

"Hey. Hey. Hey," he said. He hugged her so that her hands would stop hitting him. "I didn't mean to joke like that. But if she was on heroin then, and she still alive, she's probably a crackhead now. Just forget her. She's already good as dead."

He told her about Gerard.

"His mama's an addict. A *real* addict. She suck your dick and shit." He looked at Tia, and his eyes apologized for his language. He took out a Newport and lit it. "I give them kids money, and you know what? All them other kids buy candy and shit. They money gone," he snapped his fingers, "money gone like just like that. Not Gerard. He take that money and get on the MARTA. He buy some chocolate bars like schoolkids be selling and go to white neighborhoods. Say he's selling them candy bars for a field trip. Them white folks eat it up, and Gerard make enough money to buy himself some real clothes. Some real shoes. Not fancy ones. Just ones that fit."

Dezi gave Tia sheets and a blanket, and made a bed on the couch for her. She felt foolish for having been so worried. She remembered how the children ringed around him. Dezi didn't hurt them. He wouldn't hurt her.

As Tia fell asleep, she imagined Marcelle, in Montgomery, in her own bed. She was sure Marcelle was up to the same old trouble, but Marcelle could not top what she'd been through. Tia, in the dark of the apartment, saw Marcelle's jealous, disbelieving face. She had only one word for her, and she said it out loud in the darkness.

"Ha."

DEZI LEFT EARLY the next morning. Before he closed the door, he told Tia she was free to go, and tried to give her money, but Tia refused. Dezi paused at the door's threshold, taking her hands in his. He turned her hands, looking down at her palms, and then he was gone.

After she showered, Tia took out her clarinet and began playing *The Marriage of Figaro*. She loved fingering the succession of B-flat–C combinations that sounded like a tickle. The succession began to go up a half-scale that fluttered into a series of alternating "D"s and "E"s. Then the waterfall of the music began. The trumpets had the main part for a while, and she had never had a need to play it. In band, the clarinets sat back and played whole bars of *tut-tut-tut-tut* while the trumpets did their thing, then the flutes, then the baritones. Tia tried to play the trumpet part. She pressed variations of the silver side keys, which looked like the lazy flats they played; she tested the round fingerkeys that circuited the tube's holes in halos of thin metal. Within an hour, she had figured out the trumpet part and played it, then replayed it. She went into the bathroom so that she could look in the mirror as she played, but she was so proud of herself, she couldn't get through three bars of music without seeing a goofy smile creep up around her mouthpiece.

She left the bathroom and was about to put the clarinet away when she saw a woman sitting on Dezi's sofa. She did not know how the woman got in, but there she was, wearing a purple fitted jacket with a tiny purple skirt. Her hair fell about her shoulders in thick black waves, and her pockmarked face was covered in makeup a shade lighter than her neck. A set of keys fanned out next to the woman's thigh as if the keys themselves had had a long day.

The woman was swallowed up in the soft velour folds of the couch, her shins spread out like a colt's. She looked up at Tia, not startled so much as studious, as though Tia were an enigmatic painting.

"Who are you?" Tia asked. She realized she was holding the clarinet like a spear.

"Who am I? Who the hell are *you*? You working for Dezi now?"

Tia waited a while before answering. "No. I'm a friend of his. Are you a— customer?"

The woman pushed herself from the couch and stood up, walking into the kitchen. Water ran from the faucet, the fridge opened, and as bottles and jugs and wrapped packages were being moved around in the search for food, the woman answered. "Naw, I ain't no customer. What the hell make you think I'm some kind a fuck-up?"

She came back into the living room where Tia was still standing, still holding onto the clarinet. The woman had a good half of a bologna sandwich hanging from her mouth. Through the bread and meat she asked, "You don't work for Dezi?"

Tia laid the clarinet down in the crook of the couch's arm so the reed wouldn't get chipped. The woman was dressed as though she might have been an executive, but where one might have expected a blouse underneath the purple jacket, an expanse of chest and cleavage presented itself. Her earrings dangled, grazing her shoulders. She laid her sandwich down on the arm of the couch and began to unbutton her jacket.

"I'm *hot*. You hot?" She undid all five buttons and took off her blazer as though Tia were merely a curious pet. She stood nonchalantly in a lacy purple bra, sighed, then picked up the sandwich again. During bites she muffled, "I 'ont even have to ask if you hot. Niggas always hot," she swallowed the last bite of sandwich. "Can't get no blacks folks to cool down. No sir."

Before Tia could even acknowledge what the woman said with a nod or a word, the woman started up again. "So I guess Dezi just plucked you off the Goodship Lollipop and caged you up in here."

The woman picked up a pack of Dezi's Newports and rattled them, searching down their hole until she pried one out, crumpling up the pack of thin plastic and paper in her fist.

"No. He invited me to stay here. I'm looking for a job."

"Ohhh ho," the woman smiled as she lit the cigarette. Two columns of smoke swirled from her nostrils. "Ohhhhhh." Her head bobbed up and down, amused.

"Are you his wife? He didn't tell me he was married."

The woman laughed, then pushed Tia's shoulder as though they were longtime friends.

"Baby, you don't even know which end is up!" She laid the burning cigarette against the saucer of the coffee table plant and steered Tia to the couch, sitting her down. She sat next to Tia and made a smiling pantomime of introduction, sticking out her jeweled hand, sending her bracelets rattling.

"My name is Marie. What's your name, Miss Lady?"

"Tia. Tia Townsend."

"Alright, Miss Lady Tia." Her head made several loopy circles as she rasped, "Now, Miss Lady. How in the hell did you meet Massa Dezi?"

Tia blinked hard, trying to remember. Although it had only been two days ago, it seemed much longer. Her head flooded with many lies she could have told, but the way the woman sat, in her purple bra, her eyes the sort even liars couldn't lie to, she blurted out the truth. "I ran away from home. And I didn't have a place to stay so he said I could stay with him. He didn't seem like he was a killer or anything like that, so I thought I'd stay till I could find a job. If he's your boyfriend or something, I didn't do anything. I swear—I mean, you're not supposed to *swear*, but I *promise* I wasn't trying to be his girlfriend or anything."

Marie picked up her cigarette, staring at a framed print on the wall, then began a long series of thoughtful puffs. She turned to Tia quickly and said, "Wanna sandwich? I didn't even offer you no food, girl!"

Tia declined the offer, and Marie put out the Newport in the plant's saucer. It sizzled in the water and died.

"Well," Marie said, turning to Tia as though she was trying to make her understand something she should already know, "I *work* for Dezi. And I don't push no drugs, either."

Tia nodded her head slowly, now comprehending, but to be sure, she used the delicate term she'd heard her grandmother used. "Are you a lady of the evening?"

This sent Marie howling. Her head shook back and forth like women in church getting happy, her hair slapped the sides of her face, she smacked Tia's knee repeatedly, laughing so loudly that it seemed as though this were the finale to a TV horror movie, the bad guy cackling insanely in triumph.

"Girrrrl! I ain't heard that word used since I was in pigtails in Savannah! Who taught you that!"

Tia said quietly, "I just learned it somewhere."

Marie kept laughing until she scratched her head vigorously with the tips of her indigo fingernails, letting out the luxuriant sigh of one who's had a good time.

"Lady of the Evening," she said in bright soprano. "I like that, I like that," Marie added, trying to convince herself. "You must a come a *long* ways from home."

"Yeah," Tia said. "I guess I have."

BEFORE TIA LEFT the apartment, she folded up the sheets and blankets she'd slept in and placed them in a soft cube on the couch. She left a note for Dezi, saying that she thought it was time for her to go back home. She did not mention that she'd found out that he was not only a drug dealer but a pimp. She knew she was not going back home, but she had to tell him something to explain why she'd left. She thought about going back to the park, then going to the far south side of town where well-off black people lived. Surely someone there would take her in.

She sat in the park but hadn't the energy to play music for money. She watched for what seemed like hours as the park workers cut the lawn; in the wake of huge riding mowers, the grass stretched in a carpet of green, reminding her of the cemetery near her home in Montgomery. She looked down at her open clarinet case, the pieces of the instrument glinting limousine black in the sunlight. She was filled with a sickness and longing, wanting to hear the simple sound of air blowing through a tube of wood. The case and her backpack were getting cumbersome to carry around the city, and she tried to think of a place she could store it while she searched for lodging for the upcoming night.

Then she remembered the bus station lockers. She found out how to take the MARTA from Stanford Gardens to the bus station, and there they were in front of her, a row of lockers with combinations. She put her change into an empty locker and was about to lift her case when she saw the photocopied flyer on the next locker. "Missing," it read, and below the large lettering, despite the poor copy job, she could make out her own face, a picture of her from junior high, her smile the smile of one who tried too hard to look happy.

"Tia!" a voice called.

Tia looked around the bus station, expecting to see her grandmother, the pastor, and church members.

But it was Dezi, leaning against the doorjamb of the video arcade, wearing a black nylon jogging suit, his gold cross on display. He ran toward her, out of breath, holding roses. "Hey, baby," he panted. "Didn't think I'd find you . . . C'mon back . . . I'll take care of you . . . can't go back home . . . not after everything they did to you . . ."

But standing in the bus station with her picture facing her was enough to remind

Tia that returning home was possible. Tia remembered when Marcelle and her mother had first come to Hope and Grace. Marcelle sat next to Tia on her pew, and Marcelle's face did not ask the question, *Can we be friends?* but made the statement, *We will be friends.* Back then, Tia wanted to be mad, to send a look that said, what makes you think I don't already have friends, but Tia already knew what her own face was saying: *Yes, we will be friends. Yes.*

Tia scanned the bus station. Everyone, it seemed, was too busy trying to catch their buses, trying to find the restrooms and pay phones and food, to notice the flyers with her face on it. She stared at Dezi blankly.

"I'm sorry," she said. He threw his arms up in the air, a salesman hating to see a good offer go to waste. The roses jostled in their translucent plastic. They were the typical roses, scattered with sprays of babies' breath, the roses themselves bright red, their petal edges slightly wilted and wine-colored. He walked toward the door where taxis snailed up to the curb and waited. She wanted to tell Marcelle everything that had happened in the last two days, wanted to see Marcelle strain to hide her shock. But how could she explain that no one had ever given her flowers before? That no one had ever given her anything? At first, Tia walked slowly. Then, when the roses in Dezi's hand seemed within reach, she ran toward them.

"LOOK," DEZI SAID when they'd returned to his apartment. He turned off his pager. "I'ma only have time for you from now on." He kissed her, and his mouth smelled of smoke and Tic Tacs. She had never been kissed before, and it took her a while to understand that she had to open her mouth to receive his tongue. He pushed his tongue over hers, and it seemed to be searching out the cavities of her teeth. The vinyl-like slick of his shirt rubbed against her blouse, and his hands pushed the cotton fabric up past her bra, where tiny inelegant sprouts of elastic popped out from the straps.

She did not stop him, and there was no ceremony. Her blouse was off, her skirt was in a heap on the floor, and he had undone his pants with a single hand.

"This is how people have babies," she said. He wiped the saliva from her mouth with the pads of his fingertips. It had been a long time since she'd felt anything smooth next to her skin, and now, suddenly, so much of her skin was touched by skin not her own. He stroked a spot on the back of her neck, and it was at once frightening and mesmerizing as when she'd once seen her own hand move, without her telling it, toward a candle flame. She knew what it was that lay on her thigh, and it moved of its own accord, like a water hose flicking out of control in the grass.

"Let me," he said.

His hands, suddenly, no longer felt smooth, and she understood that he was expecting something in addition to her near-nakedness. She remembered over-hearing girls in junior high talk about sex, about how men spurted a sticky liquid into women, and how women or girls could have babies that way.

"I can't," she said, trying to sit up, but he was heavy and pressing.

"Baby," he said. His tongue flicked and circled against her neck. He whispered something and she cringed.

Tia squeezed her thighs together, but his hand found its way between them. She bolted upright, against his weight, covering herself in the blanket she'd folded just a few hours ago. He stood up and sighed. Completely naked, the muscles in his chest contracted, his gold tooth glinted.

"Shit!" He stared down at himself, and when his penis finally shrank, he whirled around and smashed the framed print on the wall. The frame clattered against the top of the stereo, and the glass, as though finished waiting for the chance to express its opinion, cracked and spilled seconds afterward.

"I'm not ready," she said, "I just—"

Dezi sat on the couch beside her, taking in an impatient loud breath before sending it tranquilly back into the air. "Shit, baby. I know you're not. I know."

TIA WOKE that evening and could not remember how she'd fallen asleep. The children still yelled and played outside, and Tia could hear the awkward dicing of Dezi making something in the kitchen. Liver and onions.

The living room light had not been turned on, and in the evening darkness Tia could feel that she was still in her underwear, covered by the blanket. She touched the inside of her panties. She could feel that she was sticky and wet, and though she had felt this way before—listening to her grandmother's snores, moving her hand between her thighs in her own bed—she was not thinking that the stickiness she now felt could be related to the kind she'd made herself. It had been a mystery to her when she felt electric waves of happiness flow through her when she rubbed herself as she lay in bed. Her hand had always drawn back, oily wet, and she had not dared mention any of it to her grandmother. She could only remember those girls she'd overheard in the junior high cafeteria talking about sex; the way they said the words "semen" and "pregnant," squealing when the boys squirted mustard on their hot dogs.

When she screamed, she could hear nothing else. Dezi came out of the kitchen and tried to put his hand over her mouth, but her cries ran over his fingers and over every noise outside. She grabbed her clothes, swinging. Buttons stung his eyes, her skirt slapped against his cheek.

"Tia!" He pinned her down.

"You raped me!"

Her legs kicked him, but she sank into the soft, endless maw of the couch. She kicked, but he held her down until her knee landed somewhere that mattered. Dezi rolled off of her and onto the floor with a low moan.

"No," he said, quietly, calmly, "No, I didn't."

She put on her skirt and her blouse, her clothes straying at haphazard angles. She swung the door open and fell; Dezi had her by the foot and yanked her into the apartment, and Tia's chin dragged the welcome mat along with her.

"I want you to repeat after me. 'I was not raped.' "

"I'm wet!" she sobbed, until she screeched at a new, high pitch, "*You raped me!*"

"What would make you think I raped you, or had sex with you. We kissed and—"

"I'm wet!"

"I did not do anything inside you. Tia, baby, I did not do *anything* inside you. You fell asleep and I started making dinner. You're probably wet because—you don't know why, do you?"

She did not know how the oily wetness between her legs had come to be there. Maybe she had fallen asleep and her hand had done it on its own? Maybe Dezi was telling the truth. Her ignorance pounded at her chest with the sharp, alert thuds of a courtroom gavel; shrieking was her only relief, an unthinking indulgence.

"Baby," Dezi said. As she continued to scream, his voice changed from the tone of one trying to calm down a woman in labor to that of someone scalded with boiling water. "Shut up!"

But Tia would not stop, and he dragged her along the shag of the carpet until her face felt the cold linoleum of the kitchen floor. She gurgled up her spit, felt blood trill down her nostrils. Her teeth locked, biting nothing, and her screams dead-ended into low grunts. The world outside faded. She could not hear the children, nor the sounds from any TV. And though she heard sirens, they were far away, and in the second she listened, they seemed to be farther away still. Then she could no longer hear them.

She opened her mouth, feeling sound about to make its way out, sound that would shatter everything, but Dezi slapped her face, and her eyes reeled until they saw the endless, happy yellow flowers of the kitchen wallpaper. He slapped her again, but his face did not match the anger of the action. He looked sad, like the pictures of starving children whose sadness becomes fragile. She could not remember getting up, her hand finding the knife on the counter. She did remember the smell of onions on it, pungent and insinuating.

There was no drama in his voice, just the word in its nudest form.

"Don't."

OUTSIDE, PEOPLE CAME into her peripheral vision, then were gone like drifting notes of music. She ran and no one followed, past the signless signs, past billboards, past the glitter of whores.

Then she ran up against a wall of soft purple and cocoa butter. Marie.

Marie adjusted herself from the run-in, her eyelashes curtsying to the man with whom she was talking. The man sucked his teeth and ambled down the street to the next flash of earrings.

Then Tia told her everything, pausing when she saw any car that looked like Dezi's drive past. Marie wiped Tia's face and rocked her, then took out a cigarette and lit it.

"Alright, Miss Lady," she said. She waved her cigarette in the air like a wand.

"See, a man got to stick his thing inside you before things start to get messed up, so I don't think he *raped you* raped you. But he ain't got no business with you anyway, see, 'cause you my homegirl. How old are you? Fourteen fifteen? That's statutory rape, right there. That's what that's called." She drew a long drag on the cigarette and kept going. "We sending you home. Yes sir. We can't have people like you running around here." She stuck her hand in her thigh-high boots and took out a thin fold of money. She peeled two bills from the top, folded them into fourths and pressed the money into Tia's hand. Then Marie slapped Tia's face. Tia touched her face with as much surprise as if she'd awakened to discover that she'd slapped herself in her sleep.

"That's so you won't forget what Dezi feels like. Wait here."

Dazed, Tia began to walk away. Marie looked over her shoulder.

"Goddammit, I said wait! That's your problem in the first place, you don't be listening when people be talking. Wait!" Tia stood still and Marie took a few haunchy, bovine steps toward the girl at the end of the block.

"Lydia," Marie called out to a girl wearing a metallic slip with matching metallic high heels. "Get over here!"

Lydia waved her limp hand like she were shooing away a fly.

Marie put her hand on her hip. "Ho, you best be moving your fat ass, I'm trying to get this church girl off and back to her peoples!"

Lydia walked over, her heels clicking with each step.

"Don't be calling me no motherfuckin' ho, ho. My pussy—"

Marie flicked her cigarette in Lydia's direction. Lydia put her hand up like a traffic cop signaling "stop." It was a slow night, three whores on the opposite side of Lydia's street heard the commotion and came over, clicking and oohing.

Marie said, "This poor child need to get her ass on a bus. She need some benjamins. What you got?"

The fat girl named Lydia looked Tia up and down then flicked her hand in appraisal.

"She got two eyes and a nose and a mouth and a pussy. She can work for her'n like I do for mine."

Marie stared Lydia down. Lydia pouted.

"Shit," Lydia said, fussing with her Oriental topknot. She undid what looked like a chopstick from her hair and out came a tiny roll of bills.

"Give her twenty."

"Twenty!" Tia expected Lydia's nostrils to snort smoke. Lydia threw the bill at Tia and it fluttered to the sidewalk.

Marie eyed the three onlooking girls wearily. "Y'all too."

One girl wore a beauty pageant–style tiara and a fur jacket, another was dressed in a skintight rainbow-striped camisole, and the third was clad in a plain black pantsuit.

"C'mon," Marie said, but the girls began to slowly walk away. "Y'all know y'all wished somebody'd a did it for you, so give it up."

Two girls exhaled deeply and turned around. The one in the rainbow dress kept on walking. When she got back to her spot she struck a pose of resignation. She smoothed down her blonde-streaked hair.

"Give it up!" Marie yelled at the two who'd returned. She cocked an eye at Tia, and her voice slid down a jazzy scale, "You know niggas don't like to be giving up no money." The girls, as if to prove Marie wrong, took out their cash with daring thrusts.

The one in the black pantsuit handed a dirty twenty to Tia.

"Thank you," Tia said quietly.

The one wearing the tiara wagged a finger in Marie's face before handing over the money. "If I get messed up cause a this, I'ma get you. *Miss Marie.*"

A car screeched, found new direction, and started up again.

"Uh oh," the tiaraed one said, "Here come the Man." Dezi careened into the corner and didn't bother to close the door after him. His cut had been wiped and cleaned, but fresh blood filled the gash, threatening to seep out. Tia remained frozen. He was holding her clarinet case.

"What y'all looking at!"

The girls began screaming.

"C'mon baby," he said, his words sounding tender, until his voice hit an angry, nervous clef as he approached her. *"Come on."* He bounced up and down like a boxer, impatient and eager to get into the ring. The girls had him, their fingernails scratching the nylon of his jacket trying to hold on him. "Baby. Come. *On!*"

The backpack she could do without, but she could not think of leaving her clarinet behind, until suddenly, she had to. Church. Home. Marcelle. All dilemmas. But dilemmas, she began to understand, are not solved so much as managed, and in a world in which someone who barely knew her could help her return home, she could possibly hope that someone at home could help her make it bearable. There would be, she thought, other clarinets.

The prostitutes were all speaking at once, their lips moving in a way she'd studied many times, trying to know what it would be like talking to God. They were holding Dezi, screaming, "Run, honey! Run! Run, honey! *Run!*"

Marie pushed Tia so hard she fell off the curb. "Run, honey. And don't let nobody lock you in no closet no more." Tia stood up and brushed gravel and broken glass from her skirt. And she ran.

recollections

WHEN I REFLECT ON my eighteen years in Iowa City, my first thought is what a very strange environment it was for a fellow who grew up in the belief that if an event hadn't happened in New York City, it hadn't happened. But what appealed to me at once about the Workshop was its function. As a book editor with a Maxwell Perkins role model I saw the Workshop scheme as similar to that of a quality publisher, seeking the best young writers, hoping to nourish and launch them, yet without that inhibiting commercial risk.

I learned that Iowa City is an island of bohemian life, a Greenwich Village, a Rive Gauche, rising out of the infinite plains and truck stops of mid-America. Its isolation has much to do with its appeal for apprentice writers. There's a commitment to going (renouncing one's familiars) and, once there, the reward of a share in the communal purpose and faith.

When I arrived in 1969, presumably for a single semester, the University was enjoying its rebellious era. The students were facing off against the National Guard and laying waste the campus to protest the war in Vietnam. The Workshop was largely male, booted, long-haired, laden with experience of the war itself or of escaping it. Psychedelics and sexual initiation were customary story themes, and if one or two young women students turned up for a discussion of the worksheet, they rarely lasted the whole session.

In the mid-1970s the women's revolution reached the English-Philosophy building (EPB) and the change was profound. Female voices, now equally distributed around the table, challenged the male authority, often successfully, occasionally inflicting humiliating damage. The ladies were not averse to sexual themes themselves but preferred the family dynamic, mothers and grandmothers prevailing on a new generation of girls.

By the end of the decade the roughhouse, I-am-the-original-egg, essentially macho attitude of its opening was shelved by the young women now arriving, fully provided with a knowledge of and passion for their literary forebears. Thus the "form course," previously the Workshop's one concession to academic order, became a serious endeavor and a sign of the neo-intellectualism that would mark the '80s.

The historic crisis that spawned the modern Workshop was the clash between the two titans, the great literary showman from Cedar Rapids, Paul Engle, and the consummate, academic statesman, John Gerber, "The Silver Fox."

Engle was a man of many gifts, and two of his most fortunate ones were his surprising ability to raise funds and his revolutionary belief that, like music and painting, the writing of first-class poetry and fiction could be taught at a university.

At the end of World War II he gathered a writing community from apprentices already used to Iowa City's long and bitter winters. He raised the necessary funds from rich acquaintances in the East and persuaded the university to let him pitch camp (Quonset huts) in the parking lot of the Student Union.

The Engle Quonset hut program promptly attracted such distinguished visitors as Robert Frost, Stephen Vincent Benét, John Berryman, Robert Lowell, and Archibald MacLeish, so that aspiring writers, many on the GI bill, flocked in to enjoy Iowa's spiritual joys and physical hardships.

Engle's success was not lost on the university, and when he complained that his "Writers' Workshop" deserved to be legitimated with indoor housing, he was offered space within the English Department, then rejoicing in its newly completed building alongside the Iowa River and the chairmanship of John Gerber.

The stage was set for confrontation between these two leaders of markedly different styles. The fulmination occurred over a trifling incident (an appointment approved while Engle was out of town), but the consequence, as I understand it, was Engle's anger. It led him to believe that the Workshop should not and could not proceed under any management but his own, and he threatened to abandon it to English Department care.

This issue proved the dividing of the streams, to Paul Engle's founding of the International Writers' Program, for which he found even more generous contributors along with an encouraging State Department, and to a Writers' Workshop formally and proudly adopted by the English Department. Unlike other writing programs, Iowa's was the departmental showcase, attracting some of its best Ph.D. candidates. Professors and scholars of the hoariest academic honors gave way in the EPB elevator for Workshop instructors who lacked even a bachelor's degree.

When I blew into town in the spring of 1969, I was oblivious of this background and not entirely clear why George Starbuck was so eager to abandon the directorship he had only just assumed nor, once I had agreed to take it on, why Paul was so indifferent to his extraordinarily successful creation.

I recall that when we decided to make a celebration of the Workshop's fiftieth anniversary, Paul remembered other plans and at first was unwilling to participate.

In fact he did attend and was at his wittiest, describing his role to the convocation of a half century's Workshop graduates as that of the corpse borne through Egyptian festivals to subdue unrestrained revelry.

One of the Workshop's virtues is that half its faculty is made up of visitors. This leads to a major preoccupation with booking future performances and hoping the current ones will work out. The search is hard because the qualities of a good Workshop teacher are rare: the prestige to attract students, an editorial sense that can foster a talent outside his or her taste and expertise, and a diplomacy that can keep student savagery from serious bloodletting. I recall the tell-it-like-it-is apprentice summarizing the worksheet of a shy classmate with, "But this is just shit, terrible shit."

John Cheever and Angus Wilson come to mind as extraordinary teachers, generous with their time and interest. Angus took each of his students to a solo lunch and kept up a correspondence with many. John saw Allan Gurganus onto the fast track at the *New Yorker*. Both men had an instinct for the sensitivities afloat in a writing community, behaved with consideration for the rest of us, and gave of themselves as though that were their own priority.

At the other extreme were the eccentrics, often flamboyant enough to attract students but emotionally needy and unreliable. I think of Fred Exley, a brilliant writer and passionate partisan of the literary life, but a determined drinker and fantasist who undertook his meandering telephone chats at two and three in the morning. I think of Dick Yates, another brilliant writer. His students were devoted, and yet he was so subject to grievance and depression that he would be overwhelmed by tears and unable to conduct his workshop.

But these frailties, a certain amount of craziness and its frequent companion of alcoholism, are no firm caveat against appointment. I think in particular of Ray Carver, as subject as any serious writer to the three-day bender, and yet the most beloved and respected of teachers as well as master of the short story. Moreover, it was Exley who brought Cheever to Iowa City (in a planeload of *Playboy* conferees, promising to get them all laid by Iowa freshpersons), allowing Vance Bourjaily and me to lure Cheever onto the staff.

In the end, it is the quality of the students more than that of the faculty that makes a good writing program. Students learn from one another, not from the hostile ones of course, but from the two or three whose work they admire and who signal approval with perhaps no more than a nod and brightening of the eyes.

Choosing which students to admit (from the ten or so who apply for every vacancy) is daunting. The admissions Walla is confronted with germinal stuff that is well structured yet derivative and germinal stuff that has flashes of originality but is otherwise chaotic. In making the decisions he hopes these two kinds of candidate will learn from the other's example.

It seems to be easier to identify likely poetry students than fiction writers. An incoming class of poets can be chosen (by the assembled faculty sorting application poems among themselves) in a single day. Judgment is not the only difference between poets and prose writers. Both tend to clannishness. After a reading in either discipline there is fraternization at the parties but actual romance is rare indeed.

I think the reason lies in the difference between the Poetry and Fiction Workshops as access to a career. The world of poetry, its publication in magazines and books, its criticism, its teaching jobs, all that Galway Kinnell means by PoBiz, is a matter of tunnels between the studies of influential poets. Admission to the Poetry Workshop is entry into the first of the tunnels and somewhat like pledging a fraternity.

Admission to the Fiction Workshop is more like joining a union. The world of FicBiz is a tractless ocean by comparison. Although connections are important in getting exposure, the short story or novel manuscript swims toward publication naked as, and with about the chances of, a spermatozoa.

And looking backward over eighteen years of the coming and going of writerly hopefuls, each with a dream of influencing the national imagination through language, seeing how few have progressed to the pages of the glossies and the Christmas list of the year's hundred best books, I wonder if there *are* dependable early symptoms of victory.

Self-styled cliques of the gifted, the "Bloomsbury Crowds," spring up either spontaneously or at the encouragement of an inspirational instructor. John Irving told me that as a student he had been in such a section (Coover's or Cassill's) and as an instructor he wanted such a one for his own. It was with this in mind that he gathered his in the back room at the Mill. But membership in these was no assurance of eminence.

Nor was critical ability. The student who can call forth comparison from Hawthorne and James and penetrate right to the heart of a narrative, voice, or character problem is enviable but creatively no shoo-in. Of course a strikingly funny or touching worksheet is always a positive omen for a writer's future, and it often seemed to me that what characterized these authors was an accurate memory along with the imagination to exploit it, to make unique experience common.

There is a truth about the Workshop experience, recognizable to generation after generation of its graduates, and Saul Maloff wrote about it in a fine piece for the *New York Times* book section. In its summary he points out that there is always a student like the one he recalls from Flannery O'Connor's class, whom everyone recognizes as destiny's choice, born a writer, brilliant, poised for the masterpiece that will mark the times and then, in subsequent years, just disappears—leaves not a trace.

But there is another truth which denies that the Workshop is a 100 to 1 shot at fame, with the vast majority of its graduates losers. If that were so, the Workshop would not have flourished and stood as a model for hundreds of such programs. I believe that everyone who serves those two Iowa City years, shares in the weekly exposures, humiliations, and occasional triumphs, emerges with a creative tempering, an understanding of his or her spiritual capacities and how they combine with will to make a core for any aspiring sort of life.

JOHN LEGGETT
DIRECTOR, 1969–1987

I remember arriving in Iowa City, standing in the middle of downtown, and asking someone, "Where's downtown Iowa City?" I remember meeting Connie Brothers, the administrator of the Workshop, experiencing the feeling that she was somehow my long lost older sister, and never coming remotely close to losing that feeling. I remember hearing my highly alliterative short story, "The Gorgeous Green of the Hedges," gently demolished in my first workshop and, upon returning to my apartment, eating bowl after bowl of mint-chip ice cream until the room spun. I remember admiring how some of my classmates had figured out how to get their own personality onto the page. At the time, I wrote like Thomas Hardy and I thought, regarding my classmates and their ability to convert their speaking voice into a narrative voice, *I can do that, or if not, I better learn.* I remember one of my classmates seeing me at a Northrop Frye lecture and saying, as a sort of accusation, "I thought I'd see you here." (My work was heavy on the symbolism.) I remember thinking nothing of knocking on a friend's door at eleven o'clock at night to get his reaction to a new story I had written; he didn't like it, so he praised, at absurd length, my delicate application of Liquid Paper. I remember becoming such a passionate fan of the University of Iowa men's basketball team that a famous writer would come to town to give a reading on the same night as, say, the Iowa-Indiana game, and it wouldn't even occur to me to worry about which event to attend; my first novel came out of that. I remember being a patient in the University of Iowa speech-and-hearing clinic and being overwhelmed by the paradox that as a writer I was learning to manipulate words but that as a stutterer I was at the mercy of them; my second novel came out of that. I remember people saying nothing ever happened to anyone in Iowa City and me wondering what in the world they were talking about. I remember, above all, during the three and a half years I lived in Iowa City, believing that absolutely nothing mattered more than writing as well as you possibly could. I still believe that, but nowhere else does everyone agree.

DAVID SHIELDS '80

MY FIRST YEAR AT Iowa I was lucky enough to draw the great visiting writer as my teacher. When he spoke in workshop it was as one of a long line, going back centuries. You could hear echoes of Tolstoy, of Chekhov, of Faulkner in his voice, of Colette maybe, but not Woolf, definitely not Woolf. His was a masculine take on the world. It was the fall semester and the big weekly event was Saturday softball. He hadn't played, he said, in fifty years, but he was a good and competitive athlete and he asked me if I would work with him Friday afternoon before the game. Of course I would, and it became a ritual.

Every Friday at four-thirty I'd meet with him and a few others and we'd take hitting and fielding practice. I'd pitch to him, tossing out bits of advice with my underhand offerings. I taught him the Charley Lau method of releasing the top hand after contact to increase bat speed, and he was a very apt pupil. At the start of the season the best he could muster were a few weak ground balls, but by the end he was really rocking that apple. In our last game he slammed a drive in the gap for a home run and there was true joy in his face as he smacked down on home plate. That, in fact, was the last hit of the season because on the very next play I slugged a liner that Billy Peterman dove for and caught, breaking his collarbone in the process: Billy Peterman's greatest play.

The visiting writer had a standing offer that anyone who submitted a story could meet with him after the workshop to discuss the work, and one afternoon I took advantage. We met in his narrow office on the third floor of the English building. We were friends by then, softball buddies, and I felt a nice equality to our relationship; Friday afternoons I taught him hitting, Tuesday afternoons he taught me writing. I was by then a little older, already a lawyer, and not so easily intimidated. We talked about softball, about the class. He complimented me on my critiques. I told him I was learning a lot. It was all very pleasant, very congenial until the question emerged.

I hadn't planned on asking it, but how could I not?

It plagued us all during our time at Iowa, the question, there was no escaping it. Did I, we all wondered constantly about ourselves, have a future as a writer? For some it seemed the answer was obvious, those like Chris Offutt, Elizabeth McCracken, Charlie D'Ambrosio, Abraham Verghese, whose work showed brilliance even then, but for the rest of us, struggling still to find a voice, it remained a torment. It was in our eyes as we sat back and listened to the others have a go at our manuscripts, it was in our greedy excitement as we set up appointments with the agents who had come to Iowa City to troll, it was in the gothic emotions of the night after fellowships for the following year had been awarded, a night of tears and violence, of overturned grave sites and wrecked pickup trucks. At Iowa, the question ruled.

So there I was, having a friendly chat with the great writer, talking calmly of the class and softball and certain issues in my own story when, almost on its own, the question seized control of my heart and told me that this man, this great writer, could finally give me an answer.

So I asked it, the question, phrased it informally, something like, "So what do you think?" something simple like that, but it was out there, the question, raw and open and so was I.

And suddenly everything in that small room shifted. It was as if I had drunk a bottle of Alice's potion and I shrank and he grew and the distance between us accelerated geometrically until it became perfectly clear exactly what he was and I wasn't.

It was an awkward moment, this shifting, for him as well as for me. He hemmed and hawed, offered some comforting platitudes, spoke about how impossible it was to judge a writer early in his career, but in the end, to his great credit, he gave me as honest an answer as he could. I can no longer summon the exact phrasing, the awkwardness of it all was too excruciating to concentrate on anything other than not falling off my chair, but the gist of it was that as a writer I was a pretty good softball player, but that was all.

His answer killed me for two days, two bad days, days spent in despair, curled on the couch. Then I got off the couch and started writing again and kept at it. This was all in the first few months at Iowa, and I was about to undertake dramatic changes in the way I wrote, in my voice, my rhythms, my subjects. He had been right of course, I wasn't then any good, and he had been right when he said he couldn't judge the future. In fact it is amazing how right he was and I've always been grateful for his honesty. I think it was one of the crucial moments in my life, when he told me I wasn't a natural and it was time to get working. And so I did, get working, and I still am.

And I'll tell you something more, I never again asked anyone that damn question and I never will.

WILLIAM LASHNER '91

IN LATE AFTERNOON the Writers' Workshop meets in Quonset huts in a kind of leveling-the-playing-field atmosphere. This is the combined session where all the students from the separate groups come together to evaluate a manuscript submitted sans name. Is there safety in anonymity? We are present that day on an errand of critical destruction. The room rapidly floods with East Coast accents committing sophisticated quips and sarcastic comments. That year there are few women in the Workshop. I belong to that minority. There are few Midwestern hicks. I claim that minority too. I am then an alien person and wonder at my audacity in even showing up.

Although it is neither snowing nor raining, still this room where we sit shoulder-to-shoulder has a constant and impenetrable smell of wet wool. This is the middle of my first year at the Workshop so I have been to these combined sessions before. I know what happens. A long table is set up in the front of the room as if judges are about to preside at a purge trial. It is there that the writing faculty sits with Paul Engle as impresario.

I am in the group headed by visiting writer Calvin Kentfield. He is young and enthusiastic. It was his request that one of my stories be presented in this combined session. And I, flattered and filled with Midwestern politeness and amiability, had enthusiastically agreed.

Copies of that story are now in all the hands around me—words multilithed and smeared blue-purple on white paper. How would I characterize the Workshop discussion philosophy that year? I guess it was similar to that of pre-med students happily destroying each other for a seat in the limited phalanx of medical school acceptance.

Would they know the story to be dissected that day is mine? I sit with face as pale as any acolyte waiting the moment of sacrifice. Was I about to be surprised? No, I was torn apart, eviscerated, expunged. Calvin Kentfield defended me as best he could, but he was outnumbered. Marguerite Young at the faculty table said no. Then two students in particular went after me—one saying that he had discerned "a woman's hand in this muddle."

It was worse than I had expected, and my tender writer's heart was broken. Afterward I went to Kenny's with friends to share pitchers of beer. They consoled me. My friends were planning to drop out and go to California in search of freedom of expression. They wanted me to come along. I couldn't. I simply couldn't.

What did I do? I'd like to say nothing, but no, I waited. I thought I knew the writing styles of my attackers. Sometimes you could tell whose story was up for the general session simply by looking for that palest of faces and that frozen stare. Yes, I waited. I honed my sharpest phrases of censure. I practiced the witticisms of humiliation. Then one of the right stories came up for discussion and I went after it—a thundering beast from the Midwest aroused from hibernation to tear into flesh. How did I feel afterward? Pretty good.

I never did that again. The need was gone. I knew that I was never destined during my years at the Workshop to be a member of the in-group—and there was one—but I was at least in the Workshop. I would like to say that my story that was torn apart that long-ago afternoon was later published to great kudos, but it wasn't. Unfortunately, I seem to have lost my last copy.

BETTE PESETSKY '59

I LOVED GOING TO the Writers' Workshop, though I saw others mangled by the experience and often felt more than a little mauled myself. The Workshop is, or can be, a notoriously competitive place, and I took my share of licks. (I still remember a fellow student, an earnest and fretful young man from Oregon, slapping a story of mine down on a tabletop and announcing to the members of our workshop, "This is just *pornography*.") I passed some bad nights in Iowa City, some even worse mornings, but more than anything else I felt enlivened by the proximity of just under a hundred other people ready to come to blows over questions involving the perfection or deficiency of particular sentences. In that economy good writing mattered more than anything, and I perversely loved the agitation it engendered in me. Everywhere else I'd been, no one cared all that much about writing one way or another.

The Workshop wasn't, of course, all combat. I met other aspiring writers who were willing and even eager to be called at any hour to hear a new paragraph I considered all but unbearably beautiful; I found I was equally willing to receive such calls from them. I actually walked around at night sometimes and stood for a while under certain lighted windows, knowing that inside someone I admired was struggling to put something down on paper, and that what was getting put onto paper might, in fact, be extraordinary. I can truthfully say that I entered the Workshop in 1978 in one condition, as some kind of nervous dilettante who felt embarrassed to be going to a writing school of any sort, and exited two years later in another condition, a far more serious and certain one, which remains in effect today. The Workshop, for me, was above all else a singular group of readers and writers, each of whom I respected utterly, all of whom had profound effects on me and my work. I still think about them. I still, in some way, write for them. All I can do, really, is list their names, with gratitude. My thanks to my teachers Rosellen Brown and Hilma Wolitzer, and to Bruce Brooks, Darrah Cloud, Peggy Gifford, Sarah Metcalf, James Shreeve, and Jan Short. They all, somehow, together, made a writer of me.

MICHAEL CUNNINGHAM '80

PHILIP LEVINE was known as a brilliant young teacher in the last couple of years I was at Fresno State College (A. B., 1960). Three years later, as a reporter for *The Fresno Bee*, I took Levine's night course in poetry writing. It was the best college course I'd ever had. I quit journalism, and with Levine's recommendation I was admitted to San Francisco State College (Herbert Wilner, Roy B. West), where, in

1964, I received an M.A. in Language and Literature with a thesis in fiction writing. Donald Justice in both fiction and poetry then admitted me to the Iowa Workshop.

I used credits from San Francisco to get the M.F.A. in 1965. I took classes a second year and in the third, taught fiction writing in the undergraduate fiction workshop alongside Eugene Garber, temporary head of the Workshop, John Irving, and Robin Metz, who still teaches at Knox College. I took a job at DePauw University in 1967 and still teach there.

When I arrived, the Workshop was housed in Quonset huts. A student needing money went to Paul Engle in person to ask about scholarships, and he personally dispensed them, or didn't. (He raised the money!) When one of my friends was falsely accused of arson after a New Year's Eve party, Engle put his house up as property bail and helped us get the best lawyer in town.

The principal permanent players in the Fiction Workshop were Vance Bourjaily and R. V. Cassill. Bourjaily was still grieving over the loss of his only daughter in an auto accident in which he was driving, and only later did he resume socializing with parties at his Red Bird farm, one of them featuring a "game pot" in the medieval style of adding to the stew whatever game someone brought. (Vance was writing the "Outdoors" column for *Esquire* and was a hunter and fisherman.) One of his parties was canceled when the talented black student-writer Diane Oliver was killed in a motor-scooter accident. Students fell into Bourjaily and Cassill camps, and stories about the parties were standard fare. Reportedly, at a Cassill party, editor Richard Barron told a feuding couple about to come to blows to "settle this orally," to which editor Knox Burger reportedly added, "I think you mean verbally, Richard."

Eugene Garber was acting head of the Workshop after Engle became head of the International Writers' Program. At Kurt Vonnegut's farewell party, Vonnegut reportedly raised his glass and said, "I want to toast the man who single-handedly is responsible for keeping the Workshop full of students." Gene Garber is said to have buoyed with expectation, at which time Vonnegut toasted, "To General Louis B. Hershey," who was head of the Selective Service System, or draft, which pulled Workshop-age citizens without a college deferment into the army to supply the army's needs in Vietnam.

The Workshop then was composed of students of widely varying ages, experiences, and geographical origins. Many of the men had been in the military, and many students were married. Readings by visiting writers had not yet become routine, and social activites centered on the parties and infrequent games of touch football, volleyball, and softball.

The atmosphere centered on writing and literature. The Vietnam War began to be a topic but was not central. When I arrived at DePauw, a history professor quizzed me pointedly about the New Left, but I had to insist, dully, that at Iowa we were passionate most about getting words on paper.

During my time there, students also included Harold Tinkle, Herb Scott, Glover Davis, Mickey Hazen, John Irving, John Casey, Jane Barnes, Francis Plimpton, David Milch, Marshall Frady, Bob Lacy, Jim Crumley, James Whitehead, Loree Rackstraw, Andre Dubus, Charles Gaines, James Tate, Jim Crenner, and Lee Winfrey. Faculty members included Jose Dinoso, Richard Yates, and Nelson Algren (who reportedly lost his year's salary at the weekend poker games of moderately high stakes. Herb Scott helped support his wife and five children in the same games.).

I think the Iowa Workshop, a launch platform for some of our finest contemporary writers, also produced two post–World War II generations of deeply committed writing teachers who transformed English Departments in the '60s, '70s, and '80s. In a note some twelve years ago, Kurt Vonnegut said, "They laughed at the MFA degree, but some of you old MFAs found yourselves among the best teachers in the country."

THOMAS EMERY '65

MY RECOLLECTIONS of the Workshop fall into what might handily be designated as glacial epochs with only a few important features in common and distinctly different qualities and fossil traces. I was a student there in the early '30s (a student in the first class Paul Engle taught after his return from England, a contemporary of Wallace Stegner while he completed work on his doctoral degree, the first given, I think, for a work of fiction). In those days probably there was little esprit de corps and a good deal of pure-hearted mayhem amid the toothless mastodons. I survived by currying favor among the jostling members of the faculty. I earned some prestige points when my stories were praised by visitors Archibald MacLeish and Stephen Vincent Benét. I suspect the prestige did more to romanticize my image of myself as a writer than to define my place as a promising writer. It became fossilized with the rest of those years when I began to declare myself as a painter rather than as a writer.

I felt the stiffness of a genuine fossil when, after the war, I returned as a scarcely paid fiction instructor. I was to become slowly but forcibly aware of the fact that most of the new male students were veterans and that they gave a rich, deep, and lasting commonality of purpose and sensibility to their work. Always after my four years of teaching there at this period, I thought of the veterans as the ideal component for a writing program. They were the found generation imparting, I think, much of the right stuff to those who were to follow them in the latest glacial epoch I worked with.

A constant urgency over all these years and among all groups was the articulated or barely hushed compulsion to publish. To publish anything of whatever quality, it seemed, though this was far from the truth. Yes, to publish was to justify oneself as part of the group, and to justify whatever anguish and effort might have brought them to the Workshop. But truly, when these syllables were uttered so recklessly often, they really meant to publish the best that one was capable of, hurling a lance that would somehow stick in the tough hide of the world. He published. She published. I published. It was a promissory code that everyone sufficiently understood. A little better than a Purple Heart, though maybe not so fine as a Congressional Medal of Honor.

The students I knew in the early '50s were not so numerous as those I met with in my last turn of teaching in the '60s. That may have accounted partly for their solidarity, though it can hardly have accounted for their high level of excellence. Somewhere I have a roll of honor of those who gathered with me in the riverbank springtime. (It does not exclude those whom I saw there later. Only blends them with heroic antecedents.)

And there were others from what I think of as the latter glacial period when I came back after an absence of six years. Of that later group I must declare what is obvious—that many were precious and successful and were doing precious and successful work, then and thereafter. I would exclude them from a place in the earlier strata, but only to make the distinctions that time and the bookkeeping aspects of publishing seem to require. Under the sweep of the glacier, faces and voices and names are nearly obliterated. Nevertheless the working and the work remain.

Even a pterodactyl history spends more on names than I can furnish. As I have indicated, Fame was the spur and Fame was won by many I knew on the passage from the "hut to the hilltop." Taking all those for granted, I turn to salute one whose fame burns with a central and specially endearing glimmer: Mary Engle.

In the years since I left off teaching in the Writers' Workshop, I have sometimes tried to amuse or irritate questioners by saying that if they wanted really to know the core realities of the Workshop, they should ask Mary Engle. Since Mary has been dead for a good while, such comment from me is bound to seem coy or merely evasive. Yet, for me, it has a runic truth not to be reduced to historic catalogues of events or names of the teachers and students who made their contributions there.

To be sure, Mary was never either a student or an instructor there. She came to Iowa City in the mid-1930s as Paul Engle's wife and they were the "Glamour Couple" among the younger faculty. As a young poet, Paul was then at what was to be, alas, the height of his fame. As his consort, Mary twinkled on the local scene and for the not infrequent visitors from the peripatetic artists and writers of the national troupe. Robert Frost particularly counted on them as hosts and missionary representatives and, as a seaboard anchor in the East, the Averell Harrimans counted them as bright courtiers from the provinces.

In summer Paul and Mary Engle removed from the sweat of Iowa City to a dowdy, crumbling mansion on a farm in Stone City built when that tiny hamlet was the limestone capitol of eastern Iowa. The mansion was surrounded by gardens, pastures, creeks, and hillocks where the Engles and their numerous visitors gardened, rode their horses, swam, while Paul at least worked on his literary projects and always immense correspondence. He worked in what I believe was the old stone water tower that had once supplied the mansion. Mary was often crouched in a corner with her needles, keeping the tack for the horses in repair or making clothes for their two daughters. Anyone seeing them in their postures of country squire and family would have seen them in a tableau of rural serenity not much interrupted by Paul's weekly trips in to Iowa City to meet his summer class and interview potential students.

This projected image of Arcadian poise would not have been misleading, I think, for Paul's physical and imaginative energy provided him throughout his life with a constructive equilibrium—as writer, administrator, or country gentleman.

Mary . . . Mary was an eerie mirror to Paul's extroverted vitality. She was not shy, but I supposed she watched us from the other side of shy. She watched Paul and the rest of us as a piece of mirror dropped in a stream running over colored pebbles. A lens not meant to record but to pass on with eerie distortions.

Already in her years of apparent vitality she was addicted to alcohol and whatever drugs were available to her. During winters in Iowa City she prevailed on the wives of young doctors at the University Hospital to sneak her codeine and morphine and other such goodies. She charmed them into supplying her, I would say, for there was always some potency of the good witch shining through her beauty and minor talents. She knew better than Paul did what he was up to, who his enemies were, and what currents in the whirlpool of Iowa City he could trust. It was a joke, and more than a joke with her, that she could cast benign and magical spells. I never believed in them, but I believed and still believe in the uncanny perceptivity she drew on to shape and aim them. She knew the people of the Workshop, faculty and students, and was as articulate as she had to be to define them all. Her eye was sharp as malice itself, though she was not given to malicious intents. She was amused, and her constant addiction to gossip was like her chemical dependencies. For a while at the last, she associated by preference with homosexuals, I suppose because of their constant supply of gossip and a taste for it matching her own. People brought her things, shiny objects from the world we all lived in while we were part of the passionate endeavors of the Workshop.

As she grew older and her good looks faded, the essential woman seemed to me indestructible. Through various hospitalizations she kept the strength to see in others what they could not see in themselves, and to express it with a candor that may have been her chief delight.

Then one winter in the '50s the mansion at Stone City burned down. This was in the midst of a time when I did not see her for several years. But thinking about her then I knew somehow that it was a sign of the arrest of her special powers. Henceforth she would live the life of a magpie with clipped wings, her visions restricted more and more to the gatherings of her past—a considerable horde to be sure. But she would have no more to tell me of the lively gossip about my contemporaries, or those I had missed in my coming and going.

The last time I saw her she was in the University Hospital, where the staff was trying to dry her out enough to withstand yet another operation on her alimentary canal still left from previous pruning. In the late afternoon light coming into her room, she looked positively chipper, though not much larger than a doll under the sheets. There was very little conversation between us and I will come right to its point. She wanted me to go fetch her a pint of bourbon whiskey, to be hidden in the reservoir of the toilet bowl out of the sight of prying eyes of nurses who did not understand her need. I knew this was a matter of life and death. The operation was said to be essential. If the alcohol could not be cleared from her system, the operation could not be performed.

I shook my head at her request. I could not and would not do what she wanted.

"Awww," she said. "Aaaaw." She frowned reprovingly. She was asking if I trusted her. After all these years did I trust her or not? As a matter of fact I did. After all, against the bidding of my better promptings, I smuggled the whiskey to her. Several days later the doctors decided she could do without the operation. So by this last encounter something was vindicated by the trust, which I have cherished to this day.

I see I have muddled from muddle to muddle in an attempt to define the indefinable witness who should be the best witness to our efforts to understand and to write.

"The horse don't talk nothing but horse," says Cary's Gulley Jimson, and I suppose that is true.

R. V. CASSILL '47

RALPH ELLISON DIED in the spring of 1994, when I was attending the Writers' Workshop and studying with Jim McPherson. He had initially decided not to attend Ellison's funeral in New York, but on the way to class that Tuesday afternoon I learned from secretary Deb West that McPherson had appointed me to direct workshop in his stead. My peers mutinied: so treasured were his insights that it was inconceivable that we hold class without him. I told myself that my impeachment was nothing personal.

The two-hour makeup workshop we instigated was distinguished by McPherson's presence in body only: as I recall, he did not utter a single word throughout. "You exercised your rights in a democracy," he explained at the end of class, "and I have exercised mine."

For years I have felt bad about having been party to robbing him of a chance to mourn his late friend and mentor without penalty. It was while reading his latest book, *Crabcakes: A Memoir,* that I came to understand that his silent protest had been predicated not on a sense of having been personally mistreated but on a larger conviction that out of respect for our very humanness, we must be permitted to honor grief and other wearying emotions with full capacity, as we would joy.

NELL BERAM '94

JACK LEGGETT ALWAYS said "nothing ever happened between four and six," so that's when the workshop met. The classrooms were so sterile and uniform it was hard to believe anything as colorful as fiction could come from them. But the real creative work was done in the hodgepodge of rented apartments we tried to call home, and the well we drew our creative energy from was much farther away than that. Even Jack's house, a big beautiful two-story gingerbread, was almost empty except for the stacks of manuscripts on the floor, placed neatly along the walls. For many of us, who came from all corners of the United States and farther, the Workshop was both a lonely crossroads and a grand central station of ideas—all in the middle of a sometimes sweltering, sometimes frozen, cornfield.

At twenty-three I was too young to digest the diversity and to know how to survive in the competitive atmosphere of so many watchful writers or to make the right choices. Having Barry Hannah as a teacher was an awkward semester for me. Three girls in a class of headstrong cowboys somehow made it difficult to keep my own ideas in focus. I never knew so many cowboys wrote novels. I began to spend less time with writers and more time playing the fiddle. I joined a yoga class, took two philosophy classes in Kant and existentialism, spent a day with the Amish, spent a day at a turkey farm, went to the Fiddler's Picnic, and found a new friend who phoned every morning with an alarm-call poem.

Still, I loved the reading classes, for which we read a novel a week and discussed it, very seriously. Readings by visiting writers were a real eye-opener too, even if a distortion of the difference between good and bad writing. Eventually we openly admitted them to be what they were—beauty contests in which the quick and clever got the applause.

Today, writing is lonelier than ever. Polished stories and poems sit quietly in various literary magazines, some with awards, little feathers in my cap. But even amateur painters and musicians get more praise, more often. It's still easier for the average punter to look and listen than take the time to open a book and read. Who really cares anymore which is more important, content or style (a hotly debated issue at the time)? I do, even though I write more intuitively and less intellectually now, with the confidence that I know how to say what I have to say. Still, I often wish that I could do it over again and take another long draught of the heady mixture that is the Iowa Writers' Workshop.

TRACY HARRIS '81

IN MANY WAYS, being at the Writers' Workshop was like being in high school again. It was a cliquish, judgmental place, where your reputation could be decided in a moment. You weren't judged on your hair or clothes, however, but on the contents of your bookshelf. My first week in Iowa City, two women, both second-year students, kindly took me grocery shopping, and afterward, foolishly proud, I showed them my book collection, ending with a small case full of science fiction. They glanced at each other, and one of them said, "I wouldn't let anyone know about those books if I were you." I started to laugh, but she wasn't joking.

Even literature departments don't take literature that seriously any more; grad students write dissertations now on *Star Trek* novels. But at Iowa, I once witnessed a fistfight at a party over—I ask you—Theodore Dreiser. It was probably the first time anybody had thrown a punch over *Sister Carrie* since Dreiser himself was in his prime. The two default writers, the ones on everyone's bookshelves, were Raymond Carver and Chekhov. Wonderful writers, of course, but there's not a lot of space between them on the literary spectrum. People who'd never read it regularly cited "Lady with Lapdog" as scripture, and people who had never met him—and none of us had—regularly called Raymond Carver "Ray." To be fair, I never heard anyone refer to "Anton."

I remember one guy who came to class every week with yet another fat Penguin Classic—Dickens or Hardy or Tolstoy. He was regarded as slightly oddball—reading work that dated from before Chekhov was not liable to win you a Pushcart Prize—though not as a lesser creature: at least he wasn't reading science fiction. I remember another guy whose bookcase was full of heavy-duty Modernists—Joyce, Mann, Musil, Marquez, Rushdie, all in hardback—who ended up giving up writing because he set his standards so high. If he couldn't write a book as good as, say, *The Recognitions*, he wasn't going to waste his time. Last I heard, he's working as a carpenter.

I don't mean to exempt myself from this kind of petty behavior. At another party I checked out our host's bookshelf and discovered that he had every single volume in the Vintage Contemporary series. I hardly knew the guy, but his stock fell considerably with me. Sure, there were some interesting titles in the series, I had a few myself, but where was his sense of discrimination? Didn't he trust his own taste? Why on earth would anyone buy them all?

At the end of my time at Iowa, after I had already sold my first book—a thriller, you got a problem with that?—I ran into the Penguin Classic reader on the street. I don't remember his name anymore, but we had a friendly chat. Then he narrowed his eyes, whether judgmentally or not, I'll never know, and said, "I hear you're writing a science fiction novel." I think I just blinked and said, "No, actually. Where on earth did you hear that?" But he didn't say, he just shrugged and walked away. To this day, I don't think he believed me.

JAMES HYNES '89

AT THE END OF the first year at Iowa, six lucky students received a Teaching-Writing Fellowship. These folks taught undergraduate writing workshops, classes that met once a week. The teacher received in-state tuition, a good salary, and an office with an actual nameplate on the door, rather than a scribbled index card. Most of all, it was a mark of high status within the program since only the very best writers were granted such honor. The Teaching-Writing Fellowship was shortened to its intials of "twf," and those students were known as "twifs."

Selection occurred during the second semester, when all first-year students submitted a manuscript. There began an embarrassing display of anxiety, boot-licking, and general paranoia. It was as if thirty people were transformed overnight into the worst sort of sycophant, utterly obsessed with who would become a twif and who would not. People spent hours discussing it, figuring out the shoo-ins and those with absolutely no chance. Naturally each of us hoped to be granted the honor of twiffery, along with all our friends.

I wish I could say I rose above the fray, that the ethical high ground was mine, that such shenanigans were beneath me. Sadly, that would be a barefaced lie. I was completely consumed with getting a twif. It interfered with my writing, my marriage, and my pool game. I observed the teachers carefully, seeking in their every gesture a secret signal that I was to be twiffed up. I gauged their slightest reactions to me with a private barometer that rose and fell hourly. I annoyed my wife no end with speculation, joy, and agony.

The real reason I wanted the award was simple—it meant the teachers liked me. Twifs got special treatment by faculty and extra respect from their fellow students. Being anointed into the wondrous realm of twifdom meant public acknowledgment that you were one of the best writers in the joint. Everyone in my class secretly believed he or she deserved the recognition.

Notification came by mail. The letter didn't include who the twifs were—just the crushing fact that I wasn't one. I began calling around, surreptitiously sounding out my buddies, until spilling the beans and sharing sympathy. Several of us met at the Foxhead that night, a gloomy, twifless bunch. In the next few days, I learned the identities of the twifs, and it was a worse blow than not getting one.

Him? I thought, surely not him! He can't write a lick. And her, I can't believe they picked her! I'm better than them. I know I am. There must be a mistake. It should have been me.

I spent the next week on the couch, furious at those students who became twifs, and at the faculty for not making me one. Mainly, I was mad at myself for wanting the distinction. It was utter cockamamie to place myself in such a vulnerable position. Six months before, I'd never even heard of a twif. Now I was flat on my back over not being one.

That summer I doubled my writing efforts, then doubled them again. Without the reward of a twif, I was forced to reevaluate my writing and go at it from a different angle, and with greater diligence. I abandoned all hope for recognition and publication. At long last, I began writing my *own* stories. My simple goal was to make them as good as I could—for myself. My standards were very high, and I decided to try and reach them instead of sitting around criticizing other people for not making the effort.

My writing changed. The work moved forward in one of those sudden improvements that you can't see at the time but is quite clear in hindsight. My voice, material, and style finally braided together to make coherent, and highly personal stories. I became a writer.

CHRIS OFFUTT '90

I WENT STRAIGHT to Iowa after four years at Yale, so I was no stranger to the way a school's *name* can affect its students. Still, it was a shock when, at the orientation meeting, a man to my right said, "Think what would happen to American letters if a bomb dropped on this room." Embarrassed by this sort of self-congratulation, I turned to the poet on my left. He seemed to be approaching the day's events with the same Gee-whiz! enthusiasm I felt. After graduation, the man to my right abandoned fiction and became a regular writer for *GQ* and other glossies. Before the year was out, the man to my left discovered that he had leukemia. He stayed in town and worked, with his wife, as a live-in parent at a halfway house for severely disabled children. Within three years, he was dead.

I think it's fair to say that my experience at Iowa was not defined by my classes (terrible, for the most part) or by my particular success story. (The first story I submitted to workshop was published in *Esquire*'s summer fiction issue.) The time wasn't even defined by my book. (As a lark, during my senior year in college, I'd decided to put to together an anthology. In the wake of my *Esquire* publication, Scribner's bought the book, *Twenty under Thirty: Best Stories by America's New Young Writers,* which quickly sold 50,000 copies.) Instead my time at Iowa was defined by difficult friendships (a roommate who decided, late one night, that I was keeping her prisoner in her room; a confidante who thought I had some nerve saying I liked her story when I wasn't using it in my anthology) and wonderful ones. Paul—the man who died—and his wife were discoveries, as was Ron, my then-boyfriend and opposite in every way, who had me dribbling basketballs in the local bar and finding a beard ("Snodgrass's beard") in one of the Tupperware containers I'd loaned him to use at his rooming house. (Snodgrass had to shave, Ron said, so he could make deliveries for the local pizza place. "OK," I'd nodded. That made a kind of sense. It didn't occur to me to ask, till later, why he had to *save* his beard.)

You need to care for people to be a good writer. Or to be the kind of writer I want to be, you need to. And for all the heartbreaks and dramas, I loved—I love—

my Iowa friends, and when I think about my education, I think mostly of the admission policy, which made for such a crazy crew, linked only by a serious interest in literature.

I was often unhappy at Iowa. Uncomfortable being the center—as I was, at times—of attention. Frightened, too, by my inability to make something more of the attention I was receiving. (The *New Yorker* wrote to ask for work, but I had nothing good enough, and knew that, in the years to come, I'd long to be honored with such a request.) But I was also often delighted: by my friends, by the writer's world (of which the Workshop is a mini-version), by broad-skied Iowa itself. One of my first nights in Iowa, I saw a harvest moon and didn't know what it was. The sun? But, of course, it couldn't be the sun. So what was it? Fat and orange. Showy. A grandstander. Moons weren't like this elsewhere in the world. Weren't so eccentric, so full of themselves, so surprisingly and wonderfully strange. By the time I left Iowa, of course, I knew otherwise. Such moons were a reliable pleasure, like all-night dance parties or a friend—at the pig farm or in the women's locker room or over drinks or after poker or in the cancer ward—pressing a book into my hand, saying, like nothing else mattered, "Debra, you *have* to read this."

DEBRA SPARK '86

I WAS ACCEPTED INTO the Workshop based on a story I wrote about a high school athlete, a wrestler, who struggles over whether or not he is gay. I was in Washington, D.C., at the time, and I had just returned from two years of traveling around the world on the cheap. I had left a girlfriend in Australia and returned to the United States in order to make some money and to apply to graduate writing schools. As a result, she and I were in the process of breaking up. However, just prior to sending the gay wrestler story to the Workshop, I sold it to a New York magazine with a big circulation, and they offered me two hundred dollars. I was thrilled about it, and it seemed as if things were looking up.

I had never actually seen the magazine, only a brief summary of it in *Writer's Market,* so I thought I'd better check it out before letting them publish it. When I went down to the Library of Congress, however, no one could find it. Five or six librarians in suits conferred. They became intense about it. They began to look everywhere for it, running back and forth, checking in. Finally after about an hour, they presented it to me like a birthday cake, crowded around and proud of their accomplishment, and we could all clearly see that on the cover was a picture of a huge cock with sperm shooting out of it. I think I said something like "thank you" and then handed it back to them and left. When I got home, I wrote the magazine and withdrew the story from publication.

It was with this piece that I got accepted into the Writers' Workshop. I arrived in Iowa City midyear, in January, and three days later faced my first workshop, still in a bit of culture shock. Three people's stories were critiqued each class and I was going to be the first. I put up a new story, freshly written. In this story, among other things, I made fun of "rich" college kids, and academic life, and for most of it the main character was at a party looking around at all the people and feeling superior and saying things like, "People with money suck," and "I bet she's never taken it up the butt." It was not a very good story. I knew that, but I also had the naive expectation that in a workshop we were expected to put up a rough draft so that we could all figure out how to make it better. I didn't realize then that my ability and my status as a writer were also on the line and that it could greatly impact whether I would eventually be able to get recommendations for fellowships or teaching positions.

Well, the story, of course, was trashed. Everyone hated it, and we went around and around the room with each person saying so. Then at the very end, the professor, a well-known writer, turned to me and in a sentence that seemed to take forever to enunciate, the meaning of which made no sense to me at the time, screamed, red-in-the-face, "AND IF YOU THINK . . . THAT BUTT-FUCKING . . . GIVES YOU SOME SORT . . . OF ENTRÉE . . . INTO MIDDLE-CLASS VALUES . . . YOU'RE WRONG!!" I could barely even make out what he was saying. "Do I think butt-fucking gives me entrée into middle-class values?" I think I repeated, incredulous. "Butt-fucking?" I said, and thought, man, this guy is nuts. Who the hell cares about butt-fucking? However, I don't think I said much more at that point. Afterward, though, a lot of people kept coming up to me and saying they were sorry, until I finally got the idea that I had clearly jeopardized something.

It wasn't long after that that I began to suspect I might have been accepted into the Workshop as the "token" gay. This would have been fine except for the fact that I was new in town, newly single, and now everyone seemed to think I was attracted to men. I also began to seriously wonder if I needed to spend this kind of money on getting this sort of advice.

I did, however, stay in the program. For a while, in public, I drank bourbon and told my most macho stories. I never put up an early draft of anything again, and I never did read the story I put up in workshop aloud, at public readings at Prairie Lights or at open-mike night at the Mill, though I was asked to. I figured dating was hard enough as it was. I also never put the story up in a workshop. Instead, I sent it out and eventually got it published in a good literary journal, though they didn't pay me anything.

PETE HENDLEY '91

IN 1964, OZARK flew planes that quivered like a dentist's drill right into Iowa City. I took a cab to my room on Brown Street, in the compound owned by Henry Black. For fifty dollars a month I got a square of concrete slab and four porous walls. Snails and spiders lived there, too. In November, ice formed outside the windows; in December, inside. Lots of writers roomed at Black's. Typewriters clacked all around me in a heady industrial ferment.

My first workshop was with Richard Yates, who taught us style. He lived alone in a freezing house on South Capitol, and that winter caught pneumonia—frightening for an ex-TB patient. We visited him in the hospital. Steve Salinger sneaked in whiskey. Immediately, Dick poured a shot for his roommate, an elderly farmer. We studied that. That was style.

I later worked with Vance Bourjaily, Verlin Cassill, R. V. Williams, David Pryce-Jones, Kurt Vonnegut, Jack Leggett, and Angus Wilson. Once, Vance brought a bunch of us, chosen for mouth, to Chicago for the filming of a special on the Workshop. In the studio, we were amazed by a mock-up of our Quonset hut classroom, with fake icicles hanging from the eaves. Amid dollying cameras, we discussed someone's story with unprecedented politeness.

The stories, the classes, the teachers, the years. Diane Oliver died one Saturday night in a motorcycle crash on Dubuque Street. The Mississippi left its banks, and some of us sandbagged in Muscatine. Bob Lacy sold a story to the *Saturday Evening Post* for $1,500.

I had two spells at the Workshop, 1964–66 (M.F.A) and 1970–75 (Ph.D.). Toward the end, Vietnam changed us; politics was crowding art. But our politics was art too. Imagination continued to rule. We had to elect George McGovern. We had to stop the downtown mall. Some freezing days, a few of us, in an action called Shoppers' Stoppage—the last word in lost causes—picketed on downtown corners, asking people to boycott commerce in the name of peace.

Some of us may have been lazy or crazy, pretentious or dull or cruel. Finally it didn't matter. The gift of the Workshop didn't depend on who our teachers and classmates were. It was a gift of legitimacy. It was a sword touched to the shoulder. It was our license to hunt life, to track and lure it within touch, and then to write our names below its trail through the snow.

JONATHAN PENNER '66

I THREW THE PARTY for Tim O'Brien my first year at the Writers' Workshop, which meant I got to pick him up at the airport and talk with him on the way through the snow-swept cornfields from Cedar Rapids to Iowa City. I had just read *The Things They Carried*, an incredible book, and here was Tim O'Brien riding into town with me in my crappy old Mazda, and treating me like a new friend.

I loved how it kept seeming while I was in Iowa that I would read a book and then meet the writer (or take a class with her), and be taken seriously by the writer because of my place in the Workshop.

Before Iowa I had been writing at my lunch breaks or early in the morning, or late at night. I was a full-time newspaper reporter, barn fires and town board meetings. I liked that when I got to Iowa that seemed fairly typical. People had come from all vocations and parts of the country. There were former actors and lawyers and social workers, doctors and journalists, carpenters, bartenders, travelers.

It is not an original statement to say that writing can be a lonely task. Iowa made it so much less so. This is what makes leaving Iowa City so hard for people. They move to Cleveland or New York City or San Francisco and they don't know very many writers in these places. I can't count how many times I've heard someone from the Workshop talk of how much they missed the community.

There are those on the outside who complain there is an Iowa mafia about, that we take care of each other. I hope that's true. I do know that I feel an affiliation to anyone who's been through the Workshop, who's lived in Iowa City, who's had a beer and played pool at the Foxhead and listened to Patsy Cline on the jukebox.

It was a very exciting time for me, a time of growth, a few frustrations, but not all that many. At Iowa they gave us lots of time to work and very few demands. There was plenty to do if you wanted. There was a built-in social life that you didn't have to work hard to maintain.

Playing pool was important. So was softball and basketball. I loved the softball games. We played fiction writers versus poets until we recognized how badly we were overmatched by the poets. Dore Anderson, a poet, said that was because "poets play in moments."

That first year, James Salter was serious enough about his softball that he organized practices the day before our games. Four or five of us would meet in the late afternoon after a long and sometimes unyielding day of work, and we might end with a quick touch football game. To this day I like to do something physical after I write.

I liked looking at the list of new writers that were arriving to teach the Workshop's semester. It was like being at a great restaurant and looking at the menu. I remember being in Meg Wolitzer's workshop when she was the least known of the visiting writers, and all of us understanding that first workshop how fortunate we were to have her as a teacher. She was so bright and funny and generous. She read whatever I finished, and held conferences with me—I think seven in the course of that semester. My other teachers were similarly generous, most memorably Marilynne Robinson, Frank Conroy, Susan Daitch, Francine Prose, and Jim McPherson.

The workshops themselves could be stressful. The group was very bright and very opinionated and it's an understatement to say that there was no hand-holding. Some of the criticism was helpful, some hard to bear. You had to learn how to listen and when to listen. There was always something in every discussion you could take with you, and there were times I resisted someone's reading of my story only to recognize later that they'd been right on, and I'd been wrong.

All said I benefited enormously from this process. Frank spoke at the first meeting that we were to be honest and that we were always discussing the work, not the person. And I think people took that to heart. We learned as we dissected. And if there were times I would have given anything to leave the room, I will always be happy that I stayed.

The worst aspect of the Workshop was the tiered system of financial aid and the stress that descended on the decision day. There were teaching-writing fellows, those who received other sorts of teaching fellowships, and then those who received nothing at all. I don't know if it can be avoided, but many good writers felt slighted.

We were told that these decisions had little bearing on future success and that has proven to be largely true.

What I loved best about the Workshop, and about Iowa City, was that it was, and still is, a place where writing is sacred, paramount. It matters more than anything else. And when you are in the Workshop, your work matters. Reading matters. Discussions are about novels and stories and books of poems. I felt like I was at the very center of things, and I felt protected from the elements, from having a job or looking for a job, from pleasing a boss, from any responsibility other than finishing the next story. What a great gift.

TOM BARBASH '91

I WONDER HOW MANY of the writers at the Iowa Writers' Workshop arrive there at a particularly difficult time in their lives. I did. My marriage had ended. My children were in college. I could no longer be the person I had been. Arriving at the Workshop was like taking up residence in a safe house where I had two years to concentrate on my writing. Except for teaching a class each semester, nothing else made demands on my time. I'd never lived in snow before, but now I look back on the times when the snow was falling with the greatest fondness. The snow amplified that sense of being cloistered.

ROBIN BEEMAN '90

I WENT TO IOWA at age twenty-one, which is on the young side, but no record. I had written two or three passable stories, just enough to gain admission. I was dramatically underread; I owned about thirty books. Some people are quite mature at age twenty-one. I was not. What little guidance I had received in becoming a writer to that point I had taken lightly. I liked language in a vague uneducated way. But if I spent any time at all considering the relationship between sentences and images, I spent as much or more time considering the trajectory of pool balls across a pool table. I was something of a player back then. My undergraduate GPA measures both my studies and the amount of time I spent in the Student Union's poolroom. Still, the moment I got into Iowa, I was jubilant and confident. I quit studying altogether, played even more pool, and almost didn't graduate.

I went to Iowa at the beginning of the summer to secure an apartment for the fall. I had a bag of clothes and my pool cue. I drove into town after sunset. The first thing I did was find a Yellow Pages and look under "Billiards." There's a poolroom in downtown Iowa City. The tables aren't flat, the balls aren't round, and the cues aren't straight, but it's a poolroom. Walking toward the entrance, I crossed paths with another man entering the hall. He was carrying a cue case just as I was. He held the door for me, and we decided to play together to split the time fee. I was hoping we would gamble. I taught him to play one-pocket, an advanced game with a lot of strategic properties. Finally, he asked me who I was. A student, I said. Undergrad? No, graduate. What department? The Writers' Workshop. He squinted at me, and nodded. "I heard a you," he said. I'd been in town less than half an hour.

The man, as it turned out, was the husband of a prominent writer, a visiting professor. My reputation as a pool player, by way of my application, had preceded me. The man quickly introduced me to Dave's Foxhead, a writer's bar with a pool table that was even less flat than those of the downtown poolroom. Here I learned Rule Number 1: do not try to find money games at a writers' bar.

It's not simply the department or the town that makes the Iowa experience what it is; rather, it's a sense of having been recognized literally and figuratively, of having been studied before you arrived, of having been anticipated. The department secretary had read the stories in my application and was familiar enough with them to discuss them. (This made her much more than a secretary.) It was a shocking thing to consider, and for the first time I began to understand the gravity of the thing I had undertaken. Iowa provides a chilling combination of vindication and indictment: it calls you by name, then takes you to task. It grants knowledge, then pokes at your kidneys. There's a lot of pressure, and not everyone comes away happy. But happiness is not the point. And of all the things it has been accused of, at least this much is true: it is an important and successful place, and it comes to feel like home.

CHRIS HALLMAN '91

I once dreamt that several of us from a small workshop section were standing around before class, in one of the Quonset huts down by the river. The door and windows were open, and sunlight angled through a window at the head of the room onto a long table spread with mounds of bright fruit and a pitcher of milk. Although the instructor was not present, the dreamer knew it was the class of George P. Elliott.

Much of the Workshop experience was a feast for a young writer during those fresh years of the Kennedy administration. Like others at other times, you discovered in Form and Theory courses how Joyce, Mann, Faulkner, Chekhov, Flaubert made words come alive on the page. You explored at the typewriter the agonizing and exhilarating process of transforming fragmented experience into unified fiction. You sharpened your critical faculty through discussing the work of fellow writers and by having your own work analyzed. Talk about writing continued over coffee at the Student Union, beer at Joe's Place, booze at Vance Bourjaily's parties, and when you weren't reading writing, hearing about writing, or talking about it, you were in the bookstores, looking at the new books of the first professional writers you'd ever known: Bourjaily's *Confessions of a Spent Youth*, R. V. Cassill's *Clem Anderson* and *Writing Fiction*, and Elliott's *Among the Dangs*. And up on the hill, in the English Department, you savored the great writing of the past: Conrad's lifetime work, the eighteenth-century novel, and the Norse *Eddas*, lovingly revealed by the ultimate pipe-smoking scholar, John C. McGalliard.

If you wanted to write, Iowa was the place to be. And once you've been there, the commitment to writing stays with you. For better or worse, richer or poorer. Which means that the longer you live after the Workshop days, the more you experience both sides of the contract. I would guess it's been for many others what it's been for me: that you struggle along with your own writing while you teach others the techniques; that when teaching jobs don't come through, and the marriage breaks, and you're unemployed, single, and broke, you get a day job, remarry, and start a new life; that no matter what, you keep writing your own stuff on the side; and that through it all, you look back to the Workshop for what Morton Zabel calls the "subject by which a writer fulfills himself and realizes his essential powers." If you live long enough and are lucky enough, you find that subject, germinated in those Iowa writings of long ago, and wonder if you would ever even have looked for the subject, much less found it, had you not feasted at the Workshop table.

JOE NIGG '63

IN A WORKSHOP with Frank Conroy a story I had written received some scathing criticism. He read my dialogue aloud, calling attention to its banal nature (it was indeed banal) and pointing out the number of extraneous details I'd used. In the two hours the workshop spent on my story, Frank lectured us on something he called "Abject Naturalism."

As I alternated between wanting to crawl under the table and wanting to turn it over on top of Frank, I felt pretty abject myself. The word conjured up a Victorian woodcut in which a father stands in a doorway, pointing a long, accusatory, and damning finger at a young girl hunched over a pregnant belly, shawl pulled across her weeping face. And it's raining.

And as Martha Graham, the pioneer of modern dance, has said, "All art is distortion." Clearly, "naturalism" was boring, banal.

To give some idea about how right Conroy was (and he proceeded at, I guess you could say, abject and detailed length to make his case): the point-of-view character in the story has just had an abortion, and she's traveled alone to the Southwest to visit some friends. I tried to show rather than tell the reader the complicated background with (I thought) sly references to the doctorlike fingers of the friend who picks her up at a bus station; drawing attention to the bloodiness of the chicken they prepare to barbecue and the shining implements with which the meat will be turned and poked. My understanding was that detail shows, therefore, detail is good, and I used lots of it.

After the workshop—hurt, aching, furious—I went through the pile of manuscripts that had been handed back to me by my fellows. I realized that while not everyone thought the story was as dreadful an effort as Frank had made it out to be, one particular margin note was extremely telling. With no sense of irony a fellow student had written: "It *does* take a long time to cook chicken on a grill, doesn't it?"

This sympathetic comment did a great deal to point out to me the actual nature of my writing problem. I pinned a piece of paper to the wall above my desk, large block letters shouting, "BEWARE ABJECT NATURALISM!" I imagined the novels I would publish, and the blurbs that would ride across their shiny hard covers:

> *Sands Hall, the founder of the school of Abject*
> *Naturalism, has done it again!*
> *Here is another of Hall's novels, filled with the*
> *minutiae of life's most mundane details!*

It took months before anything about that lecture or that devastating workshop began to sink in. But when it did, its infiltration into my writing process was thorough and widespread. In his lecture Frank had said, "As a story begins, the author makes a tacit deal with the reader. You hand them a backpack. You ask them to place certain things in it—to remember, to keep in mind—as they make their way up the hill, that is, through the pages. If you hand them a yellow Volkswagen and they have to haul this to the top of the mountain—to the end of the story—and they find that this Volkswagen has nothing whatsoever to do with your story, you're going to have a very irritated reader on your hands."

The analogy of the backpack and what we ask the reader to put into it became very useful: what do we ask the reader to observe, to remember? These items must be selected—revealed—with care. I devised for myself a filter through which a detail needs to pass: does it forward something about character? And/or plot? And/or theme? Does the detail manage to contribute something to the development of all three?

This is a great lesson, and (she admits, grumpily) worth the pain it took to learn it.

SANDS HALL '91

I HAVE THE IOWA Writers' Workshop to thank for the best mornings of my life. Blissful, inspired mornings in a fleabag hotel in Paris, in a dusty room that I shared with a pretty Irish girl who, in her half sleep, let me ride her flannel nightgown up her thighs and hold her in my arms before I climbed out of the bed in the predawn light.

It was December of 1984, the end of fourteen years at hard labor writing four novels and maybe fifty short stories that no one wanted. Fourteen years of giving the same stock answer to every question that involved the future: *as soon as I sell my first book*. Marriage, having a baby, buying a decent pair of shoes—*everything*—was held hostage to this condition, until at age thirty-four the Workshop took me in out of the cold, making me believe for the first time that I was entitled to a future that began each morning when I opened my eyes to it.

So I got to go to Paris with Colleen, who slept with the trace of a smile on her lips while I sat in the slanting light writing sentences onto the pages of a spiral notebook that began a novel called *Veterans Park*. We had just eloped in Winchester, England, where Colleen had gone to do her undergraduate student teaching while I was a first-semester student in fiction writing at the Workshop. On one of those Paris mornings I had a powerful vision that I was going to become a father who wrote books that his children would one day read.

It was the following autumn when Colleen and I walked through the leaves on Church Street to the Mercy Hospital in Iowa City where our first child, Erin, was born. The moon was so bright that night that you could see the colors of the leaves by its light, something I had never seen before and have never seen again. There was snow on Church Street when I stepped off the bus in the dark after a Workshop class on a Tuesday that winter. When I looked up, Colleen was standing at the corner with Erin in her arms. As I kissed our daughter on the top of her head, Colleen leaned against me and whispered in my ear that while I was in class a call had come from New York City to say that my novel, *Veterans Park*, had been sold that afternoon.

I dedicated the book to Erin and have always told her that some day I will take her back to Iowa City to see where her mother and I walked through the leaves in the moonlight, and where they stood that winter day waiting for my bus. Since then there have been thousands of mornings, which gave us four more books, three more babies. But there is a remarkable fitness to the memory of our days in Iowa City. When I close my eyes I can still see Colleen holding that first baby, the two of them waiting there at the corner. They were the proof that my real life had at last begun.

DON SNYDER '86

I'VE TOLD SOME of my kids about trudging through the deep snow in the dark to teach my early morning freshman Rhetoric class, how I had to stop at a gas station, then the hotel, then the restaurant at the top of the hill to catch a little warmth before sliding down past the library to the O.A.T. (Old Armory Temporary) buildings to meet the shivering freshman for a round of Rhetoric 101 or 102. I've never been back to Iowa City since I left with my degree and now ex-wife to head to California for my first teaching job in August of 1965. Going back now in this reminiscence I realize that I've forgotten a lot of names—streets and otherwise—and I suspect that at least one of my favorite bars (The Silver Spur? The Airliner? Donnelley's? Connelley's? Kenny's?) has been replaced by a high-rise parking garage or a weight-loss salon. At any rate, more than anything else I remember the strong feelings of hope that lay at the heart of so many of the discussions—in the workshops, the coffee shops, and all the rest—however bleak and downright desperate they may have been. During my stay (9/63–8/65) Kennedy was killed . . . Schwerner, Cheney, Goodman . . . Vietnam. . . . But there were still marriages—mine for one. My bride-to-be came out on the train from Michigan and we were married on a snowy day in North Liberty by the justice of the peace with his wife and the mayor as witnesses. (The mayor had been outside shoveling out his driveway.) I remember first meeting Paul Engle—we were involved in a paperwork snarl in the Workshop office. And I must say that we got it straightened out poetically. I remember Richard Yates showing up a little late for his Guest Lectureship after his car and most of his worldly belongings burned up on the way. And out on the lawn on an overcast afternoon I remember listening to W. D. Snodgrass giving an awesome reading of *The Heart's Needle.* Somewhere along the line a local character was shot in one of the bars right in the middle of town—he staggered through the double-hinged saloon doors to fall dead on the sidewalk. The cops drew a chalk outline of his body on the sidewalk and then took it away. Not particularly unusual events, but the thing is—the chalked outline of the body stayed visible for the longest time. People would stop and stare at it, many of them stepping over or around it, and some just plowed right through it. This is a good place to end this reminiscence, before I try to make something out of the image of death and tell how all the creative energy generated by people writing fiction and poems in Iowa City has carried so many of them and their readers right on through it.

TOM GATTEN '65

WE WERE ALL SITTING in the Mill on a Tuesday night after workshop when my fiancée Dena (she wasn't yet my wife) pulled me outside to tell me she'd just gotten a phone call from my parents. Back home in Tampa, my sister had died. It was totally unexpected and I left without telling anyone anything, flying home early the next morning more or less in a state of shock.

I met some of the finest, funniest, most talented people I've ever known at the Workshop, but now it was amazing and touching how quickly everyone tried to help. Craig Collins took my classes for me, Tom Piazza offered to fly down, other Workshoppers called asking if they could help in any way, and sympathy cards poured in.

We were gone a couple of weeks. When we finally got back, Connie, the adjunct mother for so many of us, pulled me into her office for a long talk, and though I can't remember all the details (and wouldn't reveal them anyway), I remember realizing that before I talked to Connie, I had seriously been thinking about quitting the whole thing. There was no question of that after our talk. That was Monday.

Jim McPherson was my workshop instructor that semester, and my first Tuesday back, workshop was held at his house. Only those who know Jim can imagine how much respect and affection we had (and still have) for him as a teacher and friend.

I was early that night, and the two of us worked at cleaning all these boiled shrimp. I was just back from Florida and here was this huge bowl of fresh shrimp he had gotten somehow in October, in Iowa, and we stood there at the sink, Jim quietly and very gently talking to me about what had happened while we deveined and rinsed. What I remember most, though, is that after everyone in my workshop had arrived, and we were past the awkward condolences and well into the shrimp, Jim stood up and talked a little about death and loss and consolation, more eloquently than I can write here, and welcomed me back home. We know you lost someone in your family, he said, but we wanted you to know that you also have a family here.

CHUCK OLDHAM '94

I'M AFRAID MY experience at the Workshop had little to do with the time, except in my reaction to the literary zeitgeist and politics going on around me. Modernism, postmodernism, metafiction—I'd never heard these things before. I'd never been in a workshop, and I'd avoided English classes because hearing stories mangled and vivisected enraged me. I'd grown up in libraries and bookstores, and thought— Forster's? Eliot's?—metaphor of writers existing in a room outside time was only sensible. I don't think I'd imagined writers could have been any other way.

Actually while in Iowa I lost a tangible sense of the time, which I'd had in Pennsylvania during both Reagan presidencies and Bush. I do mean tangible—it was a thick medium to live in, and I can still taste it. For four years I missed that—I read, wrote, and played sports in a peaceable town that had no factories, floated on a cushion of state money, and was safe inside an enormous moat of land. It was very pleasant, but I kept groping to feel where I was, and couldn't feel anything. I moved to Providence in 1997, feeling Van Winklish, and wonder now if that anesthesia wasn't a mark of the time, the main thing we've bought with this joyless prosperity. I may have thought it pleasant only because I was in Iowa.

I had an A-1 time at the Workshop; they treated me like visiting royalty, and I couldn't have learned on my own what I learned there. That first Workshop year especially I felt like that old *National Geographic* special on the human body, where they show the two-year-old's brain suddenly build this giant tangled neural network while the child learns to speak. I was used to the Workshop bluntness that upset many of my classmates—I'd been edited bluntly enough by my bureau chief and my father (letters from camp came back corrected in red ink) and by art teachers whose method was to grab my charcoal and draw over my (bad) drawings. In fact I'm still learning from my marked-up manuscripts, which contain criticisms I couldn't accept or understand at the time. What I wasn't used to—and what I hadn't expected to hear, working on my own as I always had—were arguments about what was worth seeing, and how it should be shown.

I hadn't considered that there was any question about how stories go. I thought— with a nursery-school fascism that has never quite left me—a good story had a certain sound, the sound I'd heard in the kind of books Penguin puts out in that terribly refined green. Camus, Sinclair Lewis, Bruno Schulz, Mann, writers like that. A good book had a profoundly intelligent, articulate, sensitive voice: an admirable, peculiar voice, meaning not to terrorize the reader but to strip him naked to whatever is unbearable, just as the voice's owner had apparently been stripped. The writer, especially if he was playing games, understood what mattered in the world, and what the characters' lives were. Things happened in stories, generally going from bad to worse to what I learned to call epiphany—my own if not the characters'—or it wasn't proper fiction. A book was best if you often had to stop reading because it had slipped you some rare insight.

Maybe it's not strange that I found most workshops agonizing and—being combative and awkward anyhow—I had violent disagreements with many of my classmates about what mattered in a story. Or that I was able to define an aesthetic most often against my classmates' stories. I spent most of those Tuesday afternoons scowling at the seminar table.

Much as I squirmed, though, I couldn't help but hear how carefully, how urgently these people tried to explain what they'd meant by some criticism or other, when Frank or Marilynne asked. During my first year I began to understand that some of my classmates meant something different by "story" than what I had in mind. These were visions distinctly foreign from my own, even if they weren't always fully formed. What's important in the world? How does one talk about such things? Apparently we didn't agree. Though I didn't ask such questions, not then. At the time I just thought, "Oh—they're doing something different," and was only faintly curious about what that thing might be.

One day, in my third and least congenial workshop, I sat hating the criticism more than ever. I said my piece and then scowled furiously until I was tired and cross, like a small miserable girl taken on a long ride, while we went around the room with excruciating leisure. I had reached a state of baleful passivity, idly listening and thinking "five more people," when suddenly I understood fiction as an immense, flat, broken territory, and knew I'd been living on a very small patch. I mean the land was dark brown and open, all the way to the horizon, and ran crazily, with fog and a low gray sky, and here and there were lunatic signs that someone had claimed turf. And all this time I'd been on my patch, not knowing there was anywhere else to go.

After that I began listening more carefully to stories and criticism I didn't like—still scowling, but attentive—just to see what the view was like from there, in case I wanted to work there myself someday, or lift something and strike out alone. Sometimes the notions that lived in those places were antithetical to mine; sometimes they were so alien that I didn't understand what the writer was doing at all, or whether it was doing any good. But I knew then I was looking at something I didn't understand, and that was the important part.

The best thing I got was the sense of fiction as a territory so vast and shrouded and mainly uninhabited. That was fantastic.

AMY CHARLES '95

I WENT TO IOWA right out of college, Penn State, enthusiastic about Hart Crane and e. e. cummings, not really knowing much about anything besides splendor in misery and being a smart-ass, so I collided fairly stupidly with the Poetry Workshop virtually right off the bat. Mark Strand was teaching, Marvin Bell and Charles Wright were students. Things came to a head at a conference when Don Justice threw up his hands and said he didn't know what to say about a poem I was particularly pleased about. He said it looked to him like some kind of '20s experiment. He was exactly right. I was interested in High Modernism then and now, and have always detested genteel irony and polish or merely nervous sincerity.

So I got into the Fiction Workshop, which seems sort of remarkable in retrospect. Ray Carver was a student, along with Andre Dubus and many others, people more passionate about writing, politics, and personality than about polish. Norman Peterson and Dave Roberts (who wrote *Writing Fiction* for the short-lived Iowa Writers' Workshop–*Encyclopedia Britannica* Correspondence course, for which I eventually became an instructor in fiction) were house-sitting for R. V. Cassill, and they took me in.

Norman was a former U.S. Navy pilot and an assiduous housecleaner. It turns out I was asleep and not technically present for my most vivid recollection, a properly Iowan precursor of the postmodern: Norman was vacuuming and brought to a dead halt by a crumpled pair of my underpants on the living room rug. Dave Roberts talked about it for years: "God damned Norman couldn't move!"

After that I lived at Black's on Brown Street, got married at the Iowa City Methodist Church, ate cake at the Cassill house somewhere west of the city and surrounded by cows, and lived for a year at 219 Harrison Street (I think), at the edge of a cliff and across the street from a convent: it had been Mark Costello's house, and he swore the head nun checked all of her subordinates every night to make sure they weren't trying to sleep in their cotton panties, which gave them wretchedly aromatic yeast infections.

KENNETH ROSEN, '64

I CAME TO THE Iowa Writers' Workshop in 1977 after majoring in history, coaching basketball, and teaching high school social studies, as well as subsequently pursuing a Ph.D. in U.S. history through doctoral exams. I had written stories since junior high school, but I had never taken a fiction-writing class at any level. Classically naive, congenitally oblivious, I allowed Connie Brothers, the Workshop coordinator, to talk me into putting up a story for workshop my first week in the program. Despite this fact, I managed to graduate two years later.

My memories of the program break down into two categories: that which happened in class and that which happened out. I learned how to read a short story from Frank Conroy, not how to analyze themes and detect symbols, but how to break the language down to sentence structure and individual word choice. Nearly twenty years later, Conroy's workshop remains my model, and I strive to make those writing seminars I teach at the University of New Orleans as artistically rigorous as the one he taught to me. In Frank Conroy, Fred Busch, Vance Bourjaily, and Ian McEwan, I had wonderful teachers at Iowa. But much of what I learned came from my peers, and I was surrounded by an astonishing set of classmates including Ralph Berry, Bruce Brooks, Michael Cunningham, Pam Durban, Pam Erbe, Elizabeth Evans, Chip Hannay, Jayne Anne Phillips, Janet Schofield, Stephanie Vaughn, Sarah Vogan, and Irene Wanner, every one the real McCoy.

Out of class we came together on Thursday nights for readings: among countless others John Irving, reading from *Garp* and a year later from *The Hotel New Hamp-*

shire, John Updike reading from *The Coup,* John Cheever reading "The Swimmer," Raymond Carver reading "Will You Please Be Quiet, Please?," Anne Tyler reading from *Morgan's Passing.* Jack Leggett's seemingly rambling, halting introductions were always small masterpieces of comedy. Afterward was even better for it was interactive. We gathered at someone's apartment to toast the reader, snacked on hors d'oeuvres provided by the program, and supplied ourselves with six-packs of Leinenkugel, which we nestled in snowbanks outside to keep cold (and hidden from moochers).

Sometime about halfway through my first semester, a group of us began a tradition that lasted the rest of my time in Iowa City. After workshop, often joined by our teachers, we would adjourn to the Mill to dine on hamburgers or pizza washed down by pitchers of beer that kept coming until closing. We all smoked Marlboro reds in those days, and every cigarette pack was community property. After a time we switched to Vantage, a brand ostensibly lower in tar and nicotine. We were a health-conscious lot.

Ian McEwan invited a dozen of us to the house he rented on the west side of the Iowa River. Frank Conroy played the piano, Ian the flute. A musical incompetent, I was allowed to beat time on a trash can turned upside down, Frank grimacing every time I lost his rhythm. Late that fall of 1977, Ian did the most astonishing thing: he noted my ragged clothes and wreck of a car and offered to lend me money. He'd just gotten an advance, he explained, and had far more than he needed. I was too proud (and too vain) to accept, of course. I wish I had. Had I owed Ian money we would have stayed in touch, and I would long ago have had the opportunity to convey how touched I was by his generosity, how much I admired him, the man, whom most of us know only as the artist. Iowa changed my life. I became a writer at the Workshop. A group of people who were writers, teachers, and classmates let me think of myself that way in their presence, and I've persevered in doing so ever since.

FREDRICK BARTON '79

HAVING DEVOTED my energies to philosophy until the age of twenty-six, I began suddenly and passionately to write fiction. Stories of my Mississippi childhood came pouring out every midnight, though I was supposed to be in the home stretch of an Iowa philosophy Ph.D. My friend Sena Naslund read the stories, encouraged me, and passed them to William Price Fox. Before I knew it I'd been accepted into the Workshop.

After the rigidities of philosophy, the Workshop felt wide open and wild. Seymour Krim praised student work so experimental it included handwriting over the margins of a story's pages. Bill Fox inspired extreme plots and scenes with his novel-in-progress about two Southern women performing topless gospel. Richard Yates spoke each week about a classic American novelist, choosing his words so carefully, with such love for tradition, that he filled me with respect and gratitude. And Barry Goldensohn's poetics deepened my grasp of what a single line, even a single word, might do.

These teachers made indelible impressions, each contributing to a rich whole. Of course nobody loves being a student, and the role was especially confusing in those days of the Vietnam War, the Kent State shootings, the Civil Rights movement, and political assassinations. Nightly campus demonstrations against the war sometimes spilled over into violence against town businesses, as if imperialism equaled the most humble local capitalism; to me the world was drifting without reason.

By contrast, my home revealed another side of Iowa, for I had bought David Milch's farmhouse south of Iowa City. Here among the Amish, beneath muscadine-draped walnut trees and rolling cornfields, my family and I rode horses alongside our dogs and a pet raccoon. Late at night, with the ground frozen deep and the wind howling, I continued writing my stories, feeling for true voice, working in a race to graduate.

Like many people who earn an M.F.A., I left stung by so many encounters with teachers and their acolytes. Did workshops really need to be quite so brutal? Once I moved to New York City, I knew it would take years to digest and work through that turbulent time, and to decide what Iowa meant to me. Determined to preserve the sense of intellectual excitement, I was shocked to learn how difficult this could be. Iowa City had been a cauldron, where first-rate minds appeared constantly in the brew. In New York they were spread out, self-protected, hard to find. I joined a community of songwriters which, intense and competitive, matched my need for the standard Iowa had set. And later, in my own workshops, I attempted greater kindness toward each student, along with honesty about the work. Iowa was a concentrated dream that personalized ideas, editing, and the distances between teachers and students. It remains clear and present, long after the night of that time has passed.

LUKE WALLIN '71

THE FIRST TIME I had a story critiqued I turned several shades of pink while my foolish fiction errors were exposed to all, but I learned more in that first critique than I had in four years of undergraduate work in fiction. I learned that a short story was more than a series of colorful descriptions; it was something that had a genuine shape and structure to it. Tension, too. For me, it was a revelation.

During the first few weeks of my studies at the Workshop I was too shy to go to the Mill (the Workshop bar) after workshop. When I started going, I discovered that what went on in the official workshop was only half of what I had to learn. The other half took place in the Mill, a kind of crazy equivalent to what I think the writers' salons of the '20s must have been like. There was a delicious camaraderie among Workshoppers. I had great fun with my fellow writers, a few of whom I am still in touch with these sixteen years later. I like to think the group I went to Workshop with from 1980 to 1982 was a particularly sterling bunch.

I had four very different workshop instructors while I was at Iowa. I learned from them all. But I learned as much from my fellow students, not only from what they said about my work but from seeing their work critiqued as well. There were several Workshop terms in vogue in those days. One was "skewed," which I never clearly understood, and the other was this: "it just needs a bit of fine-tuning." That I understood.

The Workshop has a reputation for cutthroat criticism, and it's true the commentary became heated at times. But there was never a finer group of souls assembled than those I was privileged to work with. We supported each other even while we dismantled each other. I sold my first short story my last semester at Iowa and made my connection with the woman who is still my agent today. I am tremendously grateful for the Workshop. Iowa City is snowy and small and sweet: my kind of town. I'm glad I got to live and study there.

KAREN STOLZ '82

ONE DAY WHILE at Iowa, I listened to a radio interview with a man who was an expert on pasta. This was the mid-1980s when pasta was chic. He spoke of grades of olive oil, cream versus tomato sauce, Italians making homemade pasta—saying *lasagna, farfalle, spaghetti,* and *al dente* with an Italian accent. I listened as I mopped my kitchen floor. I rolled my eyes. The man sounded *pretentious;* the tone of his voice was like that of someone describing the life of say, Winston Churchill, or waxing rhapsodic about the intricacies of Bernini's sculpture. I realized that it was pretentious, if not absurd, to talk of food in this way. I knew that only a year before, when I had lived in Boston, I would have listened to the man's comments and taken them to heart. Because I had been very interested in being *fashionable.* It was the era of Yuppies, and though I was a writer—an *artist,* I felt myself to be—and though we artists were supposed to be, in general, the opposites of Yuppies, everyone I had known in college in Boston or back home in Southern California was concerned with eating the right thing, wearing the right thing, listening to the right music, reading the book that everyone else was reading. It was while listening to this man on the radio that I apprehended that I had found a way of life, at Iowa, that had allowed me to look beyond fashion.

I think it was because it seemed to me sometimes that I was living in the most beautiful place on earth. The winters were bitterly cold, the spring ripe and full, the summers full of rain and thunder. The seasons changed dramatically; one day it was cold and the next it was spring, the snow had melted, the sun rose early, early, earlier every morning. I did not have a car while I was there, so I walked most everywhere when the weather permitted, and I felt the way the landscape gently rolled along, watched the river rush through, took in the green, green grass and the wide open spaces, the beautiful old houses. I remember a ride to the airport in the winter that showed me farms in the stark winter landscape: a two-story house set against the endless snow, the bitterly cold but bright blue sky, the lone tree naked without leaves. I had grown up at the beach, in seasonless weather, and I had been attracted to an urban lifestyle. After Iowa I had presumed I would go back to live in Boston, or in New York, maybe San Francisco. But being in Iowa, with its active writing scene, its affordable lifestyle, its arts events that were not impossible to get to or afford, the beautiful neighborhoods, the slower pace of life, the soul-enriching beauty of its landscape, showed me that many of the things in the urban lifestyle were trappings, diversions, often as pretentious and unnecessary as an expert's advice about pasta.

The conversations with other students were the very best thing of all. I can re-member one day sitting in a newly opened coffee shop, a transformed old house, and all day long talking with different Workshop people who happened in. The conversations flowed from one to the other, different people joined in, the group grew large, grew small. It was funny, deep, light, serious, personal, about books, the world. It always circled back to writing: what we knew, what we didn't know, what we needed to know. I had never felt so at home with other people as the ones I met there. Those conversations took place so often, in so many different places in Iowa City. There was a great camaraderie—I might run into someone on the street and join them for dinner or an Alan Ladd double feature at the university's movie theater. We may not have even known each other all that well, but we went out, talked, got to know each other. The ease with which people interacted, the open conversations—I had never found that before, and I have never found that again in the twelve years since I graduated.

The atmosphere in the workshop classes I remember as quasi-religious—a scene reminiscent of *The Nun's Story* or some such movie—the teacher always came in after we were all seated. We presented our work to the group as penitents, listened to our faults and strengths with heads bent, listened to the teacher's general statements about writing, about art, about stupidity and cliché, about originality and brilliance. We took our blows along with our plaudits. The teachers gave a lot to us—more than we appreciated at the time—and took us seriously in a way that many of us had never had someone do before. It was a gift.

I wrote a lot. I wrote every day. It was thrilling, a new freedom. I tried new things, I experimented, became more confident, went from being silent to being able to speak my mind. It was not a perfect place, of course, and many of us, myself included, went through some hard times. That was because it was a place of transformation, of initiation. As such, it brought frustration, confusion, and fear, but also it was a place that provided a time of unparalleled exhilaration, learning, and joy.

STEPHANIE BROWN '86

WHEN I WAS at Iowa, there was a lot of bitterness among the students about how little attention our work was receiving. I didn't understand it then and I still don't. I thought how much smarter than me the others must be, because to me it was far more valuable to hear brilliant people say what's on their mind—sometimes pertaining to writing, sometimes not—than to have them labor over a bungled scene in one of my stories. I remember sitting in a particular seminar of Jim McPherson's on myth and fiction and gritting my teeth in frustration as a few students kept accepting McPherson's invitation to engage him about his thoughts on the subject. What they wanted, of course, was to have their own thoughts heard. Which is normally fine, as I know that's how learning takes place and all that. But I wanted to hear McPherson. Because I'd never heard anything before or since like what I was hearing from him. I didn't want discussion, I didn't want dialogue. I wanted monologue. Ditto with Marilynne Robinson. Ditto with Frank Conroy. I'm not sure Frank ever knew my name, but it didn't matter. What was so valuable about Iowa to me was that for the first time in my life I shut up and listened. Maybe it was a coincidence that while receiving only moderate attention, both personally and in my work, I learned something about how to write. I surely didn't know anything when I came there.

I remember the people with me at Iowa. Denis Johnson's unfortunate semester-long seminar on *Under the Volcano*, after the first few weeks of which no one really knew what to say. Denis was so likable, though, we didn't much care. I remember seeing right away that some writers had something special, a gift of imagination and perspective I hadn't seen before. Chris Adrian and Nathan Englander come at once to mind. I wish I'd have had a workshop with Rick Harsch. I remember thinking how this Brady Udall character talks like he's got everything figured out, which was annoying. Then I wrote what I came to understand through Thom Jones's terminology as my breakthrough story, which turned out to be the title story of my collection, and suddenly Brady made sense; I'd just been a few large steps behind. (Though it's still annoying how often I think Brady's wrong about something, and then I think on it some more and realize he's right.) My best friend in the Workshop was Tony Fiotto, one of the only other married guys who liked to drink beer and shoot pool. Tony's writing about people connected to the law and its mysterious world was elegant and intelligent. He and his wife, Sarah, were beyond kind to me. Perhaps if I'd have known how to conduct a friendship properly, thinking of others instead of only myself, always, he and I would still be close. But my second year at Iowa was a hard one. I went there with one wife and left with the woman who would become my next. Other stuff happened in between, embarrassing stuff that kept me lying low. Iowa, for me, was about figuring things out, writing, yes, but mainly myself. It was a good place for that.

STEVE LATTIMORE '95

THE WORKSHOP was where I slowed down, just doing what I needed to get by. For a while, before Iowa, I'd tried to be a windup toy, tooling around the streets of New York City.

After college, I'd landed a job as a jack-of-all-trades for a literary agent, whose office was behind the Chelsea Hotel. I was in charge of the slush pile, and I helped some new writers get published. Another duty included retrieving the runaway office cat by climbing a scaffold in front of the Chelsea as I wore a windblown white dress. The cat had no reason to run away; he got to dine on my boss's leftover garlic shrimp.

I, however, ran away to the Workshop, where my chance to sit back, relax, and enjoy the show came in various forms. The most academic was Allan Gurganus's seminar on the short story. Anybody who's met Allan knows what a charmer he is— with his white suits, honey voice, and chockful o' nuggets way with words, a kind of gay, L-word, Tom Wolfe. In Allan's classes, we always had several hours to discuss the two short stories, from Henry James to Ian McEwan, which we'd been assigned over the week. Allan gave great detail. Oddly, the piece I remember most our lovingly examining was not a short story but a series of letters that a POW in Vietnam wrote his wife over the many years he was imprisoned. The letters were filled with aching desires and fantasies about what the man would do when he returned home. Still, less than a year after the prisoner returned to the States and to his wife, he committed suicide. Why? we asked.

In other classes, we did the Iowa thing, a combo of exchanging shortcuts and constructive criticism while slacking and backbiting. But, frankly, what happened in my classes was less important than what happened in between classes. I sometimes tell people that going to Iowa was like my experience going to summer camp, a kind of repose with a dash of see-these-people-all-the-time incestuousness. I hadn't really been part of a tribe for many years in New York, and I liked being "one of us, one of us," as the freaks say in *Freaks*.

I started Iowa in slushy January, which was pleasant because I missed the hotter-weather hoggish smell that wafts over the town. Apparently hogs outnumber people five to one in Iowa. The first day I looked for an apartment, I entered a bagel bakery with an old Victorian façade. I asked at the bakery counter if any upper-floor apartments were for rent; the front one with the big bay window wasn't, but the back one was. It was the most New York City–like apartment I saw there, with its view of chimneys, its minimalist and impractical white-painted hardwoods. Later, I had some good scuffing up of the floors at sweaty parties. That first day, I dropped by the Workshop office and met Lucy Grealy, who was neighborly at the same time she teased me about my black wardrobe.

Madison Smart Bell, with whom I'd studied in New York, came to the Workshop to teach for a semester during my second year. Madison is another generous wordsmith with energy and smarts out the wazoo. He once asked me why the students at Iowa didn't write more. Sheepishly, I shrugged my shoulders. I guess I, at least, was just *being*, practicing mindfulness. Or maybe I was just shallow and hedonistic.

Time slowed down at one of the best parts of the Workshop: the readings. When I filed into an auditorium for a reading, I noticed who was sitting with whom, what clothes people were wearing; I'd notice Poet A making out so blatantly with Fiction Writer K after just yesterday being hooked up with Teacher X. But when the Writer started reading, I stopped my fussing and went with the spell. Francine Prose read her "Tibetan Time," with the line about the ring of a gong feeling like a giant Q-tip swabbing up the character's back. One regret I have is that I didn't get a chance to take a class with Ms. Prose. I remember so many great readings: Czeslaw Milosz, Derek Walcott, T. C. Boyle, Deborah Eisenberg, Tomas Transtromer, James Tate, W. C. Merwin, and all the profs.

One of my strongest memories of the Workshop is a memory of a feeling. The only other time I'd had such a feeling was at summer camp, for a few minutes, late at night, when it seemed like everyone else was asleep. I left my bunk and ran out into the middle of an empty field. I flopped onto the grass, my back to the dampness and that grass-scent, matched only in my scent pantheon by coffee or limes. Watching the stars, I caught my breath. The feeling I had that night, I had time and time again at Iowa. It was there under the hog smell and in the slush, when I stopped, looked, and listened. It was the fine art I ended up studying.

And, okay, the classes did help.

MIRIAM KUZNETS '88

BECAUSE I WAS too broke to attend the Workshop full-time, it took me four years (1958–62) to get my M.F.A. I'd go for a semester, then work for a year, then go back for a semester, etc.

I have three notable memories of my time in IC; the Saturday softball games, where the poets and prose writers faced off; Kenny's Bar, where the writer wanna-bes hung out; and my final comps, which I was told, in error, that I'd flunked.

The softball games were played every fall weekend until it got too cold, and again in the spring. Don Justice and others were fierce players who were famous for their fanatic play. Although the games were hotly contested, they were events of innocence and passion rather than talent, since all of us were longer on emotion than ability. I played third base most of the time, but was not feared as a long ball hitter. After our daughter was born, my wife would bring her to the games, and afterward we would walk home together, since we had no car.

Kenny's Bar was, we were told when we first got to IC, the "literary bar" where all the Workshop writers hung out. We had so little money that we could rarely afford to go to a bar, but sometimes we did, just so we could be identified as writers, or at least would-be writers. What I remember most about Kenny's is that only Jerry Bumpus actually did any writing there, sitting in a booth, surrounded by Special Export beer bottles, scribbling away; all the rest of us just drank and talked about writing, but Jerry actually wrote.

There was a kind of romance associated with Kenny's. In our minds, it was IC's equivalent of the Paris bars of the '20s where Hemingway and the other Lost Generation characters hung out. All of us drinking there had the notion that we were among the future writers of America, that we were shoulder to shoulder with the literati-to-be of the last half of the century. It was a nice feeling, however false it may have turned out to have been.

My last weeks in IC, in the midwinter of '62, were notable to me because it was then that I took the comprehensive exams that were to determine whether I got my degree or not. My wife and child had flown back east, the temperatures were 15 degrees below zero, and I was living alone in our house trailer with an inch of ice on the inside walls. I took the exams with two other people and felt pretty sure I'd done well, then waited for what seemed forever for the results, and finally was told that I'd flunked the exams.

I was devastated and that night, after phoning my wife and giving her the terrible news, I stood before a mirror and shaved off my handlebar mustache (in lieu, I now think, of cutting my throat). The next morning, after sleepless hours, I steeled myself and phoned Vance Bourjaily, my adviser, to find out how I'd gone wrong. Vance said there'd been a mistake, that I'd done well. We checked the tests and he was right; I hadn't flunked, but had done better than either of the other two people. I was furious! I raved at Vance, wondering who could have mixed up the results of the exams when only three of us had taken them. He said, "Well, it was either the chairman of the department or his secretary. I advise you not to ask."

I took that advice, loaded up my car with everything I owned, and left IC and never looked back. Of course, after my anger had gone, I realized that the real victim of the mistake was the poor guy who believed he had passed and only later learned that he had failed.

I have other memories, too (Vance Bourjaily, after a morning of duck hunting, coming into the Quonset hut that was the Workshop classroom, leaning his shotgun against the wall, then conducting the class; Don Justice, at midnight, at the end of a long, boozy party, trying to get the rest of us to compose a common poem before we went home; etc.), but the three I've described here are the big ones. Now, almost forty years and a dozen novels later, I still remember them clearly.

PHILIP CRAIG '62

THE WORKSHOP in the mid-1960s was filled with bright students striving to meet their own high expectations for good writing and the standards of their peers and professors. Sometimes a prima donna–ish air prevailed, but mostly we just wanted to write well. The sections met in a WWII Quonset hut near the Student Union and occasionally several sections met together in a chemistry lecture hall. Neither location quite matched the sense of the importance of our calling as writers and as students in the Iowa Writers' Workshop.

I studied with Paul Carroll, who flew in weekly from Chicago and dressed in colorful, dandyish clothes, and with Marvin Bell who blended easily with the casual, simple Workshop norm. Both read and commented vigorously on students' work. We were encouraged to read contemporary literature as examples for technique and approaches to similar writing situations. These readings invited us to see our efforts as part of a broader artistic scene. This was daunting and humbling, but also encouraging. At least our work had a connection to better, more experienced writers.

Besides the well-known effect of the Iowa program on American letters, the presence of the Workshop and its students pervaded the whole English Department. Writing well with clarity and precision and without pretension or jargon became the high goal for all English graduate students.

DIANE PARKIN-SPEER, MID-1960S

I REMEMBER THE cold, and the thermometer at the First National Bank reading, with midwestern indifference, −32 degrees, on a day I went out to do my laundry.

I remember writing hard and well until 3:00 A.M., and throwing up.

I remember graffiti. From the Foxhead: "I'm a-peein' European, we're all 'a-peein'!" From the women's room at the Deadwood, seen at holiday time: "Three wise men? Really three?"

My first autumn, I decided, with friends, to throw a Halloween party. We were the new kids and wanted the older, bigger kids to like us and not beat us up after school; we tossed a coin, and my house lost. Halfway through the party I stepped into the kitchen and met a strong smell of gas. Somebody had opened all four burners on the old stove. A dozen people stood around this powder keg, smoking. Why we didn't all take a trip into orbit at that moment I still can't say.

And while we're at it; I remember smoking. Good god, how we could smoke!

Somebody cornered me at a dinner party the other night and demanded to know what I'd liked so damn much about Iowa. (She meant the state.) It turned out that she'd lived there ten years, and her oldest son had had some kind of bad experience. She was a bear defending her cubs, in other words, so there was no right answer, but I did my best. "It's flat," I said. "It's quiet. It's an easy place to be poor. Herbert Hoover is from there. So are Pella Windows. No one tries to sell you anything."

The morning I left was a Sunday, a morning in August. I had been up most of the night packing and cleaning the house, but the process of disassembling my Iowa life had actually consumed most of a month. The feel of that morning; the shitty smell of the fields, the drowsy buzz of the cicadas, my car packed to the tops of its windows. I had actually slept elsewhere. My lease had expired at midnight, and although I still had a key and no one would have cared, I didn't go back in. I wanted more than anything I had ever wanted not to leave, but leaving was the point, so I knew I would, too. While cleaning my house I had come across a Superball wedged behind the radiator. I'd put it in my pocket, and it was still there, so to fill the moment of my departure I bounced it up and down the sidewalk of my quiet neighborhood, saying good-bye.

JUSTIN CRONIN '89

JUST A FEW NIGHTS ago, at a Seattle Arts and Lectures event, Richard Ford was asked to name a few authors who have influenced him, and he said Richard Yates. Yates, he said, is the best unread author since WWII. Luckily, I have five of his novels on my bookshelf, most of them first editions, including *Revolutionary Road*, which appears to be the only one of his works still in print. What I'm missing is the first collection of stories, *Eleven Kinds of Loneliness*. A friend or student or ex-wife must have run off with it years ago. I've searched now in a dozen used bookstores, most of them cluttered attics and basements, and no luck. As a student in the Writers' Workshop in the mid-1960s, when I still believed good books were sacred, I had committed most of those stories to memory. I remember Richard Yates, too, of course. I remember him tall, but everything about him—face, body, eyes— seemed weighed down, like he was going through hell. I liked that about him, and I liked that he liked the little stories I wrote and always noted the details, the small truths in the descriptions of things, like a hanger snapping when you jerked a coat from it. In fact, ten years or more after I left Iowa, I saw him again, briefly, I can't imagine where, and asked if he remembered me at all, and he said yes, of course, the snapping hanger. I heard he died in a motel—in Alabama, I think. Wherever it was, Yates himself, as Ford said, was the place you went back to. There were other places too, the Iowa places I call them now, like Bourjaily and Vonnegut, who are still together here on my shelf, within reach, teaching me.

EDWIN WEIHE '66

I WAS MOST haunted by the Workshop the year I graduated. Like the last guest at a party, I lingered in Iowa City. I hung out with the new crop of students, religiously attended readings, drifted around the cramped, smoky pall of the Fox-head. In the afternoons, light slanted dully through my apartment while I labored to transform a short story into a novel, the one story that had earned a positive reaction from my classmates. Evenings, I applied for teaching jobs in the worst academic job market in decades.

I was numb. I'd come to Iowa to be elevated into a literary world I'd fantasized about since I'd first read *A Moveable Feast*. For two years, I'd brushed up against it—the heightened talk about fictional craft; the late nights drinking with famous writers; the odd rhythm of days liberated from having to make a living. Literary fame seemed plausible. Close. A visiting eminence was sure to recognize my gifts, launch my career. The Workshop would save me from the sorrow of an ordinary life.

But it hadn't, and now I spent hours in Prairie Lights investigating dust jackets and *The Best American Short Stories* for evidence of other graduates' success. One by one, friends went off to careers, marriages, other places. I spent more time alone.

I went out of my way to avoid people I knew on the streets of Iowa City, even those, who like me, had been unable to let go of the dream. One day, I slipped into EPB, the building where our classes were held, and in a dark hall, listened to the articulate voices of a workshop in progress.

My apartment overlooked the Oakland Cemetery, and each day long, ruminative walks among the gravestones led me to the Black Angel, a life-sized statue memorializing an anonymous citizen. Legend has it touching the Angel brings death; I stroked its outstretched palm and my novel died. I piled up draft after draft of the same two chapters—false starts, dead ends, revised revisions.

Eventually, I ran out of money. I took a part-time job teaching freshman composition to indifferent students at a local community college. I moved away from the graveyard and from Iowa City. I boxed the novel and put away Workshop voices, and in time, the last of my illusions about the literary life faded. In a wet Iowa summer, I married the best person I've ever known and everything changed.

What did I learn? That life goes on, with or without fiction. I work for a marketing firm these days and write fiction when I can steal the minutes. Under trying circumstances, sentence by sentence, I progress. And this is as it should be. As the first act in my writing life, the Workshop allowed me to confront my most destructive habit—getting lost in the lifestyle and not in the work.

I have a photograph of a group of us back in our heyday at the Mill, and whenever I look at it, I feel lucky and blessed. On the long list of students who've attended the Workshop, many do not survive, their faith extinguished. Frank Conroy had said over and over that "the writing life is a hard life," and I'd resented him for it. Now, I owe him a debt of gratitude and think I understand him. How difficult it must be to pass judgment on so much hope.

FRITZ MCDONALD '90

It was 1967, an hour before class, and Dick Yates was sitting in an Iowa City bar called the Airliner, in a total, cold-sweat panic. One of his best students—someone with not only a big reputation but a book contract—had a chapter up for discussion; most of us liked it but Dick thought it was lousy and had just realized there was no graceful way out. He would have to say so in class.

Would he hurt the guy's feelings? Wouldn't he just seem envious, or worse, anti-intellectual, to the students—all these overeducated kids with diplomas from Harvard or Tufts while he had none.

Glass after golden glass of Hamms beer. Cigarette after cigarette stubbed out in the ashtray. "Okay, let's go," he said, finally.

As if marching to his execution he made himself stride into the class and—as usual—in his cigarette-coarsened voice, picked apart the manuscript with such precision he left us chagrined at our own low standards. Then he left, stuffing himself into his yellow VW to drive the four miles out to the stone cottage where he lived then, convinced he had destroyed his reputation forever.

That's the kind of thing I remember about Richard Yates, now dead six years, but in the mid-1960s you could find a group of acolytes at Iowa—I was one—because of the insight informing his writing and his teaching.

We were a group hard to impress. In Hemingway's time would-be writers could head for Paris and the Left Bank; in 1966 writers needed a student deferment. Hundreds of us wound up at Iowa.

The campus bubbled with a seething mix of creative ferment and rage about the Vietnam War. John Irving was there, and Andre Dubus, Gail Godwin, Jonathan Penner and John Casey, John Wideman and Jim McPherson and Bill Kittredge and

Dave Milch—to walk into Borders these days and poke around the fiction shelves is virtually to see an Iowa alumni list from those days.

But was writing what we wanted? Our lives were dominated by Vietnam. At parties, or over coffee in the Student Union, or in our offices, we would argue about whether it was moral to even think about writing one more novel of manners when we were napalming children in Southeast Asia. Vonnegut, another good and generous teacher, told me not to worry about spending time doing antiwar work; even if I didn't write a word he had no intention of handing out F's.

Into this cauldron came Dick, back from a miserable year in Hollywood. He had been at Iowa in '64 and already had a group of fans commanded by Dubus, the burly leader of a group of older students, all veterans. Soon us younger writers joined the group.

And why not? How could you not love stories like "Builders," "A Really Good Jazz Piano," or "The Best of Everything?" with their shapeliness, mimetic dialogue, and devastating final scenes? How could you not respond to Yates's ability to create strong narratives revolving so wholly about character?

How could a budding writer not love even the little things: Yates's signature way of using a parenthesis to remind you of the essentials of a past scene ("Okay, let's go"); or the way he had of presenting the rational course of action for his character, then starting the next paragraph with "The trouble was . . ." and dissecting all the emotions that would inevitably get in the way?

Yates had no doubt that writing was important. Unlike some of the other writers on faculty—Nelson Algren, for example, who was shocked that he had to actually read student work—Dick threw himself into helping us.

By now, of course, actual conversations have long since left my brain cells. But I remember long conversations about books—why *All the King's Men* was so overrated and why *Gatsby* wasn't—and getting back manuscripts with his scrawling comments over them ("You think he'd really say it that way? I doubt it."); and listening to him go over stories as he stood draped over a lectern in the (to our minds) antiseptically bright classrooms in EPB.

We wanted him to have a happier life. I remember the way we massed outside the church after his marriage to Martha. Was it Vance Bourjaily pressing packets of rice into everybody's hands, so we, grudgingly accepting this World War II–era custom, could heave it at the two of them?

He would not have a happy life. I also remember one class session when he came in, clearly upset, his voice even raspier than usual, and stunned us with a long, rambling, only partly coherent monologue about a writer who turned out to have the luck of being a great writer—and married a woman of great wealth—the punchline of which was that it was William Styron. The next day Yates had checked into the hospital to recover from what in those days we called a "breakdown."

Once, disappointed by the neglect of his later books, he told me he thought his obituary would mention only *Revolutionary Road*. I, convinced that eventually excellence is recognized, demurred. Now, when that is the only book of his left on the shelves even of the big stores, I know better.

It's too bad. He deserves to be remembered for many more.

But I also hope people remember his character.

Yates wouldn't approve. "Who cares about a writer's character, for Chrissakes," I can hear him growl. "It's the books, the goddamn books."

Still, we don't have to remember the dead in precisely the way they want.

"I can't tell you how often," Bill Kittredge once wrote, "I have sat looking at some shabby, ambitious nonsense I just wrote, and imagined Dick Yates looking at me with those sad old eyes, shaking his head."

There are dozens—no, hundreds—of us who still have him in our heads in precisely the same way.

This wonderful writer, whose character was always thought to have inhibited his career, was also a man of great character; a man who fought mental illness to produce book after finely wrought book; who was dedicated to his students and friends and children; and who, above all, was agonizingly loyal to telling the truth, whether in one of his own short stories or in summoning up the nerve to tell a hotshot writer and a class full of his friends that he, and by implication, we, could do a little bit better.

ROBERT LEHRMAN '68

coda

A century has passed since the first course in "Verse Making" was offered in 1896 in Iowa City. For seven decades, the Workshop provided a home for writers. In its wake followed hundreds of imitators. As the new century begins, two questions must be asked: Was it worth the effort? And, should any downsides for writers be considered?

To me, the stories and reflections on writing and the writing life collected here offer an incontestable "Yes" to the first question. I find artistry not only in the works themselves but in the passions and struggles of all who have brought their talent and their hope to Iowa.

Are there downsides to the Workshop phenomenon's success? R. V. Cassill, who founded the Associated Writing Programs, reportedly stunned AWP members during a speech he gave in 1982, suggesting that AWP disband because no further good could come of writers remaining inside the Academy. As a man who was among the first graduates of the program at Iowa, as well as a teacher there and a tireless crusader on behalf of writers everywhere, Mr. Cassill, who graciously agreed to share his comments, reminds us that the first and only responsibility of the writer is to his art.

Beginning his speech, Mr. Cassill noted that, to him, Whitman's "By Blue Ontario's Shore" "continues to define the quality of the writers who belong to and serve these States." Then he proceeded to ask if the direction many writers and writing programs had taken had enhanced and vitalized the art we all strive and hope to make.

Most of us here have spent a good part of our lives and commitments of effort into bringing writing into the academic world and securing its place in the curricula. What I have to say now, to put it with extreme simplicity, is that the time has come when we must try to get it out. Extricate it. Get it on the open road again if we can't conceive another habitation. For, as I will sketch the picture, we are now at the point where writing programs are poisoning, and in turn we are being poisoned by departments and institutions on which we have fastened them.

To organize the AWP I piggy-backed around the country from school to school, getting paid to deliver a lecture called Teaching Literature as an Art. In it I argued that literary education would be leavened and brought to face its real responsibilities by the inclusion of writing programs as part of the academic curriculum. I believe that was and has been a sound idea, and much more importantly I believe that it has worked for many years. The results are in the bloodstream of many who have passed through the schools in these years. But everything has its season. The good that has been done will not justify the harms that multiply and loom ahead.

For my purposes let me come directly to what I see happening in literary education in academic circles as a result of this. The scenario I give is fictional but realistic. If nothing else can be said of it—and if it does not exactly fit the pattern you recognize at your school—I maintain it is now an altogether possible scenario. And since it is possible, it will be enacted, it will throw the advantage to those who follow the formula with fewest scruples. Those of you who know chess will foresee mate in a few more moves. Those who know Gresham's law will understand how, in this field increasingly dominated by moneychangers, the bad money will drive the good money out.

Funded with the people's [state or federal] money, a group of writers publishes their own or each other's work. Under the remnants of the 'publish or perish' policy they thus get credit for publications, which are translated into salary increments. From proliferating writing classes they muster student supporters who are paid off by student aid funds while in college and selectively boosted onto the payrolls of States Arts Councils while they wait their turn for larger grants. Along the way student publications are drawn into the phalanx by tacit or covert promises that adhering students can share in what is obviously a paying proposition, while opposition is reckless at best. Ideological covers for this double-dipping, boondoggling, logrolling exploitation are provided best by those departments dominated by young Turks who disparage 'realism' and extol 'ecriture' or those [other] proliferating critical scams designed to emphasize the aesthetic bliss of denying that language can mean what it says—structuralism, deconstruction . . . and the like. The writing programs, in their phases of decay, are appropriate accomplices of the academic gamesmen who march on the trough under the banners of criticism . . . For those of you who can still read in spite of academic miseducation, there is Orwell's terrifying thesis: That the flip side of the coin of the corruption of language is now and always political corruption evolving into lightless political tyranny.

And that . . . is the story to be told in times to come by American writers. By what agencies we were brought to this point. It is not a story that will emerge from the institutions in which we still gain our bread and try to teach.

It is the story to be told when those of us who brought writing into the academic swamp lead it out again.

In all this I have not addressed the question of who will fund the AWP or individual writers or what we call most generally *writing*. The answer seems clear enough to me. Writing will always be funded by writers. By the pawning of their lives, fortunes and sacred honor.

But, for sentimental reasons among others, I am not content to end on that note. A few words then that old Whitman sent me here to say for him:

"What I have promised without mentioning it, you have accepted, have you not?

"What the teaching could not teach, what the preaching could not accomplish, is accomplished, is it not?"

I asked Mr. Cassill to reflect on these words sixteen years after he composed and delivered them. He wrote back:

I, too, have had to laugh when I read about my turn against the AWP speech fifteen years after I had organized it and given it a slight forward momentum. But, privately I told myself I was being consistent.

In the early sixties I was optimistic about many things I saw as possibilities in politics and education. I thought that giving writers an institutional place among the teaching cadres of higher education would improve the quality of the latter and offer the security of academic status to writers involved. By the time I gave my infamous talk in Boston at the 15th Anniversary meeting of the AWP my optimism had dimmed considerably.

I supposed I saw writing programs taking on the colors of regular academic politics instead of ameliorating them. (For what I mean by such politics see Peter Taylor's "Dean of Mean" and Tobias Wolff's "In the Garden of the North American Martyrs.") The Indians were taking on the vices of the white man. Nothing was redeeming the torpidity and pointlessness of graduate scholarship. Or so it seemed to me. And it seemed to me, as heretofore, that the writer's first duty was still and always to himself and his art, rather than to any institution whatever. Like Whitman, I value institutions only as they further the well-being of the self. Better the desert than the social lie.

I guess I have a good idea of how much good work has been done by writers who have kept AWP active and flourishing. My dire predictions have not manifestly come true. Or, is it the first duty of the writer to see whether they have or not? Taking the measure of that is what I would want any writer to do. Steer always for deep water. March to the sound of the cannons.

And now, sixteen years after my sad heresy in Boston, what do I see? Things got worse in the environment of the word and those who must live by the word. Brute Clintonism and its conspiratorial cohorts on the 24-hour TV news programs have bitched us inside and outside the Academy. The blistered tongues of the ruined citizenry can hardly bend to utter the jolly old word whore—as in the epithet 'the President's whore.' Deep Throat, that funny little politico-lingual gem from the days of Nixon, can not be uttered in the cybernetic climate of their Monica.

If I were teaching now I would not dare utter such syllables for fear of the student spy system and language police. At least one student has been expelled from Brown University for yelling just three syllables in a dormitory corridor. One might say the city has fallen. Nowhere to go.

Ruminating on this I have been consoled by the French poet who wrote, "*Tu as bien fait de partir,* Artur Rimbaud." I have often been comforted by the image of that little bugger riding around Africa with a belt full of gold pounding his guts to pieces.

Iowa changed the course of American literature in the twentieth century. It has done so in a manner no other group of writers, taken as a whole, can match. I believe it's the deep ambivalence about the place of the writer in America—whether it's to be inside or outside the Academy, in the mainstream or on the margins of the culture—that has made the Iowa Workshop both a home to writers, as well an experience so intense that all writers who partake of it remain forever wary of straying too far from the desert, the place where their real work is done. The writers who make their way through the Iowa Workshop come to possess all the doubt and hope and longing that goes into making literature. And in the end, we all come to realize that the rest, as Flaubert says, "is the madness of Art."

A B O U T   T H E   A U T H O R S

Richard Bausch's books include *Rare and Endangered Species, Rebel Powers,* and *The Fireman's Wife and Other Stories.*

Pinckney Benedict's books include *Town Smokes, The Wrecking Yard,* and *Dogs of God.*

Clark Blaise's books include *Man and His World, Tribal Justice, A North American Education, Resident Alien,* and the memoir *I Had a Father.*

T. Coraghessan Boyle's books include *The Road to Wellville, The Tortilla Curtain,* the PEN/Faulkner–winning novel *World's End,* and his *Collected Stories.*

Ethan Canin's books include *The Emperor of the Air, Blue River, The Palace Thief,* and *For Kings and Planets.*

Raymond Carver's books of short stories include *Cathedral,* which was a finalist for the National Book Critics Circle Award, *Where I'm Calling From,* and *Will You Please Be Quiet, Please?,* a finalist for the National Book Award.

John Casey's books include *Testimony & Demeanor, An American Romance, The Half-Life of Love,* and *Spartina,* which won the National Book Award for Fiction.

R. V. Cassill's books include his acclaimed novels *After Goliath* and *Clem Anderson,* four short story collections, a creative writing text, *Writing Fiction,* and Norton anthologies on contemporary and classic American short fiction.

Lan Samantha Chang's stories have appeared in *Best American Short Stories* and were collected in her first book, *Hunger*.

Michael Cunningham's novels include *Flesh and Blood*, *A Home at the End of the World*, and *The Hours*, which won the Pulitzer Prize and the PEN/Faulkner award for fiction.

Charles D'Ambrosio's *The Point* was a finalist for the PEN/Hemingway Award.

Andre Dubus's books include *Dancing after Hours*, *Selected Stories*, and two books of personal essays, *Blood Vessels* and *Meditations from a Movable Chair*.

Stuart Dybek's story collections include *Childhood and Other Neighborhoods* and *The Coast of Chicago*.

Kim Edwards's *Secrets of a Fire King* was a finalist for the PEN/Hemingway Award.

Gail Godwin's books include *Dream Children*, *Father Melancholy's Daughter*, *Glass People*, and *The Good Husband*.

Allan Gurganus's *The Oldest Living Confederate Widow Tells All* was a finalist for the National Book Critics Circle Award, his story collection *White People* won the *Los Angeles Times* Fiction Prize, and his second novel is *Plays Well with Others*.

Ron Hansen's books include the story collection *Nebraska* and *Mariette in Ecstasy*, which was a National Book Award finalist.

Colin Harrison's novels include *Bodies Electric* and *Manhattan Nocturne*. He is the deputy editor at *Harper's*.

Kathryn Harrison's books include *Poison* and her memoir *The Kiss*.

Gish Jen's books include *Typical American* and *Mona in the Promised Land*.

Denis Johnson's books of fiction include *Jesus' Son*, *Already Dead*, *Fiskadoro*, and *Angels*.

Thom Jones's books include *Sonny Liston Was a Friend of Mine*, *Cold Snap*, and *The Pugilist at Rest*, which was a National Book Award finalist.

William Kittredge's books include *We Are Not in This Together* and the memoir *Hole in the Sky*.

Elizabeth McCracken's books include *Here's Your Hat What's Your Hurry* and *The Giants's House*, which was a National Book Award finalist for fiction.

James Alan McPherson's books include the memoir *Crabcakes, Hue and Cry,* and *Elbow Room,* which won the Pulitzer Prize for fiction.

Bharati Mukherjee's novels and short story collections include *Jasmine, The Holder of the World,* and *The Middleman,* which won the National Book Critics Circle Award.

Flannery O'Connor's *The Complete Stories* won the National Book Award for fiction.

Chris Offutt's books include *Kentucky Straight, The Good Brother, Out of the Woods,* and the memoir *The Same River Twice.*

ZZ Packer was born in Chicago and raised in Atlanta and Louisville, Kentucky. She attended Yale and Johns Hopkins before receiving an M.F.A. at the Iowa Writers' Workshop as a member of the final graduating class of the twentieth century. She was a recipient of a 1997 Rona Jaffe writing award, and her stories have appeared in *Seventeen, Story,* and the anthology *25 and under Fiction.*

Bette Pesetsky's books include *Confessions of a Bad Girl, Midnight Sweets, The Late Night Muse,* and *Cast a Spell.*

Jayne Anne Phillips's books include *Black Tickets* and the novels *Shelter* and *Machine Dreams,* which was a finalist for the National Book Critics Circle Award for fiction.

Tom Piazza is a noted jazz critic who has published several books on jazz, as well as his story collection *Blues and Trouble.*

Susan Power's novel *The Grass Dancer* won the PEN/Hemingway Award.

Bob Shacochis's books include *Swimming in the Volcano* and *Easy in the Islands,* which won the American Book Award for first fiction.

Jane Smiley's books include *The Age of Grief, Moo,* and *A Thousand Acres,* which won the Pulitzer Prize for fiction.

Wallace Stegner's books include *The Collected Stories of Wallace Stegner* and the novel *Angle of Repose,* which won the Pulitzer Prize for fiction.

Richard Stern's books include *Shares and Other Fictions, Noble Rot: Stories,* and *A Sistermony.*

Marly Swick's books include her story collection *A Hole in the Language,* which won the Iowa Short Fiction Award, *Paper Wings, The Summer before the Summer of Love,* and *The Evening News.*

Walter Tevis wrote *The Hustler*, the novel on which the famous film is based, as well as several other novels.

Brady Udall has published a highly regarded story collection *Letting Loose the Hounds*.

Abraham Verghese's *My Own Country* was a finalist for the National Book Critics Circle Award for nonfiction and later made into a film. In addition to several prize-winning short stories, he has written a second memoir, *The Tennis Partner*.

Joy Williams's books include *Taking Care, Escapes*, and her novel *State of Grace*, which was a finalist for the National Book Award.

Thomas Williams's books include his story collection *Leah, New Hampshire* and the novel *The Hair of Harold Roux*, which won the National Book Award for fiction.

Many authors generously contributed recollections about their experience at Iowa. Among them are:

Foremost, John Leggett, who directed the Workshop from 1969 to 1987, and is the author of *Making Believe, Gulliver House*, and *Ross and Tom*.

Tom Barbash is a 1991 graduate of the Workshop and winner of a Wallace Stegner Fellowship.

Fredrick Barton is the author of *The El Cholo Feeling Passes, Courting Pandemonium*, and *With Extreme Prejudice*.

Robin Beeman is the author of *A Minus Tide* and *A Parallel Life and Other Stories*.

Nell Beram is a 1994 graduate of the Workshop.

Stephanie Brown is the author of *Allegory of the Supermarket*.

Amy Charles is a 1995 graduate of the Workshop.

Philip R. Craig is the author of *Off Season, A Beautiful Place to Die*, and other acclaimed Martha's Vineyard mysteries.

Justin Cronin is the author of *The Short History of the Long Ball*, which won the 1990 National Novella Award, and the novel *Mary and O'Neil: A Romance*.

Thomas Emery is the Richard W. Peck Professor in Creative Writing at DePauw University.

Tom Gatten is the author of *Mapper of Mists*.

Sands Hall is a 1991 graduate of the Workshop.

Chris Hallman is a 1991 graduate of the Workshop and winner of a Transatlantic Henfield Award.

Tracy Harris is a 1981 graduate of the Workshop.

Pete Hendley is a 1991 graduate of the Workshop.

James Hynes is the author of *The Wild Colonial Boy* and *Publish and Perish*.

Miriam Kuznets is a 1988 graduate of the Workshop.

William Lashner is the author of *Hostile Witness* and *Veritas*.

Steve Lattimore is the author of *Circumnavigation*.

Robert Lehrman is the author of *Defectors, Juggling*, and other novels.

Fritz McDonald is a 1990 graduate of the Workshop.

Joe Nigg is the author of *The Book of Fabulous Beasts: A Treasury of Writings from Ancient Times to the Present*.

Charles Oldham is a 1994 graduate of the Workshop.

Diane Parkin-Speer attended the Workshop in the 1960s.

Jonathan Penner is the author of *Private Parties, Natural Order*, and other books.

Ken Rosen is the author of *No Snakes, No Paradise, A Spy in the House of the Thought Police*, and other books.

David Shields is the author of *Heroes, Dead Languages, A Handbook for Drowning, Remote*, and *Black Planet: Facing Race during an NBA Season*.

Don Snyder is the author of *Veterans Park, The Cliff Walk*, and other books.

Debra Spark is the author of *Coconuts for the Saint*.

Karen Stolz is the author of *The World of Pies*.

Luke Wallin is the author of *Blue Wing, The Slavery Ghosts*, and other award-winning novels for young adults.

Edwin Weihe is a 1966 graduate of the Workshop.

ACKNOWLEDGMENTS

Deepest thanks to Leigh Haber, a great editor, who with John Freeman came up with the idea of putting together a book on the Workshop, to Henry Dunow for championing it, and to Frank Conroy for giving his blessing, advice, and friendship.

To Connie Brothers and Deb West, who keep everyone at the Workshop, faculty and students alike, sane, thanks from all of us.

Many thanks to Bridget Garrity for tracking down the names of everyone who ever passed through the Workshop.

And to my wife, Jody, who contributed to every decision that went into the making of this book.

A B O U T   T H E   E D I T O R

Tom Grimes is the author of the novels *A Stone of the Heart, Season's End* (written while he was a student at Iowa), and *City of God,* and a play, *Spec.* He directs the M.F.A. program in Creative Writing at Southwest Texas State University.